Before Crips

In the series *Studies in Transgression*, edited by David Brotherton

ALSO IN THIS SERIES:

John M. Hagedorn, *Gangs on Trial: Challenging Stereotypes and Demonization in the Courts*

Series previously published by Columbia University Press

JOHN C. QUICKER AND
AKIL S. BATANI-KHALFANI

Before Crips

Fussin', Cussin', and Discussin' among
South Los Angeles Juvenile Gangs

TEMPLE UNIVERSITY PRESS
Philadelphia • Rome • Tokyo

TEMPLE UNIVERSITY PRESS
Philadelphia, Pennsylvania 19122
tupress.temple.edu

Copyright © 2022 by Temple University—Of The Commonwealth System of Higher Education
All rights reserved
Published 2022

Library of Congress Cataloging-in-Publication Data

Names: Quicker, John C. (John Charles), 1943– author. | Batani-Khalfani, Akil S., 1943– author.
Title: Before Crips : fussin', cussin', and discussin' among South Los Angeles juvenile gangs / John C. Quicker and Akil S. Batani-Khalfani.
Description: Philadelphia : Temple University Press, 2022. | Series: Studies in transgression | Includes bibliographical references and index. | Summary: "This book describes the rise, features, and behavior of street groups in mid-century South Los Angeles. It charts the influence of social factors on the changing culture of neighborhood street sets, describing their behaviors, customs, and values, as remembered by interviewees who were members of these groups in the 1950s and 1960s"—Provided by publisher.
Identifiers: LCCN 2021046391 (print) | LCCN 2021046392 (ebook) | ISBN 9781439921975 (cloth) | ISBN 9781439921982 (paperback) | ISBN 9781439921999 (pdf)
Subjects: LCSH: Gangs—California--Los Angeles—History—20th century. | Gang members—California—Los Angeles—Interviews. | Juvenile delinquency—California—Los Angeles—History—20th century. | South Los Angeles (Los Angeles, Calif.)—Social conditions.
Classification: LCC HV6439.U7 Q75 2022 (print) | LCC HV6439.U7 (ebook) | DDC 364.106/60979494—dc23/eng/20220304
LC record available at https://lccn.loc.gov/2021046391
LC ebook record available at https://lccn.loc.gov/2021046392

∞ The paper used in this publication meets the requirements of the American National Standard for Information Sciences—Permanence of Paper for Printed Library Materials, ANSI Z39.48-1992

Printed in the United States of America

9 8 7 6 5 4 3 2 1

We dedicate this book to

Quicker's sisters Dianne Yee and Debby Bracht,

who always had his back;

and to his sister Jane Nelson, who still does.

They taught him:

I have sisters, don't make me use them.

Contents

	Acknowledgments	ix
	Map of South Los Angeles in the 1950s	xiv
	Introduction	1
	Insiders Become Outsiders: Methodology	15
1	When the South Came West	21
2	Assemblies of Juveniles	41
3	The Discovery of Gangs in Los Angeles	63
4	Street Group Development: A Storied Evolution	89
5	Slaus Angeles, Villa Fornia 90001: Gang Capital of the World	123
6	The Big Three: Social Class, Gender, and Race	171
7	Comin'-from-the-Shoulders: Ethics, Weapons, Fights, and Violence	213
8	Malicious Mopery on a Public Highway: Crime and Punishment	255
9	Unable to Embrace the Ideology: The Rise of the Crips	299
	Appendix: South Los Angeles Sets and Car Clubs before 1965	333
	Notes	341
	Bibliography	417
	Index	433

Photos follow page 162.

Acknowledgments

I would like to thank my parents, John and Helen, who regularly allowed me enough rope during my adventures to hang myself but made sure I didn't. My wife, Diane, gets singular thanks for her unwavering support and total commitment to this project, without which it would have been impossible. Thank you to my daughter-in-law, Laura Street, whose skills at getting me the multitude of publications needed were without parallel and whose wise judgment helped smooth out rough spots opening an even larger place in my heart for her; and to my son-in-law, Erick Street, who was a rock of assurance and wealth of good humor. Thank you, Lily and Clara, my granddaughters, who often exhorted me, "Don't give up, Pop," giving me a needed boost during dark times.

To my son, Kevin Morris, whose vision for the cover was inspirational and who patiently allowed me to bend his ear, whenever the need arose, on whatever needed fussin' and discussin'; thank you. Thank you to my nieces Anne Hart and Meredith Boyd, whose comments on the plethora of inquires I sent them always came back with insights and wisdom; and to my nephew, Matt Bracht, for his computer skills that helped me negotiate technical impasses; and to my nephews, Mike Dussault and Jim and Joseph Kniest. Bird's daughter, Dai'Quiriya Martinez, has been a crown jewel. She gets extended thanks for her tireless interpretive, administrative, and negotiating skills, helping us sort through the complexities of our map, photos, and beyond. This project has been a family effort.

I want to thank the many colleagues and friends who read portions of the manuscript at its various stages and listened generously to descriptions of controversies, contradictions, and analytical complexities for their suggestions, critiques, and encouragement. These include Avery Lankford, Richard Hovard, Larry Johnson, Dan and Adrienne Garrison, Linda and Gerry Mikesell, Yank and Anne Mojo, Jeanette Barnell, and Tom Mayberry. Thank you for your help, and thank you for still being my friends. Special thanks go to my expat, retired English professor and hang-out buddy, Bill Page, whose keen-wittedness and exceptional editing skills on an earlier draft of the entire manuscript were akin to a private tutorial on correct English and writing sanity.

The countless guest speakers who spoke in my classes over the years deserve particular thanks. Police, judges, attorneys, probation officers, parole agents, gang experts, gang members, and former residents of carceral institutions all saw value in giving their time and expertise to enlighten us. Two of these experts, both deputy probation officers, stand out because of their extraordinary people skills, psychological insights, charming senses of humor, and dependable willingness to give classroom presentations: Colette Vazquez and Roland Williams. They presented detailed strategies on the profound differences in dealing with boys and girls, while emphasizing changes that were possible with good knowledge and the proper approach. I would like to thank Father Greg Boyle for the hope his numerous heart-felt class presentations, outlining artful methods that worked with East Los Angeles gang youth, gave us to believe that we too might make a difference.

I would like to thank the many intellectual giants in my life who allowed me to stand on their shoulders and believed in me, especially when I wasn't so sure. These include Ray Cuzzort, Del Elliott, Howard Higman, Herman Loether, Herman and Julia Schwendinger, Dan Waldorf, Min S. Yee, Jeff Fagan, Jim Short, Mac Klein, Joan Moore, and John Hagedorn. Diego Vigil has been particularly generous with his time over the years, regularly offering wise counsel to Bird and me, having our backs, and being there for us with great wit, kindness, and a marvelous sense of humor.

Dave Brotherton and Ryan Mulligan saw the nascent promise in our work, encouraged us, and directed us on how to strengthen our weaknesses, helping make our goals a reality. They have been unparalleled editors, giving us their solid support and thoughtful suggestions for wading through the maze of publishing logistics. Thank you to Jamie Armstrong, Gary Kramer, and the anonymous Temple copyeditors for their fine-tuning skills in helping us tidy up our manuscript.

I want to thank California State University Dominguez Hills for supporting my vision on the importance of incorporating a class on gangs in the departmental curriculum. The University also granted me a sabbatical leave as well as institutional research funds to pursue our project. Their support was essential in helping us realize our goals and in engaging my students.

Our map would not have been possible without the extraordinary skills of David C. Hoerlein, who helped craft both a valuable guide to the complexities of South Los Angeles and a work of art; and his deft ability shone in getting it to fit into so small a space. We thank him for his creation, for his good cheer, and for his patience dealing with the numerous tweaks we came up with over months of work. We thank Brian Hutchinson for his adroit design work that gave life to our cover and distinguished it, as his artful conceptualization brought out the meaning in our material.

I thank our respondents who gave freely of their time to talk with us, to hang out with us, and to invite us into their homes because they respected us and believed in the importance of our project. Kumasi, from the Slausons, was especially masterly. His poignant insights were invaluable in furthering our analysis and corroborating our facts. My students were strong motivators, candid judges, and uncompromising critics of what I lectured on and wrote about over my forty years of teaching. The fussin', cussin', and discussin' that was engaged in regularly and openly with them, from classroom to coffeehouse to pub to parties kept me honest and inspired me to appreciate the vital significance of an accurate work about their neighborhoods that was urgent, long overdue, and in need of an insider turned outsider's touch. This book required a community I am honored to be a part of.

John C. Quicker

I would like to acknowledge my parents, Chuck and Nita (as they were known to most people), for their stringent and consistent standard of upbringing. Being an only child, I was not spoiled but privileged to learn from them at an early age to see people as they are and not by what they are. And especially for instilling in me a sense of impartiality and fairness toward all people that taught me not to be prejudiced against any person, I am grateful to them. I would also like thank them for the many travel opportunities they afforded me that allowed me to see most of the western United States while I was a teenager, which created in me a uniquely diverse attitude and approach in my dealings with people and culture. And finally, I would like to thank them for their continuous support through the years of my delinquent youth and for never once turning their backs on me and for not losing faith in my intelligence and abilities.

From my teen years as a street soldier of Los Angeles, I would like to acknowledge Chinaman of Big Slauson and Roach of Little Slauson for their influence and leadership during the entirety of the 1950s; had Roach been in the military, he would have been a "six-star" general; he was just that good. I would like to thank all the guys and girls, too many to name, and all who have passed on for saving my life and being there to have my back and standing by my side when the odds were against me and nearly ended me, during the turbulent period of street gang warfare during the 1960s.

I would also like to give credit to my daughter, Dai'Quiriya Soixante Martinez, for the many days and tireless hours of helping with numerous pictures, corrections, and the map; she is a rare gem. Much appreciation also goes to Rick L. Crowell for his assistance in locating specific photos out of hundreds and being available when needed. Thanks also to the prophetic vision of the late LeRoy Box, a younger Slauson who was attending Los Angeles City College at the same time as me in 1972, for suggesting that I write a book about the streets of Los Angeles.

And to all of the Slausons, and others, both male and female, that contributed insight and knowledge to the creation of our book: Nedra Woods-Mack; Barbara J. Crooms, who was a new arrival to 1960s LA from Pittsburg, for her input regarding the phenomenon that was Slauson and the vast difference in style and attitude between the Los Angeles gangs and those from the eastern region of the United States; Sheila "Crip" Daniels, who contracted polio as a youth and, due to her disability, had the nickname "Crip" long before the existence of the Crips and Bloods; Albert James Sims, better known as "Stinky," of the Slauson Warlords, who was Quicker's favorite interviewee. And to the many others who are gone but not forgotten, I am extremely grateful for your wisdom and acuity; there are too many to mention.

I would like to especially thank Diego Vigil for his deep-seated sagacity and knowledge and for the times that we met, engaged in discussions, exchanged ideas, and had fun doing it on several occasions over the years and for the continuous advice that he gave to Quicker and myself to not be discouraged and to keep moving forward toward our objective.

And a special thanks goes to Frenchee Guliex for contributing his late 1950s and early 1960s photos to our book.

Last but not least, I would like to thank all of the transcribers, editors, map designers, and Temple University for taking the time out to read, examine, accept, and publish our book, which is something that we began close to thirty-five years ago.

On a special note, I would like to express that the book is just a small portion of the story and that the larger tale has yet to be told. . . . "For there are bystanders and those who are standing by."

Thanks to everyone who supported our vision.

Akil Saud Batani-Khalfani

Before Crips

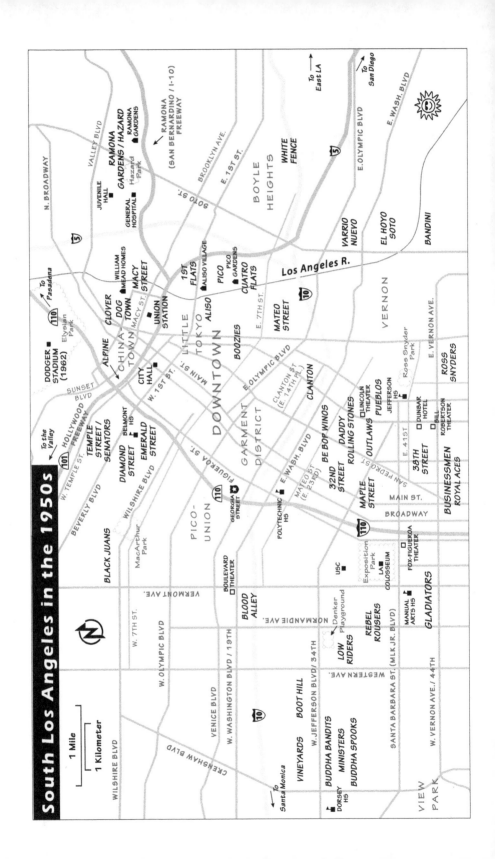

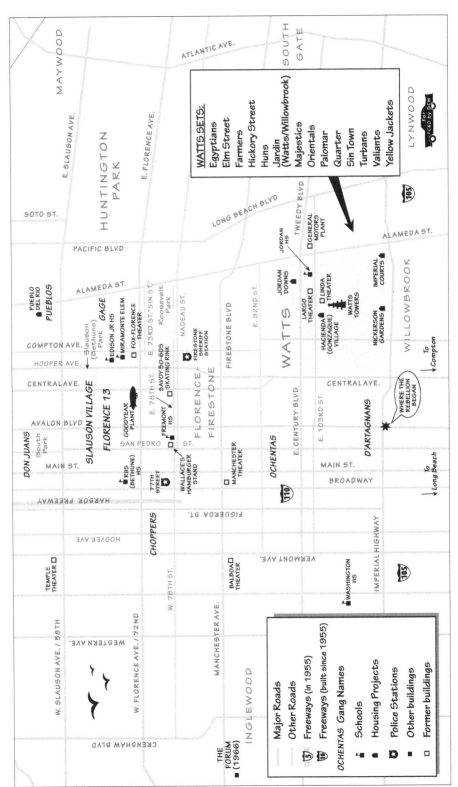

South Los Angeles in the 1950s. (David C. Hoerlein)

Introduction

You cannot describe anything without betraying your point of view, your aspirations, your fears, your hopes. Everything.
—James Baldwin, *Notes of a Native Son*

Los Angeles has created a kaleidoscope of images for its beholders. It was commonly considered a "bad town for Negroes" in the mid-1800s, because the City had been sympathetic to the cause of the Confederacy. By 1900, the City had developed a reputation as being a "good town for negroes" since it was one of the first in the nation to hire Black police and firemen.[1] In 1913 W.E.B. Du Bois claimed Los Angeles was "wonderful" for "Negroes," exemplifying a "common perception among many Black Angelenos" of a "racial paradise."[2] In 1964, the National Urban League ranked Los Angeles as the "most desirable city in America for Black people."[3] One year later, on Wednesday August 11, 1965, the South Los Angeles community of Watts broke apart in a tsunami of violence as the dam of pretense could no longer contain the City's festering racial antagonisms.[4]

Welcome to Los Angeles, a land where contradictions are the norm and ironies rule.[5] For many it is "Our Lady the Queen of the Angels,"[6] while for others it is the birthplace of racial covenants and the gang capital of America. It is a land of contrasts, a city with the greatest spatial diversity of any city in America, the ultimate "crabgrass frontier."[7] It is not the proverbial "concrete jungle." It is our city.

Called the Watts Riot, or the Watts Rebellion,[8] the 1965 violence was considered by many in the country to be a watershed moment in race relations. It was the perfect storm: a hot summer evening, a community pushed to the brink by racial and economic injustice, insensitive California Highway Patrol (CHP) officers making a series of bad decisions, and young Black juveniles being roughed up—again—by the "man."[9] Enough! The proverbial straw that broke the camel's back had been placed.

The Rebellion shattered illusions that government agencies had gotten a handle on what ailed the community, and it appeared to have marked a turning point for the South Los Angeles gangs. The perceived hegemonic transition from the pre-Rebellion street groups of lovers and fighters to the more visible, and likely more criminal, Crips and Bloods seemed like a break with the past. It has been argued that the break came out of the ashes of the Watts Rebellion and was fueled by unhealed racial wounds ripped open once more by ill-conceived criminal-justice policies. Legitimate remunerative jobs for the residents of South Los Angeles evaporated as the city deconstructed and then reconstructed in newly emerging peripheral centers.[10] These structural transformations coincided with the rise of the opportunity for residents in the core of the city to pursue the American dream through alternative means: the sale of illegal drugs, helping to fuel a turn to increased crime.[11]

An Urban Laboratory

In the aftermath of the Rebellion, California governor Edmund G. Brown determined that an urban university that served the Watts area and surrounding minority communities of South Los Angeles might help alleviate some of the local residents' problems in achieving upward mobility through access to higher education. California State College Dominguez Hills, later established as a university (California State University Dominguez Hills [CSUDH]), was born in 1966 just south of Watts, in Carson, and imbued with the hope that Brown thought higher education could provide.[12]

One author of this book, John Quicker, began teaching in the sociology department at the University in the fall of 1970, five years after the Rebellion. Offering classes in criminology, juvenile delinquency, corrections, and gangs, Quicker found that many of his students had, and continued to have, considerable personal experience with delinquency, crime, gangs, and with the Rebellion. They had relatives, neighbors, and friends who had been involved in one of these things, often all four, and many still were. Other students were professionals—such as police, sheriffs, probation officers, and parole agents—who had returned to the university seeking bachelor's or master's degrees. Many had been motivated by the federal Law Enforcement Assistance Administration (LEAA), established by the Crime Control Act of 1968, where police in the 1970s were paid to get university degrees, which could earn them promotions and salary adjustments.[13] A large percentage of Quicker's students were from South Los Angeles.

An Education of Consequence

Dominguez Hills was not a typical school for the California State system, and Quicker wasn't a typical university professor. His classes were a heterogeneous mix of equal proportions of Black, Latin, and White students,[14] ranging in ages eighteen to eighty, with the average around thirty-six. When Quicker first started teaching, more than half his students were almost a decade older than him. About 70 percent of them were women, the majority of whom were also mothers.[15] Because the students were close to the same age as him and considered him "cool," he was regularly invited to parties and various social gatherings they had. He went often and hung out with them. Occasionally they introduced him as their professor who wanted to know about LA gangs and crime. Because these were festive events on their turf, and he was considered another partygoer, they felt comfortable telling stories about their assorted deeds, both legal and illegal. These events were frequently a walk on the wild side.[16]

A majority of Quicker's students had an abundance of information from their time spent in the community. Most had lived in or worked in South Los Angeles, and many still did. These students were eager to learn. But since many were older than average university students and were sufficiently strong-willed, with opinions that had been honed by life experience, they made it clear that they were not going to accept any "bullshit" in the classroom about things they had firsthand knowledge of. And they called it like they saw it, in language they were comfortable with, ready to fuss about and discuss their views—respectfully but with resolve—with other students and with the professor. Since the discussions were about law violators and law enforcers, they were regularly lively and frequently continued in the cafeteria after class.

A Take-No-Prisoners Assessment of the Literature

In class and out, students were willing to share their opinions, whether solicited or not, particularly when they were assigned to study theories that tried to account for the behaviors of actions they had been involved with or had witnessed or had heard about and involving themselves or people they might have been related to or, at least, knew or knew of. Most striking, the experiences they shared and the theories Quicker was teaching were frequently disconnected.[17] When the students read or heard the theories presented in class, they often criticized them, with multiple examples of how they didn't apply to the people or groups existing in the neighborhoods where they lived. Student criticisms were not anomalies but everyday occurrences: the theories often just didn't fit. Quicker's students knew, from his East Coast accent, that he was not from Los Angeles, sensed he was eager to learn, and wanted to "teach" him about their city. He lectured, they listened; they spoke, he listened; and learning became an exchange.

Students were especially critical of the theorists they felt "just didn't get it," because these theorists never seemed to talk with any of the delinquents or gang members they theorized about or to understand them very well if they had. These particular criticisms were leveled at Albert Cohen, Herbert Block and Arthur Niederhoffer, and Richard Cloward and Lloyd Ohlin. They thought that William Whyte provided a lot of detail about individuals but little theory. Very perceptively too, they noted the so-called corner boys that he discussed weren't boys at all. They were men in their twenties, and "Doc" was in his late twenties: "Doesn't delinquency and juvenile gangs refer to those who are under eighteen?" students queried.

Students thought that Walter Miller's theory was racist, because the "focal concerns" he articulated were not a part of the Black community only but characterized many other people too. Black students explained knowing "White boys" who were always trying to "outwit" or "outsmart" others and how all juveniles sought out a "thrill." None of Quicker's White or Latin students disagreed with them and, in fact, often added narratives from their own lives that supported what the Black students were claiming.

Most students liked Herbert Asbury, whose writing they felt was entertaining, if mostly applicable to an earlier New York period. They were also quite positive about Harrison Salisbury, because they felt he really understood the plight many gang members faced, even though he too wrote primarily about New York. They were especially effusive in their praise for his contention as to why delinquency was so persistent through the years. Salisbury wrote that we already know what to do; ignorance is not the problem. The problem, he stated, is this: "We do not lack the knowledge. We lack the will."[18] Lewis Yablonsky's account perplexed them. They felt that little of what he had described about New York gangs applied to those they were familiar with in Los Angeles, and they believed he just didn't seem to understand gangs or find much value in any of the time he spent around them.

Interestingly, most students thought Frederic Thrasher had it going on when he theorized that gangs had initially formed as spontaneous play groups and then solidified as a result of the conflict they encountered at school, from the police, or someplace else in the neighborhood. That seemed to be just the way the groups they were familiar with formed too.[19] But students regularly added that the Chicago police must not have been nearly as racist as those in Los Angeles, since the racism Thrasher talked of was primarily gang against gang, while in South Los Angeles the racism came from the police, not the other gangs.

In a memorable effort to demonstrate just how racist the Los Angeles police were, one student interviewed half a dozen police officers, at various locations, about the gangs in their communities. His in-class report raised eyebrows, elicited some "tsk-tsking," but also brought about many nods of agreement. He wrote: "Many in law enforcement take on the attitude, 'Why get involved in a nigger[20] killing another nigger; it's only the population adjustment factor at work.'" The student wrote further that a different officer had told him, "These fucking animals will all eventually be killed anyway, and it's not worth getting my head blown off about."[21] After his presentation, the student rested his case on police racism. Nobody challenged him.

Female students initially raised questions about why the theorists, with the exceptions of Asbury, Salisbury, and Thrasher, hadn't said anything about girls. "We had our little clubs," and "we hung out with the guys all the time," they'd contend. One female student asked, "Why do you think guys do all the stupid shit they do?" This question sparked an animated discussion in this class, and in others when Quicker heuristically raised it again in them.

The consensus from those discussions was that boys will often do "stupid" (dangerous) things to show off to both the girls and their male homies, as well as to protect and defend them. Many students argued further that boys did those things simply because they were boys and that that is just the sort of crazy stuff boys do—regularly. "Why," a female student asked rhetorically, "do you think boys die more often than girls?" There was little talk of actual girls' gangs, because students felt they were anomalies in South Los Angeles.[22] But there was a lot of discussion on the regular interactions between the sexes, which occurred regardless of the boy's gang status and sometimes because of it. There was unequivocal agreement that males and females influenced one another, usually reciprocally. The Black women in class made this point most dramatically.

Often, in early conversations with students and with the guest speakers Quicker invited to class, names of street groups—neither Crip nor Blood—associated with the area just north of CSUDH kept popping up: names like the Slausons, Businessmen, Gladiators, Farmers, Huns, and others. At the time, with the exception of Roger Rice and Rex Christensen's 1965 Los Angeles County probation report, there was scant research on these groups.[23] Quicker began taking notes on the conversations because these were groups missing from the literature. The students and guest speakers spoke with confidence about these groups that preceded the Crips and Bloods, provided factual detail, and complimented and supplemented one another's stories, often unbeknownst to the other. Sometimes, the same story would be told by a different person, with a different perspective. What Quicker was hearing was an important piece of community history that had been neglected.

Serendipity Happens

In the early 1980s, Quicker introduced a new course at the University called "Gangs and Adolescent Subcultures," to be offered once or twice a year. It was very popular and always maximized available classroom space, where it generated enrollments of forty to seventy students. One of the class assignments was to do research on and then write a term paper about gangs. The paper could focus on contemporary gangs, or it could take a historical perspective; it should utilize field and library research; and it could emphasize South Los Angeles gangs. Students were very creative when interviewing respondents. As evidenced by the large number of high-quality papers submitted, many based on solid ethnographic field research with principals of gangs past and current, most students took the assignment very seriously, and most directed their focus to South Los Angeles. Findings from some of these student research papers have informed parts of this book.

In the spring 1984 class, Quicker encountered a most unusual student. It was a large class, and in such a class, his approach upon entering the room for the first time was to *read* the students. After he walked to the front of the room—and before saying a word—he would take a few moments to scan the group to look for familiar faces but primarily to determine who might be a potential problem and who would be easy to work with.

On this first day of class, Quicker saw a sagacious looking Black man, about his age, wearing a black beret and sitting in the rear of the room with his back up against the wall. It was just the way Quicker liked to sit in classrooms. He was intently looking at Quicker, and they seemed to be studying each other. Quicker suspected the student was either with the police or someone with a lot of street experience. Whichever it was, Quicker needed to find out. After the second class, Quicker positioned himself near the exit, so the student would have to pass close to him when he left the room. That would give Quicker an opportunity to speak to him. It worked easily because, as it turned out, the student wanted to meet Quicker too. His name was Bird.

Bird initially informed Quicker that he had been associated with an older Black South Los Angeles street club, had some room in his schedule for electives, and decided to take Quicker's class to check it—and the professor—out. More than merely having a club affiliation, Bird had in fact been one of the most notable members of one of the most notable pre-Crip-and-Blood street groups in South Los Angeles: the legendary Slausons. And he was just as legendary. Having lived in the same neighborhood since he was six years old, he had both met and knew the names and the faces of many of the famous and infamous people associated with the various street groups coming out of his and the surrounding neighborhoods. With an almost photographic memory, his ability to recall the names of people he had met, where he had met them, who they were, and even what they had been wearing at the time was most extraordinary.

Each time Quicker offered the course, he invited numerous *gang experts* to address the class. These experts ranged from former and current gang members to authorities from various criminal and juvenile justice agencies. On one occasion, during the semester Bird was among Quicker's students, he invited two veteran members of the Los Angeles Police Department's (LAPD) Community Resources Against Street Hoodlums (CRASH) gang unit to speak. After their presentation, and during the question period, Bird probed them on "facts" they had presented that varied considerably from what he knew. Bird was polite and respectful, and they found his questions and answers authoritative enough to make them hang around after class for close to an hour talking with both authors. The officers concurred that Bird was correct on all issues of fact. This scenario was repeated a second time that semester with two members of the Los Angeles Sheriff's Department (LASD) gang unit, Operation Safe Streets (OSS). Bird had demonstrated to the experts and to Quicker that when it came to expertise, there were expert's experts.[24]

An Incomparable Resource

Bird, whose legal name is Akil S. Batani-Khalfani, is the coauthor of this book. Bird is a nickname. It's a name he's had since he was a teen, still goes by, and is best known as. He and Quicker developed an easy rapport. During that semester, he would meet Quicker in his office or cafeteria for coffee and a soda at least once or twice a week. They would spend hours talking about gangs, delinquency, and their experiences—both professional and personal—with both. Bird wrote a superb term paper for the class, based on ethnographic field data that were grounded in his experiences and on the numerous interviews he had been able to conduct with various street people he knew.[25] His paper was the first piece of academic material to be written about the Slausons or, for that matter, about any pre-Crip-and-Blood gang in South Los Angeles. When the semester ended, but before they parted, they made sure they knew how to find each other again because they did not want Bird's paper to be the last completed piece of research.[26]

Bird's life spent in the same neighborhood since he was a young child, plus a year in Watts, has given him an intimate familiarity with his surroundings. Throughout this time, he has met, known of, heard about, or had personal dealings with thousands of people living there. He continues to be a street sage, a central figure in a neighborhood that has experienced significant change during his time there. While there are many in the community who know Bird, there are few his age who haven't at least heard of him. Each year since 1972, he and other Slausons have had annual reunions and "oldies and soul dance" affairs, which attract hundreds of people from the Slauson and other neighborhoods to get down for a few hours of revelry and to enjoy each other's company. Quicker has been to many of them. While everyone there still has allegiance to their old neighborhood and will tell you that they are a Businessman or a Slauson, their daily activity is centered on their jobs and families, not on their street days.

The State of the Debate

Rice and Christensen, as a result of their affiliation with the County's Group Guidance Project in the 1960s, interviewed thirteen gang leaders from South Los Angeles and East Los Angeles gangs and provided a variety of important insights into gang member activities in their report.[27] They did not see much distinction between the South Los Angeles and East Los Angeles gangs, perceiving both as similar to each other and to other gangs in the various parts of the United States where they had been studied. In the 1970s, Malcolm Klein made it clear that there were gangs in Los Angeles other than the Mexican groups made infamous in the Sleepy Lagoon murder case and the zoot-suit riots of the 1940s.[28] But Klein's interests in gangs were in evaluating assorted programs designed to mitigate their activities, not in doing ethnographies of the groups he was evaluating.[29] His *Street Gangs and Street Workers* had as its primary focus an evaluation of the Los Angeles County Probation Department's Group Guidance Project, which worked with pre-Crip-and-Blood gangs in South Los Angeles. Klein's research was not intended as a study of origins and activities.

Martin Jankowski's ethnographic research on gangs in three metropolitan areas, conducted during the late 1970s and 1980s, includes Los Angeles as one of his areas. His choice to not reveal the Los Angeles areas he was in or the name of the gangs he studied makes his focus unclear.[30] James Howell and John Moore's ambitious attempt to write about the history of street gangs in the United States oversimplifies and misrepresents what happened in Los Angeles.[31] Al Valdez complicates his historical analysis of Los Angeles gangs with an attempt that lacks historicity.[32] Two of the most important academic statements on Black Angeleno gangs came from Alejandro Alonzo and Diego Vigil.[33] Alonzo's ethnographic account of the "racialization" of Black youth comes close to the explanatory mark, although we question his division of gang emergence into historically distinct "waves." Alonzo's research is limited by whom he was able to interview and his time on the street with the early gang members. Vigil's account is informative, accurate, and a significant introduction although somewhat limited in scope.

Solid ethnographic work on the early South Los Angeles gangs has been done by two documentary film makers, Cle "Bone" Sloan and Stacy Peralta,[34] and by YouTube ethnographer Kev Mack.[35] Sloan's film especially provides a solid perspective on the structural conditions in Los Angeles that contributed to gang emergence. Peralta's focus gives less attention to early history because his primary concern is with the rise of the Crips and Bloods. Mack has conducted excellent interviews and, like a good ethnographer, has asked important clarifying follow-up questions of historic figures, like Bird, and a number of younger gang members in South Los Angeles. His primary weakness is that he provides minimal analysis, leaving interpretation of his data up to the viewer. There remains a huge gap concerning who these early groups were, what they did, and why they emerged. Our research attempts to fill in major portions of this gap.

In 1990 Mike Davis commented, "Almost nothing has been written about the history of South Central L.A.'s sociologically distinct gang culture."[36] Sixteen years later, R. J. Smith added that research on the effect of racism on "L.A. street gangs" is overdue.[37] This book is about that overdue, "sociologically distinct culture" and the effects of persistent racism on that culture and on the political and economic environment that fostered it. The historical analysis of South Los Angeles's pre-Crip-and-Blood gangs had been "lost, stolen or strayed"[38]—until now.

Filling a Historic Hole

A number of research projects centered on gangs have made it clear that to know where we are with the current gang situation, we need to know where we have come from. However, as John Hagedorn has argued, "much of the literature on gangs is not concerned with origins" but rather focuses on why juveniles become delinquent.[39] Since gang activity doesn't occur in a societal vacuum, we are remiss to study it as if it does. Because juvenile gangs are a piece of the overall crime problem, if we are to understand them, we must study them within that larger context. Much gang research, especially that conducted by embedded criminal justice bureaucrats,[40] directs its focus to the gang members and their immediate situation, while ignoring structural and historical institutional arrangements and the conditions responsible for creating the environments under which gangs form. Also overlooked are the power structures responsible for stigmatizing street groups with an onerous name like *gang*.

A persuasive statement on the need for a structural historical perspective is offered by David Brotherton in his critical appraisal of the state of gang theory and research.[41] He writes that gangs are "located in history" and they "have a history," and it is "crucial" to know how previous generations have understood them. Further, he notes that "renditions of the gang without history place the phenomenon at the mercy of empiricist accounts that pay scant attention to the politics" of the period or to issues of race, class and gender relations.[42]

This is specifically the case for Los Angeles. Many of the popular assumptions about gangs here are generalized renditions based on what happened with the gangs of East Los Angeles. They neglect the fact that in South Los Angeles gangs also emerged, about the same time, but were different from the East Los Angeles gangs in significant ways. Importantly, it is from the neighborhoods of these neglected South Los Angeles gangs that the Crips and Bloods emerged. There was a discontinuity between these groups and earlier ones in the same neighborhoods. This discrepancy raises questions about the generalizability of the institutionalization concept of gang development. While some gangs clearly do institutionalize, reproduce themselves, and establish legacies that upcoming youngsters adopt, such an arrangement cannot be assumed to characterize all groups, even within the same city, and especially not in one as large as Los Angeles.

Our concern is with an understanding of the gangs that existed before the Crips and Bloods so that we can make sense out of what happened next. A structural history of the early South Los Angeles street groups will help us understand how and why they appeared to desist. While the Watts Rebellion was a defining moment, one that appeared to be a culmination of fundamental changes in the South Los Angeles social and economic environment and changes in the street organizations as well,[43] it was only a piece of the evolution that had been occurring. It was a wake-up call that things weren't as rosy as they might have seemed.

Somewhat before the Rebellion, but mostly within a short time afterward, the street groups that had existed previously became increasingly less visible, producing a perceived social vacuum. Alonzo writes that "there was a lull of Black gang activity" from 1965 to the early 1970s.[44] Klein asks whether there was actually a decline in gang activity or whether it was the information sources that were on decline. Klein's suspicions were well founded, and he suspected so; it was the attention being given to gangs that had declined.[45] We theorize that this period wasn't a lull; it was a changing of the guard. The perceived lull was due to media refocusing on other more salient urban turbulence rather than an actual reduction in street group activity.[46] Concern with gangs had been overridden with concern for the nation's stability from general unrest.[47]

During the late 1960s, while many of the earlier gang members were pursuing other options, they were still visible. They were on the set but less active. New groups, like the Avenues and McCoy Boys, among others, joined them, while the nascent ideology that formed the Crips and Bloods was rumbling. The new groups were appearing in the same neighborhoods the earlier street had dominated, showing up alongside their residue and coexisting with them. But where the new groups continued some established neighborhood traditions, they also started their own.

A Macro Perspective

Davis described Los Angeles in the early 1900s, as "one of the world's great cities in the making" yet characterized by "permanent class warfare."[48] We append his analysis by also including extensive racial warfare among the City's defining characteristics. Sloan, in *Bastards of the Party*, provides a powerful portrayal of how racism had been an essential ingredient in the formation of the City's Black gangs. Others have confirmed Sloan's position,[49] while Josh Sides has argued that the culture of much of White Los Angeles, while racist in general, was specifically anti-Black.[50]

Los Angeles has one of the largest industrial zones in the world, marked by rigid segregation, including the "White Curtain" east of the Alameda industrial corridor.[51] The City was multiracial and multiethnic, where de jure and de facto racial discrimination in South Los Angeles neighborhoods led to hard feelings among all who experienced it. Moreover, many Black Angelenos had emigrated from southern states and viewed their departure from Dixie as "an escape from bondage" but now feared the "Southernization" of their city because of all the White southerners following.[52] The "Great Migration of African Americans during and after World War II" had a profound influence on the political and economic direction of the city's growth,[53] as did the large demographic increase in White emigrants.

During much of this time, the Los Angeles Police Department (LAPD) was led by Chief Davis, described as "an avowed White supremacist" who saw the "gang problem" as a function of the overall "Black menace."[54] Supported by Mayor Sam Yorty, who misled Black voters into believing he would make changes in the LAPD if they voted for him, and realtors and property owners, who determined that the economic benefits of apartheid were in their interests, the police made Los Angeles less a city of angels and more a place of devils for its Black residents. Rapid industrialization accompanied significant demographic growth, followed by deindustrialization, which produced reindustrialization in the periphery and created economic and spatial dislocations for many in South Los Angeles. It was under these conditions of disrupted lives and problems of adjustment that gangs were born, then born again as crisis-fueled phenomena, presented by representatives of the power elite who blamed the usual powerless suspects for their plight and diverted attention from systemic political and economic issues.

Utilizing the "big picture" perspective articulated by C. Wright Mills and expanded on by Brotherton and others,[55] we studied the early street groups existing in the neighborhoods where the Crips and Bloods came from. We explain how the amorphous concept of the gang became officially refined as a term to account for the behavior of non-White juveniles. We introduce the major street groups of the period, explain their origins, and discuss their behavioral patterns. We explain how race and gender identity shaped the social influences and decision-making of boys and girls alike.

We explain how the Slausons' formidability, with modest beginnings in 1952, was a result of their size and organization, charismatic leaders, neighborhood dynamics, and successful encounters with neighboring street groups. Crime carried numerous motivations and associations for different gang members that require nuanced attention, much more so than the sensationalized picture painted by institutions at the time. For example, drug sales, so prevalent a feature of contemporary gangs, were lucratively inferior to robbery. Gang involvement in the Rebellion is explained, as is the humble origins of the Crips, who began with a limp and not with a political ideology.

We show how the local, national, structural, and historical contexts shaped the environment that produced the South Los Angeles groups. We discuss the cultural, political, and economic distinctiveness of this environment and how it subsequently led to gang visibility.[56] Our goal is to explain what the early juvenile street groups were like and why they arose. There was discontinuity between them and the Crips and Bloods, unlike the gang continuity and clique "graduation" institutionalization Moore found in the East Los Angeles gangs she studied. Were the early South Los Angeles groups reprobates,[57] or were they juveniles trying to adapt the best they could to circumstances over which they had little control? Who were those people? What did they do? What happened to them? We explain.

The Dyad

We bring unique qualifications to this project. For one, our collective experience with delinquency and gangs totals over one hundred years. Second, we both have had personal experience with these phenomena as juveniles, one in Los Angeles and the other in New York. Third, both of us established professional careers: One became a professor at a university in South Los Angeles, where he did research and taught courses on delinquency, gangs, crime, and corrections for forty years. The other was both a Community Youth Gang Services worker and a counselor at a California Youth Authority facility and still lives in the same neighborhood he grew up in. Lastly, and most importantly, we are alive, conscious, and able to tell the tale.

We subtitled our work "Fussin', Cussin', and Discussin'" because the first two terms were commonly used by community adults back in the day to admonish youthful exuberance. A typical occasion for use was when a group of juveniles had gathered in a *hang-out* group and were talking and interacting, within adult eyesight and hearing range. Invariably the youths would be using language with words that would not only be inappropriate in church but were also unacceptable to the adults who couldn't help hearing them. Shortly after exposure, one of the adults would shout at the group: "Y'all quit that fussin' and cussin' now!" We added the term *discussin'* to our title both because of its rhythmic completion of the phrase and because it was a feature of what the juveniles were doing: involved in chatter, spiced up with proscribed language, along with the discussion of trivial and serious matters. They were engaged in a very common youthful interaction—fussin', cussin', and discussin'—while the adults, in accordance with their socialization responsibilities, were trying, quite successfully at times too, to keep the neighborhood respectable.

A Note on Language

Ethnographic integrity, essential to its value as a research methodology, means no word left behind. This requires an accurate uncensored description of what was seen, heard, and experienced. Researchers who make up words or ignore inconvenient language run the risk of becoming partisans. When objectivity is trumped by subjectivity, knowledge is victimized. Spinning the data is the realm of politicians, not ethnographers.

Social reality, and the language used to depict it, are rarely G-rated. In our interviews, respondents used words that expressed how they felt. To change what they said with an "expletive deleted" or a series of dashes following the first letter is to do a disservice to the speaker, the reader, and to us by writing something not spoken or meant. Changing one word loses the essence of intention. When a respondent used the N-word as a racial slur, such as the police quoted earlier, that's the way we wrote it. In different situations, with different people, this same word, when used by them, such as Dick Gregory did in the title of his book, the word meant something entirely different.[58] Context matters.

With Respect

Many of the interviewees for this work have passed away. We are not only saddened by their departure but also grieved that we will miss the opportunity we might have had for their critical insights into what we have written had they been able to read it. We trust that we have neither misquoted them nor misrepresented the spirit of what they were trying to explain to us. If we have, it has been unintentional, and we apologize. But if we have gotten it right, a little bit of them lives on in this work. For that we are much obliged.

Finally, we recognize that it's likely impossible to discuss social phenomena without having feelings or showing biases. Resulting controversy has produced numerous deliberations among social scientists on the objectivity of their work, with an eye toward making it "value-free." Brotherton has made it clear that a discussion about gangs is never just about gangs. It is about history, morality, politics, responsibility, and how the researchers view the world and the society of which they and the gangs are a part.[59] We agree with him and with James Baldwin, who noted that it is not possible to write about anything social without revealing at least some partialities. But we do believe that social science can sort through myth and misinformation and is capable of differentiating fact from fiction. That is what we have tried to do here, while also recognizing that we, like all other humans, have preferences. To put our approach into perspective, we paraphrase the eminent sociologist C. Wright Mills: we have tried to be objective; we do not claim to be detached.

Insiders Become Outsiders

Methodology

Without data, you are just another person with an opinion.
—W. Edwards Deming, *Statistical Adjustment of Data*

Our formal data collection was from the period 1987–1992.[1] On Bird's authority, Quicker was able to enter the neighborhood to speak to the people who could help us. Without Bird's vouching for Quicker as someone who could be trusted, data collection would have been restricted and would have lacked the richness of detail and accuracy we obtained. If Quicker was cool with Bird, then he had to be all right, and neighborhood denizens could talk openly to him. The people we spoke with ranged in age from their late thirties into their sixties. We gathered data on many pre-Crip-and-Blood gangs, with our primary focus being on those gangs that had formed in the 1940s, the 1950s, and the 1960s. While we collected the bulk of our formal data over a six-year period, this project has been lifelong, beginning on the streets when we were growing up. We were insiders who became outsiders. Data collection metamorphosed over the years as life got in the way and then out of the way. Additional respondents and data continued to surface, our collaboration persisted, and our understanding sharpened.

We created an open-ended questionnaire mostly using our own questions, later supplementing them with questions John Hagedorn had used in his study of Milwaukee gangs.[2] In ethnography, as in life, some people will tell you what you want to know, while others tell you less. Most of the people we talked with were very informed and informative. Our goals were to study what these street groups were all about—who they were, why they formed, what they did, why they did it, how they were organized, what their names were, what types of criminal behavior they may have been involved in, what their gender relations were like—and why the Crip and Blood gangs, which arose in their neighborhoods after them, did not continue their traditions or keep the same names. Few could answer all questions, but all could answer some.

Our last issue was particularly vexing since it has been one of the important differences noted between South Los Angeles and East Los Angeles gangs. East Los Angeles gangs are distinguished by having formed in the early years of the twentieth century, "institutionalizing" in part by having members "graduate" from one clique to another and then carrying on a number of the traditions, including the gang's name, into the twenty-first century.[3] In South Los Angeles, the pre-Crip-and-Blood gangs there, which also formed in the early twentieth century, have in many apparent respects all but disappeared. There was a discontinuity between what was and what is, and we knew that no proper analysis of these early South Los Angeles gangs could neglect this significant difference.

A Sample of Primary Sources

We began by meeting once a week, usually on a Friday evening starting around 4:00 P.M. and ending around 10:00 or 11:00 P.M. Evening was best because our respondents were most lively, having used the earlier parts of the day to complete what they needed to or to finish something from the day before. Typically, Quicker would drive to Bird's house in South Los Angeles, where we would spend the first hour or so talking together or talking with the various people who might have been there or who happened to come by later. His house was a gathering spot for many locals, who came around because it was a comfortable place to hang out for a while. It was one of our many "neutral zones."[4] It was a research setting that didn't feel like a research setting, where interviews that didn't feel like interviews were conducted.[5]

Sometimes we would spend the entire evening at Bird's house, either because the people coming through were people we wanted to talk with anyway or because we had arranged for certain people to come by when we were there to talk with us. On other occasions, after our initial discussions, we would get into Bird's "hoopty," an immaculately detailed purple 1941 Pontiac—which, at the risk of sounding redundant, was distinctive—to cruise the streets looking for people that Bird knew. Many of the people we wanted to speak to were hanging out on the street corners they frequented: so we would stop, park, and get out to hang too. Others were at home and allowed us to visit them there.

We were selective in choosing the people we spoke with. All our interviews were either with people who were key players in the gangs of those days or who were familiar with them. While this was not a random sample, there was some randomness involved in finding people who knew something and who could/would talk to us. We couldn't interview everybody we wanted to: some were incarcerated, some were unable or unwilling to speak with us, and some were not around or dead. The people we did interview, however, were not randomly chosen because they just happened to be there when we were. We interviewed people we knew we wanted to talk to, finding most of them. We reasoned we would obtain a more accurate account talking to one person who knew what was going on than distributing a questionnaire to ten who hadn't a clue but would answer as if they did.

We avoided people who were there and might have wanted to talk but who knew little or nothing.[6] A random sample would have included these people. Those we spoke with had lived or worked in the area and had firsthand knowledge of the circumstances then. Rather than guessing at who might have been whom or wasting time talking with people whose information was at best dubious, Bird's extensive neighborhood knowledge enabled us to identify and then speak with informed sources. We obtained direct first-person accounts of street-group activity in South Los Angeles from the people who had lived it—and were alive to tell the tale. Where there was the occasional and inevitable misrepresentation, it was usually an exaggeration, and we let it slide. We corrected discrepancies later in our notes.

While a number of our interviews were planned, allowing time for serendipity was crucial to gathering the data we needed. Many of the folks we wanted to talk with were appointment resistant, besides not having phones and, in some cases, addresses. At times they would get in the car with us while we rode through their neighborhoods to discuss what had happened here and there, with memories often ignited by familiar surroundings or conversation. This approach was similar to what Mike Tapia did in his research with members of some of the older San Antonio gangs he studied.[7] At other times, we would get out of Bird's hoopty to stand on the street corners with them. On yet other occasions, interviewees would join us at a fast-food parlor for some food and discussion. We had numerous neutral zones. People were cooperative because they wanted to talk, to tell their story, to people who wanted to listen to what they had to say—without judgment—and they knew and trusted Bird. No one was paid, although a few had food, coffee, or soft drinks on us while we talked.

Our interview times would range from twenty minutes to six hours or more, depending on whom we were talking with and what they had to say. Sometimes people would be a bit high on something and thus not especially lucid, so we would reschedule. Some interviews carried over into the next week and the week after that, while still others might be picked up again a month or more later. Although many interviews were taped and transcribed, many were not, depending on the comfort level of the interviewee and our circumstances. When we were together, we both asked questions, supplementing each other as well as further explaining each other's line of inquiry when needed, to make certain we were getting the information we wanted. At other times, we conducted interviews separately from each other when it was inconvenient to get together or when the presence of the other might have made the situation uncomfortable.

The greatest proportion of our interviewees were former gang members, including leaders, regulars, and affiliates. We interviewed their family members, friends, and neighbors too. We also interviewed police, sheriffs, probation officers, community leaders, and other nonaffiliated people who had been on the scene. Together and separately, we interviewed or talked with hundreds of people. In addition, our information was supplemented with historical newspaper articles from neighborhood and city newspapers, copied from microfiche, which CSUDH students helped us gather.[8] We also reviewed the literature on gangs and the historical literature on Los Angeles.

Martin Jankowski writes that he fought with his gang respondents to establish credibility by showing them how tough he was.[9] Although he states he did a portion of his research someplace in Los Angeles, roughing up respondents in South Los Angeles would not have facilitated data gathering; it would have been dangerous there. Fisticuffs with gang members you wanted to interview, where you whacked them around or got whacked around by them, would not have endeared you; nor would it have supplemented your sincerity of purpose.

Disruptions of the Natural Order

Field research, especially with gang members, invites potential elements of risk because most ethnographers are strangers in a strange land.[10] On several occasions, Quicker's presence with Bird caused a stir in the balance of community life. One time, when we were in Watts together looking for people to interview, Bird saw someone he knew who could have been of value to us. He stopped the car and asked Quicker to wait inside while he got out to see if this person was willing to talk with us. He was not. Even though more than twenty years had passed since the Slauson and the Watts street groups had been fighting with each other, this person had no interest in cooperating with anything a Slauson was involved in—especially a Slauson with a White dude accompanying him.

As we pulled up to this Watts guy, Bird sensed a bit of hostility from him before he even got out of the car. This was quite likely amplified by the guy's seeing Quicker in the car. He might have speculated, "Has Bird gone over to the dark side, now cruising neighborhoods with another cop to settle old scores by busting people?" Although he knew Bird, he hadn't seen him in a while, didn't know his current motives, and wasn't much interested in exploring them further—at least not at the moment. This was unfortunate because this guy had been on the set and could have been helpful. Fortunately, this was a rare experience.

Shortly after this encounter, we went back to Bird's neighborhood to continue our research. A few hours later, after our return to Bird's house, Quicker learned how efficiently the *palm tree telegraph* of South Los Angeles could function. Less than an hour after we were in the house, one of Bird's homeboys came by to tell him that so-and-so from Watts saw Bird down there with a "White boy" and wanted to know what he was really up to. Bird dismissed his homeboy's concern by saying that he could go where he wanted and bring whomever he wanted because everyone knew[11] he wasn't going to bring no "lame" or "poot butt" into the neighborhood. Although definitive on Bird's part on the nature of things, this was one interview we were never able to do.

Another time, Quicker was standing with Bird and about a dozen other people at a regular street hangout, in front of a liquor store near the corner of 78th Street and Central Avenue. It was a dark night, about nine o'clock, and we were all talking, when a Los Angeles Police Department cruiser passed by us deliberately slow. They checked us out, shinning a bright flashlight as they gradually passed. Then they stopped. They backed up to where we were all standing, rolled down the window, and moved the light around, illuminating the various people standing there. A number of the people became more than a bit uncomfortable, slipping to the back and trying to hide their faces by looking at the ground or away from the cruiser. But they were not the focus.

When the police saw Quicker, the light stopped moving and stayed on him, the only White person in the crowd. "What are you doing here?" one of the officers queried. Their reasoning was probably that a White male in South Los Angeles at this hour was there looking for one of two things (or both): drugs or sex. This was also during a period when police shootings of unarmed suspects had become all too common. Clearly this was a time for deference. Quicker held his position, looked them in the eye, but gave them a smile, and then replied matter-of-factly that he was talking with friends. They accepted his answer, however skeptical they may have been, and then slowly drove away, the light still on us as they left.[12] Lighthearted laughter and conversation about the incident immediately broke out for a few minutes after the cruiser's departure, which belied the previous tension but not its seriousness.

On another occasion, when Quicker was at a Slauson summer reunion in a large park, he met Eldridge Cleaver. Although Quicker had read his book *Soul on Ice* many years before and knew who he was, Quicker didn't expect to meet him at the reunion. Roach, a leader of the Junior Slausons, introduced them. He told Eldridge that Quicker was a friend of Bird's and that he could talk freely to him. A party with a lot going on when you're trying to talk to a celebrity is not an ideal place to gather data, but Quicker made the best of it. Eldridge was in a party mood, but he took some time out to give him a bit of his side on the time he had spent with the Black Panthers. Quicker learned a lot but mostly, once again, realized the value of serendipity for ethnography; experiences that just happen in the field cannot be replicated by, in Hagedorn's pithy observation, "courthouse criminology."[13]

Field research on gangs, even on older gangs and on older gang members in their own neighborhoods, is not without its adventure. Our travels to converse with the inhabitants of South Los Angeles were like that. We both took calculated risks because we believed the end product was worth it. The streets of this urban laboratory provided us with data that even the most carefully worded closed-end questionnaire from a "captive informant in a captive and alien environment" would never have been able to give us.[14] Our data were oral histories from living experientialist historians.

Our information was not spun by third-person accounts; nor were the gradations of face-to-face encounters in the neighborhoods lost, as they might have been in more controlled settings. In anonymous questionnaires, there are not only multiple and serious questions of validity, but nuances and body language are often either absent or uninterpretable. Our material came directly from the source. We were alert to distortion and checked out further anything that didn't sound right or contradicted what we understood or had heard. We were aware, as S. M. Miller and Frank Riessman made so clear many years ago, that a given response may not have "the same meaning for a lower-class respondent as for a middle-class respondent"[15] and took time after our interviews to make sure that the words we heard meant the same to both of us.

We also conferred on the material we had gathered separately, to make certain it was what we thought it was and to determine its accuracy and relevance. We were able to gather detailed information on a story that needed to be told, a complicated tale of groups that have had almost no accurate previous recognition. We were determined to not let that continue here.

1

When the South Came West

> The resurrection of antebellum southern ideology through the rise of western ideology rewrote American history.
> —Heather Cox Richardson, *How the South Won the Civil War*

Your father's gangs are not the same as your daughter's or your own. Gangs are evolving social phenomena, changing over time and place as they interact with the social environment of which they are a part. "One-shot portraits,"[1] as many researchers present, miss the gang's history and evolution. Gangs are not a "frozen form"[2] but rather are in a constant process of transformation. Frederic Thrasher emphasized that gangs were unique when he wrote that no two of them are alike.[3] One size does not fit all.[4] While gangs have many commonalities, they have many more variations. In effect, if you've seen one gang, well . . . you've seen one gang.[5]

Focusing on the historical processes of gang formation and gang behavior in South Los Angeles, this book breaks with the tradition of some of its predecessors, where these issues have not been their primary research focus.[6] In our city, the focus on gangs has most often been on how to control or eliminate them.[7] Robert Edgerton, quoting former city attorney Reiner on his frustration with gangs, makes this focus unequivocal when he writes, "You feel like the only effective way to deal with street gangs is with a flame thrower."[8] Most researchers have taken as given that gangs here have been a social problem and that our city would be a better place without them and without those associated with them.[9] This generally accepted and usually unexamined opinion is not ours; nor is it our emphasis.

Founded by Afro-Spaniards in 1781,[10] the City of Los Angeles began as the pueblo of Nuestra Senora la Reina de Los Angeles de Porciuncula.[11] Before 1850, interracial marriage was frequently practiced and sanctioned by the church and civil authorities.[12] On the opposite end, the City has also been no stranger to racial violence, and Angelenos no strangers to the use of violence when it helps them in accomplishing their goals. While Carey McWilliams suggests that Los Angeles was less of a city and more of an "enormous village" until 1925,[13] it was also home to "one of the worst race riots in American history" in 1871. Supported by the LAPD police chief, and a "leading member of the City Council," one thousand "White vigilantes" "massacred" nineteen Chinese, in the heart of downtown, because of an earlier fight between some Whites and Chinese, where a mounted policeman was shot. The news of the riot spread east, giving people there an introduction to Los Angeles and earning the City the nom de plume "hellhole of the coast."[14] With an early reputation like this, it's surprising anyone else would want to come to the City, yet come they did.

A Spatial Oasis

A feature that distinguishes Los Angeles from East Coast and Midwest cities, where gangs have been studied more extensively, is its spatial geography.[15] Christopher Rand terms it "grotesque in shape," as it stretches 40 miles north and south yet is "riddled with enclaves" throughout and within its ever-changing borders.[16] It is a city that continues to grow: from 43 square miles in 1900, to 362 square miles in 1920, to 442 in 1930, to 450 in 1946, and 470 in 2021.[17] Edward Soja describes Los Angeles as a "sprawling urban region" and, from the 1920s onward, the "most automobile-oriented city in the world."[18] City transportation was class based. There was an efficient, although range-challenged Red Car and public transportation system that sufficed when employed Angelenos didn't need to travel far to work, but it kept those without a vehicle from following the jobs when they moved from the central city region.[19]

Spread out over an area with downtown[20] on the north and Imperial Highway on the south, Vermont Avenue on the west and Alameda Street on the east, the South Los Angeles gangs occupied a huge area of the City.[21] This geographical distribution, with room to roam, was unique. Los Angeles's automobile culture and halfway decent public transportation system made gang interactions possible and made South Los Angeles feel smaller than it was. South Los Angeles gangland was a web of mostly single-family homes, with yards, lawns, family gardens, shrubs, trees, a few fences, and fewer walls. There were empty lots that nobody seemed to own, perfect for dumping bodies in,[22] numerous green parks with basketball courts, and plenty of space to hang out in. It was all connected by freeways, broad streets, boulevards, avenues, alleys, and cul-de-sacs.

Distributed throughout the neighborhoods were assorted businesses and retail shops. Since most of the neighborhoods were multiuse, and due to lax zoning regulations, there was an unpredictable mixture. Mom-and-pop shops seemed to be everywhere, operating small grocery stores, laundromats, hamburger stands, liquor stores, barbershops, and beauty parlors. There were almost no corporate fast-food joints or much evidence of corporate footprints anywhere until the Alameda Industrial Corridor. There one found defense plants, the Goodyear Tire company, a General Motors assembly plant, and various spice manufactures. A roller-skating rink, bowling alley, and numerous movie theaters added culture. With a few exceptions in Watts, residential structures were one story tall and had parking lots, with plenty of room to park. The spatial oasis street groups existed in was significant in contributing to their extensive physical distribution and in their origins and activities.

The Late Show

When it comes to world-class cities, Los Angeles was a late show. While the large eastern cities were industrializing the narrow tracts of land that defined them, Los Angeles was farming the wide-open spaces of its frontier. Soja calls the City a "peripheral outpost" until 1880.[23] R. J. Smith is not so generous, writing that Los Angeles was, in 1936, an unmistakable outpost to any self-respecting New Yorker and didn't become the intellectual and communications center it became until after World War II.[24]

World War II changed the nature of the City. The War was the event that brought the City into the twentieth century, profoundly altering it and rapidly elevating it to the status of a megacity, on a par with and in some categories exceeding New York and Chicago.[25] It was the War that helped create conditions that brought unprecedented numbers of people, White and Black, searching for jobs in growing defense-related industries. Where the first Great Migration of Black people following World War I mostly missed Los Angeles, the second one, during and after World War II, didn't. It exposed many Black people to hope, and significantly increased their numbers,[26] from 63,744 in 1940 to 763,000 by 1970. Such a dramatic demographic shift changed the political, economic, housing, educational, and law-enforcement landscapes in the City. The vast majorities of Black migrants were from metropolitan areas of Texas and Louisiana and brought with them rich southern traditions that made important cultural contributions to the City. All southern Black migrants shared experiences with Jim Crow racism, the Ku Klux Klan, lynching, and mob violence and they hoped Los Angeles would be different.[27] Hope was realized, lost, and hoped for again.

South Central LA or South LA

David Brotherton notes that "pathologizing tropes" have come to characterize many aspects of gang studies, in turn contributing to "repressive social control policies" and misunderstanding.[28] One of these tropes is the relatively recent but regular use of the concept of South Central Los Angeles (SCLA), or South Central.[29] It is increasingly used unreflectively as a poster child of minority drug and gang violence and is burdened with negative overtones. The concept has helped give the area a "ghettocentric identity."[30] Further, laden with the "pejorative du jour"[31] of murderous teen gangs, the concept has so racialized the area that its original meaning has been lost.[32] SCLA, while potentially useful, has become jaundiced and is no longer just a geographical reference but is now synonymous with gang pathology and a distraction when used.

South Central's conceptual use is derived from South Central Avenue; there is no "North Central," so the Avenue's name is somewhat redundant.[33] In 1955 it was just Central Avenue, as were all the other nearby major north-south avenues, having the prefix *South* added sometime after.[34] The northern terminus of the Avenue begins at 1st Street, the southern edge of downtown Los Angeles, and runs south for sixteen or so miles, passing CSUDH on the east, until it ends at Del Amo Boulevard. It runs through many neighborhoods but is not itself a neighborhood. Similar to what Elijah Anderson has explained about Germantown Avenue in Philadelphia,[35] there are nice parts of the Avenue and other parts that are less so. There is a range of social class families living along it, including middle, working, and poor, from a wide variety of migrant and immigrant racial and ethnic groups.

Referring to South Central as if it were a neighborhood is not only inaccurate but contributes to the negative trope and distracts from an understanding of the early street groups there. SCLA's current implication as an area of racially driven crime brings unneeded prejudice to phenomena already mired in myth, and it was a term used infrequently by the early street-group members. We will use the term *South Los Angeles* instead of *South Central Los Angeles* because of the former's more value-neutral reference. South Los Angeles suggests more or less the same geographical area, although one just a bit broader.[36]

Gangland, LA Style

Central Avenue is known as the "Great Black Way," the focal point of Black cultural development and the spine of the South Los Angeles area.[37] Referred to as "the Avenue" and "the Black Belt," Central Avenue was "like a mighty river," with street tributaries all along it, or, as a band singer once said,

"There are many avenues of the Avenue."[38] For decades, the Avenue has been home to Black residents and home to a broad assortment of various White ethnic immigrants and migrants, Filipinos, Japanese, Chinese, and ethnic Mexicans. But culturally and politically, Black Angelenos put their stamp on it. The Avenue was not Harlem, but it may have been in spirit.[39] The musical contributions of the jazz and blues greats who played there would be enough itself to distinguish the Avenue as the artistic center of Black Angelenos. The Avenue was also the center of South Los Angeles and of Black street-group activity.

Demographically and racially diverse, Los Angeles was a melting pot. McWilliams contends that the 1946 population of Los Angeles "represented important elements of every racial strain that has gone into the making of the American people."[40] Douglas Flamming argues that what distinguished the Avenue was not its "Negro-ness" but rather the "stunning ethnic and racial diversity of the place."[41] He further asserts that the majority of Black people who came to Los Angeles, at least up until 1935, were middle-class in their "values, lifestyle, and aspirations. They believed in the sanctity of home, family, and church: placed a premium on self-discipline and education; and had a penchant for thrift, savings, and acquiring real estate." After 1940 they became less middle-class. Their ambitions, strong as they were, were often "blunted" by "economic racism."[42] Up until the beginning of World War II—at least as far as their values, lifestyle, and aspirations were concerned—Black Angelenos were hardly the underclass people found in so many other cities where gangs have been studied.[43]

There had been established Black communities in areas just south of downtown and in Watts for over a hundred years. From the city center, south to 12th Street, where the B and the U street car lines intersected, Black Angelenos had lived in single-family homes since the City's founding.[44] By the late 1920s, when the Avenue had come alive with nightlife, and clubs such as the Alabam were featuring jazz greats like Billie Holiday and Duke Ellington, luxury hotels like the Somerville, later becoming the Dunbar, hosted W.E.B. Du Bois and the 1928 NAACP National Convention.[45] The Avenue's night life and grand establishments, in place around 42nd Street, helped move the Black community south from 12th Street, and then a bit south again to Vernon Avenue, which is numerically 44th Street, where another two streetcar lines intersected. From Vernon south to Slauson Avenue were "scattershot" Black Angeleno homes and assorted businesses.[46]

Slauson Avenue, between 58th and 59th Streets, was "blood latitude," the northern boundary of a mostly White enclave that extended south to 103rd Street, and was considered by some to be claimed by the Klan.[47] Referred to as the Florence-Firestone District, it had remained populated by mostly White working-class families of European descent until shortly after World

War II. There were even Gypsies within this European diaspora, made up of Armenians, Bulgarians, and Hungarians, living in trailer courts, who always had a "deal" for someone regardless of race (except, Bird notes, for when it came to fixing one's car).

When Bird first moved to East 73rd Street in 1950, his home was the only Black household on the block of about sixty-five houses. The others were five Anglo, five Mexican, and the rest European. By the late 1960s and early 1970s, East 73rd Street was all Black. In early 2020, only ten houses on the block have Black residents. Alameda Street, the industrial corridor, has also been described as a "White Curtain"[48] and a "White wall,"[49] a border for rigid segregation, with Blacks living on the west side and Whites living on the east side.

At the end of the Red Cap line, in the southeastern corner of South Los Angeles, is Watts.[50] Its northern boundary began at 103rd and Central Avenues. With dirt streets that became muddy creeks after a rain, and assorted barnyard critters, like chickens and cows, grazing in backyards and sometimes on the streets, it seemed more like a third-world country than Los Angeles. Many Watts residents called their home "Plum Nelly—plum out of the city and nelly out of the world."[51]

Watts was the most underclass of the Black Los Angeles communities. Many of the Black migrants who settled there were underprivileged rural southerners.[52] Douglas Glasgow notes that 55 percent of the Blacks there were poor in 1959, with unemployment at 25 percent among Black youth.[53] He contends that before World War II, Watts was a "polyglot community" but that its "ghettoization" began during the War.[54] A large percentage of Black Angeleno families in Watts lived in various government-built housing projects. This was one of the few residential areas of the City where there were two-story, multifamily apartment buildings, although unlike the East Coast–style multistory high-rise tenements.

Directly south of Watts is the county area of Willowbrook and the city of Compton. Josh Sides contends that Compton "underwent the most profound racial change of any city in Southern California." It transitioned from a city of mostly White blue-collar residents in the late 1940s to one of mostly Black blue-collar workers and professionals. Violence characterized much of this transition, as White homeowners were beaten by other Whites for listing their homes for sale with a realtor who would sell to Blacks. New Black residents were sometimes forced to defend their homes—with guns—from White mobs threatening violence just because they moved into the neighborhood. Compton became a new "Black suburbia" in the 1960s.[55]

There was fluidity among residents in the Black neighborhoods along the Avenue.[56] Living in spread-out extended family networks, they relocated frequently and easily. This movement contributed to families having relatives living in a variety of different sections within this expansive and somewhat amorphous area. Family juveniles joined neighborhood street groups that were sometimes unfriendly with street groups from neighborhoods other family juveniles lived in. Questions of loyalty—"Are you down with your neighborhood or your cousin?"—while potentially consequential were usually settled amicably.

South Los Angeles was divided into the East-Side and the West-Side, both by the City's maps and by the neighborhood residents. The City's maps used Main Street, which is several blocks west of the Avenue, as the dividing line, while the residents used the Harbor Freeway, now referred to as the 110 Freeway.[57] Of course the residents were aware of the official dividing line, but it often made more sense to them to use the stronger geographical barrier of the freeway as their dividing line.

The East-Side of South Los Angeles should not be confused with East Los Angeles: they were two distinct areas.[58] Flamming writes that the "West-Side meant wealthier and Whiter," and that "no one spoke of a South-Side."[59] The West-Side, particularly the West Adams and West Jefferson Districts and Baldwin Hills, became home to middle-class Blacks who, when they moved there, brought their businesses with them. Those who moved from the East-Side have been accused of "Black flight," although that's not how some of the movers saw it. They claimed they weren't running from anyplace but rather wanted to move to a "better place to live."[60]

Different Areas, Different Gangs, Different Attention

Northeast of South Los Angeles, and geographically separated by Boyle Heights, freeways, and the Los Angeles River, is the unincorporated community of East Los Angeles. Largely populated by Latinos, it is this northeastern area of Los Angeles County that has been traditionally identified with Los Angeles gangs. But a distinct cultural, racial, ethnic, linguistic, and historical chasm separates South Los Angeles from East Los Angeles. The physical barriers of freeways and the river have contributed to the areas' respective distinctiveness.[61] Gangs developed in both areas, but interactions between them were largely indirect.[62] When they did interact, it is quite likely that neither areas' groups dominated the other.[63]

Whereas South Los Angeles is a community that is mostly part of the City of Los Angeles, and therefore primarily under the jurisdiction of the Los Angeles Police Department (LAPD), East Los Angeles is part of Los Angeles

County and patrolled exclusively by the Los Angeles County Sheriff's Department (LASD). The Florence-Firestone District of South Los Angeles was under both LASD's and LAPD's jurisdiction, giving the largest sheriff's department in the world and the third-largest police department in the United States authority there.[64]

A major difference between South Los Angeles and East Los Angeles gangs has been the amount of attention given to them. The Sleepy Lagoon case in 1942, where a Mexican youth was allegedly murdered by gang members, and the Zoot-Suit Riots in 1943, where off-duty military personnel attacked Mexicans and their girlfriends, were central in establishing East Los Angeles and its gangs firmly in the minds of many. These incidents made early Los Angeles gangs practically synonymous with East Los Angeles. While much has been written documenting the racist attitudes and brutality of some of the sheriffs involved in the Zoot-Suit Riots, the possible fascist political motivations of the press and a populace needing local hate objects to substitute for a distant foreign enemy are other noteworthy considerations contributing to the riots.[65] The riots launched the terms *gang*, *crime*, *zoot suit*, and *Mexican* into the national lexicon about Los Angeles, making them practically synonymous with one another.[66]

Finally, numerous researchers have studied and written about East Los Angeles gangs for years, unwittingly contributing to the perception they were the only early gangs existing in Los Angeles.[67] Initial official attention to South Los Angeles gangs was considerably less, while academic attention was limited, making it appear as though there were no gangs there.

Unmeltables in the Melting Pot[68]

William Wilson's heuristic, "the declining significance of race,"[69] if referencing Los Angeles, would be more accurately stated as the *increasing significance* of race.[70] Glasgow notes that the primary difference between racism in the 1930s and the 1960s in Los Angeles is that it just became more hidden, more covert.[71] Cornel West offers strong evidence in his classic work on race that racism has in fact increased since the 1960s,[72] while John Hagedorn, emphasizing the crucial importance of race in gang studies, asserts that racism is an independent variable—a permanent, indestructible component of our society, showing little sign of abatement.[73]

There is no shortage of literature discussing the ways European ethnic groups have blended into America as they settled in to become part of the mixture in the great melting pot.[74] Often associated with their blend is the rhetorical question of why other groups, especially Black Americans, have been "unable" to blend too. "It must be because they don't want to" is the often ill-informed explanation given. In fact, the primary reason for European "melting" was that they were already White and didn't need to change a lot to fit: lose their accent, modify their last name, stop identifying with their native country, get hired at a decent job, get some money, buy proper clothes, misrepresent when necessary, and—boom—they'd blended.[75]

Melting in was facilitated by skin color: the Whiter the person appeared, the easier the melt. Randol Contreras explains how male Dominican drug robbers in the South Bronx tried to blend in by "improving their race" with White or lighter-skinned women whom they wanted as mothers for their children.[76] In Los Angeles, passing for White, or at least lighter skin, brought many benefits, as the history of Korla Pandit demonstrates. Passing as an immigrant from Delhi India, where his "privileged" childhood gave him a marvelous gift of gab, he hid his true origins as an African American and was able to parlay his fake background into becoming the first Black person in Los Angeles to have his own TV show.[77] Ethnic Mexicans in Los Angeles, although clearly in a category that was regularly discriminated against, were different. Their complexion placed them somewhere between a Black and White person and gave them more opportunities.[78]

Sides contends that since Whites benefitted from Mexican labor, they were considered "a necessary evil, while Blacks were both unnecessary and evil."[79] Another dose of unmeltable discrimination can be found in the case of Japanese and Black relations after World War II. During the War, Japanese Angelenos had their property confiscated by paranoid White authorities and then had their entire families locked up in internment camps in harsh environments, for years. Who would they side with after they were released: Whites or Blacks?

Before we answer this question, we should note that Little Tokyo, near downtown, the home of Japanese Angelenos, was left abandoned after their roundup and that the growing Black population coming to Los Angeles for jobs in the war industries needed places to live, if only temporarily. The Little Tokyo area, with its empty structures, became a free zone, a zone without rules, the "Wild West," where enterprising Blacks moved into, set up house, and opened businesses. Renamed Bronzeville, it became home to many Black Angelenos until the War's end. Friction marked the return of the Japanese as they evicted, fought with, and legally challenged the Black trespassers. No such friction developed between Whites and Japanese, as they accepted each other, albeit a bit warily at first.[80]

Rand has noted that the "U.S. frontier culture has always been racist."[81] Los Angeles, with its "cult of Anglo-Saxonness"[82] among White migrants to the city, had become the most "WASPish" of big cities by 1960.[83] From almost any point of view, Los Angeles's history was the essence of an urban racist environment. Not only were Black Angelenos restricted by racist housing codes, community covenants, and the underhanded tactics of realtors and banks in keeping them from living where they could afford and wanted to live, but certain public spaces were off limits to them as well. Although laws restricting them in public places didn't exist, de facto practices did. They could swim in public swimming pools only on certain days and were limited to using just a couple of beaches along the expansive Los Angeles coastline.[84] If they extended their stay on those beaches until after dark, like White Angelenos were allowed to do, the police provided an unvolitional escort off. Such arrangements were a way of life for Black Angelenos well into the 1940s.

The insidiousness of racism against Black Americans is not always easy for White people to comprehend, regardless of how they might try or how good their hearts are. After the 1965 Watts Rebellion, Walter Mosely, a Los Angeles novelist with a deep understanding of the Black community, wrote an insightful book titled *Little Scarlet*, where he tried to make sense out of the underlying elements of racism Black Angelenos understood about the Rebellion. His main character, Easy Rawlins, a wise and itinerant Black detective, tried to explain the pain of racism to a White woman who, in spite of her efforts, couldn't quite grasp the reasons why Black people would "destroy their own community." Easy explains:

> This is a tough place, Ada. You got working men and women all fenced in together, brooding about what they see and what they can't have. Almost every one of them works for a White man. Every child is brought up thinking that only White people make things, rule countries, have history. They all come from the South. They all come from racism so bad that they don't even know what it's like to walk around with your head held high. They get nervous when the police drive by. They get angry when their children are dragged off in chains. . . . Almost every Black man, woman, and child you meet feels that anger.[85]

Being Black in Los Angeles puts a "mask," "a veil of racial inferiority and servility mandated by Jim Crow laws,"[86] on Black Angelenos. It hasn't been removed.

It's Not about Money

Liberals, Flamming maintains, tend to believe that the "Negro problem" is an economic one: Whites have money, Blacks are poor; eradicate their poverty, and White racism vanishes, their thinking goes.[87] In Los Angeles, a large percentage of the Whites who migrated there from the Jim Crow south. They were characterized as "Okies," who held on to their "culture of White supremacy"[88] and helped to southernize the City with an ideology that southern Black migrants were trying to escape. White southerners migrated to the City, along with thousands of southern Blacks, giving Los Angeles in 1940 the largest Black population of any other city in the west.[89] White southern ideology held that Blacks were more criminal than Whites, were to be feared, and that the further Blacks could be kept from them and their families, the safer they would be.

Jim Crow ideology became institutional practice in Los Angeles. As southern Whites gained positions of power, they marginalized Black Angelenos even further, because of their Blackness. Black became the "most basic non-White group," the "fundamental 'other,'"[90] where their skin elicited emotions of, at best, social distance but more often hate and resentment. The ideology didn't subside, although its emergence into covertness might have made it seem so.[91] Racism continued but was repackaged in a more benign-appearing container.

A lot of racism was not covert; nor were there attempts to make it so. Cle Sloan, in his documentary *Bastards of the Party*, demonstrates this clearly regarding the LAPD. In the film, Mike Davis comments that LAPD's Chief William H. Parker was a "steadfast racist" who "declared war on race mixing along Central Avenue" and purposely recruited southern Whites for the department, especially those who had been in the military, because he felt that they supported his ideology. Chili, from the Gladiators, confirms Davis's position, stating that the police "started lynching us, but called it justifiable homicide." "We had no rights," he continues. "They called us 'nigger' and talked about our mamas." A former Black Panther said: "There's absolutely no difference between the way the police treated us in Mississippi than the way they did in California. They might not have called you 'nigger' every day, but they treated you the same way."[92]

Better is, of course, a relative term—so we always have to ask: Compared to what?[93] Smith states that well into the 1930s, Black Angelenos did better than Blacks in many other areas of the country.[94] Sides points out that in 1910, almost 40 percent of Black Angelenos in the county owned their own homes, compared to 2.4 percent in New York and 8 percent in Chicago.[95] Many middle-class Black Angelenos utilized the option of moving to "better" neighborhoods. There may have been good reason to believe that the "western freedom" Los Angeles offered was Black Angelenos' best hope.[96] After all, it was a city of abundant sunshine, warm weather, no snow, jobs, and lots of space to buy or build affordable homes. While the first Great Migration of World War I mostly bypassed the west, those Black migrants who did come to Los Angeles were city people, with a little money,[97] and they came with hope for a better life. The life they found was better, in most cases, than the life they had left. But racism lived here and hid there[98] throughout the City and still does.

Rather Be Judged by Twelve than Carried by Six

Racism was frequently accompanied by violence. Most Black Angelenos were no stranger to White violence, having left a Jim Crow south where lynching was an ever-present threat and all too common practice. Lynching didn't occur in Los Angeles, but workplace and homeplace violence did. Sides writes that the anti-Black hostility and violence among White homeowners, between World War II and the late 1960s, "forever" undermined the "relative racial peace" existing in the prewar years.[99]

There's little argument that racial violence increased after World War II, but all was not well before the War either, as Flamming notes in describing the situation Eula and Jule Deckard experienced. The Deckards were forced to defend their home on E. Fifty-Eighth Place, between Central and Hooper Avenues, in the 1920s, from a "mob" of angry Whites, some of whom were local sheriffs, intent on doing them harm because they had bought a home in a White area and had the audacity to occupy it. When the threat became imminent, Jule Deckard grabbed his World War I Winchester and rounded up a group of his buddies, who stood guard for a month at his home, until the threat ended.[100]

Black workers in the shipyards during World War II sometimes carried handguns to work to defend themselves from White worker gangs, who would jump on the outnumbered Blacks in the parking lot when they were leaving work.[101] Smith points out that Black workers were forced to carry weapons to work, especially those who left after dark. White workers, many of whom were southerners, would gang up on Blacks leaving alone and beat them, sometimes badly. When the Blacks fought back, they would be arrested for fighting or, in at least one case, shot.[102] Black workers learned to leave work in armed groups to minimize getting hurt. The famous Black writer Chester Himes, during the War years, is quoted as commenting that when at home, he kept his Winchester "within reach at all times," concerned about the potential violence that never seemed very far away.[103]

Black Angelenos understood that whether Los Angeles was going to be heaven or hell depended on them taking care of themselves, sometimes in groups, and with weapons when necessary. Bird notes that every Black family that came from the south brought the weapons they had at home with them. If they broke the law by carrying a concealed gun, and then broke it again to defend themselves, with a potential for repercussions, possession and use would at least have given them a chance to stay alive. It was far better, many reasoned, to face a trial than to face the mortician.

Rosie the Riveter: The Metamorphosis of Los Angeles

Before World War II the spatial vastness of the City minimized nonvolitional contact between Black and White people, because there was room to spread out and the Black population was "small, isolated, and invisible."[104] During and after the War, racial contact increased because previously existing empty spaces were becoming filled by changing demographics. As Sides makes clear, "virulent anti-Black racism the likes of which the city had never known" came with the War and in the following two decades.[105] Banks, realtors, tract developers, and White home sellers were in cahoots to keep Black buyers out of some areas, restricting them to various neighborhoods along the Avenue and to Watts.[106]

As a result of these efforts to contain the growing populations in racially separate areas, postwar communities became more homogeneous, and high schools and junior high schools began to lose their multiracial character, becoming both Whiter and more non-White.[107] None of these changes occurred without periods of violence, both from Whites who were resentful of losing potential profit on the sale of their houses toward Black neighbors and from Blacks defending their homes from White neighbors angry that a Black family had moved into their neighborhood.

One of the strongest cultural icons of World War II was Rosie the Riveter. While Los Angeles women of all races and ethnicities were involved in the War effort, in most depictions, Rosie was a White woman.[108] Bird, whose mother was a riveter in one of the defense plants, took notice. The War brought people of all races together to work toward a common goal of winning, but the effort was fraught with racism from the start: White workers didn't want to work alongside Black workers, and White corporations and bosses didn't want to hire them. It was an uncomfortable fit for many, especially after President Franklin D. Roosevelt passed laws prohibiting discrimination in defense hiring.

Jobs were available, and non-Whites were hired, while discriminatory practices placed them in the dirtiest, most dangerous, and least remunerative positions. The War produced labor shortages, which necessitated the need to hire Black and female workers, although where and at what pay have been less emphasized in our national memory. Laws were passed to stop housing discrimination, allowing the burgeoning numbers of Black migrants to move into previously restricted neighborhoods.[109] For those who were able to manage their money, and due to the relative abundance and cheapness of housing, homeownership was often realized. Bird's parents, for example, bought their home on East 73rd Street in 1953 and had their bank debt on it retired in 1963.

An especially alienating aspect of the continuing racially restrictive housing policies was one that allowed Blacks to purchase homes in many neighborhoods but not live in them. We welcome your money because it is green, so the ideology went, but not you because you're non-White. During the War, some of the attempts at keeping Blacks out of certain White neighborhoods were to equate Black presence there with that of the hated Japanese, just in case any White residents didn't get how odious Black people were to be thought of. These efforts tried to keep both groups out. Smith notes that Los Angeles "racism was manifest not through laws but through geography." Further, he contends, denial of homeownership was a "revocation of citizenship rights." Blacks could be kept invisible and nonproblematic if they could be kept out of White communities, where out of sight could more easily mean out of mind.[110]

"When the Truth Is Found to Be Lies"[111]

Willful ignorance rather than reasoned analysis often characterizes attempts to understand crime and gangs. A number of writers have indicated how myths, lies, distortions, and moral panics have defined the perspective many people have on crime and juvenile delinquency.[112] Joan Moore and others have demonstrated how many of these same factors have muddied the waters of comprehension when it comes to gangs.[113] When racism is thrown into the mix and blended in, the myths become just that much easier to accept and way more difficult to disentangle. Say it often enough and loud enough, and people will not only believe but will also refute efforts to show otherwise. We found this to be the case when it came to understanding crime among Black Angelenos.

Many Angelenos presumed that Blacks had a greater potential for crime and violence than Whites, due to their "natural inferiority." White criminals, the myth continued, were an exception, while Black criminals were to be expected.[114] Los Angeles "Negroes" were candidly spoken of by resident Whites as inferior.[115] Quicker used to take surveys in his classes on what students thought the typical gang member looked like to the student, as well as to members of their families and the public. Invariably, being non-White, particularly Black or Chicano, was the leading characteristic of a gang member.[116] Martin Schiesl supplemented these beliefs with his research showing that White Los Angeles police officers saw Blacks as being "predisposed" to violent crime.[117]

Helping White southern ideology to promote these beliefs was LAPD's Chief Parker's use of the bully pulpit. He and his carefully recruited officers maintained an ideological facility that understood Blacks as crime ridden. Davis argues that Parker was a "puritanical crusader against race mixing" and used this assumption to raid and shutter Black nightclubs. He *manipulated* police data, which some critics believe continues today, and used "phony crime statistics" to denigrate Blacks living in the projects as engaged in "jungle life." He "invoked racialized crime scares," "projected the specter of a vast criminal reservoir in Southcentral L.A.," and vehemently opposed the extension of constitutional rights to juveniles, Davis maintained.[118]

Davis asserts further that, along with Parker's FBI counterpart, director J. Edgar Hoover, Parker began to realize the Los Angeles gang problem was part of the "overarching structure of the Black menace."[119] Rand claims that Parker's LAPD had a worse record of police brutality against Black and Mexican people than many other cities, including San Francisco and New York. He quotes Parker as saying, "Negroes just happen to figure into most of the city's crime," and Mexicans "are not far removed from the wild tribes of Mexico."[120] There can be little doubt that Black and Mexican Angelenos and their children had two strikes against them in Los Angeles before they even came up to bat.

Ironically, there was readily available evidence to dispute, or at least raise doubt about, these allegations, which didn't seem to matter much to what a majority of Whites believed. John McGroarty, a *Los Angeles Times* editor, wrote on his popular editorial page, that "our court records show that our colored citizens are, as a rule, close observers of the written law."[121] Sides notes that Black homeowners had no foreclosures on Federal Housing Administration loans, had a delinquency rate on payments similar to Whites, and took "great pride in their property" with their fastidiousness and proper landscaping.[122] Negative attitudes toward Black Angelenos were myth driven rather than data driven. The myths were facilitated by a shared basic racism among the White populace and by persons of authority who promoted them.

Myths have at least a link or two to reality, however tenuous, or they wouldn't have a basis for belief in the first place. Black people, just like every other racial or ethnic group, had devils living among angels, and everything in between. There were people who went to church and obeyed the law and ones who didn't. Sides notes that a concentration of brothels and after-hours bars in Bronzeville added to the myth among many Whites that Blacks were disproportionately prone to illicit activity.[123] For one to believe this was a one-way ticket, one would have to ignore the fact that many of the patrons of these forbidden places were White. Sides further shows that although there was a rise in crime during World War II, the data were not broken down by race. Occurring about the same time as the rise in crime was a rise in unemployment in a number of Black communities from the late 1960s and 1970s, suggesting a possible correlation between the two.[124] While this potentiality was mitigated by weak data, it implied a simple causal relationship that helped enhance internalized racial mythology.

Industrial Change

Central among those who have established the relationship between deindustrialization and the subsequent devastation of inner city communities is William J. Wilson, with his work in Chicago.[125] Building on Wilson's framework, Hagedorn demonstrates how the disappearance of industrial jobs from Milwaukee changed the gangs there into more seriously delinquent groups.[126] In his international research with gangs, Hagedorn expands on his previous analysis of the effects of deindustrialization to conclude that demoralization and the intractability of racism compound the problem for non-Whites, contributing to increased violence in gangs.[127]

The history of Los Angeles, following the industrialization-deindustrialization theoretical paradigm explained by Hagedorn, threw in two twists that helped account for changes in South Los Angeles's gangs: *selective deindustrialization* along the Alameda Industrial Corridor and *selective reindustrialization* in the periphery. These trends began before the 1965 Watts Rebellion and continued after it. They were the "critical fulcrum" around which social and spatial restructuring revolved that created labor market segmentation.[128] Many in the Black communities along the Corridor became poorer and more marginalized, while the periphery became Whiter and prosperous.

The Rebellion was a symptom of Los Angeles's restructuring, not its cause. As blue-collar jobs disappeared from the Corridor, technical jobs moved to and were created within the urbanizing periphery, while low-paying jobs in the garment industry were newly created in the urban core. It seemed like two steps forward and then three back for the Black communities, as these structural changes were harmful to their economic well-being. The deindustrialization processes Hagedorn identified as negatively affecting Chicago and other cities around the world similarly compounded the problems for Black Angelenos in the Corridor, as their livelihoods were stripped from them, and with that went greatly reduced chances at realizing middle-classdom.

Space Makes a Place

From 1880 through 1920, Los Angeles County grew from a population of 35,000 to almost 1 million. From 1920 to 1940, another 2 million were added,[129] and by 1970 the population was over 7 million. The Black population of the City grew from 38,844 in 1930 to over 750,000 by 1970.[130] Black Angelenos experienced some of their greatest economic advancements in the twenty years after World War II, as the growth in their mainstay blue-collar jobs, which were significantly augmented during the War, continued increasing.[131] Moore notes that the defense industry supplied 40 percent of the manufacturing jobs in the 1950s.[132]

The Los Angeles urban region is an immense and sprawling area, with Los Angeles County alone comprising 4,084 square miles.[133] With few natural barriers, other than some low mountain passes, and a freeway system that provides 65 mph passageways,[134] corporations could set up shop in areas not so distant.[135] When issues in the city core became problems, corporations fled easily to the periphery and left behind unskilled workers, whose poorly functioning vehicles, or absence of them, made it difficult for many of them to follow the jobs.

The efficient and extensive rail transportation system, which stopped operating in 1961,[136] had made it possible for workers in the Alameda Industrial Corridor to travel the short distances from home to work and back. While never achieving economic or job parity with White workers, and continually battling racism in unions, many of which defended White privilege,[137] Black workers' job categories also made them ineligible to follow the industries when they restructured in the outlying suburban areas.[138] Space made a place for change that advantaged some while disadvantaging others.

Occupationally anchoring South Los Angeles before deindustrialization were the booming automotive, steel, aerospace, and rubber-tire industries. There were other smaller factories too, mom-and-pop shops, and various small businesses providing employment. During the years following World War II and the Korean War, industries that had been part of the defense effort employed Black workers who were needed in lower blue-collar jobs. In the Stacy Peralta documentary *Crips and Bloods*, Sides argues that the potential for careers at major corporations like GM, Chrysler, Ford, Goodyear, and Firestone in South Los Angeles provided a moment of realizable optimism for Black residents, who could see opportunities for merging into the middle class through their hard work. The American Dream appeared realistically within reach. But it was not to be. For Black Angelenos, the effect of the disappearance of their former blue-collar jobs and the absence of decent new ones was a game changer.

After having received massive government defense subsides and moving to the restructuring periphery, the industries "selectively reconstructed." People with the means to follow contributed to the area's urbanization by creating what Soja refers to as new "technopolitan industrial complexes."[139] The siren song of greater profit provided the motivation for the deindustrialization of Los Angeles's core and reindustrialization of the periphery.

Reindustrialization was facilitated by cheap and plentiful land, which allowed for massive plants and homes to be built at bargain prices. Soja asserts that a primary reason behind the spatial restructuring of Los Angeles was to gain better control over the labor force,[140] accomplished through a reduction of racial tensions by keeping the workforce White in industries and communities where Black people were unquestionably unwelcome. Most Black Angelenos, rather than chasing after the unappealing restructured environment, stayed along the Avenue, where deindustrialization and their changing demographic contributed to poorer, less favorable, and less diversified communities.

Black Adaptation

Black Angelenos stayed behind because many had neither the skills nor resources to follow, having been denied access to training programs—because they were Black—that could have prepared them for more technical jobs. Longshore work in the harbor area denied Black people access to apprentice programs; the aircraft industry employers believed "aircraft work was White men's work" and wouldn't hire Black employees, except as janitors; aerospace apprenticeship programs in most suburban communities wouldn't take Black applicants; and suburban communities in the San Fernando Valley and Orange County, where much of the reindustrialization occurred, wouldn't allow Blacks to obtain housing.[141]

Importantly, many Black Angelenos were uninterested in relocating to areas where they weren't wanted because they were Black and leaving communities where they were wanted, because they were Black.[142] As Glasgow argues, numerous researchers have missed understanding that Black culture has relied on its "determination to maintain a community," a propensity he believes that has both negative and positive aspects.[143] A number of extended families, like Bird's, for example, had established deep roots in the communities along the Avenue and just didn't want to tear them out to follow an illusion to remote suburbias, where they had no roots.

Some middle-class Blacks moved to West-Side neighborhoods, where the hard-fought battles of housing discrimination had become settled, as the population along the Avenue continued to grow with poorer migrants. Flamming suggests that the growing population itself contributed to a population too large to remain a single community, instead helping it evolve as separate communities of more loosely related groups with different outlooks and opportunities.[144] Such diversity made rivalries more imminent, particularly among juveniles, who were searching for identity within their communities and peer groups.[145] Community diversification set the stage for the development of *in-groupism* and *out-groupism*.

Black women, who "always worked in higher proportions than White women," had a different experience with spatial restructuring than men. Sides argues that part of the reason for this was that women appeared less threatening to employers than men. Black women made "dramatic occupational and economic gains" in the two decades after the War.[146] Their labor was much needed during the War and then afterward, especially in the burgeoning garment industry, where they had an easier adaptation to the low wages.

But it was in public-sector clerical work that Black women found some of their greatest opportunities and where they were able to gain considerable economic parity with men. Sides writes: "The rapid growth of the California state government during the 1950s and 1960s created thousands of new clerical jobs," which employed Black women and gave them financial independence. Finally, Black working mothers who found themselves without babysitters adopted communal exchange relationships with other mothers for babysitting services, thereby helping to build tight bonds with one another.[147] The powerful role Black women played in their families, especially their economic strength, enabled some women to help their families relocate to more affluent West-Side neighborhoods.

Made by Adults

We have set the stage for the environment in which gangs in Los Angeles were discovered. Understanding the historical processes contributing to gang formation is not a simple causal relationship in which change A produces result B. Social understanding is unlike understanding, say, the reactions of chemicals, where A always results in C when mixed with the correct proportion of B. Complex social phenomena are rarely so straightforward, while efforts to make it so have resulted in misunderstanding.

The stage is the world adults created for and then presented to their children. If, as the wise words of Gary Jensen and Dean Rojek dramatize, we want to understand juvenile gangs, we must "consider the behavior of the young in the context of a world handed to them by adults."[148] Juveniles inherit the world adults generate for them and do the best they can with the hand they have drawn. To be critical of what juveniles do with what they have been given, without also considering the adults and what they have been doing and continue to do, is to engage in myopic accountability.

2

Assemblies of Juveniles

The social scientist has no business attempting to "adjust" people to the moral norms of his society or any other.
—**Ned Polsky**, *Hustlers, Beats, and Others*

Over one hundred years ago, the Russian anthropologist Petr Kropotkin, in *Mutual Aid*, gave a proper wake to Hobbes's theories of "mankind" as a "loose aggregation of beings always ready to fight with each other." Life began for our species, Kropotkin theorized, as groups of families living in larger groups called *tribes*—for mutual defense, advantages in hunting, rearing offspring, or "enjoying life in common"—enabling us to prosper as a result. If we had been in constant warfare with each other, as Hobbes theorized, we never would have been able to develop the societies we have been able to create, Kropotkin countered, because we needed each other.[1]

Mutual aid worked well, so well that by the twenty-first century, and with billions of people added beyond the early paleogroups, things had gotten more complicated but also shown how successful we were at cooperating in groups.[2] If we lose sight of our fundamental social nature, we miss understanding our inherent group nature.

A consequence of being human is that we live in groups. Whether two or two thousand and beyond, we live in groups that are both bestowed upon us and those we choose. It is far easier to understand involvement in groups that are bestowed than it is to understand involvement in those we choose. We are born into an assortment of bestowed, or *ascribed*, groups; as we mature, we form and join other groups that we choose: *achieved* groups.[3] Our groups are as fundamental a part of our lives as the food we eat.

The Search for Gangs

Humans who don't group with other humans are rare. They are referred to in a variety of judgmental ways, all of which suggest maladjustment. Whether our group's opinions and behavior are right or wrong, we usually recognize, honor, and respect them. We defend our *in-groups*, while we oppose, disprove of, criticize, and battle with our *out-groups*. Our in-groups socialize us. They teach us what to accept and what to reject; our in-groups are "good," while our out-groups are "bad." We deal with our ascribed groups, while we change our achieved groups. Our groups have names, some of which we have control over, others of which we have little.

When juveniles in South Los Angeles grouped with one another, it was because they enjoyed each other's company, were the same age, lived next door, lived on the same block, lived in the same neighborhood, hung out at the same spot, went to the same schools, or were from the same racial or ethnic group.[4] Maturation and independence were key in contributing to the relationships juveniles formed: at school, the park, street corner, skating rink, hamburger stand, backyard, or movie theater.

Age similarities and geographical proximity were two of the most important criteria in the formation of juvenile groups. Similar interests created friendships that played an increasingly important role in group choice. As the number of juveniles increased, in-group choice became more selective. Racial identity seemed more important for group formation in some neighborhoods than in others but grew in importance as neighborhood demographics changed.

Numerous informal juvenile street groups formed in South Los Angeles. They ranged in size from a few individuals to many hundreds. They sometimes lasted for years, or for weeks, or for periods in between.. Most of these groups didn't have formal beginnings or founding dates scribed in historical accounts. Every group's membership was composed of juveniles: there were no adults; nor were the groups extensions of, or junior to or subsidiaries of, existing adult organizations.[5] While many youths were aware of adult political power structures and criminal groups, such groups were external to their lives.[6] Called "gangs" by the police and media, they referred to themselves less pejoratively, with names like *clubs*, *cliques*, and *sets*.

John Hagedorn writes that considerable effort has been expended searching for a definition of the term *gang* that all can agree to.[7] Since the days of Frederic Thrasher, there have been about as many definitions of gangs as there have been gang researchers. There are two general perspectives on definitions. The *control* perspective, articulated by "gang pathologists,"[8] which uses criminal justice definitions. This perspective perceives gangs as essentially different from other juvenile groups, notable by their greater amounts of delinquency.[9] A second perspective, used by ethnographers and others, seeks understanding of how gangs connect to their history, their neighborhoods, and the larger political economy. It is a search for definition based on the *processes* that form the groups.[10] Efforts to establish a uniform definition have been frustrated by the different political positions each perspective brings to the gang phenomena: the control group wants to suppress them, while the process group wants to understand them. As different as these perspectives have been, it seems unlikely they will be able to compromise without fundamental ideological compromises.

When Is a Group a Gang?

A group is a gang when those who control the definitions say it is. Both C. Wright Mills and G. William Domhoff have pointed out that the task of defining right from wrong and good from bad is primarily a prerogative of the "power elite,"[11] or the "upper class," who accomplish it directly or indirectly through their operatives.[12] Richard Quinney's seminal work offers an often overlooked and underappreciated theory of criminal law that argues all explanations of crime are both political and moral. He asserts that no understanding of crime can proceed without recognition of the existing social order.[13] Quinney asserts that the ruling groups of our society shape criminal law by defining as criminal behaviors that conflict with their interests. The formulation of criminal definitions is a political act, he contends, intended to advance the interests of a society's ruling groups.[14] We hypothesize that gang definitions, including the concept of gang itself and its application, are regulated by *power elite* ideology,[15] which serves this groups' interests and restricts support from those who would suggest otherwise. Underclass and non-White groups are the usual suspects for the gang label.

In their work on gang definitions, Robert Bursik and Harold Grasmick lead us down a tricky conceptual path with a description of what appears to be a gang-involved violent crime. After convincing the reader of the dastardly behavior of this gang, a group whose behavior fits easily into control theorists' definitions, the researchers throw in the twist: this wasn't actually a gang-involved gang rape, yet it was a gang rape, occurring at a prestigious East Coast university carried out by male fraternity members.[16] Fraternities are upper- and middle-class-based groups that, regardless of their criminality, are exempt from the gang label. For years, Bird observed the rancorous and drunken behavior of fraternities at the University of Southern California (a wealthy private university in South Los Angeles) that flew under the LAPD's radar but would have been picked up immediately if the behavior had come from a neighborhood street group.

Both the LASD and the LAPD have had groups within their gang enforcement units referred to as "gangs" by various writers and researchers, including a federal judge presiding over a class-action hearing against the LASD. Two *Los Angeles Times* writers state: "The groups—with macho monikers like the Pirates, Vikings, Rattlesnakes and Cavemen—have long been a subculture in the country's largest sheriff's department and, in some cases, an inside track to acceptance in the ranks."[17] While law-enforcement subcultures have been publicly reprimanded by departmental leadership, evidence suggests many of them not only continue to exist but are headed by department leaders who secretly sanction the group and its behavior.[18]

Official denial that these groups are gangs has been largely successful in keeping the gang label from sticking, regardless of how closely the group's behavior fits the control perspective's definitions of gang. To wit: the disgraced former Los Angeles County undersheriff Paul Tanaka was a "tattooed member of the Lynwood Vikings, a group of deputies who many assert made a sport or initiation rite out of violence against the communities they patrolled and the people they jailed."[19] Tanaka, who was also the mayor of Gardena, made an unsuccessful run to be sheriff before he was finally convicted in federal court on charges of conspiracy to obstruct justice and obstruction of justice. He was given a five-year sentence.[20] Herman and Julia Schwendinger's finding that an upper-class juvenile in eighteenth-century England, from a "maliciously violent" gang, could receive a judgeship and be knighted suggests who you are, not what you do, has ruled gang definitions for a long time.[21]

The Invention of Adolescence Begat the Invention of Delinquency

Juvenile gangs stem from two concepts whose historical roots are essential to gang research but whose influence has often been discounted: adolescence[22] and delinquency. These are the conceptual building blocks of the juvenile gang. They were created in an environment of capitalist development where all hands were on deck agreeing on the necessity for their creation.[23] David Bakan notes that adolescence was created as an intermediary period between childhood and adulthood, added to fulfill the needs of a newly emerging urban-industrial society following the Civil War.[24] Industrialization required a better trained and, especially, disciplined workforce, as Anthony Platt demonstrates, one that was able to follow the rules.[25] Adolescents unable or unwilling to abide by industrial demands posed a problem for the captains of industry who needed their labor power or, at the least, wanted them off the streets and out of public view, where their debauched behavior threatened the Protestant ethic's notion of hard work as the gateway to heaven American capitalists were promoting.

Industry captains and others of the power elite were most concerned about children of the poor. Originally referred to as children of the "dangerous classes," these classes had posed an existential revolutionary threat to the early industrialists.[26] After their threat weakened, their children still posed a problem. Platt argues that as the number of misbehaving poor children increased, they required their own special term for identification. Naming them "juvenile delinquents" was the master stroke that led to the "invention" of the concept of delinquency as a category just for them.[27] Delinquency was born out of the necessity of identifying a problem population and out of the need to give a name to an emerging group of poor children loosened from their families by industrial work requirements in urban centers and now in the streets and causing difficulties.[28]

Young poor people, by behaving young although not necessarily breaking any laws, required special control too. Problem solved: the court created *juvenile statutes*, a series of proscribed behaviors that, when adjudicated, gave the courts the same kind of control over the lives of adolescents that a middle-class parent might exercise. Juvenile statutes were comprehensive statements of morality that were so broad and so open to discriminatory interpretation by juvenile judges that any adolescent could be caught up by them and made a *ward of the court*, depending on the whims of the judge.[29]

Adolescence Is a Group Thing

Adolescence has become an important period in the progression to adulthood. There is no other period in the life cycle when peer groups are more important than they are during adolescence.[30] How many parents have had the experience of asking their teenager how their day went, only to hear a conversation stopper reply, "Okay," followed by nonverbal body language saying, *Please don't ask me anymore questions because you wouldn't understand*, then to have the teen engage in hours of interactions with their friends? During these peer periods, adolescents are involved in creating themselves, developing their identities, establishing relationships with same- and opposite-sex peers, and getting ready to assume adult roles. Diego Vigil notes that adolescence is a time of "confusion" and that, as they spend increased time with peers, they are likely to experiment with proscribed behavior, like drinking, fighting, and the "flaunting" of social norms.[31]

G. Stanley Hall, in his classic work on adolescence, found that it was a time of "ardent passions," dangerous to but crucial for the formation of character.[32] Among Hall's many findings was the nonclass and nonracially linked idea that adolescents as a group were often overaggressive.[33] "All boys," he wrote, "develop a greatly increased propensity to fight at puberty" in addition to "an unexplainable readiness to feel violent anger." Adolescents are "susceptible to envy and jealousy," and "every youngster has antisocial tendencies."[34]

Bradford Brown and James Larson note the following: the complexity of peer group relations as adolescents get older increases; peer relations are based on similar interests, backgrounds, and values; status is important among all peer groups; peer cliques have leaders and followers; peer affiliations are moderately stable; and self-perceptions are unreliable.[35] Research on adolescents supports the notion that common tendencies exist among all of them, regardless of race or class. Tendencies that *all* youth have that leads to some receiving delinquent adjudications and gang identification but not others supports our theory that delinquency and gangs are political constructs.[36]

Delinquency Is a Group Thing

Since juveniles spend as much time as possible with their peers, they rarely engage in any behavior alone, including delinquent behavior. In their research on the group nature of delinquency, Maynard Erickson and Gary Jensen affirm this: "The fundamental notion in the original development of the sociological study of delinquency [is] . . . that delinquency is a group phenomenon" and that it "is distributed more pervasively in the social structure than in lower-class male delinquent gangs."[37] Two other findings of their research were as follows: females hang out with their peers like males do, and they are involved in group delinquency rather than loner delinquency. Secondly, whether the delinquency is "small town" based or urban based, it is still group delinquency.[38]

The Schwendingers add clarity to the political nature of gang identification by demonstrating that all social classes form adolescent subcultures, often with names. The subcultures engage in delinquency, they contend, but it is particularly the lower-class "greasers" and upper-class "socialites" who violate the law more frequently than the other class-based groups do.[39] Why are some of these adolescent groups called gangs while others are not? Are gangs actually objectively identified groups of bad characters plotting mayhem during most of their waking time?[40]

Exploit the Child, Excuse the Politics

Cities were considered the "main breeding ground of criminals" and delinquent children, and rural farm family life, the key to saving them. Children were apprenticed out to "deserving" farm families or to "reform schools," where the "reformatory plan" could teach them lower-class skills and middle-class values."[41] But rather than the love of family filling their troubled little souls, they were exploited for their cheap labor power, treated more as child servants than family, and taught to accept their unequal status as the natural order of things and to behave themselves.

When industry replaced apprenticeships, industrialists' disregard for children contributed to weakening family bonds as their long work hours, sometimes as many as seventy per week, kept them from home[42] and the tutelage and love they might have gotten there. The establishment of the concepts of adolescence and delinquency emerged out of the requirements of industry to have cheap compliable labor and control of its population of urban poor, but industrialization contributed to their plight, marginalized them, and taught them the rules of exploitation.

Enabling industrialists to utilize and control juveniles was a group of professionals Platt acerbically referred to as the "child savers." These professionals, "despite their surface benevolence," were "little more than *undercover agents*" and "instruments" of the wealthy patrons, who funded the reform agencies.[43] C. Wright Mills has pointed out that the virtues of rural settings and religion as important in saving children were a moral commitment of the emerging professional group of social pathologists. He has shown that the majority of early twentieth-century researchers who studied social problems were ideologically compromised by their small-town religiosity. By using a "paste-pot" eclectic analysis, they directed their focus to individual pathologies, avoided class analysis, and avoided an understanding of the "social order."[44]

Heirs to this tradition shifted their values to accommodate the requirements of the agencies funding their research. Moneyed patrons wanted agencies to fund research that understood the locus of deviance to be defective individuals. Research that might examine the broader social issues of inequality and racism and challenge existing social structures was not funded.[45]

In his cleverly worded article, "Nuts, Sluts, and Preverts," Alexander Liazos has added that the field of deviance studies intentionally avoided consideration of power relationships. They stayed away from "larger social, historical, political, and economic contexts" and singled out the individual for focus.[46] Gang studies have been similarly characterized.[47] The majority of federal funding on gangs goes to research that supports the mission of the U.S. Department of Justice. In California, funding also supports the mission of the attorney general's Department of Justice, the district attorneys' offices, and missions of enforcement agencies. Those missions are, in a word, *suppression*.[48] The control perspective's historical roots lie deep within the political ideology of ignoring structural issues to stay focused on individuals.

On the Nondelinquent Nature of Gang Behavior

Mike Davis, in a nod to the political importance of making sense of gangs, asserts that research by traditional criminologists "was largely driven by episodic, media-incited outbursts of public hysteria over sensationalized killings . . . and heavily shaped by the priorities and biases of law enforcement and youth service organizations."[49] Joan Moore noted how two moral panics over gangs incited the public in Los Angeles, kept the attention on them long after the incidents had passed, and embroiled all groups labeled gangs in the controversy.

The first panic was during World War II, while the second, occurring in the late 1980s, involved the accidental shooting of an innocent young woman in the UCLA shopping district. As a result of her murder, news reports were filled with the tragic circumstances, day and night for weeks, while the City assigned thirty detectives and fourteen patrol officers to the case, plus offering a $35,000 reward for finding her killer. The John DiIulio theory of juvenile "superpredator"—the idea that groups of "brutally remorseless" juveniles aligned with deadly "gun-toting gangs" would soon be inundating our streets without rapid punitive changes to our laws—got a shot in the arm from the shooting-induced panic.[50] Many in the Black and Hispanic communities understood this reaction as racist, since no such effort had ever been made to find the killer of a Black or Hispanic person.[51]

In spite of the moral panics that regularly grip the public about the terror of gangs, most gang behavior may actually be quite normal juvenile group behavior. Mark Fleisher writes that since gang researchers have ignored adolescent social processes, what is frequently termed "gang behavior" is often just a common part of adolescent culture: adolescents like to hang out together, behave aggressively, dress the same, and rebel against adults. It's the way they are, and it is within the range of "predictable adolescent behavior."[52] Scott Decker and Barrik Van Winkle add that Malcom Klein's research in Los Angeles and James Short and Fred Strodtbeck's research in Chicago show the primary activity of gang members was just "hanging out."[53] Alistair Fraser reports a similar situation in the United Kingdom, writing that "gangs are very much like informal friendship networks" of young people, but they developed a public appearance that was independent of an empirical foundation.[54]

Vigil's Los Angeles research demonstrates that most gang members spend their time in nondelinquent pursuits, "cruising, partying, and socializing," but they get defined by their occasional acts of violence.[55] The idea that gang members spend a large portion of their time hanging with their homies and not involved in anything nefarious goes up against the grain of officially sponsored gang propaganda. The public doesn't believe it, university students have a hard time accepting it, and members of the LASD's gang detail, Operation Safe Streets (OSS), reject it. In the mid-1980s, Quicker gave several lectures on gangs at the Los Angeles County Sheriff's Academy to a group of OSS deputies. They were mostly receptive to the material until it came to how gang members spend their waking hours. The deputies argued that even if the research was accurate on the nondelinquent way gang members spend most of their time, during the time that they were not involved in actual crime, they were planning it. Gangs have created an indelible imprint on many as groups that are bad to the bone, and research that might show otherwise is both unnecessary and unwelcome.

A Brief History of Named Adolescent Groups

Since almost all delinquency is committed in groups of peers, the way the group is conceptualized and defined becomes crucial for understanding them. Peer groups come in innumerable shapes and sizes, identified by an assortment of names to describe them. Many of the names are very positive sounding, like *team* or *club*, while others might have a bit more menace associated with them, like *crowd* or, even worse, *mob*. Sometimes the juveniles get to choose the name of their group, referring to themselves as a *club*, *fraternity*, or *sorority* and have that name accepted as appropriate. Sometimes they get to join an existing group, like the Boy Scouts, where previous juveniles, with adult approval, have already chosen the name. Sometimes the name is imposed on the group by those with the power to do so, whether the juveniles approve or not.

Juvenile groups with names have been in existence since before the beginning of industrial societies. They may not have all met the legal definition of juvenile, yet most seemed to have been involved in some seaminess, at least sometimes. What is unequivocal is that groups of named young people have been on the planet a very long time, associated with various political economies. Geoffrey Pearson, writes about apprentice-based groups of Mummers, Summer Lords and Ladies, and the Lords of Misrule, who showed up on festive occasions, where large groups gathered, in early 1500s England. There they got drunk, belligerent, and lewd, which led to fights, rapes, and attacks on minority groups and foreigners.[56] Apprentices, he notes, were especially disorderly but were often joined by college boys in the "roaring fun" of the street battles,[57] suggesting involvement of various social classes in unruliness.

The Schwendingers contend that the "recomposition of precapitalist relationships" contributed to a "carnival of crime" in the industrializing regions of England from the 1500s through 1700s and the emergence of working-class delinquent groups with names like the Walking Morts (prostitutes), Kynchen Coes (male thieves), and Kynchen Morts (female thieves).[58] At the same time during this period, groups of upper-class delinquents also emerged, whose crimes were more malicious than the working-class juveniles and were directed to those they considered inferior. Sporting names like the Bold Bucks and Mohawks, these upper-class groups mutilated and terrorized defenseless people, especially women, because they could and because they could get away with it.[59] Their "violent frolics" also destroyed property. If they happened to kill a servant or waiter in their mayhem and acts of demolishing taverns, their "great joke" to the proprietor was, "Put him on the bill."[60]

Although Pearson uses a variety of general terms like *hooligan*, *club*, and *gang* to refer to these historical United Kingdom adolescent groups, the terms appear as interchangeable rather than definitive. Australian hooligans named larrikins were shared with the English, who also had groups called larrikins.[61] Fraser notes that the first dedicated academic studies on gangs in the United Kingdom didn't appear until the 1950s and 1960s. Other U.K. studies in the 1960s, even in London, failed to find the existence of "US-style gangs."[62] Behaviorally, the early adolescent groups in the United States didn't appear much different from those found in the United Kingdom but were defined differently, especially if they were working- or lower-class and immigrant or minority. The groups were referred to as gangs in the United States and were found in New York in the 1800s and early 1900s, in Philadelphia in the 1800s, and in Chicago in the early 1900s.[63]

Castles Built on Sand

Official data on crime in the United States are drawn from the FBI's Uniform Crime Reports and from a lesser-known survey of victims called the National Crime Victimization Survey. While both of these methods of data collection have been subject to a series of important critiques over the years, resulting in certain improvements, serious questions of accuracy remain.[64] Official data on gangs are subject to the criticisms of crime data, plus one: crime data are based on legal proscriptions, while gang data are art; its interpretation is in the eyes of the beholder.[65] When used nonreflexively, official data can produce an agency-inspired view of gangs. Sometimes this is done wittingly, while at other times it may be done unwittingly. Regardless, the power to control the narrative controls the thinking produced by these data.

Researchers' reliance on data with transient definitions, for information on gangs and gang members, renders what they construct from their source suspect, however sophisticated the construction may be. Gang researchers use official data at their peril.[66] By doing so, they ignore the prophetic words of Thorsten Sellin and Marvin Wolfgang: "A clear definition of fundamental concepts is a prime requisite for all research."[67] A definition of *gang* is necessary to have a definition of *gang member* to have a definition of *gang-related offense*.

Scott Decker and Kimberly Kempf-Leonard write that there is "no consensus on definitions of who is a gang member, what is a gang, and what is gang activity."[68] Irving Spergel expands on this by suggesting that defining gangs and gang members is not just a problem of official data but a common problem for all methods of research.[69] Moore adds that the term means different things to different groups at different times and in different places.[70] George Knox raises further questions with the quality of data collected from agencies of socialization, like schools and churches, as well as that collected from agencies of social control, like the police.[71] In a take-no-prisoners critique, Bursik and Grasmick write that the lack of an accepted definition of a gang makes estimates about them "relatively meaningless."[72] In Durkheimian theory, the myriad conceptualizations of gang raise the question of whether the term even meets the conceptual threshold of a *social fact*.[73]

Theoretical problems on the use of gang definitions are compounded when two major cities, Los Angeles and Chicago, both well known for their gang problems, use different definitions to report on the same phenomena. It would seem that an issue as compelling as gang homicide should have enough clarity to distinguish it from all other homicides, yet it does not. Cheryl Maxson and Malcolm Klein's research suggests that if Los Angeles, which uses a *gang member* definition for gang homicide, had used Chicago's more restrictive *gang motive* definition, Los Angeles's gang homicides would have been half of what were reported.[74]

In 1988, when a high rate of gang homicides—determined by using a definition likely to produce a high rate—was reported to the Los Angeles City Council, the council, believing the City was in peril, permitted LADP to launch a one-thousand-officer strong series of *gang sweeps* through many different city neighborhoods to root out gangs. Ironically, the LAPD found very few weapons, drugs, or warrant-avoiding gang members, but they managed to piss off a lot of community people who perceived the raids as another form of police harassment. Perhaps the "Gang Capital of the United States" award, which Los Angeles inherited from Chicago or New York, needs to be returned: We may not be worthy?[75] A bit of definitional adjustment might just allow the return to proceed.

Some of the most brazen acts of politically inspired involvement in gang definitions come directly from city governments. Cities will deny they have a gang problem even when they suspect they do, as Hagedorn indicated happened in Fort Wayne, Indiana, and Indianapolis. Indianapolis, it appears, was bidding for the 1992 Olympics, and, as Hagedorn quotes one official as claiming, "it couldn't possibly have a gang problem until 1993."[76] Police can be complicit in the denial as well, as Hagedorn argues they were in Milwaukee.[77] Vincent Webb and Charles Katz show how police officials in Phoenix "constructed the gang problem," so they could obtain federal funds, and in Las Vegas, police tried to link a growing gang problem with a general rise in crime to divert public attention from serious problems within their own department.[78] Spergel remarks that denial of a gang problem by police, when one exists, occurs frequently in many parts of our country.[79] *Gang* has historically been, and continues as, an ephemeral term subject to the political whims of the moment.

The rise of what Fraser terms "administrative gang research" and Hagedorn calls "embedded" criminologists[80] contributed to gang research in the United States becoming a "vast academic industry" beginning in the 1970s.[81] There's money to be made and jobs to be had imposing criminal definitions. The "Crime-Industrial Complex" spent $167 billion of tax dollars in 2001 on 2.3 million employees. Of this, $72 billion was spent on 17,000 police agencies and $38.2 billion on state corrections.[82] What chunk of this expenditure might have gone to the "Academic-Gang Complex"? How much more might this complex have received if voters could be convinced that gangs pose real threats to the security of our nation?

The Juvenile Justice and Delinquency Prevention Act of 1974 created the Office of Juvenile Justice and Delinquency Prevention (OJJDP) in 1975. In 1995, under OJJDP auspices, the National Youth Gang Center was created, which began publishing an annual report called the National Youth Gang Survey and providing grants to academicians who submitted proposals on gangs in line with the agency's mission. The data for these projects come primarily from official sources, with a small portion coming from localized self-report studies. Many published reports will acknowledge weakness in their data and then ignore or give passing reference to them later on, as they use the data to build elaborate charts and graphs with complex statistical analyses portraying the differences between gangs, gang members, and others.[83] By using a database that is ever evolving, inconsistent, weak, and full of conceptual and political holes to begin with, the portrayals of gangs constructed by embedded criminologists, regardless of their statistical and modeling sophistication, are building castles on sand.

A Los Angeles Story

Any estimates on the number of gangs and gang members in Los Angeles made before the mid-1970s were based on soft sand. In 2000, Quicker spoke with the gang expert Sergeant Wes McBride of the LASD about their gang statistics. McBride indicated that when he started with the sheriff's department gang unit Operation Safe Streets (OSS) in 1972, data were still not being collected on gang-related crimes. He indicated that it was sometime in 1976 that the department began to record crimes as gang related. Also, in 2000, one of Quicker's students spoke with Officer Buscaino from LAPD Media Relations regarding the origins of their data collection on gangs. He indicated that the Community Resources Against Street Hoodlums (CRASH) gang unit was implemented in 1977 and that LAPD began to record gang-related activity in the early 1980s.[84]

As noted, the LAPD has had a history of shenanigans creating crime statistics, with early reports on Chief Parker in the 1950s manipulating them for his own purposes. It would be comforting to believe that this was behind us and that subsequent estimates about crime and gangs by officials have seen improvement. Such a possibility would lend credibility to research based on these assessments. Two recent articles, buried in the *Los Angeles Times*, suggests this may be wishing on a star.

Richard Winton noted that a state audit released in 2016 on "CalGang," a California database maintained by law enforcement, with information on "150,000 suspected gang members," was "rife with unsubstantiated entries, names that should have been purged long ago and glaring errors." Some "gang members" were one year of age or younger at the time their names were entered into this "decades" old database, where males and non-Whites were "disproportionately" overrepresented.[85]

Adrienne Alpert, in a bit of deft investigative reporting, found that the LAPD, in an effort to establish a rationale for more officers, had been counting *nongang* members as gang members in statistics it had been submitting to the California database. Mayor Eric Garcetti, expressing requisite outrage, said: "We want more patrols, but that is no excuse to ever falsify something."[86] How many researchers, journalists, and politicians will use these uncorrected databases, wittingly or unwittingly? How many will wait for or demand that they be revised before relying on them? What these data represent is information gathered by some who are counting lions, while others are counting sheep, and then combining their counts to tell the public how many wolves there are in the neighborhood. Misinformation trumps no information in its ability to deceive.

The official portrait of a gang or gang member has produced a stereotype based on images created by researchers using reality-challenged data. Fraser notes that the term *gang* "has developed a public life independent of any empirical foundation," existing "more as an idea than a reality." He adds that gangs have been "racialized, gendered," and mired in "class-based stereotypes."[87] As David Brotherton suggests, attempting to understand gangs without history produces no understanding at all, and when done nonreflexively, a "pathologizing trope" of gang becomes the product.[88] Everyone has heard of gangs, and most view them as repositories of evil.[89] Gangs have become a convenient way to elicit public fears, by manipulating the public with a group nobody knows.

Defame with a Name

"What's in a name?" Jeffrey Reiman asks rhetorically in his insightful book *The Rich Get Richer and the Poor Get Prison*.[90] It turns out there is plenty, as he demonstrates. Criminal justice, he argues, is a "creative art," defining one act as murder and another similar behavior as an accidental or justifiable homicide. Paraphrasing Richard Quinney, Reiman contends that crime has a "social reality," not an "objective reality."[91] The definers of criminality often create definitional criteria important to their goals rather than creating them objectively. This has been the situation for definitions of *gang, gang member*, and *gang related*.

Quinney's conflict theory of criminal law formation argues that "the formulation of all criminal law is political," as are its applications.[92] Charles Reasons adds that the political nature of the law is obscured by public misperceptions about the law being value-free. It is not, he argues, but exists to protect the interests of the power elite.[93] Applying conflict theory to the formulation of gang designation, we hypothesize that the decision to impose a gang definition on a particular group or associate of that group is a political act. From Dwight Conquergood's perspective, those controlling the definition control the fears of a large and important percentage of the population: the voters.[94]

There are few names for any group that have a greater burden associated with it than the name *gang*.[95] Mike Tapia notes the name gang for most academics, law enforcement, and the public is "nearly synonymous with a delinquent lifestyle."[96] Brotherton argues that the ALKQN group he studied in New York challenged the imposition of the gang label on them because the aspersions it implied delegitimized their political ambitions.[97] More pointedly, Conquergood shows how the term has been "demonized" to terrify the middle class with fears of "alien *Others* lurking in urban shadows" to snatch innocents.[98] In the public's mind, the gang becomes the "enemy" and a "distraction."[99] Gang has served its purpose well, so well that in many ways gang has joined with other four-letter words that see use as "expletive deleted," because they are so offensive. Perhaps we should consider writing *gang* as *g-ng*?

Given official pejorative ideology on gangs, it shouldn't be surprising that most South Los Angeles juvenile street-group members did not consider themselves members of a gang.[100] While they were quite aware of the term and how it had been applied to them, most did not perceive it as an accurate reflection of who they were, what they were a part of, or what they did. A primary reason for their opposition was recognition that the term was disparaging: "It was like a bad name, it had a bad sound to it," said Roslyn of the Slausons. She felt that the older parental generation might have used the term due to its occurrence in the newspapers: "The newspaper would have it written down as a gang, and then the older people would say, 'Yes, so-and-so from that gang is responsible for doing this.'" She felt the older generation's misunderstanding of neighborhood youth groups was primarily based on misinformation from the media, and it deceived them.[101]

Whit, the vice president of the Royal Aces Social Group, said a gang was a "rowdy" group, like the Don Juans (a group not especially friendly with the Royal Aces), but *gang* didn't refer to the Royal Aces. The Don Juans, returning the compliment, would often refer to the Royal Aces as the "Royal Asses." The concept gang was a reference to "hoodlums" but not to "us," said Ameer, the president of the Baby Businessmen. "A hoodlum is one who snatch a lady's purse, beat up an old man. Every time you go in the store, you stealin' something. We wasn't no gang. The gang was a bunch of hoodlums; we wasn't no hoodlums," Ameer concluded. Acknowledging that all street groups might have had a hoodlum or two, he added that the hoodlums were "outcasts" and "exceptions," not representative of the group.

Miguel D, a counselor with the Group Guidance Project that worked with South Los Angeles gangs, was unequivocal in his comments on why the project opposed the negativity associated with the term *gang*. They didn't refer to the juveniles as gang members or their organizations as gangs: "We tried very hard not to stick an onus on a group of kids. That's why we called it Group Guidance instead of gang guidance." He added that the juveniles "never called themselves a gang as such either. 'We are the Businessmen,' they would say."[102] Miguel conducted a creative experiment with the juveniles: He explained to several groups that a person who wrote a book on gangs calls the groups gangs because of certain criteria. He then took the definition used by the author, a control-perspective definition, and let the youth read it. The juveniles were unanimous in their assessment of the definition, saying, "That's not us. We're not a gang!"

Many of our respondents believed the police were a gang. They were "bigger and worse than us," according to a member of Florence. Moreover, that same member added that it was part of the police's job: "They're getting paid to be a gang," she said. The enforcers' behavior did not conflict with the interests of those who have the power to shape public policy,[103] allowing their gang-like groups to avoid the gang moniker.

The LAPD and LASD displayed an interest in gangs a bit earlier than some of the smaller city police agencies did. Lieutenant T. of the Compton Police Department made this clear in a lecture to students in Quicker's gang class in the 1980s. He stated that a number of the Compton street groups, like the Swamps, were primarily into youthful pursuits, such as partying and throwing eggs, but not into drug use or serious crime, thus not raising much alarm. He wouldn't call them a gang, he said, because "their criminal activity was so low." They just "didn't qualify as a gang." In fact, he contended that the Compton police hadn't even begun to keep statistics on gang-related activities until after the end of the 1960s, because they had little reason before then to differentiate the groups' behavior from that of other juveniles.

We Were a Brotherhood

We asked most of our respondents: "What did you call the street organization you were a part of?" And "How did you refer to your group? What did you call yourselves?" The answers were uniformly more complimentary than "gang." They called themselves "neighborhoods," "hoods," "barrios," "clubs," "social clubs," "brotherhoods," and "sets." Most felt their group was a club, organized like any other club. Ameer said: "We were a club. We had a club mentality. We collected dues, took minutes, and held dances. . . . We were definitely a club. We had a president, vice president, and treasurer." Barry W., a Junior Businessman, confirmed this had been the case with the Juniors too: "We was a club, man. We was the Businessmen's club. We paid dues. We had club meetin's on Tuesday night. We had a treasurer; yeah, we paid dues. That's a club."[104]

Some group members took umbrage at being singled out by law enforcement to be called gangs. They knew the term was demeaning and felt it was inaccurate. *Gang*, they conceded, might be an appropriate term for a contemporary street group, but not for the older ones. "Why," they asked, should their group be called a "gang" when other groups get to be called "clubs"? Linda C., from the Florencitas, of Florence,[105] makes this clear in her angry words about her group being called a gang:

> Oh yeah, we were a club! We had a lot of activities. We use to go to the mountains; we use to have dances at the park; we use to go to the show every Sunday. We went cruising. We use to have meetings, mostly at Roosevelt Park. They [group members] always called them clubs; they never said gangs. That came way later, and then law enforcement put that on us. I don't know what gang means, all right, because the YMCA could be a gang. It's very degrading to me; and it's meant to be. But we had clubs. That's who we were.

When asked if there were any other terms in use then to refer to her group, she said: "We didn't call them gangs. We said 'homeboys' or 'neighborhoods' or 'barrios.' And there were the Pachucos too."

Moore notes that in the early years of the East Los Angeles gangs she studied, the community didn't use the term *gang* either to refer to the local street groups but called them "the boys from the barrio."[106] Vigil found that the members of the Los Angeles groups he studied considered themselves like a family, helping each other out, having friends, and being a part of something larger than the individual.[107] Bird didn't mince any words in his commentary on the use of the term *gang* by neighborhood juveniles: "I have never in my life asked somebody what gang they were from." Even more clearly, he exclaimed: "See we didn't call it no gang. If you heard a person say that, you knew he was a square motherfucker or something was off."

In his 1960s field research on the Chicago-based Vice Lords, R. Lincoln Keiser found himself regularly using the term *club* when he referred to the Lords, because that's what they called themselves.[108] On the first page he writes: "It is generally stated that the Vice Lord Nation—[is] referred to by [the] Vice Lords as a 'club,' not a gang." He argues that an important reason why the Lords called themselves a club was that they had a leadership hierarchy. They had a president, a vice president, a secretary-treasurer, and so on.[109] David Dawley, who joined the Lords for two years to do research on them in the late 1960s, also referred to them and to the other neighborhood groups as "clubs," throughout his 1973 book *A Nation of Lords*. In a rare divergence from the media's refrain, Pye, writing in a 1963 *Los Angeles Sentinel* article on various South Los Angeles "teenage" street groups, contends that the term "club" might be a more accurate and "acceptable connotation" than "gang" to refer to them.[110]

Roger Rice and Rex Christensen, in their study of pre-1965 Los Angeles gangs, repeatedly refer to them as "clubs" and "sets." In the quotations they provide from gang leaders, the leaders regularly referred to their groups as "clubs"—until the researchers began referring to them as "gangs." Then, the leaders began to use "gang" too rather than "club" as the interviews continued.[111] The concept gang seemed infectious: easily caught, easily transmitted, and difficult to get over.

In his coming-of-age tale in Los Angeles during the 1950s and 1960s, Luis Rodriguez makes it clear that he and his homeboys formed a group they didn't consider to be a gang. His description of his group and their name adds meaning to the vast power differences between those in a position to create a definition and those in the group being so labeled. Rodriguez writes:

> We didn't call ourselves a gang either. We called ourselves clubs or *cliqas*. In the back lot of the local elementary school, about a year

after Tito's death, five of us gathered in the grass and created a club—
"Thee Impersonations," the "Thee" being an old English usage that
other clubs would adopt because it made everything sound classier,
nobler, *badder*. It was something to belong to—something that was
ours. We weren't in boy scouts, in sports teams or camping groups.
Thee Impersonations is how we wove something out of the threads
of nothing.[112]

There was a chorus of agreement among South Los Angeles juveniles
that their organizations may have been many things, but a gang was not one
of them. Chinaman, the leader of Big Slauson, felt the term was plainly inaccurate when used to refer to groups in existence before the mid-1940s. It
characterized neither who they were nor what they did. He stated, "The
early groups called themselves 'lovers'; they liked the girls and the parties."
Ameer, when asked about his group, said: "It's funny you should ask that.
We never did consider ourselves a gang; we consider ourselves a brotherhood. We were brothers. We would die for each other." Roach, a leader of
the Little Slausons, said they were a brotherhood, the "Slauson Brothers."
The High Priest from Slauson said, "We were clannish," suggesting a familial type of relationship. Roach added that Jerome, the president of the Little
Slausons, called the Slausons "Slauson Village" or the "Villa," and said that
Jerome was the first to begin writing "SV" on the walls of buildings in the
neighborhood. The High Priest said: "In graffiti, I never personally wrote
'gang.' My thing was Slauson Village. I never painted on the walls 'Slauson
gang.' I was from the neighborhood."

What It Was

The most common way the South Los Angeles youth groups referred to
themselves during the 1950s and 1960s was as a "set."[113] The High Priest
said, "We used the term *set*, not *gang*, in reference to ourselves." Commenting on a number of the various South Los Angeles groups, Roslyn exclaimed:
"The Slausons were a set. It's just like the Gladiators were a set, or the Businessmen were a set, or the guys from Compton were a set, or the guys from
Watts, the Farmers—that was a set." Cardel from the Slausons observed that
a typical question, upon meeting someone for the first time, would be:
"What set you from?" Bird added that the term *set* could also refer to one's
location, as in, "Let's see who's on the set." This might mean, "Let's see who
was around," or who was on the corner or over at the hamburger stand.
"Lame, get off the set," would mean that since you weren't a "regular," you
can't hang with us here. *Set* might be used in a question, as in "Where's the
set at?"—meaning, "Where's it going on?" or "Where's the action at?"

Set could also be used more generally to refer to the entire neighborhood. "A set is the neighborhood. We didn't call ourselves a gang; the police started it." Bird emphasized:

> We ain't never said gang! I can't find a person to say "what gang" they was from, but I can show you all the ones you want to see, tell you what set they was from. That's what they would say, "set." "Fool—what set you from?" We didn't even use *neighborhood* that much, cause we use to call this [the community] the Neighborhood.

The concept of set then was a very inclusive and general term that could refer to either the group or the entire neighborhood.[114] The term *gang* wasn't used in intergroup discussions to refer to their group or to any other group. Bird emphasized: "It's always, 'What set you from?' 'What barrio you from?' And never, 'What gang are you from?'" Whereas the term *gang* offers a pejoratized and limited reference, the community terms imply significant complexity and are far more benign than the scornful box the gang pathologists were trying to squeeze the street groups into.

The fact that most of the individuals in South Los Angeles groups referred to their organizations as clubs or sets should not be interpreted to mean that they did not at times think of themselves as gangs or some of their members as gangsters or their fights with other groups as gang fights. They did. The term *gang* had become an acceptable and ubiquitous part of American nomenclature, used regularly and unreflectively in public discourse. Set members had been called gang members and their groups called gangs by the media and the police since at least the 1930s. They also recognized that other street groups, as well as their own, were, on occasion, engaged in enough criminal behavior to perhaps justify the use of this name. This was the case when they mobilized to confront another group over a perceived wrong; the confrontation was termed a "gang fight," not a "set fight."

A Consideration for Self-Reported Data

In his analysis of the state of gang knowledge, Spergel is concerned about the lack of good data on gangs. As a consequence of poor data, contradictory statements on the state of the youth gang problem are often a result. He quotes the 1976 National Advisory Committee on Criminal Justice Standards and Goals writing that "youth gangs are not now or [*sic*] should not become a major object of concern. . . . Youth gang violence is not a major crime problem in the United States." Spergel then notes that Walter Miller, after conducting a national survey on gangs in major American cities in 1975, "concluded that the youth gang problem of the mid-1970s was 'of the utmost seriousness.'"[115] Both conclusions can't be right. Which one do we choose, and why? Is the choice we make based on science, or is it a political decision?

When the reviews on self-reported data's value for research began coming in, in the 1950s, they were consistently positive. Issues of reliability and validity notwithstanding, self-reported data were seen as a significant improvement over official data.[116] The Schwendingers argue that this new data source posed a "theoretical crisis" since all previous research had been based on official data, biases and all.[117] The new self-reported data were indicating that delinquent behavior was much wider spread in the class structure than official data had been suggesting, drawing new attention to some of the already known biases of official data.

Using self-reported data in gang research continues to raise validity questions that have yet to be fully addressed. Fraser found evidence that some youth boast about being gang members when they may not be, just to boost credibility with their peers.[118] Bursik and Grasmick add that some nongang juveniles will adopt gang symbols as a sign of rebellion and that their graffiti might lead to a public perception of more gangs than there actually are.[119] Juveniles who may be gang members might say they are not because they don't trust the anonymity claims of the researchers. We asked several respondents how they would respond to an anonymous questionnaire on their street activities and associations. Their responses are best summarized by the comments of one: "Shiiit, are you kidding? I ain't telling someone I don't know shit. Who are these motherfuckers? They could be the man for all I know." We concluded that the lack of trust our respondents had for anonymous investigators wouldn't have worked out well for their research.

On another level, if a self-report survey had been given anonymously to a group containing early South Los Angeles gang members, and the question asked whether they were a gang member, if they told it like it was, the responses would have been a consistent no, because, although street group members considered themselves group members, they did not consider their group a gang. But if this same member had been asked a different question, if they were a Slauson or a Businessman or a Gladiator or . . . , and if they were being up front, the response would have been yes. If self-report is the best we have, Spergel's concerns on the weakness of data on gangs is justified.

They Say *Gang*, We Say *Street Group*

An important question for our research became how we should refer to these early South Los Angeles street groups to most accurately represent what they were, while at the same time not ignoring generally accepted terminology, even if it might be flawed. Myths prevail in the fields of crime, delinquency, and gangs, regularly supplanting fact; we did not want to make a contribution.[120] We marinated on this question a bit further.

Socially, South Los Angeles street groups behaved more like fraternal organizations than like any other kind of group. But they were as far from being Greek-letter-based university fraternities as they were from being predatory groups of marauding youth who spent most of their waking moments either thinking about, looking for, or exploiting victims. Most accurately, they were self-selected assemblies of juveniles organized to help one another, like a "band of brothers."[121] They were societies of juveniles associated in a "brotherly manner," as for "mutual benefit" and aid.[122] They were friends, partners, relatives, and "road-dogs";[123] they were homies drawn together out of a commonality of interests. Moore notes that the reference of street youth to one another as "homies" suggests a bond and a trust, like family members.[124] Neither saints nor sinners but with elements of both, these volitional peer groups were similar to yet different from both fraternities and the stereotypical gang.

Hagedorn argues that gang authorities like Jerome Needle, William Stapleton, Walter Miller, and Malcolm Klein have criminalized the definition of gangs by operationalizing it to mean that a "gang is any group of youth police call a gang." He finds this unacceptable, since these gang authorities "leave little room for critical analysis when they ask what a gang is, tell us how those concerned with law enforcement define 'gangs'; then conclude by saying, since this definition is the 'contemporary usage,' we should adopt it too." We agree, such usage is sociologically unsound. But we would add that the term *gang*, regardless of how it might be cleaned up sociologically with efforts to place it within a community context to achieve a more process-related understanding,[125] continues to be so fraught with negative connotations that its use misrepresents what many street groups are, especially the pre-1965 groups of South Los Angeles.

It would be disrespectful to the social reality of the group culture of South Los Angeles to refer to the groups there by names that would further misunderstanding. Not only was the term *gang* not theirs, but they rejected it because it distorted who they were and what they did. These were street groups of juveniles with names, often organized with designated positions of authority.[126] They fought with individuals from other groups; less frequently, they fought with individuals from within their own group, and they fought as a group with other street groups. While some members were delinquent or criminal some of the time, they were so as individuals or in small subgroups. Sometimes, though, they just behaved like a gaggle of immature adults—like juveniles. These were not criminal, conflict-oriented, or retreatist subcultures like Richard Cloward and Lloyd Ohlin theorized were in existence then.[127] Their reason for existence, their organizational purpose, was not to break the law—but sometimes they did.

At times, street-group members[128] and community people referred to the street organizations as gangs, either because they believed they were or they behaved like they were or because common vernacular was momentarily, and perhaps unreflectively, accepted. To prevent confusion and to respect the groups we studied, when the media or a justice agency or an interviewee or any other reference uses the term *gang*, we will too, but with the caveat that it is their term, not ours. *Gang*, *set*, or *street group*—we'll let the context of the discussion establish which term fits best for our use at the time. We will use *gang* where it is rhetorically appropriate, although *street group* most accurately characterizes the juvenile assemblies of early South Los Angeles, and it is our preferred term.

3

The Discovery of Gangs in Los Angeles

Speaking like this doesn't mean that we're anti-White, but it does mean we're anti-exploitation, we're anti-degradation, we're anti-oppression.
—**Malcolm X**, *The Ballot or the Bullet*

There have been reports of juvenile "gangs" in South Los Angeles since at least the 1920s,[1] many decades before the emergence of the Crips and Bloods. Some recent accounts suggest it was not until the late 1950s or early 1960s that gangs "really got underway" there and that when South Los Angeles gangs did emerge, they copied the traditions that had been established in East Los Angeles a generation earlier. These studies further contend the Watts Rebellion of 1965 helped initiate a transition that then paved the way for the rise of the Crips and Bloods.[2] These theories oversimplify or neglect the rich complexity of street-group life that had developed in South Los Angeles before the Rebellion and the structural changes that had been taking place.

Making the Scene

Before 1942, little had been written about South Los Angeles gangs because, presumably, little was known.[3] The dearth of attention suggests that whatever gangs may have existed here were involved in activities of such insufficient newsworthiness that neither the police nor the media nor academics nor anyone else saw much reason to bother with them.[4]

When attention was turned to South Los Angeles's juvenile problems, the focus was on delinquency, with the term *gang* rarely appearing in print. Indeed, with some notable exceptions, street gangs in South Los Angeles were regularly ignored by the media and police until after the 1965 Watts Rebellion, once the Crips and Bloods became newsworthy. When pre-1965 gangs were mentioned in association with crime, identifying information was usually not given, so it was often unclear whether the focus was on an organized street gang, an organized adult criminal gang, or a group of juveniles who might have ganged up or grouped together to do something newsworthy. *Gang*, for the Los Angeles establishment, was a term searching for a referent and for a definition.[5]

Abetting the search were two early incidents. Both involved groups of minority youth that drew national attention to the Los Angeles "gang problem," through repeated and often sensationalized media attention: the first occurred in 1942/1943 and the second in 1953. The first incident helped establish Los Angeles's credentials as a city with gangs, while the second brought renewed attention to Los Angeles gangs after a ten-year hiatus.

In 1942/1943, the Sleepy Lagoon case and the military-versus-Mexicans Zoot-Suit Riots thrust East Los Angeles and its zoot-suited Mexican "gang hoodlums" into the national spotlight.[6] They gave Los Angeles the dubious distinction of having finally arrived with its gang city predecessors, New York and Chicago. It took the concepts of gang, crime, Mexican, and zoot suit and made them essentially synonymous. Carey McWilliams, writing for the *New Republic*, noted: "The constant repetition of the phrase 'zoot-suit,' coupled with Mexican names and pictures of Mexicans, had the effect of convincing the public that all Mexicans were zoot-suiters and all zoot-suiters were criminals; ergo, all Mexicans were criminals."[7]

As officials became more involved in portraying Mexicans in a negative way, antagonistic public attitudes, supported by sanctioned propaganda, were highlighted by the naming of the so-called Zoot-Suit Riots. Perhaps the greatest irony of these riots was that most of the confrontations were initiated by groups of sailors, who were egged on by civilians, with the sailor and citizen roles then later misrepresented by officials. The effect was to portray the zoot suiters so negatively that they, rather than the sailors, received the public opprobrium. Racism dripped from these depictions. The zoot-suiter groups, not the sailor groups, were identified as gangs. The public chose sides, not on the basis of what actually happened but on the spin provided by most official accounts.[8]

The riots left no doubt that gangs now existed in Los Angeles: Mexican gangs. Also clear was the official position that these gangs were the most negative of organizations. They were characterized as "predatory packs," "wolf packs," and "rat packs."[9] Class and racial biases became established too, as the press took pains to differentiate the group behavior of upper- and middle-class juveniles from that of working-class Mexican juveniles. For example, the press reported a group of Beverly Hills boys who had shot out the windows of a sixteen-story building as "vandals," while reporting Mexican youth committing similar acts as "mad dogs."[10] After attention to the Zoot-Suit Riots ran its course, the press and criminal-justice sources dropped their focus on Los Angeles gangs for the remainder of World War II. The second incident, the Cluff case, occurring in 1953, reinforced the image of a gang-infested Los Angeles and further emphasized the City's emerging similarities to New York and Chicago.

With Cluff There Was Enough

William D. Cluff, who lived in an "expensive Hollywood Hills apartment," was the fifty-six-year-old president of the Western Chemical and Manufacturing Company, when he made a fateful decision to intervene in an altercation between some military men and Mexican juveniles. While window-shopping one December day in 1953, at 7th Street and Broadway in downtown Los Angeles, Cluff witnessed the fighting and jumped in to aid the military men. He was punched and, according to all reports at the time, died as a result of the punch when he fell to the ground and struck his head on the pavement.[11]

The reaction by the media and public officials to Cluff's death was immediate, dramatic, racially charged—and wrong. More designed to fire up the community than to accurately account for what had happened, official response was consistent with their reactions ten years earlier to the zoot-suiters. Newspapers came alive to condemn the Mexican "hooligans" and "gang" members for their acts of "terror."[12] Article after article focused on Cluff's innocence and the domination of the City now by "rat packs" of youth. Extreme situations like the current one require extreme measures, the arguments went. The following editorial in the *Los Angeles Times* exemplifies this opinion:

> The harsh facts are that brutal hoodlumism is on the loose, that it is growing and spreading in open defiance of the law and the courts, and that unless the most prompt and stern measures are immediately taken nobody's life is safe at any time on any street.... There is only one way to deal with the rat packs. It is to summon up the entire strength of the community, moral and physical, and impose the extremity of justice on every hoodlum that steps an inch out of line.[13]

This was an early illustration of zero tolerance.

The youth were from the dangerous class; they were violent and morally depraved. By dramatizing the Cluff incident, it gave the power structure reason to justify a more potent police presence to prevent further episodes.[14] In his plea for more officers, LAPD chief Parker—in a theatrical exaggeration—compared the fight police were being asked to wage against domestic juvenile gangs to the communist takeover in Russia. He claimed, without evidence, that "there's a criminal army of 6,000,000 in the United States—a larger force than the Communists had when they captured Russia. You are losing the war against crime."[15]

The melodrama continued, with others apparently trying to not be outdone by the chief. The president of the Los Angeles City Council, John S. Gibson Jr., explained his position with these words: "I feel this is one of the most shocking things that has happened in the history of our city." The president of the Los Angeles Police Commission, Frank J. Waters, said: "It is shocking and reprehensible almost beyond belief that cowardly hoodlums could come into the heart of the city like this." Police Commissioner John Ferrero added: "I am shocked, and cannot understand that at an intersection such as Seventh and Broadway there was no protection for a citizen who was *ganged* by hoodlums."[16]

Cluff: An Excuse for Control

In his successful effort to use the Cluff case to expand the LAPD, Parker complained about the "department's lack of manpower." He opined that the incident "represented a serious problem that police of this city have faced for some time," primarily because the department itself is "seriously undermanned, with 265 vacancies still unfilled."[17] He added that "juvenile gangs" had been a problem in the San Fernando Valley, but most of the problems were now "solved" through "stronger police methods." About a week later, Parker "ordered additional police into duty to combat juvenile gangs."[18] Demonizing juvenile street groups, enhanced by various shades of racism, had worked to advance social control.

The Cluff incident served notice that gangs were now firmly established in the City. They were a menace to public safety, the situation was serious, and they would no longer be ignored. Gangs had been rediscovered in Los Angeles, never to be lost sight of again. From this point on, the police, the press, and various public agencies gave much more attention to gangs—and gave it more systematically—than they had before, although it was primarily Mexican gang members from East Los Angeles that were the focus.

More gangs were recognized after this incident as the dynamics of a city on the rise changed. Cluff was the catalyst that brought fresh attention to Mexican groups, which had slipped under the official radar for ten years. The groups were now excoriated for what appeared to be a vicious crime. While Cluff brought renewed awareness, the increase in the number of street groups had been ongoing, a consequence of urban development, demographic growth, and the changing socioeconomic structure. Mexican gangs became the new public menace because they were an easily identifiable and readily condemnable group of dark-skinned people with accents and little political power.[19] Barry Krisberg notes that World War II took attention away from street gangs until its conclusion. Afterward, the "fighting gang" came to symbolize urban violence and, as a result, received the lion's share of delinquency-prevention efforts.[20] Los Angeles is a good example of where this happened.

An ironic twist to the sordid saga of Cluff was that the wrong culprit was blamed for his death. The media frenzy surrounding the incident blamed his death on the fight and the "vicious hoodlums" who attacked him. Reports of the attack provided the media and the police with enhanced credibility to incite the citizenry with assorted references to Los Angeles "gangsters," "wanton gang violence," "hoodlums" in the street, and the "powder-puff treatment" that had given rise to "gangsterism." Moreover, it enabled the police to promote the need for additional officers to deal with the gangs. The frenzy also justified pleas for the public to support a get-tougher-on-crime approach.[21] For officials, the Cluff incident had been the perfect storm.

Two years later, after three Mexican youth had been convicted of manslaughter and were serving time in prison for Cluff's death, three justices on the court of appeals ruled that the judge in the original trial had failed to present the defense theory to the jury in his instructions. The justices' summary, supported by the results of two autopsy surgeons, stated: "The actual injuries sustained by Cluff were minor and . . . he died from a brain hemorrhage." Their theory held that his death was brought on by a blood vessel rupture caused by "high blood pressure." Thus, Cluff had died from a stroke and not from the fight. To add insult to irony, the exculpating article was short—somewhat over a one-hundred-word piece—and appeared in the back pages of the newspaper, where few would notice it, much less read it.[22] Accordingly, myths about gangs, generated by a plethora of misinformation and promoted by an overzealous press and control-oriented criminal-justice system, took root. Why bother with facts when the course of action is clear?[23]

Holy Molokans

It appears that the earliest Los Angeles street groups to be identified may not have been either Mexican or Black but rather Russian Molokans. The Molokans were "peasants and pacifists who had left Russia on the eve of the Russo-Japanese War," to come to Los Angeles in the early 1900s. A large population of them, some five thousand by 1905, settled near the current Men's Central Jail on Vignes Street, just east of downtown. The first generation of Molokans was "the one group of newcomers which was not welcomed by the Chamber of Commerce." Perhaps their snubbing had something to do with the "homogeneous nature" of their colony or their schism with the Russian Orthodox Church or their maintenance of strong traditional ties, including the wearing of native costumes and beards by the men. Adherence to their native customs and their own language didn't ease their entry into American life.

Although little has been written about the Molokans' Los Angeles history, what has been published makes it clear that their second generation formed adolescent street groups that were called gangs. They had aroused enough antipathy within the Los Angeles criminal-justice system that "by 1929 the Molokan boy-gangs of 'the flats' had the social workers busy making studies, charts, and graphs" to try and manage them. These actions were for naught, because by the mid-1930s the older peasants had disappeared, while "most of the youngsters had married outside the group, and Los Angeles had forgotten all about its Molokan problem."[24] The Molokans, being racially White, left their culture at home and blended.

Sundry Groups, Some Quite Early

The downtown area was the point of origination for South Los Angeles street groups. Our oldest respondent, John S., who was born in 1920 and lived at 28th Street and Central Avenue, remembers street groups existing there as far back as the 1930s. His recollection was that Clanton was the first group he had heard of in the area. It "got started in the early 1930s" and had a racially diverse membership of White, Chicano, and Black.[25] The group members all lived in the neighborhood, went to school together, and hung out with one another. In the beginning, their primary activity was associating at dances. By the time World War II broke out, Clanton had about one hundred members and was about 98 percent Chicano, according to Frank M., a Black member of the group.[26]

Four other street groups appeared nearby about the same time as Clanton: Macy Street, Mateo Street (a.k.a. 23rd Street), Maple Street, and Temple Street. Writing in 1953 for the *Los Angeles Times*, Will indicates that the "heaviest concentration of gangs" was in the "Central, Eastern, and Northeastern sections of the city, where such gangs have been in existence for at least 30 years." He also remarks that the Macy Street[27] gang is one of the oldest in existence, "well known and going strong as far back as 1923 and 1924."[28] While it is pointless to try to determine which group was first, the evidence suggests many were in existence before the 1930s and most likely present in the early 1920s.[29]

Mateo Street and Clanton were quite large, with perhaps as many as one hundred members each. They both emerged out of the same junior high school and, in the beginning, were each other's main rivals. Some of their members attempted to distinguish themselves by their hip clothing styles. The wearing of "drapes"—baggy coats with long pants, similar to zoot suits and worn by a number of members—were especially distinctive. Frank M. observed that some of the older members of Clanton dressed in all-black clothing and wore thick-soled shoes that could be used effectively in fighting.

A Boozie Clan

Robert Jackson and Wes McBride have identified another South Los Angeles street group emerging around the same time and in the same vicinity as those mentioned above called the Boozies.[30] They state that the Boozie gang was "very active" in the 1920s around Central Avenue and 18th Street.[31] The attorney general's Youth Gang Task Force seconded this when they indicated a gang called the Boozies had been around "as early as the 1920's."[32] Our research indicates the Boozie gang was a group of twenty-five to fifty young Black males, many of whom were related—brothers and cousins— that was around in the 1930s and 1940s.[33] Ted W., who was born in 1923 and lived in South Los Angeles since 1937, was a member of the Boozies. He remembered that the founders of the group were a number of brothers whose last name was Boozie, and their group consisted of a lot of relatives from their extended family, plus friends.

All respondents who knew the namesake Boozie brother, agreed he was tall, good-looking, a fashionable dresser, and "nice." He was never "rowdy, but was always smooth and cool with his locks over his eye." This was the distinctive-looking "Boozie curl," a hair twist that came down below his eye brow. Other group members copied this style: "It was one way to tell if you were a Boozie; we had to have a string of hair come down over our right eye," noted Ted W. Dressing neatly in black and white clothes, with dress pants and a white shirt, they wore white tennis shoes to complete the style. Most Boozie members either worked or went to school. Ted W. remembered that Boozie probably died from tuberculosis, and the group "dispersed after WW II." Although existing in a racially mixed neighborhood, there is no evidence the Boozie group had any non-Black members.

Their crimes, while bothersome, were neither serious nor gang-like. Ted W., who later became a Watts community leader, recalled: "Mostly their thing was hustling nickels and dimes, drinking wine, and smoking some pot. That was the extent of it; they were basically looking for a good time." Stealing cars and fighting were some of their most serious offenses, which they did as individuals rather than as a group. Frank Miller, who hung out with 18th Street when the Boozies were around, wrote that the Boozies were "street fighters" and "party crashers." In spite of this, he reported that Mayor Bradley's office referred to them as the "good gang," because their offenses paled in comparison to what the gangs of the 1980s were into.[34]

Many Boozies had "nice" and legally obtained cars, while other member's cars were stolen. The group formed out of a gym in the area, where they would meet and hang out. All of them were "good with their hands," having honed their boxing skills at the gym. The fights they did get into were generally over women and did not involve killing anyone or even leaving any one seriously injured.[35] There is no evidence that any of their fights were gang motivated or organized. All of the Boozies drank and enjoyed parties: those they gave, those they were invited to, and those they invited themselves to. Criminality, when it arose, seemed linked to obtaining the wherewithal to enjoy themselves or as a consequence of enjoyment getting out of hand rather than in defense of a territory. It takes a considerable stretch of the imagination to conceive of this group as a gang, since they primarily behaved like a social club, albeit a sometimes rowdy one.

The Nifty 50s

Other street groups with names emerged in the 1940s, south of downtown, in the blocks known as the "20s."[36] Some of these groups had names that reflected their street origins, such as 22nd Street, 23rd Street, and 18th Street,[37] while still others were referred to more generically as "the 20s," making the area and the groups often indistinguishable from one another. A number of these groups, like the Boozies, had all-Black memberships, while others, though primarily Black, had some Mexican, Chinese, Japanese, and even White members, like Glen Castleberry, a tough White dude from the Slausons. Some of these groups had names that reflected their mixed racial composition, like the Black Juans or Wongs, the Buddha Spooks, Buddha Bandits, and the Spook-a-Pinos.

Some groups in the 20s neighborhood, like the Daddy Rolling Stones, the Golden Ear Rings, and the Bebop Winos, emerged from several different junior and senior high schools in the area. The Roman 20s, emerging in the late 1940s, started a pattern of name development, utilizing a cool or rhyming name associated with an area. As the Black populations spread farther south from downtown, new names appeared. These street groups included: the Dirty 30s, the Naughty 40s, the Crown 40s, and the Nifty 50s.[38]

By the mid- to late 1940s, a number of groups began emerging in areas even farther south along Central Avenue,[39] in areas that had been primarily ethno-European enclaves. The street groups that developed in Watts, an older agricultural area, were both larger than the earlier downtown groups and more conflict oriented. In Watts, a.k.a. "Mudtown" because of its dirt roads and open tracts of land, a group called the Farmers arose. The Farmers distinguished themselves by a clothing style that both set them apart from and was symbolic of a proud reflection of where they came from. Their style was bib overalls, whose large pockets were also a handy place to carry hammers, which could be used against rivals. Some of the other Watts groups established reputations as fierce fighters, like the Huns, while still others, like Sin Town, were more into the pursuit of illicit pleasures.

Slausons, Businessmen, and Gladiators

North of Watts and adjacent to it, in the largely White European working-class Florence-Firestone District, on the East-Side, one of the largest, longest-surviving, most powerful, most established, most feared, and most complex street gangs in all of South Los Angeles arose—the Slausons. Ted W. stated that the Slausons "were one of the biggest gangs in south-central Los Angeles until 1970." While they fought with many different gangs during their tenure, their archrivals during most of their history were the Watts gangs.[40]

Farther north, between Central and Broadway and the upper 40s and Santa Barbara,[41] another powerful East-Side street group from South Park emerged in 1957, called the Businessmen. Initially, this group was an amalgamation of individuals from various other sets that had formed earlier in the area. On the West-Side, a number of other street groups emerged, the best known of which was the Gladiators.[42] Their home ground was near the University of Southern California (USC) and close to the Coliseum.[43]

Individuals from the various cliques of the Businessmen and the Gladiators would occasionally have differences with one another that would be settled with fists, although for the most part, they were friendly. The president of the Baby Businessmen[44] told us they considered the Gladiators to be "West-Side Businessmen." Friendship was not in the cards between the Gladiators and the Slausons. The mere mention of the other's name could get blood to boil.

How Many Street Organizations?

Nobody knew how many street groups there were, an apparently minor issue since it did not deter widespread speculation. Even the venerable Frederick Thrasher, with his sanctified numbers of 1,313 gangs with 50,000 members in Chicago in the mid-1920s, may have manipulated, or been manipulated to put forth guesstimated numbers. It's curious that researchers have not raised issue with the symmetry of Thrasher's numbers or where he got them. But George Knox did, in an often overlooked magnum opus on gangs.[45] Through interviews and examination of historical records at several universities, Knox draws the following conclusions about Thrasher and his data: he was an "amusing and likeable fellow" but "asked questions carelessly" and "would have been forced to run for his life" had he entered any of the "three empires of gangdom in Chicago."[46] Gilbert Geis, in a nod to the value of history from the source, suggests the 1,313 number was given to Thrasher as a prank by research assistants, because it was part of the address of a brothel near Thrasher's gang project.[47]

Thrasher's field research proceeded with an opaque methodology, according to Knox. He probably spent no more than one to two years in the field, and he couldn't have had direct or even indirect contact with all 1,313 gangs. He relied on the police and crime commissions and the YMCA for much of his data and included "any club" that was not socially sanctioned, as well as more delinquent and criminal groups, as gangs in his count.[48] Thrasher's contributions to gang research have been enormous, but as Knox notes, he had little idea of how many gangs there were when he counted as gangs groups that met his definition as well as those that didn't.[49] He appears to have counted lions and sheep, to tell us how many wolves there were.

Statistics on South Los Angeles street groups are more complicated than the headlines suggest.[50] While the data on how many street groups existed in the years before 1965 remain elusive, a lot of numbers, from assorted sources, are available to choose from. The Los Angeles newspapers uniformly suggested the number of street groups and their members increased from the 1920s to the 1960s, following the significant demographic expansion in the areas where the groups were found.[51] This is a reasonable assumption. Plus, the increased official attention the groups received all but assured that many guesstimates would remain newsworthy topics for decades to come.

Formal statistics on the numbers of these groups don't exist because, as noted, they were not being kept by either the LAPD or LASD before the 1970s.[52] Also, because the newspapers and news articles of the period left the definition of the group up to the articles' authors, who in turn offered estimations based on questionable data sources, it's often unclear what kind of a group they were writing about. Nonetheless, the following material should be interesting.

Go Figure

Dick O'Connor, in a series of articles written in the *Los Angeles Herald and Examiner*, claimed 138 youth gangs existed on the streets of Los Angeles by 1953. He indicates that some of these were "roving squads of vandals and party crashers," but others were miniature armies with up to five hundred members.[53] A *Los Angeles Times* article, also written in 1953, stated: "There are some 5000 boys and young men in Los Angeles who belong to the gangs."

Some of these gangs were from East Los Angeles, but an undisclosed proportion of them were from South Los Angeles. At least one of these downtown gangs included "Anglos and Negroes, as well as youths of Mexican descent."[54] Gene Sherman, in a three-part series for the *Los Angeles Times*, writes: "Juvenile gangs in Los Angeles have increased from 209 in 1961 to 258 last year [1962], capturing the concern of law enforcement agencies, sociologists and the citizenry at large."[55]

One writer speculated the number of gangs in Los Angeles in 1960 ranged from 130 to 311, many of which were in South Los Angeles.[56] If car clubs are considered as part of the gang scene, there may have been as many as 2,000 of them with some 25,000 members during that same year.[57] In the following year, a *Los Angeles Times* article estimated the number of gangs at 336, with a membership of nearly 20,000. The racial and ethnic composition of these gangs, according to this author, was as follows: "Mexican American, 147; Negro, 73; Caucasian, 23; Oriental 17; Mexican-Negro-Caucasian, 6; Mexican-Negro, 5." The number of gangs in East Los Angeles was 54, while the number in South Los Angeles was 137.[58] The number of members per group was speculated to be from around 15 or 20 to as high as 200.[59]

Numbers from our respondents suggest no shortage of willing conjectures either. Billy P., a probation officer at the 77th Street LAPD station, who was born in Los Angeles in 1935 and had either been involved in or been working with gangs for most of his life, offered some informed estimates. He felt that the "first generation gangs," those that began in the mid-1940s to the early 1950s, like the Yellowjackets and Don Juans, were relatively small, with about ten members each. The Royal Aces, Ambassadors, and Crusaders were somewhat larger, with twenty to thirty members each. In general, he believed the early groups were smaller than those that followed. Evidence from the Serfs car club adds credibility to Billy P.'s evaluations. It was one of the first car clubs in Los Angeles, according to Lefon A., a sagacious Serfs member who joined in 1954. He estimated they had about twenty members at any one time during his tenure.

Barry Wa., from the Junior Businessmen, thought there were around 75 to 100 Junior Businessmen. He said these were the youth who were around most of the time so that you'd probably see everyone at least a couple of times a week if you were on the set. If a big party happened or a fight came down or they wanted to hang out at the park and play basketball or other sports, 150 might show up, usually on a weekend. Ameer, the president of the Baby Businessmen, estimated there were about 150 Babies at the height of its membership but a much smaller number of Senior Businessmen, somewhere between 20 and 50.

With somewhat different numbers, although following a similar pattern of a smaller number of members in the early cliques to larger numbers later on, the early Slauson cliques—Senior, Junior, and Babies—resembled the Businessmen. Bird estimates there were five hundred Slausons in the Babies at their zenith, when he joined in 1955. It was the largest of their cliques. He said that even though he had never seen more than ten Senior Slausons, he knew there were more.

By the early to mid-1960s, after the Babies had begun dissipating, numerous other Slauson cliques had formed. The leader of the Village Assassins clique of Slauson estimates there were about 180 of them in 1963. Florence, a Mexican group sharing the same neighborhood with Slauson, may have had 75 to 100 members of the Florence Midgets then, according to Rick C., a member of the Midgets, a number he thought remained consistent for five years. But the Slausons were likely the largest of the pre-Blood-and-Crip gangs, with perhaps as many as 5,000 members at their peak.[60]

Although most of the South Los Angeles street groups and cliques followed the pattern of small initial numbers of members to larger numbers as they grew, there is more uncertainty about the Watts street groups.[61] They began earlier than those directly to the north of them, because they had been in an established neighborhood longer, and they were centered within the housing projects. By the time groups like the Slausons and the Businessmen came on the set, the Watts groups had already been recognized, with clusters that were often quite large. Bird knew that they not only had many cliques but that each clique had a "healthy helpin' of suckas." The Watts street groups were powerful, their neighborhoods insular, but their mobility was limited because they lacked the cars that groups like the Slausons had. To some extent, their limitations were probably due to their greater poverty—no money, no cars.[62]

The picture of Los Angeles's juvenile street groups portrayed here suggests that the City and county have been home to them since at least the early part of the twentieth century. The groups were geographically widespread, varied considerably in size, varied in their activities, were socially rather than criminally organized, were racially and ethnically diverse, and were quite numerous. Nonetheless, South Los Angeles sets failed to attract much attention even after the 1953 Cluff incident. Although the incident happened in South Los Angeles, the gang focus continued to be kept on East Los Angeles and Mexican gangs.

The Main Events

The industrial restructuring of Los Angeles had accomplices. World War II[63] and its aftermath led to dramatic demographic changes in South Los Angeles for Black Angelenos, as those who had come to work in the booming war-related factories stayed on, while others who were stationed here or had spent time here as a result of military commitments returned to live, often with their families. Ron Eldridge, a South Los Angeles Fire Department captain, dubbed the demographic change accompanying World War II and the Korean War "the great Black migration to L.A." He writes:

> Black military servicemen stationed on the west coast during the wars found a better place to live than the segregated South. They wrote home and sent for their friends and families to come west. Due to WW II and the Korean War there were an abundance of jobs in factories and plants like Douglas, Lockheed, and Hughes Aircraft.[64]

Besides job availability for the men and the existence of a different kind of racism than where they came from, Black women found jobs too: "Black mothers could work for rich White movie stars, doctors, businessmen, and lawyers, and not be oppressed like in the segregated South. . . . Blacks came west looking for jobs and a better way of life," Eldridge pens.[65]

Associated with this westward migration was the re-creation of a lifestyle they were familiar with. The people who moved to Los Angeles brought their relatives with them or encouraged them to follow later, creating large extended family networks reminiscent of those they had been raised in. Eldridge notes: "Fathers would come first, then send for the mother and kids. These families would send for other family members who wanted to live close by." Circumstances sometimes led to overcrowding among certain families, with "as many as three to four families living in one home."[66]

Many families moved into the existing Black communities near downtown and into those in Watts. Due to such an unprecedented migration and because of a shortage of affordable housing, various government housing projects, designed in part to house servicemen and their families, were built to accommodate the newly arriving immigrants. Many of these projects were located near the downtown area: William Mead Housing Project, Ramona Gardens, Rose Hills, Estrada Courts, and Aliso Village. Others, such as Jordan Downs, Imperial Courts, Nickerson Gardens, Hacienda Courts, Palm Lane, and Pueblo Courts, were located in Watts.

Servicemen with GI loans and families with some money bought single-family homes in the traditionally White Florence-Firestone District, along Central Avenue, which separated the downtown Black community from Watts. Some of the families moving into the district came from other states, while others moved from the two largely Black areas mentioned. The Florence-Firestone District provided decent employment opportunities for those whose homes were now close by. Homes in this district were "nice," "clean," and with no housing projects, large apartment complexes, or tightly clustered homes present. As Batani-Khalfani writes:

> Not a single project or apartment or cluster of homes was present. These homes had big front yards and back yards. Most of them had hardwood floors and some had fireplaces. There was an array of different varieties of trees present, including hundreds of palm trees on some streets. With the presence of Goodyear Rubber Company and numerous other small factories, job opportunities abounded. This area provided an attractive incentive to spur Black families from the northern and southern sections of Los Angeles to migrate into this section of South-Central Los Angeles.[67]

The Florence-Firestone District became a mixed-race working-class area of South Los Angeles and an area, similar to those north and south, that developed street groups.

After the Watts Rebellion of 1965, the street groups that had formed earlier were not as newsworthy as they had been. Harry S., a life-long resident of the Florence-Firestone District, explained the perceived reduction in street activity like this: "After the Rebellion, I thought that the gang stuff kinda died. I'd say from '65 till about '72 or '3 you didn't hear much." It is convenient to conclude that the Rebellion itself was the primary factor contributing to this decline of street activity, but it is also an oversimplification.

The Rebellion was definitive but not causal. Its influence on the community and street groups was profound, but it was another factor among the social dynamics contributing to the decline of the early groups. Bird summarizes: "The Watts Rebellion was one thing, but it was the trend of the times." It occurred during the time numerous other social forces had been gathering momentum for several years, providing alternative opportunities for street-group juveniles. Bird continues:

> The Watts Riots—they called it the Uprising, the Revolt, the Rebellion—was at the center. It was right in the midsixties, 1965, dead center. Okay, but you've got to take into account everything that happened from 1960 to '65. Like, understand that Martin Luther King was running around, Malcolm was running around, Elijah Mohammed, and, okay, Ali. He becomes an Olympic champion in 1960, and then he becomes the heavy weight champion. Then he announces that he is Muslim, and he started propagandizing and saying Black is beautiful, you know. "I'm pretty."

The Rebellion was chronologically positioned in the center of great social change and given more credit for the change than was warranted.

The Black Power movement and the Civil Rights movement siphoned off a number of important street members who found greater purpose than the set in the emerging political struggles. Their absence from the street left irreplaceable gaps in the group structure there.[68] "See, you had the whole movement, Black Power, Civil Rights, and by the Rebellion coming down in the center of all that, you had many things," observed Bird. Ameer added:

> 'Cause see, I came to the Nation of Islam in 1965. I was gonna be a Muslim 'cause Malcolm X was my idol. I dug Malcolm X, since 1962. When Malcolm died, I cried. I was mad! And there were a lot of brothers who became Muslims; some joined the U.S. organization, some became Black Panthers, and like that. The gang thing kind of dropped; it went down.

Ameer indicated that more formal city-based organizations, like the teen posts, were a contributing factor in apparent decreased street-group activity because of their emphasis on nonviolence within the Black community. He continued: "They had teen posts at that time, and they were teaching you how to have brothers come together. Their thing was all about peace in the Black culture, which I was interested in."

Also transforming the community was the criminal-justice system—it removed numerous key players through incarceration. Out of the way and out of contact with the new groups of juveniles arriving on the scene, the deleted could not provide the tutelage they had been capable of providing earlier. Alonzo, more forcefully, writes that Black consciousness was eradicated by the end of the 1960s, with the FBI's COINTELPRO "neutralizing" Black political leadership and their efforts to ameliorate social problems harming the Black community.[69] J. Edgar Hoover saw the Black Power movement as the greatest threat to America and spared little in his relentless efforts to eradicate it.[70]

Notable figures who had remained on the streets aged out of street activities, as families, children, and jobs took priority. A leadership vacuum, created by the absence of guidance from the early leaders to the youth starting to come of age, contributed to a discontinuity between the pre-1965 street groups and those that followed.

A brief anomic period followed the Rebellion, seeing new groups emerge until the first Crip sets appeared in the late 1960s. Somewhat later, Blood sets appeared. These new organizations represented a break with the past, as they seemed to be different from the groups that had preceded them. Perhaps most distinguishing was the new groups' greater ideological commitment to crime. While the earlier group members had become involved in crime with quick economic gain as their primary motivation, the new groups began to increasingly appreciate crime as a lifestyle and a reason for group existence. Whereas violence had previously been occasional, it was now being reported as commonplace.

Class and Race Rule

Early Los Angeles newspapers and national news magazines before 1942 used the term *gang* infrequently when referring to Los Angeles juvenile social problems. After the Sleepy Lagoon case and the Zoot-Suit Riots, its use became more common. In one notable 1953 treatment by the *Los Angeles Herald and Express*, for example, the author stated "that they [gangs] constitute a terrorism whose reign is Los Angeles' No. 1 police problem."[71] For most of the Los Angeles media, though, the term *gang* did not have a clear referent. It could be used interchangeably with "group," and group crime might be called "hoodlumism of irresponsible elements."[72] A gang's clearest referent before 1953 was to figures in the criminal underworld: Mickey Cohen, Bugsy Siegel, and Benny the Meatball, among others, were the primary Los Angeles "gangsters" running the City's "gangs," according to both the local and the national press.[73]

After the 1953 Cluff incident, there were attempts to link juvenile street groups to organized crime by referring to some of the juveniles' more nefarious behavior as a "juvenile gangland slaying."[74] The evidence for these claims was little more than unsupported official analogies. While some respondents had been involved in serious offenses like murder and armed robbery, it was never as part of an organized adult enterprise. Many respondents were well aware that there were organized criminal gangs in the City, having heard about them from the media or neighborhood elders. South Los Angeles juvenile street groups were neither structurally nor functionally affiliated with them, having developed independently.[75]

The Cluff incident precipitated the more frequent appearance of the term *gang* in the media's accounts of juvenile delinquency. One article in the *Los Angeles Times* titled "Youthful Gangs Active in All Parts of the City for Many Years" tried to make it appear as if Los Angeles had been plagued for a long time by violent juvenile gangs committing the most vicious of crimes:

> There is probably no crime on the books that Los Angeles gangs have not committed. Murder? Sure . . . Assault with a deadly weapon? Happens every day or so . . . Narcotics peddling and addiction? Gang activities are rife with use and sale of all types of narcotics . . . Assaults against women? The young gang members boast of such conquests.[76]

Mexican juveniles were the scapegoat. They were all described as bilingual, perhaps as a way of distancing them from law-abiding people. The *Times* writer continued: "And since the population in these [gang] areas is largely of Mexican descent, it follows that the largest single group in the gangs is made up of youths of Mexican descent. Completely bilingual, these youths habitually use Spanish when conversing with one another."[77] With little evidence and with a dubious commitment to historical accuracy, this first in a series of analytical *Times* articles following the Cluff incident helped to sensationalize, exaggerate, and mislead with its opinions on youth gang behavior.

Rather than gang activities being "rife" in all parts of the City as claimed, it was the media that were suddenly rife with its reports of these activities. There is no question that juvenile street groups had existed for years before 1953; nor is there any issue with Mexicans being a part of them. But Mexicans, at least those in South Los Angeles, did not have proprietary rights to gang membership, and many were not bilingual. Motivated by their parents, many Mexican juveniles were trying to acculturate, and those within the Black community were significantly influenced by Black culture.[78]

A threat of potential physical harm to the public from gangs, as suggested by the media, raises the question of what was the actual danger that gangs posed compared to the perceptions of that danger. The dearth of media material before the Cluff incident suggests that both the actual and the perceived danger from gangs were probably quite low. Racial separation, due to the spatial nature of Los Angeles, was still considerable, keeping conflict minimal, while deindustrialization was just in its infancy.[79] It was the "dramatization of evil," as represented by the Cluff case,[80] that opened the Pandora's box to perceived danger and fear from Los Angeles street groups rather than any sudden increase in predatory gang activity.

A Pejorative Assembly

The post Cluff discovery of gangs evolved haphazardly. Much of the time, officials were not clear in their statements as to whether a youthful street group interaction was a *melee*, a *brawl*, a *riot*, or a *gang fight*, carried out by a *faction*, a *club*, a *fraternity*, or a *gang*, as the terms were seamlessly used interchangeably when referring to these groups and their activities. The following example, taken from various incidents occurring at the beach, is illustrative:

> Torrance and Redondo Beach police reported yesterday they broke up a riot of 15 to 18 youths. . . . Three members of the 'muscle' fra-

ternity at Long Beach received County Jail terms for their parts in a beach brawl.... Police and lifeguards yesterday broke up a minor gang fight between two youthful factions on the Long Beach strand.[81]

It is quite possible that these incidents, occurring in primarily middle-class White communities, received less opprobrium than they would have had they happened in a lower-class minority community. Perhaps the term *gang* might have been too harsh a label for this news source to reference these activities and too unacceptable to its readership.

Increasingly though, the word *gang* began to take shape in more clearly defined ways. Its usual referents were non-White juveniles, involved in fights or assaults, occurring in a lower- or working-class area or implicating lower- or working-class participants. When weapons were found, and when one or more participants wound up being hurt seriously enough to require either a doctor's or, more rarely, mortician's care, *gang* was there. These examples from the *Los Angeles Times* (1954–1958) are illustrative:

Homer Ray Johnson, 147 E. 77th street, ganged upon and severely stabbed in the abdomen and the lower part of his back.... Carmen Garcia, 18, of 4127 E. Zola St., Pico, was shot in the right arm and stabbed several times with an eight inch butcher knife early yesterday in an apparent outbreak of hoodlum gang warfare.... Four persons involved in a gang fight during which an El Toro marine was stabbed to death were filed on by the district attorney.[82]

Another but less frequently appearing context for *gang* began to occur when the groups involved were identifiable by a name. A name provided a solid basis to classify the group as a gang, with or without corroborating evidence: "Five teenage boys, asserted members of gangs, attending local and junior high schools, were arrested last week after a fourteen year-old youth was attacked and severely beaten.... Others arrested said that they were members of the 'Roman Twenties' and 'Agitators' gangs."[83] Names, as markers for deviants, have a rich history in labeling theory, where they dramatize evil and facilitate control by imposing stigma.[84] As symbols, gang labels designated a group with organization and gave the public a conceptual category and a definable enemy.

The group's behavior may have involved criminal activity, as the case above suggests, but then, it may not have. If the group had a name, irrespective of whether their behavior was criminal, they were a gang according to many officials. As the following example suggests, a named juvenile group became a prime candidate for gang status: "Members of the Compton and El Jardin gangs—who have been at odds for the past several years—sat down at conference tables last night to 'iron out their problems' in the gymnasium of Centennial Senior High School, Compton."[85] A name differentiates a group from a mob, crowd, or any other nonorganized entity with its suggestion of union.

Gangs became defined by media reports that were enhanced by police and other criminal-justice agencies' input in Los Angeles during the 1940s and 1950s.[86] The essential characteristics that emerged to distinguish gangs from nongangs became race or ethnicity, social class, violent behavior, and a name. In a casual dismissal of the need to examine further what constitutes a gang or a gang member (because it should be so obvious to even an untrained eye), some justice-department officials would often derisively use the following refrain: "If it walks like a duck and looks like a duck, it must be a duck." Bird deftly upended this sweeping generalization with the following observation: "A goose walks like a duck and looks like a duck, so is it a duck?"

To add to the growing list of pejorative characteristics of gangs, there were attempts to portray those who joined as being social misfits.[87] In Los Angeles, Saul Bernstein, using categories provided by the Group Guidance Project of the Los Angeles County Probation Department, described three different types of gangs in existence between 1961 and 1962, as follows: (1) "chronically gang-oriented," representing 14 percent of the gangs; (2) "situationally gang-oriented," representing 62.8 percent; (3) "non-delinquent," representing 23.2 percent.[88] Admitting ignorance of and questioning the validity of the conceptual and methodological rigor employed in arriving at these constructs, Bernstein nevertheless continued to conduct his analysis of gangs as though the characterizations are probably accurate. By doing so, he contributed to building the castle, using a foundation that even he suspected was built on sand.

Of special interest was Bernstein's focus on the "chronically" gang-oriented boy. The boy was termed the "gang psycho" and "gang war butch," a juvenile with a history of family "psychopathology," who was a school dropout, with a poor work history, living in a family with "frustrating" relationships.[89] Such negative ad hominem terminology did little to promote objectivity but probably did a whole lot to contribute to the condemnation associated with juvenile gangs and gang members.[90] We found little evidence to support any of Bernstein's pejorative contentions.

With the exception of organized adult criminal gangs, the references to White gangs in Los Angeles were limited.[91] This omission, in all probability, helped contribute to the solid public notion of gangs as organizations of minorities.[92] Although never clearly articulating what a gang was nor how it might have differed from a group, a mob, a football team, Alpha Lambda Phi, the Girl Scouts, or the Elks Club, the term, with its derogatory connotations, became established in the public lexicon and imagination as named groups of poor minority youth engaged in crime—or at least up to no good. In Los Angeles, rather than focusing on racism, it seemed more expedient to focus on gangs. Rather than demonizing prejudice and inequality, its victims were blamed, as gangs were demonized.

Grab Another Non-White Group

Durkheimian theory holds that social conformity is facilitated when there is a group of deviants to cast aspersions on.[93] Erikson adds that societies need deviant groups to serve as a bond to hold the society together and that societies create institutions, like prisons, to guarantee the production of criminal groups.[94] The gang has become one such group although its origin was rather humble. It is a term whose English roots date to around 1400, where it refers to a "band of men," or "group of men," often, "work men."[95] David Brotherton adds that the term was applied to criminal groups in England displaced by the industrial revolution and that by 1900, it had become a derogatory concept in Europe. In a nod to the powerful influence of the *American gang industry*, and the American search for a "universalized definition of gang," Alistair Fraser notes the early English definitions lacked the current "malignant overtones" found among many American gang researchers.[96]

When the term *gang* came to America, it could refer to a group of slaves for sale and to working-class thieves.[97] American English added a *-ster* suffix to *gang* around 1900 to create the American term *gangster*,[98] enhancing the original English meaning. Americans further reworked the term by taking out its root, *gang*, and then transforming it to be more compliant with the new Americanized concept of a gangster. The gang was reborn in America as a violent criminal group with gangsters as members. Further American refinement has racialized the term and "encoded it with class-based stereotypes," as concern among many researchers grows that the dominant voice among gang researchers will become firmly in control of those who are "embedded in law enforcement."[99] Although having English roots, the term should properly be stamped with the label *Made in America*.

At times in America, gang was treated lightheartedly. *Our Gang* was a group of mischievous youth—Spanky, Alfalfa, and Buckwheat—of the 1920s and 1930s. The group was later reborn as *The Little Rascals* when TV became more ubiquitous in the 1950s. The *Dead-End Kids* made their debut in a 1937 film of a similar name, becoming the *East Side Kids* in the 1940s. Another name change in the mid-1940s to the *Bowery Boys*[100] had them in the public eye until the mid-1950s, when they became popularized in a number of films. *Kool and the Gang*, another variation on the aberrant innocuousness of the term, was a musical group formed in the mid-1960s. But the halcyon days of gangs ended.

Researchers, since the 1950s, using aggregate police data or self-report data, have found similarities in their conceptualization of gangs that resemble what the early Los Angeles media constructed. Accordingly, gangs are described as groups of youth, mostly minority, mostly male, and primarily from the underclass or lower class. Gangs are found to be involved in a disproportionate number of crimes and statute violations and are often recidivists.[101] Finn-Ange Esbensen and L. Thomas Winfree Jr., note that it wasn't until the 1950s that "commentators" began to identity gang members by race or ethnicity,[102] while we wrote earlier that "racialization," as used by Alonzo,[103] was a process that began in Los Angeles during the World War II years.[104] As the idea of gangs took shape in America in the late 1800s and early 1900s, a "foreignness" theme,[105] differentiating them from everyone else, characterized them. This theme later transitioned to non-Whites, as the non-White population increased while White foreigners became less foreign by blending.

John Hagedorn is unequivocal in his assertions that an understanding of racism is essential for an understanding of gangs. "Black is dangerous," he notes.[106] And Black males are the "embodiment of the predator," Elijah Anderson adds.[107] "The deracializing of gangs is one of the most egregious errors of Western criminology," Hagedorn continues.[108] Joan Moore suggests, "Perhaps the image of 'gang' to include Whites as well as Blacks and Hispanics would be to make Anglos think too much about gangs as ordinary adolescents, like their own children, not like 'them.'"[109] When the dangerous classes included assorted unassimilated White European ethnicities, such as those studied by Frederic Thrasher and Herbert Asbury, calling these groups gangs was acceptable. But the European ethnic groups melted into White America, departed from the dangerous classes, and abandoned the opportunity to continue to be labeled gangs, bequeathing the name to non-Whites.

Brotherton notes that the efforts being made to universalize gang as a negative phenomenon seem to be an American penchant.[110] Fraser adds that gang meanings are being removed from local historical contexts and then "re-imagined as a global universal." Such pathologizing by power elite agents is part of an effort to define gangs as dangerous by collapsing popular fears of non-Whites into them so that gangs can be better controlled.[111] By focusing on the control of gangs through fear, a second function is achieved: shifting attention away from other, even more serious—although less threatening to societal hegemony—issues. We worry about gangs and not the crimes of the power elite.

The alien Other, a concept used to describe the disparagement of Blacks and the way they have been vilified as people to be fearful of, has jumped genres: from Blacks to gangs and gang members. Good citizens can rally; they can feel solidarity among themselves while focusing on the wicked—the gang. Some gang researchers are pushing the theoretical envelope by broadly generalizing gangs in an effort to draw parallels between juvenile street gangs and the newest moral panic—terrorist groups.[112] The reduction of gang to the alien Other is being universalized,[113] with the most nefarious behavioral examples of Los Angeles and Chicago gangs serving as the model for gangs elsewhere.[114] Localized historical development is being overridden, as research on the pathologized gang becomes the focus, with its consequent dependence on government funds.[115]

Anderson has shown that people in the Black community perceive the criminal justice system to have a double standard: one for Blacks and one for Whites.[116] Moore concurs, affirming that law enforcement in Los Angeles has used "racist explanations" for decades to account for the problems of Mexican American youth.[117] Black Angeleno juveniles are another non-White group whose problems are explained the same way. We hypothesize that the control perspective on gangs, by pathologizing them as malevolent organizations, has become the essential ingredient in the transmogrification of the concept of the gang from the early English version to gangs as a "fundamental social evil."[118] The term *gang* was pejoratized and racialized on this conceptual journey and is now well established as synonymous with groups of inherently no-good—even hopeless—non-White juveniles of the underclass. *Gang* has become a "pathologizing trope"[119] in its unreflexive evolution, so that it has now become an acronym for *Grab Another Non-White Group*.

"We Ain't No Delinquents. We're Misunderstood."[120]

Understating a problem can be just as harmful as overstating it. Juvenile groups appear in an infinite variety of shapes, sizes, and organizational arrangements, with enormous variation in their behavior. Few are saints while many are sinners. Juveniles break the law, at times willfully and at other times inadvertently. Sometimes their behavior is understood well, and sometimes it is not. We do not want to minimize the personal harm or property damage juveniles are involved in or excuse it. But to lump together curfew violators with killers and terrorists because they both happen to be non-White and have a connection to the same named group is to engage in a fallacy of misplaced concreteness: demonizing all because of the actions of a few. When the control perspective homogenizes non-White street groups by calling them gangs and then uses the worst among them as the archetype of all, punitiveness is facilitated.[121] Homogenization is enabled when fear is stoked.

While being a gang member in California is not exactly a crime—yet—criminalization of the term is in process. The California Street Terrorism Enforcement and Prevention Act, or the STEP Act, of 1988, was passed because the legislature found the State to be in a "state of *crisis* which has been caused by *violent* street gangs."[122] This finding justified the legislature adding gang enhancement penalties to anyone gang affiliated and convicted of a crime. The Act mandated that if a person could be adjudicated a gang member at the time he or she was found to have committed the felony or found to have assisted a gang member in the commission of a felony, anywhere from one year in a county jail to as much as ten years in a state prison could be added to whatever sentence they might receive for the crime(s) they were convicted of.[123] The felony could be as serious as murder or as nonserious as theft. Regardless of the Act's alleged good intentions of protecting society, the latent consequences have been to guarantee that those labeled gang members go to prison.[124]

A Threat to the Social Order

A Grand Canyon–size political chasm exists between what the public believes to be true about crime and the data-driven social reality of it. Crime in American society has been and continues to be ubiquitous.[125] By the amount of attention given to street crime, and especially crime involving juveniles and street gangs, it would be reasonable to assume that it is the most frequently committed type of crime and that it represents the greatest threat to the social order. Political leaders and their agents promote the myth that delinquency and gangs pose a serious threat to the well-being of our nation. Alfred Regnery, an OJJDP administrator, wrote that juvenile crime is a "grave problem on a national scale," "staggering" in range and intensity. A Florida congressman stated that juvenile offenders are "the most dangerous criminals on the face of the earth." Add to this the media's refrain of "youth crime plagues" and "remorseless teens" "running amuck,"[126] and the myth is easily internalized.

A 1994 Gallup poll found that 72 percent of the public viewed "the growth of youth gangs" as an important contributor to violence in America.[127] Quicker regularly conducted surveys in his large lecture classes on the first day, asking students to indicate what they thought were the ten most serious threats to the well-being of our society. The results became quite predictable over the years. Juvenile delinquency or juvenile street gang crime consistently appeared in the top five, often in the top three.[128] When he pointed out that youth crime was only one dimension of the larger crime problem, and a minor one at that, since the number of juveniles at any given time is a fraction of the overall population, their most regular response was, "Really?" When they discussed gangs, he would point out further that only a small percentage of juveniles considered themselves gang members,[129] a minority of a minority, and that it would be statistically improbable for them to be engaging in the majority of crime. Again, he would get another, "Really?"

While juvenile groups are involved in a wide variety of crime, they are minimally involved in the plethora of crimes adults are.[130] Such adult crimes like political crime and organized crime may see a smattering of juveniles, while one of the most pernicious crimes, white-collar crime, has even fewer.[131] White-collar crime is mostly associated with crimes of the middle and upper classes, where it continues to benefit from a public perception as relatively benign, if even criminal.[132] Yet conservative estimates put the economic costs of corporate crime at $400 to $500 billion a year in the early 2000s, which was more than thirty times the cost of street crime. When it comes to violence, the number of victims of street violence pale in comparison to the victims of corporate violence. In the early part of the twenty-first century, the average number of people who were the victims of murder was around 16,000 annually. At the same time, over 100,000 people died on average each year from preventable injuries at work, unsafe consumer products, and environmental pollution.[133]

Crime can pose a serious threat to the social order, but not juvenile crime. Juvenile crime is a symptom of the overall level of the social ills of a society: it is a dependent variable. This is not the case for white-collar crime. As former attorney general of the United States Ramsey Clark stated in 1970, white-collar crime "is the most corrosive of all crime."[134] C. Wright Mills emphasized that its existence created a "higher immorality" in our society.[135] James Coleman adds that white-collar crime, whether measured "in terms of financial losses, deaths and injuries, or damage to our social fabric . . . is the greatest crime problem of our age."[136] Victor Kappeler and Gary Potter write that corporate crime unequivocally "does more damage to the social fabric, health, and safety of the country than all the murderers, rapists, terrorists, and property criminals combined."[137] White-collar crime is enabled by political complicity. The power elite are involved in, benefit from, and facilitate white-collar crime and have the resources to prevent prosecution and even association with these crimes.[138]

Crimes of the power elite can be concealed from the public when the criminal hides behind street crime and street criminals. Using crimes by despised gang members works especially well, as Eric Alterman argued happened in New York in the middle part of the nineteenth century.[139] As initially documented by Asbury in *The Gangs of New York*, and then again by Martin Scorsese in 2002 with his film of the same name, immigrant gangs of violent adults, driven by racism, were battling in the streets. Excluded from both accounts was the gang belonging to William "Boss" Twead and his hardened Tammany Hall thugs. Known as the "Twead Ring," it used the city's warring gangs as physical enablers in its corruption, while remaining mostly hidden until its scandals threatened the larger power elite.[140]

Herman and Julia Schwendinger, in an important heuristic on crime, tried raising the bar a bit higher on the political nature of definitions of crime. They argued that criminologists, by accepting the current legal definitions of crime, without considering other acts that are just as socially injurious, and in many cases more so, are using science to defend the political and economic order rather than to promote a more just society. By ignoring considerations of issues such as imperialist wars, poverty, sexism, and racism as crime, and those who commit them as criminals, criminologists are acting as defenders of existing power arrangements.[141] When gang researchers unreflectively consider juvenile street groups as independent variables and associate them with the worst social evils, without studying their association with the larger social order, their histories, and their local contexts, they too run the risk of becoming "defenders of order" rather than "guardians of human rights."[142]

4

Street Group Development

A Storied Evolution

We need histories that teach us how societies learned to imagine themselves as threatened by conspiracies of the marginalized.
—David Nirenberg, *The Impresarios of Trent*

S treet group formation in South Los Angeles occurred among juveniles who enjoyed one another's company, as evidenced by their hanging out together. *Hanging out*, or *hang-out group*, describes them better than Frederic Thrasher's term *play group*.[1] Hang-out groups spent their time *fussin', cussin', and discussin'*, some while engaged in various activities, such as playing a sport. Hang-out groups were usually part of larger in-groups where fighting was common. Since certain types of fights are considered criminal, it could be argued these were criminal groups;[2] but this is a stretch of logic that does not contribute to a better understanding. Each group was distinctive yet with notable similarities to the others. Social phenomena are complex: what is generally true is often specifically false.[3] The nuances are what confound organizing social life into tidy categories.

Skinny Turnips and Pyramids

A detailed description of the complexity of gang structures is provided by R. Lincoln Keiser in his analysis of the Chicago Vice Lords. The "Vice Lord Nation," he argues, is divided into territorially based "branches," with their own name and set of officers. At least one of these branches, the City Lords, was further divided into a subordinate subbranch, or "section," also with its own name and leaders. Most branches were subdivided into "age groups," like the "Seniors," "Juniors," and "Midgets," with their own additional set of officers. Branches and sections were subdivided into the "basic units" of the Vice Lord social system: "cliques." Cliques, Keiser writes, are "running partners" whose membership may cut across age groups. Many of these cliques have their own names. While other researchers have found gang structures divided into various subgroupings, none has found a system as complex as the one Keiser describes. Keiser notes that the Vice Lords—similar to the South Los Angeles groups—referred to their organization as a "club," not a gang.[4]

Malcolm Klein's research found the most common gang structure was a "skinny turnip," where the oldest and youngest cliques were at the top and bottom and were relatively small in comparison to the larger middle cliques. The "gang clusters" he described were composed of two to five age-graded subgroups, which represented various cliques.[5] John Hagedorn found Milwaukee gangs to be composed of a "coalition of age-graded groups," with their own main group, and "wanna bes." These gangs, he argued, did not have the "bureaucratic pyramidal shape" that the police pictured.[6] The police analysis seemed more influenced by, and more representative of, a police department's own organizational structure than a gang's.

Diego Vigil describes Chicano gangs as having numerous cliques of the same age. Usually these cliques of thirty or so members seldom acted as a group but rather spent the majority of their time relating in dyadic and other small-group formations. Weekends and special occasions, like weddings and baptisms, were exceptions, bringing the whole "cohort" together to join in the festivities. Normally, Vigil contends, the average number hanging out with one another, at any one time, seldom exceeded five to ten members.[7] South Los Angeles street groups were similar.

In South Los Angeles, the most common structural form the largest juvenile groups assumed was the shape of a crudely formed pyramid with rough, uneven sides. This was not the bureaucratic pyramidal shape rejected by Hagedorn but rather a form displaying the increasing number of clique formations and the larger size of the cliques, as the group aged. At the top were the Seniors or the Bigs, such as the Senior Businessmen and the Big Slausons; these were the group founders.[8] If the founders groups survived long enough for younger cliques to form, and they recognized the founders as originators, the group became a set.[9] Each subsequent group became a clique of the set, with the founders' clique usually being the smallest. As new age cohorts emerged in the set's neighborhood, each successive cohort tended to be larger than the preceding one. Cliques formed within those cohorts, under the banner of the set, until there were so many cliques the set became too large to recognize itself as a group. Set expansion contributed to increasingly diffuse central control, to a loss of structural definition, and to a loss of name identity after 1965.[10]

To Clique or Not to Clique

Larger sets in South Los Angeles usually had cliques. Cliques from the larger sets often had more members than some of the smaller sets. Very large cliques continued the process of subdivision by forming numerous smaller cliques within a similar age range. Cliques that subdivided or split off became new cliques rather than forming any other named subdivisional unit. Though numerical size was an important factor in clique division, because there were so many cliques and sets of varying sizes, size was not a factor differentiating a set from a clique.[11] Sets and cliques were sometimes distinct, while at other times they were not.

Given the multiple meanings of the concept of gang, the above should not be surprising. One writer's gang might have been another's clique, club, set, crew, fraternity, or soccer team. In South Los Angeles, the groups that formed were far more complex than a collection of predatory delinquent youth scouring the City looking for victims. The early sets were from and identified with a neighborhood. So closely aligned were the concepts of set and neighborhood that members would regularly use the terms interchangeably when referring to their group. Also reflecting the closeness that set members often felt toward one another was the use of an even more intimate term for their group: *family*. "My set was like my family," was repeated regularly in our interviews.[12]

Age, as researchers looking at other cities found, seemed to be the single most important factor for clique formation in the groups they studied.[13] This was the case in South Los Angeles too. Most sets that had been around for two or more years subdivided into cliques that were composed of juveniles who were within one or two years of each other in age. When age-graded cliques got too large, they subdivided further into additional cliques based on mutual interests. The clique's name could be modified while keeping allegiance to the larger groups. The Baby Slausons, for example, developed smaller cliques of like-minded individuals from within the Babies, such as the Warlords, who continued their allegiance to both the Slausons and the Babies: they were the Warlords of Baby Slauson.

When a set had cliques, the primary factor uniting them was identity with the larger set. Many cliques had names that reflected their neighborhood affiliation, like Little Slausons and Baby Slausons or Senior Businessmen and Junior Businessmen. When cliques took names, the clique name usually preceded the set name.[14] Cliques had various degrees of independence, but they generally adhered to the norms of their neighborhood. The norms were not written but were understood. They were established, maintained, and enforced by the older respected members of the set. No matter how many cliques formed, they never lost sight of the larger whole of which they were a part.[15] Cliques unable to demonstrate set fealty either became new sets or disbanded altogether.

Determining which came first, the set or the clique, must consider social context. Often the nascent sets appeared more like a clique than a set, while considering themselves neither. Whether clique, set, or social group, some lasted less than a year. Some changed their name, added or deleted a few members, and then emerged as a new organization for a time. For sets like the Slausons, the original Big Slausons were a small group of perhaps a dozen youth who came from other neighborhoods to hang out at Slauson Park, or the Park. They considered themselves to be "the guys of Slauson Park" because they hung out there together. They didn't become a clique of the Slausons until after the Little Slauson clique was formed. The original group became the Big Slausons clique by default since they were first, and because the younger group had established name recognition as Little Slausons, the earlier group had to be "Big."

Street groups that formed without developing cliques often disappeared after a few months but could last longer. The Senators were such a group. With about forty-seven members, they lasted four or five years before "fading away."[16] They had their beginnings sometime before 1957 in the Temple Street neighborhood.[17] According to their president, Jasper, they were initially just "a social club: a bunch of guys hangin' around; there was no gang in our thoughts." They behaved that way too, like a club or college fraternity. Jasper said that their reasons for existence were to "give parties, hang out together, go to the beach together, low-ride together, catch chicks, you know, just a bunch of guys." They had a president, a vice president, and a treasurer. Group cohesion waned as the members got older, got jobs, got married, and started families.[18] The Senators considered their group a club, although they also recognized that their occasional conflict with other groups might qualify them as a gang in the eyes of many.

Essay or *Ese*: Mexican Sets on the South Side[19]

Cultural influence was often reciprocal among people living in South Los Angeles, and it blurred racial differences, especially between Blacks and Chicanos. When Poop from the Little Slausons was fourteen or fifteen years old and was an Eagle Scout, he was asked to write a five-hundred- to one-thousand-word essay on why he wanted to be a fireman. The assignment confused him: How could he write a Mexican?

The two terms *essay* and *ese*, while often pronounced similarly, are spelled differently and have different meanings. "Essay" to Poop meant *ese*, a Spanish word that translates as "that" or "you." *Ese* was the term Mexicans in his neighborhood regularly used to refer to one another. Following their lead, Blacks did too. Poop was being requested to write a five-hundred- to one-thousand-word *Mexican*, he reasoned, an assignment that didn't make sense and that he was too embarrassed to inquire further about. As he thought when given the assignment: "What kind of shit is this? You know what 'essay' meant to me, a Mexican. The reason Blacks called them 'eses' was because every time a Chicano would say something in them days, they say 'ese.' 'No, ese,' and 'ese this' and 'ese that.' We started calling them eses. Yeah, essays to me were Mexicans." Familiarity in this case bred cultural ignorance, then fear, and consequently no career as a fireman.

South Los Angeles north of Watts was a racially mixed neighborhood, originally composed of White European households; as Black and Mexican families moved in, most Whites moved out, and those that remained became the minority. Black and Mexican youth found themselves living alongside each other and going to the same schools together, like it or not. Racial harmony between them became the norm, especially in the earlier years when social class differences were few and both found themselves unwelcomed by the Whites. Blacks and Mexicans even joined the same sets, especially before 1940. As their populations grew, their sets became increasingly homogeneous and often overlapping.[20] The largest Black and Chicano sets in the Florence-Firestone neighborhood, Slauson and Florence, shared the same original neighborhood in a mostly peaceful manner.

Linda C., a founding member of the Florencitas,[21] explained that the reason why there were few racial antagonisms between Blacks and Chicanos was because their life experiences were similar: they shared their cultures and battled the same adversaries as they faced the same barriers.[22] In her words:

> We've gone hand and hand through life. We've gone through the same struggles, the same bullshit. We've had the same enemies, okay; we've gone to the same schools. I mean, we had families living next door to us that were Black. My best girlfriend, Ana Jean, was from one of them. I use to eat at her house, she use to eat at mine. That's why I know about soul food.

Linda adds that South Los Angeles Black culture had more influence on their lifestyle than Chicano culture, giving the South Los Angeles Chicano groups more in common with them than with East Los Angeles Spanish-speaking gangs. She continued:

> See, that's why I say our identity is so different from East LA: just by our talk, our rap, our culture, our walk, our music; it's just about ev-

erything. It's so different and unique from them that we would never be able to get along. When you go to the penitentiary, just by the way you talk, they can tell where you from: Sur [south], East-Side, or whatever. But Black gangs and Chicano gangs have always been right there, okay, hand and hand, walking through the whole thing—together.

Whit, the vice president of the Royal Aces, concurred with Linda C.'s analysis, adding, "The Mexican and Black kids got along really well back then. You never heard of a Mexican jumping on a Black; they were always friendly with the Blacks." Besides having similar foes, there was another common element that contributed to their racial harmony: marijuana. For Blacks who enjoyed it, Mexicans would oblige them—for a price, of course. As Whit makes clear: "The Blacks use to go and cop weed from the Mexicans a lot of times 'cause they sold their weed so cheap and it was some of the best." This cooperation was a natural outgrowth of parties attended by both Blacks and Mexicans, where interracial mingling and dating were not uncommon.[23] Marriage and having children together were unexceptional in the neighborhood.

Racially One Way, Culturally Another

Where Mexicans outnumbered Blacks, Blacks adopted a lot of Mexican culture, reducing the differences between them to one: race.[24] As Whit explains, "The Blacks that lived there, lived like the Mexicans themselves. They spoke Spanish, ate Mexican food, and the only thing was that they were Black." Correspondingly, among the Florence set members living around a large number of Blacks, the situation was reversed: the Mexicans adopted many Black traits. In addition to listening to predominantly Black musical artists and dancing with Black aplomb, Mexicans talked with Black street accents and fought like Black boxers. Rick C., a White member of Florence, wanted to make it clear that his set was more like a Black set than an East Los Angeles Chicano gang. He explained, "We wouldn't talk like a Mexican gang in East LA. You would talk, and you would sound Black."

Frank M., who in the late 1940s and 1950s lived and hung out with the guys from Clanton and Mateo Street,[25] all mixed groups of Blacks and Chicanos, saw no racial antagonisms either.[26] He said:

> We lived real close together, and we did things together. We'd have little boxing matches. We went to grammar school with them, went to junior high; we were pretty friendly. See, they had Black guys in

their gangs too. Like we had Mexican guys in our gang, so we didn't get into a racial thing. We had Chinese too. Race didn't enter into the picture at all.

Frank did acknowledge that Blacks and Chicanos would sometimes fight with each other, usually having to do with ownership rights of items or personal antipathies, but not race. He expounded:

If we'd see a Mexican guy that we didn't know that had something we wanted, we'd take it from him. We'd see a Black guy or Mexican guy that had something, or we didn't like him, we'd beat him up and take whatever he had. We wouldn't just beat him up because he's Mexican. If we beat him up, it was because we just wanted to beat him up and take something.

As Frank M. explained, to understand that there was racial harmony is not to suggest there was complete accord. Antagonisms between individuals, and more general antagonisms between respective cliques, occurred and did lead to fights. But the causes were largely personal. Linda C. summarized the fighting this way:

I would say it was for a reason, but not race. If you were a snitch, or you messed with somebody's old lady, or you hurt somebody. It wasn't because of where you were from. When somebody did get down, you knew why. He did something wrong, or he robbed somebody, stole something from somebody; you could pinpoint it.

Bird elaborated on Linda's conclusions, adding that his clique of Baby Slausons and the Tiny Florence clique had some ongoing battles over a variety of personal annoyances, some of which might have been petty but none of which were racial. If the antagonisms had been racial, Bird reasoned, there would have been a more general struggle involving a diverse assortment of people from both races rather than just two different cliques.[27] As he explained:

As far as Blacks and Chicanos warrin'... Okay, when I was in junior high school, we warred with Tiny Florence all the time, but it had nothing to do with race. It was two cliques that didn't get along. See, 'cause you always had somebody who said something or done something or bumped into somebody at school, and he went and got his homie, you went and got yours, and then words would pass, you know. Call it whatever you call it, slurs and stuff, but it still wasn't a racial thing because all of the Chicanos didn't get into it. It was still with the same age group. And nobody really got hurt—no blood was drawn.

An Accord

While individuals from Florence and Slauson sometimes fought with one another, and cliques from each set sometimes got into it, both sets had a common enemy: the sets from Watts. Curiously, it was an agreement in 1957 over the danger from this common enemy, with the understanding that they shared the same neighborhood, that eventually led to a lasting truce between Florence and the Slausons. Two venerable leaders, Mariano from Florence and Roach from Slauson, agreed that it was in their best interests to put a halt to their quarrels, so they could unite against their common foe. Bird clarified:

> By '57 we stopped fighting, mainly because of Roach and Mariano. See, Watts came to fight Florence at the same time Slauson comin' to fight Florence at Roosevelt Park. You know, and Roach, bein' a general again, told Mariano: "When all them dudes from Colonia Watts come up there to fight Florence, man, your dudes outnumbered. If we jump on you and Watts jump on you, you gonna lose." And Mariano—he didn't really care, you know; he was a hellified fighter. And Roach said, "I tell you what, man, we been squabbling all these years about bullshit and everything; we live in the same neighborhood, man." He said, "We're fightin' Watts, Black dudes from Watts, and you're fightin' the Mexican dudes from Watts." He sayin', "You know the Mexican dudes—they ain't none of our friends," and everything.

Roach understood the concept that Malcolm X articulated later, that "the enemy of your enemy is your friend." Bird, quoting Roach, continued, "'We got the same enemy, man; we got to stop. So I'll tell you what, we gonna help you guys fight these dudes today, and from now on, no more hassles; it's just Slauson and Florence.' And ain't been one [fight] since."

Florencitas Precede Florence[28]

It was a hang-out group of girls in the Florence-Firestone neighborhood who were the principal founders of Florence.[29] Their beginnings had to do with fun and romance. About fifty Mexican and White girls, who went to junior and senior high school together, used to hang out after school to enjoy themselves. Their locales included their schools, a hot dog stand, a park, and numerous movie theaters. Local boys viewed the neighborhood girls as magnets that gave definition to the emerging Florence set by attracting the boys from their own and various other neighborhoods. Linda C., born in 1936, and an original member of the Florencitas, provided the following account of Florence's founding:

> Florence was known at first for just girls. That's all there was there on Florence when it first originated; it was just girls. This was in '48 or '49. We had White girls, we had Chicanas, but no Blacks. There was about maybe a good fifty girls then. No men, no guys. So we started hanging at Edison, we went to Edison Junior High School, then I went to Fremont [high school]; we were all hanging. I remember hanging at Roosevelt Park and the Gentry and the Fox, the Florence show. By the Fox, they use to have a hangout named the Wigwag, a hot dog stand. And all our girls would be there. That was on Graham and Florence.

The girls were quite mobile. They were having fun "hooking up" with boys from an assortment of different neighborhoods, having neighborhood parties, or "jumps," and traveling to other friendly neighborhoods to party. Linda C. continued:

> And because there was so many girls, all kinds of guys started coming out to this little hot dog stand. We had guys from Wilmington, San Pedro, Jugtown, East LA, Maravilla. We had dudes from Flats, from Primera Flats, from 38th Street, and from Clanton. And we use to go cruisin'; we use to go cruisin' a lot. As long as they had cars, the thing was cruisin', you know, not sex or drugs; it was partying and cruisin'. Drinking, yeah, but mainly partying and cruisin'. We'd end up over there at the beach somewhere, or we'd go to East LA and go out there to their parties or wherever; we partied a lot. We maintained a club which was the Florencitas.

Establishing the Florence set was a process that unfolded naturally. It was the result of a number of synergistic factors: a collection of young females who knew one another, enjoyed each other's company, and were interested in meeting and partying with young males; their mobility, which in turn attracted guys from various other sets to their neighborhood to hang out; the attention of guys who had familiarity with set connections in their own neighborhood; familial relationships facilitating set participation; and adopting the name of the neighborhood the girls lived in as the name for the set, making it easy to identify with. Linda C. explained further:

> Florence territory was Florence. See, Florence-Firestone is a district, that's its name; we combine it. And we had dudes come in from 38th Street, from Jugtown, from all over, and some that were living there in the neighborhood. Then they started claiming Florence, but it wasn't really Florence yet because we had a lot of guys from 38th and Jugtown. Then we got entwined somewhere with 38th Street and a lot of 38th became Florence. A lot of [the] people [who] lived in Florence became Florence, the dudes especially. Florence is a lot like a family: we know everybody; some are related.

Florence Cliques[30]

Florence developed numerous age-related cliques during the 1950s and early 1960s,[31] some of which had names similar to those of the Slausons. Among those were Big Florence, Little Florence, Baby Florence, and Midget Florence.[32] There were also the Diablos and Santos, Peewees, Termites, Tinys, Jokers, Dukes, Gangsters, Night Owls, Locos, Tiny Locos, Miramonte Boys, Cherries, and the Toakers.[33] Linda C. believes that there were about sixty in Big Florence and forty to fifty in Little Florence. Rick C., a member of the Midgets, thought there were seventy-five to one hundred youth in the Midgets. Estimates of the number of members in each clique are guesstimates, since no one actually conducted a census. Membership could be ephemeral—in one clique, then another, then back again, or into yet a third clique.

There were two cliques of Midgets: the original and a group that formed in the 1960s. The 1960s Midgets had a more formal founding than the other Florence cliques. This clique was established by an older Florence member called Rowdy Frank, a member of the first group of Midgets. He left the set for a while to attend college, only to return later to involve the set in a project for a class he was taking and to try to help some of the neighborhood youngsters stay out of trouble. Rick C., of the second Midgets group, recalled their founding:

> What he [Rowdy Frank] did is, he went to college and changed his last name. He came back to the neighborhood, and he seen that we were just a bunch of kids getting into a lot of trouble. So he needed college credits anyway, you know, for his sociology class or whatever he was taking. So he got with us for the meeting with us. He says, "We're going to be organized from now on. You guys are going to be able to

have parties without law enforcement busting you down. We're going to do things properly to avoid confrontation with law enforcement." So there came an organizing period for a minute.

This second group lasted quite a bit longer than a minute, in fact longer than most sets without cliques, lasting about five years. Rick C. contended it was their sponsor, Rowdy Frank, who kept them organized for such a long period; that was his goal.

Florence has traditionally been a South-Side set. Before 1965, there was no East-Side Florence or West-Side Florence, only Florence, South-Side. Florence was one of the first sets to begin using a number in its name when members would put their monikers on walls. Curiously, the numerical form of the number wouldn't be used, but instead a letter was substituted to signify the number. *LFT*, for example would mean *Little Florence Thirteen*, or *BFT*, for *Baby Florence Thirteen* (or *Trese*).[34] Sometimes the *thirteen* would be written out, such as *Florence Thirteen*. Other sets followed with numbers written out too, such as *Choppers Twelve* and *Clanton Fourteen*.[35] Numerals appeared later.

East-Side, West-Side, All along the South-Side

Racially mixed street clubs in the 1940s and 1950s, between downtown and Slauson Avenue, whose neighborhoods radiated along Central Avenue, took their names primarily from the streets and parks in their neighborhoods. Their boundaries varied, but as Jasper, president of the Senators, said, "You couldn't go ten blocks and you was in another gang's neighborhood, walkin' down Central." There is no way of knowing the specific reasons why all the South-Side street groups formed. Clearly though there were geographical boundaries, socioeconomic factors, and racial and ethnic commonalities, as well as neighborhood and school-related affinities contributing to their ingroupism.[36]

Street-group members went to the same schools and lived in the same neighborhoods. They initially clustered in play groups, social groups, or hang-out groups of homies, because it was easy and convenient; they were comfortable with one another.[37] If they got better organized, a likely reason was conflict between individuals or small groups of in-group members with out-group members. But the circumstances of group formation had to do with the specific conditions surrounding each set in each neighborhood during the period in which they formed, as the beginnings of Florence demonstrated.

Groups like the Boozies formed to party and then dissipated after a few years. Clanton Street, which was considerably larger than the Boozies, formed for self-defense. Frank M., an intermittent member of Clanton,[38] explained their formation this way:

> Los Angeles was dangerous for little kids, you know. If you went to the store, there was somebody there to beat you up and take your money. If you went to the swimming pool, there was somebody to beat you up and take your money. When you went to school, somebody was going to take your bus money. It was more or less—you could say—mutual protection. And if somebody bothered you, all you had to do was go round up somebody. Everybody had to be together to stop that. . . . You had to kind of stick together.

Significantly, the juveniles who would be initiating the accosting were often in groups of three or four and usually not from the same neighborhood as the juvenile(s) being accosted.[39] It was typically not a racial thing but an opportunity to take advantage. A lone juvenile was vulnerable when *he*[40] was in an unfamiliar Chicano or Black neighborhood, while one with neighborhood comrades was less so. His in-group would protect and defend him and might get more organized in the process and organized yet further if challenged by others.

Conflict Rules, Sometimes

A number of sets did form following the classic developmental pattern explained by Thrasher, beginning as a *spontaneous play group* of friends and then becoming united into a more organized group, or "gang," as a result of the "disapproval and opposition" they "excited" through conflict with an out-group.[41] The Senators were that kind of group: they were united by conflict. Jasper, the president, and a light-heavyweight champion at the YMCA, was very pleased with the social direction his group had been going in—until the day one of his homies went over to the West-Side and was jumped on by guys from an out-group, the Head Hunters. Afterward, a chain reaction began. Jasper recalled: "He came back and told us. At first, he said, 'Nah, what the hell,' but then he got his partner who was another Senator. They went back on the West-Side and kicked their ass." From here, things began to escalate between the Senators and the Head Hunters. Jasper continued:

> And so then, from there stuff began to jump off, and then it really jumped off! I had a fight with some Head Hunters at a house party. They locked the door, kept my boys inside, leave me and one more Senator outside. One of the guys from the other club [the Head Hunters] was outside jumpin' up and down, 'cause he was gonna—I

knew he was gonna fire on me [throw a punch]. And he was blowin' a lot of air and talking a lot of shit, so fuck it, I just fired [a punch]. And he went down. And another guy [from the Senators] hit the other guy [from the Head Hunters], and I'm tryin' to get the hell out of there. And I kicked the guy's head. There was a brick porch; I kicked his head against the loose bricks, and the bricks fall on top of the guy, and right away Geronimo [Jasper's a.k.a. then] became somebody.

The other members of the Senators were proud of Jasper for showing his mettle in the face of adversity, so much so that they took up a collection to buy him a new jacket since the one he had been wearing got ripped during the fight. The Senators were reborn—from a social club to a group of street fighters.

The Senators grit brought them popularity with a number of other clubs that wanted to align themselves with them—but the Senators weren't interested because the clubs seeking to become a brother club were "weak" and would be a liability. This was especially true of the clubs from the 20s, according to Jasper: older, Black clubs that had seen their membership numbers fall. But the Senators made an exception for the Black Juans from J-Flats, because Jasper liked their leader, an Asian guy with fierce looks.[42] In Jasper's words:

> The Black Juans were our brother club. We had that trouble with the Head Hunters; we had that fight. So the president of the Black Juans comes to me and talks to me by Belmont High School. This little cat was the most notorious-looking Japanese. He looked like—out of World War II, a kamikaze with these glasses with no rims, the round ones. Geez, I say, "Where did they get this motherfucker from, the movies?" Shit, he was made for it! You know, he looked like he started it, like he started World War II. He looked like he was still pissed off.

Jasper took an immediate liking to the Black Juans' president—not only because he looked dangerous and was tough but also because Jasper had grown up in a downtown neighborhood called Little Tokyo, which was a racially mixed grouping of Blacks and Japanese. "I played with the little Japanese kids, because kids don't know color," Jasper explained. He learned martial-arts techniques from some of the kids he played with; so the Black Juans, with their intense-looking leader, made for a viable in-group association with the Senators.

The Black Juans, with their proximity to the racially heterogeneous downtown, are a good example of a racially mixed set. Bird explained what cultural street-group heterogeneity was like when in the mid-1970s he encountered a group of Black Juans at a party: "All them old Black Juans come to the party. They had Black dudes, Filipinos and Japanese, and some White dude Black Juans, and a couple Chicano Black Juans too. Dudes that came to that party looked like they were from the '40s."[43] Jasper added that all of the Black Juans acted and talked like Black dudes. He noted that when he was with his girlfriend one time, downtown at the Paramount Theater viewing Jimmy Dean's car, which was on display, they encountered a White guy that his girlfriend knew. Jasper continued: "Me and my girlfriend, who later became my wife, were standing there looking at his car when a dude came up behind us and I started rappin' with him. He was a White dude in the Black Juans. 'That cat sounds Blacker than me,' I told her later."

A Notable Two

The Businessmen and Gladiators were notable because of their size, complexity, and longevity. Businessmen cliques included the Seniors, Juniors, and Babies, separated by an age range of one to two years. The Seniors originated from Ross Snyder Park, on East 41st Street, adjacent to but just east of Jefferson High School. This eleven-acre park had a history as a gathering spot of various sets and cliques, like the Royal Aces, Royal Deuces, Connoisseurs, Don Juans, and Park Boys, all of whom hung out there. Juveniles from these groups formed the Senior Businessmen. Ameer, the president of the Baby Businessmen, thinks there were about fifty Seniors and one hundred plus Juniors.

South Park, located at East 51st Street and Avalon Boulevard, a few blocks southwest of Ross Snyder Park, became the Businessmen's primary gathering location. They called themselves Businessmen because there were "some particular dudes who were always dressed up in suits and stuff, trying to be players and pimps and stuff."[44] Set porosity was on display when Chinaman, who was already a Slauson leader when the Businessmen began, was recruited by Shug, the president of the Senior Businessman, to be their leader because he was so well liked. Chinaman declined, since he had internalized the idea of Slauson as family and wanted to preserve that group of which he was now a major part. "Man, I been hangin' out with these dudes over here," he said, "and this is where I belong." "He already had a base," Bird observed. There were no hard feelings between the two sets over this.

Other Businessmen leaders included James P., president of the Juniors, and Ameer, the president of the Babies.[45] The beginnings of these cliques were unremarkable, coming from Ross Snyder to South Park, where numerous other sets gathered to hang out and play various sports. The Seniors and Juniors, some of whom went to Carver and Edison Junior Highs and knew each other, began about the same time in 1957, but they were separated from each other by a few years of age. Their exploits were limited, as was their longevity, with both cliques more or less disappearing around 1959.[46] Soon after, the Babies, the most notorious and largest clique of the Businessmen emerged. They formed from three smaller sets, the Bossmen, the Pharaohs, and the Mafia, who all used to play football together at South Park.

The Babies formation involved a Junior Businessman who, hanging around the park one day watching these juveniles play football, gave them their name and identity. According to Ameer, this Junior, observing the group's esprit de corps, said, "'Y'all must be Baby Businessmen.' We said, 'Why not?' And so we became Babies." At their peak, there may have been as many as 150 regulars in the Babies. There was some discontinuity between the Babies and the two previous cliques. Beginning a number of years later, the Babies emerged after most of the Seniors and Juniors had left the scene. Their continuity with the previous cliques was South Park, the schools, and their acceptance by an older clique member as successors. The Babies were "close clubs" with the Outlaws and the Pueblos, while their "archenemy" was the Roman 20s, said Ameer. This antagonism with the Roman 20s is especially interesting because some of the Businessmen had previously been members of the 20s. While rivalries existed between the Businessmen and the Slausons, they were never serious enemies as clubs.

The Gladiators were the Baby Businessmen's "brother club." Their closeness was partially due to a few Junior Businessmen moving to the West-Side and helping to form the Senior Gladiators. It was also due to some Gladiators and Businessmen having been together previously in a small East-Side set called the Cavaliers.[47] Many Slausons, recognizing this relationship, referred to the Gladiators as West-Side Businessmen. The Gladiator area was west of the Harbor Freeway, east of Western Avenue, and south of the Los Angeles Memorial Coliseum, primarily in the blocks between 59th and 50th Streets.[48] John Muir Junior High School, at 59th Street and Vermont Avenue, was dominated by the Gladiators; "it was a Gladiator school." The Gladiator neighborhood, established in the vicinity of the University of Southern California, was considered a "clean" neighborhood, characterized by lawns that were kept up, houses that were nicely painted, and the absence of graffiti.

Many of the original Gladiators were from Aliso Village on the East-Side, but they didn't take the name Gladiators until their families moved to the West-Side. Little Bird, from the Slauson Flips, explained that the original cliques of Gladiators were more like a social club, into partying and girls, but that the younger group, the Baby Gladiators, did all the fighting.[49] They began as a small club or clique called the Del Vikings, later becoming the Baby Gladiators. A group of Babies that were in juvenile hall had decided that the Babies needed a name upgrade and changed their name to the Descendants. Lasting about a month, the name never got purchase and was changed back to the Babies. There were some younger cliques, like the Basimbas and the Unborn Gladiators, who, while having written their names on walls, were small and relatively short-lived, never gaining the dominance of the Babies or the lasting power their wall ink had.[50]

On the Effects of Mobility

While the Businessmen and Gladiators could show unity and force together, having been allies in a major fight against some Venice gangs in 1960 that involved the use of "gas bombs," antipathy existed between the Gladiators and the Slausons. In his oft-used expression, Kenneth Folk of the Baby Slausons perhaps best captured his club's relationship with the Gladiators when he said: "I'm a Gladiator hater and a Gladiator getter." Along with the Watts and Compton clubs, the Gladiators were among the Slausons' least favorite street groups. Bird emphasized: "All Gladiators were enemies to all Slausons, regardless of which clique you were from." One factor contributing to their initial antagonisms was a middle school attended by Gladiators and by some Slausons: John Muir Middle School. In the center of Gladiator territory, this school was naturally dominated by them. The arrangement put Gladiators and Slausons in direct contact with one another, permitting disagreements to develop, fester, and to stick.[51] The young Slausons at John Muir were out of their neighborhood, in a school with a club that had heard of them and was enviously aware of their reputation.

Street-group mobility was paramount in the event considered definitive in creating permanent hostilities between the Slausons and the Gladiators. It began on Memorial Day in 1959, at Lincoln Park, a neutral location in neither group's neighborhood but readily accessible by car, where many different neighborhood cliques had gathered to celebrate the holiday. By this time, the Slausons had established a formidable reputation due to the many battles they had been in and won, especially with Watts. To do battle with a Slauson, Little Bird remarked, win or lose, was a way to enhance one's own reputation.

The event began when a large group of Gladiators and juveniles from Aliso Village encountered a smaller group of young Slauson Flips and Little Renegades.[52] Before this, the Slausons had not had much interest in the Gladiators, much less trouble with them. Happenstance created an opportunity for the Gladiators "to jam" the Flips in a way to enhance their own status as giant killers.[53] Since the Gladiators had never encountered the main cliques of the Slausons, they incorrectly inferred that these fledgling cliques included most of the Slauson set. Problems, as a result of this miscalculation, soon followed.

The Gladiators went after the Slausons when Floyd, the "bold" leader of the Babies, "called the Slausons out" and then, along with other Gladiators and Aliso, ran them off. Afterward, the Gladiators began bragging that they had run the Slausons out of their park, suggesting that they had defeated the main body of Slauson rather than just a few members from a couple of their younger untested cliques. Of course, this didn't go over well with the other Slausons, and it initiated an antagonism that remained for the duration of the Gladiators' active existence.[54] Bird indicated that following this incident, the Slausons began to actively search for Gladiators, often going into their territory to seek them out.

After the Memorial Day incident, Little Bird, who was doing time in the California Youth Authority, overheard some Gladiators boasting about their exploits against the Slausons. Not one to allow baseless claims against the Slausons to go unchallenged, Little Bird—in his inimitable style—challenged the braggarts with this comment:

> I'm the littlest and youngest guy in the Flips. I can't whoop anybody in my club. None of you guys can whoop me. So tell me when you defeated my whole club? I can take on everybody standing here and win. Now tell me when you went—you and who else—and defeated my entire club of guys, who I don't even belong with, because I'm younger than them? I just had the heart to be with them.

It may be redundant to add that Little Bird's challenge silenced the group, but that's what it did.

Geographic Ignorance and Heart

Adding fuel to the enmity between the Slausons and the Gladiators was a juvenile justice agency decision that created regular occasions for conflict: the location of a probation office, on the west side, in the center of the Gladiator's neighborhood, one block from their pool hall and donut shop hangouts. This was the probation office where Slausons who were on probation were required to go. Bird surmised: "All them dudes, when they was on probation, had to go to the probation office on 53rd and Vermont. Now, what kind of shit is that, 'cause the Gladiators' stronghold was 54th and Vermont? Now, how is it you gonna go in the probation office without a Gladiator seein' you?" Bird continued:

> They would assign you to that probation office like they can't put you nowhere else in Los Angeles to see a probation officer. They would

put you in this probation office knowing you was gonna get in trouble. No way in the world could my homeboys go to 53rd and Vermont to go see a probation officer and tell them, 'I'm doin' good, I'm gonna piss in a bottle today, I wasn't smokin' no weed,' or whatever, and not get in a fight.

Running into Gladiators became unavoidable; fights were inevitable, and sometimes they could get pretty nasty, resulting in incidents like a Slauson named Onionhead experienced. He had gone to the probation department to see his probation officer when some Gladiators there exchanged a few unpleasantries with him and then jumped him. Though outnumbered, Onionhead fought back, the fight being ended by the probation staff after Onionhead "got thrown through a plate glass window." Then there was Garland from Slauson, who "goes to the probation office and Gladiators see him, and Floyd [Gladiators] and them jump him. That's when he [Garland] cut Floyd with the straight razor." Both wisdom and information appear to have been lacking in the decision to locate a probation office in an in-group's neighborhood for them and out-groups to meet in, resulting in too many incidents like the preceding, which went a long way toward keeping these two sets far from the peace table.

While the Slausons and the Gladiators regularly saw red in each other's presence, many Slausons nonetheless had respect for the Gladiators' bravery and tenacity. According to Little Bird, losing whenever they came up against the Slausons didn't seem to deter Gladiator efforts to try and try again. He explained:

> The thing they had that they had goin' for them most was that they were bold. They were real audacious. Almost every time they come up against us, there was no chance of winning, but they were persistent. One time they came up to Fremont to fight the Slausons, and they had these chains with a ball with the spikes on them. Like, you know, you've seen in the movies: gladiators, the Romans, and some barbarians fighting with these chains with the balls hanging off the end with the spikes on them. So they came to Fremont to fight, and they got whooped to shit.

On another occasion, a Gladiator named James R. came up to the hamburger stand, a regular hangout in the Slausons' neighborhood, to write *Gladiators* on a nearby wall. He was caught, whooped, and sent on his way. To demonstrate further hegemonic clarity, Bird and several Slausons went back to the Gladiator stronghold, where they encountered a much larger group of Gladiators who were taken aback by the Slausons' boldness. Bird then made a cheeky move. What happened next is best told in his words: "We were at 54th and Vermont at the donut shop. There were five of us and like twenty of them. I drank a chump's apple juice and bit into his sweet roll and kissed his ol' lady—just like that." In shock, the Gladiators remained motionless. Bird and the Slausons just turned and left—unscathed, with no repercussions, their reputation enhanced.

Watts: A Surviving Power

Watts became the Black ghetto of Los Angeles by the late 1930s. Created as a result of racial discrimination, it was characterized by numerous public housing projects, high unemployment, low educational attainment, and high rates of public dependency. John Howard and William McCord contend that Watts, from the late 1930s to 1969, was "a Black island in the city."[55] Nicknamed "Mudtown," for its unpaved streets that became muddy during the rain,[56] and "Nigger[57] Heaven," because of the availability of inexpensive land, the area had previously been a mixed-racial enclave of White, Japanese, Mexicans, and Blacks, living alongside each other and getting "along fine."[58] Housing covenants, cheap land, and cheap housing attracted the Black migrants who poured into the City from rural areas in the South;[59] many of whom went to Watts.

As Black families moved in, other families moved out, contributing to a growing homogenization of the population.[60] Chinaman, who began fighting with Watts set members in the early 1950s and knew the area well, claimed that many of his adversaries there were desperate people, motivated by poverty to commit crime. As he put it: "They were righteous cutthroats, rebels, destitute, hungry, surviving people with thirteen/fourteen kids in the home. There's gambling, drugs, prostitutes, the whole thing there." Almost thirty years later, George Tita and Allan Abrahamse second Chinaman's analysis of the dangerous nature of Watts with police data showing it to be the "first or second most violent place among the 18 LAPD Areas," from 1965 until at least 2001.[61]

The "ghettoization" of Watts was begun when it was annexed to Los Angeles because many, including local Ku Klux Klan members, "feared the community would become a Black town" and thus more capable of controlling its own destiny if it was allowed autonomy as a separate city.[62] Ghettoization was accelerated by the construction of public housing projects, the first of which, Hacienda Village, opened in 1942. By the end of the 1950s, "over one-third of Watts' total population" lived in the housing projects.[63]

Most of the projects were built for World War II factory workers and then opened for public housing after the War. This distinguishes Watts: it has more public housing projects than any other area of Los Angeles. With some notable exceptions, most of the project and nonproject Watts youth went to the same middle school and the same high school.[64] Since many of the juveniles were grouped together in the projects, the projects became architectural agents of social conditioning, offering imposing socialization that readily contributed to a natural sense of in-group and out-group identity. It was from the community of Watts that some of the earliest and most powerful Black street groups came.[65] Their existence in South Los Angeles created antagonisms with many other Black street groups, especially in the 1950s and 1960s.[66]

Some of the earliest Watts sets were composed primarily of Mexican youth. These included groups like Jardin Watts, Colonia Watts, Elm Street, Hickory Street, and Palomar. When the Black sets came along in the late 1940s and early 1950s, most were associated with specific projects. The Valiants, Sir Valiants, and Orientals came out of Imperial Courts; the Huns were from Nickerson Gardens; the Royal Genies, from Hacienda Village;[67] and the Farmers,[68] although associated with Jordan Downs, were mostly from Palm Lanes.[69]

Generally, the projects were large, containing hundreds of family units, with the Nickerson Gardens, at 1,054 units, "the largest public housing project west of the Mississippi River."[70] Some street groups, like the Farmers and the Huns, were dominant for a while in their projects. But because there were so many youths in the various projects and because street-group organizational skills were limited, most projects had more than one group. Groups often replaced each other in the same area and at times overlapped. Other nonproject street groups like the Orientals, Yellowjackets, Majestics, and D'Artagnans[71] had project group affiliations. Watts had a lot of sets and cliques, and each of these groups had a "healthy helpin' of suckas," during the 1940s and 1950s when it was strongest, Bird noted.

Setting the Stage for Enduring Conflict

The rivalry between the Slausons and Watts is legendary. Sharing a common but porous and ambiguous boundary contributed to these antagonisms. But sharing a middle school the Slausons considered theirs sharpened the battle lines, while the class variance between the groups helped to make attitudinal differences inevitable. First, the boundary: city maps have 92nd Street as the northern boundary of Watts, while many Slausons considered Firestone Boulevard, which is 86th Street, six blocks north of 92nd Street, to be that boundary. That leaves a half dozen blocks between these streets that were mingled territory—technically not a part of Watts, although affected by Watts. Bird noted, "All the cats that live on the south side of Firestone were Watts influenced." The other boundaries of Central Avenue on the west, Alameda Street on the east, and Imperial Highway on the south were not borders of dispute.

Edison Junior High School, at 6500 Hooper Avenue, in the heart of the Slausons' territory, was considered the Slausons' school. Many of the juveniles there had known each other since grade school at Miramonte, were currently attending middle school together, but were now in classes with youth who had gone to various other grade schools. A considerable portion of the juveniles who attended Edison came from Russell Elementary School, located on the north side of Firestone Boulevard, east of Hooper Avenue, and thus adjacent to the mingled territory.

Juveniles from Russell had divided loyalties. Some, like Little Bird and his friends, were Slausons; others, like Bunchy Carter and his friends, sided mostly with the Slausons but had an orientation to Watts; the third group was the Watts partisans, who, despite the Slausons' dominance at Edison, remained loyal to Watts. Many of these partisans came to Edison from an area now served by Markham Junior High School, opened in 1957 on 104th Street, east of Compton Avenue and west of Grandee Avenue. Before 1957, juveniles from the Markham area, which is deep in Watts, had many opportunities to encounter the Slausons at Edison—time during which animosities formed. Juveniles from the area served by Jordan High School in Watts, with grades 7–12 and was overcrowded, had the option of going to Edison for junior high school and Fremont for high school or staying at Jordan, since the early 1950s.[72]

John C. Fremont High School, in the 7600 block of San Pedro Street was, like Edison, in the heart of the Slausons' neighborhood and was their school. The Watts loyalists there had a chance to marinate further on their antipathy with Slauson. Established in 1924, Fremont received juveniles from Edison, and also hosted other junior high schools with their own neighborhood affiliations, including Jacob A. Riis Developmental School, located on 69th Street in Slauson territory.[73] Riis was an all-boys school of juveniles who had had trouble in a regular school or had had trouble with the law.

Juveniles from Gompers Junior High on Imperial and San Pedro Streets, just west of Watts, had been coming to Fremont since the late 1930s, and Markham Junior High on 104th Street in Watts followed suit in the late 1950s. Bird believes that antagonisms with Watts developed because so many of their juveniles were regularly bused to the Slausons' neighborhood for so long that they "automatically" became enemies. The non-Edison youth who came to Fremont weren't "punks, or poot-butts, or rumkins," as Bird clarified, but "different" from the Slausons, with dissimilar behavior and attitudes. "They weren't the same cut as us," he opined.[74]

Watts juveniles established a reputation among the Slausons of being a wild bunch. For those who rode the school bus to the Slauson schools, their unruliness was worsened by the effect of time spent on it. Bird asked: "Can you imagine a couple hundred or more students comin' to enemy territory? They been ridin' the bus, messin' with each other all the way up here, actin' rowdy and crazy? They were comin' to our school, and they were rambunctious." He estimates that three overcrowded busloads came from the Watts region every morning to deliver their passengers to Slausons' schools. The congestion on the buses was a major part of the problem. These were not buses where two people sat comfortably in a seat together but "crowded busloads." Bird explained:

> What I mean by a busload is chumps standing in the aisles, squeezed all up against each other; guys feelin' girl's asses, squeezin' their titties; fights on the bus all the way 'n' everything. Suckas be hangin' out the window, bus drivers so nervous, you know, shakin' like a duck shittin' persimmon seeds. I seen it in '55, 'cause that's when I got to junior high, but I knew it was before that."

As Bird and other Slausons understood it, Watts juveniles were disrespectful. But there was something stronger implied in "they were different from us." They would do things many of the Slausons found inappropriate, thereby further separating and alienating themselves. On one occasion, a Watts youth named Terry F. stole a school bus full of students at Edison, drove it back to Watts, and provided personalized bus service to everyone's door. "See, he started a fight on the bus from Edison and drove it all the way to Watts, took everybody home," Bird remembered.

Some Watts dudes were just "real bad and outright fuckups," like Rule B., who would hang out the bus window and snatch the hats off the heads of strangers, just because. One time, he took a peanut butter and jelly sandwich and threw it from the bus window onto the dress shirt of a man waiting on the corner. Some of the Watts girls were reputed to be morally loose—indeed, loose enough that they would have sex on the bus traveling between the schools. Bird concluded: "See, we didn't do that kind of stuff." It was undignified and suggestive of juveniles who might not have known any better, adding to the Slauson perception that Watts juveniles were members of groups for which it was easy to not have respect.

Despite these contrasts, there were other Watts juveniles who earned respect from the Slausons by their boldness and toughness. Two of these legendary individuals were Marvin M. and N. D. A former Watts set member told us that as late as the early 1980s, adults in the Will Rogers Park area remembered both of these juveniles well, including some of their exploits. N. D., when he lived on 83rd Street, would come out in the morning on his front porch, stretch, and then shout "*W-A-T-T-S!*" so loudly that many neighbors heard him. He boastfully proclaimed himself to be the "Mayor of Watts." Both of these youth died before they reached their twenties, depriving Watts's street groups of strong potential leaders.

Some Effects of Architecture

In multiple ways, the housing projects in Watts made club formation and interactions different from other areas of South Los Angeles. The projects gave insularity to the sets that both created antagonisms among them—they fought each other—and prevented the Watts neighborhood from ever developing the kind of unity that characterized the Slausons.[75] Roach, from the Slausons, who repeatedly fought with the Watts juveniles, observed that groups from the projects were "territory oriented" and "splintered" by them. Individuals or groups from the outside might be friendly with a particular Watts set or various set members, go to their neighborhood to socialize with them, and then get jumped on by another Watts group on their way home, due to the company they kept. One's visit, for example, could be to the Huns, who might have been at odds with the Valiants, who in turn either witnessed the Hun visit or knew you were friendly to them, making you an enemy by association. "That's what's so cold about them," Roach concluded.

In spite of the antagonisms existing among some Watts sets, it was not the Hobbesian war of all against all; allies did exist. These allies would unite, under the right circumstances, to form a larger group to oppose a force they needed to contend with. They would "team up" in groups, or individuals from one group might help individuals from another group that they were friendly with. In contrast, any incursion into the Slauson neighborhood was taken as a threat to all by the Slausons, to be met with by a response from the entire group.[76] As Bird contended, "When you come in my neighborhood, we'd call out everybody. Yeah, see, we'd blow the bugle then, and people come out."[77] The Slausons' united neighborhood response was one of the factors contributing to their notoriety.

There was no evidence to suggest that the Watts sets served any purpose other than as a place where juveniles could find an in-group identity, friends, and safety. Bird observed that most Black residents who lived in Watts had emigrated there from rural parts of the South.[78] If they came to Watts as an older teen or young adult, they were not interested in joining a street group that held no economic benefit for them. They wanted jobs so that they could pursue a better life. Bird proffered:

> If you found one [a youth] that had already gone to high school or junior high school and came from the South, they're not going to be gang members, 'cause they got too much more on their minds and

too much to do. He's coming to get a job and to make money. He ain't got no time to stand on the corner in front of nothin', doin' nothin'.

On the other hand, if a juvenile was of school age when they arrived, especially if they went to junior high or high school in Watts, there was a good chance that they would join a street group. "If he came out here and grew up out here, did his schooling here, he'd be a gang member. It's usually the guy who ain't got nothin' to do. If he ain't got nothing to do, then eventually he just goes 'fuck it' and joins up," Bird summarized.[79]

By the mid-1960s, the Watts groups had lost much of their specific set identity. Youth became less likely to claim they were from a certain set and more likely to just say they were from Watts. Publicly proclaiming themselves to be from Watts was not as benign as claiming, say, Beverly Hills, as your home. A Watts declaration had an edge to it and helped create the potential for consequences. To assert—with attitude—"I'm from Watts" symbolized a neighborhood affiliation they were ready to defend. In Bird's analysis, social settings could produce conflict just by the way someone identified himself. He observed: "If they went to a party somewhere, and we're enemies with Watts—they say, 'We from Watts'—that was enough for us. There's gonna be a fight whether you a gang member or not."

Juveniles without Borders

Regardless of neighborhood boundaries, the borders for certain individuals were characterized more by porosity than by impermeability.[80] The freedom of movement they had was the result of personal reputations built on characteristics that enabled some to cross into other sets' areas with minimal repercussions. Slauson notables Chinaman, Roach, and Bird, as well as Watts notable N. D., were examples of juveniles who could more or less go where they pleased with minimal set repercussions, because of the respect they had established.[81] Although well known as skilled fighters, they conducted themselves civilly where they went. Chinaman said, "I had a rep across town and didn't know anyone there." He thought that it was his right to venture wherever he wanted to without incident. He believed, "I didn't have no boundaries. Ain't nobody in the world can tell me where I could or couldn't go."

Billy P., who grew up on 36th and San Pedro Streets and became a California Youth Authority counselor in 1961, remembered two well-known pugilists, both nonset members, who could go anywhere they chose: Chubby Dukes and Horseshoe.[82] These juveniles were tough, having demonstrated how skillful they were with their fists in front of numerous audiences. They were like "one-man gangs," according to Billy. Horseshoe, an all-city fullback from Jefferson High School, was "real tough," having been fighting "grown men since he was ten years old." Neither Chubby nor Horseshoe was a bully. They just had "no fear" and, with their reputations preceding them, had no boundary restrictions. They didn't go looking for trouble and didn't want trouble, but they would come out on the winning end if trouble found them.

Ameer was another set leader without borders. He was able to carry off these adventuresome feats because no one harbored any grudges toward him, even though some of his own Businessmen homeboys were not comfortable with his travels. As he explained:

> I could go anywhere, my personal self, anywhere on the East-Side. Because see, my club got mad at me 'cause I use to hang out with the Ross Snyders. I played football at another park, with a different clique, and we won the championship. Okay, what happened see, some Businessmen saw me walkin' out of their [Ross Snyders's] park. They said, "You hangin' out with Ross Snyders, man?" So I said, "I live in the area, man. I can go where I want to. I can go to the 20s, to the Pueblos. I can go anywhere."

Ameer appended that such travel was not a guaranteed set benefit, available to all. It was a personal thing, available to a few: "I know a guy from my clique; when he go on Central Avenue, he pay people a dollar to go with him. His reputation was so bad; he had enemies. I didn't have no enemies."

The Power of Love

The fundamental reason neighborhood boundaries were breached was the adolescent males' inexorable quest for girls. To Ameer, this was so obvious that it was hardly worth explaining. He said: "Of course [they entered other sets' territory]; they had women. Women, that's the main thing—that's the only reason to go over there—to go anywhere. I mean, there was no other reason." Indeed, there were other reasons, such as sports, as he had already pointed out—but none as compelling as the chase. Participation in the chase could and often did lead to problems with males in the breached neighborhoods. Frequently the problems remained interpersonal, between two individuals, but when they became more complicated, they could require set involvement.

Another important factor contributing to boundary breaches, and one with an extra element of legitimacy, was the "record hops." These were dances put on by professional disc jockeys (DJs) at various parks and high schools, which, on the surface, were open to all. A popular White DJ, Hunter Hancock, who had a reputation for both understanding and promoting Black artists to a mostly Black audience, conducted many of them.[83] Sometimes the record hop locales worked well, accommodating juveniles from a variety of sets, while at other times they worked less well, serving to exclude rather than include. Those that were held at Jefferson High School are an example of the former, whereas those held at South Park are an example of the latter. The Businessmen considered South Park their park and required sets who wanted to attend record hops there to ask their permission. The "Gladiators and Pueblos always asked permission," claimed Ameer, and were allowed entry, but they would not allow the Roman 20s and others to attend.

In Watts, the record hops were held on Saturday nights at Jordan High School on 103rd Street and were an enticement for juveniles from all over Los Angeles. Differences would frequently arise, especially between Watts and non-Watts individuals and sets. Although these festive occasions were supposed to be for dancing in a neutral zone, the attendees often made the record hops a place where seeds of conflict were sown or where seeds previously sown germinated into yet larger issues. Various male set members would attend, often with their homeboys, and then stare across the dance floor at one another while at the same time taking notes on the girls. Looking at, talking to, or dancing with the wrong girl—especially dancing too close—led to most conflicts. "You lookin' at me? Nah, man, you lookin' at me," and it was on. Sticks and stones—and looks—could break bones.

Joining a Set

Prominent gang theorists of the 1950s and 1960s claimed that harsh social pressures, stemming from an inability to achieve middle-class status, despite high aspirations to do so, compelled juveniles to join gangs. Gangs afforded them an alternative solution but were "sour grapes": a second best to the middle-class status they really wanted but lost out on because their lower-class position inadequately prepared them for competition with the better-prepared middle-class youth. Another theorist of this genre contended that adherence to the norms of the lower-class lifestyle is in itself conducive to participation in gang delinquency.[84] Over the years, these theories have been subject to numerous revisions, critiques, testing, and retesting, with the majority of the research concluding that the theories' explanatory power is minimal.[85] We add our voice to this cacophony of critics.

Joining a set in South Los Angeles could not be explained by the above theories: no one joined because it was their second choice. The range of reasons for joining and the degree to which one was committed varied widely. Some joined inadvertently, by default, while others had an official joining ceremony involving an initiation. Some joined existing cliques, while others started their own cliques within an existing set, and still others began new sets. Many joined the early street groups, established to party, for revelry, while others joined for protection. Some joined for a few months, while others joined for longer. Some, now in their sixties and seventies, still considered themselves to be members. Finally, those interested in playing a sport or who just wanted to hang out, sometimes found themselves caught up in an in-group that unexpectedly became more violent because of a new challenge by an out-group. Initial in-group involvement for fun now bound them by loyalty to a group that, out of necessity, had become violent.

Regulars and Off-Brands

Associated with joining was whether one was considered a neighborhood *regular*, *lame*, or *off-brand*.[86] A regular was someone who was part of the "regular army, the regular troop, the main cadre, the light foot soldiers," claimed Bird. Regulars were juveniles who lived in the neighborhood, were part of the neighborhood, had friends who were set members, would back up a member if called on, and would fight if necessary—but were not necessarily set members. Within the neighborhood, the regulars were the guys who could be counted on when the chips fell. They were the "down homeboys." Regulars were accorded set privileges regardless of set membership.[87] Herman B. was such a person. He went to school with the Slausons, hung out with them, was tough, and would always side with them in a dispute. He was a neighborhood regular, but he was not in a set.[88]

In contrast, Bird notes, if one was a *lame* or an *off-brand*—a "Paul Willy Lump Lump sucka"—he could have been from the neighborhood, may even have been in a clique, but wasn't one of the regulars.[89] Bird explained, "You got Kerns or Knott's Jelly; then you got plain wrap.[90] That's an off-brand, you know. Everybody else is drinking Coke, and you drinking Nehi; you're an off-brand."[91] Lames were often uncool juveniles, but they were also youth who just may not have been liked by members of a particular clique. "You didn't like the fools, they were chumps. They were always trying to bogart,[92] then begging you, trying to pressure you out of something, trying to do things their way," Bird clarified.

There were also *punks* or *cowards*, guys who wouldn't fight when they were needed. Punks were unwanted by the sets because they lacked *heart*, running from rather than facing up to adversity. It was not necessary to be tough to have heart either, as Bird asserted: "You didn't have to be as tough as everybody, but you just had to show you had some kind of heart. Even if you wasn't that tough and somebody tried to jam you that was tougher, and tried to bogart you, somebody else would say something." There might have been one or several others who would have had your back, to get you through the danger then or later. Youth with heart could be depended upon to do the right thing and were accorded reciprocity.

Peer Influence: The Default Motivation

Pressure to join a group, when there was pressure, came from one's peers—although more accurately, it was *peer influence* rather than peer pressure. Geronimo, the president of the Senators, explained: "You don't have to join no gang. You can know some of the guys, and you was cool. You joined a gang 'cause you wanted to, not because you had to." Chinaman concurred, stating, "There was no peer pressure; you didn't have to belong." Willie C., who grew up on "Sin Street," in the heart of Slauson territory, felt the influence of his immediate neighborhood put pressure on him to be successful, not to join a gang.[93] He explained: "On Sin Street I wasn't pressured by my peers to become a gangbanger, you know. See, peer pressure play a major role in a person's life; and on our street, it was the pressure of being successful and not goin' out and hurtin' people." He added that his sense of independence, which led him to want to take care of himself, also deterred him from joining. Joining would have compromised his values: "I wanted to be my own man. I don't want to have to rely on this person to protect me, you know, to fight for me. I'm not a follower."[94] No one in South Los Angeles joined a set because he was disappointed that he didn't have opportunities to join the middle class.[95]

Liberal attitudes of most set members toward nonjoiners permitted people like Willie C. to follow set principles without being considered a pariah for not joining. Nonjoiners were excused for not joining if they were cool or if they had a good excuse. Ed B. grew up on Sin Street too, but his divorced mother didn't want him to join the Slausons. As he noted: "My mother was a mother and a father for us, and I figured, why put extra pressure on her when she taking care of me and my sister. I had respect for her." Bird approved of his reasons for not joining: "It wasn't necessary because he was already in the neighborhood. Why join and put pressure on your mother?"

Ed B.'s mother was neither anti-Slauson nor was she anti-Bird; she just didn't want her son to join. His mother was quite aware of who Bird was but liked him all the same. Ed B. stated, "I ran with Ernest [Bird] because he respected my mother and my mother respected him. She knew what he did, but they [the Slausons] always had a lot of respect for her." Ed B. was a Slausons' regular, but not set member. His decision not to join was acceptable, understandable, and reasonable; he was cool.

Falling into a Street Group

For many neighborhood juveniles joining a set was a natural, taken for granted, process that was done as casually as going outside to hang out with one's friends when the sun was shining or hanging together inside when it wasn't.[96] Ameer explained: "If you grow up together on the East-Side, you always be in a gang; it's second nature." Cardell from the Baby Slausons believed that joining may not even have been a volitional act for some; it simply happened as a result of where you were from and the company you kept. He contended: "It wasn't decidin' you gon' get in. It was just a thing that if you went to Slauson Park, that's where you was from; you was from Slauson. If you went to South Park, you was from the Businessmen."[97] Joining was an unintended result of actions normally engaged in during the course of the day. Cardell continued: "It wasn't the idea of like you joinin' the gang. You just automatically—if you was from this neighborhood—this was where you was from."

Rules about joining or not joining existed, but they had such great variation that a general theory applicable to all set members throughout South Los Angeles, from the early part of the twentieth century until 1965, is untenable.[98] To assume otherwise would require bending, forcing, ignoring, or torturing the data so that fiction would be the result. These youth were not following negative values unique to their social class by becoming set members; nor were they on a quest escaping the pursuit of unattainable goals. Juveniles joined a set because they wanted to.

Initiation

An initiation involving some form of fighting was but one of the many ways of being officially admitted to a set or clique. Initiation varied according to who you were, the group's rules at the time, and whether you were a founder or joined later. The Big Slausons, originating in the late 1940s, not only lacked an initiation but became the Big Slausons by default, after the younger clique of Little Slausons formed. Street groups that developed in the 1920s through the 1940s, primarily for social purposes, like the Boozies, did not have an initiation. Even some of the later street groups, that were more combative than the early social clubs, didn't have a sanctioned initiation.

Initiations were rare until the early to mid-1950s. Frank M., a Clanton member in the late 1940s and early 1950s, wasn't even aware that sets conducted initiations, since it was not a requirement to become a member of Clanton or any of the sets Clanton interacted with. Indeed, the process of joining, as well as of leaving, had an informal naturalness to it, as Frank M. made clear:

> It was just a matter of saying, "Hey, you want to be in Clanton?" You say, "Yeah, okay." "Okay, you're in; we'll see you at so-and-so." You're in the gang. They might not see you for a week, but you're still in Clanton. Then the next time, you might say, "Hey, man, I'm out. I don't want to be in anymore." If they want to get in our gang, they just hung around us. You didn't even ask to get in; they were just more or less in the gang.

"Float like a Butterfly, Sting like a Bee"

Once initiations began, the most common form involved the initiate being punched around for a couple minutes or so by one or more of the members.[99] The punches were not intended to cause injury but to produce some hurt, to see if the initiate could take a bit of physical pain without whining.[100] Cardell's initiation into the Baby Slausons is illustrative: "The initiation, you know, was like body punching, no hitting in the face. We just body punched, from stomach to chest. You had to body punch with somebody that was already in Slauson." The initiate was usually allowed to punch back or to push or shove his initiators, but this was not a fight. This was a straightforward process to test the fortitude of the prospect, to see if he could take it, not to see if they could whoop him.[101]

Junior Businessman Barry Wa. confirmed what Cardell said about the body punching, and the intention to do no real harm to the initiate. He also noted that, at least for his set, the initiation was no cake walk either. If you wanted to join, you were going to have to demonstrate that you were worthy. He explained the initiation:

> A bunch of them, not one, would jump on you. They don't hit you in the face or nothing like that; they beat you in the body. They beat you real good. You sore, you sore the next day. They ain't gonna hit you once; you gonna take a butt whoopin'. You know, they ain't gonna mess over you, but you gonna get hit eight, nine times. It ain't get hit once, you want to quit, and it's over with. No, it don't go like that; you had to fight.

Barry Wa. added that the reason for such a strenuous initiation was to separate the men from the boys, especially to weed out the punks. He said: "The whole thing was, we didn't want no punks. You hit a punk, he gonna punk out real quick." Bird concurred: "What it was also was to see if you was qualified to be with the rest of them," that you had what it took. It separated the tough from the weak, the worthy from the unworthy; it determined if you had the right stuff.[102]

When Poop became a Little Slauson in the early 1950s, initiations for his clique were rough. Prospects chose their initiators and could fight back, or at least they could try to prevent themselves from being hit too hard, even though they were put upon by some of the hardest-hitting members of the clique. As Poop observed:

> When you get initiated, they tell you, you had to choose. You know, they made sure that whoever you chose were the toughest guys; they was gonna whoop you. It was gonna be four or five guys jumping you. But then, you know, we didn't have no weak ones—everybody was tough. Either they thought they was or had to act like it, or they couldn't be wit' us anyway.

Initiations became a way of weeding out those engaged in what Max Weber theorizes is "hypocritical loyalty" from joining.[103]

In and Out and In

Diego Vigil provides an important analysis of the complex factors associated with leaving the Chicano gangs he studied,[104] many of which were similar to South Los Angeles. For the Slausons, during the late 1950s and early 1960s, when the number of cliques were increasing due to the arrival of more juveniles, a youth would occasionally join one clique and then leave that clique for another. This was not a sign of disloyalty but rather a transition into another group that was more appealing. When there was a clique transition, a new initiation might be required, but then again, it might not. Sometimes a group of individuals would form a subclique of a larger clique, taking on a name that followed the clique's name. Within the Baby Slausons, there was a group of forty-two "hand-picked" guys who were real tight with each other; they became the Bellbottoms, then the Pharaohs, and then the Warlords.[105] When they were the Warlords, they were the Warlords of Baby Slauson.[106] There was a selection process for membership in this subclique but no initiation, just the name change.

Geronimo provided yet another twist: the Senators had no formal initiation for juveniles they wanted in but did for those they didn't particularly care for. The idea was that if you wanted to join badly enough, you'd return after you were jumped. Returning was a sign you might be all right and could now be accepted. As Geronimo explained: "If somebody didn't like you, a couple of his partners[107] would just fire [punch] on you upside your head. If you came back and you still wanted to be a member, you can get in. But if you just punked out, you punked out; you wasn't ready." Geronimo's attitude regarding the prospect's return was very matter-of-fact: the way it was was the way it was. "And if you didn't come back, I didn't feel nothin'. Wasn't no thang, because that's what you had to do," he concluded.

As initiations became more common, initiation conformity did not. Sets continued to do it their own way. Some juveniles were able to join because they were just present, became known among the set members, expressed a willingness to join, were cool, and were in; the formalities were skipped. Lafayette was one such person. He joined the Slausons by association, not initiation. He hung out in the neighborhood, went to some of the Slauson schools, would frequent the Park, and was known and accepted by Bird. After several months of steadily hanging out at the Park, as he stated: "I was from the hood; I was from Slauson." In another twist, after Lafayette became a Slauson, he founded a clique called the Village Assassins. Those who wanted to join this clique were initiated into it.

Generally, the founders of a set or clique were youth who knew each other and who had likely grown up together; they did not initiate one another into the group they were founding. Those who joined after the founding probably had some form of initiation. As Bird indicated about Oliver Cool and the founders of the Little Flips Slauson clique:

> See, he [Oliver Cool] grew up from four years old here. So, say him and Punkin and Lonnie and all them grew up together, and they sit down and form a clique. Okay, those first initial dudes don't necessarily have to be initiated, 'cause they the ones that originally started it. But everybody else that come along got initiated.

After group formation, the founders usually dealt with leadership issues amicably and democratically. Group leaders could change during the clique's existence, depending on things like the group's longevity and changes in the leader's popularity or presence on the street. Leadership had nothing to do with psychosis, as argued by Lewis Yablonsky, but rather had to do with who exercised the greatest degree of influence over the others. Juveniles who were popular had a far greater chance at leadership in South Los Angeles than those who were crazy.

Curiously, as rough as some of the initiations were (and some of them did leave bruises and draw a bit of blood), there were usually no hard feelings once they were over. While occasional member exuberance might produce some initial bitterness, it was quickly replaced by new feelings of camaraderie. The youth were all now members of a group they had chosen to join, and with people who wanted to be with them. After the initiation, the occasion might call for festivities to celebrate. As Barry Wa. of the Junior Businessmen explained, "Oh yeah, 'cause other homeboys say, 'The man's all right. You fought him, it ain't no thang, ain't nobody not party with you.'" They had been accepted into and were now part of the in-group. It was a happy beginning.

Neighborhood Alternatives

There were a number of options available to neighborhood youth besides joining a set that would afford status as a regular. These alternatives included joining the military, participating in sports, and having an interest in school. A Slauson called O. C., for example, had an older brother who had been very interested in the military throughout his high school days and upon graduation joined the navy. He was never interested in joining a set and was never bothered by set members to do so. Another juvenile, the oldest in his family, was fourteen years old when his family moved to the Slausons' neighborhood. Although his younger brother became a Slauson, he did not because he didn't grow up with youth in the neighborhood and worked a part-time job after school to help his family. While he was known and respected in the community, he didn't have the time to hang out with the other youth. "It wasn't necessary for him to join," claimed Bird; there was "no pressure."

Tommy, who went through grade school and high school with the Businessmen, became friends with the president of the Baby Businessmen during this period. He was always good at sports, becoming a "track star and basketball star" in junior high and high school, but was too busy with his sports career to consider joining. Tommy was cool, and his athletic abilities praiseworthy; he became a neighborhood regular but never a set member. Barry Wa. of the Junior Businessmen felt that juveniles who placed a high priority on school should be left alone. He said, "We believe that if someone was trying to get an education and better himself, we didn't interfere with that." In fact, protection was often afforded the athletes and scholars because their success impacted the whole neighborhood, portraying it positively. What was good for them was good for their community.

During the 1950s and 1960s, involvement in political causes, like the Civil Rights movement, could be legitimate justification for not joining a set. Woodrow C., a Los Angeles County probation officer who grew up in Compton, believed that gangs were a stage of life that youth outgrew as other opportunities became available. He felt there was so much to do during this time that gangs took a back seat to other activities. He observed: "What's neat about the '50s and '60s is that you really didn't have to belong to the damn gang. You could live in the area. But the guys respected you if you doin' something progressive, 'cause that's reflected on the neighborhood."

By the end of the 1960s, many of these alternatives had changed significantly. In Stacy Peralta's 2009 documentary, *Crips and Bloods: Made in America*, Kumasi stated that the killing of Black leaders like Martin Luther King Jr. and Malcolm X was a serious blow to the hopes of a brighter future for the Black community and a major factor contributing to the rise of the Crip and Blood gangs. Opportunities for street groups to change was authorized by the power elite when it suited their interests, but withdrawn when it violated their hegemony.

5

Slaus Angeles, Villa Fornia 90001

Gang Capital of the World

Wherever I may go, wherever I may be—there will always
be a Slauson there, even if it's me.
—Kenneth Folk, Baby Slausons

On one of his thirteen visits to jail, this time to the new county jail on November 1, 1963, a young man wrote on the wall of his cell: "Bird, Slauson Village, South Central, Gang Capital of the World."[1] At the time he wrote this, he was one of the most respected and feared notables of the largest and most powerful pre-Crip-and-Blood gang in South Los Angeles: the Slausons.[2] The Slausons were such a dominant group in the City then that they felt justified in renaming it. Lafayette, the founder of the Village Assassins clique of Slauson, noted that "Slaus Angeles" was the term many Slausons used wherever they went, to tell all they met that Slauson ruled: "We wouldn't just say, 'This is our set.' No, we'd say, 'This is Slaus Angeles! Yeah, the whole City is Slaus Angeles.'"

The Villa

Established in 1952, at Slauson Park, or the Park, as it was referred to in the community—a modest working-class neighborhood of mostly White European immigrants—the Slausons grew to encompass an area that now contains over twenty-five different Crip and Blood gangs.[3] Slauson Park was the only park in the neighborhood where non-White youth could gather with minimal friction because it was the "Black and Chicano park." It was here that Bird met Chinaman and Roach, older original members of the set, who discovered this youngster to be as tough as he was smart. The Park became an oasis for Bird and the Slausons in a neighborhood whose demographics were changing from various shades of White to darker hues.

From a small group of youths in the late 1940s to the early 1950s, the Slausons grew to a commanding size of over one thousand by the early to mid-1960s.[4] Roger Rice and Rex Christensen note that the "population" of the Slausons was "put in the thousands," "the biggest gang organized in the whole Los Angeles." Further, Rice and Christensen's respondents contended that there was an "almost mythical flavor in the references to this group."[5] During the Slausons' time, they battled the Watts and Compton sets to the south, the Gladiators to the west, several others on the north, and formed an alliance with Florence, a Mexican set sharing the same neighborhood. At their peak, the Slausons' territory had the following boundaries: Slauson Avenue on the north, Manchester Avenue / Firestone Boulevard[6] on the south, Harbor Freeway on the west, and Alameda Street on the east.

Within the Slausons' neighborhood were a variety of businesses, which could provide enough of the necessities of life to give logical merit to the youthful perception of their neighborhood as "self-sufficient" and a "complete" society, Bird notes. Goodyear Rubber Company was there, as was Tampico Spice, the Eskimo Radiator Company, furniture stores, a lumber company, restaurants, a library, grade schools, a middle school, a high school, clothing stores, a supermarket, and numerous mom-and-pop shops. There was also a post office—their post office, in Los Angeles Zone 1. When zip codes were established in 1963, the zip code in the heart of their neighborhood became 90001. Many Slausons saw this as their destiny—to be number one. So impressed were Slauson youngsters of being granted number one status by the federal government that one of the homeboys, Kenneth Folk, said: "Yeah, and I'm that one! We're zone one. And why are we zone one? Because we're number one."

In addition to the numerous businesses in the neighborhood, it was also the home of the Goodyear Blimp: the huge, slow, but highly visible elongated flying bubble with brightly colored, illuminated lettering on the sides that could be seen for miles when it was in the air. The blimp gave the Slausons additional bragging rights that no other neighborhood could claim. These rights were used against Watts, whose neighborhood contained the debatably less important Watts Towers. This arrangement gave the Slausons a sense of self-importance.[7] Bird explained:

> Watts dudes would tell us, "You Slausons, all you got is a little wading pool up there" [Will Wright swimming pool]. I said, "Old raggedy fools, we got a blimp!" I said, "I tell you what, you keep your Watts Towers over there. I'm going to go get in the Blimp and come into Watts and throw bombs and missiles out of the Blimp on the

Watts Towers." I said, "Chump, the Blimp goes all over the world. What do they know about the Watts Towers? I'm going to get the blimp to write Slauson in the sky and let it come over Watts and high-side."[8] I said, "The Blimp parks in the neighborhood too, fool."

Given these attributes, it's not difficult to understand why Roach, viewing his surroundings, could reason that this was more than just another neighborhood, this was a village—"The Village," "Slauson Village," "The Villa."

The Slauson community became a tight-knit neighborhood of hundreds of families and thousands of family members with strong personal affiliations with one another.[9] While not everybody there was a Slauson, everybody was a member of the Slauson neighborhood. Their pride is reflected in Bird's words written in his county jail cell on his visit in 1963 and in Kenneth Folk's words at the beginning of this chapter. To many Slauson juveniles, this was their City in their State: Los Angeles, California, had become "Slaus Angeles, Villa Fornia."

A General for a Minute

It facilitates the control perspectives' position to be able to cast street groups negatively. Race is one way, while a second way is to denigrate their leadership. Researchers who have discussed gangs of this period emphasized that they were organized groups with well-defined leaders who were often the most delinquent juveniles of the group.[10] Lewis Yablonsky's extreme view argues that the leaders of "violent gangs" are the most "sociopathic" members of the group; the more pathology one exhibits, he claims, the higher one's status. He contends that their need to exercise their pathology is enabled by the almost constant state of violence the gang finds itself engaged in.[11] This view is misleading. None of the "leaders" we interviewed were sociopaths or even the most delinquent in their group.

Max Weber's theory of "charismatic leadership" is a more accurate way of understanding Slausons' notables.[12] As Weber theorizes, notables were "born" out of the systemic "suffering" most juveniles had experienced and became "heroes" to them by virtue of their exploits and "exemplary characters." Concurring with Reinhard Bendix, we suggest that Slauson leadership was an individual response to crises in "human experience,"[13] where juveniles "trusted" the notables to have the group's interests in mind when offering a directive. Slauson notables were charismatic, intelligent, tough, and bold. Popularity not only trumped sociopathy in every instance, but "leaders" often rejected the title of *leader*.[14]

Notables within the sets may have had the title *leader* conferred upon them, may have accepted it, and may have even identified themselves as such, but they were not "shot-callers."[15] They were people of influence, with titular references to leadership positions. Notables were usually sanctioned by a majority of their group, but with a term limit that ranged from a few minutes until group dissolution.[16] Bird summed up the idea of leadership with these comments:

> No one gave orders. No one led anything. We just moved on impulse and moved on, you know, spontaneously whenever necessary. When we had to run or we had to duck or we had to dodge to get out of the way, that's what we did. Anyone could have called the shots for that moment; everybody had a chance to be a general for a minute.

We use the term *leader* with reservations. It is a convenient way to refer to someone who appears in a position of power, although conferring a definition that distorts who they were, what they did, and for how long. There were recognized positions of president, vice president, and treasurer, but these were informal roles without any rules for terms or succession. Leadership during this period was often ephemeral, varied greatly, and is characterized best as Weberian charisma.

Chinaman from Mexico

The legendary and undisputed notable of the Slausons was Chinaman. Born on September 18, 1937, in Mexico, Missouri (a town so small it wasn't even on the map when he arrived in South Los Angeles at the age of seven), he was the son of a military man. His nickname came from his Asian appearance. He was once called "Chinaman" by a man and his wife at a church he attended because of his facial features, especially his eyes: "That Chinaman thing has stuck with me. And there's nobody else I've heard of with that nickname," he claimed. Chinaman felt special: "I'm so unique: a Black guy named Chinaman from Mexico, Missouri."

Chinaman distinguished himself as a juvenile by knocking out a "Mexican guy" at Riis Junior High who had proclaimed to him, "I'm the toughest guy in school." Besides the skill he regularly demonstrated with his fists, Chinaman was also academically minded enough to graduate from high school and attend California State University, Long Beach, for a year and a half. Although he often got into various types of trouble, he did not see himself as a troublemaker: "I was a rebellious kid. I was grown, and I didn't even know what grown was."

Chinaman's family life provided him structure. At home he appeared well behaved: "When I got in the house, I was one of the best kids in town." He had what he termed "stubbornness" about him, although it appeared more as independence, with a clear sense of what it meant to be a "man." These traits gave him an inner strength that he attributed to his family, especially his father: "I had a strict father. I had strong family relations, aunts and uncles. I was given direction and standards to live by. My father is a strong man, and maybe I govern my action in ways behind him. I mean if he say no, it's no; it's that strong rearing. See, I was given direction; I was given a choice."

Chinaman spent many years of his early life in and out of federal prison, mostly for bank robbery. He went to school there, played bridge, pinochle, chess, and joined the Toastmasters during his incarcerations. On one of his stays, the prison administration, recognizing his leadership skills, asked him to be a liaison to help keep the growing tension between Los Angeles and San Francisco Black inmates from getting violent. He agreed, believing that he could both help the other Black inmates avoid further trouble and improve his own chances for an earlier release through his cooperation. On the streets, when the Businessmen, who also admired Chinaman's leadership skills, asked him to become a leader in their group, he turned them down because of his relationship with the Slausons.[17]

In the late 1940s and early 1950s, Chinaman hung out at the Park with a number of guys who casually referred to themselves as the "guys off of Slauson Park." They were a loose-knit group of young Black males who enjoyed each other's company in a park where they were mostly left alone, and where they were somewhat removed from other neighborhood dynamics. Bird has dubbed Chinaman a "hellified character," a person who continued to garner respect from all in the neighborhood during his lifetime. While he was not the oldest member of the Slausons, he hung with the oldest members, and his charisma was such that he is recognized as its originator. He is held in veneration by all Slausons.[18]

Field Officer Roach

The coruscating leader of Little Slauson was Roach. He got his nickname somewhat inadvertently from a group of people he was hanging around with sharing a bit of marijuana. As the joint was smoked down to a small "roach" size, Roach took it, "Bogarting" style, and slipped away from the group with it.[19] Someone in the group yelled out, "Hey, come back here with that roach, Roach," inventing a name that stayed with him until he peacefully passed away, over fifty years later.

Roach was born in 1940 in Los Angeles and was raised in foster homes because his father had left for Chicago, where he was later killed, while Roach was still quite young. Roach and his "brother" Jerome gave greater definition to the relatively loose group of Slausons that had begun hanging around the Park with Chinaman.[20] Sensing elements of commonality that had formed among this group, Jerome began referring to this park community as the "Village," and writing "SV," for "Slauson Village," on the walls of neighborhood buildings.[21] Jerome became the first president but was arrested shortly afterward and removed from the community. Roach felt that Jerome was well liked not only because of his strong, silent disposition and his wise decision-making but also because his mother allowed the juveniles to gather at her house, where she fed them and left them alone. As Roach saw it:

> He was a quiet dude, but when he say, "Let's ride," we're ridin'. And sometimes when he say, "Don't shoot the guy; don't stab a guy," or something like that, they stop. He'd give guys play. Everybody respected him, everybody loved him, 'cause his mother was damn near a saint: Miss Davis. We'd come over there and get ready to go to a party, and his mother would cook up a whole bunch of stuff. We could basically hang out at his house, you know, play cards till about twelve o'clock, and she never complained or nothin' like that.

After Jerome was arrested, Roach claimed, "I took over from there," becoming the president of Little Slauson.[22] Bird added, "He was the one with the bugle call." He was the most visible, enduring, and recognized leader of this clique.

Roach felt there was powerful solidarity among the Slausons and a unity with his homies that was shared by many others. He explained:

> I'm gonna tell you two things: it [being a member of the Slausons] was a loyalty that you had with your brothers, your brotherhood, peoples that was raised in the Village; and it was basically religious. That's how dedicated it was. Guys use to say: "When I die, bury me in Slauson Park, or take some grass from the Park and throw it in my coffin." That's how funky it was; that's how deep it was. Well, it's no doubt we had a unity LA had never seen before.

He had "heart" too, although at times the fearlessness he showed could have been interpreted as foolhardiness. To some, he was a bit of an enigma. Bird noted:

> He had his own ways. Like, I seen him one time on Florence and Hooper. I thought he was crazy when I first seen him, 'cause he was talking all the time, you know. But I kinda knew him, see. I asked him where he was going. He said he was goin' on the West-Side; some

dude's supposed to be lookin' for him. So he went on. Okay, a couple days later I heard that Roach went on the West-Side and jumped on this dude and hooked up a couple other ones too, and that's like fantastic.

This was impressive to the fourteen-year-old Bird, witnessing such behavior. "It takes a lot of heart, or you was crazy. In them days, that's what they say: 'You got heart.'"[23]

Wild Willie Poo Poo

Wild Willie Poo Poo, or "Poop," as he was usually called, offered an extended version of the founding of Slauson from a first-person perspective. Born in Buffalo, New York, around 1941, his family moved to South Los Angeles in 1945, then to 56th Street in 1948, where he lived for two years until they moved to 73rd Street. When he was nine years old, he joined a small club called the Cavaliers, with about fourteen members, because "We saw guys in other clubs, and we wanted to form us a club." His older brother Charles was in the Daddy Rolling Stones and having fun going to sock hops but wouldn't let Poop join because he was too young.

The Cavaliers split up after a year or so, with former members joining a variety of other clubs, such as the Businessmen, Gladiators, Pueblos, Roman 20s, Boss Bachelors, and Slausons. Like Poop, these juveniles joined new clubs after leaving the Cavaliers because their families had moved to different neighborhoods where they went to different schools and associated with the youth they met there. As Poop saw it, "I couldn't live on 73rd and be a Cavalier, and nobody else could either. We was in Slausons' neighborhood. Others couldn't live in their areas too."[24]

The Founding of the Slausons

Poop became a Slauson when he was twelve years old in 1953. He said: "I was there when they started." He knew Chinaman and Roach well, especially Roach because they were in the same clique. He remembered the Slausons' founding being due to a fight Chinaman and some of his homeboys from the Park got into with a Watts set at a party over a girl.[25] His recollection of these events is particularly poignant, because he was in the second car at the fight, not having been allowed to accompany Chinaman in the first car with the older group. Poop recalled the events:

> Chinaman, Melvin Ayers, Bobo, Herbert Bellinger, Otis Dawson, Charley [a.k.a. Dracula], and some others went to a party at the Nick-

ersons [Nickerson Gardens, a Watts housing project], where the Yellowjackets were having a party. They [Chinaman and his homeboys] weren't a gang or nothing, just a bunch of guys from the neighborhood. They was going out there to jump on these guys. We didn't get out of the car; we stayed in it. Chinaman and them got out, walked up on the porch, knocked on the door, and the door opens. Don Jordon, John Hall, and somebody else reached out and snatched Chinaman in the house and closed the door. They beat him real bad; they damn near killed him. Then they opened the door and threw him back out, and everybody in the party came out behind them. They [the Yellowjackets] jumped on the rest of them [the Slausons] and ran them all away and us too.

This confrontation was not taken lightly by Chinaman and his homeboys, who were now in need of a solution to their new problem: they had to decide how they were going to respond to this indignity. They understood that part of their difficulty was they were not only outnumbered by the Yellowjackets; they were also unorganized. The next day they met at the Park to discuss both what had happened and how they were going to respond. It was at this meeting that the Slausons were born. According to Poop, the Park proceedings occurred as follows:

I remember because they didn't tell us to go away. And they were talking about it, that what happened wasn't right. They talked about what they were going to call themselves, what they was gonna be; they was getting organized. There wasn't enough of them to do what they went out there to do, you know what I'm saying? They was tough enough, but it wasn't enough; there was twice as many [Yellowjackets as Slausons at the party]. So what they was really doin' that day was create the Slausons, so they can have something to join. Instead of just bein' in the neighborhood or the Park Boys, they thought they was gonna be Slausons. That's basically how I remember it started.

Slauson was organized as a group through the efforts of a number of people who hung out at Slauson Park. Chinaman and his homeboys considered themselves just Slausons—no prefix. The battle in Watts, attended by two different age groups of Slausons, arriving in separate cars, produced the Big and Little Slausons. Chinaman's group became Big Slauson by default, because they were older, after the younger group began calling themselves the Little Slausons.[26]

Frederic Thrasher and John Hagedorn have demonstrated many of the street groups they studied in Chicago and Milwaukee began as play groups that were then united into gangs through conflict. This is similar to the Slausons, but they were a hang-out group. What began as an unorganized group of young males hanging around a park together resulted in these youngsters creating a more organized group as a consequence of a confrontation with a larger, better-organized group. The Slausons were born from a need to defend themselves so that the next time, they would be ready.

Babies Aren't Babies

There were three original cliques of the Slausons: Big Slauson, Little Slauson, and the Babies—all beginning between 1952 and 1953. Bobby Moore, who became the president of the Babies, originally lived in Watts, but soon after arriving in the Slauson neighborhood, he joined the Little Slausons due to his closeness in age with them. He remained a Little Slauson a short while before he and a number of other Little Slausons left to form the Babies. Their departure was due to the expansion of Little Slauson and the leadership struggles that had been going on since its founding. In Bird's view:

> Bobby Moore was a Little Slauson. And there were so many Little Slausons and so many tough guys and too many leaders in the same group. What Bobby Moore and them did was broke away—broke off from Little Slauson and started up the Babies—so therefore he could be leader. Yeah, you take a step down and start up a new one and recruit some more men, then you can lead.

Bird joined the Babies in 1955 when he was twelve years old, becoming the youngest member of the clique. "Babies" sounds like a bit of a misnomer; it meant different from, younger than, and junior to Big and Little Slauson. When Bird first considered joining the Slausons, he was similarly uninformed about the Babies, expecting youngsters. He explained what he discovered:

> Okay, I came up there in 1954 to join the Babies—me and Little John. I was eleven years old, and we ask, "Who were the Baby Slausons in here?" Lobo and all them dudes were in there, with glasses on and stuff, and I look at them, and they said, "We Babies." Shiiit! I came back in '55 and that's when I joined, because them dudes wasn't no babies. Them suckas was old!

All three original cliques were organized around age when they formed, with no more than a few years separating them from each other. Ages overlapped among the cliques, while within them there were smaller differences of a year or two. All the cliques were composed of juveniles. The Babies, who were in their early teens, were too young to be Little Slausons, who in turn had been too young to be Big Slausons.

Thunderbird: The Cynosure of Slauson

Bird adamantly asserted: "I never said to anybody, in my entire life, that I was the leader of Slauson. That got put on me."[27] His leadership skills and his ability to thump, while ample, were played down by him: "I got pointed out and took to jail because I'm supposed to be a leader of all them fools, and no, I wasn't even the baddest. I can name a hundred guys off the top, right now, all who could whoop me." In the same way that Chinaman never claimed he was the leader of the Big Slausons, having had that title imposed on him by Jerome and other Little Slausons, Bird became a notable through his exploits and his charismatic personality: "It was something I inherited," he observed. Although insistent he was not *the* leader, he was *a* leader; he was the archetype of a leader and the heart of Slauson. A Slauson named Rashad said of Bird, "He was the soul embodiment of the Slauson institution."[28]

Bird, who accepted a directing role as a matter of necessity,[29] has an unpretentious style. Besides not considering himself a leader, he felt that he wasn't a joiner either—having joined "but two things in my entire life: the Boy Scouts and Slauson." He was smart, tough, independent, well organized, and bold. He never backed down from any confrontation where he believed he was right. Whereas he began as a youngster from the neighborhood associating with the "originals," his intelligence, good judgment, sharp memory, and fearlessness elevated him to one of the most memorable symbols of Slauson ideology. Bird was the cynosure of the Slausons; without Bird, they would have been a demonstrably different group.

An only child, Bird was born on May 11, 1943, to working-class parents whose marriage lasted until death took them late in life. He lived on Central Avenue in Watts until the age of seven. Then his family moved to 73rd Street, in the heart of the Slauson neighborhood, where he spent his active Slauson days. While his parents were able to provide him a comfortable lifestyle, outside his front door was a world of discomfort. There he was introduced to racism, to the rough life on the streets, and to other youngsters who were experiencing similar things. He related well to the other juveniles, those both older and younger and those of the same age. He became a member of the "original stock" of the Slausons through his associations, although he was too young to be a founding member.

In addition to the modest material comforts his parents were able to provide him, they were also a strong force in his character development.

Bird's mother understood the importance of a proper education, insisting, for example, that he wait until he got out of probation camp to graduate from a proper high school because the camp diploma was "not a real diploma." Although the camp diploma was a legitimate high school diploma, and he could have graduated with it a semester earlier, Bird followed her direction, graduating from Fremont High School in 1961 a few months after being released from camp. From his father, he learned to develop his identity, to be strong, to deal with racism, and to never be intimidated by it. As he saw it:

> See, I understood who I was early in life, 'cause I had to. My father was a good image of that because of me going to the South when I was young and seeing my father fight these Whites there. It was racist stuff. And seeing him and my uncles literally wear all the motherfucking skull caps off their heads. And they told them they didn't take this shit. I had all this to grow up under. I had men to grow up under.

Bird was eloquent and smooth—qualities that served him well and got him into trouble. As he expressed it, "I didn't fuck up; I spoke up."

Bird was well traveled by the time he was eighteen years old, having been to numerous states in the United States. As a child, his parents frequently drove with him back and forth between Los Angeles and Texas and Oklahoma to visit various relatives. There, on both sides of his family, were other strong male role models, including grandfathers, uncles, and older cousins who continued his education on the nastiness of racism and how best to deal with it. His exposure to racism was pervasive, as was his understanding of its offensiveness. "I saw racism and prejudice every day in the South: seeing those signs 'White Only' or 'Colored'; seeing two water fountains, one in front and one out back; going to the movies and getting taken out by the usher and put upstairs." It was at the separate water fountains that the young Bird had one of his most impressionable experiences with racial injustice:

> Growing up and going to the South and holding on to my mother and father because White people had called me a nigger.[30] I remember, I asked my mother and father one time when we went to a place to get some water, and they had two water fountains. I could read, and I knew "colored" and "White." And I stood back and looked at it. I said, "Daddy, isn't the water [for both fountains] coming out of the same pipes?" And he shook his head and said, "Yes." I said, "Then how come they got this one here and that one over there?" I really did get an attitude as a little boy.

A Nickname with Traction

When Bird first joined the Slausons, he didn't have a nickname that fit him, having been variously referred to as "Outlaw" or the "Bubblegum Kid." It wasn't until 1957, when he was fourteen years old, that his nickname—the result of an error—took hold, staying with him his entire life. He was hanging out with some homeboys by a liquor store they weren't permitted to enter any more, but he could. The homeboys' shopping list for him included a "short dog" (a small bottle) of Italian Swiss Colony white port wine, the preferred wine on the street at that time, which Bird was to liberate. Instead, he took a short dog of Thunderbird wine, much to the chagrin of his homeboys, who were eagerly awaiting him. "Look at that fool, Thunderbird wine [indeed]!" they exclaimed. It turned out they liked the wine and began calling him "Thunderbird" for his starring role in introducing it to them.

Two other serendipitous factors helped concretize his nickname: his choice of snacks and a coat. Bird used to enjoy eating sunflower seeds, corn nuts, pumpkin seeds, and peanuts, loose bits of which he would hold in his hand and nibble on. Noticed by some of his older homeboys, they concurred, "Yeah, he kinda look like a bird." The coat came by way of his father, who bought him a Thunderbird coat. Named after the Ford Thunderbird car (the 1955–1957 models were emblazoned, even then, with *classic*), the coat took on some of the car's panache and was arguably about as cool a coat as you could have at fourteen. "Thunderbird" was a righteous name for this well-liked youngster. The name stuck, and Thunderbird, abbreviated to "Bird," was born.[31]

Boldness Is Preceded by Wit

From South Los Angeles to Guadalajara, Vera Cruz, and Acapulco, Mexico, Bird wrote or carved his name wherever he went: on walls, in buses, in courthouses, in jails, and in fresh cement. Reminiscent of the GIs in World War II who wrote "Kilroy was here," he left few places unsigned in the areas he frequented. His writing was so prolific that his name became ubiquitous in some circles. In 1967, when Bird was in Los Angeles County Jail, he had an encounter with a younger White male that initially appeared as if it might develop into something nasty instead of the amity that resulted. As Bird told it:

> In '67, I was in the county jail, and this White boy kept lookin' at me.' He kept looking at me for about two days, man; and when a sucker's lookin' at you for two days, something's wrong. I never seen this dude before in my life, plus it's a White boy looking at me—oh

no, this is gonna be some shit! So I'm scheming, until one day the dude comes over with his hand out. He said, "Bird?" I say, "Yea." "I'm John Adams from Torrance, man. I know you don't know me, but I just want to shake your hand." I say, "Well, why is that?" He said, "I feel like I know you." He's ten years younger than me, been going in and out of foster homes and juvenile hall. He said the first time they threw him in lockup, he saw "Bird Slauson" on the wall. He said he went all over juvy [juvenile halls] and found it in other places too. He said he rode on county buses where he saw it too. I've been to the Torrance courthouse before too, and he saw it there.

Bird's reputation began early, when he was in grammar school, sparked by his encounter with Chinaman. This was a huge bump up in the eyes of his peers—he had seen the legend. Bird explained: "Growing up in the same neighborhood, all I ever heard was Chinaman. When I'm in grammar school on the day that I saw him, it was like going to a summit, meeting Kennedy or Khrushchev and five-star generals all in one." Their meeting was a chance encounter; there was no conversation, but it gave Bird bragging rights among his young classmates. He had actually witnessed the phantom in the flesh, an experience few had had because of Chinaman's troubles with the law resulting in extended absences from the community. When Bird arrived at school that day, he told the story of his encounter to a rapt audience: "How'd he look?" they all wanted to know. Bird reveled: "He's about seven feet tall, with dark Chinese eyes, and he had a cast on his head!"

Chinaman was not seven feet tall, but Bird had their attention, and he glowed. It turned out that Chinaman's bandaged head was due to a concussion he had gotten from a fight he had been in with some Watts dudes. One of them had whacked him with a pipe wrench, knocking him to the ground. He managed to get back up and, with blood streaming down his face, whooped both the dudes he was fighting. Charisma is a hard-won thing. To impressionable children, this bigger-than-life legend had been seen by one of their own—in warrior garb—a feat incomparable to anything they had done. This gave Bird élan, a medal he could place at the top of his list.

The eleven-year-old Bird first encountered Roach in 1954 in the Park. This was another rarity because of Roach's own issues with the law that took him off the street for different periods. It was an encounter that left Bird quite impressed, especially with Roach's sartorial style and discursive skills, which were on full display at the time. Bird related:

> Then, up comes Roach. I seen him with these blue denims on, with Black stitches down the sides, and a white shirt. I mean, we're wearing old JC Penny's [a basic clothing store] stuff or whatever to school,

and here's a cat with a white shirt and those kind of denims they don't even make anymore. Those were some clean denims. He had on some Florsheims [classy shoes], and they were shined. He had on a black derby hat and a bamboo cane and a coat draped over his arm. I said, "Who's that?" "That's Roach, man." I said, "He sure do talk a lot." He was parading back and forth, and he was talking properly, using proper English.

Over the next few years, Roach spent a lot of time in and out of lockups. In 1957, he came back to the neighborhood, where he showed up at the Park and once more put his oratory skills to work. People would come listen to him as he laid out the ideology of Slauson, established strategies of who was going to be fought with, by whom, and when and where. Bird was at the Park regularly, watching and listening to Roach. "He's a strategist," Bird said, "and I picked up a whole bunch from him. Not only from him, 'cause there were a lot of other dudes around, but mainly him. See, I was an observer. I was too little to be trying to fight anybody." Roach was aware of Bird early on and respected him.

A clearer understanding of the nature of the early relationship that was established between Roach and Bird, and an illustration of the values Roach was espousing for the Slausons to follow, is demonstrated in this next anecdote involving Bird and an older, bigger member of the Little Slausons, Ralph Chestnut.[32] Roach felt the Slausons shouldn't prey on one another, especially on the younger members. He believed that they should be organized and should treat each other like family; they needed to be respectful among themselves. On this occasion, the fourteen-year-old Bird arrived at the Fox Theater nicely dressed, with a resplendent corduroy jacket, to join a group outside waiting for the movie to begin. As Bird recalled:

> One day in '57, I had on some white khakis, French toe shoes, and an olive-green corduroy coat fresh from Silverwoods [a classy clothing store]. It still had the smell of new in it. I had on my little stingy brim hat. Oh man, I was clean and weighing a hundred twenty pounds, five feet nine inches tall. I fall up to the Fox; I come out for the show. And Ralph Chestnut and them are standing out front and he say, "Hey, Thunderbird." I say, "What's happening?" And so Ralph Chestnut says, "Man, that sure is a clean jacket; let me check it out." And he tried it on. He was a muscular dude 'n' stuff, but I had the frame but not the rest of the meat to go with it, so the jacket could fit him. He said, "Oh man, this is nice! Shiiit, wool lining and everything." He said, "Thanks."

> I said, "No, man, you can't have my jacket." Then he pushed me. When he pushed me, I ran a set [a number of punches] on him—boom, boom, boom, boom—and he pushed me back. No way I could whoop this dude, but I mean we gonna do something up there today 'cause my mama just bought me the jacket, and I couldn't go home without it. I couldn't say, "Some boy took my jacket." My father would say, "You let somebody take your jacket?" I said, "Man, you gotta give me my jacket."
>
> Then Roach came out the show, and we scrambling, you know. And Roach said, "What's going on?" And I said, "Man, this dude's got my jacket." He said, "Oh, Ralph, let him have his jacket." So they started having a few words, and Roach said, "That's Thunderbird from the Babies, man. You don't be messin' with the Babies, man. You leave the Babies alone; they are the future Slausons." And Chestnut took off the jacket and gave it to me. So I looked at Roach and nodded, and I went on about my business.

Bird's boldness in the face of this threat was an early display of the heart he had that so endeared him to his neighborhood. Bird was right; Chestnut was wrong; Roach confirmed it; and everyone present understood it this way.

On a second occasion, Bird once more found himself in a dilemma. Again, he stood up, demonstrating further the strength of his character when challenged by yet another bigger, older, and stronger opponent who had wronged him. Bird had loaned his "tam" (a tam-o'-shanter, a beret-type hat) to Frank Gentry, who, in turn, rather than giving it back, sold it to Zey, who wore it one time in Bird's presence. When Bird found out where Zey had gotten the tam, he put out the word he was looking for Frank Gentry. As Bird told it:

> So I went down to the Park, okay, and no one seen Frank Gentry. He's bigger than me and a year older too. And I said, "Tell him that I want my tam, a dollar and a quarter, or an ass whoopin'." I said, "It don't make no difference which one 'cause I want something. So everybody put out the news: 'Thunderbird lookin' for Frank Gentry.'"

This happened when Bird was still fourteen years old and about 120 pounds, while Frank Gentry was fifteen but 150 pounds and from a family of tough fighters with a dangerous reputation. Bird's audacious actions caught the attention of many in the neighborhood, who were anxious to see what would happen when the two met. They did not have to wait long, because two weeks later Bird found Gentry at the gym playing basketball with his homeboys. With sixty people present, Bird confronted him, with these results:

> Frank Gentry said, "I heard you lookin' for me. I heard you say you wanted a dollar and a quarter, an ass whoopin', or a tam." He said, "I ain't got the tam, and I ain't got no dollar and a quarter!" So I fired on him [hit him with his fists]. Well, what was I gonna say? If he ain't got the tam, and he ain't got the dollar and a quarter, ain't but one alternative, you know, and I fired and the shit was on.

The fight that ensued showed observers the amount of soul Bird had, as he demonstrated again the charismatic qualities that endeared him to his neighborhood. Bird ruminated on the fight:

> Now, he don't know that he had busted my lip all on the inside, 'cause I kept swallowing blood; I wouldn't spit it out. Now, we fought from Slauson Park all the way to 70th and Hooper. We fought three consecutive times. We'd fight, and we'd back up, and we'd fight, and we'd stop. We was gettin' tired. We was getting tired of walkin' and fightin'. The fight was a hellified fight, because everybody remembered that fight, because it lasted so long and I wouldn't give up.

These early experiences, with audiences looking on, helped to define Bird in the community. His powerful male family role models gave him a sense of what manhood involved. His socialization by the founders of Slauson made him a younger part of the original set. He not only accepted the values of the neighborhood that Roach taught but readily internalized them as his own and then expanded on them. He stood out among his peers because of his intelligence, experiences, and principled exploits, which distinguished him as someone who was a cut above the ordinary.[33]

A Legend Takes Root

There was continuity between the Slausons' junior high school, Edison, and their high school, Fremont, that was absent between Fremont and the other junior highs. Most of the students from Edison had also gone to elementary school together and were now attending the same high school, in their own neighborhoods, with students they had been with since kindergarten. Bird recalled:

> We were going to school in our neighborhood, in the center of the neighborhood, the original neighborhood. We were all family in the

sense that everybody went to the same elementary school and the same junior high school. And everybody lived in proximity to each other. The closest high school for all those cats that lived across the freeway [on the west side of the Harbor Freeway] and in Watts was Fremont.

This arrangement gave the Slausons an organizational advantage: they could affect juveniles from all the other neighborhoods now attending Fremont. Fremont became an amalgamation zone for the Slausons, a melting pot of juveniles from nearby neighborhoods whose education now also included learning about the Slausons. While none were forced into joining the Slausons, the opportunity to join was there. Many chose not to join. Those who did join did so not only because of the Slausons' dominance but because they liked what they saw and understood that to be a Slauson was to be cool.

From the early to mid-1950s to the early 1960s, the Slausons' leadership was mostly associated with Chinaman, Roach, Jerome, Poop, Eugene, and Bobby Moore, who were regularly engaged in altercations with the Watts street groups. In 1957, Chinaman went to the penitentiary for robbery. Roach followed a similar path several years later when he was incarcerated in 1962. Whereas Chinaman's incarcerations were for so long they essentially kept him out of the loop, Roach's confinements, while not as long, were frequent enough to keep him from ever establishing any greater leadership role. Other Big and Little Slausons were also either imprisoned or, having gotten older, found new pursuits (such as families) more appealing than continued street activity. Bird explained that Bobby Moore, a "fifties guy," was one such person, getting married and "settling down," only to be killed in 1967 in a car accident. By the summer of 1962, he noted, those who had founded Slauson ten years earlier were off the streets: the "real dudes that Watts were having problems with were all gone." "Almost all the dudes that was Little Slauson or Big Slauson was either married, moved out of the neighborhood, in the penitentiary, or something," Times were changing for the Slausons, save for one youngster who knew the score and who remained in the neighborhood: Bird.

Bird didn't settle down; nor did he leave the streets. With the exception of a number of relatively brief jailings, he was there reporting for duty. He also kept up a regular correspondence with Roach while he was in prison. It was a connection to the Slauson legacy that was absent from the other Slauson juveniles. Roach was very interested in what was happening in the neighborhood, and Bird was committed to keeping him informed. The original Slausons in prison knew that "Bird was out there holding it down," that he was keeping the Watts sets from marauding in Slauson territory and "taking all the girls" or crashing the parties.

Associations with the originals contributed to Bird's charisma. He became an authority by his exploits, his tenacity, and his link to the originals.

As he remarked: "I'm from the old set, from the '55 set, and I had all of that Big Slauson, Little Slauson, and older Baby Slauson. I'd seen all these guys, and I had some of those ingredients, and I knew certain things to do and what not to do, when and where." These connections distinguished Bird from his peers with an influence other juveniles lacked.

The Bird era, beginning about 1959 and continuing through the Watts Rebellion of 1965, brought greater definition to the Slausons. By the late 1950s, Bird had spent time at Riis Developmental School, from 1959 to 1960, and in juvenile probation camp until December 23, 1960. At both venues, he distinguished himself by his regular involvement in fights with juveniles from a variety of different street groups. His capable pugilistic exploits earned him continued praise from his homies but enmity from his rivals. A lot of people who had never seen him before knew about him from the stories about his escapades coming back to the streets. His fearlessness and skill with his fists, and his reputation as a member of the Slausons and a member of the "original stock," contributed to continuing awareness on the streets that the Slausons hadn't lost their edge—it had been sharpened. *Bird of Slauson* became ubiquitous in many parts of South Los Angeles, enhancing the reputation of the Slausons.

The Matchmaker

The antagonisms that had originated between the Slausons and the Watts street groups not only continued after the older founders left the street, but Bird made certain that the Slausons would never forget their archenemies. Convinced that the Watts groups would have dominated and even taken over the Slauson neighborhood if the struggles initiated by the founders were not continued, Bird "rallied the troops."[34]

Bird made sure the juveniles his age and those a few years younger knew about the old antagonisms and were prepared to deal with the current ones. In his words, "I was one of those youngsters who had grown up under all these generals and learned all their tact. When those Watts dudes started coming, I roused up those young Slausons and told them who was who." Bird had learned not only tactics from the founders, but he also knew about the fighting skills of various individual Watts combatants. As an accomplished fist fighter, he was able to serve as a matchmaker, matching skilled Slausons with those of comparable skills from Watts, but also wise enough to give advantage to the Slausons.[35]

> I knew those Watts dudes. I would say, "Man, that's so-and-so; you could whoop him." I could pick out who could whoop who or who

could give them a hell of a fight. I knew. I had studied them all 'cause we had been dealing with Watts ever since I was a little boy. I had heard all their reps, and I read into it, and I listened to all the stories that everybody had told. I knew whether they were left-handed or right-handed, and I could tell them, "Watch this dude 'cause he drags his leg Archie Moore style" [a World Light-Heavyweight Champion boxer]. I knew all of that. I had a file in my mind on a sucker.

Bird made matches between rivals and continued with a lot of his own fights, where he was the winner. As his growing reputation brought him greater recognition, it also brought him increased animosity from his foes, especially Watts. Bird's emergence as a force in Slauson marked him as a trophy to be taken. The person who could bring him down might be able to gain praise, respect, and maybe even some of his power. But it had to be done right. This idea seemed to escape the would-be assassins, who instead screwed it up. The two attempts to kill him, rather than leading to his demise, permanently cemented his status as the essence of Slauson. His legend grew.

From an Enemy with Intent to Kill

On March 13, 1962, Bird went to the old Manchester Theater on Manchester Avenue, between the Harbor Freeway and Broadway, to see a film. There were other juveniles there from various street groups, including a Watts-oriented group called the D'Artagnans, all of whom had come to the theater for a variety of reasons. Some had come to see the film, while others were there to see who else was there and to just hang out. And then there were those who might have come looking for trouble—or, more specifically, looking for Bird.

A few nights earlier, several Slauson Renegades and some Huns (Watts) had been hanging out together in a group called Set Seven.[36] They had been partying with the D'Artagnans when a fight broke out. Some of the Set Seven members claimed they were from Slauson, bringing responsibility for them back to the Slauson neighborhood. Eugene, from Little Slauson, felt that the Slausons were obliged to defend them: "Man, they from the neighborhood, and we got to back up the neighborhood," he asserted. Bird felt it was the clique's business, and they had to take care of it themselves: "They got to ride their own beef." Bird had grown weary of regularly defending the Renegade cliques, which would continue their pattern of partying and fighting and then drag all of the Slausons into an unnecessary confrontation. But he was overruled by an older Slauson, who convinced a number of other

Slausons, and eventually Bird too, to return to Watts to take revenge. Bird narrated:

> I didn't want to fight, period. Because I wanted Charles Wright and them [Renegades and Set Seven members] to ride their own beef. See, they was from a different clique, and they always out partying, hangin' with them dudes from Watts. And once something go down, the main body end up fightin' for everybody else. That's what I was trying to express. But see, Eugene, he was older, he said, "Well, no, we got to go down with 'em."

Eugene was trying to spread in-group solidarity, while Bird was trying to limit it. Bird felt he shouldn't argue further but instead needed to honor Eugene's decision.[37] Bird and a number of the Slausons then went down near Watts to confront the D'Artagnans.[38] The Slausons fought with them and got the best of them, as Bird explained:

> Charles Wright was arguing with Billy Kent, Chevalier, and them [D'Artagnans], and we standing there listening. Richard Stebbins [Slauson] is standing over here on the side, and Billy Kent says, "What you got to do with it?" And Stebbins says, "Well, I got a lot to do with it. I'm from Slauson, fool." Just like that. And Billy Kent fired [punched] on Richard Stebbins, and when he fired on Richard Stebbins, I fired on Billy Kent. I beat Billy Kent all the way down the slope. Then Chevalier struck out running, and PotTea [Slauson] whooped Chevalier all the way down 122nd and Main, all the way down to San Pedro Street. In fact, PotTea ended up with his [Chevalier's] overcoat, a green-and-Black-checked trench coat. Whooped him out of his coat.

By defending one of their dissident cliques and beating the Watts-oriented clique in their own neighborhood, the Slausons had shown a commitment to their unity. They had distinguished themselves, but they also embarrassed their Watts rival and worsened an already strained relationship. Embarrassment in one's home court, in front of those who know you, is the worst of embarrassments.

After Bird arrived at the Manchester Theater on March 13 and the "fussin', cussin', and discussin'" had commenced, eleven shots were fired, most of which went in harmless directions, except for the three that hit Bird.[39] At first, Bird was unaware that he had been hit, until Foot, one of his homeboys, saw blood on him and said, "'Man, you're bleeding!' I looked down, and I was more pissed off than anything," Bird exclaimed. He went into the theater's men's room with his homeboys to see how badly he was hit. It turned out that it was bad enough that an ambulance was called, and Bird was taken out of the theater on a stretcher to a hospital. It was his exit from the theater that excited the crowd. It dramatized the bravery and essence of character Bird had become known for and had now demonstrated—even in the face of death. Bird explained what happened:

> When they were bringing me out on the stretcher, blood was coming through the sheet, and everybody was like, "Oh man!" And some people were like, "All right, man." [We're going to take care of this.] One of my arms was hanging out, and my homeboys Italian and Tommy Tuck came up and said, "Man, what's going on?" I said, "A fool shot me," and I told them who shot me. I said, "They shot at me with two guns." So as they're getting ready to put me on the ambulance, I said, "Tell all them dudes from Watts, next time they come after me, tell them not to send no poot-butts and punks. Send a man!" Then I threw up the V.[40]

Word on the street spread fast that Bird had been shot. Spreading too were many exaggerations of what had actually happened. Some contended that he had been shot eleven or thirteen times. Others contended that he was standing there holding up the V while two guns were blazing on him. Bird was not certain how many people saw him exit the theater but guesses it was at least fifty—each of whom had their own perspective on what had actually happened. "That's fifty people who go fifty different directions with fifty different stories," he noted.

Be Careful What You Wish For

The effect the shooting had was to bring Bird's name into households with a vitality and significance that exceeded what any newspaper could have done. The close web of community affiliations made the spreading of the shooting personal. To them, this was a gang-related incident, concerning gang-related antagonisms, which took down a popular youngster from the neighborhood. But Bird's fall was temporary.

A week or two after his shooting, Bird came back on the set in dramatic fashion. He attended a sporting event at Fremont High School, dressed to make a statement to his supporters and enemies alike: he was back, visible, grander, and more powerful than ever.

> After I'd been shot and I'd been to the hospital, been home, rested a few days or a week or whatever it was, I go to this game. I got on brown biscuits [shoes], brown slacks, sport coat, brown stingy brim

hat, shirt, and I got this brown cane. I was cleaner than a mother. Okay, PotTea and me fall to this game at the stadium at Fremont. This was a big old-fashioned stadium with a lot of seats. And somebody says, "There's Bird!" Some people had never seen me before in their lives because they were still in high school and I had gotten out already. Okay, when they said, "There's Bird," the whole stadium stood up, and they threw up the V. Everybody on the track field quit running. That's when they said, "The Villa!" I said, "Yeah, all right."

Contributing further to Bird's legend at this event was the car he drove to it: a spotless 1949 convertible Chevy that he had gotten from his father, who had customized it, including the addition of a chopped top.[41] The car had been artfully lettered: "The Fiend in the Bat Machine," by "Dirty Ernie," a skilled car-sign painter Bird had met in a class at Los Angeles Trade Technological School.[42] His car had become well known in the South Los Angeles neighborhoods, because once seen, it wasn't forgotten. Arriving in this car at this event contributed to the mythologizing of Bird among hundreds of youths who may have only heard his name before. It was a momentous occasion. The shooting had made him fabled; his arrival at the stadium made him real. Rather than killing him, the shooting had lionized him. As he described it, "When I got shot, my name shot up 177 percent."

During the remainder of 1962, Bird led the Slausons on many of their forays against the other street groups of South Los Angeles, especially against Watts and the Gladiators. As the Slausons' reputation grew as one of the most powerful street groups in all of South Los Angeles, with Bird as their very visible director, so too did their list of enemies. With a few exceptions, the detractor groups comprised all the other street groups, especially those geographically closest.

On June 23, 1963, Bird got married. Less than one month later, on July 12, he was at a record hop at Jefferson High School with several other Slausons when they were attacked by a "goo-gob" (large number) of guys. Although outnumbered, they fought back until Bird got stabbed from behind: "I got hit in the back with a bayonet, two times. I got kicked, stomped, spit on, and almost got hit by a car while layin' in the street at 41st and Naomi. They were trying to kill me," he recounted. This incident, which almost cost Bird his life, led instead to a strengthening of his star. He was injured badly, with a pierced lung and a punctured bowel. In the hospital he had tubes in most of his orifices, including IVs in both arms. He remained there eighteen days; much of the time in intensive care, the rumors flew on the street that he had been killed. But he had so many visitors, both family and other Slausons, that it soon became clear that his injuries, while life threatening, had not been fatal.

After a lengthy recuperation, Bird returned to the streets in early September 1963, only to be arrested again on September 23 and sent to jail where he remained until March 1964. During this time, his persistent inquiries—both with other inmates and through homeboys on the street, into who had shanked him—paid off. It took almost a year of detective work, but he found out. He had known all along that it had been someone from either the Ross Snyders or the Businessmen, but he didn't know who specifically until a homeboy told him. It turned out that Calvin, the younger brother of Cecil, the tough president of the Baby Businessman, was the stabber. Bird had whooped Cecil in an earlier fight, and Calvin was out to avenge his brother. But Calvin wasn't man enough to confront Bird directly, so he and his homeboys "rat-packed" Bird when they had him and his homeboys outnumbered.

Once Bird determined who had stabbed him, he acted. In late May or early June 1964, when there was a sports event between Fremont High School and Jefferson High (the Businessmen's school), at "Jeff's" stadium, Bird gathered the Slausons together at Wallace's hamburger stand on 78th and San Pedro Streets. Again, Bird was dressed to make a statement: "I had on a black-and-green herringbone sport coat with the leather patches on the sleeve, with leather buttons and trim. I had on black high-top biscuits and black pants, a black-green shirt with a tie, and a black hat." He exhorted the gathering forces at the hamburger stand with both wit and determination: "I'm goin' up to Jeff to get down. All of you who don't want to go, who ain't goin' to fight, don't come. If you're gonna get down, let's get on." He got 100 percent compliance. "Everybody was goin'. "Everybody wanted to be able to say: 'I rode with Bird.'"[43]

As the many carloads of Slausons were arriving at the Jefferson stadium, people began to take notice, creating an unease that spread throughout the crowd. Bird recalled:

When we pulled up at Jeff, some girls in the bleachers said, "Whoa, look at all those niggers." And everybody looks out at us and says, "Goddamn!" I don't know how many of us there was, but we took on the whole stadium. We called out all the Businessmen, the Ross Snyders, and everything on that side of town.

When Cecil and his homies came out of the stadium to investigate, Bird made his intentions unequivocal. He asserted:

Man, when I was down here before, there was five of us. Y'all were rat-packers, and I got stabbed. Now I got all my homeboys here, and you have all your homeboys. I tell you what: All you Businessmen, all you Ross Snyders, and whatever you other motherfuckers are on that side of the street—we here to get down. I'll show you that y'all's a bunch of punks. Y'all rat-pack five, but you don't want to get down even steven.

Bird's oration chased many from the other street groups, who, out of concern for their well-being, tried to sneak away to their cars. Noticing this, Bird, refusing to lose the moment, revised his offer: "I'll tell you what. Get fifteen of your best, your tops, and we'll get fifteen Slausons, and we'll get down." But this offer was refused too. "They couldn't hang." So again, Bird made Cecil yet a third offer: "Okay, I'll tell you what. Me and you had a fight; then your brother stabbed me in the back. Here's what we're gonna do. You, your brother, and your best, and me, Little Bird, and Baby Bird, we gonna fall at it. Just we get down."[44] But Cecil and his homeboys weren't going for the third offer either. They knew they were going to get whooped no matter how things were arranged. So rather than fight, they chose to lose face: they slunk off.

This incident at Jefferson High further augmented Bird's stature. His fame went up "200 percent" as a result. Contributing to Bird's supremacy was the fact that he not only had the charisma to organize carloads of Slausons and the audacity to take the fight to enemy territory, but when he challenged his would-be assassins in front of their home crowd, their response was a meek refusal to go "head up" in a fair fight. That this scenario played out publicly in front of their women cemented Bird's hegemony. "What it boiled down to was they're a bunch of punks. And see, this is in front of girls and bystanders, who knew their guys was the ones who stabbed me. Then they see an opposition come and punk their guys out." As Bird is fond of saying, "We were there for a cause, and they were there because." He had the high ground, held on to it, and everyone knew it. His demands for respect were met by cowardice.

The Soul of Timing

Bird was the most dominant and visible embodiment of Slauson throughout the 1960s. Chinaman didn't want the leadership mantle but reluctantly accepted it. "I was just there," he said; the leadership role was "branded on him," he complained. But he also ran afoul of the law early, having been convicted of enough serious crimes to spend much of the mid- to late 1950s and early 1960s in prison. While many people knew about him, few had ever seen him. Jerome faded quickly because his reserved demeanor and legal troubles didn't bode well for a leadership position. Eugene, a Little Slauson who also had leadership potential, was killed on May 20, 1962. By the time the 1960s began, most people on the streets didn't even know who Bobby

Moore was, because of his early marriage and automobile accident death. Roach wanted to be leader, and indeed was a leader for a while, but his legal problems kept him off the streets too often for him to command the day-to-day activities for very long. He was nevertheless one of the most visible leaders, second only to Bird.

Bird came from the original set of Slauson. He was in the right places during the right times with the right personality to step into the void and assume the duties that were presented to him. His emergence was serendipitous rather than planned or desired. He had been "awakened" through challenges and "tested" by circumstance.[45] As he observed: "There were ninety-nine dudes that were tougher than me, badder than me and everything else, except the difference was they weren't out there." He stood up "in times of trouble," when demand for leadership was greatest.[46]

Bird remained somewhat detached from conventional commitments, was able to avoid extended confinements, and stayed loyal to the Slausons. The time he spent in jail only enhanced his status. He was probably the only one remaining in the community who could gather the youth together to confront a problem. As Little Bird explained it, "He was the only one left who could muster all the troops." He was a natural orator and someone who had the ability to "bluff a sucka in a second," when he needed to.

Something else endeared Bird to his peers: he was not a troublemaker. While he never backed down from a challenge, and he led the Slausons against other sets for perceived wrongs, he didn't go looking for trouble. Trouble seemed to find him. This phenomenon was recognized by Chinaman, who, regardless of lengthy prison stays, remained tightly connected to the neighborhood. In comparing himself to Bird, Chinaman observed:

> By me being the type of person I am, I always came out on top, just like Bird. I've never heard nothing bad about him, and I never heard him start nothing. That's the same; I never started nothing. You can go around Los Angeles and talk to a million people—people back during my time—I never started nothing, but I always came out the winner.

Chinaman also recognized another characteristic of Bird's that gave him leadership qualities: his intelligence. Chinaman believed this trait was shared with other set members who survived the challenges of neighborhood life: they combined the best of being both tough and intelligent, with brainpower getting top billing.[47] As he recalled:

> I'm going to say this here too: the guys like Ernest [Bird] were tough guys, and they could fight. They were smart guys too, very intelli-

gent. They're the guys that could pull us up and down these streets. Most of them were well educated, were going to school, and were very intelligent. It's a survival game, and in order for you to survive it, you gotta have some intelligence too, okay?

Bird was the epitome of this.

One other significant Slauson requires mention here—Bunchy Carter, a member of both the Slausons and the Black Panther Party. He has been termed "the former head of the Slauson gang, five thousand strong, originator of its feared hardcore, the Slauson Renegades," by Elaine Brown in her memorable book *A Taste of Power*.[48] While Bunchy was one of the best known Slausons, he was never their leader.[49] He was the leader of a large, distinctive clique of the Little Slausons, rightly identified, by Brown, as the Renegades. Although he was a person of considerable charisma whose allegiances—mostly to Slauson—were mediated by his connections to Watts, he never commanded the overall neighborhood respect that Chinaman, Roach, or Bird did. Bunchy's political appetite led him to leadership in the Black Panthers rather than any further commitment to the Slausons.

Cliques Were In-Groups with Names

The Slausons' era occurred over a couple of decades and across a large geographical area. During this time, a number of cliques emerged whose formation was based on age, proximity, mutual interests, friendships, the schools they went to, or the activities they shared. Throughout the 1950s, the most important factor in forming the cliques was age. Bird remarked, "A year in age could make the difference of what clique you were from." Age determined who you grew up with, what school you went to, the classes you took, and with whom you primarily hung out. Later, as the neighborhoods grew with more juveniles and an increasing number of cliques, factors other than age became significant in clique formation, producing yet further clique differentiation.

While there were physical similarities between juveniles of different-aged cliques, the juveniles in the older cliques were generally bigger and tougher. This difference was usually sufficient to prevent a younger juvenile from provoking a confrontation with an older one, since he would then have to deal with the more formidable juveniles in the older homeboy's clique. Bird explained, "If you jammed them and whooped them [an older juvenile], then their righteous homies would say, 'You have to whoop me now.'" As the Slausons grew, the cliques took on distinguishing names.

There was a core of neighborhood juveniles associated with the Bird era that presided over the Slausons' development. Although the core expanded, it was chronologically connected to Bird's maturation from childhood into young adulthood. The closer a juvenile's relationship was to Bird, the more he was a central part of the core. Bird became the hub of the wheel of the Slausons' development. As he observed, "We [the core] were the center of the neighborhood, the original neighborhood. We were all family in a sense that everybody went to the same elementary school, the same junior high school, and the same high school. Everybody lived in proximity to each other." While those juveniles who came from other elementary schools and other junior highs were able to join the Slausons, they were generally more peripheral to the core.

By the mid-1960s, clique formation had mostly ceased and everyone became just Slausons. Slauson became such an "umbrella" concept that juveniles rarely identified themselves by clique. If a specific inquiry was made from another neighborhood member into where a Slauson juvenile was from, the youth might give his clique's name, but mostly he simply said, "Slauson." When a juvenile gave the clique's name, it led to some other neighborhoods thinking that Slauson was smaller than it actually was, because they mistakenly identified the whole neighborhood with one of its cliques.

The Slausons changed. According to Bird: "We got older, we grew up. See, the littlest dudes in the neighborhood are eighteen or nineteen now [by the mid-1960s]. We had been Baby Slauson, Little Slauson, and such 'n' such and so on." It was the core of cliques associated with the originals that had gotten older and moved on. The frequency of the core's interactions with one another, "hangin', bangin', and partyin'," was reduced because of interests in more adult pursuits. Maturity trumped clique identity. Younger juveniles, subsequent to the core, saw themselves as just Slausons until newer groups, with a distant connection to the core, arose.

With a few exceptions, the Slauson cliques were porous and variable. Juveniles could change cliques or branch out and start new ones.[50] They could leave one clique to join another, and yet another and then return to their first clique.[51] Juveniles from different cliques might also hang out together. A clique might have several different leaders, as the Littles and Babies did. A leader from one clique could leave that clique to start another clique or change the clique's name. The whims of clique organization were a reflection of neighborhood dynamics, as demographic growth increased the number of juveniles, and the originals grew up.

Interclique fighting, especially among some of the later cliques, was not uncommon. The Little Renegades and the Flips for example, could be counted upon to regularly get into it with each other and to "stay into it." A party was often the occasion where previous "beefs" were revisited, sometimes for the entertainment of others. "Individuals would stay into it, see; they already had their man picked out. You'd be at a party a week later and the same lame you was fighting with would be there. They just had to get into it, and everybody would come to see the fight," Bird recalled. When these fights occurred, it was usually during times the older dudes were not around. Weapons were not used, and deaths did not occur, although injuries might. The Slausons resembled a large extended family and, like such families, had interpersonal issues that increased as the neighborhood grew and diversified.

After Bobby Moore founded the Babies in 1953, they grew quickly to become the largest clique of the Slausons. Bird estimates there were five hundred Babies by 1955. As the number of Babies grew, the group became unwieldy, with rising discontent creating factions. Bird and a number of other Babies started their own clique in 1958, the Warlords, with Onionhead and Robert Manual as leaders. This clique was a tight group who had been organized because of their toughness. In Bird's words:

> There were too many Babies, so we cliqued off. We wanted Onionhead and Robert Manual because we dug them. We narrowed ourselves down to forty-two, which was hand-picked. We never got whooped, by nobody. Whoever we went up against, however many it was, our clique never was whooped.

Bird became the "War Counselor" of the Warlords.

Names with Meaning

Clique names were influenced by a variety of factors. Some names came from areas where the members lived, like 109 Slauson, Manchester Park Slauson, and West-Side Slauson. Some came from words that just sounded cool: Warlords, Ambassadors, Village Assassins, Cut-Downs, Les Messieurs, New Breeds, Pharaohs, Sultans, Vigilantes, and Village Brothers. The Flips were a clique whose members were distinguished by their athletic skills, as were the Little Flips and Royal Flips. Another clique, the Forgotten Eras, was a group of nine members who owned classic customized cars, such as a 1939 Buick, a 1938 DeSoto, and a 1939 Olds. A television series called *The Untouchables* produced a Slauson clique with that same name. The Bell Bottoms were a sartorially oriented clique from the pre-Warlord days (before 1957). A few younger cliques took their name from an older group with which they had similarities and wanted to show affiliation. These would include the Little Warlords, Baby Assassins, Little Flips, and Little Renegades. Several clique names were adapted from Florence, the large Mexican street group who shared the neighborhood with the Slausons. Two of these cliques were Tiny Slauson and Midget Slauson. The Soul Brothers were the last clique from the Park.

A Slauson clique requiring greater attention because of its unique position in the neighborhood is the Renegades. Even their name suggests this group might be different from the other Slauson cliques. The Renegades dissented from the originals with an ideology more varied than any other clique and took a name to match.[52] Located in the southeast section of the Slauson neighborhood, south of Nadeau Street, north of Firestone Boulevard, between Central on the west and Alameda on the east, they were adjacent to Watts. Proximity to Watts meant that many Renegades had gone to grammar school and junior high with Watts juveniles, some of whom they liked. This connection set the stage for loyalty testing when the Renegades had to choose sides in a struggle between a Slauson clique and a Watts clique. The Renegades' mixed loyalties—partying with Watts one minute and then claiming association with the Slausons the next when disagreements arose—created situations that often led to problems, such as Bird's stabbing.

Most of the original Renegades, as well as their leader, Bunchy Carter, had been Little Slausons. In 1957 Bunchy left the Little Slausons with a group of followers to form the Renegades. He seemed to generate great loyalty, both from the Renegades and later from the Black Panther Party. Many of the members of his clique had gone to Russell Elementary School on Firestone Boulevard in the Slausons' neighborhood and to Markham Junior High on 104th Street in Watts. It is therefore not surprising that the Renegades would have some loyalty incongruities as a result of their neighborhoods' location and their schooling.

For much of their existence, the Renegades regularly interacted with the Watts cliques by both partying with them and having hassles. "They were too close to Watts for us," Bird observed. They also partied with the West-Side sets too, at times appearing to prefer these groups to the Slausons. This varied from the norms of the other Slauson cliques who kept their partying primarily in the extended Slauson neighborhood. As Bird described it:

We just didn't go out of our neighborhood to party. The neighborhood was so big, parties be sometimes two or three house parties on the same block. We had no need; we had enough of everything right here. That's why it's 'Slauson Village.' But they [the Renegades] had certain affinities, and some of the dudes in Renegades use to be from Watts, and we never got that clear.

The factor that seems to have particularly irritated the Slausons was that fights inevitably broke out at parties between the Renegades and Watts. Afterward, the Renegades would claim they were Slausons, which now "automatically involved everybody from Slauson." Bird and most of the other

Slausons got worn out bailing them out, since the Renegades would then turn around and go back to hang out with the Watts cliques again. In addition, the Little Renegades and a more central clique of Slauson, the Flips, were often adversaries. Renegade dissidence from Slauson made them a rogue group throughout their existence.

Another anomaly in the Slauson neighborhood was an area called Boptown. This was an arrangement of about six to eight two-story apartment buildings, whose residents included members of different sets. Located near the Riis Developmental School,[53] the families of juveniles from Watts, the Gladiators, the Businessmen, and the Slausons all lived there, although the majority was from the Slauson neighborhood. Boptown was neither a set nor a clique. It was a distinguishable group of juveniles who shared commonality in their living quarters, making them all "pretty tight" with one another, according to Bird. Boptown serves as an indicator of the absence of comprehensive organizational control in the Slausons' neighborhood. Youth who lived in Boptown were free to come and go to their homes, while their families were left alone by the Slausons. Boptown unity came from their living arrangement rather than from set association.

"Sin Street"

The strong leaders of the Slauson cliques that formed before the mid-1960s never saw clique identity as a threat to neighborhood unity, except Roach. But his legal problems prevented him from carrying through on many of his unifying efforts. He did try, however. On one occasion, when a tight-knit group of youth from 73rd Street proclaimed themselves the "Sin Lords from Sin Street" and began writing "Sin Street 73rd" in visible places, Roach stepped in to admonish them, asking, "What's all this Sin Lords, Sin Street shit? What's that all about?" He continued: "Y'all know where y'all from. Y'all from the neighborhood. You can't have a set on a set." Roach perceived this group to be dissidents, trying to establish themselves as a separate entity within the Slauson neighborhood.

"Sin Street," between Central and Hooper Avenues, was a unique area of the Slauson neighborhood. Sin Street was never a Slauson clique but was rather a tightly knit community containing large numbers of juveniles who were close in age and who knew one another well. It was also the street that Bird had grown up on, and it was a group in which he played a central part. He named it Sin Street in 1959, calling it, "A set within a set." A major contributor to the unity of this street was the departure of White families and their replacement by Black families who developed an in-group through their acknowledgment of racial commonality. Also, the relatively even sex ratio of male and female youngsters meant that neither gender had to go very far to find friends. If there was a soul to the Slauson neighborhood, it was here.

Bird promoted the area by writing "Sin Street" on many walls in the neighborhood, often with arrows pointing in its direction should anyone be interested in finding it. One person who was very interested in finding it was Roach. Initially, he perceived its existence as a threat to overall Slauson unity, but he changed his mind once he went over to the street and discovered he could regularly socialize with girls there.[54] As Bird observed, "Roach started coming out there damn near every day 'cause, you know, he could see things that would benefit him, so he just dropped it [his concern]." Sin Street never posed a threat to Slauson unity, becoming instead an integral part of the neighborhood.

Although some Sin Street juveniles joined cliques, the street had in-group qualities that were powerful enough to insulate them from joining if they chose not to. Those who were from Sin Street were considered regulars in the neighborhood and had the backing of all the other juveniles who lived on the street, as well as many of the Slausons, if they found themselves requiring support. Bird explained how this worked in his analysis of Ed B.:

> Being a regular in the neighborhood and not being from any clique, you also had your own set of friends. If you were someplace and got jumped on, then you go tell those friends who were also regulars. If you all couldn't handle it, then you come back and tell the homeboys. See, he [Ed B.] lived on 73rd Street. And when they jumped on him, they jumpin' on somebody from Sin Street. So you had to fight people who come off Sin Street, and therefore you fightin' people who were from Slauson. It didn't matter; you got some backup anyway you go.

Ed B. was a gymnast whose training and participation in sporting activities precluded involvement in most Slauson activities. His athletic skills, his mother's wishes for him not to join, plus his residence on Sin Street kept him from officially joining the Slausons. He was three years younger than Bird, and Bird knew him and his family well. Ed B. said that he did not become a Slauson because "I was never forced to join. Just because I lived in the area, they just took it for granted that I was a part of it." His relationship with Bird served as an additional insulator: "By me being with him [Bird], being seen with him, everybody took it for granted I was part of it." As he makes clear, Ed B. was right where he wanted to be in his role in the neighborhood:

> It was fun being a part of it. I was like fifteen or sixteen years old, and it was like a macho thing being seen with him [Bird]. I did live

in the area, and they really truly never initiated me, and everybody took it for granted that I was a part of Slauson. It was fun being with Ernest [Bird] because he was like a legend. It was good to be seen with him. You know, you're young and you in the car with him, and it was impressionable on everybody: "Ed B. is with Bird."

Sin Street was Bird's creation. He lived there, named it, advertised it, partied there, and established the rules of organization. Even the petulant Roach, whose initial opposition was strong, came to see the value in its continuation. Neighborhood adults, who may not have understood or approved of certain adolescent activities, were often won over by Bird's charm. Some of the things he was involved in might have been unacceptable, but it was okay for him personally to hang out with their children. Bird's high approval ratings had deep roots within the community.

"Dirty" Slausons

As a group, the Slausons were formidable. There were a lot of them, they had a history of in-group loyalty, they retaliated in force, and many of them were tough fighters. Little Bird, who had spent a significant portion of his youth in and out of various institutions, encountered many juveniles there, from an assortment of different sets, all of whom knew of the Slausons and all of whom shared the belief of their intimidating nature. Many used to brag about their having fought a Slauson, a claim that became of even greater value if they had won. Little Bird thought that, win or lose, fighting a Slauson was "the test of manhood for everybody in LA." As he explained:

> They used us as their virility rights. I don't think they thought they were men until they went up against the Slausons and survived them and were able to boast, "One night we had a fight with some Slausons." Even if they got whooped, they were so proud to admit that they had had a hassle with us.

The community perception that the Slausons may have had this kind of power led to an assortment of strong assertions about them—some deserved, some less so. One dubious epithet was that they were the "dirty" Slausons. It earned them such broad ill repute that Pittsburgh Slim, when she was new to South Los Angeles from Pennsylvania, and before she had become familiar with and then part of them, remembered first hearing about the Slausons as "those dirty Slausons." Her introduction to the Slausons came from her brother-in-law, who thought the more nefarious deeds of a few of their members were cool. As she emphasized:

Okay, well, when my brother-in-law was telling me about the Slausons, he told me about an incident that happened at the country club, Fox Hills Country Club; but it's [the club] gone now. Anyway, there's these three guys robbing the country club, and one of them killed the bartender or the janitor or something like that. But they blew his head off! Now my brother-in-law thought that was just great.

Pittsburgh didn't concur with her brother-in-law's assessment, feeling that he was somehow living "vicariously" through them, enjoying their alleged exploits. After listening to his analysis, she began to take greater notice, because the term "dirty" often preceded the Slausons name. She explained:

This is when I really started hearing about the name. I would hear that people in LA referred to the Slausons as those "dirty Slausons." That was the name all the time, those "dirty Slausons." And so I couldn't imagine what they did and what they were about. And nobody really got into detail other than "Those damn Slausons chased me off."

Pittsburgh's initial perspective gave her a "dim view" of the Slausons. After she had been in South Los Angeles for a while and learned more about them, her perception changed to one of greater understanding and appreciation. As she found out more about them, she saw them as a club with rules and with a sense of loyalty to one another that she respected:

From what I learned about the Slausons, they seemed like a club, that they started out as a club and you had to work yourself up. And once a Slauson, always a Slauson. You just never stopped being a Slauson. Once I learned about them, I got a different opinion of them, that they were together for a purpose, you know, of comradery, enjoyment, and, I guess, in a way, territorial, keeping others out.

She appreciated that some of the times the Slausons fought was to defend or protect their girlfriends and that they were far more multidimensional than her initial impressions of "dirty." Also, they had created the dance craze called the "Slauson Shuffle," a popular dance routine she was familiar with, which had aired on American Bandstand.[55] In her words:

The fighting part of it that I used to hear about was interesting also because some of it seemed to be based around somebody's girlfriend—somebody saying the wrong thing to one of the girlfriends and they [the Slausons] would come down and gang up on them. I didn't know that their fights and all this was behind their girlfriend or that they went to picnics or that they had dances. I knew that they had created a dance called the Slauson Shuffle. I was shown that when I first came out here, at a playground.

Pittsburgh's awareness of how the Slausons wound up with that pejorative label first came about after she had been around them for a while and noticed that they were winning fights not only on their home court but when they visited other neighborhoods too. Of course, the Slausons were hated and called names; they were making the other groups look bad, at home—embarrassing them in their own neighborhoods, in front of all their homies. As Pittsburg explained:

> They [the Slausons] were so well organized that when they went somewhere for a fight, they always kicked ass in somebody else's backyard. You know, that's not really where you get your ass kicked at; it's usually at the other person's backyard. I can't understand why they called them dirty. I mean, I thought their tactics were pretty good myself: that if one guy got jumped on, because he was coming through Watts, he would go back to the Slausons and tell them what happened. And they would all caravan back to wherever it was and beat up whoever was around. But they [the Slausons] had more members, and they seemed to be so well hated because they were so organized and they seemed to always come out ahead on the fights. On top of that, they just didn't seem to be easily intimidated. They seemed to be hated all over.

While there were assorted explanations for the reputation of being dirty, Pittsburgh's account comes closest to what we heard from most others. Quite likely it was Watts who gave this name to the Slausons, at least as far back as the 1950s, for their fighting prowess. The Slausons not only retaliated in strength against Watts and "did a job on them," but sometimes an errant Slauson, or two or three, would return after the retaliation to get in a few more licks. This was not sanctioned by the other members, as Oliver Cool explained:

> Now, say we might have a fight. It's over with us far as we're concerned. But we always had them little snakes, punks, they want to come back and catch one person by their self, you know. They [the errant Slausons] either jump out of the car and shoot 'em or jump out the car and stab 'em. And then suddenly we become "dirty Slausons."

Wild Willie Poo Poo believes the dirty Slauson reputation came from the Baby Slausons' frequent encounters with Watts. He felt that the Watts gangs would often rat-pack the Babies, who would fight back hard, giving kind for kind: "They would rat-pack you. So, you know, Bird and them got forced into doing that back. You know, you had to do them like they do to you." After an encounter, the Watts groups would often refer to Slauson as dirty because they had been whooped; they had been beaten, often in their community, and not because the Slausons did anything in particular that was wicked. The beaten ones may have rationalized to others that the reason they lost was because the Slausons didn't play fair, although the evidence doesn't point to unfairness. Most likely they lost to the Slausons because of their absence of skills or numbers rather than anything dirty the Slausons might have done.

A Flip named Big felt that the Watts groups were just jealous of the Slausons' prowess, calling them dirty as a putdown. They would have been a Slauson if they could have, but they didn't have what it took, he felt, so they continued to be jealous, "even today" (1989): "You can talk to some people fifty years old, and they'll say 'the motherfuckin' dirty Slausons.' But if they could have been from Slauson, they would have." Another Little Slauson, Percy Mack, echoed Big's position, saying it "was jealousy; they envied us." Then, rather than seeing the designation "dirty" as a source of shame, Percy Mack turned it around and claimed: "I take pride in that."

As might be expected, the Watts street-group members had a different perspective. Woodrow C., a Los Angeles County probation officer and former member of a small 1950s Watts set called Sin Town, felt that the Slausons were mostly social isolates, having no friends at all: "Nobody got along with Slauson. They had their own little world." Since "none of the other gangs got along with Slauson," from his perspective, "dirty" was an appropriate name, because it could explain their perceived isolation. While none of the Watts groups got along with Slauson, other non-Watts groups did. The Slausons were no angels, but they weren't pariahs either.

Adding to the reputation of being dirty were the activities of a couple of members of the Little Slausons, who had teamed up to commit various robberies. Because these individuals hung out at the pool hall on 78th Street and Central Avenue, where many other Slausons hung out too, the behavior of these two may have given an undeserved reputation to the entire group. If there were rotten apples in the barrel—and there no doubt were—the whole barrel must have been bad, the thinking might have gone. Most likely, the label "dirty" came from envy and shadowed them because of jealousy.

The Swastika

FBI agents came into the Slauson neighborhood during the 1950s because of two issues: first, they were looking for Chinaman, due to his suspected connection to the robberies of FDIC-insured banks; and second, swastikas had been discovered drawn on the walls of buildings, and the Slausons were suspects. The bank robbery allegations have been noted, but the swastikas require explanation. Before the arrival of Black families, the Slauson neighborhood had mostly been an area inhabited by European immigrants from Poland, Lithuania, Italy, Russia, and Germany. These families shared the neighborhood before gradually moving out as Black and Chicano families began buying their homes. Some of these European homeowners were Jewish, with all too vivid recollections of what the swastika had symbolized during the recently ended World War II. Its appearance on walls in their neighborhood was alarming, particularly when it was accompanied by "Slauson Village" written alongside of it.

A few of the Slausons were in fact responsible for the swastika graffiti—but it emerged from ignorance, not hatred. Bird explains that the Slausons might have known what country the remaining immigrant families were from, but their religion was not a Slauson concern:

> We knew what they [the immigrant families] were, but we didn't know what church they went to. We knew some of them were Catholic and some were Protestant, but we didn't go around and ask, "Are you a Jew?" We didn't have time for that. We weren't interested in that. We were too busy doing what we were doing. We didn't know what effect it [the swastika] had on them.

Chinaman thought the swastika was primarily Roach's creation, something he did for "recognition." Its appearance on neighborhood walls had nothing to do with anti-Semitism, Chinaman explained; it had to do with its regular portrayal on the newsreels in the movie theaters the juveniles attended and with a youthful interpretation of its implications for power.

Along with a variety of other names and symbols that the Slausons found "cool," many, like the swastika, came from media the juveniles experienced. Hanging out and watching films at movie theaters was a significant source of entertainment in youthful lives at this time. In the mid-1950s, neighborhood juveniles would go up to 7th Street and Broadway to the Newsreel Theater, later renamed the Tower Theater, to watch films. The films were always preceded by newsreels with news about the world and about the nation. There Slauson juveniles learned about exotic things like the *Orient Express* and mysterious characters like Charlie Chan and became infatuated with words like *Budapest* and *Trieste*. They learned about concepts like espionage, the Iron Curtain, and communists. They also saw images of Hitler marching around Europe in a sharp uniform, surrounded by military equipment, with the ever-present swastika adorning their flags. Juvenile impressions of these images were less concerned with the havoc Hitler was causing than they were with how potent these guys were and how it might relate to them.

Hitler was perceived as neither a bad guy nor as a good guy but as a powerful guy. He commanded armies that wore crisp, well-fitting, and good-looking uniforms. He had power, and it was this power that the youthful movie viewers related to. Bird noted: "It was what that swastika meant to Hitler, in their militaristic drive and the force the Germans had. We zeroed in on that, and said, 'Yeah, I'm gonna use that.' It was a symbol of force and power." In addition, Bird added, "No other neighborhood was using any kind of sign in those days." The swastika's symbolizing of strength to the Slausons was adapted from newsreels and then written on the walls to let all who saw it know that this group was a force to be reckoned with. "Beware," their rationalization went, they had arrived and were not taking shit from anyone.

The established European families in South Los Angeles and the newer non-White families moving in did not form tight bonds with one another. People from these groups tried to be courteous to each other, when they could, but racial distance kept them apart and kept them from understanding very much about each other's political, cultural, or religious heritage. Whatever empathy there may have been regarding each other's respective plights was minimal. Under circumstances of unfamiliarity, it's easy to offend when no offense was intended. That is what happened with the swastika: the European families and the FBI ascribed to malevolence the flaunting of a symbol that was a result of ignorance.

Symbols Have Roots

Street-group symbols, particularly those involving hand portrayals of ones' set, emerged in the early 1960s a short time after the swastika. Bird contends that the Slausons first began using hand signs when they threw up the *V*, which meant "the Villa," to designate Slauson Village. They took this sign from the television commercials for Viceroy Cigarettes, where actors formed a *V* with their fingers for Viceroy. Bird asserted that no other South Los Angeles set had symbols before 1961. About the same time as the Slausons established their sign, other sets did the same. Watts had a *W*, and the Businessmen had a *B*. The Gladiators used two thumbs down. They took this symbol from the film portrayals of Caesar, who would hold two thumbs down during the gladiatorial events at the Roman Coliseum when he wanted the vanquished to become the dispatched. The Vineyards set, who would naturally gravitate to a *V*, couldn't use it since the copyright was held by the Slausons. The Vineyards symbol became a *V* with the thumb held in the middle. Group symbolizing for organizations like the Lions Club, the Elks Lodge, and Rotary Club, a standard practice for years—long before the Slausons—had trickled down to South Los Angeles street-group life.[56]

The Slauson Legacy

The Slausons came into existence in a neighborhood that was in transition from working-class European immigrants to working-class Blacks and Chicanos.[57] Families from established Black communities in the City moved there as did new Black immigrants, all seeking a better life through good jobs and homeownership. Immigrants from Mexico and other parts of the City and country came for the same reasons. Juveniles from these families found community, forming in-groups of like-minded seekers. As the number of juveniles increased, so too did the number of their in-groups. Youth met with each other on their blocks, in school, in the Park, at the skating rink, at a party, at the record hops, at the movie theater, at the hamburger stand, or on the corner.[58] Young people were attracted to anyplace other young people gathered or lived. The Black juveniles in the Slauson neighborhood named themselves after Slauson Park and then solidified their in-groups into street groups, under the Slauson banner, as conflict with the surrounding street groups increased. Charismatic individuals emerged who provided leadership to the nascent street-group formations. The original leaders left the scene early, either voluntarily through maturity or involuntarily by court order.

The story of the Slausons is a tale of developing juvenile cohorts caught up in the dynamics of rapid urban evolution. Complicated by racial transitions, but many with sufficient family means to purchase their own homes, most of the Slauson juveniles came from the new families in the area. To endure, the youth formed alliances with one another; to flourish, they fought back against those who would deny them. One youngster, Bird, was able to sustain the idea of the Slausons into an enduring whole. He became the soul of Slauson, a role model to many, and a catalyst for their qualitative transformation. One of Bird's homeboys, Big, admired him so much that he claimed, "We use to call him 'Mr. Bird.' He's a legend in his own time, more important to us than Muhammad Ali."

Without Bird, the Slausons would have had a very different history. They would have been more like other Black street groups in South Los Angeles, without the unity and organization these Slausons had. As adult interests and responsibilities became more important to Bird, he spent less time in the youthful pursuits of neighborhood defense. Bird and many other Slausons still live in the neighborhood, still consider themselves Slausons, and have a notion of unity that is reflected by the numerous dances they continue to hold throughout the year and their August picnic, often attended by hundreds. The survivors are older now, but they still form a community and remember and regularly honor the many that have departed. The way it was is remembered fondly.

Miramonte Elementary School 6th Grade Class, 1955. Future set members of Florence 13 and Slausons. Captures the demographic diversity of Bird's elementary school. Bird is *top row, fifth from right*. Alongside Bird, on his *right*, is Joe Nelson Bridgette, Bird's first friend from the neighborhood, who was killed in the Watts Rebellion, ten years later, shooting it out with the LASD.

Bird at sixteen years old, showing the importance of physical strength, by making a muscle. Note the high-waisted pants. Probation Camp 7, 1960 Mendenhall, Lake Hughes, CA.

Right: Harry Miyagi, Black Juans. Probation Camp 7, 1960 Mendenhall, Lake Hughes, CA. Miyagi was one of three Asian males, out of one hundred youth, at the boy's camp.

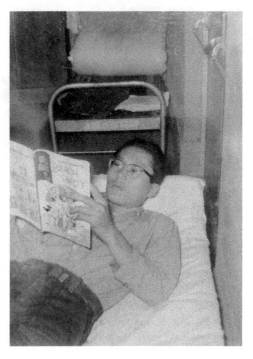

Below, from left to right: Lizard from Vineyards, Mouse from Slauson, and Wendel Harris from Watts. Getting along, for the moment, as they cope with a common foe—the juvenile justice system. Probation Camp 7, 1960 Mendenhall, Lake Hughes, CA.

SHIRLEY STARK - FREMONT HIGH SCHOOL - 19
HOLDING THE "SLAUSON V"

Above: Big and Little Slausons, early to mid-1960s, at 78th Street and Central Avenue, a major hangout corner for the Slausons. The KEDREN's building, in the background, formerly housed the Savoy Skating Rink, a hangout spot for various sets.
(Frenchee Guliex photo)

Left: Shirley Stark holding up the V for Slauson Village in 1963. This is the first known photo of anyone holding this hand symbol, which was adopted in 1961 from the commercial for Viceroy cigarettes.

Florence set members at Griffith Park, Los Angeles, summer 1969, reflecting male and female youth together to hang out.

Little Slausons, 1950s: Frank Gentry, James Huntley, Robert King (in shades), Dorothy Rat, and Treetop (*far right*, the tallest). (Frenchee Guliex photo)

Above: Kumasi (*left*) and Bird (*right*) with iconic photo of the 1965 Watts Rebellion between them. Note the Slauson youth in the background of the photo holding up the Slauson V. Just to Kumasi's right is Crook, of the Slausons.

Left: Bird and Janey at her prom, 1967, demonstrating the impressive Slauson sartorial style.

Right: Bird (*left*) and Fish from Florence (*right*) gangster stylin', representing the comradery between the Slausons and Florence. The liberated street signs of Holmes Avenue and Florence Avenue between them, were a major hangout spot for Florence.

Below: Cover from a poster promoting the Lloyd Thaxton national teen dance show, on television during the 1960s, headlining Slauson-style dance hits, including "Do the Slauson."

Roach (*left*), the Village Regulator, with Slaus Angeles T-shirt, at a late-1990s Slauson picnic reunion. These regular reunions, begun in the early 1970s, continue into 2021, with entire extended families coming together to enjoy each other's company.

Slauson reunion, with Slauson placard. Bird is in the light-colored suit, wide-brimmed hat (*lower right*).

6

The Big Three

Social Class, Gender, and Race

Black folks can't change because white folks won't change.
Ask for what you want and be prepared to pay for what you get.
—Maya Angelou, quoting her mother's advice,
 The Heart of a Woman

Research conducted on street groups has varied historically on the theoretical importance of social class, gender, and race. Class has been given the most consistent attention, especially in the work of early researchers. Gender and race were late bloomers, mostly lost in the early work on gangs, although there was evidence to suggest their analytical value. Perhaps gangs, then, were different enough to justify initial theoretical negligence? Gilbert Geis disagrees. He suggests that Albert Cohen, Richard Cloward, and Lloyd Ohlin, were "armchair social philosophers" and Walter Miller was "blaming the victim," with the result being that they "oversimplified" a more proper understanding of gangs and missed the political meanness that makes gang membership "virtually a crime."[1] Recent research is more sophisticated, has involved more ethnography, and has recognized political associations, helping to create a better, albeit more complex, understanding[2]—with a weakness: the relative dearth of area-specific historical analyses of what was. In this chapter, we fill in some gaps.

Danger Lurks among the Poor

A euphemism used to characterize the class street groups come from is the *lower* class. It is a pablumized way to refer to a class that has historically put fear into the hearts of ruling groups. William Wilson's work on the *underclass* changed serious ethnographic gang analysis by highlighting a concept that then became almost impossible to ignore.[3] Wilson argued that the underclass in the inner cities was a result of the growth of industry, which changed the class and racial structure there. The concept of the underclass provided a social category into which most gang members seemed to fit.[4] David Brotherton and Luis Barrios make it clear that John Hagedorn and Joan Moore note the theoretical importance of the underclass in the postindustrial era as "the main reason behind the 'astounding proliferation of U.S. street gangs.'"[5]

In the mid-1960s, Michael Harrington called attention to a large preunderclass group he termed the "other America." Although his focus wasn't on delinquency and gangs, he made it clear that the other America was a fundamental part of the "seamy side of the affluent society," often "invisible" to better-off Americans, and a function of industrial growth. The other America is another name for the group of poor people gang concepts come from. Existing in every city in America as an "economic underworld," where "tens of thousands of hidden people labor at impossible wages," the other America remained "immune to progress."[6] They are "hidden" from the classes above them by ignorance and neglect.

Before the other America and the underclass had been identified as social phenomena, another group, not only older but more durable, called the "dangerous class[es]" had been recognized and proven to be a valuable concept.[7] Identification of this class served the class interests of the ruling groups, who wanted to hide from the mess their industrialization had made. Concerned about the dangerous class's revolutionary potential, the ruling groups sought to marginalize it, by discrediting the class as a group of "parasites" and criminals, "violating the fundamental law of orderly society." The dangerous class was defined as a "morally depraved" group, a "race apart" from themselves, and "detached from the prevailing social conditions."[8] Lumped into this class were a host of groups often derogatorily referred to as "social junk" or "social dynamite," depending on the group's level of need or potential for violence.[9] John Irwin, focusing on these same groups, notes that many of them were perceived as social "rabble" and were the residents of our nation's jails.[10]

Split-Level Delinquency[11]

By emphasizing problems of life in the lower class and neglecting to consider life in other classes, early researchers were able to establish considerable initial credibility for their theories. Mayhem no more characterized lower-class life in the inner city than *Father Knows Best* families characterized the middle-class suburbs.[12] Regardless, many held those clichéd views of life in these two environments. While early researchers based their theories on the lower class having proprietary rights to gangs, there was available evidence to suggest gangs existed outside this class.[13]

William Whyte, in his 1940s study of "Cornerville" groups, identified "gangs" among the non-college-bound juveniles of the "slum" and "clubs" among the "socially mobile" but college-bound juveniles from the same slum. He observed that clubs could form out of gangs when the group's orientation changed from rowdy to more covert behavior—like trying behind the scenes to squeeze local politicians for money or favors. Blurring the line between gangs and clubs, whoever joined a club, whether a former gang member or not, could help the club achieve the *appearance* of legitimacy by getting it a "charter," a sanction to exist from the city. Then, they could engage in White-collar crime, a middle-class act, with little worry about the prosecution that resulted from the blue-collar crime of gangs.[14] Whyte's position was influenced by class favoritism. If it was *street*-based crime, it was a lower-class or gang act, but if it was *suite*-based improprieties, it was middle-class club behavior, a more acceptable type of crime. The change from street crime to suite crime followed a class change.

The idea that gangs could be transformed into clubs after adopting middle-class standards of behavior was not lost on the Los Angeles Group Guidance Project of the 1960s. Their emphasis was to change the gang so that its activities were "redirected into socially approved patterns" and that the gang's energies were redirected toward "socially sanctioned goals."[15] Project ideology emphasized that by changing the gang into a group that functioned under appropriate middle-class norms, the gang would be converted into a club.[16] Presentation of the street group as a group adopting sanctioned middle-class behavioral patterns was a key determinant in this analysis as to whether the group was to be termed a gang or a club. Absent from this framework was a consideration of the evidence that the middle class not only had delinquency but also had gangs.

Class Privilege

Harrison E. Salisbury, a Pulitzer Prize–winning journalist, emphasized that middle-class juveniles, who were engaged in a wide variety of delinquency, some of which was very serious, often did it in groups that had names. From shoplifting and vandalism to rape, murder, and even terrorism, juveniles from families wealthy enough to live in the suburbs were shown to be just as dangerous as inner-city urban juveniles. Their behavior was hidden by their wealth: not talked about, not prosecuted, and not punished. Quoting Professor Robert MacIver of the New York Delinquency Evaluation Survey, Salisbury writes:

> There is much more upper-class gang activity than is realized. There is more delinquency. But it is covered up. It's almost impossible to get statistics on. We know that it exists. . . . But it is all nicely covered up.

> A middle-class child has to act much worse than a poor boy before his conduct becomes the subject of notation on the police blotter.[17]

Some researchers were quite aware of the emerging evidence on middle-class delinquency but dismissed it as "petty," infrequent, easier to control, and with little police data on its occurrence.[18] If middle-class deviance was not part of the public record, the reasoning went, it either didn't happen, was so minor it didn't require further attention, or happened so infrequently that it was not worth paying any further attention to.

Although published years after early researchers offered their lower-class theories of gang behavior, Herman and Julia Schwendinger left no doubt that, at least in England, there had been considerable evidence around for a long time that juveniles from wealthy families, in the sixteenth century, had formed gangs that were involved in serious crimes of violence. The Bold Bucks and Mohocks, for example, were White gangs of "Young Gallants" who were "maliciously violent," mutilating women with knife cuts on their faces and beating them "without provocation." Not only did these youth remain above prosecution by the law, at least one of them *became* the law—a lawyer—and then was later appointed a judge and knighted, his early youthful crimes conveniently forgotten.[19] The Schwendingers also suggest that the middle-class American groups they studied, such as "academics," "surfers," and "gremmies," exhibited gang-like behavior.[20]

In the late 1950s, objective evidence emerged that group delinquency was not a lower-class monopoly. Termed "self-report studies," this research revealed delinquency was far more widespread within the class structure than official police data suggested.[21] Lower-class boys and girls were doing it, but so were middle-class juveniles of both genders, with some studies showing that they were doing it the most. Salisbury made it clear that Albert K. Cohen, James F. Short, and Kenneth Polk had all written easily obtainable papers on the demise of the myth of delinquent domination by the lower class. Whatever ignorance may have fueled earlier theories had now been called into serious question by data that were difficult to ignore. The alleged lack of these data on middle-class delinquency could no longer be relied on as an excuse for misunderstanding. Yet the data were snubbed.

Self-report data shook up the study of delinquency but seemed to have less of an impact on the study of gangs. In 1967, Edmund W. Vaz edited a book titled *Middle-Class Juvenile Delinquency*, as part of a series on social problems. Although the book didn't create much of a stir in the academic world, articles in it by Howard and Barbara Myerhoff and Vaz offered weak references to the existence of middle-class gangs. Other articles in the book made use of self-report studies to open wider the discussion of middle-class delinquency.

William J. Chambliss's classic 1973 study "The Saints and the Roughnecks," on middle- and lower-class gangs, demonstrated that both groups, although engaged in different kinds of delinquencies of more or less equal seriousness, received wholly different community responses. The middle-class Saints, viewed by the community as "good" boys, could do no harm, while the lower-class Roughnecks, seen as troublemakers by the community, could do no good. The Saints got away with their delinquencies, while the Roughnecks got clobbered.[22] His research added to the clarity that group delinquency was as dependent on interpretation as it was on actual behavior. Theories relying on selectively chosen data were intellectual exercises rather than reliable accounts of street life.

Although the question of which class is the most delinquent is controversial, the issue is resolved in the research and theory of a large body of serious gang researchers in the academic / juvenile-justice community: the lower class has the monopoly; get over it. In 1995 Malcolm Klein and associates began publishing the *Modern Gang Reader*. This authoritative compendium of the most relevant articles published on gangs is now in its fourth edition in 2014. In none of these editions is the issue of social class raised as a theoretical concern. Neither William Sanders nor James Howell and Elizabeth Griffiths, in their recent gang texts, discusses any other class than the lower class to explain gangs.[23]

Mean streets can produce mean people, while the police and media can exploit what may or may not have occurred there for their own purposes. At the same time, privileged folk, with access to private attorneys and insurance or power-structure figures who can "fix" things, can hide what goes on in their neighborhoods.[24] Failure to consider this will limit our understanding. In sum: the role of lower-class status in gang formation has been overplayed while middle-class gangs/groups have gone unnoticed. Social class can account for who gets arrested much better than it can for why juveniles join groups; the types of delinquencies juveniles will be involved in more than whether they'll be involved in delinquency; the types of groups juveniles will join more than whether they will join a group; and the types of names the groups will be given by the larger society. Without a critical re-examination of the political issues of class, myths about gangs will grow. Working-class South Los Angeles juveniles were far less worried about frustrations in becoming middle class than they were about girlfriends and racism.

Wagging the Dog: Female Set Affiliations

"Girls have been a part of gang life for over a hundred years,"[25] yet early researchers mostly ignored them when they tried to explain the actions of gang males and the causes of delinquent behavior.[26] More contemporary researchers have contended that girls were not given serious research attention as possible gang members until the mid-1970s.[27] It is likely that early theories minimized consideration of gender because the police data they used showed males to be the most frequent contributors to delinquency and the most seriously delinquent gender, which continues to be the case.[28] Meda Chesney-Lind and Randall Shelden argue that there were built-in biases to studying girls and gangs, driven by media stereotypes and by male researchers relying on male gang members for their data.[29]

In 1974, Quicker documented the existence of female gangs in East Los Angeles and discussed their groups and their relationship to the boys' groups after interviewing self-identified female gang members.[30] Before this research, when girl gangs were considered in other parts of the country, there was typically inordinate attention paid to their sexuality and attractiveness.[31] Researchers were not concerned with the "functions of the gang for girls" as Quicker was.[32] Current research is more analytically sophisticated, as girl gangs have become a concern for humanistic researchers. While Joan Moore and Diego Vigil have since expanded on Quicker's work in East Los Angeles and on other Los Angeles Chicana groups,[33] scant attention has been paid to early girl gangs and gender relationships in South Los Angeles.

It might seem simple to resolve the questions of how many girls are gang members and how many girls' gangs exist, but attempts to do so have produced a flurry of estimates reminiscent of the responses to these same questions when asked about boys. Gini Sikes notes that in 1992 New York City, the police claimed there were no female gangs, yet in 1984 Anne Campbell writes that of the four hundred gangs in that city, 10 percent were female.[34] In New Mexico in 1996, Dana Peterson got responses similar to Sikes when she interviewed the director of a multiagency task force. He asserted that "there aren't any female gang members" in the area.[35] Chesney-Lind found that in Oahu in 1991, 7 percent of suspected gang members were female.[36]

Closer to home, Moore estimated that in 1985 a third of the gang members in East Los Angeles were female.[37] Malcolm Klein and L. Crawford found that 26 percent of gang members in Los Angeles in 1967 were female.[38] The 1991 GREAT database put the number of Los Angeles gang females at 6 percent.[39] Given the range of these estimates across time and geography, numerous conclusions are possible. Three stand out: (1) Researchers' and law enforcement's "gendered habits" have made female gangs "invisible,"[40] thereby jaundicing an accurate count. (2) These numerical differences are a reflection of the variance in female gangs in different areas over different periods. (3) No one knows.[41]

Girls on the Set

South Los Angeles male street-group juveniles did not live in a "single-sex bubble."[42] Girls in the neighborhoods were on the set "21/7."[43] While females did not have the same troubles with the police males had, they hung out with them, influencing them and being influenced by them.[44] Girls were key players in much of the activity, both directly and indirectly. They partied with the boys, watched them fight, encouraged them, went to school with them, rode in cars and buses with them, and became romantically involved with them, and they had babies together. Most adolescents in the neighborhoods had considerable concern about what members of the other sex thought about them, as well as what members of their own sex thought.[45] To diminish the influence of these gender relationships on juveniles is to ignore the fact that juveniles sometimes do the things they do because they care what their peers—of both genders—think of them.

"Gang" girls or girls in the "gang," were discovered by the Los Angeles media in 1963 when provocative front-page second-section articles, written by Mary Ann Callan, with titles like "Lives Smashed in Girl Gangs" and "Girl Gangsters Thrive on Hate," appeared in the *Los Angeles Times*.[46] As might be expected from such terms of endearment, the articles' content focused on the girls' alleged violent and predatory behavior. They were described in the articles as wearing "fighting clothes" and being "defiant," "unreachable," "incorrigible," "vacuous-faced dolls." The media claimed they were drug-addicted sex delinquents, whose purpose was to "terrorize" other youth, and that they had "whacky" relationships with their weak supervising parents, who had generated offspring that were "miserable human being[s] ready to explode in the pressure cooker of adolescence." These characterizations bore little resemblance to the women we encountered in our research.

A few months before those articles appeared, a more temperate article by Gene Sherman was published in the same newspaper, discussing the paucity of research on female gang activity and the importance of gathering data on it. One purpose of his article was to explain the reasons for funding that was earmarked for the University of Southern California to conduct necessary research. Sherman states: "If the full scale study is undertaken, it will be one of the first directed totally at girl gangs, about which data is extremely scanty—as might be expected with a recently emerged problem."[47] The emphasis of the research was to develop prevention strategies for working with boys and girls, since it was assumed—finally—that girls influenced boys to do things they might not otherwise do.[48] This assumption is spot on but should have included the following corollary: such influence cuts both ways. Girls were influenced by male behavior as much as they influenced it.

Girls have played central and dynamic roles among males and within the street groups of South Los Angeles for many years.

In a word, *interdependence* characterized the relationships between them. They relied on each other for mutual aid in navigating the vicissitudes of urban life. There was an agreed upon division of labor based on gender roles, with explicit, though marginally overlapping, expectations for both genders. Informal female *clubs*, whose primary purpose was social, formed throughout the neighborhoods, usually affiliated with a specific clique of a male set and often using a feminized version of the clique's name as their own. Girls' clubs were often referred to as cliques in the neighborhood but not referenced as gangs or even as sets. Girls in the clubs were generally the same age as the boys in the clique they were affiliated with.

Peterson's review of the literature considers the deleterious consequences experienced by girls as a result of their gang membership. She notes how the "social injury" hypothesis explained by Moore, Hagedorn, and Terrance Thornberry contrasts with the "liberation" hypothesis and "gender oppression" hypotheses of Chesney-Lind, Brotherton, and others. Her conclusions are that gang membership for girls generally has potentially "deleterious effects."[49] Set affiliation and club membership in South Los Angeles did not have these deleterious effects during the period we studied. What deleterious effects did accrue to girls was more a result of their class and especially because of their race.

Female clubs were smaller than the male groups, with more fluid membership, and usually did not have initiations. Often girls from their club would date males in the affiliated clique, but it was not a requirement. Males dated whom they could, while the females dated circumspectly. As expected, dating outside one's neighborhood—for both genders—was often a precursor to individual or clique-involved squabbles. Girls who had boyfriends or brothers in a street group were protected by both. That protection was extended to girls even when their boyfriend or brother was physically separated from the set, as, for instance, when he was in prison.

Cliques with Girls

While many male cliques had female clubs affiliated with them, others did not.[50] Whit, the vice president of the Royal Aces, contended that his set was composed of "lady's men," with no female club affiliation. A few of the girlfriends of the Royal Aces would socialize with one another but were mostly unorganized and just not interested in creating something more formal. Whit explained: "Some of the steady girls use to hang out together, but they never got strong enough to have a name for themselves. They were just the girlfriends of the Royal Aces."

The Royal Aces, beginning in 1946, were similar to other sets of that period, all of which lacked female affiliates. Female club formation was more a phenomenon of the 1950s and 1960s than it was of earlier times. Some sets of the mid- to late 1950s, like the Senators, were alleged to have female affiliates, but even the president of that set, Geronimo, knew little about them. When asked about the "Senates," the purported female affiliate to the Senators, he said: "I know nothing about them girls. I just heard, like other people heard, but I never seen any." His account is consistent with findings by other researchers on the relatively short-term existence of girl street groups.[51] The existence of a name for a group doesn't always mean the group existed—or, if it did exist, that it lasted much longer than a minute.[52] Chesney-Lind and Shelden point out that once police include a juvenile in their database, it becomes permanent, regardless of desistance.[53] This finding could help explain the large discrepancies noted previously in the counts of gangs.

When female clubs did form, they were usually associated with a specific male clique, showing their affiliation by adapting the clique's name so that it was suitable for a female club. Thus the Renegades' girls club was Miss Renegades. When the Renegades became the Apostates, the girls club became the Apostenettes. The Warlords had two female groups: the Warnettes and the younger group of War Sisters. Before the Baby Slausons emerged, there was the Slausonettes, most likely affiliated with Little Slauson but quite possibly Big Slauson too. They were the "old ones," Bird contended, with "Mary Ann S. and all them." The Flips' girls tried to be the Flipettes, but the name just didn't sound right. They became the Charlenettes instead, taking a name that worked.[54] Girls in the 20s neighborhoods appeared to take on a more generic title of the Twentiettes, if they were affiliated with any of the street groups in that area.

The Farmers had the Farmerettes, while the Junior and Baby Businessmen, breaking categorical consistency, had the El Social Playgirls.[55] Florence cliques had the Midget Locas plus the Midnight Locas, Gangsta Locas, and Tiny Florencita. Sometimes the girls took the set name instead of the clique name: the Rebel Rousers had the Rebelons; the Gladiators, the Gladiettes; the Del Vikings, the Del Viqueens; the Senators, the Senates; and Florence had Florencita.[56] At times, the girls' groups were referred to as "sister clubs" and familiar to most set members, while at other times, key male club members may never have met any of the supposedly affiliated females, although they might have heard of them.[57]

Joining for Fun

Sherman quotes Klein as writing, "These girls are themselves organized into gangs or quasi-gangs with leadership elements, power figures and other evidence of organizational structure."[58] Roger Rice and Rex Christensen contend that Los Angeles's girl groups were "girl-affiliate groups or gangs" and that the girls' groups are "sometimes a formal and recognized part of the gang and sometimes are associated only because of proximity to the male gang."[59] The female groups we found in South Los Angeles had little organization, being no better organized than a teen friendship clique with a name. Rice and Christensen saw the girls as "instigators" of delinquent activities, causing fights and being "trouble makers."[60] Mary Ann Callan suggests that girls who join female gangs are psychological misfits, who are headed to "social oblivion" but find redemption in the gang because it "gives them a status beyond themselves" and an escape route by providing "a framework of discipline."[61]

While a female connection to males and to their fights is practically universal, it's an oversimplification to argue that the girls' only links were as instigators or because of mental or sexual issues.[62] We found no evidence that any of the girls in the clubs had psychological problems outside the ordinary issues facing their nonclub peers.[63] The range of personality types in the clubs showed a variance similar to the range found in other female adolescents in the community. Their reasons for club affiliation were not particularly strong. They were not running away from abusive homes;[64] they didn't lack parental supervision;[65] nor were they poor students;[66] nor did they come from gang member families,[67] as researchers have found to be the case with more contemporary gangs. They joined for fun.[68] The girls' clubs were mostly social groups of like-minded juveniles who thought that a name for their small assemblage might be cool, especially if one or more of them might have had a boyfriend or brother in the neighborhood male clique.

Ominous Connections?

When a female affiliate club began, it was frequently uneventful. Nedra, of the Warnettes, described the inauspicious beginnings of her club this way:

> When I was growing up, we just started hanging together, and we said, 'We should start a club.' Two or three girls was going with Warlords, and I was just a part of the group, but I wasn't going with nobody then. I was well protected by my brothers, you know; I didn't have to join for that.

The Warnettes activities were about what you might expect from a group of Girl Scouts or a high school sorority. Nedra continued: "We had club meetings and stuff over at people's houses. Basically, it was just a gathering of friends. We hung on the porch talking about . . . stuff. We wore the same colors and dressed alike—and all made sure we wore the same colors to the show and stuff like that." Then, sensing that she might not have responded clearly enough previously, she added: "We never, as far as I'm aware of, none of us ever got into a fight because we were Warnettes. But there were some rowdies, and they got in fights, in their own right, all the time." Clubs would form, exist for a while, and then fade with about the same amount of fanfare as they had started. There were no obvious characteristics, psychological or physical, that distinguished club members from nonmembers.

The clubs' activities included dressing alike and organizing parties. Club membership was not necessary to be an organizer, although a number of the organizers were members. As Bird saw it:

> The girls mostly ran around together, wore sweaters, and associated with the Slausons. Some were in clubs, some weren't. They'd party, and they'd give parties. Or whenever there'd be a picnic or something, the girls would set it up, and they'd get all the food. We'd come up with some money from a club meetin', and they would get all the food, and we'd go to a weenie roast, or we'd go to a beach party.

Ameer, the president of the Baby Businessmen, concurred with Bird, adding: "They partied with us. They'd provide the dances; the girls organized it. They did the shoppin', they bought the food, and they prepared the food. Yeah, we gave them the money." Roslyn, who was not a club member, carried on like members did, by holding parties at her auntie's house, with Slauson clique members and club and nonclub girls in attendance.

A Place for Independence

While the above clubs had independence from the male clubs—or, as Bird observed, "The dudes didn't run the girls"—there were other girls' clubs whose names and activities suggested even greater independence. This was characterized by an absence of fealty to a male set, although they usually had a variety of male social affiliations. Two of these clubs were the Conservative Young Ladies[69] and the Monza Club.[70] The Conservative Young Ladies were from the Rebel Rouser neighborhood, on the West-Side, but they weren't Rebel Rouser connected. Some of them had boyfriends and brothers who were Rebel Rousers, but that did not stop a group of them from partying with the Slausons. Their conservatism seemed related to their style of dress and not to the people they hung out with. The Monza Club was from the Slauson neighborhood. Some members may have been related to each other, but, as Sheila D. noted, they "did their own thing," facilitated by having their own Monza cars, which gave them an independence many other girls lacked.

There was a web of social affiliations between the male sets and the girls' clubs that would be a challenge to quantify, diagram, or otherwise describe sociometrically. Important as it is to operationalize and then quantify social phenomena, compromises, usually established arbitrarily, are required to create categories, which can then miss important nuances. The following narrative of interaction between some Slausons and Conservative Young Ladies demonstrates a few of those complexities. It begins with a Slauson homegirl, Diana F., who moved to the West-Side and became familiar with some Conservative Young Ladies, telling Bird about a party in the Rebel Rouser neighborhood where there were girls.[71] As Bird reported:

> Diana F. tells us about a party on the West-Side in the Rebel Rouser neighborhood with all these girls. We ain't met these girls yet, Diana had just told us. Okay, we fall to the party, nine of us in four cars. The party is full of Rebel Rousers, you know: Jay Bird and Tiger, Dice and Dirt, and Tramp—all of them was at the party. We looked at them and said: "What's happenin'," blah, blah," and we talkin' to them and all that. They got a paid security guard, a big ol' brother, on the door to keep the peace. Okay, we get to talkin' to the girls real good. I'm sittin' over in the corner talkin' to Lynn F., lyin' like a big dog. Okay, Gloria O. is Billy J.'s sister-in-law, and Lynn is his cousin. So I'm talkin' to Lynn, and everybody talkin' to Cheryl S., Andrea V., Rosemary S., Linda, Gail S., Beverly, and Janice S. There was twenty-three of them.

Bird and his homeboys befriended this large group of girls and got cozy with them, only to discover that the Rebel Rousers, who had brought the girls to the party before the Slausons arrived—and for reasons that are unclear—decided to slip away, leaving the girls stranded a long way from home. Bird continued:

> So finally we get kinda friendly with them. And as the night progresses, and the party's comin' to an end, suddenly they don't have a way home. We said, "Well, how did you all get here?" They said: "Well, Tramp and all them brought them all here." We looked out, and there ain't no Rebel Rousers left. The dudes were all gone. I don't know why they left them; maybe because they [the girls] started socializing with us? It wasn't that they was afraid of us, 'cause we didn't have a beef with Rebel Rousers. And they was some pretty tough dudes too, the ones that was there. They wasn't no punks or nothing, but they just went on and left them.

Being gentlemen, the Slausons couldn't just abandon the girls they had spent the last few hours entertaining; they felt a responsibility to help. Not wanting to take undue advantage, they did the chivalrous thing: they came to the rescue, with unexpected results. Bird concluded:

> Anyway, they said: "How we gonna get home?" They looked outside, and it was foggy. You know, it looked like the Boston Strangler was to come out and everything, like Scotland Yard might be around. So we said: "Well, how many of ya all is there?" They started countin'—boom, boom, boom—there was twenty-three. So I said: "There's nine of us; we'll take you home in the hoopties." They said: "*Hoopies*?" I said: "No, *hoopty*." They said, "What's a hoopty?" I said: "Come here." We walked outside and showed them, and they said: "Them's gangster cars!" And we took all of them; we put twenty-three girls and nine dudes in four hoopties and took 'em home, took 'em to their individual houses. Then the whole West-Side, down to 35th, started hearin' about the Conservative Young Ladies runnin' with the Slausons.[72]

Unaffiliated, affiliated, running with the Slausons, girlfriends to the Slausons—none of these categories are quite accurate yet all have a bit of truth. The relationship the Slausons had with the Conservative Young Ladies had shades of assorted involvements, some subtle, some less so, but they were not easily subject to categorization. The absence of clear categories was not unique to this connection but was generally more characteristic of gender associations between the sets and clubs than not. The relationships were complex, convoluted, and elusive.

From the Neighborhood

Female club formation, rare to nonexistent before the early 1950s, was consistent with patterns of traditional gendered relationships. Male youth felt that there were things they shouldn't do around girls or with them and that there were things girls shouldn't do at all. Having street-group affiliation was one of them. Frank M., from Clanton, said that the males "didn't cuss around the girls" and "didn't like the girls to be rough." They "didn't like the girls to cuss," and they "didn't like the girls smoking grass." When the guys talked about sex, they didn't do it in front of the girls. Girlfriends weren't sexual partners but companions they were later going to marry.[73] The girls weren't tomboys.[74] Frank emphasized that he never saw the girls carrying weapons for the guys, although he had read about it in the newspapers.[75] He'd also heard about girl gang members but never saw any himself and knew Clanton didn't have any. From his perspective, the guys wanted to keep the girls away from any of the fighting or deviant things they may have been involved in: "They didn't want them in any mess at all." The women we spoke with agreed.

In the early Chicano sets, especially those existing closer to downtown before 1950, female affiliation was rare. This was most likely a consequence of the more traditional gender relations in existence in those communities then. When asked about female association with the 1940s gangs like Clanton and 38th Street, Frank M. commented,

> Definitely not. Now, like Clanton, there might have been one or two [girls] you might have heard a little about. But basically, Mexican guys didn't cuss around the girls, they didn't like the girls to be rough, and they didn't like the girls smokin' grass. I didn't know any of them who did. But I'd seen it in the papers, where there's girls that have knives and stuff, but basically that was just something that just didn't happen.

Boys found girls who went against this grain to be less acceptable as dating and marriage partners, according to our respondents.

By the mid-1950s, gender relations began to change, together with an increase in more neighborhood clique and set formations. But girls were still not considered gang members; nor were their clubs considered gangs by them or anyone else in the neighborhood. Girls' clubs became more commonplace but were not well organized and were more exclusive than inclusive. Girls were not coerced into joining a club. Roslyn, from the Slauson neighborhood, said: "We were never pressured. Everyone already knew what I was about. Guys did their thing, and girls took care of girl business." Bird remarked, "Girls didn't have to join nothin'. They were already here; they were from the neighborhood." Linda C. noted that Mexican girls in Florence were "courted in" if they came from outside the neighborhood but were "automatically in" if they lived there. She added that "automatically in" didn't include all neighborhood girls, since there were some who weren't especially well liked.

Relational Benefits

Sheila D. was a member of the Laquinians' Drill Team, a Veterans of Foreign Wars–sponsored group. She was familiar with some of the female affiliates of Slauson but never felt a desire to belong to any of them because she already belonged to a group. She was "cool," she was from the neighborhood, and she could participate in the available activities.[76] The Slauson female affiliates were not considered girl gangs; nor were the girls in them considered gang members by anyone she knew in the community. They were girls whose boyfriends were in Slauson, and as Sheila said: "We all went to parties and different functions that we had together."

Having a boyfriend or a brother in a set provided protection. Sheila D. continued: "If a guy found out you were going with somebody from Slauson, they would have to answer to whoever the boyfriend was and all his club members."[77] Geronimo said that his girlfriend wore his club jacket, a sign that she was "taken"; she had a boyfriend, and prospective suitors had best keep their distance lest they face his wrath. Such an arrangement seemed acceptable to both parties. Geronimo explained:

> See, my girl wore my jacket. Bein' her goin' with me, nobody would mess with her. She could go where she wanted because, "That's Geronimo's woman." You know, if cats would hit on her, she would jerk away, tell them, "I'm Geronimo's woman," like that. They'd say, "Oh, okay." And she had—it was protection. There was a blanket over her wherever she went, that she used.

Such affiliations provided a wide variety of benefits, but they weren't necessary to enlist neighborhood support. Just being from the community was sufficient to offer girls protection from any predatory behavior inside or outside their neighborhood. Ameer, from the Businessmen, suggested there was consensus, a general unwritten law, that girls in the neighborhood were extended protection just because of their neighborhood affiliation, regardless of whether it was formal or informal. He noted:

> We had a girl that use to go to junior high school with us. We'd stop by her house to see if anyone messed with her, 'cause she was a far-out kid, and she walked to school with us. No guy would disrespect her, no girl mess with her, 'cause they got to deal with us. It was called an unwritten law of protection. She was protected because she was from our neighborhood. She hang around with us, she come to our park, she come to our dance, so therefore she was a regular.

Neighborhood attachments ran deep, had a spiderweb of associations, and were strong. Club membership was superfluous, a luxury, and unnecessary for neighborhood backing. If you were cool, as Bird described, you were a homegirl with benefits:

> If you lived in the neighborhood and you were so-and-so's cousin or whatever, or you lived there and everybody saw you every day, and

you weren't a poot-butt, you were still from the neighborhood. And if someone saw somebody jammin' you or something happen to you on the other side of town, but you were cool, they [the homeboys] would still come over and take care of it. But see, somebody might have seen you and said: "Yeah, she live over there in Slauson." But they [the girls] weren't from the neighborhood as far as being in the club, but they were from the neighborhood because they were a part of the community. They bought at the same grocery store we did, or their mother might have worked there, or they might have owned it, so they were still from the neighborhood.

Neighborhood protection benefits didn't expire for girls whose boyfriends were in prison or jail: they were expected and continued. Bird remarked:

I had to whoop this sucka behind Hazel. Zay was in the penitentiary, and this dude kept messin' with her. I said: "That's my homeboy's old lady; don't mess with her." "Yeah, well, where's he at?" I said, "Well, he's not here right now," and he [the sucka] said, "It ain't no thing." And I said, "No, it is a thing. I'm ridin' his beef." 'Cause you know, if it'd been the same thing and he'd done something to Hazel, and Zay hear about it, and Zay turn around and ask: "Well, who was there?" "Bird was there, and so-and-so, and you allowed this?" I had to whoop this dude, you know, 'cause see, she was a homegirl and Zay was a homeboy.

Hazel wasn't a kept woman; she was protected. Demonstrating the autonomy that she held and the importance of neighborhood connections, Bird added:

I mean, Hazel, she want to mess around, that's her business. But she was tellin' the dude to freeze up, and he kept on talkin' that stuff. He wuddn't from the neighborhood either, no way. Number one, you wuddn't from the neighborhood, fool, so you really ain't got no business talkin' like that. You can dance and all that, but you ain't got no business going further.

Nedra nodded her head in agreement with Bird's analysis. Then, to demonstrate how serious some of these relationships were, she added: "And that's another thing: the women, if their man went to jail, they would wait. I mean serious wait—no sex. Like, you go to the party and everything, and everybody knows whose woman you were, and everybody knew what penitentiary your man was in."[78] But there was lady's choice: an expectation that she would wait but not a requirement—dalliances did occur.

Neighborhood slang suggested a variety of proscriptions associated with dating more than one person at a time or having sex without involvement. "Playin' double and lookin' for trouble" was one such comment. It suggested a two-timer, usually a male who, in dating two women at the same time, was opening himself up for a world of hurt if caught. "Crummin'" was another term that referred to a male who was trying to mess around with a girl other than his girlfriend. Bird noted, "Crummin' is when you creepin'—like you got a girlfriend but you creepin' with somebody else's.'" "Dippin' and tippin'" was a male having sex and then leaving, without further entanglement. Regardless of the prohibitions associated with multiple sex partners, escapades happened. These were, after all, adolescents, not saints.

An important factor keeping girls out of club affiliation was an even higher priority: pregnancy and child-rearing responsibilities.[79] With courtships often short, and youth marrying young and having children early, girls frequently had little time for club affiliations and hanging with the homies.[80] The traditional attitudes toward sex that many girls held—sex out of wedlock was improper, and being a "good girl" was important—led to early marriages. As Nedra explained: "All my grandmother ever told me was: 'Keep your draws up and your dress down,' and that's what I did. Well—mostly."[81]

Nedra's sister added that it wasn't easy following their grandmother's instructions, but at least some of the time, they and their friends obeyed the rules. As she recounted: "It wasn't so much that we didn't want to, or they didn't want to; it was what we were taught, and that's what we did. I mean, we use to kiss and rub bodies and all that; 'scrunchin' and grindin'' we use to call it."[82] Exceptions occurred, when situations just got too hot to handle any other way than full on getting it on. Then too, there were the loose and lascivious neighborhood females—known of and talked about by many—who could have given the other women a bad reputation. Although it would have been simple for the media or a casual observer to interpret their promiscuity as the norm, our respondents felt that it was not.[83]

Romance Rules

When a girl did choose someone to date, she chose a person she liked or could benefit from—whether a clique member or not—but not because he was a clique member.[84] A number of girls began dating male clique members before they even knew anything about their membership, often finding out about it after they had become involved.[85] The discovery was never a reason in itself to end the dating. Interestingly, some girls noted that clique membership enhanced the guy's appeal, making him even more attractive. A few women told us they preferred those who were set connected, because they were "cool." Lafayette added: "If you were a clique member or from a certain set, and you had a reputation, shit, the girls come lookin' for you." Rick C. noted: "Some of the ladies liked the gangster look. They were there because they liked the way he dressed, the way he talked, the way he carried himself. That was their attraction."

Parents, when they discovered that their daughters were dating set members, were frequently not supportive.[86] But their efforts to intervene and to discourage further association were often for naught. Roslyn's mother, for example, after meeting Bird, told her: "I am gonna kill you if I hear that you're talking to that person again or even thinking about it." Shortly thereafter, she married him—and is alive today.

Where being a set member was rarely a reason not to date a guy, a double standard held: boys rarely preferred their partners to be club members. Geronimo explained that a lot of guys liked "square" girls, girls loyal to them and not to a club.[87] Although both males and females dated people from outside the neighborhood,[88] neighborhood proximity made things convenient. It was far simpler to date someone who lived on your block or around the corner and whom you saw at school than it was to date someone from another neighborhood. Logistics and attraction had benefits: they often overruled clique or club membership.

Girls would occasionally fight over guys. Ameer thought that whenever the girls did fight, it was usually over a guy: "Mostly, the girls jump on other girls 'cause the other girl try to take her boyfriend away. That's the main culprit." He felt further that any group the girls might have been involved in was not a fighting group. Fighting was primarily a male activity: "The girls' gang, per se, wasn't no such thing; girls wasn't in gang fights. It was a man thing then; it was man against man at the time. The set was a macho thing," Ameer claimed. Fighting was certainly not unknown among girls in the neighborhood, but it wasn't the norm.[89] With due cause, girls would fight, although not on the levels of or for the reasons usually reported in the media.[90] Even more infrequent than female fights might be the appearance of a weapon—like a nail file—that could do damage. Media reporting of a weapon usually did greater damage than the weapon ever did.[91]

Some girls rejected the male idea that they would fight because of the guys. Girls like Nedra, for instance, brought a very independent attitude to their relationships with males. While Nedra agreed that other girls might fight over a male, she refused to; she understood that the male she had just gotten through battling over might not want her anyway. She clarified: "I never did fight. One time this girl was gonna jump on me about Bobby M., and I told her, I said, 'Hey, you know what, if he wants you and you want him, you can have him—ain't nothin' for us to fight about.' I said, 'But if he wants me, you should just leave me alone.'"

Nedra's web of personal affiliations was another important factor in keeping males or females from "messin'" with her very much. She was not a club member, but she was the sister of a Little Slauson, the girlfriend—at different times—of two leaders of Slauson cliques, and eventually the wife of another powerful member of the Slausons. As strong as these affiliations were, they didn't insulate her completely, as she pointed out:

> One time, this girl came over to my house, named Pat. She wasn't from the Park or anything like that. She was the person who liked this guy who liked me. And I didn't even like this guy, but we were friends. And she came over to my house and jumped on me, whooped me. She hit me, and I just started cryin', and she chased me around my own house. She told me to leave him alone, and she better not see him in my house no more. And I'm wonderin', "Wow, why didn't she do it to him?" I mean, I ain't gonna get him and make him come to my house.

Nedra's sister Davetta, who was a Warnette, indicated that she never fought either, over men or otherwise, although she knew of girls who did. Her friend Johnetta "could whoop anybody and was afraid of nobody." Her skills provided automatic protection to whoever hung out with her, because few had the mettle to challenge her.[92] Davetta and Johnetta hung out together.

Neighborhood girls could be assertive. If a girl loved a guy, she would cut him a lot of slack. Regardless of his behavior, she would stand by her man—hang in with him *until the wheels came off*.[93] But when they came off, especially if he had wronged her, by doing something that she thought was improper, he could be in deep trouble. In one case, Little Bird recalled witnessing a guy at a record hop bragging about all his conquests—pity him—in front of a girl he had recently dumped. After he completed his display of braggadocio, she said, so all could hear: "Yeah, you a lyin' motherfucka'; you're full of shit. You begged to eat my pussy, and I was on my period." Redundant though it may be to say, she effectively rained on his parade.

Romance ruled, but some guys were abusive to their women. These circumstances were not the norm. But they received more notice than their frequency would justify, because their outlandishness brought exaggerated attention. When problems between the sexes did occur, they were rarely left unchallenged, as this situation of abuse involving Nedra reveals. Her situation involved marriage to a guy who treated her badly until she made him an offer he couldn't refuse. In her words:

> Mac use to lock me up. And he'd stick a piece of paper in between the door and jam. He would leave; and when he come home, if that

paper not there, he would whoop me, beat the devil out of me. We were livin' in his mother's house, but she had a live-in job. And one time, he locked me in for the evening. And his mother came home, and she opened the door, and the paper fell out. But his mama went out with some of her friends before he came home, so when he got there, he whooped me for goin' out, and I hadn't done it.

Nedra continued to discuss other abuses she experienced at his hands until finally, she had had enough. He was too large and strong to challenge physically, but she found another way. She continued:

One time he came home—he had been gone two days—and it was like three o'clock in the afternoon, and he just walked in the door and walked up to me and just slapped me. And he slapped me from one end of the couch to the other one. And he said, "Now, bitch, get me something to eat!" So I got up, and I went and fried some chicken and rice. And everything I cooked I made sure you could put pepper in it, 'cause I knew he liked pepper. And we had this rat poison that looked like pepper—and I added just enough to make him sick, sprinkled it on his food. I wasn't tryin' to kill him; I was scared to kill anybody. And he ate it, and he went and laid in his bed. He use to call me "Sweets," and he said, "Sweets, my stomach is hurtin'." I said, "What you want me to do? Do you want me to get you some ex-lax?" "No, it's a different kind of hurt than that kind of hurt." And his stomach started crampin' and everything, where he couldn't move, where he couldn't get to me. I said, "Now, motherfucka', this is the last time you gonna hit me and lock me in this house. You gonna live, but you gonna hurt." I'm not sayin' he never hit me again, but he thought about it more than once before he ever did it again.[94]

None of the girls reported they felt taken advantage of by the males.[95] They understood that the world they lived in had perils they needed to be wary of. Danger increased with lack of affiliation, although joining a club just for protection was a weak motivator. Primarily, safety came from having friends, male and female, or families. Davetta's experience at a party illuminates this:

We knew Score and them 'cause we live around the corner from 'em. So they had a party, and they invited us, and we went. There was me, Nedra, Brunetta, and I think Baby Sister. So all night long these guys was sittin' over in the corner watchin' us: Rob R., Floyd H., and

Danny H., and I can't remember all the rest. And Nedra says, "Well, you know, they lookin' at us kinda funny." So I went and told Jimmy H., and he said, "Well, I'll let them know who you are." So he went over and said, "These are Larry's sisters and cousin." Rob R. said, "I don't give a fuck who she is. I want the one with the red hair." So we left. We walkin' home, and they following us. Then Treetop and Larry [Little Slausons] are drivin' up to the party, and they saw them follown' us. They stop the car, get out, say somethin' to them, and they turned around and just went back to the party.

While females did fight other females over males, males were far more likely to fight over females than the other way around. Sometimes the male fights would be with one's homeboys, as when the older guys from the Little Slausons would hustle the younger girls from the Babies, but more likely the fights would be with members of another set. If a guy met a girl at school, the skating rink, a movie theater, record hop, or another part of town, and they liked each other, phone numbers would be exchanged and visits arranged. When guys traveled to another neighborhood to date a girl, the guys there were not accommodating to either the outsider or their homegirl, who risked in-group hostility over dating outsiders. An appeal that might have been made to a girl considering an out-group liaison would have been, as Barry Wa., a Junior Businessman explained, something like this: "Whatcha doin' messin' with them Rebel Rousers? There are guys already here" . . . "When they go to jump on us, they find out we hell. We wear their ass out."

On Jealously

A probation officer who grew up in South Los Angeles and spent his career there thought a lot of girls did go outside their own community looking for boyfriends and that it always led to problems with their own homeboys, a stigma that was not likewise extended to boys willing to cross neighborhood borders for their romantic partners. Girls dating outside their neighborhood weren't necessarily looking for trouble; romance just happened, he thought. The record hops, "where everybody there was from somewhere," were particular hotbeds of friction. While they were supposed to be "neutral" gathering spots, they were instead venues where juveniles from various neighborhoods would meet and jealousy would surge.

Jealousy was the primary reason why males fought over females, whether in the same neighborhood or another.[96] Jealous adolescent males settled with each other by an action they knew best—"throwing down" (fighting). Terming it "in-house fighting" when males from the same neighborhood fought over a girl, Bird argued that the battles could often, ironically, be for naught since the girl always had the last word. As he explained:

> There were individual neighborhood fights because of jealousy. Someone said they were badder than you, or you thought you was tougher than them, or you all likin' the same girl and you was gon' settle who was gon' get the girl, and she might not want either one of you fools in the first place.

When the fights were between members of the same neighborhood, they were personal, and other in-group members made sure they stayed that way. On the other hand, when the fights were between members of different sets, they could become what the media termed a "gang fight." A lover's quarrel, magnified and intensified by in-group loyalties and out-group enmities, could be the start of a long period of feuds between neighborhoods.

Interneighborhood dating raised another contentious issue. Many homeboys took the view that women in his neighborhood were not available to the outsider male in the first place—just because he was an outsider. A likely scenario might develop this way, according to Bird:

> See, a dude from another neighborhood cannot stand an outsider comin' to the neighborhood getting something he couldn't get. He see the chick every day. He's been out there for years, and you pop up on the set—outta nowhere—and walk straight through the door. Oh no, see, that's out of the question.

Neighborhood males felt they had proprietary rights to all the females in their neighborhood, regardless of what the females might have thought. Male A from one neighborhood, "wronged" by male B from a second neighborhood by dating a girl male A liked from his neighborhood, would often go to his set, provide an explanation of what had happened, and enlist his homeboys for an encounter with the male(s) who had wronged him. This wrong could be the root cause of an extended antagonism between one neighborhood and another. Ironically, the wrong was often later forgotten by both neighborhoods and, thus, forgotten too were the reasons as to why they were enemies in the first place.

Woodrow C., a probation officer in South Los Angeles during the 1950s and 1960s, felt that the records hops, especially those held at Jordan High School,[97] were a source of potential gender friction and made significant contributions to male confrontations because the events brought together youth across neighborhood boundaries. He felt that a girl who went outside the neighborhood for a boyfriend and then brought him to a record hop held at a high school in her neighborhood, knowingly or not, was the source of a problem.[98] The mix of outsiders with insiders at record hops, combined with the inevitable flares of jealousy, as well as the potential for settling past grievances, often destroyed any notion of neutral ground, while both created and expanded on animosities now requiring a settlement—usually with a fight or two or more.

Not surprisingly, boys had a different understanding than girls about why girls dated males from neighborhoods other than their own. Girls contended they did it simply because they found someone there that they liked and wanted to see again; there were no ulterior motives.[99] Nedra used to make it a point to date someone outside Slauson, after breaking up with a Slauson, just "because." While the neighborhood boys might have had problems with this, since the outsiders had to come through their neighborhood to her house to see her, there were no contradictions for her; her position was "get over it!" A number of boys thought the girls did it intentionally, to cause friction. Rick C., from Florence, made the male position unequivocal:

> A girl from the neighborhood might get into an argument with a homeboy. And then they go to another neighborhood to try to get revenge on this homeboy by being with another neighborhood guy. Then he might do something to her, and then she'd go back to the [her own] neighborhood and tell them. They [girls] were just trouble. They would start fights at parties where other neighborhoods would show up. Or they would talk bad to some guys from someplace else and would use your neighborhood name. "I'll go get my homeboy" or "I'll go get my brother." They started a lot of shit.

This was, not unpredictably, another double standard. Most males thought it was okay for them to date girls from other neighborhoods but were much less accommodating when it came to homegirls dating outsiders. Romance gets complicated.

Holsters or Companions?

In an oversimplification, the "official perspective" across the justice system, academia, and the media contended that girls both fought a lot as well as instigated fights and that they were often gun molls for the guys at their fights.[100] More designed to inflame than inform, media claims like the following, at the very least, misled:

> But some [girl gangs] equal the boys in ferocity. There have been incidents lately of girl gang fights that go beyond the hair-pulling stage—

fights with razors and knives. . . . But there is increasing evidence that she [the gang girl] is often the aggravator, the impetus for boy gang fights, the carrier of weapons and narcotics, the emotional undercurrent for the excitement and the violence of the rumbles.[101]

Partly truth, partly fiction, such accounts spun the dramatic and the predatory, whether true or not.

Woodrow C. argued that female gangs were rare but that the girls, while not necessarily fighting themselves, "created a lot of gang conflict." If they were dating a set member, they had a personal advantage, because they could and did play one set member against another. As he understood:

If they [the girls] goin' with a gang member and another guy would say something to them, and they didn't like it, then the girl come cryin' that "Such-and-such called me a bitch," or "touched me." "He done this," or whatever; then you got a carload of dudes comin' at your ass after school. This is bad, man. I mean this upsets him, callin' his old lady a bitch. Oh man, yeah, a guy's got to deal with that.

Linda C. explained that girls were so powerful they could actually stop a fight, if they wanted: "I know because I've done it." Girls used this power, she believed, when it suited their interests, which often coincided with those of the guys they were with. Since girls who accompanied guys in their cars—or who might be walking on the street with them—were most likely dating them, there was a strong likelihood the girls would help them if needed. This was not quid pro quo but an example of the universality of commitment often found in a relationship and, in this case, a neighborhood.

Before 1965 there were few female law-enforcement officers and none on the streets of South Los Angeles.[102] A male officer could not search a female, especially an adolescent, giving girls a security clearance males didn't have. If the male happened to have a weapon in his car or on his person—and the girl agreed—he could give it to her to hold if he was in danger of being stopped by the police. Bird contended: "Yeah, see, most police were men, and they couldn't search a woman, so that's how we got away with stuff." Some might argue—with good cause—that the males were using the females, although the girls did have the right, and often used it, to say no. Bird continued: "Okay, and if you want to say we used the girls, then you could say we used them for that, but that wasn't no everyday thing. You have your gun in your car or someplace you want to get to it. Plus the girl might not put it in her purse, tell you no, or she might panic." Sheila didn't feel used when requested to hold a boyfriend's weapon; she felt that it didn't happen very often, and when it did, she wanted to help. In her words:

The guys wouldn't go lookin' for no fight, but if one happened, we do what's necessary. Like most of the guys, when they carried guns, they would always have them in their trunk or in their car somewhere. They didn't go around gunslingin', all in their pants and that type of thing. But like sometime, we were at a party, in a neighborhood where we had no business being or where there might be some trouble, then they would give us the guns. Or if the police came, they would give us the gun, 'cause back then the police didn't search women; they would never bother us.

The girls who held weapons for the males were not gun molls. They were helping their homeboys, dates, boyfriends, husbands, or brothers who found themselves in a situation where their help was needed.

In providing cover, girls provided neighborhood continuity; they were *counterparts* to the guys. They were the second half of the mutual aid quotient keeping community interactions flowing in an acceptable direction. When the girls needed help, the guys were there for them, and when guys needed help, the girls returned the favor; they had each other's back. It was an expected and accepted part of life in the community. The existence of a gender-based division of labor did not imply inequality. It was an acceptance of the strengths and weaknesses traditionally established by gender. Girls weren't weapons mules: they weren't engaged in regular fighting, and they weren't gang members, because that was not what girls were about in this community.[103]

By the mid- to late 1960s, things had started to change, for both the Chicana and Black girls in the neighborhood: they had become more involved in fighting and with weapons.[104] Rick C., of Florence, described the arrangement:

> The girls would have razor blades in their hair and stuff. So if your set was fightin' with another set, and if the other set's girls were there, and yours were there, then they would get into it also. Some of these girls you could really depend on, because they would back you up. They would hold your gun or your knife or whatever. They would help you if you're getting whooped. They'd jump in and fight with you. Some of them would.

Bird concurred that he had begun to see these changes among the Black sets, as girls began to play a more active role on the streets.[105] Greater female involvement with the sets and in activities previously exclusive to males was no doubt part of the change in gender roles occurring generally in the larger society. This was the 1960s, when women were becoming more involved in many actions formerly viewed as male-only.[106]

Attitudes, behavior, and language changed for some girls, who became more aggressive and less respectful. Some treated older males with derision. This seemed especially true for males who would offer the kind of advice girls might have gotten from elder relatives. When Poop was in his late forties, he was shopping in a convenience store, where he overheard a group of teenage girls talking loudly and disrespectfully to an employee. His polite attempt to put the girls in check with a suggestion of being more respectful was met with the following comment from one of the girls: "Why, you ol' motherfucka', you can kiss my once-a-month bleeding pussy! Mind your own fuckin' business." Poop went on about his "own fuckin' business" without further ado. Changes in female set involvement and delinquency occurred along with neighborhood changes and with changes among the males, brought on by overall economic and demographic shifts that affected the entirety of South Los Angeles. Juveniles and their groups changed because their social structure was transformed.

Forces for Unity: Racism and Prejudice

Consideration of race and racism to explain gangs has a short history. Hagedorn's critique of the theoretical failure to include these concepts is noteworthy; his concern is unequivocal: "It would seem foolish to look at the emergence of minority gangs and neglect racism and the minority experience of inequality, but almost all academic studies do just that."[107] He observes how in most scholars' assumptions, contrary to his own findings, social class trumped race as the key driver of youthful motivations. Certainly, social class is important, but it is frequently not clear whether it is social class or race that prompts certain types of behavior. To neglect race is to guarantee that theories of gangs will come up short. In South Los Angeles, racial discrimination was a fundamental part of adolescent life and an indispensable factor contributing to street-group membership.[108]

Researchers who have examined racism during the time of these early sets agree that Los Angeles, and in particular South Los Angeles, had plenty of it.[109] Housing covenants and bank redlining concentrated Black Angelenos in communities where they were allowed. Institutional racism created concentrations in specific areas, while leaving other areas primarily for White people.

While Los Angeles's brand of racism may not have been as obvious as that existing in the southern states from which the greatest number of Black Angelenos had come, it was the same racism marketed differently. Spatial diversity and late entry into the nation's megacities provided initial inoculation. Black juveniles were spread out in racially segregated communities, out of sight and out of mind. There was no need for "colored only" drinking fountains in Los Angeles because the fountains had been replaced by entire Whites-only neighborhoods. Racism inured Black juveniles and was an essential factor in in-group development.

Race provides a natural category for in-groupism. It facilitates a phenotypical simplicity determining which group one belonged to.[110] Being Black in Los Angeles was supplemented by sharing historical cultural commonalities: mostly southern and mostly traumatic.[111] Enhanced by migration patterns where entire cohorts arrived in waves from the South—traveling the same routes, meeting each other, sharing stories about their voyages, exchanging the names of relatives and friends from where they came to see who knew who, giving those groups a camaraderie and feeling of "We're in this journey together"—makes it easy to understand the unity Black migrants arrived with.[112] When they got to Los Angeles, the patterns of segregation and racism they experienced helped to solidify the already powerful sense of in-groupness they had brought with them.

Shared commonalities resulted in some creative behavioral innovations that were known only to in-group members. One of those was a 1940s–1950s mutual-aid system that mostly all Black people, especially those using public transportation, were involved in. Frank M. recalled:

> But see, like the Blacks, when I was a kid, we had a camaraderie. We'd ride the streetcars, and you'd pay seven cents, and you'd get a transfer. You could go anywhere you wanted to on the transfer. Every Black person that got on a streetcar would get a transfer and stick the transfer in a telephone pole where somebody could see it. They could pick it up and use it themselves. That was common. You'd go to a transfer point, and any transfer point that you went to, you'd look and see if you could find a transfer that you could use. That was common; it was everywhere, everywhere in the Black neighborhood that you went.

For many Black people in South Los Angeles during the 1930s and 1940s, the race-based exclusionary practices of businesses were not much different from the ones they had grown up with in the South. Ted W. of the Watts Labor Community Action Committee, who came from Mississippi in 1939 when he was fourteen years old, was reminded regularly that he was not as far from home as the geography suggested. The main social activities for local Black residents then were centered near the vicinity of the Dunbar Hotel at 4225 Central Avenue, as Ted explained: "Very little was happening on any other major street in the City because at that period of time Blacks were barred, even on Avalon Boulevard and Vernon, from going into the bars and pool halls that were frequented by other people in the community." The Woolworths and S. H. Kress 5-10-25 Cent stores in the community, as well as numerous other businesses along Central Avenue, wouldn't hire Black workers, according to Ted.[113] He concluded: "Our feelings at that time were that we had our place, and our place was not to intrude in any way against White people."

Not for a Cause, but Because . . .

Mike Davis writes, "It seems probable that the first generation of Black street gangs emerged as a defensive response to White violence in the schools and streets during the late 1940s."[114] Years later, Alejandro Alonso notes that intimidation from White groups "led to the early formation of Black social street clubs."[115] In 2010, Alonzo adds that Black clubs expanded in the 1950s as a "direct reaction to the growing violence by White gangs," until "the balance of power shifted and Black residents were no longer intimidated by White residents."[116] White intimidation of their Black neighbors is part of the historical record; but nowhere has it been changed by Black street clubs, and there was no balance of power shift as a result. We wrote earlier that South Los Angeles was deindustrialized by corporations that fled the area to reindustrialize in the periphery. Whites left too, following the lucrative jobs, leaving behind the Black neighborhoods and conflict. Migration of new Black and immigration of other mostly non-White residents changed the demographics, while deindustrialization changed power relations.

Defense was an important reason why some sets formed, and intimidation by White groups occurred. But street groups of Black juveniles already existed before confrontations with White juvenile groups began. Loose hang-out groups had been fussin', cussin,' and discussin' long before White groups, like the Spook Hunters[117] came on the scene.[118] When groups such as the Slausons became more organized, it was initially in response to a confrontation with Black street clubs in Watts and then solidified further in confrontations with other Black groups. None of the Black sets formed to fight White racists, although they certainly fought back when confronted by them.[119] Group comradery has a long natural history. While the overall experiences of racism were potent factors contributing to the sense of ingroupism within the neighborhoods and sets, attacks by White groups were contributors, not *the* cause.[120]

South Los Angeles sets were not merely neighborhood defense groups; they were sanctuaries where juveniles, who were abused by the racism of the larger society, and its members could find acceptance for who they were, the way they were. Identity with one's own race in the set, even with those whom one was not especially fond of, was facilitated by shared commonalities and experiences. Suffering similar racial indignities produced a powerful force that pulled set members together and held them there. Stokely Carmichael is quoted as observing: "What unites Black people today . . . is the very issue from which their oppression stems: their Blackness."[121] Racism motivates its victims directly and indirectly, causing both immediate and delayed responses. Its insidiousness can deplete the soul and motivate its victims to do things they otherwise might not do.[122]

It oversimplifies the motivations for joining a set to claim that racism was the sole cause—it was not. But to ignore or misrepresent racism's power in set formation invites misunderstanding. Racism's effect on set development varied according to the period and the neighborhood where it was found. In the downtown area, the sets were racially mixed because the neighborhoods were racially mixed.[123] White racism there helped unite various groups of non-Whites who were also experiencing it. Their shared commonality was they were non-White.[124]

In Watts, concentrations of Black and Chicano people living in insular areas were an important factor in the homogeneity of the sets. Housing differences between the projects in Watts and the Florence-Firestone areas' single-family homes resulted in closer bonds between Black and Chicano residents in the Florence-Firestone area than in Watts.[125] The projects divided the community. But in the Florence-Firestone District, the demographic transition from White to Black and Chicano was accompanied by hard feelings from the departing Whites toward the newly arriving non-Whites, resulting in strong identification among non-Whites with each other because of shared feelings of discrimination.[126]

Bird summed up the relationship between racism and the American value structure as contributors to set membership by observing that South Los Angeles sets were not imports nor were they dropped from the sky; they were made in America. As he explained:

> We were more or less forced to be where we were anyway because of racism and prejudice. If you live in America, you were told to belong to something. You needed to be part of the Woodcraft Rangers, the Boy Scouts, the Elks or the Moose Lodge, the Knights of Columbus, or, you know, be a fireman and join the Firemen Association. Look at the signs out there to join the LAPD—earn so much—here is your future and your career. Well, we were told the same shit. So we were bred to be what we was gonna be. We were bred to be cliqued up, except we chose one another—our own army outside of what they wanted because racism and prejudice dictated the circumstances at the time.

Set formation was affected both by personal experiences with racism and by the more ingrained institutional forms of it. Bird continued:

> You're talking about the first half of the '50s, last of the '40s, when people was runnin' around calling us names cause we were Black. They had us segregated in a certain section of town, and when we moved to where White people wanted to live, they ran off and moved someplace else. You know, White *fright*, before they started callin' it "White *flight*." They moved someplace else, so we all ended up together.

All of our respondents mentioned at least one experience they had had with someone who had discriminated against them because of their race. Everyone had had many experiences. They experienced the discrimination in a variety of ways, often at different times during their youth, and had numerous examples of how the experiences had affected their lives. Being called "boy" was an especially nasty but common expression used to malign young Black males. Almost all our respondents had heard the term used derisively, at least indirectly and often directly at them. Bird noted that one retort he used to an ill-mannered name-caller was: "Boy plays with Tarzan, Tarzan plays with Jane, and I play with your mama, muthafucka'!"

Why Not Join?

Racism is violent whether it is physical and produces bodily injury or mental and produces anger and psychological damage.[127] For most juveniles, the experiences of racism were personal. It started when they were young, involved people they didn't expect it from, and left indelible scars of hurt and bitterness. Racism came from "friends," teachers, and the Boy Scouts. It came from places expected too, such as the police, who often blatantly called them an assortment of offensive names. The police would frequently justify their actions with racially charged ideology and use explanations that contended that the juveniles were getting what they deserved.

Occurring in many forms, institutionalized racism was an additional humiliation. It came from assorted businesses that wouldn't serve non-Whites, either because of policy or because of clothing styles they disapproved of; it came from segregated living areas; and it came from nascent TV programing, which reinforced the idea that Whites were superior to everybody else. But there were two significant primary social groups for juveniles that were devoid of racism: their family and their set. Sets allowed them to join with others who had experienced similar racial antagonisms; sets permitted understanding, friendships, acceptance, protection, and access to members of the opposite sex. Welcomed by other juveniles who identified with their plight, the set became a refuge and a sanctuary that, for many, was like another family.[128]

A clichéd question, regularly asked by researchers and social policy makers is, "Why would they join a set (or a gang)?" A plethora of answers to this question have shown little traction in research or effectiveness in policy decisions. A much more productive question is, "Why not?" The larger society had marginalized them,[129] disowned and disparaged them. Why would they join a group like the Boy Scouts or aspire to be, or respect, a police officer when people in those groups had treated them badly and unfairly because of their race—something they had no choice in and couldn't change—when they could join a group that welcomed them? The sets provided an appealing social organization in a society that rebuffed them while offering few acceptable alternatives. Sets were an asylum where juveniles could find solace in a group that wanted them. Set in-groupism provided a safe harbor in a storm of rejection and a sea of indignity. In the set they were beautiful. Why shouldn't they join? Joining was a rational act.

Sanctioned Child Abuse

Racial discrimination, beginning early, left indelible lessons for recipients. The maliciousness of this discrimination let children know they were different from the larger White society; they were unequal, unworthy, and unfit because of what they looked like, not because of anything they might have done that would have generated the same disparagement against others. For some who had White "friends" as children, the scorn often came as a surprise. Nedra got up close and personal with racism from a White friend she knew in grammar school, whose mother wouldn't let the friend play with her once the mother found out Nedra's race. Nedra related the experience:

> My mother taught us that people are people, you know. And I liked everybody and got along with most people. When I was in grammar school, I had this little White friend. Her name was Joy. And she walked me home one day and asked my mom could I go over to her house. And so she walked me home, and then I walked her back home. And my mom says it was okay, and she was happy that I had a little White friend. And I went to her house, and her mother wouldn't let me in the house. And whatever her mother told her, she wasn't my friend no more. I was so hurt.

Though her feelings had been hurt by the rejection she received, Nedra was still a child, and it wasn't quite clear to her why her little friend's mother had treated her so coldly until one day her former friend clarified things: it was because Nedra was Black. Nedra continued:

> I didn't understand. And then my mom asked me why I was home, and I told her because Joy's mom wouldn't let me in the house. She told me, "Don't worry about it; it's just some White folks is like that." And, you know, it didn't bother me no more until one day she [Joy] called me a "nigger."[130] And it was like, "You know my name. Why would you call me that?" And she said, "Because my mother said that's what you are." And I said, "Well, when you go home, you tell your mother that my mother said she's stupid." And she cried. I mean, I didn't hit her or anything like that, but my mother told me that people who feel like that are stupid. And that's what I told her. I don't know what she told her mother, but she never spoke to me again after that. No more.

Bird's early experience with being called names had different results. When he was a child, his family was the first Black family to move onto East 73rd Street. For a while, if he wanted to play with other children there, he had to play with White kids. That was fine with Bird until one day one of the White kids he had played with regularly was instructed by his mother not to play with Bird anymore because he was the wrong race. In Bird's words:

> I was the only Black child on 73rd for a year, and the only kids I had to play with were White. See, it was okay for them to come in your yard and play in your yard with your toys and your balls and stuff. And I played with a little boy down the street named Charles. We was real cool. We played together every day until his mama got sick at work and came home early one time and seen me playing with him—we never played together again. He called me a "nigger" one day after that. The next day, it was trash day, and he took some grass from the trash can and got it all over me. I waited for him the next day, but he didn't come out. I got him two days later; I beat his ass.

Yet another shade in the variety of forms early exposure to racism came in can be seen in the following experience involving Little Bird. He first encountered the injustice of racism at an even younger age than Nedra and Bird: in nursery school, when a White kid called him a "nigger." He had never heard the word before, didn't know what it meant, but could tell from the White kid's expression that it wasn't a compliment. So Little Bird said back to him: "No, I'm not a nigger; you are." The White kid went home and told his mother that Little Bird had called him a "nigger," neglecting, of course, to tell her who had started things. The mother promptly told the school authorities that Little Bird had called her son a "nigger." *Judiciously*, the school expelled Little Bird for his behavior.[131]

Racial in-groupness begins early in life, not only for non-White children but for White children too. Where does a young child learn to call non-White children names but at home? When Bird was a teen, he and some of his friends were walking in an almost exclusively White neighborhood when they became aware of a White woman and her young daughter walking behind them involved in an impromptu discussion of race, designed for their ears only. It didn't quite work out that way. As the words grew audible, they became public, providing a bit of embarrassment for the woman when she realized Bird's group had overheard them. In Bird's words:

> See, in 1958, Billy J., Mack K., George W., and Larry W. and me was walkin' up to Huntington Park, walking to go get something. There was a little White girl and her mother and some more people walkin' behind, and the little White girl was pullin' on her mama: "Mommy, mommy, mommy, look." The mother looked, and the little girl said: "Real niggers!" I looked at her and the lady said, "Oh, I'm so sorry." I said, "That's alright." I said, "That's what you taught her."

These anecdotes lend clarity to the origins of racial in-groupness.[132] Things taught at home, especially things understood to stay at home, have a way of spilling out of the nest at inopportune times; kids may say the "damnedest things," but they speak what they are raised to believe, unvarnished by the social niceties that can obscure their parents' own racism.

Reaping What Is Taught

Mid-twentieth-century American culture encouraged youth to join groups, albeit those considered appropriate for good citizenship. One of those respectable groups young males were encouraged to join was the Boy Scouts. When he was twelve years old, Bird tried to do just that. He tried joining a troop that was only a block from his house, with the following unexpected results: "In '55 I tried to go to Goodyear to be a Boy Scout. I was not allowed 'cause I was Black and it was an all-White troop: one block from my house! 1955! And I had to go all the way to 49th and McKinley [about twenty-five blocks away] to be a Boy Scout; and I only lived one block from where the closest troop was."

Bird persevered; he joined the distant Boy Scout group and the Woodcraft Rangers, too. His Boy Scout troop had a number of non-White members from other sets, who managed to get along with each other while in the troop. Once, in an effort to fully participate in the scouting experience, Bird went with his troop on an overnight camping jamboree. There he found additional forms of racism from the White Boy Scouts. He explained: "Half my Boy Scout troop was from different sets, see. And we went to a jamboree in Griffith Park, and the White boys cut our tent 'n' stuff. And we had a big ol' fight in Griffith Park." This was a fight because of race; it was not a gang fight: an in-group of White youth fought with an in-group of Black youth. But because youth from assorted South Los Angeles sets were involved, it could easily have been labeled a gang fight, dependent on who was doing the labeling.

From an early age, Bird took pride in the way he dressed. Sartorially resplendent at fourteen years old in his selection of styles and colors, it got him desired attention from numerous young women—plus some undesired attention from a carful of White juveniles. It was another dose of racial disdain, an indignity that embarrassed and angered him. In Bird's words:

> Yeah, see, I got a cola thrown on me in 1957 on St. Andrews and Florence. It was from some White boys in a '57 Chevy. I got on White khakis, a White jacket, a purple-and-white checked shirt, my tam, and I'm clean as a broke-dick-dog. I was standin' on the corner talkin' to some girls, and someone said, 'Hey niggas!' And pow, a whole cola, man, right on me! It washed all down that white jacket and pants, and it looked like I'd peed on myself. And I had to catch the bus, and the bus didn't come for another half hour. I'm standin' out there with all them girls and kids, and I got on White pants with a brown wet stain. I looked like I got pee on myself. I'm fourteen years old, and I'm pissed off, man! You know, these was White boys ridin' down Florence.

School, as a primary socializer of youth, was where the early lessons of discrimination were often enhanced. For most neighborhood youth, the school experience was a continuation of racial injustice. As Bird explained, when he was a child, he observed that the books used at the schools he attended appeared older and more worn than those used by White children in their schools. He also noticed differences among the characters in the children's books based on race. "You got to remember, Jack and Jill were White. Any Black characters you'd have was Little Black Sambo, and we didn't like that shit." Bird's deduction might be dismissed by some as an inadvertent school misstep, but to an intelligent young Black child, there was nothing inadvertent about it. The racism was clear, and though perhaps indirect, it hurt.

From the perspective of numerous non-White juveniles, neighborhood schools promoted racism by discouraging them from pursuing their dreams and then belittling them when they tried. Although many of our respondents had had problems with various teachers and principals, overt racism was less obvious at school than it had been from their playmates, perhaps because of the absence of explicit racist name-calling.[133] Such absence might have been a sign that racism just wasn't there. It might have signified that whenever any discrimination occurred, it was not based on race but on simple discrimination, perhaps because the teacher just didn't like them. Our respondents felt otherwise, interpreting much of the discrimination they experienced as racism. The effect of perceived racial bias did not endear respondents to the in-groupism schools were trying to promote, making acceptance of school values difficult when the promoters also gave evidence they didn't accept the students for who they were.

Sometimes the experience was subtle, as when Poop and Bird recalled having their interests in science and literature discouraged by teachers who instead encouraged them to take shop classes. Other times, the experience was less subtle, as when Frank M. remembered being humiliated in grammar school after he sang a song by Louis Armstrong instead of another more situationally appropriate song. As he explained:

> I was very young. I couldn't have been over five. The teacher was telling the class to go up and sing a little song. And everybody would sing, and then she got to me. Well, I had heard Louis Armstrong sing "I'll Be Glad When You're Dead, You Rascal You." So that's what I knew. So I got up, and I started singing, and she said, "What? Go sit down!" And everybody just laughed and laughed and laughed, and I was real ashamed.

Then, sometimes the experience lost almost all of its subtlety, as Frank M. found out from a teacher in a high school drafting class whose rebuke was devastating. He recounted:

> I had a drafting teacher, Mr. Hill, and for some reason, he wouldn't teach me. And when I'd make a little mistake, he was really, really, really hard on me. And there was another kid in there that was Black, but he was almost White; he was very light-skinned. And I noticed he [the teacher] really took him under his wing. But I learned drafting really good. All I knew was I could draw that stuff real good, and I could visualize what the other side would look like, stuff like that. It came so easy to me. One day, the teacher put this drawing on the board to do. And I did my drawing, and I took it up to him. He just stood there. And then he shouted, and he screamed, and he hollered, and he banged on the desk, and he just went through a real tirade with

me. So I took my drawing, and I went back to my chair, and I never asked him another question. I never did another drawing. I went there, and I spent my hour in there, and he never said one word to me. When the semester was over, he gave me an F, and that was the end of it.

But it wasn't the end of it; the experience was remembered long after its occurrence. It's possible Frank's drafting teacher was an unstable sort who just took out his problems on Frank, or he might have simply been jealous of Frank's skills. A more likely explanation, Frank believed, was racial: anger at a Black juvenile, a perceived inferior, who had demonstrated superior skills.

Youth not only learn academics in school, but they are also encouraged to join a variety of school-sponsored activities and clubs. The one area where school in-groupism worked, where the schools accepted certain non-White juveniles, was sports, especially basketball and football. Here, the juveniles were made to feel welcome, a part of the team, and a part of that in-group. They were encouraged and supported and applauded when they did well and the team won. Whether the athlete was a set member or not, other set members encouraged their participation in this in-group, even protecting the athletes from neighborhood dangers, believing that any accolades their skilled athletic homeboys might earn was a positive reflection on the entire neighborhood.

With Justice for Some

The most consistent and flagrant racism in South Los Angeles came from the police.[134] Direct and deliberate, it was designed as both a humiliation and an unequivocal statement on who was in control. As noted, Los Angeles's policing agencies have had a long and sordid history of racial problems, with limited and varying degrees of success in dealing with them.[135] From the 1920s, when the Los Angeles County sheriff and Los Angeles police chief were members of the Ku Klux Klan, to Chief William H. Parker, the longest-serving chief in the history of the department (1950–1966)—"an avowed White supremacist"—these agencies have been regularly criticized for their handling of non-White residents.[136]

It's not surprising to hear that their behavior toward South Los Angeles juveniles was often characterized by brazen racism, contributing further to the youthful perception that their set was a safety net, an almost necessary primary in-group. Bird recalled:

> We use to stop the car and park whenever we saw the police stop somebody White in the neighborhood. We use to sit there and look. We wanted to see what they was gonna do, 'cause we wanted to see if they done them like they done us. And I told you before that the

police made damn sure in those '50s, especially in the first half of the '60s, that everybody from down here had some kind of jail record. Your name was down for something you were doing.[137]

The juvenile perception of justice became: sometimes there's *justice*, but most of the time it's *just us*.

Barry Wa., a Junior Businessman, recalled the paucity of Black police on the streets before 1965, a rarity he noted with these comments: "There were no Black cops at that time. Yeah, they weren't on the streets; they weren't dealing wit' street problems. You just started seeing Black policemen in the '70s."[138] No other respondents disagreed. One of the rare Black LAPD policemen on the street from 1940 to 1961 was Tom Bradley.[139] Frank M. remembered Bradley well, due to a number of encounters he had had with him, all significantly different from those he'd had with White officers. Bradley treated him like a person, as if the stop was a stop in a wealthy White neighborhood rather than in the inner city. Frank M. explained: "I had Mayor Bradley[140] stop me several times, pick me up and carry me home and chide my mother and tell her that she better watch me. He knew me by name. He'd seen me out after curfew, and he'd pick me up and throw me in the car and take me home." Bradley's effort on behalf of the juveniles was exceptional among the LAPD or LASD.

Most of the White police on the streets treated the juveniles badly, calling them names and making certain they had arrest records whether they had done anything to deserve them or not. The following incident that happened to Poop is representative of the experiences other set members had and a form of police punishment we heard about regularly. In Poop's words:

> One time I got stopped by the police. And before he asked me what I'd been arrested for, I told him, "I ain't never been arrested." And he says, "You never been arrested and you twenty-two years old?" I said, "Yeah, I never been arrested." This police told me, "You a goddamn liar!" He said, "Ain't a nigger in the City of Los Angeles that's gets as old as you and ain't been arrested." I said, "I never been arrested." He said, "You won't be able to say that tomorrow, nigger, 'cause I'm gonna arrest you now." I said, "For what?" He said, "Suspicion." I said, "Suspicion of what?"

Poop never got an answer to his question—a particularly important query, since he hadn't been doing anything at the time to be arrested for. But he was arrested nonetheless.[141]

Often the racism experienced on the street was continued at the police station, where the only witnesses were other police. Black juveniles were called names, lied about, and put in fear. The wedge between their racial in-group and that of the police was driven deeper, as the power differential was made explicit. Frank M. recalled a time when he was walking on the street with several homeboys when the police pulled up on the other side of the street and, for no obvious reason,[142] started pummeling a Japanese juvenile. A White lady witness started screaming, frightening Frank and his homies, who split up and ran off. Shortly thereafter, Frank and the homeboy he had run with were stopped by the police on suspicion and taken to an LAPD station. As Frank recounted:

> So when we got there, the lady and the kid that got hit hadn't shown up yet. So we—we're sitting down, and the detective was talking to us. So he said, "Did we hit him?" I told him, "No, I didn't know anything about it." Then the big motorcycle cop came in, the one that hit him. And he had his hand all busted like he had hit somebody. And so he said, "What did these niggers do?" So they said, "Beat up a little White kid." He said, "Well, what the fuck's the matter with them; kick their goddamn asses." He said, "You Black motherfuckers."[143]

When the White lady and the Japanese juvenile arrived at the station, they explained that Frank and his homeboy were not responsible for the youth's injuries. They were released, without an apology but having suffered enough racial indignities to confirm to them the value of their in-group. Both Frank and his homeboy were set members, but they were not at the police station because of set membership. They were there because they—like Poop—were guilty of being Black in public.

As equal-opportunity racists, the police didn't confine their racism to Black set members or Japanese juveniles; they spread it around to other ethnicities, as indicated by the following anecdote from Poop about a Mexican set member he knew:[144]

> I knew this Mexican dude named Manuel, and he lived out in Boyle Heights. And he's over by the Coliseum with me at this house. The police watching us 'cause we had some drugs. So Manuel and Charro come in the house, and the police see this and rush the house. And they had us all sittin' around handcuffed and shit, searchin' the place for drugs. And they asked Charro how he got over here, you know. It's a long way; and he [Charro] said, "We took a cab." And he said, "I just come from work." And the police say, "He's a goddamn liar! Ain't a Mexican in LA got enough money to take no cab over here." Yeah, that's how they thought about us.

Rick C., a White member of Florence, remembered being belittled by the police when they pulled up in a patrol car while he was hanging on a corner with some of his set members. As he told it:

> The most racist comment I ever heard was through law enforcement. They'd pull up and say, "Oh, a White boy with the Mexicans and niggers. You must be a bad motherfucker." They'd get out of the car and make an example out of me. Get in my face. They took me to jail one time. They put a hurtin' on me, slapped me around, beat me up, put me in the hospital. Yeah, they were scary motherfuckers.

Not limiting themselves to racial epithets, the police mixed in other innovative racial slurs and overt discrimination. Bird recalled a time one of these slurs was used on him by the LAPD as he was leaving their station after having been detained for several hours. They let him go because they couldn't find anything to charge him with, but they showed their disdain as he was exiting. In his words:

> Okay, I'm at the 77th Street Station in 1962. As I'm walkin' out past the desk sergeant, out the back door, he says, "Good-bye, spear chunker, jungle bunny, burr head." I said, "What did you say?" And he said, "Spear chunker." I said, "Ain't that a bitch." I had to laugh; I hadn't heard that shit before.

In the early 1970s, a bookish young Black student at the University told Quicker a story about a time when, as a teen, he was impeccably dressed in a tie and sport coat to go on a date. On his way to meet his date, he was stopped by the police, handcuffed, and then made to lie facedown on a street wet from a recent rain while they searched his car. They found nothing and let him go, but rather than apologizing or explaining the stop, they gave him smirks. Experiences of racism from the police before 1965 for non-White youth abound, making it clear the police played a central role in fostering the in-groupism non-White juveniles felt for each other. "Justice" was a hollow concept in their community, with little relationship to street experience.

Racism's Ubiquity

Other forms of institutionalized racism confronted non-White South Los Angeles youth every day, from restaurants that wouldn't serve them to television programing that took aim at them as inferiors. Frank M. remembered a drugstore on 55th Street and Central Avenue that, in the 1950s, wouldn't allow Black patrons to enter: "If you were Black and tried to go in, they would usher you out." He also recalled a café on Georgia Street, near LAPD's Georgia Street Station,[145] with a sign in the window that read: "We do not serve negroes." The police in many neighborhoods too, like some areas of downtown and Baldwin Hills, would "tell us to get out if they saw us there," he recalled, because they said that we "didn't belong there."[146]

Racism on television could be more elusive, perhaps more difficult to understand, unless you were Black—then it became unambiguous. Famous television heroes like Hopalong Cassidy and Tarzan regularly demonstrated White superiority in their adventures. Poop used to watch those shows until he recognized the putdown they demonstrated to non-White people. "Yeah," Poop said, "Hopalong Cassidy and them guys, you know, they whoop a whole tribe of Indians by dey self. And Tarzan, he was chasin' all the Africans through the jungle.... Now what kind of shit is that? What they tellin' us?" The message of *us* versus *them* on television had one side White, the "good guys," and the other side non-White, the "bad guys"—making a strong statement on group favoritism. The White guys always won and were always the heroes. They wore white cowboy hats, rode white horses, and took action to rid their White communities of evil—which was everybody else.[147]

Bird noted that the vast majority of actors on television were also White until around the mid-1960s:[148]

> The first television commercial that I saw with Black people in it, they were chewin' Doublemint gum. And that was during the second half of the '60s. Then Blacks started drinkin' Cokes. I been chewin' gum and drinkin' soda all my life, but you didn't see that on TV. Okay, psychologically what does that do? You got a baby, okay. You go to the store, and all the babies on the Pampers box are White. Yeah, see, baby be layin' in the crib looking over there at the Pampers box and see all that kind of shit. It's shit we took notice of.

The notice confirmed for many that, in Bird's words, "We are not part of this in-group, because the people here are White and we're not. The people on TV are part of a group that doesn't include us, doesn't seem to want us or may want to hurt us or may not know or care if we even exist." Bird felt that television programing in the 1950s and 1960s, in spite of its biases, was instructive because it contributed significantly to the idea of having a tough-guy image and encouraged juveniles to be physically capable. Television taught them the racists weren't going to be any tougher than they were.

While racism was a prime factor in creating a strong sense of in-groupism for the South Los Angeles sets, as a group, racism was not something the sets promoted. As mentioned, many of the sets, especially the earlier ones, were racially mixed. Certainly, juveniles from different non-White racial and ethnic groups would fight with each other, sometimes leaving one another bloody, but the clashes were mostly personal, not usually racially motivated. The exceptions were the loosely organized all-White groups with the not-so-subtle name of Spook Hunters existing in and around the non-White communities. They were a diverse grouping of car clubs or assorted groups of football players, whose raison d'etre was their general contempt for non-White people. Racism united non-White and White groups, although in very different ways.

The Spook Hunters were gangs for a minute, organized to accomplish a task that, once completed, temporarily ended their unity—until the next time. Existing in the 1950s, at least one of these groups had blue, sports-affiliated letter jackets. On the back was a logo depicting a big foot in what was obviously a "negro's bloody face," according to a Slauson juvenile called Skillet. Spook Hunter groups were found in such diverse city locations as the Clanton area south of downtown, Watts, all up and down Alameda Street, on the West-Side in Sportsman Park,[149] and on the corner of West Century Boulevard and South Western Avenue.[150] They also came from primarily White communities, such as Lakewood and Bellflower, and would drive to the Black communities looking for vulnerable youth.[151]

Although scant, the evidence on the Spook Hunters suggests they arose in opposition to Black families moving into their neighborhoods and from general racial contempt. There were individual and small group clashes between them and some Black youth but no large-scale battles or gang wars. Evidence to suggest that Spook Hunter groups on one side of the City may have been affiliated with similarly named groups on the other side hasn't been found. Their name was a title for what they did and why they existed, not a symbol of organizational unity.[152]

Social class, gender, and race are connected in a complex web of affiliations with one another that contribute to set membership. Ignoring or minimizing their importance limits our ability to understand the pre-1965 sets. Comprehension of what occurred in early South Los Angeles will help us understand what is happening there now—although it might not be a blueprint for other cities. But, an accurate understanding of what occurred elsewhere, then and now, would benefit from taking these factors into account. Doing otherwise risks incompleteness and contributes to misunderstanding. Street groups are social entities formed from assortments of building blocks that create other social groups. The existence of sets is not an aberration, but is a result of the structural ordering of certain blocks. South Los Angeles street groups did not drop from the sky; they were made here.

7

Comin'-from-the-Shoulders

Ethics, Weapons, Fights, and Violence

People should be taught what is, not what should be.
—**John Cohen,** *Essential Lenny Bruce*
  (quoting Lenny Bruce)

There are regular reminders in the news and on the street that gang violence is frequently deadly, with claims that it is worse than it has ever been. Innocents are killed, while gang neighborhoods get characterized as war zones. Most reports conclude that weapons have become more powerful, more visible, and more frequently used, as inhibitions against use have steadily evaporated. These appear to be reasonable assumptions, but until we know what it was like, how do we know how much worse it has become? More violence—compared to what? There is little research into what weaponry was available to the pre-1965 groups or how willing they were to use what was available or the reasons why certain weapons were or were not used.

Various weapons have been available for long periods in South Los Angeles, with willingness on the part of some to use them. But there was also a general attitude before 1965 opposed to the use of weapons, stressing instead a "fair fight." Great respect was granted to those who were good with their hands. To fight with your fists, to go "head-up," "one-on-one," "mano a mano," or "toe-to-toe" with someone, is to *come-from-the-shoulders*. Manhood was often determined by how well somebody fought or by how much "heart" he showed when facing adversity and by their eschewing of weaponry. Any punk could use a gun, but it took a man to go head-up. To come-from-the-shoulders was the pinnacle of manhood, especially if one was good at it.

In this chapter, we explore a number of the issues related to the amount and kinds of violence that existed among the early street groups. We will examine the concept of comin'-from-the-shoulders, the ideology that produced it, and the ethics that governed confrontations between individual set members and between the battling sets. We discuss some of the notorious fights that took place between legendary neighborhood figures, explain the circumstances involved in the various street-group fights, and assess the actual amount of injury associated with them. Finally, we show what weapons were available, where they came from, how often they were used, and under what circumstances. We keep in mind that the participants were male adolescents, who, like male adolescents everywhere, didn't possess the cognitive negotiation skills that enable adults to avoid physicality. The juvenile ethos is *fight first, talk later*.

The Importance of Being a Man

Gang researchers from around the country have shown the almost universal significance of machismo, masculinity, heart, rep, and status in the lives of male gang members. These are recurring themes in much of the pre-1970 work on gangs[1] and were behavioral and ideological commitments of early South Los Angeles street groups. A come-from-the-shoulders ideal of manhood, combined with other community values, contributed to less weapon use, thus less serious injury and fewer deaths from interset altercations in the neighborhoods. As Oliver Cool, from the Slausons, explained, when asked if guns were used a lot:

> No, 'cause what we were doin', like I said, if we had a problem with somebody, it was about goin' from the shoulders. That was an era of manhood; it was moral indoctrination. The reason I didn't kill him is that I know his mother, Mrs. Mitchell. I'm not gonna kill him. Comin'-from-the- shoulders was a prestigious thing.

In a broader sense, coming from-the-shoulders not only meant how well you could fight with your fists but how well you could take a whoopin'. While there was clearly honor in winning, many fought knowing they might not win, because losing was honorable too—if you fought well and showed heart. Barry Wa., a founder of the Businessmen, put it this way: "Getting whooped—that made a better man out of you. Oh, he'd be mad, but peoples around him let him know, you got your butt whooped. It's a sorry man can't accept an ass whoopin'." In a fistfight, juveniles could get hurt, but they would heal—they wouldn't die, and families and the community remained intact. Barry Wa. continued:

> Fistsfights wasn't nobody getting' hurt: black eye, swollen lip, or something like that. Put to sleep, but you'll wake up. No mother lost their kids. No mother had to cry for death. Then when the guys get through fightin', they sit down and start drinkin' wine.

Miguel D., a longtime member of Los Angeles County Probation and a former leader in the Group Guidance Project, agreed that losing could still be honorable because there was group support whether you won or lost. The primary goal was to show you were not afraid to fight:

> There's honor in fighting and no dishonor in losing. And that's always been the case. Because when you fought as a gang member, either by yourself or in a group, and then you get with your fellows, the word would already be out as to whether or not you ran or stood your ground. If you'd get there all beat up, the guys would say, "Attaboy," you know, in spite of it. So your ass isn't really whipped because your boys are telling you that. You had the guts to hang in there and to say your name and to stand up for your gang.

Miguel D. agreed with Barry Wa.'s contention that an added advantage to a fistfight was that there was rarely permanent damage: "The beauty of that at the time was nobody pulling out a gun and blowing you away," Miguel D. noted. You may have lost the fight, but you won the war because you showed heart; you didn't punk out. Pugilists showed they had "cojones."[2]

Winning Wasn't the Only Thing

Fistfights also meant that you could come back later to have another go and possibly win this time, because you might have just barely lost the last time. Barry Wa. continued: "You might have to fight again now, but that's not like getting shot. 'Cause you fought so hard the first time you might of lucked up and won that first fight. That don't mean you gonna win the next day, 'cause you barely won that day." In addition to getting another chance, a message was sent, a statement was made, whereas both would have been lost if a gun had been used. Donny H., who lived the first thirty-two years of his life on 73rd Street (Sin Street) in the Slauson neighborhood, concurred: "The gun: if somebody did something to you and you use a gun, you'd kill him, and that's no gain. If you whoop him, they gonna remember that. That's gonna be a well-earned memory, you know. They'd be around to carry the message."[3]

Knowing how to fight well gave confidence to those who might find themselves in situations requiring self-defense. According to Frank M. from Clanton, there were at least two situations where self-defense was going to be a necessity: going into other neighborhoods and attending parties. Frank explained:

> You see at that time what you wanted to do was be able to fight so good that you could go in any neighborhood you wanted to go to, and you were known and nobody would dare, you know, would dare. Like, if there was a party—okay, sometimes somebody would turn the light out and hit somebody—that nobody would dare do that to you. That you felt, that you knew that you were rough.

Showing heart by comin'-from-the-shoulders, standing firm in the face of adversity, and showing you were a man who could both take and give out a whoopin' had another essential benefit: it enhanced the males' reputation with girls. There is social standing within one's gender and outside, and each presents its set of incentives. The guys who showed the most heart felt entitled to "the pick of the crop," Bird asserted. A guy's sex appeal was enhanced by his demonstration of heart, not an insignificant reason to face adversity "head-up." Joan Moore adds that fights like this established a "pecking order" among the males.[4]

Occasionally there would be weaker individuals who would befriend tougher ones, then benefit from the reputations the tougher ones had established. Weaker ones were often consequentially indistinguishable from their stronger buddies: if you messed with them, you were going to have to deal with the buddy too. Bird termed it "riding somebody else's rep," or coattails. He explained:

> Ridin' or livin' off somebody else . . . See, a lot of dudes ran with dudes to live off their rep. "That's so-and-so; he run with Johnny Irons." So you don't mess with him 'cause he run with Johnny Irons. See, if you whoop him, you got to whoop Johnny Irons. So you didn't want none of Johnny Irons. . . . He'd beat all the eyebrows back off your forehead.

Riding a rep was not encouraged because it demonstrated little courage and emboldened the rider to do things he might not otherwise do. Bird continued: "See, we didn't like dudes like that either. You knew they wasn't nothin' but who they ran with, but you couldn't bother them. And they pulled a lot of shit, you know, 'cause they ran with a real tough guy."

To be considered a man meant that juveniles not only demonstrated fighting prowess and fearlessness in the face of adversity, but they also had to "hold their mug" and "ride their own beef." They couldn't be a snitch and had to take responsibility for their actions. Even when involved in something inappropriate, it was a sign of weakness to seek support from "the man," the police. A real man would suck it up and accept his culpability for his part in the deed. Although many individuals represented this ethic, the epitome of it was a legendary juvenile named Horseshoe.

Horseshoe: A Legend in His Time

Horseshoe, "the legend of all clubs," was one of the toughest and most respected individuals in South Los Angeles in the 1950s but was not a street-group member. "He was a loner. He got his name from when he was a little kid: he fell off one of the streetcar trolleys and hit his head on the tracks, with the injury leaving a scar that formed a horseshoe on his head." He was a tough, no-nonsense fighter, formidable and afraid of no man or other juveniles. Horseshoe also happened to have a teasing and playful nature, which was on display on an occasion that led to the following incident, narrated by Whit, the vice president of the Royal Aces:

> I remember one day, we were in South Park during the summer. And Horseshoe like to play a lot. And there was some guy—I don't even remember who it was—come over that day all dressed up. And he and Horseshoe were playin', and the guy told Horseshoe to let him alone. He said, "I don't feel like playin' today," 'cause he was dressed up. He had a suit on or something. And Horseshoe felt like playin', and the guy kept tellin' him to leave him alone. Horseshoe pushed him, pushed him in the pool with his suit on. And the guy cut him, cut him real bad on the shoulder. But when the police came and all, he never told them who did it. Horseshoe never told who cut him, 'cause he knew he had provoked the guy, and so he just took it.

Taking responsibility for his behavior by not snitching to the police were esteemed neighborhood values that elevated Horseshoe's reputation even higher.

Although fighting was a common activity involving many of the juveniles in the South Los Angeles neighborhoods, at least some of the time, it was also a behavior most tried to keep secret from their parents. This was particularly so for the more serious fights, which could bring the greatest rebuke. As Poop, from the Little Slausons, described:

> Most of our serious fights started in the evening, in the Park, and not in the open. We kept it away from home. The only time our parents would know that we were about this stuff—maybe they would hear us talkin' or something like that or one of us got hurt, come home wit' a bloody nose. They knew we were in these clubs 'n' stuff.

Coming-from-the-shoulders permitted mistakes to be made and then later rectified. It permitted the wronged to retaliate without fear of deadly retribution, if the retaliation was within the accepted neighborhood guidelines.

Strong Role Models Provide Guidance

Most leaders of the early South Los Angeles street groups were strong-minded individuals with clear perspectives on what it took to be a man. As David Riesman's theory of inner-directed man explains, they had clarity and focus, knew what they wanted and where they were going. Their perspective stemmed both from unequivocal family values plus strong family role models, "implanted early in life by the elders."[5] Chinaman, the legendary leader of the Big Slausons, explained:

> It wasn't about me being bad or nothing. It was about I was stubborn enough or I had something in me that said ain't nobody in the world can tell me where I can go and where I can't go. My daddy don't even tell me where I can't go. I got to die doing something; I just as well go on and live and be a man. That was part of being a man; that's all I can say. My whole attitude was to be a man. Most of the times it's that strong rearing, but if he going to do something, that's what he do, regardless of consequences.[6]

Chinaman learned what was right and wrong from his father, who taught him to do the right thing, the moral thing, so that any subsequent consequences were inconsequential: "But it ain't never no consequences, 'cause it all be in line." By following his father's philosophy, imaginable consequences became a small price to pay for doing what he knew was correct.

Perhaps as important as parental influence in emphasizing the come-from-the-shoulders ethic were other significant adult role models juveniles had growing up in South Los Angeles. These were often sports figures, most notably, boxers, who were heroes in the community. The best boxers, the most notorious, the ones whose names everybody had heard of, were primarily African American. They had demonstrated class and courage in the ring, a fear of no man, and a skill with their fists to be emulated. These were powerful figures to young Black males in the City, as Bird made clear:

> See, we came up at a time when sports was a great thing, and boxing was one where you still had Sugar Ray Robinson. Okay, you had Archie Moore and Sonny Liston being able to go from the shoulders and showing how good you was during the 1950s and stuff. Everybody was a potential boxer in his own right. Showing how good you was in the shoulder was a prestigious thing for your own manhood.

So if you ran and got a gun, knife, or something, you was called a sissy, a rum, a punk, and rooty-poot 'cause you couldn't hang. It was a prestigious thing to be able to go-from-the-shoulders, stand your ground under any circumstances, any conditions.

The president of the Senators, Jasper, claimed the ethic these fighters established became so ubiquitous in the community that all the youth were copying their style:

A kid growing up in the '40s and '50s—you gotta remember that Joe Lewis was still around, Sugar Ray Robinson was still around, Archie Moore was around, Jersey Joe Walcott was around, and all these dudes were boom boom boom. And everybody, you know, had the step. And everybody wanted to be one of the above. See, and everybody was seeing how good the left hook was, the right cross, and everybody had the dance step or something—everybody.

Bird added, "Guys were copying the Archie Moore slide with their feet when they walked, because he was tough and cool, and we could be too."

In at least one neighborhood, the youth grew up around several men who were professional boxers. These men were focal points for the neighborhood juveniles, who would hang out at their houses to learn real boxing skills. It was not to discover how to hurt somebody but rather an exciting learning environment to develop important life skills. Frank M. noted:

See, the guys on my street, when we came up, there were four or five boxers that were professional fighters that were around. And we would just box you know. It wasn't that we did this because we thought we were gonna beat up somebody; it was just like a pastime with us. Like people throw a football or play basketball, boxing was a pastime with us. That's what we did it for. Like, when I would get out of school, I'd go in this guy's backyard and we'd just box, box, box. His father would come home, and I'd box with him.

After a while, some of these youth became quite skilled and developed enviable reputations. Lesser-known rivals from other neighborhoods, who wanted to see just how tough they were and enhance their own reputations, would occasionally challenge the skilled ones—often well aware that their chances of winning were slim. Frank M. continued:

But that's what we would do. Sometimes five guys would stand around, and we would just hit. That's how our particular crowd became really, really known. Because they knew that everybody, just about everybody, from around here could fight pretty good. And see, people from different neighborhoods would come around sometimes and try to box with us. But it really wasn't much of a contest, you know. Clanton or whoever came round, it wasn't much of a contest. And they knew that.

A Place for the Equalizer

Not every young male thought he was a Sugar Ray Robinson. Some juveniles, especially the smaller ones, found other ways to get respect. The "ol' equalizer," a gun, irrespective of its overall poor image in the neighborhood, could nevertheless be a useful way of both getting respect and keeping the skilled fighters away. This was especially valuable for those who were not only armed but also considered crazy enough to actually use the weapon, as explained below by one of the smaller Slausons when asked about his fighting prowess:

> Basically, I was not challenged because my jacket, per se, was "crazy, dangerous." If I was in another neighborhood, why would an individual want to throw his hands up and say, "Let's fight," when I'm gonna pull out a .22 and shoot him? A big ol' dude, just out of camp [Youth Authority or probation], eighteen-inch arms and things, and they would want to grab me and knock me out. But in the back of their mind: "He's gonna pull a gun; he's gonna pull a gun." It wasn't a cowardness. It was the fact that if you were gonna disrespect me or insult me or try to hurt me, then I was gonna be deadly.

Another Slauson dealt with his diminutive size by being quick and fearless, counting on these skills to do at least some damage early on. As he explained: "I just have a light ass, but I was quick; I was fast. Motherfucka' didn't get out of the way, I be there punching ten times, and by the tenth one, he's hurting on the ground."

Lacking organizational control over the behavior of many set members and having inadequate cultural norms to sway them, some juveniles just went their own way, especially when it came to guns. Bird felt each neighborhood had exceptions, members who carried guns regularly with a greater than normal tendency to use them. "In every neighborhood, they have their shooters and their killers. See, Little Skull, he's a killer, and he kept a gun." In spite of a general tradition that required a proper reason for deadly violence, there were juveniles who were violent for little reason. Bird explained: "I know some chumps will kill you for breathin' the same air in the same space. I know some chumps will pull a gun on you for high-siding and never pull the trigger; gun might not have anything in it."

Sometimes the reasons were justifiable, as Bird continued: "See, Marvin, when he got killed, he went home and got a shotgun, a chrome brand-new shotgun. And he came back up and confronted Reggie with it. Reggie had a gun, and he had to shoot him." Reggie was not considered any less a man than were other come-from-the-shoulders juveniles for using a gun. The special circumstances of this situation permitted the action that was taken: it was self-defense. Marvin was out of order, and Reggie needed to stop him—or be killed or hurt badly.[7]

Why Fight?

The ideology of comin'-from-the-shoulders, along with the widely accepted attitudes of the inevitability of confrontation, contributed to regular adolescent involvement in fistfights. Rather than walk away from combat, many South Los Angeles youth would face the challenge head-up, with fight rather than flight. In addition to neighborhood norms, they were inspired by the ideology of the times, the effects of World War II and TV and movie heroes, which showed them that fighting was an honorable way to settle problems. Bird explained:

> You got to remember that what we talkin' 'bout is the first half of the '50s. World War II was just over. Everybody was pushin' that soldier stuff, and everything you saw on TV had something to do wit' the tough guy 'n' such 'n' so on. You had Errol Flynn sword fighting people, John Wayne whoopin' everybody. Everybody saw that kind of stuff, and people pushed you to be tough.

Poop elaborated on Bird's account by mentioning additional characters socializing them by demonstrating toughness. He asserted: "Yeah, Hopalong Cassidy and them guys, you know, they whoop a whole tribe of Indians by their self. And Tarzan was chasin' all the Africans through the jungle 'n' shit. And I know how tough Tarzan and Hopalong Cassidy was, and they wasn't no tougher than we was." Poop had developed an early understanding from his neighborhood of how important it was to be tough. He added: "Yeah, and it was about tough guys, you know, and we was tough guys. When we was growing up, we use to have this saying that 'We wasn't scared of no old man, no little niggers,[8] and no White boys.' 'Cause we didn't think a little guy, a White guy, or an old guy couldn't whoop nobody." Bad to the bone, whether one was or was not, was an attitude to take and goal to strive for. No one pushed Hoppy or Tarzan around. We're as bad as they are, so no one is going to push us around either, the reasoning went.[9]

Numerous situations had the potential to produce arguments that could lead to fights, but a main cause was disrespect. While disrespect can be interpreted in many ways, when it was experienced, the results were predictable: somebody was going to pay. In the following anecdote, Lafayette, the High Priest, who started the Slauson clique of the Village Assassins, explained that even people in authority were not off limits if they were out of order. When asked about the cause of most fights, he replied:

> Disrespect: in my opinion, it was disrespect. Now, I got kicked out of Dorsey for hitting Mr. Davis. Mr. Davis is a big ol' ex-football player. He was the boy's VP. Okay, I'm comin' down the hall at Dorsey—this is in '61, and I got a mohair sweater on. I got a red mohair sweater on, some red mohair socks—'cause see color wasn't our thing, but matchin' was—and some biscuits [a high-top shoe]. I got short pants, some gloves, and a stingy brim, and he said, "You look like a sissy." And I hit him 'cause he was disrespectin' me. He was disrespectin' my set.

Wolfin' Skills Can Make Juveniles Weep

Disrespect was sometimes done inadvertently, through ignorance or accident, but it was frequently intentional. One form of intentional disrespect, requiring adroit verbal skills, was called "wolfin'." Wolfin' is a clever use of unrehearsed rhyming denigrations designed to humiliate and disparage. Adept wolfers left little doubt that words were equal contributors with sticks and stones to broken bones. "If I'd a had change for a quarter, I'd been your daddy" and "I screwed your mama on the moon, and no one can get her but me an' Calhoun" are examples. Bird felt that wolfin' was "universal among Black people all across the states." A Junior Businessman, describing how a scenario might begin, added: "See somebody come walkin' down the street. Somebody say to him, 'Hey, boy, whatcha doin' with your mama's shoes on?' Then it would start." In other places, wolfin' has been referred to as "doin' the dozens." A particularly gifted wolfer might even get hired to wolf for a fee for someone less resourceful, although he often required protection from his employer when the wolfee got too angry.

An especially skillful wolfer was Rickie H., who grew up on the Slausons' Sin Street. His motto could have been "Have wolfin', will travel." He was so good that he was often sought out for his skills and paid for his services. "I was kind of like the king of wolfin' at Edison. I'd be way off to the other side of the school, man, and there'd be guys at the other end, and they'd come get me. They'd give me their lunch money to talk about a guy and his mama." Rickie noted how dangerous his services might be:

> I had talked about this one guy at Edison, man. This dude—he gave me seventy-five cents just to talk about this one dude. So I did not hit him with everything, but I hit him with enough to make him so mad he wanted to jump on me. I already tell them before they come to me and give me the money and stuff, I said, "When I talk about this mothafucker, he's gonna get mad; he's gonna get pissed off. Don't let him, you guys, don't let him touch me!"

Rickie's skills created a dilemma for the wolfee: Does he fight, flee, or melt? At times, Rickie could demean the guy so badly he had no choice—anguished tears just flowed:[10]

> I talked about that one guy. I talked about him bad, man; he was ready to fight. And homeboy, he said, "Man, no you can't put your hands on him [Rickie]; you can't touch him." So I left, because I felt I had wolfed him so good. . . . Like, I get into what I'm sayin', you know. Like, I talked about this one guy so bad, man, he started cryin'. They said, "Come on, Rick, lighten up on him." So I didn't say no more about him and stuff. So this other dude, he kept talkin', so I started talking about his ass. I talked about him so bad he started cryin' too.

Rickie H. considered himself a lover, not a fighter. He understood that to get along was important and knew there were rational reasons to avoid fighting, such as when outnumbered. As he described:

> If I was outnumbered, then I was gonna play it cool, you know. If I'm outnumbered man, I ain't stupid, you understand? See, I'm not gonna sit up there and talk a whole bunch of shit to ten motherfuckers when I'm there by myself. So I really relied on my rap, whether it's a man or a woman or whatever.

Since Rickie was well respected, was smart, came from a street that was itself a tight clique, had numerous friends, and would help others when they needed him, his particular mannerisms enabled him not to lose face among his peers. He was exceptional, though not an exception.

Snipin' and High-Sidin'

A veteran South Los Angeles probation officer, who grew up in Compton, discussed a form of fighting for hire he called "snipin'." A "sniper" was a person who could, in a nonchalant way, slip up behind someone and then unexpectedly hit him so hard with his fist that he would knock him out. Snipers would snipe someone for themselves or for someone else, as the probation officer explained: "Some kids were real good at this. You let a sniper know who you want to get, he'll snipe him for you." A sniper would choose his moment, have a getaway plan, and usually manage to get away without getting caught or hurt, while the snipee might not even know who hit him.

"High-siding," or being a smart ass, was done by juveniles who were often pompous, full of braggadocio, and pretentious show-offs who seemed to be looking for trouble by exhibiting behavior they knew others found offensive. Many juveniles could walk away from such braggarts, while some, often braggarts themselves, would accept the challenge: "Fool draw a fool. If you out there high-sidin', you can find somebody else out there high-sidin' too. You goin' north, they goin' south," Bird noted. Interestingly, "most of the baddest dudes never high-side," although they could get drawn into it when it involved someone from the neighborhood.

A Part of Neighborhood Life

An area especially conducive to demonstrations of toughness, with a high likelihood of producing a fight, was in situations involving girls. Jealousy led the way, primarily concerning males attempting to establish hegemony over other males. Some of the most dangerous confrontations occurred at parties and dances, locales of both regular and infamous reasons for hostilities. As Big from the Village Brothers clique of the Slausons suggested: "All this would start over a dance or a party behind somebody dancin', probably too sexual, with another girl from another set."

A common situation for a fight scene occurred when somebody said something or did something to someone else's girlfriend, which was then perceived by her boyfriend to be disrespectful. Most girls approved of male defense of their honor, while many also believed they had the power to control a confrontation before it began. When they intervened, it gave the males an acceptable way out of a battle that might have been dangerous for them, and they may not have wanted to engage in the first place. Linda C., a founder of the Florencitas, when asked what the girls thought about the boys fighting over them, explained it this way:

> It's an everyday thing; it's accepted. It's not looked down on or frowned on or whatever. I mean, if they're going to fight, it has to be for a reason.... I've told my old man, "If you go, I'm gonna cut you loose." And he goes, "All right, all right, I won't go." Maybe I saved his life

by him not going that night. I wasn't successful all the time, but I still believe I might have been able to save his life a few times.

When a female lived in a neighborhood different than her suitor, fights could erupt between the neighborhoods or between the boyfriend and some others in the neighborhood, based on the terms of endearment the parties had with one another. When terms were good, hassles were minimal, but if terms soured, both the boyfriend and the girlfriend might be in trouble. Ameer, president of the Baby Businessmen, when asked about the cause of fights, replied:

> Over a woman—that's the main thing. Like, I use to love a girl who lived in Ross Snyder territory, but I had no problem with Ross Snyders because I was kind of tight with them. . . . But I loved a girl who lived in the Roman 20s territory, and I had a problem. . . . And the Roman 20s would go on to the bus, and they'd threaten the girl.

Probation officer and longtime resident Billy P. thought relations between the sexes were important but that they might have been secondary to school rivalries in contributing to fights. When asked how girls figured into the fights, he explained:

> I'd say, you know, somebody thought one guy might be dancing with his girl or something, and something might start. But I really think that was just more or less an object for him to focus in on than the reason. The most common reason is what school you go to. I was taking a girl to Compton one night, on a date, and she wanted a hot dog from this stand that use to be on 130th and Compton. So I got out of my car and went and got her a hot dog and a soda pop, and while I'm walking back to my car, some guy asks me what school I go to. I said Jefferson, but then I started thinking, "Hell, I'm in the Jordan High School area." So I took a whoopin' behind the school I went to. It had nothing to do with her; they knew I wasn't familiar to them.

Clearly, school rivalries created in-groups and out-groups and fostered antagonisms between them; such rivalry was frequently reason enough to fight.

Something Serious

When serious fighting took place, it typically occurred between individuals or between groups from different neighborhoods. Within the neighborhoods, general harmony could be broken by petty quarrels.[11] Similar to families, neighborhood individuals occasionally had personal issues with one another; but as in many families, they were usually settled with words or fists rather than with weapons.

There were also fights between the cliques within a neighborhood. While combatants might end up a bit bloodied, and the feuds might be drawn out, there was no killing. Often the fights were over important issues, as when an older clique tried to muscle in on the prerogatives of a younger clique. Such squabbles happened between the Little Slausons and the Baby Slausons over who could do what to whom, when, and where. Bird explained:

> Yeah, see, Baby Slauson and Little Slauson got into it all the time. We had to fight; we had to jump Little Slausons. We had to jump them because they always come over trying to run things and talk that shit, you know, trying to take people's money and stuff. Go tell us they're goin' to come to our parties and try to take the chicks and all that kind of stuff. So we laid for them at the Park one day, and there were fifty or sixty of them. Little Slausons, shit, we had a hundred and something. We jumped on them; we threw some in the trash cans.

A similar situation happened with the Businessmen in 1964 when a number of the Seniors were getting out of jail and trying to reclaim hegemony from the Babies, who by this time were the dominant clique. Ameer concluded that the disagreements were resolved peacefully, but they were not settled without some sharp verbal exchanges. In sum, the primary causes of fights were demonstrations of being a man, displays of being good with your hands, efforts to get a little respect, being in the wrong place at the wrong time, and male proprietary rights over females.

Neighborhood vs. Neighborhood

Interneighborhood battles occurred frequently, usually involving many participants, and were potentially the most dangerous of altercations.[12] While some observers and participants describe these battles as "wars" or "rumbles" or "gang fights," others suggest they were little more than community border skirmishes.[13] A *Los Angeles Sentinel* article's headline, "Shots Fired as Teen Gang War Flares on W'Side," blamed the "Black Juan Gang" for the altercation. While bats and chains were the primary weapons, three shots were also fired, although nobody was reported to have been hit.[14]

Sometimes the "gang war" might be termed a "fete" by the news, where the "war" was nothing more than a fistfight.[15] On other occasions, there could be blood, as this *Los Angeles Times* article indicates: "Rival Gangs

Erupt in Bloodiest Fight in Years; 3 Seriously Hurt, 10 Booked."[16] At times, the combatants may have just gotten lucky, with no one getting hurt. As this next *Los Angeles Sentinel* headline suggests, in spite of their ferocity or intentions, there were no injuries: "Easter Miracle: None Hit . . . Three juveniles, riding the range . . . emulating bad men of the old Wild West . . . sprinkled Compton neighborhoods with hailing lead."[17]

Conflicts could erupt over both seemingly trivial issues and more serious matters, with blood, when present, most likely to come from scrapes, cuts, and bruises rather than from death or grave injury. Of course, when weapons, especially guns, were used, the chances of someone being seriously injured increased dramatically. Some neighborhoods had long-standing hostilities with one another and could be depended on to renew their grievances when opportunities arose. Due to a variety of reasons, many of these antagonisms existed up through the Watts Rebellion of 1965, discussed in Chapter 9.

Depending on the neighborhoods involved and the period for the struggles, the confrontations ranged from fistfights to major battles with weapons. Generally, the earlier the period, the less harm and injury occurred in the conflicts. Neighborhoods of the 1940s were more likely to be involved in less serious and more informal confrontations than neighborhoods of the 1950s and 1960s.

In the late 1940s, certain individuals could pick and choose the neighborhood fights they would participate in without losing face for nonparticipation in a battle that may have been against their personal interests. Frank M. recalled that he would, without repercussion, not participate in fights where he knew or liked the guys his club was fighting. In his words:

> They'd [Clanton] say, "Hey, man, we're gonna go over and fight. You want to go?" And I'd say, "Yeah, okay, I'll go." Then [another time], fifteen or twenty guys would come by my house, and I'd say, "Who you guys fightin?" "Ah, we're gonna fight the Twenty-Thirds." "I know those guys. I don't want to fight them; you guys go on." They'd come back, and they tell me what they did. It wasn't you chicken 'cause you didn't go; they knew why I wouldn't go.

He felt some street groups would fight for little or no reason, but his homeboys had good reasons when they went to battle: "If we did something, we more or less had a reason; somebody would hit one of the guys or take something from him. We'd catch him and beat him up and stuff like that. But, like, most of those guys from Clanton would fight just for anything; it didn't matter; they just wanted to fight."

Things had changed by the 1960s. Two groups, the Businessmen and Gladiators, were far rowdier then than the 1940s Clanton Street club. Ameer noted that the Businessmen and Gladiators combined forces against a Venice group in 1960 and "burned down a whole block." A gang war, to Ameer, meant the heavy artillery came out; people often got hurt, sometimes seriously, as the two sides confronted each other: "A gang war is like a declared war, and you fight to the finish. Everything comes out: guns, gas bombs—you name it. You fight till it ends." The gang war, as Ameer explained, between the Businessmen and the Roman 20s in 1963, illustrated how dangerous these battles could be:

We had a gang war with the Roman 20s in 1963 that was a brutal gang war. That, I've got to admit, was the most vicious fight I've been in. Both sides had their tire irons, and they merged at night under the streetlights. It was vicious, and guys was cryin', and you can hear the jack handles clingin' in the air—cling, cling.

Because of their relatively larger sizes, their proximity to one another, and many unresolved grudges, one of the most bitter and longest lasting of South Los Angeles's neighborhood wars was between the Slausons and Watts. The Watts street groups, beginning in the late 1940s, had already established themselves as the southern power to be reckoned with before the Slausons had come together as a neighborhood. Once the Slausons became established in the early 1950s, many of them saw it as their duty to keep Watts out of their neighborhood, lest Watts should dominate all of Los Angeles. Bird described the situation this way:

If it wasn't for us, like I keep telling everybody, if it wasn't for Slauson, Watts would have ran all LA. Watts would have ran over LA, like Attila the Hun. But they [Watts] had it wrong. They made enemies with us too soon, and we kept fightin'. We had been fightin' them since the first of the '50s, all the way, you know, until the Watts Riot came.

Watts was not popular with many of the other neighborhoods, but Watts was often more powerful and better organized, thus less likely to be stopped. To get to many of the other neighborhoods, the Watts groups had to go through the Slausons area, giving the Slausons an advantage. Bird continued: "But they had to come through us, and so we short stopped them. See, and I mean they were fightin' other people too, but we were the main force against them 'cause we were the only ones that would really go and attack them." The Watts groups were aggressive, acting on the premise they could go anywhere and do anything, but when Watts came to the Slauson neighborhood, the whole community showed support against them. Bird explained:

> Dudes from every place else in LA had fights with Watts, 'cause in them days Watts dudes use to leave Watts and go all over town. They beat up a neighborhood and take all the girls and tear up the house and do all that stuff. They come down here—they get ran all the way back to Watts by our youngsters, because the whole community come out on 'em. And see, so we had the best defense against Watts.

As a younger member of the original Slausons, Bird felt that it was his duty to carry on the traditional struggles with Watts that had been established by older Slausons. It was up to Bird to "rally the troops," to socialize other Slausons into comprehending who the enemy was and what they needed do about it. Bird explained:

> Curly was in the penitentiary; Joe King was in the penitentiary; all my clique was gone. Everybody was either in the penitentiary, YA, or camp or the county jail or something. Poop and them were older than me. They were still from the neighborhood, but they was out with girls or workin'. By me being an original member, when the Watts dudes come down, I was able to muster up the troops and get them to fight. See, what I did is took all them dudes that was younger than me, and I was tellin' them, "So-and-so from Watts, he ain't nothin'; you can have him." I made them dudes face up and fight these dudes.[18]

Bird believed Watts would have dominated all of South Los Angeles had it not been for the potency of the Slausons. Yet there was respect. Respect from your enemy is among the most esteemed. Some Watts people felt that the Slausons were more than just a gang—they were a phenomenon. A former Watt's gang member, Louis Tackwood, commenting on the rivalry between Watts and Slauson in his 1973 book, *The Glass House Tapes*, confirmed Bird's position that Watts could not defeat Slauson; nor could they undermine its power, regardless of how hard they struggled:[19]

> But the Slausons really got us tangled up. We fought and fought and fought but you see, ours was the violent thing. We conquered by violence, we had no ideology or nothing. The Slausons was an idea. They didn't wear no jackets. They just considered themselves Slausons and that was it. . . . But the Slausons were sharp dressers and their old ladies were good-looking too. We were trying to kill an idea, jus' couldn't do it.[20]

Coming Home from School

From another perspective, seemingly innocuous incidents between groups with long-standing unresolved grievances, like the Slausons and the Gladiators had, could evolve quickly into eruptions of combat. One time, when Bird's girlfriend Roslyn and her friend Brunetta were walking home from school through the Gladiator area, some Gladiators told them not to cross a street they needed to cross to get home. Roslyn phoned Bird to tell him they could not get home because the Gladiators were preventing them from crossing the street. This call led to the following escalation, as Bird explained:

> They [the Gladiators] told Roslyn and Brunetta, "Y'all better not cross 54th street," as they was walkin' home. See, Roslyn lived on 57th and Normandie, and Manual was on 42nd and Vermont. There's no way you can leave from 42nd going south and get to 57th without crossing 54th. I'm at the pool hall when she called. I said, "What's happening?" She said, "Yeah, we up here at Manual, and Gladiators are talking that shit." I said, "What shit!" "They told us we better not cross 54th." I said, "Who's up there?" She said, "Me and Brunetta."[21]

Then, the web of Slauson affiliations intensified the situation as the phone bank came alive, turning an innocent attempt by two Slauson girls to cross a street in another street group's neighborhood into a major incident. Bird continued:

> I said, "All right," and I called Eugene. And Eugene was Brunetta's boyfriend. And Wild Willie Poo Poo is Brunetta's cousin, okay, and these [two dudes] are Little Slausons. And Lee Hutchinson and all them—man, we come up to Manual. But see, when that phone call was made, when I got off the phone, Poop called Jimmy Fuller at home. Jimmy Fuller call Freddy Rat; Freddy Rat called so-and-so and told everybody, "Meet us at Manual."

In a show of force, the Slausons went up to 54th Street and demonstrated their domination by giving the Gladiators a lesson on respect. Bird concluded:

> And that's when we fell out. And I told Roslyn, and Eugene told Brunetta, to walk across 54th Street. And Roslyn, you know, you tell her somethin' like that, you got to believe she's a fool. Yeah, she strutted right across 54th; they just walked across. What's gonna happen? I said, "Who's the lame told y'all that?" She said, "That's him over there." He sittin' back on the ledge of the window by the donut shop.

I walked up to him, and Roslyn walked up, and I said, "Man, did you tell her not to cross 54th?" "No, man." "What?" I said [to Roslyn], "Slap that lame's face." Right there, she took her hand, drew back, and slapped the spit out of his mouth. He reached for a gun in his waist. I grabbed his hand and stuck a .25 in his mouth and said, "Go ahead, fool; if you move, you lose." And Lee Hutchinson was in the middle of the street with a chrome shotgun 'n' stuff, and he said, "I don't want to see any more of you young lames up here in the streets no more."[22]

In the face of the Slausons' muscle, the Gladiators had been confronted and then humiliated in their own neighborhood. They backed off, the girls crossed the street, and the situation was resolved, for the moment. As with Watts before them, there were many other struggles between the Slausons and the Gladiators. Some were large group confrontations; others involved individuals or smaller groups. While these street groups never made peace with one another, as they got older and went through life changes, the war cries had been reduced to whispers by 1965.

The overwhelming majority of street-group fights that took place occurred between racially and ethnically homogeneous rivals.[23] That is, African American sets fought other African American sets, and Chicano sets fought other Chicano sets. The Slausons and the Mexican set Florence shared the same geographic boundaries yet were generally tight with each other. It was not always that way, because in the mid-1950s Tiny Florence and Baby Slauson were fighting regularly, although not over racial matters. Their beefs involved two sets that just did not get along with each other. As noted, their battles were eventually ended by the Roach-Mariano truce of 1957.

The major exceptions to the amelioration phenomenon were the confrontations with White "gangs," all of which were associated with racism. These confrontations were fewer, were issue specific, and, while sometimes violent, rarely involved loss of life.[24] White groups' antagonisms were directed at Black Angelenos because they blamed them as threats to their way of life and because their phenotypical visibility made them convenient targets. Mark Hamm has written that White racist subcultural continuity has become commonplace in America, especially extending their focus to non-White immigrants, as white groups have become more organized, more terrorist, and more deadly.[25]

Individual Fights

While neighborhood-versus-neighborhood battles were a fundamental part of life in South Los Angeles, many fights also occurred between individuals.

They might be set members in sets that had a beef with one another or between individuals from competing cliques within the same set. The fights were frequently over non-gang-related issues, having more to do with personal issues, which were most likely compounded by intraset or intraclique or interclique relations.[26]

Often large factions of the neighborhoods would be directly involved as spectators and fans, and not as participants. Some fights were like "gladiatorial" contests, where time was allowed for an audience to form to see the combatants go at each other. These could be memorable events. Percy M. told of a time he was watching a couple of homeboys fight, when Zey from the Slausons threw the punch heard around the City.[27] In Percy M.'s words:

> I think the thing that really fascinated me the most of all of the past was when I seen Zey knock that brother out of his shoes. I mean, four Muhammad Alis could not hit as hard as this one man [Zey] could hit! And when this man's shoes was tied up on his feet, and he [Zey] hit him, and his shoes was in the middle of Central Avenue ... I mean shiiit, it was unbelievable!

Fights between individuals were opportunities to demonstrate the style, heart, and status of the combatants. Sometimes a fighter knew he faced insurmountable odds—"He was gonna get his ass whooped"—but fought anyway, on principle. It was about "being a man," a concept that was not limited to street-group members: it was understood by neighborhood residents as well as by others. Perhaps surprisingly, certain police officers who worked there shared this ethic. Chinaman, from the Big Slausons, explained:

> Back in my time, we basically dealt with our strength with a man's attitude. It wasn't about killing; it was about who was the better man, based on manly moves.
>
> I had a friend who got in an argument with the police: two sheriffs. And one said, "If you whoop me, I'll let you go." He took his gun off, his badge off, and everything and gave them to his partner. And they got into it. But what he didn't know was that my friend had just come out of training, and he was real tough. He [the friend] whooped the man, and after he whooped him, they let him go. Okay, this was man against man; he wasn't disrespecting the law or disrespecting the neighbors or the people.

Chinaman's tale is a reflection of the complexity of relations that existed between police and juveniles. Similar stories from police officers confirmed what he said had happened had also happened elsewhere. But there is also little reason to think fights like this, between street juveniles and the police, were commonplace; they were not. Racism ruled, while exceptions occurred.

A Clash of Titans[28]

All individuals have a history, a reputation that, as Bird expressed, is "like a hump on a camel's back"—it follows them wherever they go. Two individuals, Roach from Slauson and N. D. from Watts, were juveniles of such epic proportions that when they fought, they created neighborhood lore, remembered by some residents even today. It was a classic "clash of the titans."

Judging by the accounts of those who knew him, N. D. was the "baddest dude Watts ever had in his time period." He was large, powerful, and not averse to physical combat to determine right from wrong. Roach, commenting on N. D., noted: "The guy was bad; he was huge." N. D. lived on 83rd Street and Hooper Avenue in Watts and, as noted, considered himself its nominal mayor. N. D. had a lot of respect in the community plus a reputation for being "pleasant" if he was not drunk or angry. But when he was, he was dangerous, having beaten a security guard to death, with his bare hands, for killing a friend of his.

Roach was tough, too, with more than enough heart to make up for his smaller stature, being several inches shorter than N. D. Roach was solid, with broad shoulders, powerful muscles, and bulldog determination. Bird calls him a "red-eyed squabbler." Roach was also mischievous, ready to defend a homeboy in a second, and not opposed to seeking out a bit of adventure during slow times. As Roach told it, on the eve of the big fight, he and some of his homeboys had had words with some Watts dudes at the hot dog stand on 103rd Street and Compton Avenue in Watts.

It could have ended then, but Roach and a few homeboys escalated things by going farther into Watts and busting up and shooting up some things, among which was N. D.'s car. N. D. tracked Roach back up to 68th Street and Central Avenue, the Slausons neighborhood, where they confronted one another. Roach pulled a knife and was going to cut him, but then, because Roach was a "man" and N. D. was a "man," and a knife was not manly, Roach reconsidered. "I knew him. We use to run together when I was in the Zebras. So I threw my knife on the ground; we just start to fighting," he proclaimed.

It took a lot of heart for N. D. to come into the center of the Slauson neighborhood to look for someone with as fearsome a reputation as Roach had, and it took a lot of heart for Roach to decide to go-from-the-shoulders with a dude as big and bad as N. D. was. When N. D. first arrived on the scene, he encountered the formidable Chinaman. Aware of Chinaman's fabled reputation as having never lost a fight, N. D. displayed no fear. He announced to Chinaman that he was N. D. from Watts, and he was looking for Roach.

Chinaman wasn't worried about N. D. and suspected that Roach had most likely done something to deserve this visit. But he also understood this was Roach's problem and that he would remain an interested observer. Besides, it had taken "monster balls" for N. D. to come all the way to the middle of the Slauson neighborhood, by himself, to look for a mega character like Roach, and Chinaman respected that. Within a few minutes, Roach appeared, and he and N. D. "got to talkin' and then got to arguin' and then to squabblin' and then to fightin'." The full flavor of this fight can best be appreciated from Bird's eyewitness account:

> These dudes was fightin'. I mean, this is a classic; this is just like in the movies. Okay, there was a hotel called the Gateway Hotel sittin' on 68th Street, across from the Red Dragon Saloon. I'm talkin' about a saloon! And it actually had some doors like in the cowboy pictures on it. It had a closing door, but it also had the swingin' doors. They started fightin' on the street in front of the Red Dragon Saloon. They fought all in the Red Dragon Saloon, fought all over the tables and shit, back out of the Red Dragon Saloon, fought up 68th goin' east to the Gateway Hotel, and they fought all this side of Gateway Hotel. You remember those old Coca-Cola machines, look like a old refrigerator, with no window? It had a lever and a chute. It was a great big ol' heavy sucka. These fools fought up a stairway on to the old Coke machine, knocked it over, rolled on the ground, and fought all out in the street and said, "Hah, yeah, it's all right, man; get you on the next one." See, basically they fought to a draw.

Roach and N. D. fought two more times, once in Watts and once at Fremont High in the Slauson neighborhood. N. D. got the best of Roach in Watts, and Roach returned the favor at Fremont. It has been said these two were "archenemies," could have easily killed one another, but did not because they respected each other, as men. Their rivalry illustrates what the concept of coming-from-the-shoulders meant. Their demonstration of manhood also disambiguates why they were leaders and able to command the respect they each received, from their own and from each other's neighborhoods.[29] From the control perspective, proponents might assume this rivalry constituted a "gang fight," since it involved two formidable street-group leaders. But it remained a personal rivalry contested only with the fists of the two combatants, going to show how respect was won and maintained within the culture at the time. This point could have easily been lost by lumping the personal into a gang-conflict category.

Another memorable fight involved the time Dudley B. from the Slausons whooped Floyd from the Gladiators. This was a fight of considerable proportions because, although Dudley B. was tough, Floyd was the heart and soul of the Gladiators. But Dudley B. was not afraid to battle with the best, even when he thought he might have been outclassed. Bird remarked: "Dudley B. whooped Floyd from the front of Fred's Burger stand across the street from John Muir, head-up. Whooped Floyd from there all the way back to the freeway. See, Dudley B. was cold with his fists—we called him 'gangster.' Floyd was their main dude." On a subsequent occasion, even after getting beaten, Floyd posed such an intimidating figure to Wallace of the Businessmen that Wallace used intoxication as an excuse not to fight him. Thus, although Floyd had lost a fight to a formidable foe in Dudley B., the loss did not diminish the respect he carried. It may have even enhanced it, because he had shown the heart to fight.[30] Other potential adversaries, who were perhaps a bit short on heart, continued to give him deference.

Horseshoe, as introduced, was, according to a probation officer who knew him, "a tough kid" with endearing charms, who was granted many liberties anyplace he traveled. He went where he wanted to go without reprisal. As Whit, the vice president of the Royal Aces, noted:

> Nobody bothered him, nobody. Everybody knew him all over the City—he was God. He mostly ruled—he controlled South Park, gave orders over there. He could go to Ross Snyders and survive. Now Ross Snyders is known for its cutthroats. Just about any place he went and hung out for any length of time, he controlled.

Horseshoe's fighting prowess, as well as his belief in protecting the vulnerable, earned him neighborhood respect. Los Angeles County deputy probation officer Billy P. knew him and had this to say about how capable Horseshoe was at comin'-from-the-shoulders: "He was real tough. Horseshoe was fighting men since he was ten years old; he was just a legend. He wasn't so much a bully, but he was just a guy that could fight, and he didn't have any fears."

A Touch of Warmth

A great curse of research on street-group life using institutional data is statistical abstraction. Treating street-group members as numbers omits the concrete human dimension of real people. Horseshoe, the feared lone wolf, whose fighting ability made people take pause before tangling with him, is illustrative. Considered as a statistic of violence, the warmth he showed toward those in need of protection would be lost. But it was a characteristic where his strong traditional values endeared him to many. To wit: on one occasion, a teenage girl he knew, who later married Whit, went with two of her friends to the 20th Street playground for a summer's night dance. Horseshoe saw her there, watched over her, then pulled her aside, and told her to go home because he knew her parents would not approve of her being there. Whit's wife recalled the experience: "He came over there, picked me up, and said, 'What are you doin' down here?' I said, 'I just came to the dance.' He said, 'You go home.' I left 'cause that was not where I lived and he figured that was not where my mother or father would want me to be." Whit offered this account of why Horseshoe had acted so chivalrously toward his future wife:

> He knew her family. He knew her brother; he knew she come from a nice clean-cut family. She wasn't one of the rowdy young ladies that would go anyplace and do anything. He told her to go home so nothing would happen. He knew that her family wouldn't approve of her being down there.

Earlier we explained why perceptions of in-group propriety rights will often cause boys to fight over a girl crossing a neighborhood boundary to date an out-group person. We expand that analysis to emphasize that an exceptional individual, a multidimensional person—such as Horseshoe—could enter an unfriendly neighborhood to visit a girl or to conduct other business if they did it properly. While there was no one standard of correctness, the following illustration shows how another juvenile, LaHunter from the Roman 20s, visited his girl in a hostile neighborhood and not only carried it off but earned the respect of those he encountered in the process. As Bird described:

> Here's an archenemy from an archenemy neighborhood, LaHunter. He's from enemies individually and groupwise to Businessmen, 'cause he's from the 20s, but he came to see a girl. He didn't come up there lookin' for no Businessmen. He didn't come up there talkin' no shit. But when he was confronted by a whole corner full of Businessmen, he didn't turn and go away; he crossed the street and came over. That's a hog with big nuts. Now, he might of had a bazooka, but he didn't flash or nothin'. He came to state his business. And he was saying, "I'll go where I want to go." There was respect. Now, they could have just whooped him and pulled his legs apart, but you know, he was cool. And see, in them days, characters was judged by how much heart they had.

In addition to having heart, LaHunter was tough, but it was not about that. It was that he had the unmitigated gall, the cojones, to leave his neighborhood, come into enemy territory, and stand up to a group of his neighborhood's enemies without any backup. While it is proper to conclude that in South Los Angeles people were judged on the basis of where they came from, of equal importance was that they were judged by who they were, what they were doing, what they were likely to do, and how they were conducting themselves. In LaHunter's case, he was a set member, on personal business, in an enemy neighborhood, who was accorded safe passage because he demonstrated the heart to gain the respect of those who could, but would not, hurt him.

Some Serious Whoopin's

There was another type of violence that occurred in South Los Angeles before 1965, a kind that happened circumstantially before escalating dangerously through happenstance.[31] The first example concerns Poop, who, when he was seventeen in 1958, was mistreated by a man ten years his senior. In the days before the existence of the now ubiquitous cell phone, when public pay phones ruled, this man felt he had a right to a pay phone Poop was using. Poop disagreed. The following narrative, on how the dilemma evolved, reveals just how easily misunderstandings and thoughtless behavior could lead to dangerous injury in a culture whose come-from-the-shoulder ethic encourages the defense of oneself when disrespected. According to Poop:

> This must of been the beginning of '58. And at the time that this happen, I was talkin' on the telephone in front of this bar on McKinley and Florence. I had been talkin' for quite some time; I was talkin' to my girlfriend. And this guy kept comin' out the bar to use the phone. Not just this one guy—a lot of people kept coming out the bar to use the phone. But I stayed on the phone because there's a telephone directly across the street in the gas station. So most of these people seen this youngster on the telephone, so they went on across the street and use the telephone and go on back in the bar and keep on partyin'.
>
> And this one guy came out there, and he was a little tipsy. And this was the first time he came out. And he stood there and waited for me to finish using the phone. But after he's been there about five minutes or so—I'm laughin' and jokin' and carryin' on—he tells me to get off the phone. I just look at him, you know, "Fool," and turned my head and keep on talkin'. He touched me on the back and told me to get off the telephone again, and I tell him, "Man, there's a phone

across the street." He says, "I'ma use this phone." And he get to cursin' and calling me a "little young motherfucker." He was a Black guy, and he was talkin' really kind of rough to me. And I said, "Man, you better go on and take your old ass on away from here 'fore something happen to you." And I turned my back on the guy again.

And he slaps me. You know how you pop people upside the head? He pop me in the back of my head. So pissed off, I turn around and pick the telephone up and throw it at him. Well, the phone only go so far, right? So when it gets to the end of the cord, it jumps back and bust me in my mouth. I am truly mad now, and me and this guy get into it. I just jump on him, rush him. We fall out in the street, and we fight. We're doin' some serious fightin'; like, I was seventeen, and the guy was twenty-seven.

Anyway, the guy worked for the railroad, and he was a big ol' strong guy. And I said, "Damn, I made a mistake rushin' this guy. I should have boxed him." We fell out in the middle of Florence Avenue, and a bus came and almost hit us, and some people pulled us apart. The guy was stronger than me, and he was gettin' the best of me, and he was hurtin' me when he hit me. When they pulled us apart, I just snatched loose, and they was still holdin' this other guy, and I kicked him and fired him up a couple times. And he broke loose, and I broke and ran.

I just lived around the corner, and I was headed to the house and some help. 'Cause I knew if I could get him around there—I always had a yard full of Slausons—'cause I had five sisters, I'm gonna get this chump killed. So I was runnin' around the house, and when I jump on the porch, there's a bat. Now there's nobody in the yard, which is surprising, but the house is full of people. And I slide to a stop. And I picked this bat up; and this man is chasin' me; he hot on my ass and jumpin' up on the porch behind me.

He never did touch it [the porch]. He jumped, and I swung that bat, hit him across his stomach. You could hear the air go out of him; he fell back on the ground. I don't know how that man got up from there, but I went to poppin' him with that bat. My mama came out and grabbed me. He was out there hollerin' and screamin'. I was wearin' his ass out, and my mama grabbed me, and he staggered around the corner.

The beating Poop had administered left the man with a broken jaw, fractured shin, broken arm, fractured collarbone, broken ribs, and a concussion—and it caused Poop trouble with the law—but nobody died. The come-from-the-shoulders ethic both necessitated the fight and probably kept the combatants alive. What might have been easily and amicably resolved—a dispute over phone rights—turned quickly into a brawl that not only became injurious but could have quite easily resulted in a death. Neither person was capable of quitting until outside intervention kept the dispute from turning into tragedy. The masculinity ethic ran deep in South Los Angeles, not only internalized by street-group members but also by nongroup members and by many adults. The ethic disposed them not to choose weapons, especially not guns, as the first option in a dispute, but the tenet encouraged a fight.[32] "Whoop or be whooped" reigned.

At times, injury was a mishap away from being serious or fatal. Occasionally preventing this was the serendipitous intervention of a third or fourth party that kept injury from becoming a 911 call. The following anecdote shows how Bird, in trying to protect his cousin from an older sexual aggressor, wound up in a potentially dangerous situation. The intervention by his aunt would have made matters far worse had it not been for the quick actions of a clerk who prevented a shooting and possible homicide. Bird explained:

> In '61, I had got cut in the throat and stuck in the ear by a man right here on Florence and Mace Place, by Fine's Market,[33] 'cause he was messin' with my cousin. She was like fifteen, and he kept tryin' to hit on her. We were washin' clothes, and I say, "Man, don't bother her; she not but fifteen years old." And I was eighteen, and he was probably about thirty years old, maybe older. He said, "I'll cut your throat, little young punk; you ain't gonna do shit."
>
> And so we left and went to the store. And we had come back from the store, and the dude is standin' on the side of the laundromat. He said, "Yeah, little ol' punk." I said, "Oh, there you are again." Just like that, you know, and he jumped out and tried to swing on me, and I sidestepped him, and we start fightin'. And he had a pocketknife in his hand, and he was swinging, and he stuck me right here in my ear and cut my throat like he said he was gonna do.
>
> See, in them days, they use to have them newspaper stands sittin' like an A-frame, with the little tube down the side. And you put a dime in; it had a lock at the bottom. I picked one of those up and beat him all down in the middle of Hooper. I whooped his ass right out there. And right where the childcare center is use to be a market. Okay, when we first start fightin', my cousin ran from there to my house and got my mother and my aunt, and they came round. My aunt was a real dangerous person; she always carried a gun.
>
> Okay, when my aunt comes around the corner and comes in the store, the dude had run all up in the grocery store, and I had whooped

him all back in the meat department. And my aunt came in and said, "You motherfucker, you gon' cut my nephew?" And she pulled a gun, and she had actually pulled the trigger. But the White dude named Morrie, that worked in the meat department, when he had seen her pull the gun, he ran and say, "Hey, lady," and hit her hand, and the bullet went into the ceiling. And that was the only thing saved that fool. And after that, that sucker broke outta there.

The come-from-the-shoulder cultural prerequisite for being considered a man was gendered; women functioned under different rules.

Sometimes We Get Lucky

The preceding incidents about Poop and Bird showed how set members could get caught up in nonset situations and injure or be injured under circumstances that could have justice-system ramifications. Poop's situation in fact did lead to police involvement, with assault charges brought on him. But the charges could have been homicide, for Poop and Bird's aunt. These incidents show how close to the surface potential injury was and how easily severe harm could have occurred. Both Poop and Bird were fortunate in these situations to avoid anything more serious than what they actually experienced—they got lucky. They were street-group members involved in non-street-group-related violence, which could have had ramifications for their group had the criminal-justice system and media become more involved and provided "gang" definitions to what had occurred.

Whit, from the Royal Aces, explained how Lucky Strike cigarettes helped him get lucky and prevent a skirmish from becoming a homicide, when he was walking home from the Coliseum through the Don Juans' neighborhood, with his girlfriend, and wearing his club jacket:

> The Don Juans pulled up next to us, and one says, "Hey, royal ass! Hey, royal ass, I'm talkin' to you!" I looked in the car; there was about six guys, and one of them had a switchblade. I told the girl, if they stop the car, to go ahead and start runnin', you know. And I guess the Lord must have been with me, man, because when they pulled up and figured to get out, friends of mine named Floyd Dennis and Pee Wee, both of those guys were from the Ross Snyders, recognized me. They said, "Hey, Whit, got a cigarette man?" I said, "Hey, man, I got a whole pack of Lucky Strikes. I'm just opening it up now." See, they knew. The Don Juans knew Pee Wee and Floyd from the Park, man, and they didn't want no part of those guys. They really saved my life, 'cause I think they would have cut me up.

Luck is a variable as important as any other in determining whether a confrontation will be a simple assault or a homicide and whether a juvenile ends up in the arms of the law or not. Luck has not been given the scholarly attention it deserves.[34] When one person swings a bat at another, and the swung bat is deflected from smashing into the head of the intended victim, hitting the body instead, the victim may be hurt but is still alive, and the swinger, as well as the swung upon, had good luck on their sides for that swing.[35]

Good luck is inversely proportional to the deadliness of the weaponry; good luck decreases as the weapon's deadliness increases. Most respondents had tales of how luck had prevented a difficult situation from becoming worse. At least one of Roger Rice and Rex Christensen's respondents recognized how important luck was in keeping him from being arrested. As they report, "He considered 'luck' to be the most important element" keeping him outside the sheriff's station.[36] Being fast enough to get around the corner or close enough to it to get around it before the police arrive is good luck. Being too slow or too far away from it is bad luck. Whether we term the phenomenon "luck" or perhaps something more academic, like a "causally unmeasurable phenomena," it is an essential part of life.[37] Luck is difficult to measure, easy to understand, and important enough not to be denied.[38]

Weaponry

Myths about weapons run deep, especially when comparisons are made between the pre-1965 street groups and the present-day ones. In 1979, Rose Nidiffer, from EL Centro Del Pueblo, a Los Angeles community organization serving youth, described the difference. When testifying before the California Senate Select Committee on Children and Youth, Juvenile Gangs section, she suggested that the earlier gangs had few weapons in contrast to the firepower of today's gangs. She said:

> Gang life is something that is history. It has gone from generation to generation, except today the gang members' weapons are a lot more sophisticated than years ago. Before it was garbage can lids and chains, today it's 357 magnums, sawed-off shotguns and even hand grenades.[39]

The same point has been made repeatedly by other commentators on the differences in weapon use and availability between the early juvenile gangs and the contemporary ones. A current assumption is that the early gangs had just a few weapons, and those they had were primitive. Guns were something they had especially limited access to. Even one of our respondents, Ed

B., who never joined a street group but who grew up among them and hung around with various group members, including those in the Pueblos housing projects, echoed these sentiments: "Nobody had a gun I knew. . . . I might of seen a gun once, but use it, no. It wasn't like that."

Official sources from the 1950s and 1960s implied something entirely different. In the news accounts, there was no shortage of sensationalized media claims about gangs in South Los Angeles having a plethora of weapons they were willing to use, with regularity, where people were often hurt. The following headline from the *Los Angeles Sentinel* in 1963 is illustrative: "Teen Gangs Flare; Two Leaders Shot . . . five carloads of youths, brandishing guns, tire-irons and jack handles . . . blasted [a youth] in the forearm with a .22 caliber rifle."[40] Speculative rather than evidence-based assessments rule when weaponry comparisons are made between the early street groups and the current ones.

There is considerable misinformation about what weaponry was available to early South Los Angeles street groups and how, why, and when it was used. While we found evidence of chains being used, the use of garbage can lids never came up, although Bird did indicate that someone hit him with a garbage can during a fight. It is a mistake to think there was a dearth of weapons available to the street groups. They were there, were accessible, and were generally the same weapons obtainable by the community at large, mediated—in both situations—by technology. Uzis, assault weapons, or fully automatic weapons were either not yet invented, extraordinarily expensive, or so much on the cutting edge of technology that they had permeated neither the larger community nor the early street groups. But among the neighborhoods, during the period we studied, there was an abundance of weapons that grew both in number and sophistication as the times changed.[41]

Guns Were Ubiquitous

Los Angeles newspaper articles on youthful violence indicate the use of guns was quite rare until 1954. Before that date, most violent acts involved fists or knives.[42] By 1954 the use of guns and other assorted weaponry began to appear in these articles. One mid-1950s altercation, for instance, involved a major disturbance at the Coliseum. There, authorities searched two to three thousand juveniles, arrested seventy-five, and in the process discovered a number of guns, clubs, "small pistols and long knives."[43] Throughout the remainder of the 1950s, guns appeared on a regular though infrequent basis in articles where violence and juveniles were associated. The guns that were written about were all of small caliber, such as .22s, both rifles and pistols, and .38 caliber revolvers.[44] On one occasion, a .410 caliber shotgun appeared in the arrest of five seventeen-year-olds,[45] and on another occasion, a "zip gun"[46] was found among some juvenile gang members in a gang battle.[47]

While the news reports on the use of guns suggested that it was a relative rarity, other weapons were reportedly used more frequently. These included knives, bricks, clubs, chains, blackjacks, bayonets, brass knuckles, jack handles, iron bars, pipes, wrenches, and razors. These weapons were mentioned in more articles than guns, suggesting they were a more familiar sight and probably used more often.[48] One of the most dangerous weapons reported during this period was the Molotov cocktail, or gasoline bomb, but it was rarer than guns.[49]

Relative to what had existed, media articles in the 1960s suggested that South Los Angeles experienced a mini arms race, especially for guns and Molotov cocktails. With a few exceptions, the articles contended that the guns remained of small caliber but were accompanied by a notable increase in the use of large-bore shotguns, often sawed off for concealment and maximum dispersal efficiency. On two different occasions in the late 1960s, two high-powered rifles, a .270 Mauser and an M-14, appear in articles associated with criminal but not juvenile street-group activity.[50] According to media reports, other weapons available in the 1950s continued to remain available in the 1960s and were supplemented by an increasing variety of more deadly ones.

Our respondents confirmed what the newspapers reported on guns: they were rarely used before the mid-1950s even though various other weapons might have been. Frank M., who was active in street groups of the late 1940s and early 1950s, explained, when asked about using weapons: "Well, most of the guys had knives, but they were seldom ever used. We'd get into a fight with somebody, and one time, I seen a guy pull a knife and just stick a guy a little bit but never just stab him." A further inquiry about the use of guns during this period brought this comment:

> I know one guy that carried one, and he shot a couple guys. And I heard of one other person, but I didn't know him. But they told me he had a gun. And that was something that you just didn't hear about. It was something that we didn't—we wouldn't . . . It just didn't enter our minds to have a gun. Oh, wait a minute! Once I did have a friend that beat a guy up and pistol-whipped him, pistol-whipped him pretty bad.

The former vice president of the Royal Aces, who was active in the late 1940s and early 1950s, confirmed the rarity of gun use. He pointed out that the assortment of weapons that were available got used every so often, but use was often guided by pragmatism:

Knives, we kept those things in the car. We didn't want to accidentally use them on anybody, not the Royal Aces. We kept them just in case. We kept chains. We kept things you couldn't get arrested for. Anybody could have a chain in the trunk of their car. Bumper jacks, baseball bats, you know; naturally knives, you know, but never any guns. *Never any guns!*

An ethic of pragmatism and wit worked quite well for Bird on an occasion when he was stopped and questioned by the police. They were especially interested in the contents of his trunk. He noted: "See, like, there was the police who stopped me once when I had four bumper jacks. Cop asks me, 'What you doin' with four bumper jacks?' He said, 'You only need one.' I said, 'I got four tires.'"

Miguel D., a probation officer with the South Los Angeles Group Guidance Gang Prevention Program, believed that when groups of juveniles traveled from one neighborhood to another, at least one would carry a "backup gun." This gun was most likely a .32 caliber "Saturday Night Special," to be used only "in a dire emergency."[51] As he explained: "If they walked over to another set or rival set and they were scared that they weren't going to be able to get back without getting screwed up, then they always had the gun." The gun was not necessarily a pistol either but might have been a rifle or shotgun; it was carried as a type of insurance policy.

To suggest that guns were used rarely in street-group member confrontations during this period should not be taken to imply that it was due to their unavailability: guns were readily available. Many respondents contended they often carried a gun or could get one quite easily if needed. Guns were obtainable from various sources, both legal and illegal. They could be bought or traded for on the street, from someone who had stolen them or owned them legitimately; or they might have been borrowed from the homeboy's own home, from a relative who often never knew his gun was missing; or they could have been stolen from a store.[52]

According to Miguel D., some juveniles could be quite creative when it came to transporting guns from one location to another. As the following example of a group of Businessmen, walking through an area where they were vulnerable to attack or arrest, demonstrates, their creativity was amplified by street smarts:

They had to go from Businessmen's territory to this other gang territory, and in between, there was Jefferson High School. They were going to do the gang fighting, okay, and they didn't have cars, so they were walking. At Jefferson High School—I was there—because they were having some kind of awards ceremony, with people, kids, cops, and everything else; but they [the Businessmen] couldn't go around, so they had to go through that area. What they did was to dismantle the shotgun that they were carrying, and everybody carried a piece of it. They walked through the police lines to the other side where they were going. They did what they had to do. They stopped and talked to me. They even stopped to talk to the cops. What they were doing was setting up an alibi.

Shooters and Chumps

Guns were used when circumstances required it. Bird acknowledged that he regularly had a gun available, often a .22 caliber pistol, sometimes hidden in the trunk of his car. His police record shows he had been arrested for carrying a concealed weapon but, as he proclaimed: "I wasn't a shooter." He explained:

> Yeah, in those days, we could get guns if we wanted, but that was something that never crossed my mind. We had them; we had guns, but we didn't use them. You know, it had to be absolutely necessary, somebody really done something wrong and shot somebody or shot at somebody. Then we'd come out with the arsenal. We always had a gun.

To have a gun was one thing, but to use it was something else. And how it was used was different yet again: there was "shootin' at" and "shootin'," Bird remarked. There were plenty of opportunities to shoot someone, if that was your goal, because at least somebody in the crowd had a gun close by. But much of the time, many of the juveniles who had guns would just shoot in the air with it to scare people off, to break up a crowd, or to get them to take notice. Bird claimed that the primary purpose of a gun was as a *dispersal apparatus*; shoot it, and you got everyone's attention. A warning before shooting might be, "You better get hat," which meant to grab your hat and run. Or the warning might be, "You better get steppin' before I get the weapin'."

While most youth wouldn't shoot people, there were "shooters": juveniles who were far more aggressive with their guns. Some of the shooters seemed to be easily provoked, while others just seemed willing to pull the gun out as a threat but not to shoot. Then there were those who would go a bit further and make good on the threat by shooting, even though they never hit anyone: "Well, Lafayette, he was just a shooter, but he never did really shoot anybody. He shot at them," Bird observed.

An escalation in deadly weapon use in the 1960s, as described by the media, happened, but relative to the inactivity of the 1950s and earlier, weapon use may have seemed greater than it actually was. Structurally, more weapons were available in the 1960s than before, while moral proscriptions on their use, although remaining, were weakening. Lafayette, the High Priest from the Slausons, contended that the escalation in use of deadly weapons began in the early 1960s, but it may also have been more situational than indicative of a new trend. He, for instance, was considered by others and by himself to be dangerous, because he always had a gun: "I always knew that I was Jessie James and that I was dangerous. If it came down to it, you know, then I would kill. But I didn't want to kill nobody. It depends on how the disrespect came and how the aggression came towards me."

The former vice president of the Baby Businessmen suggested another option to consider: the use of deadly weapons may have been more characteristic of certain cliques than others. He mentions two occasions when the Baby Businessmen went into the Slausons neighborhood and shot up the pool hall and then returned to shoot up the skating rink, both Slauson hangouts. On a different occasion, when his homeboy had been shot, presumably by a Slauson, the Baby Businessmen retaliated by going into the Slausons' neighborhood, ready for "serious war," but were stopped by the police before things could get going. In the trunk of their car were "three handguns, one chrome sawed-off shotgun, and twenty-four gas bombs." Had the confrontation taken place, it would have been a major media event.

Poop indicated that guns were often available at gang fights where they may or may not have been used. Use was conditional:

> No, we didn't use them if we went to a gang fight. I've used a gun before in a gang fight, like if it's going to be a rumble. If we just happened to go through somebody's neighborhood, we didn't need to carry guns [but might have, just in case]. If they came, we just fight, you know. We had bumper jacks and baseball bats and stuff like that. A lot of guys had knives maybe, but we didn't take guns. We didn't just carry guns.

He confirmed that the guns in the neighborhood were easily obtained—either by purchasing them, as he had done, or by stealing them in a burglary or by "snatching" them from somebody.

Poop was one of the best-armed Slausons: "Well, I had one all the time, a .38 and a .32, Smith and Wessons. And I had a 30-30 Winchester up under the hood of my car—always, every time you saw me." For Poop, these weapons were occupational tools, primarily for professional use rather than for gang activity: "I carried a gun all the time 'cause I was an armed robber. That's how I made my living, so I needed my gun." If gun violence was expected at a particular event, participants often arrived at the event "packing" or having their guns readily accessible someplace. They brought revolvers, rifles, and shotguns. Most people with access to shotguns reported they could obtain large-bore 12-gauge shotguns, which were specifically designed for maximum firepower at relatively close range. Molotov cocktails were used in a limited way, most notably in the hands of a few individuals rather than as a general street-group weapon.

Guns from a Way of Life

Availability of, easy access to, and comfort with guns among South Los Angeles residents and neighborhood street groups should not be surprising. Many of the people who had migrated had southern roots, where guns were commonplace—used for hunting as well as for protection. When they came to the City, their guns came with them. In addition, many residents were World War II and Korean War veterans who held on to some of the weapons they had been issued after returning home. Donny H., a long-time resident, explained it this way:

> If we're talking about the first of the '50s, the Korean War had occurred; a lot of people came back from Korea. Okay, now guns, almost every daddy had a gun. The WW II guys still had their service revolver. The daddys comin' back from Korea still had their service revolver. They might of had more than one gun. Some people, especially if the guys come from the South, who like fishin' and huntin' and stuff, most of them had rifles and everything else.

Los Angeles County probation officer Woodrow C. (W. C.), who lived all his life in South Los Angeles and was a member of a Watts street group in the late 1950s and early 1960s, recalled that the most common weapons used by all residents were knives, razors, pipes, and bumper jacks. Sawed-off shotguns were the most potent weapon and were readily available but were used infrequently. Some street-group members would keep them under the hoods of their cars by the radiator. Zip guns, he noted, were also in evidence, but they were few and used even less frequently than manufactured guns because they were both inaccurate and dangerous to the user. He contended that one reason guns were used sparingly was because of the opprobrium they could bring on everyone in the neighborhood from the police. "They [neighborhood residents] were frightened, knowing that a gun could get them all in trouble."

Most of the guns present in the community, according to W. C., came from the set member's own home or from someone who had taken the gun from their home.[53] He felt that the southern nature of many of the older residents pretty much guaranteed there would be a gun in the house. "All old people were known to have a shotgun. I mean, that was the gun from Tennessee to the backwoods of Mississippi; everybody had a shotgun." Further, household guns were not hidden away in some inaccessible place but were frequently in known, easy-to-get-to locations. "Old people didn't hide their guns. They'd leave them layin' up under their beds or in their closets; they were very available. That's just part of their way of handling guns, coming from the South," W. C. continued.

While guns were commonplace in households, so were baseball bats, chains, knives, and other assorted weapons. Practically anyone who wanted a gun could get one. Availability was facilitated by marketing, by southern lifestyles, and by two wars. Their use was determined by the values of the set/clique culture and by neighborhood norms. We contend that weapons, especially guns, were used infrequently because to do otherwise would violate the come-from-the-shoulders ethic dominant in the community. When they were used, it was because of circumstances that could not be handled with fists alone—or that they were used by a small number of individuals with personal proclivities to using them. Most of the time, guns were the choice of last resort.

Injury and Death

When people fight, especially with weapons, eventually somebody is going to get hurt, some seriously, and some will die. Guns, more than any other weapon, heighten the probability of serious injury and death. Most of the time, fights in South Los Angeles left people with lumps and bumps, although periodically people would be hurt more seriously and, on occasion, would perish from their injuries. In this section, we try to put these issues into perspective.

Newspaper articles suggested that injury and deaths were rare events among youth in the 1940s and 1950s but that their occurrence picked up the pace some during the 1960s. The *Los Angeles Sentinel* reported two stabbings in 1946 among South Los Angeles youth and a homicide in a "gang war" in 1947.[54] In the 1950s, every year, two to four incidents were reported in which a juvenile was injured in a gang or youth-group incident; every other year there was a story about a juvenile who had been killed. During the 1960s, with the exception of 1965 (the year of the Watts Rebellion), four to eight incidents of injury per year occurred, with the deaths of at least two juveniles reported almost every year. Some articles were less clear. They indicated that weapons were used but did not reveal what kind, or whether there was any injury or how serious the confrontation may have been.

Perhaps a more detailed examination of a daily paper like the *Los Angeles Times* might show more incidents than we found in the *Los Angeles Sentinel*, but we doubt it. When the *Times* did report on violence, it often wasn't clear in which area of the City it occurred. A careful examination of LAPD and LASD statistics on these phenomena might be more fruitful—but, since data on gang-related incidents were not kept until the 1970s, separating killings between gang and nongang juveniles would be difficult.[55] We suspect that further analyses of a daily newspaper or the discovery of accurate law-enforcement data would not change the overall theme we found in the *Sentinel*: mostly low incidents of serious injury and death in the early years, increasing gradually as the years progressed.

Supporting our conclusions are verifications by community people, who largely confirm the *Sentinel* reports of low death and injury rates. Barry Wa., from the Junior Businessmen, and county probation officer W. C., commenting on the 1950s and early 1960s, both observed that people were "seldom killed," although stabbings or cuttings were somewhat common. The idea was not to seriously harm someone but to make a statement—often enforced by the set—to let your opponent know you had beaten him but to do it in a manly way. The cowardly use of a gun was a negative reflection on the individual as well as on the neighborhood. W. C. elaborated:

> The intention was to break somebody's jaw, but not to take somebody out. To hurt a person to where those bruises is gonna reflect on his particular image in the neighborhood—he got his ass kicked. But to kill somebody, I mean, a lot of people within your own group, they say, "You coulda dealt with that better than that." Even a lot of gangs, when they see certain members of the gang fight in a coward way, they put him down.

Shooting someone may have been prevented by the southern Christian religious values of many residents, holding to the doctrine of "Thou shall not kill." W. C. felt that "the religious base took death very seriously." Shooters might be shunned by their community or by their friends, who "would back away" because the shooting "tears the gang down" and tears down all who might be associated with the shooter. "Gangs didn't do a whole lot of cold-blooded killing," and what killing they did do was often unintentional. While a stabbing could lead to death, it did not have the same certainty that a shooting did. W. C. noted that when a killing took place, there may have been "some intent," but there was "no premeditation." From his perspective, killings took place in the heat of passion, without forethought, due to a fight that got out of hand and that may have been facilitated by alcohol.

Probation officer Billy P., also a long-time South Los Angeles resident, concurred with W. C.; the killings were few. But he added a twist. He suggested that killings of neighborhood juveniles increased in the mid-1960s, not so much as a result of the gangs getting more violent but as a result of the police shooting gang members who they believed may have been involved in the increase of neighborhood crime: "Death started coming up more or less in the mid-'60s. I think a lot of that was also due to the fact that the gangs started robbing and doing a lot of other things. A lot of them were getting killed by the police." The observations of residents in the neighborhoods about their community are consistent with the data on violent crime nationwide. According to the Uniform Crime Reports of the FBI, most crime, including violent crime, was on the rise during the 1960s, and law enforcement took more aggressive actions to deal with these increases.[56] Violence is often reciprocal.

It was neither rare nor was it the norm for badly injured bodies to remain after street groups fought. Dead bodies were rare. The occurrence of either badly injured or dead attracted attention and left memories and reminders of the danger of fights. Ameer, from the Businessmen, discussing the aftermath of some of that bruising on his brother, suggested that he resembled a wounded warrior: "My brother Wallace—he's a gangbanger. He's been stabbed and shot. He got battle scars on him like a killed guy. He got a bullet in his foot; he got a bullet in his hand; he got a bumper jack scar across his forearm and got stab wounds in his neck."

A factor that may have kept Wallace and others in the neighborhood alive was the relatively small size of the communities and the subsequently large degree of personal ties and interactions among the people. There was a web of group affiliations[57] spread across a significant number of neighborhoods affecting not only the families of the combatants but also those who knew them. A death to one was felt throughout the neighborhood and mourned by many. The death was of a person others recognized and perhaps loved: it was somebody's son, someone's lover or husband, someone's father, brother, uncle, cousin, or friend. The dead were not simply detached, disreputable, or anonymous no-name somebodies no one knew, who just happened to be in the neighborhood at the time of their demise. The killings were of real people, who were much more than a dehumanized statistic to their communities.

Neighborhood Role Call

Of the neighborhood members who died before 1965, some died because of gang fights, or as a result of the aftermath of those fights, in a retaliation, but many also died from personal, non-gang-related behavior.[58] We have compiled two tallies, one for neighborhood members who died as a result of gang-related issues, the other for neighborhood members who died over non-gang-related issues. These tallies make no attempt to be complete; nor are they intended to comport with the assorted police definitions of "gang-related" killings but rather are indicative of the circumstances under which known people died and how even some of the most notorious community fighters often died ignominious or, simply, natural deaths.[59] The death of a street-group member should not be considered, by default, gang related.

  I. *Gang related deaths:* Bird estimated that approximately ten Slausons, out of several thousand members, were killed from the beginnings of Slauson in 1950 until 1970, due to gang activity. These include the following:
     1. Treetop: Chinaman's first cousin, killed in May 1962, stabbed by set members from Watts. He bled to death waiting for the ambulance.[60]
     2. Roger Casey: killed in 1961, by a Compton gang.
     3. Pumpkin: killed in 1961, by a Compton gang.
 II. *Non-gang-related deaths:* These include gang members who were involved in personal non-gang-related issues, suicides, or from natural causes:
     1. Chinaman: Big Slauson, died of natural causes while in prison, early 1990s.
     2. Horseshoe: killed in 1967, shot in the back, near the pool hall on 42nd and Central, in an apparent gambling quarrel.[61]
     3. Charlie Pitts: from Watts, shot in Temple City by a White man who thought Pitts was pimping the man's wife.
     4. Lawrence Sanders: a.k.a. Spartacus, a president of the Gladiators, died of a drug overdose.
     5. Crump: from Slauson, drug overdose.
     6. N. D.: from Watts, shot in the mouth in 1965, by someone running from him who shot back over his shoulder to hit him.
     7. Floyd: from the Gladiators, killed in 1965, by someone at a party.
     8. Eugene: Little Slauson, May 20, 1963, killed in a robbery.
     9. Bobby Moore: Baby Slauson, killed in a car accident in 1967.
     10–14. Babe Brother, Wolf, Jerry Ellis, Eddie Davis, and Jeff Vercher: all from Slauson, all suicides.
     15. Luku Wise: Ross Snyders, died peacefully in New Orleans in the mid-1980s.
     16. Roach: Little Slausons, died from natural causes in 2016.
     17. So So: killed in a robbery.
     18. Edward Fuller: Big Slauson, killed in 1960, personal.

From Bottles to Bullets

What about drive-by shootings, a phenomenon that dominated the front-page headlines on gangs in the 1980s?[62] While cities like Chicago have had many well-documented cases of gangster drive-by assassinations, beginning in the 1920s, Los Angeles was spared that kind of carnage in its early years. The first reported drive-by in Los Angeles was most likely not a shooting at all but was more accurately a *throw-by*. It involved a bottle, not a bullet, which was thrown from a moving car at a group of youth on the street.[63] A member of the Slausons added the following comments on the infrequency of drive-by shootings before 1965: "Back then, you know, you didn't have to worry about walkin' down the street and a damn car pullin' up and shootin'." Bird elaborated:

> You could walk down the street, and the worst thing you had to worry about was a car pull up with some dudes jumpin' out on you. You had a chance: you could run, you might get away or you could fight, or they might shine it on when they see that you wasn't the one they was lookin' for.

Los Angeles graduated from bottles to bullets in just a few months with a "gang-style shooting" in 1954.[64] Both the *Los Angeles Times* and the *Los Angeles Sentinel* record other instances during the 1950s and 1960s where either shots or Molotov cocktails were dispersed from cars at standing targets. None of this violence was on the order of Chicago's gangster decades; nor did it seem to be especially widespread. Drive-bys were occasional. Bullets from cars broke with the norm for the pre-1965 sets.

Several reasons may account for South Los Angeles's lower incidence of serious drive-bys before 1965. First, the city did not have organized adult-criminal gangs waging wars against one another but rather had juvenile street groups with no connection to the criminal gangs.[65] Second, when the street groups fought, it had little to do with financial issues and far more to do with who did what to whom, when, and where. Fighting was about establishing one's position in a pecking order, and a sneak attack from a car would have been a negation. Confrontations concerned disrespect, not territorial or economic gain. Dispatching a rival from a car did nothing to improve on one's respect. Third, the come-from-the-shoulders ethic held that there was honor in fighting but little honor in shooting.

Finally, there was respect between parent and child, where juveniles were concerned about parental and community disapproval of inappropriate behavior. Lafayette, a Slauson, gave the following response when asked how neighborhood adults viewed the activities of the street groups:

Every now and then somethin' would occur, and they would say, "Oh, why did you all do that?" Like when I got arrested for the gang shooting down on Central and 47th in 64, and my father had to bail me out, and he asked me: "Did you do it, and why did you do it?"

Respect was not lost with proper cause: "But it wasn't a real disgraceful type of activity because the person that was supposed to get shot got shot."

Serious injury and death from interpersonal relations in early South Los Angeles, were relatively infrequent. When they did occur, they involved individual as well as street-group-related issues. The come-from-the-shoulders ethic, though not without its own dangers, both promoted and prevented serious injury and death by encouraging juveniles to respond to acts of disrespect in a manly way—using fists—and by discouraging the use of deadly weapons. Before 1965 juveniles had respect for themselves, their homeboys, their neighborhoods, and their families, and they demanded it in return. It was a time when a strong code of behavior regulated the norm for those who lived in the community.

Cultural norms, social circumstances, and the dominant come-from-the-shoulders ethic contradict the violence-amelioration theory, which, as articulated by Steven Pinker, posits that as our society has matured, our "inner demons" have been silenced, while the "better angels of our nature" have surfaced.[66] Violence in South Los Angeles has not declined, as theorized, but has increased, although "demons" versus "angels" seems a shade hyperbolic.

8

Malicious Mopery on a Public Highway

Crime and Punishment

> Persons of the upper socioeconomic class are more powerful politically and financially and escape arrest and conviction to a greater extent than persons who lack such power, even when equally guilty of crimes.
> —**Edwin H. Sutherland,** *White Collar Crime*

In the early 1960s, Bird was stopped by the police as he was walking on the sidewalk. After a few questions, it became clear that he had not been stopped for anything in particular—rather, it was a *just because* stop. It was soon evident to the police that Bird knew his rights and that they were going to need to come up with a reason other than *just because* if they intended to detain him much further. His query as to why he was being stopped was finally answered with this charge: "Malicious mopery on a public highway."[1] It was as ridiculous a charge then as it seems now, but with serious overtones. He was detained but was soon released, with no record of the encounter. Both Bird and the police knew the charge was absurd, knew it would not go much further than those moments in the street, but also knew that it was a way of reminding him that, despite his popularity, there was still a power greater than his on the streets.[2]

Rare was the respondent who denied involvement in at least some type of illegal or statute-violating activity as a juvenile. Rarer still were the respondents who failed to observe that there was not a lot of crime, especially not a lot of serious crime, on the streets then.[3] There was no denial that crime was a problem before 1965, although, without exception, respondents claimed that the problem was much worse currently than it had been when they were young. Given the "historical amnesia" older generations often suffer when comparing their activities as youth to those of the current generation—a thinking process that makes older generations regularly believe that the current juvenile generation is a lot worse than their own was—our evidence supports their contentions that there was less crime in the years before 1965 then there was at the time of our interviews.[4]

In this chapter, our focus will be on street crime rather than on *suite* crime, or white-collar crime, since, with a few exceptions, most of the crimes committed by set members and those they were aware of were street crimes. There were exceptions. One involved cases of petty fraud in gambling, such as confidence games like three-card Molly, where the goal was to cheat the player out of his money after first convincing him he had a chance to win.[5] These games could end violently when the victim tried to reclaim his money from the cheater. The results often added to the street-crime statistics on assault and robbery and sometimes homicide. A "victimless," though not white-collar crime, was prostitution. Of the two, street gambling was more likely to involve violence, particularly when there was cheating. Both of these victimless crimes were committed so infrequently by juveniles that it would be a distraction to consider them further.[6]

Neighborhood street crimes ranged from juvenile statute violations to petty property crimes to murder, with many more examples and occurrences of the less serious offenses than the more serious ones. There were no offenses that were unique to the neighborhoods; nor were there neighborhoods free of those offenses that existed elsewhere in other large cities. South Los Angeles criminality was likely a microcosm of what was occurring in other working-class neighborhoods in American cities with similar demographics.

How Much Crime and by Whom?

The accuracy of the information on crime in America and its demographic distribution before 1965 receives—at best—an incomplete grade. Researchers examining the history of crime even have trouble agreeing on which period over the last couple hundred years was the most violent.[7] The data are no better for Los Angeles. Numerous books have been written about crime in Los Angeles during the early part of the twentieth century that include reports on murder among political and business figures, labor violence, bombings at the *Los Angeles Times*, racial violence, and mob violence.[8] Excluding our previous discussion on violence among juvenile street groups, there is minimal other research that specifically examined juvenile crime.[9]

Anecdotal media reports on juvenile crime and on crime attributed to youth gangs can be readily found in Los Angeles newspapers and some national publications, suggesting Los Angeles was not immune to being linked to these crimes. Less clear is how much these crimes contributed to the City's overall crime problem and how the data indicating juvenile crime were gathered. At times, the data were weak or speculative. Sometimes speculation was dramatized and authenticated by those with expertise in one area but with no particular qualifications to extrapolate on crime. For example, Donald T. Forsythe, the president of Kiwanis International in 1953, while not commenting directly on juvenile gangs but instead on juvenile delinquency, used his position of authority to claim: "Juvenile delinquency is not only on the increase... but it is now an epidemic and appears to be the worst wave of lawlessness among youth since the Zoot-Suit riots of 10 years ago." He continued: "Youths steal automobiles to commit crimes in them; people are robbed, beaten up, shot, and stabbed." Then in a comparative statement of just how out of control it had gotten in Los Angeles, he commented: "I don't know whether Los Angeles and Chicago are the worst cities now," since he felt all cities were awash in juvenile crime, with one as bad as the other.[10] How did he know? His comments were epistemologically challenged.

Forsythe did not indicate how he gathered his data, except to say that during his Kiwanis years he had worked with clubs that worked with boys, thereby presumably giving him a license to guesstimate. His conjecture was not supported by the official data of the time, since police and social agency estimates put the number of youth from "areas of dense, substandard housing and poverty-stricken people" in Los Angeles who are in gangs at 5 to 10 percent, with only half of those being "really active."[11] With such a small number of gang juveniles being "really active," one has to wonder who the youth were that were committing all the crime Forsythe perceived.

Regardless, the portrayal of juvenile and juvenile-gang crime, by Los Angeles officials, was that they constituted serious and recurrent problems. These depictions were relatively infrequent before 1965, progressively increasing as the City matured. Media narratives on juvenile crime and crime attributed to gangs were primarily based on local justice-agency reports. They usually gained greater traction when they were presented after a dramatic or destructive event or as part of a crime wave, where, like the Zoot-Suit Riots and the Cluff incident, they could arouse "moral panics."[12] Further complicating the picture of who was doing what to whom, when, and where was the limited nature of the justice statistics the media had to work with. In addition to having an inconsistent idea of what constituted a gang, the police did not seem particularly interested in identifying crime by gangs until well after 1965. A brief examination of some of the newspaper accounts that were published before 1965 provides an appreciation of the official position, but likely not a very accurate view of crime.

Talking the Talk without Knowing the Walk

In male prison parlance, "Talking the talk without walking the walk" means that a person talks as if he's cool and down for the cause, but when the time comes to do what he's been talking about, the talker is AWOL. Like a dog that barks loudly but runs the other way when the time for action arrives, the inmate is all talk with no follow-through. This term aptly describes the pattern the officials followed in their gradual discovery of increasing delinquency and gang-related crime in Los Angeles. They barked loudly that delinquency and gang crime were on the rise and then showed almost no follow-through when it came to offering adequate data to back up their claims. While there seems little reason to doubt that youth crime was increasing during the pre-1965 period, information on how much, what kind, and how serious was left to the realm of speculation.

Los Angeles's officials began focusing quite early on the problems juveniles were causing, at times suggesting a city where calamity was near at hand much of the time, if not already present. In 1927, a *Los Angeles Herald and Examiner* article warned that juvenile hall had more cases than it could handle due to a "300 percent" increase over the previous six years.[13] Ten years later, in an effort to prevent delinquency, the same newspaper reported that the "new Los Angeles County Morals Education Committee" was advocating five "preventive rather than curative measures to curb juvenile delinquency."[14] The idea was that through "leadership, training and other character building activities," delinquency could be nipped in the bud, "eliminating" it, or the need for it, "before it occurred." A 1942 article, quoting Chief Probation Officer Karl Holton, made it clear this scheme had not worked, claiming instead that delinquency had increased 22 percent in the past year, 8 percent among girls.[15] Characteristically, the nature of those delinquencies was left unstated. Were they curfew violations, or were they murder, or perhaps something in between? It was left to the reader to impute the spin.

The Los Angeles Herald and Express concluded that by 1941 the police had declared "open war against juvenile delinquency." Necessitating this war were such heinous offenses as the following: a large group of males and females, ranging in age from twelve to twenty-three years old, sitting together in a café near Vernon and Vermont Avenues, drinking soft drinks, while the older youth had liquor on their breath. Mayor Bowron, commenting on this moral outrage afterward, "declared . . . that juvenile delinquency constitutes one of the city's major problems and asked public and police cooperation in checking its increase."[16] One is left to contemplate how much greater depravity might have existed in the City than young adults—with liquor on their breath, sitting with Pepsi-sipping juveniles, since this "crime" seemed unworthy of such furor.

It was not until the 1950s, following the Cluff incident, that the local media began to report a significant escalation in the criminality of juveniles. Lurid front-page headlines like "Hunt Thrills in Dope, Wild Knife Brawls," followed by a subheading stating "Violence and vandalism have reached alarming heights among some of the youth of Los Angeles," were spun to get the reader's attention. High school boys and girls were enjoying "a pop of heroin" together and then using the "deadliest of modern weapons, the automobile," to "tear down the street" together with their "knives, guns, iron rods and Blackjacks." The causes of this alleged serious increase in juvenile crime, according to this report, were the "cold war" with its "spirit of nihilism" and the flourishing of anarchy, "wearing the masks of Fascism and Communism."[17] These headlines might have reaped sought-after attention, titillated the imagination, and sold newspapers, but their melodramatic imagery, in conjunction with spurious etiological explanations, did little to accurately inform the citizenry.

The 1950s experienced increased attention directed to the criminal activities of groups, or "gangs," of juveniles, who, it was argued, were compromising normal social discourse by their criminality. Their behavior was primarily portrayed in the most disparaging of fashions, using jaundiced adjectives that left no doubt as to group's "evil" ways:

> In the streets at night youth has its fling, not with the exuberant revels of time past, but with the violence of gang fights that are really miniature battles, of homes mobbed and invaded by kids as wild-eyed as dervishes conked to the eyebrows on hashish, of girls kidnapped off the streets and criminally attacked, of roving gangs looking for trouble and usually finding it.[18]

A grand jury investigation was begun to look into the "terrorism" the "youthful gangs" had created. Something needed to be done about these "howling mobs" who "stormed" private parties high on the "toxic drug of violence."[19] Other incendiary reports focused on the "harsh facts" that "brutal hoodlumism" and "wanton gang violence" were on the loose while the community "meekly" and "passively" endured it and law enforcement gave it "kid-glove enforcement."[20]

Blame the Communists

Within the communities, the propaganda continued: "Everyone is afraid of the gangs," while "no one dares cross any member of the gang or he may be waylaid and beaten—and even killed—in retaliation."[21] While most of the time gang life is "boring," it was claimed, the gangs do have a "favorite outdoor sport" with rules as follows: "Then begins a pushing and hauling operation in which the victim is shoved from one gang member to another, and the shoving gets progressively rougher until the gang falls on the victim and beats him into unconsciousness." So as to not lose the enormity of the moment signifying the brutality of gangs, the author states that this is "practiced by *all* of them."[22]

Some officials determined that a number of these groups, or "gangs," were preoccupied with what was no doubt an even greater evil than their violence: an alleged connection to communism. An article titled "Commies Stir Up Street Gangs" cited a Captain Ben Stein who—with no documentation—contended, "Communist agitators have done their best to stir up the street gangs." He further stated, "The purpose of such agitators is to create racial tension and destroy faith in democracy."[23] We found no evidence to corroborate Stein's beliefs but solid reasons why such assertions were not only conjectural but probably wrong.[24] Many of the early set members exhibited characteristics similar to what James Short found among Chicago gangs; they were primarily apolitical.[25] A notable exception to this was the affiliation, by some in the 1960s, with the Black Power movement.[26]

Estimates on the amount of juvenile involvement in crime and on whether the crimes may have been gang related varied widely. Hampering these estimates were both the absence of an agreed upon operational definition of what constituted a juvenile gang—or a juvenile-gang or gang-member crime—and specific record keeping by law enforcement on gang-related crime. Regardless, the reports were suggestive of violent and rapacious behavior, as these *Los Angeles Examiner* articles indicate: "25 Youths Held in Wild Gang Battle,"[27] "Youth Gang Shooting Jails Six,"[28] "One Beaten, 6 Held in Youth War."[29] The *Los Angeles Times* adds: "Five Gang Youths Held after Stabbing of Boy 13,"[30] "200 Teen-agers Battle with Fists, Clubs and Knives at Hollywood High,"[31] "75 [juveniles] Jailed in Drive by Crime Prevention Officers during Relays."[32]

A *Newsweek* article published in 1959 elevated Los Angeles's lawlessness above that of New York and Chicago: "Los Angeles . . . is the most crime ridden of the nation's three biggest cities." Without specifying the age of groups involved in Los Angeles crime, although implying that the lawlessness was due to juveniles, the article quotes FBI director J. Edgar Hoover on the City's crime: "The rate of increase in juvenile crime was above the national average."[33] In another *Newsweek* article titled "Who the Teen Killers Are: The Gangs of New York," the authors, when referring to Los Angeles, point out that "a well-organized police intelligence unit watches gang leadership, and when trouble looms, arrests are made selectively."[34]

In 1961, a *Los Angeles Times* article, using data collected by the Group Guidance Section of the Probation Department's Delinquency Prevention Services, gave an estimate of the number of "gang incidents" occurring by area in 1960. Ranging from "minor fights to murder," although not specifying how many of each or what the particular offenses might be, the article reported the following number of incidents:

East Los Angeles—30; Southwest—43; Bellflower—34; Van Nuys—23; El Monte—17; Torrance—15; Huntington Park—14; Long Beach—12; Metropolitan—10; Glendale—1.[35]

In addition to not knowing whether the incident estimates were petty or serious, there was no way to tell what might have actually constituted a gang incident. For example, if a gang member gets into a fight with a nongang member over a girl they both thought was their one and only, is that a gang incident? Suppose both males are gang members—is that then a gang fight? Readers were provided official hypothetical nudges to help them decide. Officials did their best to cast aspersions on the activities of street youth groups and their members, in the most disparaging of ways, utilizing weak references which lacked the clarity necessary to determine just what or to whom they were alluding. They reported conjectural information as factual and imparted credibility to individuals with status who may have had their own agenda or been misinformed.

An Official Perspective

Relying on the mass media for accurate material on crime among youthful street group members before 1965 gives us a picture that is at best suspect and is most likely misleading. The dramatic and predatory images created by them of juvenile street crime achieved such verisimilitude that it is not surprising that some citizens developed a cynical view of group members. An official source of information about crime in the City during this period, the Uniform Crime Reports (UCR) of the FBI, suggests the media may have overstated their case.[36] Table 8.1 is a distribution of offenses reported by the police to the FBI about crime in Los Angeles during 1934–1965. Since the UCR were a work in progress during these formative years, the various changes that were made in its data reporting rendered some crime categories incomplete or modified, creating analytical problems comparing data over the years examined. Several of these issues were encountered creating this table.[37]

The table's data show the total number of offenses reported increased from 1934 to 1965. This could be a reflection of an overall increase in the criminality of Los Angeles residents, although, and most likely, the crime increase is explained by the overall growth in population. That is, there were simply more people around to commit crimes—thus, more people means more crime.[38] A report titled *Migration and the Southern California Economy*, for example, showed the net immigration to Southern California added almost three-quarters of a million people between 1955 and 1960 alone.[39] Josh Sides, in his trenchant historical analysis of Los Angeles's African

American community, writes: "The growth rate of the Black population in Los Angeles from 1940 to 1970 was 1,096 percent."[40]

It is logical to assume that as the City's population increased, so too would the number of crimes. An increase in the reasons for committing additional crime, following growth in the complexity of social relations, could be expected as well. LASD data for homicide, among all of its jurisdictions, indicate the homicide rate increased from .32 in 1960–1961 to .45 in 1964–1965, demonstrating that, at least for homicide, there was a slight increase in incidence per person throughout the County among all age groups.[41] We also found that among the street groups, there was an overall increase in crime and its severity following various social changes associated with urban growth.[42] We hypothesize that change in the criminality among the street-group members was a result of the structural changes they experienced in their neighborhoods.

Data for violent crime in Table 8.1 suggest few of these crimes were committed before 1965. This is especially the case for homicide, which did not even reach triple digits until after the mid-1950s and then stayed below two hundred until 1965. There was a considerable jump in all crime in 1965, quite likely partly due to the Watts Rebellion. The most frequently occurring crimes from 1934 to 1965 were nonserious. They were property crimes, especially burglary and petty theft. While the significance of the growth of crime—and its consequences—should neither be understated nor neglected, these data do not offer a portrait of a city under criminal siege. What crises

TABLE 8.1 NUMBER OF OFFENSES KNOWN TO THE POLICE FOR THE CITY OF LOS ANGELES, CA, 1934–1965

Year	Homicide	Forcible Rape	Robbery	Aggravated Assault	Burglary	Larceny / Theft over $50	Larceny / Theft under $50	Auto Theft
1934	65	228	1,413	490	8,247	2,716	11,825	6,456
1935	93	269	933	462	7,369	2,551	9,519	6,081
1940	86	N/A	2,169	684	10,022	4,337	21,497	8,424
1945	91	N/A	3,776	1,721	11,654	10,088	17,185	10,613
1950	63	N/A	2,280	2,042	10,610	11,210	19,120	4,543
1955	95	N/A	3,049	4,639	17,184	12,873	24,117	7,417
1958	136	1,028	4,622	6,354	31,123	22,513	32,626	13,215
1960	154	1,085	6,068	7,565	36,256	21,417	36,321	15,085
1961	159	1,156	5,729	7,973	35,409	20,912	35,191	14,862
1964	177	987	6,740	8,900	43,362	26,453	40,902	19,532
1965	249	1,268	8,016	9,211	50,771	29,708	42,600	22,136

Source: Compiled from the Department of Justice, *Crime in the United States*, 1930–1969.

were reported by the various social and justice agencies seem to have been more a function of the agencies' agenda than a data-informed crisis.[43] What emerges from the UCR data is an image of crime, in one of the fastest growing cities in America, that did not appear to be much of a problem before the mid-1960s.[44] Our respondents helped confirm the official picture.

White Port and Lemon Juice

Whit, the vice president of the Royal Aces Social Club, described his choice for getting high in the late 1940s and early 1950s:

> WP and LJ, white port and lemon juice—that's what we use to drink when we were young. You drank just what they call the "poison," on the top. You pour a can of lemon juice [real lemon juice, not lemonade] inside the bottle [of port wine] and shake it up, and you had a terrific drink, man. And you get a terrific high till the next morning. In my little clique, it was about four or five guys, and we flipped [a coin] to see who would get the poison. The odd man get the poison, and you better not drink no more than your share. Fine times was comin'.

Such imbibing was a socially acceptable behavior for his clique, as it was for other cliques, although it was an activity primarily engaged in by males.

We do not want to underestimate the gravity of the effects that alcohol and drug use played among some set members by suggesting the sets were organizations that primarily held tea parties as their major social activity. This is as detrimental to an understanding of them as are the claims that their main goals were to generate murder and mayhem when they were high on an assortment of controlled substances. Without exception, all of our respondents indicated that alcohol, as well as various drugs, were present in their neighborhoods when they were growing up. All were aware of the existence of hard drugs,[45] of their effects, and of people who used them. South Los Angeles was hardly a place of abstinence before 1965.[46]

John S., who was born in 1920 and lived near 28th Street and Central Avenue, explained that there was a lot of marijuana around when he was growing up: "For five cents, you could buy a joint as big as a cigar." It was rolled in brown cigarette paper and looked like a cigar too. Much of the available marijuana then was grown in someone's backyard rather than being imported. The first time John S. was aware of the "hard stuff" though was when he heard about the actor Bela Lugosi dying of an overdose in 1956.[47] That you could die from hard drugs was enough to deter John S. from experimenting with them, although not enough to keep him away from marijuana. A respondent from the Slauson neighborhood recalled being aware of the following drugs when he was a teen in the early 1960s: "red devils, truinal [sic], weed, bennies or whites, goofballs, gorilla biscuits, stumblers, and 'ho-makers.'" But he added, "I didn't know nothing about no cocaine." Before 1965, cocaine, which was marketed then in its powdered form, was relatively rare in all neighborhoods.[48]

Most respondents asserted that when they were young, they did not use hard drugs, and smoked cigarettes sparingly,[49] but they acknowledged considerable familiarity with alcohol and marijuana.[50] Two teetotalers told of having very difference experiences in the presence of friends who smoked marijuana. One, a nonset member, who grew up in the close-knit community of 73rd Street, or Sin Street, was self-described as "not easily influenced." His friends would often taunt him, by blowing smoke at him and trying to give him a "contact high." The other person, a Baby Slauson, who contended he "did not participate in any form or fashion with smoking, drinking, or drugs or anything," asserted that his friends would not smoke marijuana around him because they had too much respect for him. "All I heard they did was drink ale and wine. But they would keep the weed from me if I would come in the house or if they knew I was coming. They wouldn't smoke it.... That's how much respect they had for me," he claimed. While neither of these experiences necessarily characterized the norm between users and nonusers, the experiences do suggest considerable neighborhood variability existed.

Drug News as Histrionics

As director of the Federal Bureau of Narcotics from 1930 to 1962, and with pharmaceutical company blessings, Harry Anslinger led the charge to criminalize non-Whites, especially Blacks, for drug use.[51] With comments like, "Reefer makes darkies think they are as good as White men" and "Marijuana causes White women to seek sexual relations with Negroes,"[52] he left no doubt about his racist motivations. While he was largely successful in developing myths about the associations between non-Whites and drugs, serious research has not backed any of his claims, including our study in South Los Angeles.

Drug use among the Slausons was limited, while a few also denied their use of beer and wine. Chinaman explained, "Back then, didn't nobody mess with drugs. Their main high was white port and lemon juice and Rainier Ale. Drugs wasn't even introduced into the community." One female respondent, who had been partying a lot during the 1960s and early 1970s, in the company of members from various sets, added that beer, wine, and some occasional weed were in use by some Slausons at the club's parties in the early 1960s but no hard drugs. She claimed, "I didn't see anything other than the drinking of beer and wine and maybe some weed. If there was anything other than what I saw, I don't know. I didn't even see any hard liquor."

Justice department officials we interviewed from two different agencies confirmed these observations and suggested that limited drug use applied more generally than to just the Slausons and other sets; it was a community thing. Long-serving deputy probation officer and street group expert Miguel D. understood that drinking problems were much more common than drug problems among the people he worked with: "Drinking was evident everywhere, but drugs were rare." E. V., an LAPD officer in the neighborhood for more than twenty years, remarked that "narcotics weren't that heavy, and coke wasn't around," although "heroin and weed" were, but "not that much."[53]

Local officials took considerable editorial license in proclaiming there was extensive drug use in South Los Angeles, especially by juveniles and by gang members. Bird remarked that the media created an impression, accepted by the public, of all set members being substance abusers: "They think that all people who were gang members drink, smoke cigarettes, smoke weed, drop pills, shoot heroin, and everything; and that's a lie."[54] But the association of gangs with drugs was an early indelible image created with tactics designed to have it take hold with bulldog tenacity.

A few examples from the media's reporting on drugs and gangs makes their position clear. When a twenty-seven-year-old man on Central Avenue was shot and caught with $32,000 worth of heroin, the headline was: "Dope-Peddling Suspect Shot and Captured."[55] When five seventeen-year-olds were found to have "several thousand sedative pills" in their car, the headline was "One May Die from Using Pills."[56] After several young men were arrested by the Newton Street police with "marijuana cigarettes" in their possession, the headline read: "Police War on Narcotics Jails Seven." The next line began: "Continuing a relentless war on dope peddlers and users of the drug." The article explained how the "war" was progressing.[57] Finally, this: "L.A. Teen-Age Gangs Feed U.S. Dope Rings."[58]

We are not questioning whether these events happened but are suggesting that the spin put on them helped to cast drug involvement in the most pejorative of ways, was an additional criminalizing label for non-Whites, and benefited from the racist invective propagated by Anslinger, attempting to make it appear as if drugs were ubiquitous in the community. We found the situation among street-group members to vary considerably from the images portrayed in the propaganda.

While practically a teetotaler, when he did indulge, Bird rarely consumed anything stronger than an occasional beer. He was not alone, as he discussed in his own experiences with substances and then compared them to the experiences of another righteous Slauson:

> I never smoked cigarettes, never smoked weed, and never used drugs. I had a taste of whiskey about twice in my life, and I didn't like it; and my nickname is Thunderbird too. I drank some wine, but I quit drinking wine by '59. I know Crook's the same way; he never done none of that.

Bird's eschewing of intoxicants was another reason why he attracted so many admirers. By suggesting strength, and by demonstrating value in being in command of one's faculties, he was his own man. He could be counted on to be present when required and ready to take care of business. As he proclaimed, he was as "clean as a broke-dick dog."

Peeling the Grape[59]

Experience with alcohol varied widely among set members, from regular drunkenness to abstinence. A Los Angeles probation officer who grew up in Compton with the street groups felt that excessive alcohol use among juveniles was a major problem and it had a negative impact on families: "Yeah, drunkenness, there was a lot of drunkenness. Parents were always at the police station picking up kids. My brother use to lay out all the time drunk; parents have to get him." Most street groups did not want as members those who drank heavily and could not be relied upon; nor was such behavior condoned in most families. The president of the Baby Businessmen explained that the family position on excessive drinking was one of intolerance: "My brother came home drunk one time, and she [their mother] busted him in the head with my boxing trophy." Bird added: "Shiiit, I was thirty-one years old before any of my relatives ever saw me drinking—and that was a beer."

Roslyn said that neither alcohol nor drugs were involved when she was a teen at informal Slauson gatherings. These were typically school ditching parties held by her and Bird's friends at her auntie's house, when her auntie wasn't home: "We wore my auntie's rug out dancing and waiting for the guys to come by. And we weren't involved in drinking or smoking or no drugs or anything like that." Some adults permitted these parties because the attendees were respectful and didn't break things, do illegal things, or tear up the house.

Larger parties had greater diversity, where various substances were in fact often evident. Although used by some, their use was by individual choice rather than being an overriding characteristic of the party. Assertions that these were drug and alcohol fests carried on by neighborhood gangs where everyone was loaded are flawed. Drugs and alcohol were likely present, but their use was far more nuanced than many reports might have us believe, whether ditching parties or otherwise. Some used, some didn't, as Bird explained:

> Ditching parties was always at somebody's house whose mama wasn't home. You'd go there and meet so many girls and so many guys. Somebody would go to the store and get the beer and wine. Somebody would come in and have a roll of red devils. Somebody else had weed or something. Certain people had certain things. Some people didn't do none of it but drink water. So, you know, when they say juveniles or as a gang member they all do this and that and the other, that's a lie. You can't say that because it's not true. I can fill up the Shrine Auditorium with people who did none of the above. The worse they ever done was smoke a cigarette.

Bad News Drugs

Concomitant with adult disapproval of alcohol and drugs for their juveniles was another central reason why these substances were often eschewed: they could render the user pathetic and unreliable.[60] Observing a wasted tough dude get made a fool of when he was high made a permanent impression on the young Bird. It convinced him never to be in a position to display the kind of weakness he had witnessed. He explained:

> I saw enough of other people taking those red devils. I saw an incident when I was in the eighth grade in '56. A dude came to school loaded off red devils. And I hadn't seen a red devil before. I did not see a red devil until '61. But they said he was loaded off "reds," you know. He was a bad dude. But he came to school that day and was messin' with this little ol' poot-butt, and the poot-butt wore him out. And I was thirteen years old, and I was a little guy; and I weigh no more than about 105 pounds or something. This dude was one of the toughest dudes in school. But he was loaded, and I said, 'Gol-leyyy!" And he got all beat up. I had seen him fight before, you know; he was a bad motherfucker.

Further confirmation of the inherent debilitating effects of drugs came when Bird saw this same bad dude return to school a few days later, now sober: the results were dramatically different. Bird recounted: "About four or five days later, he came back. Man, he damn near killed the dude that had whooped him. And then I'd seen that his condition had changed so much, and I said that whatever that was that he had, I don't want any of that stuff.

I don't ever want to be like that." A respondent from Sin Street, discussing the reasons why he didn't use reds or any other drugs, endorsed Bird's position: "I see guys, they was dropping reds at the time, and they'd be so fucked up that the littlest cat on the block could whoop their ass."

Bird took a comparable position on cigarette smoking. His dislike for them had less to do with their pharmacological toxicity than it did with their disabling nature. In his words:

> I always kept myself in prime condition. See, I noticed that dudes who smoked—I seen them fight, and then I seen them run out of gas. They was whoopin' the shit out of a dude, and the dude was like finished, and then he [the smoker] would run out of gas. The dude lost the fight because he was short winded. So I figured a lot of this shit out early.

Poop was a bit more sanguine when he talked about drugs and alcohol use. Describing what he did on a typical summer evening, he commented: "Well, you know, actually man, we stand on the corner and sing and drink Silver Satin and Kool-Aid and maybe smoke a little weed." He was well aware of the various drugs available on the street: "Well, I can tell you exactly what kind of drugs were around when I was a kid: red devils, yellow jackets, truinals, bennies, and marijuana." But he did not use any of them. He began using drugs in the penitentiary and was twenty-seven years old before he smoked his first cigarette, also in the penitentiary. Poop's understanding of the debilitating effects of hard drugs echoed Bird's. He noted:

> One time, Shackdaddy got full of these red devils. And this guy we know name of Duck was down in front of the Savoy Skating Rink. And Shackdaddy kept bothering Duck, and they got into a fight, and Duck whooped him. I mean, Duck beat him up, but Shackdaddy kept on fightin'. You know, it's [red devils] a pain pill, and he [Shackdaddy] didn't know he was getting his ass whooped like he was getting it, 'cause he couldn't feel it. And so he kept comin' back at Duck and kept coming back at him. So Duck picked him up and threw him down on the sidewalk, and his face was all bleeding and stuff. And Duck said, "Man, I'm gonna beat him up for so long so many times. I'm gonna go home before I have to kill Shack." And Duck started walking away. Then Shackdaddy found this big rock and threw the rock and hit Duck in the back, and he [Shackdaddy] said, "That's right—run, you coward, 'cause if you come back, I'm gonna give you the same thing." And Shackdaddy standing there bleeding, nose broke, bleeding like a pig.

Curiously, Shackdaddy wasn't considered a pariah by his peers for his excesses but was tolerated as someone with problems. Duck did what many others would have done—he punished Shack for irritating him but left before he had to hurt Shack worse than what he already had. The punishment was not because there was any glory in whooping someone who was so messed up or even teaching a lesson but because it was necessary to stop him.

Almost everybody agreed that alcohol use, but especially drug use, was primarily done by males with male friends and that females were far less likely than males to use either. The vice president of the Royal Aces noted: "You could count the girls on one hand that did dope." Bird added, "You could count the girls that smoked cigarettes or drank alcohol like that." There were certainly females who used drugs, alcohol, and smoked, but when they did, they did it with a male they were involved with and rarely or never on their own or with girlfriends.[61] These values began to change in the early 1960s, especially after 1965, as the opprobrium associated with usage weakened.

An Indefinite Number of Drugs: A Differential in Use

Association with drugs in the neighborhood, especially hard drugs, had temporary in-group qualities to it, but drug users did not constitute a separate subculture.[62] There was no evidence of any street group before 1965 organized around the use or sale of hard drugs. As Whit explained: "Only a special selective group of people fool around with heroin and cocaine." It was a small group, sometimes no more than two, "a very, very select group," who would often "disappear" somewhere for a while and then later rejoin the larger group or party. Not everybody knew what the departees were doing, although those who did know let it slide as something they just did. Drug users formed groups of convenience, developing for a minute[63] to consume or sell among themselves and then disbanding once their agendas were completed[64] to participate again in the larger community, albeit sometimes with stigma.

Many in the neighborhood were aware of the existence of heroin, but it was used by none of our respondents or any of their associates. Poop's discussion of heroin was typical of what we found:

> When we heard about heron [sic], the only people we knew about who knew about heron was Charlie Parker and Lady Day [Billie Holiday]. Then, I remembered when somebody told me that Ray Charles was hooked on drugs or heron or something. That stuff didn't faze us. We didn't have what you call hard drugs. I remember when Tim-

othy Leary made that acid 'n' stuff; you know, we didn't mess with that stuff. We always thought it was a White boy's high. I found out later on that a lot of Black people started using heron. Maybe they had been doing it all the time, some of them. After I got out of the penitentiary, and when I came home, cocaine was getting kind of popular.

Heroin appears to have been used by a few non-street-group people. Those who were thought to use heroin were considered neighborhood pariahs, especially if they were believed to be "hypes." Whit explained: "A hype wasn't accepted on the social level with the rest of us because, you know, nobody want to sit around someone nod and slobber at the mouth, scratchin' 'n' stuff." Whit added a second reason to account for the pariah status of hypes when he noted that bringing them around invited theft of your things: "You didn't want to bring a hype into your house; they steal. They rip off their own buddies sometimes."

Frank M., who was born in 1928 and grew up on 18th and San Pedro Streets, observed that there were a lot of drugs around in his neighborhood. "There was heroin, yellow jackets, and something they called 'bobbytods,'" which he understood to be a mixture of heroin and cocaine. He knew of a few people who used heroin, but he stayed away from it because he had read about its dangers: "When I was a kid, I use to read a lot. I had read about heroin and mostly morphine, and I'd heard about doctors on morphine. I knew people could get hooked foolin' with that stuff." He knew that heroin was used by both Black and Mexican people in his neighborhood but that most stayed away from it due to their awareness of its harmful effects. "People sort of looked down on using heroin; we called the persons 'hypes.' We kind of looked down on them because most of us thought it was stupid, and we realized it was habit-forming, and those guys were stealing, and you couldn't trust them."

While drug sales were neither a street-group activity nor a reason for their existence, this was partly due to sales not being a lucrative endeavor. Poop explained that the primary reason he didn't sell weed was because he couldn't make enough money at it, fast enough, to satisfy his needs. Drug sales were an individualistic entrepreneurial process. There were those who were considered "big dealers," but their sales were usually transacted with people they knew, thus minimizing the risk of arrest and, consequently, limiting their market. As Whit observed:

> Now the dealers in those days wasn't actually big dealers. You had your big dealers—but if a guy bought a big quantity of drugs and marijuana, well, he knew enough guys in his clique that he could

buy enough for himself and spread the rest around to guys he grew up with. There was no chance of getting busted because you didn't sell to nobody that you didn't know.

While not large, proceeds from these sales seemed sufficient for the sellers to continue selling.

In sum, an assortment of hard drugs was available for a long while, but they were used by relatively few of the residents. Ignorance and wariness, as well as general indifference, seem to have characterized the attitudes most juveniles had toward hard drugs. This includes cocaine, with no one using or knowing someone who did.[65] Our data suggest hard drugs played a minimal role both in the neighborhoods and in the lives of street-group members before 1965.

A Ubiquitous Herb

Hard drugs were one thing; marijuana was another: it permeated most South Los Angeles neighborhoods. Frank M. observed, "Just about everybody you saw, Mexicans and Blacks, all smoked weed." It was "prevalent; everybody had it, and you could get it anywhere you wanted to." The circumstances under which marijuana was consumed suggested a nonstigmatized neighborhood acceptance: "It would be just somebody had some. You could be gamblin', or you could be walkin' down the street or on your way to a party or goin' to the beach. It was just anytime you felt like it and somebody had it, you would just smoke it." The one notable exception to where it was not used was around girls: "In fact, we tried to hide it from them; we didn't let them know," Frank stated.

Marijuana was sold in two different forms: either loose in a can or in individual joints. Half a can cost around six dollars, but there was a discount on a full can, only ten dollars. Empty Prince Albert tobacco cans were the cans of choice, producing thirty-five to forty joints that could be sold at fifty cents each. Shorting a customer with less marijuana than negotiated was considered an egregious error, with consequences: "If you didn't get between thirty-five and forty joints, you go lookin' for the guy. If you came up short and if you came up with twenty-five joints, you go lookin' for him, and he better produce it," Frank M. asserted. Proper packaging required the marijuana to be tightly packed in the can. Sellers knew that, and they knew when they were shorting the customer; it was deliberate and readily punishable in a community with a close web of group affiliations.

Another mistake, similarly punishable by a thumping, was to sell poor-quality marijuana, as Frank continued: "It had to be good, see. If somebody sell you something bad, they had to stay out of sight. And they knew you were lookin' for them." Money was tight. While economic motivation was the primary driver for sellers, cheating created real problems for the frauds: "See, we didn't have a lot of money, and everybody, or maybe two or three guys, would put in a couple of dollars apiece or somethin'; then everybody would go lookin' for him [if the quality was poor]." When the cheated buyers found the seller, either he righted the wrong, or he got an "ass whooping."[66] As a neighborhood entrepreneur with a limited market, a negative sales report would discourage potential customers. In neighborhoods where there were few strangers, this was an effective deterrent for many sellers.

Lowriders' Discretion

Lefon, a member of the Serfs car club and elder statesman in the community, reported that lowriders did not use any drugs but would drink beer on occasion if it was Rainier Ale. Born in the 1930s and associated for most of his life with cars, car clubs, and such community car club legends as "Big Red," Lefon was a neighborhood sage. He explained, "Drugs were around but not around lowriders." According to Lefon, drug use was most prevalent among "dudes around pool halls and night clubs." It was the atmosphere, the music in those establishments, that was conducive to drug use, especially by musicians. Lefon observed: "If you were influenced by jazz, then you was basically gonna smoke weed or heroin, because that type of musician, they seemed to think, made them better. Musicians did the heavy drugs 'cause it took them to another dimension, the fifth dimension, or the twilight zone." Obviously not all aficionados of jazz used drugs, but many of them did, and one is often found associated with the other in much of the literature. South Los Angeles wasn't much different than other areas with a significant jazz culture. Lefon's perception of this relationship was no doubt influenced by his proximity to the jazz center of early Los Angeles, Central Avenue.[67]

Although it seems obvious that driving while loaded would be a primary motivation for lowriders to teetotal—which it was—Lefon identified two other factors of equal importance in making this decision: religion and parental disapproval. In his words: "In those days, they had strong religious beliefs and the fear of God put in them, so they were afraid of drugs. Our parents influenced us too; they protected us from drugs." Both of these ethical checks were mentioned by other respondents as deterrents not only from drugs but as more general deterrents from things morally inappropriate and criminally wrong. These proscriptions should not be interpreted as commanding neighborhood religiosity or powerful family structures, as much as just an overall respect for the church and parental authority.

Rather than finding South Los Angeles to be an area rife with alcohol and drug usage generating numerous related crimes, we instead found neighborhoods aware of these substances but with considerable variation in their use and acceptability. Respondents were unaware of drunken criminal rampages or rampant drug-induced criminality there, while among powerful sets, like the Slausons, drug abusers or problem drinkers were not welcome. Drug-related crimes, including selling or using controlled substances and petty theft to support usage, existed, with alcohol and marijuana being the most commonly used substances. Alcohol was sometimes used to excess, mostly by males, with the associated belligerence occurring in predictable ways, while marijuana produced pleasurable experiences—again, for primarily male consumers. Driving while intoxicated or high occurred but with consequences difficult to determine.[68] When females used any of these substances, they did so in the company of their main man rather than in a group setting.

There was no evidence for drug sales as a large money-making enterprise; nor did any of the sets or cliques—as a group—engage in sales. Selling drugs was a low-incentive individual endeavor because of small profit margins, engaged in by either set or nonset members. Given the opprobrium associated with hard drugs, it would be illogical to conclude that street groups were joined to get access for use or markets to sell them or for protection from other sellers. Regardless of official theatrics, with the exception of marijuana, illegal substance abuse and use flew under community radar before 1965.

Forced Sex

From 1934 through 1965, the UCR data indicate that "rape" or "forcible rape," often termed "forced sex," was an offense juveniles throughout the nation engaged in infrequently. For example, there were national totals of 237 arrests in 1934 of juveniles for "rape" and 1,946 arrests of juveniles for "forcible rape" in 1965. We do not know what percentage of these numbers involved South Los Angeles adolescents, but if it was proportionate to the juvenile population, it was a small number and consistent with the dearth of agency reports on its occurrence.

We found limited evidence of forced sex among street-group members.[69] There were at least two reasons why this may have been the case: first, rape was a public display of failure in the all-important world of adolescent cool, and second, it was considered morally repugnant.[70] Homeboys who were successful "ladies' men" were respected by their peers, both male and female, for their suavity and for their endearing personalities. Those lacking these abilities were accorded less esteem than their more socially adept associates. As explained by one probation officer: "I wouldn't say it [rape] was nonexistent; it just wasn't popular, because it was sort of like admitting that you didn't have the social skills to seduce a girl on your own."

The second reason why forcible rape was uncommon is related to the respect accorded families. To rape someone was to violate not only the person but her family as well. The violation was perceived as one that could have been against one's own family or one's relative or friend's family; it could have been personal. Such defilement was communally condemned. A Junior Businessmen explained the community condemnation this way: "That man had to be a weirdo. You know, 'cause everybody got sisters, aunties, cousins, a mother. . . . We had better morals about ourselves than takin' something from somebody like that."

Many neighborhood women feared forcible rape, understanding it as a graver threat than males did. One woman felt that the risk of rape was greater for unaffiliated females than for those with boyfriends or brothers in a street group. As she explained: "If you didn't know somebody, you stood a chance of being raped during that time." An experience she had had at a party where someone "grabbed" her and "threw [her] in a car" gave substance to her worries. The assault stopped quickly, as soon as the perpetrator found out who she was: she had both a boyfriend in a Slauson clique and an older brother in the neighborhood.[71] In this capacity, the street groups offered protection for females, by enforcing sexual morality for those with a street connection. Mess with one of the groups' women, lose face and get whooped, perhaps badly.

There is another reason why rape might have appeared to be so infrequent: the matter of definition. Behavior that might have legally been termed "rape" might not have been perceived as such among some neighborhood residents, thus not something that needed to be reported. A forty-three-year-old probation officer who had grown up in Watts and Compton said he was aware of a behavior that sometimes occurred at parties, often preceded by considerable drinking, called "rat piling." His description of the behavior seems to fit the legal definition of rape, although the participants did not appear to feel it was criminal. As he recounted:

> Rapes were not rapes, as in the form as they describe rapes. Particularly, you know, in light of the fact that many of the girls during that period knew the guys that raped them. They would be at a party, and they'd been drinkin', or . . . and, you know, three or four guys rat piled them or rat-packed them, pulled a train on them. It was not really like rape. It was not like cold rape. But it was a form of rape, a form of gang rape.

Such behavior was seldom reported to the police because it seemed to fall within the range of community norms of acceptable sexual activity, albeit at the far end of that range. In addition to not trusting the police to do anything about it, and the well-known efforts of the justice system to embarrass the victim, there was another twist: a community norm accepting the notion that the girl(s) involved must have had at least some complicity in the sexual encounter, or it would not have occurred. As explained by the probation officer: "It's the sort of thing that everybody knew about in the community. The old people would look at it like, you know, your daughter was raped and she must have had something to do with it." Most residents considered forced sex with a stranger to be rape but were reluctant to use this term to describe the varieties of adolescent sexual activity occurring within their community among juveniles who were familiar with one another.

This rationale was not limited to South Los Angeles but occurred in middle-class White communities as well; to think otherwise is to misunderstand how behaviors we shun are more easily essentialized to groups viewed as "other" than to those recognized by the dominant political structure as "us."[72] Was forced sex rare, common, or nonexistent in South Los Angeles? We may never know. Mostly, it was not talked about.

An Occasion for Violence

Violence came in many forms. The justifications for violence were rooted in community values of appropriateness, which at times tolerated violence but at other times did not. Sometimes violence followed a pattern of escalating passions that resulted in eventual police intervention and formal punishment. Poop was one of those youngsters who seemed capable of finding occasion for its use somewhat more frequently than average. On one of those occasions, when he was sixteen or seventeen years old, a fight erupted between him and a doorman at a movie theater over a disagreement on the appropriateness of his return to the theater. The altercation was serious enough that someone could have been hurt badly, if not killed, had events evolved a bit differently.

Poop had taken his little brother and sister to the movie and then exited the theater for a moment without them. He expected to be let back in at no charge because this had been the norm, but this doorman chose to differ and not let him back in. Poop became upset, concerned that his younger siblings were now in there without him because of the doorman's unreasonable actions. "We started arguin' and carryin' on, and I called him a bunch of names 'n' shit. He wouldn't let me go back in there and get my brother and sister out," Poop proclaimed. The argument soon escalated into a fight, which in turn led to a battle, and then to a mini arms race. As Poop recounted the events:

> Then he [the doorman] pushed me, and I pushed him back. He was a bigger guy 'n' stuff like that, but I didn't care. The security guard

came, and he told me to get off the property. And I said, "Man, I'm not goin'. My mama sent me down here with my little brother and my little sister, and I'm not goin' without them." And the guy pulled his billy club out and commenced to whackin' me on my legs 'n' shit with it, you know. I couldn't allow this, so I rushed him, and we got to fightin' and carrying on—got into a serious fight. So the leg thing [whacking] wasn't working no more, so he went to popping me upside my head. And I couldn't fight that; he was a man; I was a teenager. He was a big ol' strong man with a club in his hand, and I had to break and run. So I split and, um, left my little brother and sister. I came home, and I was cryin' and carryin' on and got the baseball bat and went back up there. My mother kept trying to stop me, and I ran off back up there; she followed me up there.

I gave him a serious ass whoopin'. After I got through whoopin' him, the police came up there, and they had me. They broke us up, but they didn't take my bat. I was still hurt, you know. I had knots 'n' stuff growin' on my head by now, and I was cryin'. And I was embarrassed more than anything else: he whooped me in front of them girls. I was really hurt too. He [the security guard] had a gun too. When he pulled the gun, the police got in front of us. And they was talkin' to the guy and tellin' him to put the gun up or they was goin' to shoot him. Matter of fact, they took the gun from him. And they was still talking to him. And I'm standing back there still crying and interjecting stuff. And I'm so pissed off at this man; I hadn't done nothin' to him. When the police came, he was goin' to be a tough guy now.

Anyway, both of them [the two sheriffs] turned their back on me. So I eased up and stepped between these two sheriffs. And I could see this guy between them. He was lyin' on me, and I knew I was fixin' to go to jail, right? He had the authority, and I was on the property, and all that ol' shit. So I eased between these two sheriffs, and I let him [the security guard] have it: I tried to knock a homerun wit' homeboy's head. It sound like—oh, man, it sound like a homerun. The hat went flyin' one way. I mean, I liked to knock the top off his head. Before the police could grab me, I hit him about five or six more times, on his body and shoulders. Oh, I messed him up real good!

Poop got lucky again, because the man didn't die. Since Poop was still a juvenile when this happened, and the sheriffs decided to be solicitous, he was taken to the Firestone sheriff's station where he was "threatened" by the sheriffs with juvenile hall. But they finally agreed to release him to his mother because he had no other record at that time. This narrative not only shows how dangerous spontaneous violence could be but also demonstrates how easily a street-group member, involved in a non-gang-related battle, could have simply been jailed as a gang member for a violent gang crime if the definition of terms had been different. This was a personal fight over personal issues.

On-the-Job Training

Robbery was not infrequent. It ranged from petty offenses like theft of bicycles and theft of small change from peers to serious acts like armed robbery.[73] Although none of these crimes was committed as a street-group activity, when two or more people were involved, the chances of the involved parties being from the same street group were considerable. The primary motivation for the more serious types of robbery was the promise of quick money—usually much more than could be made from a job or drug sales. One of the more successful and verbally adroit robbers was Poop. He began his delinquent career with significant tutelage from his older brother-in-law Mac, who had previously established himself as a proficient robber.

Mac's explanation to Poop of what he needed to do to rob a restaurant, with people in it, was not particularly detailed: it was an on-the-job training exercise, fraught with potential mishap. Poop detailed his tutelage: "The dude [Mac] didn't tell me shit. He just told me to go in 'nere, and just . . . He was teachin' me how to be a bandit." When asked if he tried to hide his identity from his victims, Poop's reply clarified the spontaneous nature of this robbery: "No, I didn't plan for them to see me no more. No, we didn't wear a mask 'n' stuff like that; that some television shit there."

Poop's first robbery was not a smoothly orchestrated event but rather a serendipitous escapade imbued with the possibility that things could go wrong in a heartbeat. He was not even certain he wanted to go through with it when the time came or quite sure how to go about it, until he received some rather forceful encouragement from Mac. Poop continued:

> I went in 'nere, and all these people was in the restaurant. I came back out, and I told Mac, "Mac, there's about fourteen, fifteen people." I went in and came back out, you know. Then I went in and came back out again: "Man, go in 'nere and take care of business," [said Mac]! Him and another dude is sittin' in a car in front of this place waitin' on me. So I go back in 'nere the third time and come back out again. Then I said, "Man, that about fifteen, sixteen people in 'nere." So he [Mac] said, "Well, rob 'em all, nigger![74] You come back out that door again, I'm gonna shoot your ass." So, you know, he wasn't bullshittin'. I believe Mac would of shot me, or at me anyway.

As frightened as he was to commit his first robbery, Poop was even more frightened of what might have happened to him if he backed out. As his tale continued, an unexpected but major chance for failure loomed large. It was even greater than anticipated because of the web of community affiliations:

> So I went back in 'nere and pulled my gun and was scared to death. An' I pulled my gun on these people and make everybody get up against the wall 'n' stuff. And the lady workin' behind the cash register is Pat W.'s mama—the girl who I liked. I use to be in this woman's house. But I didn't know she had this job in this place, you know. And, um, she didn't recognize me, but I knew who she was. And, ah, I had her put all the money in the bag.

Poop prevailed. He collected the money from the cash register. Then, as advised by Mac, he began to rob the patrons until another incident almost turned this robbery into a homicide. Poop explained:

> This one guy was sittin' in a booth wit' his girl. He was one of dem pimp-type guys, you know. His Cadillac parked outside, and he tryin' to hide his diamond ring. He bent over to stick it in his shoe—'cause they already know that soon as I get this money out of the cash register, I was going to come around wit' the bag. Homeboy was trying to hide his diamond ring. And I see his hands go outta sight, and I'm thinkin'—gun! I turned around and shot a .45 automatic. Like, I tried to shoot him, you know? You know how those ol' big puffy seats with vinyl? Cotton shit flew everywhere! I put a big ol' hole in this thing, and that's what made me leave outta 'dere with just the cash register money. I rushed him [the pimp]. I went over 'dere, and he got to snivelin' 'n' cryin' 'n' stuff and said, "Here, man, take it—the ring." And I just left. I had the money out of the cash register. Anyway, that was the first time I robbed somebody.

Poop's guardian angel had hung with him. Nobody died or got hurt, although the possibility of both happening was high throughout the drama of this theft. Poop's share of the proceeds from this first job was considerable, providing the incentive he needed to pursue his robbery career. During some of his thieving, he partnered with other set members, but their behavior was never approved of by set leadership—nor was it disapproved. The robberies were accepted as the robber's business. Any money acquired during these robberies was shared by the participants but not by the street group itself. These were crimes committed by individuals, some of whom also happened to be street-group members, for personal gain. Describing the individualism characteristic of group members then, Bird explained: "We had individual think, not groupthink."

Luck is not a reliable phenomenon to depend on when one is regularly involved in dangerous pursuits. Over the course of the next six years, two of Poop's partners were killed committing robberies. While Poop was never busted for any of his robberies, he ironically wound up being busted for a robbery he didn't commit, although he did supply the guns for the robbers. He was "snitched" on, "railroaded," in his opinion, causing him to spend five and a half years in the penitentiary. Luck has an expiration date.

Do Your Own Thing

Two other members of the Slausons had reputations as armed robbers: Chinaman and Lafayette. They robbed banks. Chinaman's criminal and prison careers began when he was young, giving him his first federal stint in 1957. He returned to prison in 1964 and again in 1972. Lafayette's decision to rob banks was pragmatic: it was lucrative. As he noted: "I was never into robbin' poor people, 'cause there was no money there." He saw himself as "criminally oriented," with a record that supported his image: "By the time I was twenty years old, I had been busted twice for guns in my locker at Manual [High School], one attempted murder, two assaults with a deadly weapon, and a robbery." Lafayette received federal time for the robbery. The principle connecting the bank-robbing activities of Chinaman to those of Lafayette was Lafayette's awareness of Chinaman's exploits. Chinaman, having come before him, had left behind a reputation of legendary proportions.[75] Though they were members of the same set, there was no tutelage. Chinaman and Lafayette were Slausons from different cliques, who also happened to rob banks, doing so as individuals rather than as members involved in group-sanctioned activities that had been passed down.

As the fabled founder of the Slausons, Chinaman carried a lot of juice, but even he could not sway another one of the powerful Slausons, Roach, to join him in robbing banks. Roach had higher priorities. Chinaman said to him: "Hey, man, you don't need to be out there bangin'. Why don't you come on down to 68th and Central and hustle with us?" Roach felt the offer was not as attractive as the position he already had with the Slausons and turned Chinaman down. As Roach explained, "The neighborhood is my life, man. I feel like I have, like, a father's responsibility." Chinaman's independence and monetary focus kept him from the kind of neighborhood attachment that Roach had developed. Within the same street group, there were key players who went in different directions; yet, as different as they were, they were still respected and recognized as righteous leaders of the set. Leadership among street groups is a complex variable.

Lefon, discussing crime among his car group, supplemented our theory that criminal behaviors were carried out by individuals, acting on their own accord or with an associate or two, for reasons unassociated with street group membership. Lefon's club was not criminally organized: "Everybody had their private things that they did, but when we were together, it was clean." Bird added, "We had some dudes who would rob, but that had nothin' to do with us." Expanding on the absence of a collective involvement in crime, Bird continued: "It wasn't like we sat down and held a club meeting and said, 'Okay, we're gonna go pull a robbery up there on such 'n' such, or we're gonna go murder this dude over here.' If you wanted to pull a robbery, that was your business." We found no South Los Angeles street groups existing before 1965 that had been organized for the purpose of committing crime. But we did find numerous situations where street-group members, who had had various involvements in assorted criminal activity, often did so with another member or two from the same group.[76]

Goods obtained illegally, especially money, were the property of those who had acquired them and were not shared with other street-group members. A group member's money, wherever it came from, was his. Group members might use their money to help their family, give some of it to a homeboy(s), or spend some of it on selected friends by buying a bottle of wine, but they didn't divide it up among their set or clique. Whit explained: "Our club as a whole did not thrive on robbin' and stealin'. We had members in the club that did it on their own, but they didn't bring nothin' or money back to the club." Bird added: "Yeah, they didn't pull a robbery and put it in the club treasury."

What the Police Knew and How They Knew It

Police records on juvenile street crime probably recorded different amounts of crime than what we found because the police had a different raison d'etre: agency rule enforcement rather than research. They would arrest set members and then release them, sometimes with and sometimes without filing charges. Their data could indicate there was a higher degree of criminal involvement than our respondents claimed. Police records reflect agency record keeping rather than an objective rendering of set member criminality. As Bird related: "I got four robberies on my record, and I ain't never robbed a person in my life—but I got busted with a gun. If you got busted with a gun, you automatically got a robbery." Bird never went to the penitentiary, a likely possibility had he in fact been involved in four robberies. More plausibly, he was caught up in police profiling, being seen as a potential suspect, due to his visibility, regardless of his proximity to the offense. He offered this example:

> I was on 88th and Central at eight thirty in the morning, in front of the El Blanco Motel, getting a traffic ticket for something on my car. It [the ticket] had a time and date on it. Okay, I went south to 92nd and Central and then turned and headed west toward Broadway. The police are comin' east on 92nd, and they see my car. I had a chopped-top '49 Chevy, the one I called the "Bat Machine." The police make a U-turn, come around, get me, and take me to the 77th Street police station for a robbery of a pet shop on 97th and Figueroa at eight thirty that morning. Okay, it [the robbery] happened that morning. I show them the ticket and everything. I said, "Man, I was gettin' a ticket on 88th and Central at eight thirty—here it is." They said, "Naw," and took me to jail, booked me, ran all kinds of makes on me, and after four hours released me.

Bird's eventual release did not come before "suspicion of robbery" appeared on his record for an offense that would have been physically impossible for him to have had anything to do with. Other set and nonset members told us of occasions when they too were brought to the police station and booked, only to be released later with no charges. But the official record had been created.

Another time, when Bird was questioned about a different robbery, he displayed his wit and his discretion, when the policeman told him he was being stopped because he "looked like a robber." Bird inquired, "How does a robber look?" When the officer described a robber as being about five feet eight inches to five feet nine inches tall, black hair, mustache, goatee, wearing a black hat and leather coat, Bird realized he was not only being described, but so were half the males in the neighborhood, and that this was a discussion he wasn't going to win. As Bird understood, it is wise to say nothing in situations where the logic is on your side but the power isn't. Might, after all, is always right—even when it isn't.

A World War II veteran who was the director of Roosevelt Park and lived on the northern boundary of Watts offered an opinion on crime in Watts that was supported by other perspectives on the area. He suggested Watts was much more violent and criminal than the Florence-Firestone area, a position he sustained with his view on the LAPD's directive to enter with caution. He observed:

> LAPD would never go below 103rd [a bit north of the middle of Watts] because it was so hot [dangerous] below there. One cop would never

come down there. They came down in twos and threes. And I stayed down in there too. People was wild and crazy. Most people used razors, knives—that kind of thing. You didn't hear of pistols too much, but shotguns was everywhere.

It's quite possible the criminal situation we have been describing for most parts of South Los Angeles was different for Watts. Material presented previously indicated there were considerable differences between Watts and other neighborhoods, making this conclusion reasonable. Watts was an area more characteristic of the urban blight generally associated with higher levels of street crime than other areas were. Watts's history reflected a greater structural marginalization,[77] an arrangement that continues.[78]

Many South Los Angeles people understood that loose lips sink ships: what went on in the community stayed in the community, in spite of police efforts to find out otherwise. A likely factor contributing to perceived community ignorance of neighborhood criminality was a code of silence to authorities.[79] It's not that people didn't know what was going on, because they often did, but they were not about to be a snitch.[80] As Whit expressed it: "If somebody told you something in those days, you didn't dare tell nobody. Not because you were gonna get killed either, but it was just the code of the streets." Also, there was certainty in the belief among community residents that the police could not or would not help them. Authorities were rarely notified; nor were they given much assistance during their inquiries about what was perceived to be neighborhood business.

One Slauson reported there was extensive criminality around him much of the time, and he considered many of those involved in it to be his friends. He never felt compelled to participate, was not pressured, and had no thought of saying anything to authorities.[81] "My friends, that I ran with, they been in jail for robbery and everything else, you know. When we leave the Park, they say, 'Well, we gonna go and do such 'n' such.' I go home." Rather than being looked down upon for his reluctance to participate in something he didn't believe in, he was thought more highly of because he was principled—he was righteous. His independence and his silence were rewarded. As he noted: "You were looked at as being strong that you wouldn't participate in wrong. You didn't have to do wrong to be all right with somebody." Neighborhood juveniles didn't have to go along to get along.

The dearth of peer pressure to take part in things set members felt were inappropriate or perhaps illegal is another example of neighborhood individuality and helps account for the absence of criminal subcultures. Do your own thing, be cool, lead if you can, or follow if you want to were more thematic of the community than was collaborating in a criminal lifestyle. Likewise, it is possible some robberies were committed by people who kept their activity secret because they knew they might be expected to share if their homeboys found out.[82] As one Slauson explained, "If they did pull a robbery, they would never show us the money. Yeah, because we would have to split it up." Bird summed up set member criminality this way: "The majority of us weren't criminals," even though various set members had regular brushes with the law that gave them police records, jail time, and even prison time.

Bird noted there were at least two rational reasons why set members kept their distance from those involved in serious criminality. First, there was little a set member could do about it. One could not make the other do things they didn't want to do, especially if the other might be as tough as or even tougher than the member proffering advice. "You might have a guy in your club, but he's just as strong as you, and you can't tell him what to do and what not to do. You can't make him quit doing nothin'," Bird proclaimed. A second reason may have been even more compelling: if you were ignorant of another's criminality, you were of limited value in a police inquiry. As Bird explained: "If the police come, they gonna get them, not me. I didn't wanna ask no questions." This attitude is reminiscent of the proverb "See no evil, hear no evil, speak no evil." Sometimes, what you don't know can't hurt you.

The Slicksters

Kumasi[83] was an observant and critical witness of his surroundings. Having spent time on the street as a Slauson Flip and time in numerous state penitentiaries, his skills as a good listener and gifted orator gave him access to information often denied to or ignored by others. He noted there were several groups of adults in the 1950s and 1960s who were "not actually a mob" but rather a "loose confederation of dudes from the neighborhood who were hustlers," primarily oriented to making money. He called this group the "slicksters." The slicksters were criminal figures who used street thugs as enforcers for the onerous tasks: "The slicksters take the toughest and the baddest from the tough guys on the street, and they used them as bullies to keep everybody else in line," he noted.

There was no progression from street thug to boss among the slicksters; it was a caste system: thugs always kept the "role of flunky," contended Kumasi. Slickster thugs were among the most marginalized of youth, appearing as a group of permanently disenfranchised males.[84] The thugs were in and out of prison, lacked job skills, often had drug problems, and perceived their street work as the only thing they could do to maintain a semblance of material comfort in their lives. They were essentially unfit to do much else. Their criminal bosses treated them this way too: as disposables, to be used as needed, discarded when not. Kumasi's metaphor comparing them to prostitutes put the slickster thug/boss relationship in perspective:

> So when they [the thugs] get broke or go to prison, and he's back on the street, if somebody else wants to pick him up, they do. This happens until they die. In the meantime, they [the slicksters] hook him up, like you do a prostitute that you want to work for you all the time. You get her loaded; you keep makin' her drinks, dress her all up. You keep the best champagnes and liquors up under her belt; she becomes an alcoholic. Or you keep feedin' her pills, or you just give her straight-out hardcore drugs and make her think she's livin' the high life. She's doin' what nobody else can do. Now she's hooked in. And now she needs you to supply her. Yeah, but you don't need her no more. You dump her ass. This is what happened to all these dudes [the slickster thugs].

A slickster might know set members or might have been or still be a member, but *slicksterism* was never an activity a set was organized around. Nor is there any evidence the slickster bosses were anything more than street hustlers. They were using up and then "junking" the less fortunate,[85] which, after all, is the spirit of American capitalism.[86]

A Lot of Petty Crime

Without exception, our respondents knew people, many of whom they were related to, who were delinquents or criminals. Most respondents had also participated in a variety of petty juvenile crimes or statute violations. Some respondents knew people who had been involved in serious crime, as they also had. When respondents and their acquaintances transgressed, they did so as individuals, frequently in small groups of two or three. Often their offenses were neither set orientated nor set involved but were behaviors they got caught up in because of who they were or where they were at the time the opportunities arose. Petty crimes give police opportunities to detain and arrest those they choose, as Richard Quinney contends in his theory of the social reality of crime, and can lead to increases or decreases in crimes and criminals as administrative needs require.[87]

Unwritten rules of right and wrong existed, but exceptions appeared often enough to suggest there was no neighborhood central command. One example is purse snatching. There were strong proscriptions against it, with the Slausons and the Businessmen both condemning it and anyone who might do it.[88] For some, their antipathy to purse snatching was because of the beloved women in their lives who could be potential victims. Barry Wa., from the Junior Businessmen, made this ethic clear when he exhorted: "How they gonna snatch that lady's purse, and I got a mama? She struggle to make things happen for us. We tear a sucker's ass up for snatching a woman's purse." Bird agreed with Barry Wa., adding that bothering old people was also "out of the question." Barry Wa. expanded on his previous comments by noting there was always someone in the set who would break the rules. Especially in a large set, there was always a "fool" who couldn't be contained or whose behavior went undiscovered. "It's like this: say out of fifty guys, you might have one that's an asshole, might of did some stupid thing, might of bothered a little girl, rob an old man. We wouldn't know nothing about it, 'cause we wouldn't allow it," he explained.

A member of Clanton indicated a number of the guys in his group had more criminal tendencies than those of the Slausons or the Businessmen. Similarly, though, when Clanton members broke the law, they also did so as individuals, since Clanton was not organized enough to orchestrate these behaviors as group activities. He noted, "Some of the guys held up gas stations and stuff like that; they would strong-arm." He pointed out that some would snatch purses. The example he gave for purse snatching was of a businesswoman with a business in the community but who didn't live there. She was known to take home large sums of cash in her purse on Fridays. It made her an easy and lucrative target but one without personal community ties. The juveniles who robbed her got away with three to four hundred dollars— a sizable amount then—in a crime involving a nonresident, who was not related to or a friend of any of those living in the community.[89]

This Clanton member was also aware of some "older guys" who were "bunco artists," adults who used a series of street scams to liberate the ignorant from their money. These scams involved assorted con games, like three-card Monte, designed to trick people into betting on things they had little chance of winning. Upset that they lost or were cheated, embittered victims were the fuel for potential violence. One scam, involving two or three people working together, would get an unsuspecting victim to lay out money on the ground alongside the scammer's money. Dice were then rolled to determine who got to keep the money. Before anyone could "win," and after a sufficient quantity of money had been put down, one of the scammers would pull a knife while another would grab the money, with both then running off in different directions. The scammers would meet up later to divide the proceeds. These con men did not actively recruit but saw themselves as "doing a favor" by providing tutelage through observation for certain neighborhood youth, who then might take up the business themselves at some point.

Another potentially violent activity was street gambling. When it involved alcohol, which was frequently, the gambling could quickly get out of control. But because it was sometimes quite lucrative, there was pragmatic justification for the risk.⁹⁰ Baby Bird, for instance, won his first car, a 1954 Pontiac, in a dice game at the Shrine Auditorium, where the Temptations were playing. Such a large coup was an exception, but the potential of opportunity arising from it—however improbable—made it seem more possible for others. For the most part, at the street level, the risks of gambling usually outweighed the rewards and contributed more to neighborhood violence than to personal gain. Gambling was a gamble older juveniles and adults of many ages were willing to take.

Probation officers' views on the types of offenses committed in the community varied, but they generally sustained the notion of a considerable amount of petty crime occurring among set members. One probation officer said, "Stealing was their primary source of income." He knew that strong-arm robberies and home burglaries happened but thought they were infrequent and not an important income source. He also understood juvenile theft was supplemented with income from various petty jobs like work in gas stations. A second probation officer felt that strong-arm robberies and burglaries were more common than the first probation officer thought. Both concurred with our previous assertions that these offenses were committed either by individuals or in groups of two or three. Putting in context the gravity of one particular group's activity, the second probation officer provided the following example of a "gang robbery":

> One time there was a *gang* of kids, and they were walking by the Allied Pie Company, maybe about ten of them. And then this one particular guy says: "You know what, we ought to go in there and just steal all the pies we can." 'Cause they used to have the trucks [with the pies] that would drive up, and they would load them on the platforms and stuff like that. And so, you know, he got them all excited about that. And I remember the words still because the guys told me afterwards. And this guy says, "Come on, *gang*." And they ran at the docks, and everybody just scrambled to get boxes and everything else. They got the pies and took off. Well, it's kind of a robbery type thing. [Emphasis added.]

The probation officer concluded that this "robbery" was a "spontaneous act."⁹¹ Since the pies were stolen from the dock, not from a person, this was actually a theft and not a robbery, but possibly a grand theft. More importantly, though, this was an opportunity that was just too easy to pass up. While a lead participant did use the term *gang* to refer to his group, this was hardly the sort of group behavior one imagines when considering the dimensions of a gang robbery. This was a serendipitous act carried out by a peer group of juveniles, some of whom may have been in a set, all of whom were in the right place at the right moment.

Ted W., who grew up in Watts and was a member of the Boozie club, remembered that Central Avenue had an "affluent sports group" in the late 1940s to mid-1950s, who were connected to the hustlers, pimps, prostitutes, and gambling houses. These were adults who wore "big diamond rings and big gold chains" and drove "black Cadillac cars." They had names like "Black Dot" and "Speck." They were no more organized than necessary to make money from their activities and did not have any group names or even the recognition of being anything more than a group for a minute—a fleeting unity to get the money and go. This group of adults did not provide tutelage to the juveniles.

Crime Thrills

On the national level, the offenses youth were most frequently arrested for were nonserious behaviors. Burglary and larceny/theft were the top two offenses for juvenile arrests from 1934 to 1965. To give some perspective, a few statistics from the Uniform Crime Reports on the offenses juveniles were arrested for—nationwide—should be helpful. In 1934, 149 juveniles were arrested for "criminal homicide," but 4,851 were arrested for burglary, and another 4,266 were arrested for larceny/theft. By 1965, the arrests for all of these offenses had increased proportionately: 542 for "murder and nonnegligent manslaughter," 84,698 for burglary, and 191,037 for larceny/theft.[92] Throughout the nation during those years, the UCR data confirm that crime for all juveniles was similar to what we found to be the case in South Los Angeles: relatively few serious crimes compared to a lot of petty crime.[93]

When status offenses were introduced into the UCR arrest records for juveniles during the early 1960s, such offenses as runaway and curfew violations became the predominant reasons for juvenile arrests. Some respondents saw curfew violations as police harassment rather than as youthful crime, since the police seemed to selectively choose the juveniles they wanted. Police would then transport the juveniles to another neighborhood, where they would release them, forcing them to make their journey back home the best way they could.[94]

Occurring late in the evening, in the days before the arrival of the now ubiquitous cell phones, such neighborhood drop-offs could cause the juveniles a lot of pain. Barry Wa. explained:

> The biggest thing they got us for was curfew. The police just take you over there [another neighborhood] and make it hard for you. They

know you don't have any money in your pocket, number one. They take you ten miles out your neighborhood; you have to get back the best way you can. Who you gonna see you know at nine or ten at night? It was dangerous, man!

The president of the Baby Businessmen believed the police knew by the way juveniles were dressed and the manner in which they conducted themselves whether they lived on the East-Side or the West-Side. The police confirmed their suspicions of residence after they stopped you, he contended, and then took you to a neighborhood that was distant from your home.

Numerous other petty offenses occurred. One was stealing bicycles, usually in other neighborhoods, and then selling them for their parts. This often involved several youngsters, typically from the same street group as the perpetrators. Another offense a respondent described as his "job" was "rippin' off" the hubcaps from cars that he would later sell, earning him forty to eighty dollars daily. One night, a group of juveniles were out drinking, under age, and were arrested, after a couple of them were seen by a neighbor urinating on a fence, who then called the police. Other petty offenses included thefts from residences when no one was home. One rather unusual theft involved a desperate youngster who took dirty clothes. "Leon stole the clothes; he stole the poop-stained drawers out of the dirty-clothes hamper," Bird recalled.

Two of the more common forms of neighborhood theft were stealing auto parts and "junkin'." In addition to hubcap theft, a few car club members would steal "anything they could find for a car." Even the insignias on cars, if they were cool looking, were fair game. These items would be either sold or used on their own or on a friend's vehicle. Junkin' was the theft of saleable items, especially metals like brass, copper, and aluminum or auto parts, usually from a junkyard or other private property. Old lead car batteries or vehicle radiators were targets, since these, along with the materials mentioned, could be sold back to other scrap yards for a certain amount per pound. In effect, these juveniles were early recyclers, albeit illegally. Interestingly, no thefts took place at the home of a regular.

None of our respondents were seduced into committing thefts like the middle-class students Jack Katz interviewed for his *seductions of crime* theory.[95] There was nothing "sensual," "propelling," or "game like" about committing the offense; nor did anyone necessarily participate in it because it was fun,[96] although some did use what they had procured illegally to have fun with, such as buying the wherewithal to party with.[97] Need[98] and opportunity trumped most other motivations for the theft South Los Angeles juveniles were involved in.

Gender Differentials

With few exceptions, male respondents did not mention involvement in shoplifting, but several females did.[99] One woman talked about her shoplifting career beginning when she was fourteen or fifteen years old, occurring with some regularity for a year or so and then intermittently or as needed afterward. She stole items for herself, family, and friends and would often give them away as gifts. She said: "I was good at it. I use to steal shoes for my brothers and my sister, my mama, anybody. I'd steal clothes or whatever." When she was eighteen and planning to marry, she discovered that the cost of wedding dresses she liked priced her out of the market—so she stole hers. She wanted to make it clear that all her stealing was to help the people she knew who were in need and that she was not a *booster*: "Boostin' is when you're making money at it, and I wasn't sellin' nothing."[100]

Vandalism was common, especially graffiti marking. While the use of graffiti by street groups was relatively unknown in South Los Angeles before the 1940s, what began as a whisper progressed slowly at first and then by 1960 had become a scream.[101] Bird was one of the earliest and most prolific of the graffiti artists, getting great enjoyment out of leaving various messages around town, especially in wet cement. He would imprint his initials, those of his girlfriend, or various iterations of Slauson in many locales throughout the neighborhoods and in the numerous other places he traveled.[102]

Bird wrote on the walls of buildings but never on people's houses or cars. He explained: "I was a wall sprayer, but I had some morals and principles," and to do that would have been wrong. When done within the moral parameters outlined by Bird, there seemed to be little community opprobrium associated with the early street expressionists. Graffiti developed like a street newspaper, as others began using it too as way to communicate. By 1965, its usage had greatly expanded, as had the sophistication of applicators.[103]

Like most neighborhoods in Southern California, South Los Angeles had a wide variety of fruit trees growing in people's yards. Sometimes the branches hung over into public spaces, making the fruit fair game for passersby, although most of the fruit was in the owner's yard, making it the owners' property. Theft of fruit—apples, pomegranates, apricots, peaches, and all sorts of citrus—from these trees when it was in the owner's yard was common and was usually tolerated by the owners, especially those without fences. On occasion though, the theft was not tolerated, with tree owners either calling the police or, more often, settling it themselves when sufficiently irritated. Lefon, from the Serfs car club, elaborated: "We could run fast because we had it down. When we go stealin' peaches and apricots, okay, this dude goes up in his house and gets his shotgun. By the time we hit the ground, he shoots up in the air. We get home our fastest. All we had to do was hear the 'pow.'"

There was a range of those who were involved in property crimes, from occasional to regular. Regardless of where they fell on the range, they did not boast about it, keeping instead "low profile," particularly when they were with their homies. Others in the neighborhood, who knew about or suspected their involvement, accepted the juveniles "like normal people," mainly because they usually conducted their business in other neighborhoods. It was understood that "some guys went out and stole because they wanted to, and there were other guys [who] went out and did it to survive," opined Whit. There was nevertheless wariness toward those who were perceived as thieves, out of concern the thief might steal from them. As one set member explained, "A thief would burn anybody, you know. If there was a thief in the group or neighborhood, everybody knew who it was." Survival theft and theft for personal gain were tolerated, but the thieves were kept at a distance.

Injustice Is Served

With serious criminality relatively low in South Los Angeles before the mid-1960s, we might assume that imprisonment would also be low, but we would be mistaken. We found there were no more than one or possibly two degrees of separation between people in the neighborhood and the incarcerated. That is, respondents and their associates could be described by one of three—and frequently by all three—of the following characterizations: they had been in jail or prison themselves, they were related to someone who had been, or they knew someone who had been. Rick C. from Florence indicated that about 75 percent of the males he knew had been incarcerated. Ed B., one of the few respondents who had not been to jail or prison, wanted to make it clear that although incarceration was an uncomfortable fact of life in the neighborhoods, "a lot of us never went to jail." He was proud of that, even though he knew many people who had been incarcerated. Jail or prison were ever-present factors influencing the lives of just about everybody who lived in South Los Angeles.

State-raised was the term used to refer to people who, as juveniles and young adults, had been in the state correctional system for such long periods that much of their socialization occurred there. Chinaman gave us another term. Having spent over ten years of his life in various federal institutions, starting at twenty years old, when he was the youngest inmate at the McNeil Island Federal Penitentiary, he considered himself "federally raised." He took advantage of his federal time to stay clean and sober and to get educated, only to discover, upon release, that his record kept him from decent employment. Robberies are what had gotten him into the federal system in the first place and then kept bringing him back. This vicious cycle eventually disqualified him from the requirements of life necessary on the outside, regardless of the symbols of middle-class sophistication he had developed during his repeated stays. The cycle of imprisonment, return to the street, and then more imprisonment was a common refrain in South Los Angeles before 1965.[104]

Imprisonment, especially for long periods, sucked life out of the community. For women like Roslyn, it meant growing up without a father because he had spent most of his life, especially during her adolescence, in prison. While incarceration took some criminals off the street, it also removed many whose deletion was due to factors other than their criminality. Rick C. observed that modest family means, such as those with a little bit of money in contrast to those with none, produced a bias that was primary in determining who went to jail. As he noted, "It's strange because here all the kids who come from families that don't have money, most of them end up in jail at one time or another."[105] Barry Wa. believed his mother kept him out of jail because she would do what she could to borrow money for lawyers when he got in a jam. Bird concurred, adding that if he had gotten all the money his mother spent on lawyers, fines, and bail, he could have bought "a brand-new car—cash." Incarceration changed families by removing the males,[106] and it kept potential set leaders from realizing their potential. Sometimes the incarceration was justified, but often it was not.

Neighborhood juveniles had contact with the juvenile justice system as a consequence of both serious and less serious behaviors. They could be railroaded as a result of being in the wrong place at the wrong time. In one case, a number of youth were jailed as a result of police being called to a party because of loud music. As Bird explained, it appears the police contributed to the problems they were called to solve, which in turn provided them with even greater justification to arrest:

> He [the person hosting the party] turned the music down, but the police come up there anyway. His sister Beanie had on a short miniskirt. And what she had on was real short. Okay, the police up there talkin' and everything, and one cop, man, actually felt her [Beanie] on her legs! Beanie said, "Motherfucker!" then fired on [punched] the police. Then everybody start fightin', gonna whoop the police. [Of course they didn't, the police won.] Beanie went to jail. That's when Esther went to jail and cried like a baby. I think Sheila went to jail, Clyde went to jail, Sonny went to jail—about six or seven of them went to jail.

This illustration adds further credence to the contribution various justice agencies made to the perception, and existence, of more crime in South

Los Angeles than respondent data suggest. Bird and numerous others believe the police were on a crusade to stigmatize most of the youth.[107] As Bird opined, they "made sure all of us had some kind of record." Unintended consequences from situational circumstances cannot be ignored in efforts to understand crime data in South Los Angeles, any more than they can be depended upon to produce uncontroversial information. Their occurrence may be difficult to quantify but not difficult to appreciate.

Organized Crime

Mickey Cohen, the legendary organized-crime figure in Los Angeles during the mid- to late 1950s, whose exploits have been enumerated in books and in film, had some of his operations on Central Avenue in the Slauson neighborhood. While many Slausons were aware of these enterprises, we found no evidence to suggest they were involved in them. Roach explained, "Especially on 68th and Central, they had prostitution goin' on, they had gamblin' shacks goin' on, the pool halls goin', and the drugs and all that shit goin' on." Chinaman and other Big Slausons had knowledge of the activities there but were so offended by the racism they encountered from the Cohen group that it turned them away from further contact with them.

Evidence of a "Black mafia" or "ethnic succession" into criminal enterprises among the set and nonset juveniles, such as Francis Ianni found in his New York research,[108] was lacking in South Los Angeles, as were the economic connections Carl Taylor found in his research on Detroit's Black juvenile and adult gangs.[109] John Hagedorn's discovery of an unknown relationship between Chicago's Latino gangs and an Al Capone–type mafia was absent here as well.[110] Individual set members may have had personal associations with some of the organized-crime figures, although no one we spoke with had; nor were any respondents aware of other juveniles who might have. There was no evidence to suggest organized crime played a role in set formation, ideology, organization, or perpetuation before 1965 in South Los Angeles.

Crime: Why?

There were at least three reasons why neighborhood residents became involved in crime: out of need, out of material desires, and because it could be fun. First, parts of South Los Angeles were sufficiently economically deprived during these years that crime, especially theft, was a means of getting by. For juveniles like Percy of the Little Flips, "I did what I had to do" to survive. "I never did nothin' to really hurt no one," he continued, though he stole cars and their parts to sell. While the theft might have deprived someone of his vehicle or its use, because no one was physically harmed, Percy was able to justify it. Frank M., whose father had passed away, thus denying his family paternal support, described his rationale: "What we did was mostly out of necessity." Frank M. worked at various jobs and then supplemented his income with thefts of bicycles, which he could sell later. He too felt that because he didn't physically hurt anyone or steal from someone who could not afford it, his behavior was morally appropriate. Further rationalizing his theft was that he did it in other neighborhoods, from people he didn't know.

When discussing some older youth he knew, Bird added a nuanced complexity, showing how the lack of jobs and existence of racism contributed to their more serious robberies. He explained:

> See, put it like this. Okay, Shug and Chinaman—they was grown. They were about eighteen or nineteen. They needed to be put out of the house. They didn't have no job, didn't have that much money—see, them dudes didn't have nothin', really. So they had to do somethin'. Plus, they wasn't going to take no abuse and racial abuse and anything else. So they said, "Fuck all this," and so they started robbin'. [Their reasoning was] real simple.

Rather than Shug and Chinaman's robberies contributing to the development of a criminal gang subculture, their robberies kept them off the streets and away from their sets. Street-group activities were one thing, something done when younger, while robbery was something considered when older and with different priorities. Bird noted: "They [the Businessmen] wanted Chinaman to be president of the Businessmen. But Chinaman said, 'No,' because he didn't have time for that bullshit. They [Chinaman and Shug] wasn't gang fightin' and that; they didn't have no time for that." Maturing out of set participation as material needs became more dominant yet unable to get jobs where they could make decent money provided sufficient motivation to consider robbery as an attractive option. And robbers didn't have to pay taxes like those who were "workin' their ass off all day at a greasy hamburger joint, smellin' like grease, for nothin' [little money]."

"Oh, Lord, Won't You Buy Me a Mercedes-Benz"[111]

A second reason for criminal involvement was as American as keeping up with the Joneses: an internalizing of the fundamental American value of material possessions as a sign of success and a perception of appropriative crimes as a way to get there. Thorsten Veblen theoretically identified the powerful role materialism played in American life in his important work *Theory of the Leisure Class*. His term for America's pursuit of material things and their visual display, "conspicuous consumption," became a recognizable part of our lexicon over one hundred years ago.[112] That such materialism was adopted by South Los Angeles youth was a result of being Americanized.

Consumptive crime was not survival crime but crime committed so one could participate in the pursuit of the American dream and then display one's success at it through a conspicuous exhibition of possessions. Robert Merton was spot on when he supplemented Veblen's work with his oft-quoted theory that American culture is characterized by a "heavy emphasis on wealth."[113] The path to wealth, he theorized, is *innovation*, using whatever means are available, legal or not.

Merton intended his concept of innovation to be a general theoretical explanation for appropriative crime that was engaged in by all social classes, not just the most deprived, as it has been reprogramed to suggest.[114] Innovation, as he explained it, develops from "great cultural emphasis" on "success," defined as achieving "wealth and power." This goal is "adopted by people in all social strata." Commenting directly on the behavior of the captains of industry,[115] Merton quotes Thorstein Veblen: "It is not easy in any given case—indeed it is at times impossible until the courts have spoken—to say whether it [an innovation by a captain] is an instance of praiseworthy salesmanship or a penitentiary offense."[116] So right and wrong, innocent or guilty, is determined by the courts. This determination is in itself dependent on the financial resources and political connections the accused are able to muster for their defense. Justice is more ideology than political reality.

South Los Angeles juveniles did not need to be set members to partake in the pursuit of materialism. In fact, there were assorted examples where set membership might have been a liability rather than a facilitator for certain crimes of acquisition. Poop made this clear when asked if his robbing activities were gang connected. He emphatically exclaimed: "No, that had nothin' to do with it; it was about money!" A follow-up question concerning whether he was motivated or encouraged by the Slausons to rob again produced denial: "No, it came from profit and the want of things. We [the Slausons] didn't do that shit. I guess I just like nice things," he proclaimed. For Poop, the best way he found to be able to *live large* was robbery.[117]

Poop was adamant that his criminal career was unrelated to street-group influence. At sixteen years old, he was tired of being poor, tired of working at jobs requiring lots of time with little pay, and tired of dealing with long commutes to jobs that left him almost as poor as when he started. One day, when Poop was complaining to his brother-in-law Mac about the paltry sums to be made selling weed, another idea about a way to make more money came up. "It had nothin' to do with gangs. We was talkin' about money, and Mac said, 'I'll show you how to get money.' We needed faster money than sellin' weed, 'cause we like cars. We had our own tailor, Tip. We had our clothes made." Poop's share of the take on his first robbery was seven hundred dollars—big money for a sixteen-year-old in the late 1950s. He spent some of his money on clothes, dressing well enough that at one point he and his cohorts were called "the well-dressed bandits." In a manner typical of many Americans, Poop was showing off how successful he was through his conspicuous sartorial display.[118]

Having Fun

A third reason why some juveniles engaged in certain delinquencies is because they enjoyed it. Condemning illegal behavior by arguing how socially unacceptable it is makes explanations for delinquency more comfortable for some researchers to express if the juveniles can be seen as forced, either by individual or gang circumstances, to participate in something they would really rather not do. From this perspective, it can be reasoned that our social system is not at fault for the misdeeds of its citizens because the rules are so fair that almost all are willing to obey them. To transgress requires more effort than to follow; that is, transgression requires a deviant mindset. Those who deviate must do so because they are either supported by a deviant subculture or have psychological problems. Thus, engaging in delinquency because of group pressure or mental issues becomes a more suitable explanation—more fitting with the idea of, "We're okay, but they're not"—than participation in illegal activities simply because they're fun. How could it be fun if it's illegal? The "nasty gang" becomes the ultimate out-group to the rest of law-abiding society, the dominant in-group. Maybe it's fun because it is illegal?

Contrary to requiring a deviant mindset, the fact is that for some juveniles, their involvement in certain delinquent behavior was precisely because it was just that: it was fun.[119] While theft may not have had the fun associated with it that Katz describes, for neighborhood juveniles, participation in assorted "victimless crimes," like gambling, certain types of sexual deviance, and the use of illegal intoxicants, was perceived as fun. As discussed, set members rarely gambled; but gambling, although potentially dangerous, could be a thrilling as well as lucrative experience. The fun part of adolescent sexual experimentation—from petting to intercourse—while having certain statutory proscriptions is easy to understand. With hormones raging, many male and female juveniles were more interested in investigating what they might be able to do about that than they were in heeding moral restraints for why they shouldn't.[120]

Getting high can lead to an abundance of troubles, but it can also be a pleasurable experience, especially when engaged in with homies on festive occasions or on occasions made festive because high.[121] We found considerable evidence that those juveniles who were getting high were doing so because it was an enjoyable way to spend some time. They weren't desperate; they were having fun. As R. C. from Florence put it, "We were just a bunch of kids that would do anything for excitement." Getting high was a hoot. "The hell with those who say we shouldn't," was the guiding principle for those who chose to get high. Subcultural memberships or mental issues were not necessary for South Los Angeles juveniles who wanted to enjoy the pleasures of some "bud" or the "grape."[122] When addiction is involved, the circumstances for use are very different—but there was limited evidence of addiction.[123]

Deciphering Deterrence

Having a job, being swayed by religious morals, and being influenced by certain features of the family and the community deterred some juveniles from delinquency, while others, who were also similarly associated, were not deterred. It's not clear why some were deterred while others weren't. This important discussion needs to be had at a different time and in a different place with additional data. The examples below of how these associations worked to deter were contradicted by other instances of how they did not. Nevertheless, these examples should provide insight for that discussion.

Many of our respondents had assorted legitimate jobs. While all the jobs were low paying, their effects in deterring delinquency varied.[124] In some cases, where the jobs did not pay enough, income was supplemented through criminal activities, but in cases where they were paid *enough*, they may have been deterred.[125] For Cordell, a Baby Slauson, it was evident the jobs paid him "enough," most likely deterring him from delinquency. He credited his work ethic as the insulator keeping him out of troubles with the law. "Like I say, I've always worked. From the time I was like nine years old. I had a paper route all the way through the eleventh grade. After that, I was working at the candy company. I didn't have no reason to commit no crime for no money." His only involvement with the law came when he and another Slauson received jaywalking tickets together. Cordell went to court, paid his fine, and never had another brush with the law.

Religious values as a deterrent were found infrequently. Willie C., from Sin Street in the Slauson neighborhood, was one who credited his reform to his faith in God. He had gotten in trouble while young with drugs, which controlled him more than he controlled them. He credited God primarily—

and a drug program secondarily—for his ability to get off them, as well as kicking his nicotine habit. As he explained: "Throughout my drug uses, I prayed, and I asked God to get me off it. He showed me the way, which was the drug program. I read from the first chapter of Matthew to the last chapter of Revelation. Every time I got the urge to smoke a cigarette or use [drugs], I would read the Bible. . . . I fear God." Although community church preachers railed against the evils of crime, at their often well-attended Sunday sermons, we found little evidence of the effectiveness of their exhortations.

Willie C. was also helped to desist from crime by the third deterrent factor, family and community, although in his case, it was a departed family member, his father. Willie's father was killed while Willie was still young, which both contributed to and then deterred him from drug abuse. In Willie C.'s words: "Well, at first it [his father's death] had something with me going deeper into it [drug use], but then, after a while, I started thinking, 'Hey, my father wouldn't like this.' He didn't want me to be like this, and that's when I started comin' out of it." Respect for his father's wishes was instilled early, and it was strong enough to pull him out of the emotional slide he suffered after his father died.

A number of respondents emphatically drew attention to the separation between their street activities and any information they might have shared about those activities with their relatives. What happened on the street stayed on the street because family adults would not have approved. Cordell observed, "You didn't let your parents know anything then. You'd been in deep shit if you did." He even refused to get some pills for a girl he liked because he saw a friend of his father's at the time he was about to procure them and knew the friend would report him to his father if he did.

Parents seemed to have multiple ways of discovering what their children did and where they did it. A South Los Angeles probation officer explained that the neighborhoods were small enough then and the web of individual affiliations extensive enough that it was very difficult for juveniles to do things that could be kept secret from their families. Somebody somewhere was going to see them. When seen, word often got back before they did, to relatives who took a dim view—there was nowhere to hide. In his words:

> The neighborhoods were more cohesive then. I couldn't play hooky from school. Where am I going to hide? You know somebody's going to tell that I wasn't in school that day. You know, I couldn't go hide out at the neighborhood theaters; the shows didn't open. It could have been the family values. I think that the whole societal values were different. School was an expected necessity. You went to school 'cause your folks had to go to work. And they had truant officers in those days.

Juvenile criminal activity in South Los Angeles before 1965 was largely independent of set membership. A causal link between sets and crime was weak, with each being generated by other social dynamics. Violence in fights frequently had set connections but was mediated by an ideology eschewing the use of weapons.[126] While serious crime was present, its exaggeration by officials gave it an appearance of regularity that was not supported by our research.

Crime is normal, Emile Durkheim theorized, "because a society exempt from it is utterly impossible." He wrote that crime is a "social fact," and it is found in "all societies of all types."[127] Crime in American society is and has been ubiquitous. Clearly, crime in our society is, in the Durkheimian sense, a social fact. It exists among all social classes, all races, and all ethnicities. Former U.S. attorney general Ramsey Clark has written that American crime "has many faces."[128] The face of juvenile street crime in South Los Angeles before 1965 was, in Durkheimian theory, normal, where media-based accounts to the contrary were overstated.

9

Unable to Embrace the Ideology

The Rise of the Crips

Power concedes nothing without a demand.
It never did and never will.
—Frederick Douglass, speech, Canandaigua, NY, August 4, 1857

Most accounts of the American 1960s portray it as a time of social turbulence, fueled by various powerful social movements. Los Angeles was at the forefront of many of these movements, whether they came from students, the universities, or the streets. South Los Angeles added its own twists: significant population increases, the Civil Rights movement, increased racial harassment by the police, a major rebellion, the emergence of Black Power groups, and the rise of a larger-than-life street group—the Crips.

Los Angeles's unrest during the 1960s "set the night on fire," according to Mike Davis and Jon Wiener.[1] In 1990, Davis argued that the period 1959–1965 was a "winter of discontent" for Black youth. He demonstrated that their median incomes declined in South Los Angeles while Black unemployment rose to 20 percent and reached 30 percent in Watts. Further, he writes: "Every attempt by civil rights groups to expand job or housing opportunities for Blacks was countered by fierce White resistance."[2] Mayor Sam Yorty rejected federal antipoverty funds because he couldn't control their distribution and felt they represented a threat to his power, leaving Los Angeles as the only major city that failed to "organize effective anti-poverty programs."[3] The major restructuring that Edward Soja reports, beginning around 1960, involved a significant shift in the social, economic, and political life that reconfigured the City. Old secular trends were broken or fell apart, while new ones were created in their place.[4]

As the pre-1965 street-group juveniles matured, their priorities changed, their range of interests expanded, and time on the street decreased. Their new priorities, in conjunction with the turbulence of the period, were magnified by an even greater force: unprecedented demographic growth, "the fastest-growing Black population outside the Southeast, three-quarters of it concentrated in South L.A."[5] All the street groups were shaped by this growth and by the social movements and aging cohorts of street group *elders*[6] who, willingly or not, found other things taking priority over their previous fussin' and cussin' lifestyles. Some of the elders began participating in social movements; others got married, got jobs, and started families, while still others were imprisoned or had died. Fussin', cussin', and discussin' were things they had done for a while, when they were juveniles—but they grew up and gave it up.[7] In their maturity, they had to face adult realities, in a world changing around them.

Then came the Crips. From humble beginnings, the phenomenon of the Crips soon became ubiquitous. In relatively short order, after their South Los Angeles origins, Crip gangs were discovered in the California cities of Sacramento and San Diego; the western cities of Phoenix, Las Vegas, Portland, and Denver; and then in East Coast cities, as well as in various cities in between. Law-enforcement groups soon began presenting evidence of their existence in European cities too.[8] By many accounts, a gang originating in South Los Angeles had spread all over the country—perhaps all over the world—creating images and symbols of all that was terrifying about the City's gangs. More than any single phenomenon, the Crips helped Los Angeles garner its moniker of "gang capital of the world."

To the media and in the popular consciousness around the United States, it seemed a small campfire had become a conflagration, fanned by western winds to inflame the country and beyond. Whoever they actually were, in the public mind the Crips quickly became the *baddest* of the bad and the worst of the worst, a plague of criminality that had taken over our nation's public spaces with an unprecedented ferocity. They were akin, it seemed to these observers, to a virus that had started in Los Angeles and was now infecting innocent communities everywhere by spreading through the waterways, the highways, the flight routes, and in the west-to-east trade winds. Lost in the rhetoric about the Crips was any careful analysis of who they really were and how they had originated. Gang myths about them rose everywhere, missing a central element: it was the contagion of the name that had caught on. While new groups did develop, it was because of political and economic changes rather than an organized Crip conspiracy. The Crips gangs that cropped up in far-flung cities were not coordinated South Los Angeles offshoots but imitators attracted to the fear, respect, and cultural cache the LA Crips had accumulated through their mythology. This chapter will offer a sober look at how the neighborhoods the Crips came from had changed to produce such metastasized phenomena.

The Winds of Change

The extraordinary demographic growth Los Angeles experienced might have been enough in itself to shake up the lives and social groupings of people in the area. By whatever measure of growth is chosen, the rate and absolute numbers of increases in the population from the end of World War II to the early 1970s were unprecedented. Growth in the Black population was greater than in any other large city in the United States.[9] When the significant increases in the Latino, Asian, Iranian, Guatemalan, Columbian, Cuban, and especially Salvadorian populations are included,[10] it becomes clear that the orderliness of life and whatever community stability there may have been were bound to be dramatically changed. Soja argues that the new arrivals were "peripheralized" and marginalized, as the expanding White populations moved out of the central city following the best jobs, leaving behind an environment developing with even greater political and economic struggles.[11]

As the new arrivals—strangers to most—moved in and then moved out again, often in rapid transitions, and relatives and acquaintances left, South Los Angeles neighborhoods lost the close camaraderie they had had. Various unfamiliar languages with many dialects were now being spoken in the community, while a lot of new youth, without the familiarity and comfort shaped by the binding ties of prior schooling and neighborhood affiliations, began appearing in schools and on the streets. And there was more.

"Blacks were always open for advancement and progress. Whether they did it or not, well, they were always open for it," noted Bird. Among South Los Angeles Black families, there were regular family relocations from one neighborhood to another. To better themselves, older siblings or younger siblings and parents might move from the neighborhood they were in to one offering greater opportunity. Or they might move because they were encouraged by external forces: schools that didn't want them, local law enforcement harassing and threatening them, or acquaintances ready to do them harm.

For all the tightness South Los Angeles held for Black families, it was a neighborhood in flux. When people moved, the new location was frequently an upgrade, but settling in was disruptive. New locations required a period of adjustment: getting used to new schools, new shopping routines, new friends, and new opportunities. Neighborhood fluctuations contributed to the loss of community closeness as demographic expansion accelerated.

Quoting Rap Brown's famous 1967 comment that "Violence is as American as cherry pie," the authors of *The History of Violence in America* write:

"Americans have always been a violent people.... It is nonetheless clear that the 1960's rank as one of our most violent eras."[12] In Los Angeles, violence increased too, just as it had in other large American cities, but an LA peculiarity saw the City's reputation as a gang center bloom in the 1960s. Mass media accounts of increases in crime, delinquency, numbers of "gangs," and "gang" violence were becoming commonplace, as local news became regular contributors to the idea there was more violence from more gangs.[13] During the 1960s, reports on violence that had previously been occasional now became a quotidian ritual—"If it bleeds, it leads" news became dependable headlines.[14] Gang issues titillated, and the public became conditioned to believe that gangs were among the top two or three social problems the country faced.

In an ambitious effort to reduce gang delinquency in South Los Angeles by using community outreach workers to intervene in gang members' lives—and make them better people—the Los Angeles County Probation Department launched a four-year project in 1961 named the Group Guidance Program.[15] LAPD's Chief Parker, termed the "warden of the ghetto,"[16] was not impressed and was not supportive. Although praised by reformers, parents, and community leaders as vital to turning gang members' lives around because arrest wasn't working, it was criticized by the heads of both major Los Angeles law-enforcement agencies as contributing to criminal behavior. The program was born into and remained in turmoil throughout its existence.[17]

An evaluation of the program by Malcolm Klein and colleagues contended it had led to an increase in delinquency among gang members.[18] When added to the already intense debate about the program, this criticism became a sledgehammer the program was not able to survive. The effort by community leaders to try something new and positive was an acknowledgment that the repressive actions of law enforcement not only weren't working but may have made the situation worse. But the new approach did no better. It was not only because of its controversies that the program failed but also because it was mired in the Band-Aid solutions of the interventionists. Their idea that middle-class reformers could somehow transform juveniles—whose issues were structural, not personal—without structural change was dead on arrival.[19] Many of our respondents were aware of the Group Guidance Program, and a few had participated in it—but none praised it.

Los Angeles became part of a concerted effort in the 1960s to reduce racism by changing its housing practices. In an admission of the impropriety of previous housing policy, the California Fair Housing Act (the Rumford Act) was passed in 1963, making it illegal to discriminate against people based on race in public and private housing.[20] Not everyone agreed with the need for this act, particularly the California Real Estate Association, which immediately launched a repeal campaign. Their effort resulted in Proposition 14, a successful, with two-to-one voter support, 1964 referendum to rescind the act. Rumford was later restored in 1967 when the California and U.S. Supreme Courts concurred that Proposition 14 violated the Civil Rights Act of 1866 and was unconstitutional.[21] The eventually successful effort to reduce some forms of institutional racism seemed to have little direct impact on the South Los Angeles street groups, but the contention that the City's housing bias was racist did serve as fact-based ammunition for the growing Black Power movement.

The Vietnam War, though dividing large parts of America into pro and con camps during the 1960s, seemed to have minimal impact on the South Los Angeles street groups.[22] Chinaman noted that he didn't know anyone, friends or family, who joined the military. Bird observed: "Almost no one we knew went to the service." When Bird tried to enlist in 1962, he was denied because he was on probation. Some of the guys who did enlist "were fresh out of high school and square," Bird asserted. He knew of a few others who did enlist but believed they were the exception. Of the enlistees who went to war, some of those able to return home smuggled back guns they were issued or had found there. While these guns were not a major source of neighborhood weaponry, the few that did show up on the streets helped to inform the citizenry of how far weapons had come since the days of zip guns and Saturday Night Specials. From the War and elsewhere, new and sophisticated weapons began showing up on the streets—a contribution by the weapons industry to the neighborhood arms race that followed. An ode to the violence the industry's technology helped spark might be "We couldn't have done it without you."

A Sense of Power

The Black Power movement (BPM) provided encouragement for a number of South Los Angeles people. Its peak years in America were from 1955 to 1965.[23] Charismatic leaders like Martin Luther King Jr. and Malcolm X emerged with a message of hope, encouragement, and eventual prosperity for Black people. Their oratory eloquence was inspirational, while they served as role models for what one could be or do. Grassroots Muslim groups, inspired by legendary figures like Muhammad Ali, began appearing on street corners and in prisons encouraging young people to join and to take back their lives. It was a cathartic, though brief, period when many hoped the wrongs of the Black experience might be made right. But the LAPD and the FBI saw the Black Power movement differently—as the greatest threat to the internal security of the nation—and unleashed all resources at their command to undermine it.[24]

The Black Panther Party (BPP), beginning in Oakland in 1966, was founded and organized on the premise that power must come from within the Black community through organization, unity, and the knowledge and exercise of constitutional rights.[25] Kumasi,[26] a Slauson Flip, said the Panthers "were able to take social fuck-ups and put them on the streets to do something, until the Movement was crushed."[27] The Black Power movement, as articulated by the BPP, brought real hope into people's lives. In the Party's analysis, racism was not only unacceptable; it was unconstitutional. Blacks had a right to defend themselves against it and a Second Amendment right to bear arms.

Bunchy and the Teen Oost

The Panther message spread quickly to South Los Angeles when a magnetic leader, Alprentice "Bunchy" Carter from the Slauson Renegades clique, met Eldridge Cleaver, the minister of information for the Panthers, in Soledad prison. Cleaver was so impressed with Bunchy that he told Huey Newton and Bobby Seale, the founders of the Panthers, about him. Cleaver told them that Bunchy was a Slauson and how tough he was; he was just the kind of person that the Panthers needed in Los Angeles to start a chapter there. Newton and Seale agreed and accepted Bunchy into the Party.

Bunchy started the Los Angeles chapter[28] and obtained the rank of deputy defense minister, a position he held until he was killed at a Black Student Union Forum at UCLA on January 15, 1969.[29] While a number of Slausons became Panthers, Bird believed that the "main body of the neighborhood" did not join them. He explained: "We were individuals who could function within a group, and we already belonged to something," the Slausons. People who had done time or were Renegades or followers of Bunchy were the most likely to join the BPP, according to Bird. But there is no denying Bunchy's appeal, his intelligence, and his ability to attract supporters.

After Bunchy got out of prison, he and Wilbert T.—a non-Panther and "Bunchy's righthand man"—ran a teen post in the Slauson neighborhood that attracted a lot of youth.[30] Among those juveniles who attended were Craig Monson, Jerry C., T. T., Dusty, and Raymond Washington. They were teenagers at the time, all some ten years younger than Bunchy, who was Bird's senior by seven months. These youngsters would later form various age-related cliques in the Slauson neighborhood, one of which would become the Crips.

In addition to Bunchy's charm, the juveniles were attracted to his status as a Slauson and as a Black Panther.[31] They were impressed with the Panther sartorial style of blue shirts, black pants, black leather jackets, and black berets that looked so good on Bunchy.³² Though Bunchy and Terry were charismatic, Bird felt they had more of an influence on neighborhood youth because of their group affiliations than because of their personalities:

> They definitely controlled and influenced all of the youngsters in the neighborhood. That means from Firestone to Slauson and from the freeway [Harbor, or 110, Freeway] to Alameda, the original neighborhood. See, they controlled in a sense of the way they thought and acted, which has nothin' to do with just Terry and Bunchy bein' in control. It has somethin' to do with them bein' from Slauson and then becoming Panthers.

Interest in the Nation of Islam was also high in South Los Angeles during the 1960s. The president of the baby Businessmen and a Malcolm X type Muslim, Ameer, believed the Nation attracted juveniles because it offered them spiritual, mental, social, and economic improvement and ways to help their communities. Gardell's subsequent research adds that the Nation in fact had a positive impact on many Black juveniles, earning it respect for its critiques of violence.³³ This encouragement inspired juveniles—some of whom had been set members—to understand that they too could help themselves and their community by joining.³⁴

Ameer converted to Islam while doing time. After his conversion, he was on the streets briefly before going back to jail over some traffic tickets. While there, he shared a cell with Raymond Washington, the juvenile from Bunchy's teen post, who is credited with being the founder of the Crips. Ameer and Raymond began discussing who they were and where they were from. Raymond told Ameer that he was from the Slauson neighborhood and "the one who started the Crips."³⁵ Ameer thought Raymond might have been a young Slauson,³⁶ because Raymond said he knew Bird, even though he didn't think Bird had anything good to say about him.

Ameer and Raymond got along well together despite their age difference of almost ten years. Ameer found the young Raymond to have a great interest in Islam and that Raymond wanted him to tell him more about it. In Ameer's words:

> Man, we got tight. Me and Raymond was real tight, man. "Get in touch with me man; make sure you get in touch with me," he told me. So he gave me his number, man. He wanna come; he wanna join. When I got out, man, I had so much to take care of. I had my own thing to get together. When he got killed, I felt really bad. I never did get in touch with him when I got out.

As Raymond declared, he was from the Slauson neighborhood. He had met Bird before he met Ameer, and as suspected, Bird did not get a very good first impression of him. On that occasion, on the street where Bird's mother lived, Raymond was behaving so poorly that it not only caught Bird's attention but required Bird to put him "in check." As Bird explained:

> One day, I came home from LA City College, and Raymond Washington was sittin' down by the fireplug—there's only one fireplug on 73rd down there—and he was drunk or loaded or somethin'. He was probably about fifteen years old. This was before he became Raymond Washington. Okay, well, he was Raymond Washington, but he wasn't *the* Raymond Washington. When I saw him, he hadn't gotten big yet. And he was sittin' down, cussin', and he was talking to Helen Walker. And I told Helen—I said, "Who's that?" She said, "That's Raymond," which meant nothing to me. But there were kids out there, and I told him, "You're gonna have to get off the street. You can't be sittin' here cussin' like that in front of these kids."

Bird didn't encounter Raymond again until 1976, when Raymond's "number one boy," Craig C., was killed by Little Stevie, whom Bird knew.[37] By this time, young Raymond had become *the* Raymond Washington, the notorious founder of the Crips, and well known by many, including those who only knew about him.

South Los Angeles Panthers and Muslims had sufficient neighborhood influence that a number of set and nonset juveniles joined their ranks. A third BPM group, the United Slaves Organization, or US,[38] formed in Los Angeles with deep roots in the community. Its presence was less dominant than the Muslims and Panthers, in part because of its connections to the White power structure.[39] The Muslims and Panthers didn't have this connection, but they had a strong presence in the California prison system during the 1960s and attracted a lot of their early recruits from those behind bars. Besides the appeal of their messages, the Muslims and Panthers also tried to provide various levels of support for inmates upon release and for children, with their breakfast program.

Organizationally, the Black Power groups attracted set members based on their set affiliation; many Businessmen became Muslims, while none joined the Panthers.[40] Bunchy had so much influence on the Renegades that a number of them followed him wherever he went. They followed him into the Nation of Islam when he joined and then followed him again when he left the Muslims to become a Panther.[41] Some Watts set members became Muslims, though few joined the Panthers or US. US got much of its set support from the Gladiators, archrivals of the Slausons and a factor in Bunchy's assassination at UCLA in 1969. It appears there were at least two motivations: gang and political.

Bunchy was first a Slauson and later a member of the Black Panther Party. He was shot, allegedly, by a person who was first a Gladiator and then later joined US.[42] The Slausons and the Gladiators were historical street-group enemies, while the Panthers and US were political rivals. Bunchy's assassination was facilitated by his membership in a street group that was an enemy to the street group of his alleged assassin, although his death was most likely due to his political association with a group that was enemies to the political group of his assassin. Gang killing or political killing? It was a little of both. If the circumstances of the killing were statistically forced into either category, many of the gradations of what actually happened would be lost.

A Riot Runs through It

In a study of the history of American violence, Richard Brown asserted that the "racial conflict between Caucasians and Negroes is one of the most persistent factors in American violence, extending far back into the 18th century."[43] Los Angeles was no stranger to racial violence, having experienced it in a variety of forms for many years before the 1965 Watts Rebellion. Sometimes, the violence got nasty. When the White mob attacks during the Zoot-Suit Riots of 1943 became especially violent, street groups of Blacks and Mexicans teamed up to fight the White instigators. One time, after a pack of one hundred servicemen had held down a twenty-three-year-old Black male and "gouged out his eye" with a knife, five hundred youth from Watts, Clanton, 38th Street, and others joined together in a united front of Blacks and Mexicans to confront the mobs of soldiers, sailors, and Marines in a showdown the following night.[44]

Closer to the occurrence of the Watts Rebellion, Elizabeth Poe pointed out that "two hundred Negro teen-agers and young adults rioted in Compton, near Watts, in 1961."[45] John Howard and William McCord report that on Memorial Day 1961, there was a "racial incident in Griffith Park"; then a year later, there occurred a police-involved shooting with Black Muslims in April 1962, plus numerous small-scale riots in 1964 at Jefferson High School and Central Receiving Hospital.[46] Also, in 1964, the assistant attorney general, recognizing the extent of the racial powder keg in Los Angeles, warned that further demonstrations there could be joined by the "entire negro community," causing millions of dollars in damage. The warnings were ignored by the mayor, the chief of police, and the governor.[47] With a past like this, and with little having been done to ameliorate seething racial tensions, it should have come as no surprise that Los Angeles remained home to numerous riot potentialities and was a straw away from breaking the proverbial camel's back. Yet surprise it did.

Daryl Gates, the LAPD "field commander" during the Watts Rebellion, expressing the sentiments of many, questioned how it could have happened in such a wonderful community as Watts, where the problems Black people faced were not nearly as bad as those faced by Blacks in eastern cities. He wrote: "Reporters who came out from the east [must have] ... had difficulty understanding how so much violence could erupt in a neighborhood with leafy trees and tricycles parked in driveways." Gates added that the neighborhood was, after all, a place where "kids playing in the park would go into the police station to buy candy bars out of the vending machine"; it was a neighborhood with a "small town" feel to it.[48] Further, Gates left no doubt that in his opinion racial injustice was blameless for what happened: "Say all you want about social causes, I don't believe they accounted for what occurred." In his view, the causes for the Rebellion were clearly the fault of the people who rioted.[49] He seemed to believe that had the people been more grateful for how lucky they were to live where they lived, under the conditions they were so fortunate to have, they would never have rioted. Gates miscalculated.

Perhaps if Gates and the others who expressed the mystified view of "How could it happen here?" had been listening to the comments of LAPD's Chief William H. Parker, who said the participants behaved "like monkeys in a zoo," they wouldn't have been so oblivious.[50] Perhaps if they had been aware of the insights reported by Robert Conot in his penetrating study titled *Rivers of Blood, Years of Darkness*, they wouldn't have been so clueless. Perhaps if they had had just a little sense of history, they would have been aware that ugly clashes between police and Black Angelenos characterized most of the City's past.[51] Perhaps then they would have understood that *justice* meant "just them" to the people of Watts, and not *us*, since the *us* in *justice* excluded most non-Whites. Then again, perhaps they wouldn't.[52]

The LAPD had accomplices in their racist accusations. During the Rebellion, with LASD deputies shouting, "Run niggers,"[53] as they chased people from stores with broken windows, or a deputy who complained, "I'm tired of you niggers messing with me," as he whipped a girl "around the thighs," it was obvious some deputies were on a mission.[54] Had Field Commander Gates been aware of this—or had he even paid attention to his own officers at the 77th Street Station, who shared the acronym "LSMFT"[55] derisively spoken by one officer to others with this accounting, "Let's shoot a motherfucker tonight!" and comments like "Got your nigger knocker all shined up?"—he might have seen more clearly that all was not well in leafy green Watts.[56] But Gates, Parker, and other city leaders seemed to have skipped over this chapter in their civics lessons.[57]

Volumes have been written, including a *U.S. Riot Commission Report*, on the 1965 rebellion. The role that structural and personal racism played in its occurrence has been unequivocally documented, yet 90 percent of people nationally believed the police were too lenient.[58] In sum: the six-day riot killed thirty-four people and wounded another 1,032; police killings were called "justifiable homicide'" while everyone else was charged with crimes.[59] The Rebellion caused $40,000,000 in property damage and accounted for 3,952 arrests, of which 500 were juveniles,[60] most of whom were booked for loitering and curfew.[61] At the time, the Rebellion was the most deadly and expensive battle between citizens and law enforcement in the history of the City. There were few among the 6,000,000 living in the entire county of Los Angeles who were unaffected by this near war.

Street-Group Contributions

What has not been examined is the connection of the South Los Angeles street groups to the Rebellion.[62] Little has been written on how the Rebellion was affected by and in turn affected those groups and the new street groups to come afterward. Conot does write about a 77th Street police officer's awareness of the street groups' role at the Rebellion with these comments:

> As Mac Benton went out he saw that all the gangs were out in force, riding around flashing the V sign of the Slausons, the thumbs-down fist of the Gladiators, the open fingered O of the Businessmen, the W of the old Watts gangs. As they passed each other in cars they would be cheered—old enemies forgetting their grudges to go and get Whitey. The Outlaws, the Rebel Rousers, the Parks and Boot Hill—all had representation.[63]

Although Bird sarcastically referred to the Rebellion as "a lot of shootin' and a little lootin'," he understood it was a major neighborhood event, profoundly affecting all who lived in Watts, the surrounding areas, and in the City.[64] The Rebellion was more a piece from a general process of socioeconomic transformation, already in play, than it was definitive for street groups. The Rebellion was about racism and against the injustice that everyone knew. In its breadth, it caught up all who had had enough, were mad as hell, and weren't going to take it anymore.[65] But the "old enemies" among participating street groups Conot had referred to had not forgotten their grudges.

The Watts Rebellion, beginning near Imperial Highway and Avalon Boulevard, didn't start in Watts; it started in an area a few blocks from Watts where the D'Artagnans street group hung out.[66] The D'Artagnans were enemies to a number of the Watts sets, like the Huns, thus generally not able to generate much sympathy from the Watts groups for something that happened to them in their own neighborhood. That the Watts groups joined the D'Artagnans, as well as joining with other street groups who had had previous antagonisms with Watts and with each other, makes it notable the street groups perceived a greater enemy than they were to one another. They understood that they were there to confront a common foe: the police. As Bird explained about the Slausons' involvement: "We didn't come to loot; we came to get down. We came to fight the police." The appearance of unity among the street groups was an easy error to make.

Antipathy toward the police had been building for a long time among street groups for the injustices they felt the police had shown them. The inappropriate handling of Marquette and Ronald Frye, by the highway patrol, on the fateful day of August 11, 1965, when the brothers were stopped for "erratic" driving, was the catalyst: it was the spark that lit the flame to the Rebellion. The sequence of escalating events to follow—especially the perception of great disrespect by the police toward the Frye family—was the cause that generated street-group engagement. From the perspective of street-group members, this was another wrong by the man—it was his fault—but this time the man took things too far. As Bird expounded:

> The worst thing you could do is put a uniform with a badge, a gun to back it up, on an idiot. See, and that's what they've done. Now they [the police] feel like the hog with the big nuts. You gettin' these chumps all the way from Tennessee to come on the police force that don't like Blacks, no way. See, I know. If you rode in as many police cars as I have—police and sheriff—been to jail as many times as I have, you'd know. And see, 75 percent of the time the police are out of line. That day they stopped Marquette and Ronald down there, the highway patrol, they stepped out of line. Had they just gave the dude a ticket for drunk and allowed his brother or his sister who came down there or his mother to drive the car home . . . "We just live around the corner. Okay, go ahead and take him to jail, and let my other son go, and we'll take the car home." See, no, they didn't do that. No, they got to be police. They got to be, "No, you just shut the fuck up; you get out of the way." They [the police] put their hands on them [the Frye brothers and their mother].

Word of the escalating confrontation spread to the various street groups through the neighborhood telegraph: a complex network of phone calls and word-of-mouth communications that make Twitter seem slow by comparison. The Slausons became involved early on because the mother of one of them lived on East Imperial Highway, where she could see the gathering of people through her home's window. As the crowd gathered, she knew something big was up. She phoned her son, who, in turn, alerted another homeboy, who alerted yet another, until word had spread this was an event requiring everyone's attention.

Cooperation, Not Coordination

Slauson and Watts sets were some of the earliest large groups on the scene. While it was the first time they had ever been on the same side for anything, they were not—nor did they become—an organized force following central leadership and cooperating side by side to help each other. Bird clarified: "We did things with our own neighborhood, and they did things with their own. See, we still cliqued off to our own. We fought during the Rebellion with our own troops." There were good reasons for this absence of coordination. They were together for a common purpose against a common enemy, but they were also historic enemies who were not about to coordinate. Bird explained:

> If we'd have mixed with Watts, then they would have been tryin' to call some kind of shot or somethin', or they would have gotten in our way. See, we didn't run with those dudes. And we knew who our guys were, and we knew who we could depend on, you know. We knew when to move and who we had to ride back with. See, we were out of our neighborhood. We were far out of our neighborhood, so we ran with our own homeboys.

At times, when members of the groups might have had a single focus, the distrust and lack of mutual familiarity with one another caused problems. In an incident between a Slauson member and a Watts group, when a bundle of cash was being divided up, wariness was confirmed. At that time, Bird was nearby when some Watts dudes had opened a safe and were making a grab for the money. Bird grabbed too, but then the situation deteriorated, and he found himself in a jam. He elaborated:

> I got trapped on 103rd by some dudes from Watts that wanted to jump on me, 'cause they had tore a safe open and was gettin' money out of it. I stuck my hand in there, and I had money, and they said, "Man, you from Slauson, man." You know, and I had a fist full of dollars. And Big Freddy Everett from Watts said, "Man, he needs some

money too." Just like that. And me and Freddy Everett was always tight. He's a great big muscle-bound dude, with about twenty-inch arms. But because I was from Slauson, them dudes from Watts said I wasn't allowed to get any of the money.

In the end, Big Freddy's juice prevailed, and Bird was allowed to keep the booty he had grabbed. Had Big Freddy not been there and had Bird not been friends with him, things would have no doubt turned out differently.

Although, as Conot wrote, other street groups participated in the Rebellion, all were more or less involved in the same way Slauson and Watts were. Noted gang researcher Lewis Yablonsky, after interviewing some of the juveniles involved in the Rebellion, thought that one possible outcome would be peace prevailing among the "Negro gangs" while they "trained their sights on," and organized against the "real enemy," "Whitey."[67] He seemed to have misunderstood that this was not a confederacy of gangs. While those street groups that did participate might have extended the length of the Rebellion through their internal organization, no group went to Watts to help Watts or became united in the process. The groups came to fight the "establishment," especially as it was manifested in the police: "They came together to get down but not together with each other," Bird emphasized.

Many other street groups at the Rebellion also had long-term antagonisms with each other and had developed deep antipathies that didn't change just because they were now battling a common foe. Members from these groups took items from the broken window fronts because they were readily available; they were there for the taking. Mostly it was opportunistic theft, but theft was not the primary reason the street groups were there. The Rebellion was a battle that had been a long time coming, and now that it was happening, the street groups were taking advantage. Since many in the community had accepted the righteousness of the Rebellion, it was relatively easy for them to defend the involvement of the participants, if not directly, then at least indirectly.[68] The Rebellion provided an occasion for temporary community solidarity that was stronger than any other unifying force had been in a long while. But it was no street-group *kumbaya*.[69]

Power structure authorities, who continued to misunderstand the nature of the Rebellion, thought that by bringing in Black celebrities to address the crowds, they would be able to calm things down. Authorities reasoned there might have been outside agitators organizing the people, who would change allegiance to the Black celebrities once they heard from them. What the authorities had missed was this: no one was in charge. The Rebellion was not an organized conflict; it was a free-for-all. It was a spontaneous combustion that had caught up diverse elements as it spread, uniting people and bringing them together because of the ubiquitous sense of outrage felt by so many.[70] Bird explained: "I've heard that someone orchestrated this or set that off. That's bullshit! Ain't nobody came in and told nobody to do nothin', 'cause wasn't nobody runnin' nothin'! I didn't want to hear Martin Luther King or Dick Gregory tell me, 'You all be cool.' He had to get on. Someone shot at him [Dick Gregory]." The cluelessness of the authorities on the causes and their lack of preparation were quite likely factors prolonging the Rebellion.

Before 1965 began, many members of the street groups, including those who participated in the Rebellion, had already begun to reduce their time on the street with their group. They had moved on. The Rebellion had given them a brief opportunity to put their differences aside for several days, as the real enemy became momentarily visible. For most set members, the Rebellion had provided some transitory excitement, but it also portended a new era. Whatever improvements against injustice that were made after the Rebellion ended represented a pyrrhic victory for the participants. A lot of blood had been shed for a few fleeting gains. A flurry of post-Rebellion studies pointed out that the unmet needs and legitimate complaints of the people were left to history.[71] To be accurate, some peace did follow in the community subsequent to the Rebellion. Teen posts opened, more Blacks and Chicanos were hired by local businesses, and the Black Power movement—offering hope—seemed to gain some momentum.

One manifest consequence of the Rebellion was to alert power structure authorities of how ill prepared they had been to deal with an uprising of this magnitude. Since authorities were convinced that another riot was imminent, they were determined not to be unprepared again. Great energy was expended to shore up the community presence of the criminal-justice system by providing the police with the modern technologies they would need for prevention and early containment of future insurrections. This meant more police with better training and greater fire power. It did not mean new long-term programs for amelioration of the conditions that produced the Rebellion in the first place.[72] The criminal-justice system became tougher, not more just.

After the Rebellion, those who were active in the street groups of the 1950s and early 1960s continued to develop the interests they had been involved in before it had begun: other more meaningful or necessary pursuits. Many were married, were starting or had started families, had jobs, or were in college and needed to take care of adult business. Some others, who might have been unemployed or uninvolved in any meaningful activity, went back to that. Still others took advantages of the mixed new opportunities the Rebellion had created. The Rebellion had brought them together for a minute because it was there. When it was over, life resumed. The Rebellion came, it happened, it ended. In its wake, a new and very different kind of normality began to settle into the communities, as the altered realities reflected by these changes occurring around them asserted themselves.

In Their Time for a Time

Street-group affiliation involving fussin', cussin', and discussin', for the pre-1965 Black South Los Angeles residents, was a phase in their lives, not a lifetime commitment. It was neither cool nor appropriate for Black males to remain on the street with young street homies by the time they reached their early to midtwenties. Deputy Probation Officer Woodrow C. argued that most gang juveniles saw gangs as a "stage in life," a "temporary" place, something to do when you're young, not when you reach adulthood. When gang juveniles started getting into their twenties, they just got out of the gang, he believed. "You're still doin' this at your age?" might be a reproach from some "older folk," he argued, reminding the juveniles that it's time to put childhood activities behind them. Bird summed it up: "You'd look mighty damn stupid at thirty still runnin' around tellin' about you still a gang member."[73] In adulthood, pre-1965 set members were motivated to put aside youthful differences their groups might have had in their now mutual pursuit of money. Legal or otherwise, the quest for pecuniary resources became a common denominator for the pre-1965 Black males as adults. As time went on, they went on. They grew up and aged out of street activity.

Families were often influential in limiting street activities by issuing powerful mandates. When a twenty-something Black male got married, his wife didn't want him out on the streets with his homeboys, especially after they became parents. It was his job, and usually hers too, to find work and to support the family. Some people could get preachy about the necessity of being off the streets and bringing home money. Roslyn exhibited this attitude. Although "converted to the neighborhood," as Bird contended, when she became a mother, she got a job, and she "didn't come back to the streets with that gang shit. In fact, she got on other people's case about that." For Lafayette, it was his father who told him, "Enough." He was going to be on his own if he got arrested again for gang activity. As Lafayette explained:

> My father told me, "Look"—because I had been arrested three times in like nine months for gang activity, shootin' 'n' stuff—"I'm done gettin' you outta jail." He says, "I understand you say you a Slauson and you gon' be Slauson till you die and all that. I understand that shit. But I'm not gon' get you out of jail no more for gang fightin'. I'm done."

Lafayette also had an older brother who seconded his father's mandate and put additional pressure on him to stop his troublemaking ways.

The ephemeral nature of street-group involvement for some juveniles can't be easily categorized. For many it just "sort of ended," like a moment in time that gets over without definitive closure marking when or even how it happened. But an ending of street activity, especially for the Slausons, did not mean complete separation from the group. A Slauson was a Slauson for life, though not a street denizen for life. Cardell explained his reduction in street activity this way:

> Like with Blacks, when you get a certain age, you just sorta like vanish. As we get older, we just gradually fade out, like no mo'. So if we know who's a Slauson, and when we see each other, we throw up that two fingers, meaning for Slauson Village, we still recognized as being homeboys from the Park. But as far as it's a gang still going on at Slauson, no, it's not that way. As you get older, things fades without you knowin' it.

Cardell also had a job, sometimes two or three at the same time, which put increased demands on his time. The jobs paid well enough that he honored his growing commitment to them, as he slipped further away from active street involvement.

Don't Pass Your Vices Back

Pre-1965 street-group Black males held to another ethic that was self-defeating for group institutionalization: most felt it was inappropriate to pass their "vices" back to the younger generation. When those vices included behaviors that might cause trouble for the youngsters if copied, the vices were not boasted about in situations where their tender, though tuned-in, young ears could hear. Bird reported that his two older sons did not know he was a Slauson until they were in their teens. They just happened to find out one day when they were with their mother and ran into a homeboy, who inquired about Bird.[74] The boys overheard the conversation, asked, and were told that this was one of their daddy's homeboys. Later, when they saw Bird, he confirmed what they had heard.

Sometimes one's homeboys were not even familiar with each other's younger relatives. When chanced upon, the situation could become awkward, particularly if the younger kin were boasting. Such was the case when Roach met Bird's son in jail. Roach didn't know him but was not about to let this youngster claim Slauson connections that he might not have had. As Bird explained:

> See, okay, Dante met Roach in county jail. Roach called me on the telephone to ask me, "You got a son named Dante?" I said, "Yeah." Roach say, "'Cause I was sittin' up here talkin', and I said something about Slauson, and this youngster come up and started talkin' about

you." He [Roach] said, "I had to put him in check, or I had to check him out." I mean, Roach took his twenty cents that he could have used for somethin' else, and he called me to verify that this dude is who he says he was. Although he [Dante] had all the right answers, but that don't mean nothin'. He could have been hangin' around me, or he could have heard it through the grapevine. But Roach went out of his way and called to verify whether this dude was my son or not. And if this little dude was wrong, Roach was gonna kick his ass. But see, you can't go around droppin' them logs unless you are who you say you are. That was a standard rule in our neighborhood. It was standard in most neighborhoods.

During the time the originals, like Roach and Bird, were on the set and the set was relatively small, the originals had considerable control over membership. They didn't encourage family member participation, neither their own nor from the families of homies; nor did they permit imposters.

Offspring were especially not welcome. Younger family members were even discouraged from attending parties where the goings-on were considered detrimental to their well-being. According to a park director, who had spent a lot of time with neighborhood juveniles, they were instead given guidance, shown proper morals, and issued a warning to not be like me. As is often typical of younger generations, these admonitions frequently fell on ears unwilling or incapable of hearing the message. While the juveniles no doubt found some direction from their elder's exhortations, they were influenced more by the elder's behavior and by the circumstances they found themselves in. Usually juveniles, preoccupied with their peers, did their own thing; they didn't share with family adults. But street-group participation and formation remained a viable option for young people in an environment that continued marginalizing them. Not only had the circumstances for street-group association in South Los Angeles not changed for the better; they had worsened so that getting socialized into street groups was going with the flow.

A Makeover

By the mid-1960s many things had changed for the Slauson originals: maturation, incarceration, and moribundity had depleted their ranks. Bird was now in his early twenties, with "gunselin'" no longer holding the same attraction for him it had during his teens.[75] For a number of the other originals, similar circumstances prevailed; those who had forged the Slauson ideology out of common antagonisms had, through various exits, left their street activity behind. While most continued to closely identify with Slauson traditions, and many had either stayed in the neighborhood or moved to adjacent ones, their role in street-group organization and cohesion had diminished.

Gang activities, especially large-scale gang fights, were relatively few after the Rebellion and continued to be rare right up through the late 1960s, according to Ameer and Bird.[76] There were "skirmishes" but no major battles.[77] Some juveniles chose not to be involved with street groups at all. Their primary interest was to follow various traditions of being "players" rather than members of a named street group.[78] While change was underway before the Rebellion, the Rebellion contributed to—and accelerated—further change. Bird observed: "A lot of stuff was tore down and rebuilt or not rebuilt. A lot of people moved, Black and White, and they started rebuilding. Attitudes changed." Black studies programs and Black student unions were created at universities, while California State University Dominguez Hills was opened just a few miles south from where the Rebellion had taken place. Local businesses hired more Blacks, and a lot of federal money flowed into the community for assorted projects and improvements. Opportunities, however temporary they might have been, emerged for many.

Reducing the odds for these opportunities to be realized were many of the changes made in the criminal-justice system. It had been caught *slippin'* and unprepared for the Rebellion.[79] A growing public sense that crime, juvenile delinquency, and gang violence were getting out of hand and needed to be treated with tougher criminal-justice tactics had emerged before the end of the 1960s. Relying on these sentiments and the demonstrated weaknesses of gang intervention programs, new criminal-justice strategies of *suppression* began to replace the earlier efforts of *prevention*.[80]

Two major problems with this new get-tough criminal-justice approach were that it was the "least effective response" to gang problems and that it was most likely to "exacerbate the racial disproportionality of arrest."[81] The proposed cures not only failed to improve the problems, but their implementation made the problems worse. Los Angeles was one of those cities where getting tough on gangs became the norm, guaranteeing more severe gang-related complications for its non-White youth. The police, whose tactics had been singled out by the early street groups as especially egregious, responded with even harsher strategies.[82] Rather than amelioration, South Los Angeles got deterioration.

As neighborhood populations grew, they were transformed from communities of more organized social networks where people knew one another and had histories together to places more anomic. New kids on the block came from everywhere. They migrated and immigrated, in different age cohorts, fitting in some places but not in others. Set elders not only didn't welcome the new arrivals into their sets; they often didn't even know who they were.[83] The elders became protective of their set's name. Bird insisted that the Slauson name was like a "U.S. patent." He continued: "See, had all of us stepped off the set, it might be different, but we weren't. You couldn't be a Slauson 'cause you said you were a Slauson. You had to come with credentials or a passport. Someone had to speak for you; you had to be tested. We needed to see you in action."

PotTea, who became Bird's "runnin' partner," passed his Slausons admissions test when he whooped George C. from Watts in front of Eugene, a Little Slauson. Eugene, who was initially leery of befriending PotTea because he didn't know him well, gave his "stamp of approval" when PotTea showed "how good he was with those things [fists]" and how fearless. Although not an original, PotTea was acknowledged as a righteous member of the Slausons. But as the 1960s progressed, new PotTea-type youth joining the Slausons went from rare to extinct.

Peaceful Coexistence

To make a legitimate claim on Slauson membership or to have formed a genuine new Slauson clique required permission from an original, or at least not opposition.[84] Anyone who became a Slauson during the 1960s, like PotTea, although considered an elder, was not from the original set. Since most of those from the original set—the "main dudes"—were gone, few remained to grant admission. Too many new youth were arriving too quickly for them to directly, or even indirectly, approve or disapprove of everyone.

For most of those who came to Fremont High School during the 1960s, permission to become a Slauson was not necessarily denied; a lot joined, but their connection to the original set was weak to nonexistent. Bird noted that there was always an elder around to keep those who claimed to be Slausons in line. As he explained: "If you gonna use somebody's name, you had to stay in line. That's like usin' a family name. There was always someone around to put you in check." Why would the next successive group of juveniles claim that name and risk needless friction? "See, now you can claim any other name you want to and be an idiot if you want to, but you don't carry the name Slauson, because you'd been out of order."

There were other juveniles, in different parts of the Slausons' neighborhood, who, while recognizing they were from the neighborhood, were not particularly interested in claiming fealty to a group of Slausons they knew little about, irrespective of its previous glory. Further, the Slausons were a group they had less in common with anyway—a group of "old guys"—than they did with their peers. Besides, why would they want to adhere to a bunch of standards and rules they had no part in making and that might run counter to their interests? The old guys wouldn't understand the problems the new dudes were facing, and they would be judged unfairly. On top of this, the aspiring juveniles, in most cases, would have been denied permission anyhow had they even requested it.[85]

Permission denied didn't mean the aspirants went away sulking, with bowed heads and hands in their pockets, abandoning their desire for street-group affiliation. They hadn't come begging and didn't leave dejected. The aspirants started groups with their peers, their own motivations, and activities and then coexisted with the elders from the earlier groups.

Coexistence among the various pre-1965 street groups, the new street groups, the Panthers, and the Muslims became the new norm during the late 1960s. Sergeant T. of the Compton Police Department recalled new gangs in the Compton and Watts/Willowbrook areas emerging in the late 1960s and early 1970s with names like the Piru Boys, the Canal Boys, the Carver Park Boys, the West Side Boys, the Campanella Park Boys, the Willowbrook Boys, and the Avalon Boys. New groups in other areas of South Los Angeles such as the 76th Boys, the McCoy Boys, and the Shack Boys emerged as well.[86] None of these new groups received sanctioning by the pre-1965 groups; nor is it evident they actively sought it or put up much of a fuss when it wasn't forthcoming.[87]

Differences between the new sets and the pre-1965 sets were sufficiently great that the best they could do with each other was to stay out of one another's way. While this approach worked well enough between them, it worked less well among the new street groups. The new groups developed antagonistic relationships with each other and became rivals. They were peers who might have initially been together and cliqued off because of differences. Their group might have started up as a response to an already existing peer group, or they might have started up for an assortment of other reasons.[88]

When hostilities developed among the new groups, they usually followed an incident(s) that may or may not have been remembered or even known by all the members. What the juveniles remembered, especially the later joiners, was who their enemies were, regardless of why. The development of enemies was a function of in-group membership, not necessarily a rational process. Enemy creation followed the well-established patterns of in-group/out-group associations; groups disliked each other "because . . ." Antagonisms could easily develop more sound rationales when the initial dislike was later accompanied by actions that were considered offensive. An offense that produced a reciprocal offense could escalate tensions and generate out-group enmity with reasonable justifications for respective animosities.

Contributing to changes among street groups in the Slauson neighborhood was a formal name reform. Los Angeles officials have a history of changing the names of various landmarks that street groups took their names from, hoping it might diminish the group. Slauson Park's name change is an example. The Park's name was changed in the 1960s to Mary McLeod Bethune Park. The formal reason given was to more clearly respect the community, which in the case of Slauson Park had merit. But changing the name of their park also denied the Slausons a principal connection to their neighborhood. As Cardell clarified, "Although Mary McLeod Bethune was Black, which was better for us because James Edward Slauson was White—that was our park, regardless. See, by them changing the name, it took away our label, our identity." While the Park continued to hold its importance for the older Slausons, it lost its meaning for the neighborhood juveniles coming up after the name revision. It was no longer a landmark that gave unity to the neighborhood or had a history the youth could relate to—it became just another park that happened to be nearby.

A Street Group of Avenues

One of the earliest and better known of the new South Los Angeles street groups was the Avenues.[89] Beginning about 1968 or early 1969 in the Renegades' neighborhood, the Avenues hung out in Roosevelt Park.[90] Although they were from the Renegades' territory, the Renegade Babies, the youngest Renegade clique, wouldn't allow this new group to clique with them. The Avenues founded their own clique and created their own name, taking it from the north-south avenues in their neighborhood: Hooper, Central, Parmelee, and Zamora. They were known for their muscular physiques. Their leader, Craig Monson, a former member of Bunchy Carter's teen post, had assembled a group of about fifteen young dudes into a clique.[91] Among the members of Monson's original clique was Raymond Washington, who was an Avenue before he became a Crip, although he also considered himself a Slauson. More precisely, Raymond, like Monson, was from the Slauson neighborhood. Neither Monson nor Raymond became Slausons, but Raymond joined Monson's clique of Avenues before he began his own clique—the Crips.

When Bird first met Monson, he noted how large he was. Bird exclaimed: "This motherfucker was bigger than me! He was six feet tall and had big ol' hands. Man, his wrists look like Billy clubs, you know, little tree stumps, a big ol' tree-stump dude." Around six or seven years Bird's junior, and about fifteen or sixteen at the time, Monson was from a different generation than Bird. Bird noted that Monson was trying to dress cool, with a humbug hat and a black leather coat, like a Slauson or a Panther might wear. Bird and the Slausons were not happy with Monson and his homeboys because they were hanging out in Slauson (Bethune) and Roosevelt Parks and rumored to be doing things—like stealing leather coats after assaulting the owners to get them and extorting money—that the Slausons disapproved of. One day, Bird confronted them, with this result:

> And see now, Monson, Teddy Bear, and Donny Boy were comin' out real heavy at Roosevelt Park. Okay, we jammed them one time, and we asked them, "Why you guys out here runnin' around doin' all this stuff?" I said, "I hear you been runnin' round takin' people's coats and stuff?" He said, "No, man, what you talkin' 'bout?'"

Monson knew who Bird was and knew that he carried a lot of juice. He showed Bird respect, and the encounter ended peacefully. They understood each other and knew there was no need for further discussion. As Bird explained, "And you know what they told us? 'Because.'" Monson was the leader of a new set from the old neighborhood. Composed of juveniles who had grown up there and others who may not have, they had become the new kids on the set.

In their early years, some of the Avenues were on the high school football team because they were large and muscular. Bodybuilding to look strong and fearsome was a shared activity among most of them. Since looking fearsome was a major part of their unifying theme, it appears they didn't abuse alcohol and probably didn't use drugs—at least, not in the beginning.[92] As they got older, things changed, with a number of them getting strung out on "sherm."[93] As Bob M., the director of Roosevelt Park, explained, "A lot of the Avenues were smokin' the sherm, and it just affected their brains. They had strokes and are just old men now [1989]." The Avenues were more like a clique than a set, not lasting long enough to form age-graded cliques. They existed within a community of assorted other cliques, older sets, Black Power groups, and the nascent Crips. Some of their greatest differences were with the Crips, with whom, at times, they were often confused.

Tales from the Hood

With a phenomenon as sensationalized as the Crips, the rise of multiple folktales to explain them is to be expected. The reason behind most of the explanations is political, primarily seeking to advance the agenda of the explainer. Several accounts have assumed that Crip is an acronym for something ominous—associating the name with its ability to threaten or cause harm, giving it a frightful awe. Other versions have disrespected the group by claiming the name stands for something derogatory. But the majority of legends attempt to embellish an image of the group as dangerous, menacing, and powerful.

Perhaps the most persistent myth of how the Crips developed their name is that they took it from the British film titled *Tales from the Crypt*.[94] This horror film portrayed a series of five stories of deceit and mayhem, providing a fitting example of Crip treacherousness by association. The fact that the film used the term *Crypt* rather than Crip and that there is difference in spelling and meaning of the two words offered little problem to proponents of this myth. They dismissed the discrepancies with such rationalizations as "Well, these kids can't spell so well anyway" and "Diction is not one of their strong points." Since both the Crips and the film occurred more or less at the same time, it seemed evidence enough to sustain their argument. However, it is only by ignoring the actual sequence of events that their contention holds up. The Crips began in the late 1960s, while the film wasn't released until 1972.[95] Since the Crips' founding predates the film's release by several years, it would have been impossible for the Crips to model themselves after something which had not yet happened.[96]

Another legend of the Crips' name involves an alleged connection with the substance called "kryptonite." Fictional kryptonite is the stuff that even Superman can't defeat. If the Crips can be portrayed as more potent than Superman, they have more than enough power to "cripple" any opponents who even think about messing with them. Again, the differences in the spelling and the meaning of *Crip* and *kryptonite* seemed of little concern to those arguing this position, once more dismissing the discrepancies by blaming them on the weak intellectual abilities of the youth.[97]

The fable of the Crips' taking their name from their ability to cripple is an accurate assessment of their capabilities—mess with them at your risk—although not of the origin of their name. While many of their opponents have ended up crippled or dead after a confrontation, the evidence to suggest the name Crip originated because they crippled rivals or saw themselves as cripplers is weak.[98]

Treating *Crip* as an acronym has produced a number of wild and mostly partisan post hoc associations. Two of the more interesting ones are: "*C*owards *r*un *i*n *p*acks," and "*C*ontinuous *r*evolution *i*n *p*rogress."[99] The first acronym came from the police while the second came from a Crip defender. Both came after the Crips had established themselves and had created a reputation that impressed people—differently, it turns out, depending on their in-group membership.

A noteworthy account of the Crip's name comes from Danifu, the author of the "Crip Constitution," as reported in the 2005 documentary film *Bastards of the Party*. Danifu claims he and Raymond were looking at a baby's crib when Raymond experienced a transcendent moment in which the name Crip just came to him. Crip then transmuted into "Community *r*evolutionary *i*nterparty *s*ervice." The strength of attachment to this name became evident sometime later when the Crips attempted a symbiotic affiliation with the mayor's office. To make the group more acceptable to the mayor, city officials, and others the mayor had to do business with, the Crips readily replaced "*r*evolutionary" with "*reform*" so that it would be, well, more politically appropriate.

These accounts are salient but not exhaustive. Myths often have obscure origins, which lose relevance in their entrenchment. Myths have an inverse relationship to reality; the further they are from it, the more imagination is required. Most partisans probably don't know where their tale for the Crips came from but have accepted the fable popular in their in-group. Political expediency has allowed the myths of Crip origins to remain shrouded in mystery. Myth, after all, sells more newspapers, generates more TV market share, and can be more effective in shaking loose funding from competitive fiscal budgets to fight gang activity than evidence some might not want to hear. Myth can be transformative for gang members, who can lay claim to a name that in itself is sufficient to strike dread into even the bravest of hearts. But we're gang researchers, not partisans, so we dug deeper.

Innovations in Black Slang

Black people have a long history of linguistic innovation.[100] Certain words, which have been part of the argot for decades, have emerged because they are descriptive or express a feeling or rhyme or because they simplify and make intelligible some trait or behavior. Black slang is another way to express in-groupness: if one is Black and hip, one is an in-group member and understands. Slang contributes to distinguishing one's in-group from a society that hasn't treated them well. Sometimes the slang will be interpreted by outsiders as offensive. At times the slang will be offensive, while at others it will be complimentary, and at still others just matter-of-fact. What determines the meaning is the context in which the slang is used. Intonation sets the stage. The same word in different contexts can be either an insult or an expression of warmth: members of the in-group will know right away which it is.

Most people are familiar with the word *cripple*.[101] While considered an offensive term when used as a noun in politically correct parlance, in the Slauson neighborhood, this term was used as a verb—crippin', when disabled people were limping or otherwise displaying their disability. According to Bird: "Whenever you see anybody when you was growing up that was limpin', we would tell them, 'You crippin'.'" In discourse, the brevity norm shortened the two-syllable word *cripple* to the one-syllable word *crip* to refer to people who were crippled. For many, cripple, or crip, was not derogatory—it was just a way to state an obvious fact.

In the Slauson neighborhood, the term had been applied to a much-respected homegirl who, as a child in the early 1950s, had developed polio, resulting in a limp when she walked. While she was often called by her given name, she was also frequently—and affectionately—referred to by her nickname, "Crip." She no doubt was not the first or the only person in the community with this nickname, but she may have been the first set member from the Slauson neighborhood to receive it. Thus, she was arguably the first "crip" from the Slauson neighborhood, though she was not a Crip but a Slauson. But she was a crip before there were Crips—just like any others from the neighborhood who sported disabilities would have been. This account of origins loses melodrama but gains accuracy.

The Infamous Raymond

Raymond Washington left the Avenues, either because he was kicked out or because he had honored an agreement between him and Craig Monson to leave. By some accounts, Raymond left because he was considered a "fuckup" by Avenue notables and was not a good fit. His departure may have been accelerated by a scuffle with them.[102] Regardless of specifics, it appears that Raymond was in search of a proper fit somewhere. He had been expelled from Fremont High School and then sent to Washington High because of his behavior. He was a poor student, dropping out of high school before graduation without the ability to read or write very well, if at all. Bob M. noted that the Avenues had a bit "more style" than "Raymond and them," who were more "rowdy." Donny H., who was Raymond's contemporary and knew him, said that he had a difficult time establishing rapport with peers, choosing instead to hang out with younger juveniles who were impressed by his physical size and prior affiliations.[103]

Around the time he left the Avenues, Raymond and some of his partners got into a fight, which caused enough injury to his leg that he limped afterward. Shortly thereafter, Darryl, Tony S., and Billy W., from the Slausons' neighborhood, ran into Raymond and his entourage, several of whom had also been injured in the fight, walking down the street toward them. Darryl shouted out to the group, "You all are a bunch of cripples. You nothin' but out here crippin' together." Crippin' Raymond and his injured pack suddenly were identified with a name that took on legs—the name stuck. They were crips who had now become the first Crips.[104]

Raymond admitted as much to Ameer when they shared a jail cell together and Ameer thought Raymond might have been a Slauson. Ameer's inquiry as to who he was generated this reply from Raymond: "'I'm a Crip, man. I'm the one that started the Crips.'" Ameer continued: "He [Raymond] said he was on crutches and somebody was sayin', 'Yeah, I see you crippin' around here.' And that's how it went from there." Raymond Washington, the youth who couldn't live up to the neighborhood rules established by the elders and had been dumped by a street group he sought affiliation with, now had a new identity with his recently named group of beleaguered warriors. It was not because they were skilled fighters that they became the fearsome Crips but because group notables were limping and on crutches and were called cripples.[105] Raymond Washington was another crip from the Slauson neighborhood whose crippin' gave definition to the Crips. The Crips' name began with a limp but not with a wimp.

There is a mistaken perception among some gang researchers that Raymond Washington and Bunchy Carter formed the Crips together.[106] They did not. Bunchy and Raymond knew each other as mentor and student from the teen post Bunchy briefly ran before being assassinated. Bunchy and Raymond were ten years apart and never peers. Bunchy was a Slauson and then a Black Panther but never a Crip. Although Raymond came from the Slauson neighborhood, he was never a Slauson but an Avenue and then a Crip. The Panthers were a political organization. They had developed numerous self-empowerment programs in the Black community, starting with defense from the police and later with breakfast programs for children, which were perceived by the LAPD and the FBI to be serious threats to the stability of power structure arrangements in the country, thereby justifying their systematic decimation.[107] The Crips were not a political movement and were not ideologically linked to the Panthers but rather began as a group with a circumstantially developed name that was readily adopted by other Black street groups in Los Angeles and in other areas of the country.

A Name Gets Purchase

The first group of Crips was a clique from the 70s Street area of the Slauson neighborhood. Although some youth in the early Crip cliques were known to the pre-1965 set members, the Crip youth never became a clique of those sets because those sets were dissipating, not adding new members. Jerry C., Raymond's "road dog," told us that the juveniles who became Crips didn't grow into Slausons because "they wouldn't let us." An important reason why the new street juveniles were denied Slauson membership was because of their cohort's behavior: many of the Crips and the Avenues were thieves, stealing leather coats from weaker youth. They were unruly too, involved in "unnecessary" rowdiness.[108] This behavior wouldn't have been acceptable to the pre-1965 sets if these juveniles had seriously tried to become a sanctioned clique of one of them.[109] Kumasi succinctly summarized the philosophical differences between the Slausons and the new cliques when he noted: "They were unable to embrace the ideology." Bird added, "They couldn't live up to the neighborhood rules."[110]

The Avenues and Crips in the 1960s were nascent cliques within a mature set, without fealty to that set. While occasionally put in check by older Slausons, the new groups had a limited connection to the original set and its elders and mostly made their own rules.[111] They were from a different generation. The limited connection between the old and the new was not a serious problem for either of them. There was mutual recognition of and then acceptance of the fact that they were different from each other. Many of the members of the new cliques were related to members of the pre-1965 cliques, but many were not. Some new clique members had lived in the neighborhood all or most of their lives, while others were recent arrivals. The new cliques represented a reordering among the street groups within the changing demographics of the neighborhood. They were cliques from the Slauson neighborhood, but they were not cliques of the Slauson set.

After Raymond's group formed, other cliques with the Crip name started to appear. Tweedy Bird, who ran with Raymond but lived in an apartment building near East 71st Street, became one of the founders of the Castle Crips, taking their name from their apartments, which looked like a castle. Tweedy Bird was impressed with Raymond's prior affiliations and his clothing style of black berets and leather jackets. Raymond was a role model.

The oldest Crip set still existent in 2021, still using the same name, is the Kitchen Crips. Beginning around 1972, near Manchester Avenue, they took their name from the Kitchen Liquor Store in their neighborhood. During the remainder of the 1960s and into the early 1970s, the emerging Crip cliques were new street groups from the old neighborhoods, with little more in common with each other than the Crip suffix in their name. They kept a low profile for their first few years.[112] There was no East-Side or West-Side name associated with the cliques, even though there were Crip cliques from both sides of Central Avenue.

The Usual Suspects

Crip beginnings around 1969 were modest.[113] A few cliques arose here and there, before there was the "Big Bang"—an event or events that launched them, with increasing regularity, into living rooms on the nightly news and into kitchens in the daily newspapers. On a 1972 LAPD "Gang Territories" map, there were a half dozen Crip sets depicted, as well as depictions of eight other non-Crip sets.[114] If we assume these sets were all or most of what the LAPD knew about the new street groups, then Crip sets were not only few but were slightly outnumbered by the non-Crip sets. Crips sets, along with other sets the LAPD might have been aware of, plus those that had not yet crossed their radar screens, were forming in the territories formerly dominated by the pre-1965 groups—and replacing them. The 1972 map might not have accurately represented all the sets police were aware of, but then again, there is little reason to believe otherwise.

Between the time this map was created and the end of 1972, the Crips metastasized into street groups that were dominating the news, where they were being portrayed as dangerously violent gangs of "mad dogs." Mike Davis writes that in December 1972, "Cripmania was first sweeping Southside schools in an epidemic of gang shootings and street fights."[115] Did youth suddenly just start flocking to the Crips in late 1972 because of things as simple as, say, a Black Friday–type fire sale where the attraction of free breakfast programs and cool leather coats, plus the opportunity to get guns and act menacingly, was something that Crips all over the City were offering joiners, and the juveniles couldn't resist? Or did something else happen? The smart money is on something else.

On March 21, 1972, the front-page headline in the *Los Angeles Herald Examiner* read: "Sunset-Vine Murder; Gang Kicks Youth to Death in Street."[116] The Los Angeles Coroner's Office summarized the killing as a "Beating— Fists and Feet." Not to be outdone by its rival, the *Los Angeles Times* met the *Examiner*'s "glaring headlines" with headlines of its own to show just how horrible the killing had been because of how nasty the gangs had become. Dramatic claims that the boys who did the killing were a "gang of hoodlums" and that the boy who was killed was an attorney's son, "stomped and beaten to death" because he refused to give up his leather jacket, exploited class differences and made hot headlines burn even hotter.

All of the boys tangled in the killing had been at a well-advertised concert in Hollywood, at the Palladium, where young people from all over Los Angeles had come, to attend the first *Soul Train* award ceremonies. After the concert ended, crowds of people were spilling out into the street, leaving the area, when a brawl erupted between two groups of juveniles, where one was killed. The two groups connected in the brawl were adversaries because of the high schools they were from—one from the West-Side and one from the East-Side, which was enough to cause friction. But that was not the way it was portrayed. It was sensationalized as gang involved, even though gang membership was secondary to historical school antagonisms. Had the media reported the brawl as the result of feuding high schools rather than gang related, the depiction wouldn't have aroused the attention it did.[117]

Shortly after this incident, as police were searching for witnesses and attempting to round up the usual suspects, a grandmother entered the LAPD Hollywood Homicide Bureau with her grandson, an apparent witness to the killing. After some persuasion, the grandson told the detectives, "It was the

Crips" who killed the boy. The detectives he told hadn't heard of the Crips before, although some other police at the station had. In a nanosecond, the Crip name moved from relative preincident obscurity to a gang that was suddenly on the front pages and into the public vocabulary, symbolizing all that is terrifying about street gangs. The name emerged from relative unimportance into the public's living rooms and into their lives at warp speed. The Crips' fifteen minutes of fame pushed them into years of infamy. An attorney's son being murdered by a remorseless gang because they wanted his leather coat helped give the media a new purpose in the 1970s, after having had a bit of respite from the previous decade's continual front-page violence.

From a Whisper to a Scream

Commenting on how rapidly the Crip name spread, retired investigator for the district attorney's Hard-Core Gang Unit, Ken Bell, contended that the Palladium incident made the Crips. He felt that it focused a spotlight on a small diverse cluster of street groups with "Crips" as part of their name, giving them a magnified image beyond anything they had ever had before. Bell observed: "It was definitely a landmark killing. Nobody doubts the impact of this killing. That killing has become the status of the shot heard round the world in terms of killings. We had entered into a different world."[118] Michael Krikorian adds: "In the way that the killing of Archduke Franz Ferdinand of Austria sparked World War I, the war between the Crips and Bloods was ignited by the killing of Robert Ballou, Jr."[119]

A second event in August 1972 contributing to setting the Crips name on fire and helping it to spread was "the biggest all-Black gathering in American history," the Wattstax music festival at the Los Angeles Coliseum.[120] Attended by 100,000 people, including Crips dressed in their finery and looking tough, various street groups saw Crips like Tookie and knew they needed to be Crips too. Kumasi noted that Crip members were asked to provide "security," elevating them to even greater visibility among their peers, especially when asked by a staff member on a microphone, so all could hear, to keep order on the field. Providing media attention to the Crips gave them "prestige and pride," with the baddest group being determined by how much attention it got, Kumasi summarized.[121] The idea of *crip* being a cripple lost meaning and *crippin'* was no longer *limpin'* but now a reference to a way of life that was grand and marked by being tough and fierce.[122]

Given the enormity of quick attention associated with this name, notoriety could come cheaply and easily to any other street group willing to embrace it. With a built-in reputation for fierce to a group with "Crip" in its name—without actually having to do anything to earn that reputation other than make your name known—what name are the cliques of juveniles coming up or already on the street going to choose if they want to get their fifteen minutes of fame right now and be taken seriously? Will they choose the Chillicothe Chicksters or the Eight-Trey Gangster Crips? Will they choose the Pickle Ball Swatters, or will they choose a name variation that has "Crip" as a suffix? Names matter.

A name that had gotten purchase as something dangerous spread quickly, being readily and easily adopted by other juvenile groups. It gave "local" street groups a "cosmopolitan" identity[123] but not unity. They fought among themselves with such verve that contiguous groups often became each other's worst enemy. Crip groups behaved locally in accord with their historical-structural environment, while high-siding along with official promoters about their cosmopolitan identities. The name made street groups of juveniles infamous and provided them with ties to myths of power they never had.

Tempting as it is to put all the blame for the rise of the Crips on the infamy generated by Ballou's killing and the subsequent notoriety, it would also oversimplify neighborhood dynamics and permit the real culprits to get away. Undoubtedly the media gave the Crips' name a huge national boost by dramatizing it as a symbol of violent Black adolescents. It's difficult to imagine the Crip reputation being promoted with any greater efficiency than by being front-page news. But the media was one cause of the rapid development of the newly named groups in Black street-group areas. Numerous factors had been there before the Crip name received widespread attention, while yet others both accompanied and followed the name.

Raymond, Tweedy Bird, Tookie, and other Crip notables didn't lead the Crip growth; they were figureheads for it. They could be blamed and pathologized by authorities, which easily individualized Crip growth and ignored structural issues. In Los Angeles, the Crips metastasized because conditions were ready for them. Their seeds had been planted on fertile soil in a nurturing environment. Emerging political and economic forces had deepened the unresolved conditions the pre-1965 street groups faced, providing solid reasons for the development of new, more violent street groups. Young males, who experienced daily the evaporation of legitimate options to become proper men and who bore witness to Black leaders being assassinated for speaking the truth, saw the incipient sets with "Crip" in their name as pathways to what they needed most: identity, manhood, power, and money.

"Gangsta" Culture's Boost

At least seven structural changes were occurring around the same time as the Watts Rebellion to limit the options for juveniles in South Los Angeles and promote the growth of a "gangsta culture."[124] First, many good jobs left town when deindustrialization moved them to the periphery so that by the

1980s most solid manufacturing jobs within the Black population had disappeared or gone overseas.[125] The industries took people's livelihoods—both from those who worked directly in them as well as from those who provided services to families with industry jobs. Deindustrialization took hope. In the wake of the industries' departure, the debris remaining left increased unemployment and denial of a fair and legal shot at the American Dream, especially for young people.

Second, the men and women who came home from World War II had an important social safety net that gave them unprecedented access to achieving the American Dream: the GI Bill. The bill provided them with a basic prerequisite for security: a low-interest loan to buy an affordable home. The bill also provided resources for veterans to go to college while raising their families. Those who came back from Vietnam in the 1970s had much weaker federal support for those things, but they had a greatly improved chance of going to prison because of drug addiction.[126] Third, gang prevention policies among criminal-justice agencies were reorganized in the 1960s to change their focus from intervention and deterrence to suppression. This intensified racial antagonisms and guaranteed more correctional attention and control, denying families completeness by removing breadwinners and the bread they bring home.

Fourth, the Black Power movement was destroyed. Law-enforcement efforts, magnified by continuing racism on the national and local levels, to deny Black people the right to work toward establishing political parity further alienated cohorts of young Black people.[127] Another dream deferred or, in this case, erased. Fifth, state repression was personalized by the assassinations of multiple Black leaders, both locally and nationally. Bunchy Carter was shot at UCLA. Malcolm X was shot in New York City, Fred Hampton was shot in Chicago and Martin Luther King Jr. was shot in Memphis. The message of "challenge the power structure and die" was unequivocal.[128] Righteous role models for young Black men and juveniles, and the hope from their words, were snatched from before their eyes. Kumasi said in *Crips and Bloods*, "After they killed all the leaders, sent others into exile, a new element rose up called the Crips. And the shit started again."

Sixth, the inflow of large quantities of drugs into the South Los Angeles neighborhoods created new opportunities for employment. Young people who might not have been able to get jobs in the automotive industry could, with some luck and a bit of buy-in money, attempt to realize the American Dream by starting their own business: a drug franchise. Never mind that it was illegal. Many great fortunes have been made in America by bending, distorting, changing, or disregarding the law.[129] Unlike the robber barons of the early part of the twentieth century who made their fortunes using questionable techniques and the robber barons and politicians who persist today, those who sold drugs on the street were often killed—or sent to prison, if they survived and were caught.[130] But the money was good while it lasted, and death was something that happened to the other guy.

Finally, the Los Angeles justice system formally conceptualized gangs and gang crime, something that had not done before the 1970s. Newly created categories for these phenomena became available to be filled, with rewards for agencies able to fill them in the form of grants, new equipment, and departmental growth. Agency growth increased ruling-class power by strengthening the criminal justice system to serve their interests of additional control of unruly non-White groups led by menacing notables. Official recognition gave credence to gang existence and their criminality, with new definitions, however ephemeral, situationally utilized or scientifically compromised, permitting previously amorphous social phenomena to be enumerated. To no surprise, gangsta culture was accompanied by increases in gang crime.[131]

Made in America

One way the Crips and Bloods distinguished themselves was by the colors they wore: blue for Crips, red for Bloods. These particular colors most likely had their origins at the California Youth Authority, where different colored bandanas are issued to youth as part of their institutional haberdashery. Red is a logical choice if you're a Blood, and blue is cool if you're a Crip. Distinguishing in-groups from out-groups by identity with a color, particularly blue and red, has deep roots in American history. During the Revolutionary War, the British wore red, earning them the name "Redcoats." Not to be outdone by his adversary, George Washington had his revolutionaries wear blue. The Crips and Bloods were subscribers to long-standing American traditions, utilizing traditional colors, which were enabled by state institutions.

The power structure did all the wrong things in trying to ameliorate the situation of South Los Angeles juveniles. It contributed bad decisions and misunderstanding to their existing but unresolved problems and then sat around and wondered why the gang problem got worse. Missed by the power structure was a basic tenet of the Hippocratic Oath, historically sworn to by all medical doctors: "First, do no harm." Juveniles' difficulty in improving their plight worsened when they were handed further disenfranchisement, while the attractiveness of an in-group willing to help them became more appealing, regardless of whether membership led to further marginalization.

It is beyond the scope of this book to delve further into the dynamics of how these structural changes functioned to make the Crips—and the Bloods, who came along in the early 1970s—into the organizations they are today.[132]

The pre-1965 street groups were involved in different things and were less violent than those that followed. The earlier groups were lovers, partiers, club members, mopers, and fighters, but the new ones became more criminal. By now, the reader should have a good sense of how the first happened and a burning curiosity about what happened next. Kumasi gives us a clue:

> The original Crips came out of our neighborhood. They were the children we passed by every day and paid no attention to. But they watched us. We had something to attach ourselves to, to connect with—the great personalities of our parent's generation—but they didn't. They were born in a state of suspended animation, totally disconnected, like a planet out of orbit. They were made in America.[133]

And that's the way it was. From lovers to criminals, from street fighters to killers, the Crips and the Bloods were unable to embrace the ideology that preceded them because their neighborhood had changed around them—without their consent.

Appendix

South Los Angeles Sets and Car Clubs before 1965

This appendix is a compilation of sets and car clubs that existed in South Los Angeles prior to 1965. This list was established through our interviews, neighborhood and justice agency contacts, and experiences. Many of our respondents knew of or about the different groups in their neighborhoods from their street and school contacts. Additionally, a large portion of our respondents had been in jail or prison, amalgamated melting pots for street groups from all over the City. Groups they hadn't met on the streets or in school they might have met there. Bird, in particular, having been in and out of Los Angeles youth facilities, jails, and lock-ups numerous times, paid close attention to those he met. He would inquire at length about where people were from, who they knew, where their neighborhoods were located, and what these neighborhoods were like.

Other South Los Angeles melting pots, where youth from neighborhoods all over the City had time to meet each other and decide how they felt about one another, were the schools for youth in trouble. There were two that had the greatest impact: Jacob Riis School, on 69th Street between Main Street and Broadway, and Andrew Jackson School, on East 7th Street in Boyle Heights. Termed by the Los Angeles Unified School District as "opportunity" high schools, these were all-boys schools for juveniles from seventh through twelfth grade. Youth who had difficulty in regular junior highs or high schools and those who were on probation and parole were assigned to attend one of these schools for a semester or more; the period was usually established by the court. Many juveniles who went here were set members. Fights were common, especially at Riis, which became known as a school for "warriors." Often the fights were so anticipated by the students that the expectation of one or more happening was an incentive to attend classes that day to experience the drama. The effect these schools had on set solidification and ally and enemy formation was significant.[1]

The appendix represents an effort to comprehensively list the various South Los Angeles sets and car clubs in existence before the first Crip and Blood gangs later emerged in these same areas.[2] In addition to the East-Side and West-Side sets, the list also includes downtown sets, those a bit north of downtown, those in Boyle Heights, and those in Compton. Some sets, like the Zebras from Willowbrook Junior High and the Royal Greeks adjacent to Slauson, are omitted because they were around for such a short while that they may have been cliques. It's quite possible we have identified a clique as a set and included it here. This was unintentional but unavoidable, given their unstable nature and subsequent fluidity.

This list purposely omits groups from East Los Angeles, Wilmington, the San Pedro projects, or the San Fernando Valley. It also excludes the numerous cliques of the larger sets that emerged in the 1950s and 1960s. Some of these cliques lasted for a brief period, perhaps no more than a few months, while others may have lasted for longer periods. To try to include these would have made this summary imponderably long and given greater authority to a subset of the larger set than warranted. While many differences such as size, longevity, and racial and ethnic composition distinguished the listed sets from one another, they were all sets rather than cliques of larger sets. Finally, numerous groups not included here emerged after 1965, before the first Crip and Blood sets had established name recognition. They are discussed in Chapter 9.

TABLE A.1	SETS OF THE 1940S AND BEFORE			
Name	Location	High School	Race	Miscellaneous
Alpine	North of downtown[1]	Various in Chinatown	Predominantly[2] Mexican in the 1940s	
Boozies	Downtown	Various	Black	One of the oldest and best known
Clanton Street[3]	South of Downtown	Poly/ Jefferson	Mixed[4] Mexican, Black, Asian, and White	a.k.a. C-14; 1930s to present
Diamond Street	Downtown	Belmont	Mixed Black and Mexican	
East Side Clover	Northeast of downtown	Lincoln/ Cypress	Mixed Black and Mexican	
Emerald Street	Downtown	Belmont	Mixed Black, Mexican, Asian	
Lafayette[5]	West of downtown		Predominantly Mexican	
Macy Street	Between downtown and Boyle Heights	Belmont/ Roosevelt	Predominantly Mexican	
Mateo Street	Between downtown and Boyle Heights	Belmont/ Roosevelt	Predominantly Mexican	
Rob Roys	East Side[6]	Various	Black	
State Street	Boyle Heights	Roosevelt/ Lincoln	Mexican	
Temple Street	Downtown	Belmont	Mixed Black and Mexican	1923–
White Fence	Boyle Heights	Roosevelt	Predominantly Mexican	Oldest LA gang in continuous existence: since 1910

(Continued)

TABLE A.1	SETS OF THE 1940S AND BEFORE (Continued)			
Name	Location	High School	Race	Miscellaneous
1st Flats[7]	Boyle Heights	Roosevelt/ Lincoln	Mixed Mexican and Black	a.k.a. Aliso Village and Aliso Flats
7th Street[8]	South of downtown	Poly[9]	Mixed Mexican and Black	
38th Street[10]	East-Side	Poly/ Jefferson	Mixed Black and Mexican	1930s–

1. Our reference to downtown includes some areas north of Washington Boulevard.

2. We use the term *predominantly* to refer to groups whose primary racial or ethnic composition was that listed. There were usually a few members of other races or ethnicities within a group, given the heterogeneity of the neighborhoods, but they were not significant as a group. A smattering of White juveniles, often no more than one or two, could be found associated with all sets, according to Bird, where they adopted the dominant culture of the group.

3. This set was named after Clanton Street, a street south of downtown, and renamed East 14th Place, probably in the 1940s. It ran between San Pedro Street (to the west) and Central Avenue (to the east). Frank, a member of Clanton, explained that city authorities believed they could weaken or eliminate the Clanton Street set by depriving them of street identity through renaming the street. The Clanton Street set still exists, although they now call themselves East Side Clanton, because a West Side Clanton started up in 1964. The infamous 18th Street gang emerged out of the West Side Clanton neighborhood sometime in the 1970s. It was started by a couple of White dudes from West Side Clanton who branched off. It is currently reputed to be among the largest, most diverse gangs in Los Angeles.

4. When we use the term *mixed*, we mean that significant portions of the group were composed of different non-White ethnicities or races. The mixed sets were often in or near downtown, where neighborhood demographics were similarly mixed. Wherever the groups emerged, social class seemed to be more important for their organization than either race or ethnicity. The youth lived in the same neighborhoods with each other, went to school together, worked and hung out together, and sometimes dated and married partners from each other's racial or ethnic group. Families had similar annual incomes. Racial or ethnic dominance was unusual downtown, while racial antagonisms among the sets appeared to be primarily sidelined. Bird noted that sets even as apparently homogenous as the Slausons and Florence had some racial variations too.

5. This was a small group that was around for a short time in the 1940s with all Mexican members except for one White member. They were from a street called Lafayette Park Place, but it's not clear whether they used *Street* in their name. Other small groups also emerged in the 1940s for a few years near downtown, like 23rd Street, that identified with the street many of its members were from. Since these were racially mixed streets, the group reflected that mixture.

6. East-Side and West-Side were geographic designations in common usage among set members of the 1950s and 1960s. In order not to confuse our designations with East Los Angeles, which was, and on occasion still is, referred to as the "East Side," our reference is to the East-Side and the West-Side of the South-Side, that is, South Los Angeles. Main Street is the South Los Angeles dividing line: streets west of Main have a west prefix while those east have an east prefix. Set members were quite aware of this designation but used the Harbor (110) Freeway, a stronger landmark, that was a few blocks west of Main Street, as their east-west dividing line.

7. In some cases, where two different racial groups were significantly represented in an area, one might have used one term while the other used a different term to refer to the same area. In this case, the project the Mexican group came from was Aliso Village. The Black group referred to it as Aliso or Aliso Village, while the Mexicans referred to their group and the project as Flats or First Flats, because the project was on First Street and had flat roofs.

8. 7th Street was quite likely a clique of the Clanton neighborhood.

9. "Poly" refers to Polytechnic High School, 1905–1957, on Washington Boulevard and Flower Street, just south of downtown. In 1957 it moved to the San Fernando Valley.

10. There is no longer a 38th Street on the East-Side of South Los Angeles. A powerful, predominantly Chicano set took the name 38th Street in the 1930s, giving the street a recognition not enamored by city officials. The street was renamed East 41st Street for much the same reason Clanton Street was renamed.

TABLE A.2 SETS OF THE LATE 1940S, CONTINUING INTO THE EARLY 1950S

Name	Location	High School	Race	Miscellaneous
Bebop Winos	East-Side	Jefferson	Predominantly Black	
Connoisseurs	East-Side	Jefferson	Predominantly Black	From Pueblos
Daddy Rollingstones	East-Side	Jefferson	Predominantly Black	
Don Juans[1]	East-Side	Jefferson	Predominantly Black	
Golden Earrings	East-Side	Jefferson	Predominantly Black	
Hazard	Boyle Heights	Roosevelt/ Lincoln	Mixed Black and Mexican	a.k.a. Ramona Gardens
Pueblo Players[2]	East-Side	Jefferson	Predominantly Black	
Purple Hearts	Boyle Heights	Roosevelt	Mixed Black and Mexican	
Royal Aces[3]	East-Side	Jefferson	Predominantly Black	
Royal Deuces	East-Side	Jefferson	Predominantly Black	
Syndicators	East-Side	Jefferson	Predominantly Black	
Yellow Jackets	Watts[4]	Jordan	Predominantly Black	
32nd Street	East-Side	Polytechnic	Predominantly Mexican	El Nino Community Center was a major hangout

1. Whit, the vice president of the Royal Aces, recalled the Don Juans as a group he had encountered one night walking home from a track meet at the Coliseum. He did not know too much about them, except that his encounter with them was confrontational and might have gotten him hurt had he not gotten lucky.

2. This group came from the Pueblos housing project, which not only had numerous cliques within it, like Conquistadors and Condors, but also seemed to be a source of youth to other sets like the Slausons.

3. Whit emphasized that his set was a "club" that "gave dances, nice clean social dances, and naturally all the girls would go to any dance they would give." Prior to being the Royal Aces, however, they were the Social Playboys, a group of athletes who were also good students. The original Social Playboys began in the early to mid-1940s but changed their name to the Emersons, before becoming the Royal Aces, because the playboy concept detracted from their image.

4. In its earlier years, Watts was also referred to as "Mudtown," probably due to one or both of two factors: first, the large proportion of Black people living there, or second, its unpaved streets that became muddy after a rain. The area referred to as "Little Watts" was also part of the lexicon. It referred to the city of Hawthorne, which in the late 1950s reminded a Slauson named Bay Bay, who was living there, of Watts, where he had lived before Slauson. Hawthorne's dirt streets were often bordered by weeds.

TABLE A.3 SETS OF THE 1950S

Name	Location	High School	Race	Miscellaneous
Avenues[1]	Highland Park	Lincoln/ Cypress	Predominantly Mexican	
Bartenders	West-Side	Manual Arts/ Dorsey	Predominantly Black	
Black Juans	Silver Lake District	Marshall/ Belmont	Predominantly Asian	a.k.a. Black Wongs
Blood Alley	West-Side	Manual Arts/ Dorsey/LAHS	Predominantly Black	
Blood Brothers	East-Side	Jefferson	Predominantly Black	
Boot Hill	West-Side	Dorsey/LAHS	Predominantly Black	

(Continued)

TABLE A.3 SETS OF THE 1950S (*Continued*)

Name	Location	High School	Race	Miscellaneous
Buddha Bandits	West-Side	Dorsey/LAHS	Mixed Black and Asian	
Buddha Spooks	West-Side	Dorsey/LAHS	Mixed Black and Asian	
Chiefs	Various	Various	White	Car club
Choppers 12	West-Side	Manual Arts/Fremont	Mixed Black, Mexican, and White	
Coachmen	West-Side	Dorsey/LAHS	Predominantly Black	
Coasters	West-Side	Dorsey/LAHS	Predominantly Black	
Compton Varrio Tres	Compton	Centennial/Compton	Mexican	
Constituents	West-Side	Dorsey/LA	Predominantly Black	
Dirty 30s	East-Side	Jefferson	Predominantly Black	
Dutchmen	Various	Various	White	Car club
Dominators	Silver Lake District	Marshall/Belmont	Predominantly Asian	
El Hoyo Soto	Boyle Heights	Roosevelt	Predominantly Mexican	
Elm Street	Watts	Jordan/Fremont	Predominantly Mexican	
Excellos[2]	Watts	Jordan/Fremont	Black	
Happy Valley	Boyle Heights	Roosevelt	Predominantly Mexican	
Hickory Street	Watts	Jordan/Fremont	Predominantly Mexican	
Largo	Compton/Willowbrook	Centennial/Compton	Mexican	
Ministers	West-Side	Dorsey/LAHS	Mixed Black and Asian	
Mongolians	Watts	Jordan	Black	
Naughty 40s	East-Side	Jefferson	Predominantly Black	a.k.a. Crown 40s
Nifty 50s	East-Side	Jefferson	Predominantly Black	a.k.a. Boss 50s
Ochentas	East-Side	Fremont	Mexican	
Outlaws	East-Side	Jefferson	Predominantly Black	a.k.a. Agitators[3]
Palm Lanes[4]	Watts	Jordan/Fremont	Predominantly Black	
Rebel Rousers	West-Side	Manual Arts	Predominantly Black	
Regents	Inglewood	Inglewood/Morningside	White	1960s car club
Roman Pearls	East-Side	Jefferson	Predominantly Black	
Roman 103s	Watts	Jordan/Fremont	Predominantly Black	
Roman 20s[5]	East-Side	Jefferson	Predominantly Black	

(*Continued*)

TABLE A.3 SETS OF THE 1950S (Continued)

Name	Location	High School	Race	Miscellaneous
Ross Snyder	East-Side	Jefferson	Predominantly Black	
Royal Syndicators	West-Side	Mural Arts	Black	
Senators	Downtown[6]	Belmont	Mixed Black, Mexican, and Filipino	
Spook Hunters[7]	Various	Various	White	Car clubs / football players
Swamp Boys	Compton	Centennial/ Compton	Black	
Vineyard	West-Side	Dorsey/LAHS	Predominantly Black	
T-Timers	Inglewood	Inglewood/ Morningside	White	1960s car club
Tortilla Flats	Compton	Compton/ Centennial	Predominantly Mexican	
Treintas	East-Side and West-Side	Polytechnic	Predominantly Mexican	
Willowbrook 13	Willowbrook		Predominantly Mexican	
39th Street	West-Side	Manual Arts	Predominantly Mexican	

  1. This group of Avenues has no connection to the group of Avenues that emerged on the East-Side in the mid-1960s. These two groups were both geographically and racially distinct from one another. We do not list the latter group of Avenues here because they were post 1965 and are discussed at length in our last chapter.
  2. Some of the Farmers later became the Excellos. Shedding their trademark overalls, they took this new name from the wine they drank, Excello wine.
  3. Before becoming the Outlaws, they called themselves the Agitators.
  4. This set had a reputation of being one of the "baddest" sets in Watts.
  5. The Roman 20s came from the streets whose numbers were in the 20s, like 21st Street and 23rd Street, just south of Washington Boulevard, thus south of downtown.
  6. Jasper, the president of the Senators, indicated that the Senators were from the Temple Street neighborhood. Most of their members were from north of 7th Street, but some came from as far south as the 20s.
  7. The Spook Hunter name was intended to sound racist. It was an umbrella term reflecting the organizational ideology of the group's members: hostility toward Black and Mexican families moving into their neighborhoods. The Spook Hunters were not a set but may have been minute cliques: numerous small, mostly independent groups of Whites who would seek out yet smaller groups of or individual non-Whites to jump on and pummel. Spook Hunter groups were primarily located on the West-Side and up and down the Alameda corridor. The term *spook* is a derogatory term used to refer to Black people. This racial slur, used this way, is toxic. We quote it because we believe the reader needs to know what was said, not what we might have liked them to say. Speakers and writers need to take responsibility for their words.

TABLE A.4 SETS BEGUN IN THE 1940S AND CONTINUED INTO THE 1960S

Name	Location	High School	Race	Miscellaneous
Aliso Village	Boyle Heights	Roosevelt/Lincoln	Mixed Black, Mexican, and White	
Dogtown	Downtown	Roosevelt/Lincoln	Predominantly Mexican	Northeast of Chinatown
Hazard	Boyle Heights	Roosevelt/Lincoln	Predominantly Mexican	
Jardin	Willowbrook/Compton	Fremont/Centennial	Predominantly Mexican	
Huns	Watts	Jordan/Fremont	Black	
Palomar	Watts	Jordan/Fremont	Black	
Quarter	Watts	Jordan/Fremont	Mixed Black and Mexican	From Colonia Watts
Ramona Gardens	Boyle Heights	Roosevelt/Lincoln	Mixed Black, Mexican, and White	
Tree Tops	Compton	Compton/Centennial	Black	

TABLE A.5 CAR CLUBS OF THE 1950S AND 1960S

Name	Location	High School	Race	Miscellaneous
Caravans	Various[1]	Various	Black	From Compton
Coachmen	West-Side	Various	Black	
Conservatives	Various	Various	Black	
Evil Angels	Various	Various	Black	
Highway Men	Various	Various	Black	From Pasadena
Khans[2]	Various	Fremont/Various	Predominantly Black	
Latin Gents	West-Side	Various	Black	
Low Riders	Various	Various	Black	
Men of Status	Various	Fremont/Various	Black	
Road Devils	Various	Various	Black	
Satan's Saints	Various	Various	Black	
Serfs[3]	East-Side	Jefferson	Black	
Superior Trays	Compton	Various	Black	Lowriders from Compton
Van Dykes	Various	Various	Black	From Compton
Voodoo Men	Various	Various	Black	

1. The Los Angeles car clubs were often made up of members from different sets as well as those who were not set affiliated. Membership required either car ownership or a good friend with a car. Organization was based on their interest in cars. Since members were older, often nonjuveniles, had cars, and were mobile, they had opportunity to recruit from geographically diverse areas. Thus "various" best sums up their location and high schools. Neighborhood association was secondary to an interest in cars.

2. A good proportion of Khan club members came from the West-Side.

3. The Serfs car club was a group of twenty youth between the ages of sixteen and twenty-one, who drove lowered Chevrolets. They considered themselves lowriders. They had flags for their cars and jackets with their insignia on them. In existence from the mid-1950s until early 1960s, their Chevys were all "primer" colors: powder blue, black, gray, baby blue, pink, and yellow. Lefon, a former member of the club, drove a powder blue 1937 Chevy.

TABLE A.6 SETS OF THE 1950S AND 1960S

Name	Location	High School	Race	Miscellaneous
Blocks	Compton	Compton/Centennial	Black	
Businessmen	East-Side	Jefferson	Predominantly Black	a.k.a. Dodge City
D'Artagnans[1]	Watts	Jordan/Fremont	Black	a.k.a. Dartanians
Egyptians	Watts	Jordan/Fremont	Black	
Farmers[2]	Watts/Willowbrook	Jordan/Willowbrook[3]	Black	a.k.a. Excellos
Florence 13	East-Side	Fremont	Mostly Mexican and a few White	
Gladiators[4]	West-Side	Manual Arts	Predominantly Black	a.k.a. Roman Gladiators
Grandees	Compton	Compton/Centennial	Black	
Hickory Street	Watts	Jordan	Black	
Majestics	Watts	Jordan/Fremont	Black	
Orientals	Watts	Jordan/Fremont	Black	
Saracens	Watts	Jordan/Fremont	Black	
Shandus	Athens Park	Fremont	Black	Watts affiliated
Sin Town[5]	Watts	Jordan/Fremont	Black	
Sir Valiants	Watts	Jordan/Fremont	Black	
Slausons[6]	East-Side	Fremont	Predominantly Black	
Spartans	Watts	Jordan/Fremont	Black	
Swamps	Compton	Compton/Centennial	Black	Possible 1940s origin
Turbans	Watts	Jordan/Fremont	Black	
Turks	Watts	Jordan/Fremont	Black	
Valiants	Watts	Jordan/Fremont		

1. The D'Artagnans, on the edge of Watts, was a Watts-oriented group because many members used to live in Watts. Their territory was Avalon Boulevard on the east, Harbor Freeway (110) on the west, Century Boulevard on the north, and El Segundo Boulevard on the south. Significantly, it was a member of this group, whose interactions with the California Highway Patrol, initiated the Watts Rebellion.

2. According to Woodrow C., whose brother was a member of the Farmers, this set was the dominant Watts set. Woodrow C. said: "It occupied almost all of Watts, having fifteen to eighteen hundred members. I thought they were very organized," he opined with authority.

3. N. D., one of the most notorious members of the Farmers, went to Willowbrook High School.

4. The Gladiators' territory was near the Los Angeles Coliseum, which is adjacent to and south of the USC campus. They took their name from their proximity to the Coliseum and its titular association with the Coliseum in Rome, where gladiators fought. This set called themselves the Roman Gladiators, though most of the time it was shortened to Gladiators.

5. According to Woodrow C., a member of Sin Town, this was a large set of as many as 150 youth that overlapped with Compton and Willowbrook, in addition to Watts.

6. The original Slausons are discussed in detail in chapter 5. At least two other groups have used Slauson in their name but have no relationship to the original group. One was a group of 1980s youth who lived near Slauson Avenue and referred to themselves as the Slauson Boys. Members of the original Slausons would have never used the term *boys* in reference to themselves. When they did use the term, it was always in a scornful or disparaging way: "Who's that, your boy?" "Boy" referred to someone who was a chump. The second group referring to themselves as Slausons was a clique from the Rolling 60s Crip gang. They were from an area near Crenshaw Boulevard and Slauson Avenue.

Notes

INTRODUCTION

1. Los Angeles's attitude toward Black Angelenos was a reflection of the "opinion in California," according to McWilliams, 1988: 324. Good town and bad town for "negroes" is McWilliams's take on how the perspective of the City had changed from the mid-1800s to 1900. Ibid.: 324.

2. Sides, 2006: 11.

3. Sides, 2006: 4.

4. We will use the concept South Los Angeles throughout this book instead of South Central Los Angeles for reasons to be explained.

5. Soja, 1989: 221, describes Los Angeles as a "concatenation of paradoxes."

6. Flamming, 2005: 20.

7. K. Jackson, 1985.

8. The 1965 Watts Riot has at times also been referred to as a rebellion, revolution, revolt, and uprising. From the perspectives of those describing the seven-day conflict, these terms served to help them make their points. We will use the term *rebellion*, because the actions were purposive among those we interviewed, and it was the term they used most often and preferred.

9. Conot, 1967.

10. Soja, 1989.

11. Peralta, 2009.

12. Los Angeles Southwest College, a community college built on a seventy-five-acre site at Imperial and Western Avenues, was opened later than CSUDH, in the 1970s, with a similar goal in mind of providing academic as well as vocational training for local residents, most of whom are Black. Sides, 2006: 189.

13. LEAA/OJP, 1996.

14. There was a small percentage of Asian and Pacific Islander students at CSUDH in its early years, which increased as a percentage of the whole as the University matured.

15. A considerable percentage of Quicker's male students were also fathers, but were not nearly as forthcoming about that as women were about motherhood. Women wanted to make sure their status as mothers and role in childrearing were recognized. Since many of the women had teenage children, with teenage friends, they often used personal experiences to make their points. Male students were less likely to do this.

16. One of Quicker's students was a Samoan woman whose husband was a debt collector for a wealthy South Los Angeles drug dealer. At a party, her husband asked Quicker if he would like to meet the dealer. He informed Quicker that the dealer surrounded himself with some bad dudes, all ex-convicts, who wouldn't think twice about permanently incapacitating anyone who even thought about bringing harm to their boss. Easy call: Quicker said yes and learned about as much as he needed to know at that time about the risky business of drug dealing in the early 1980s. To learn any more than that would have put him at a greater risk than he was willing to take on. Danger was pervasive at the meeting, especially fears of the police, who might bust the house and arrest everyone there, possibly shooting a few, and secondly from other drug dealers, who might decide now was the time to kill and rob the dealer and anyone else who was there. Guns were visible on most people at this meeting.

17. This disconnect between the theories Quicker was teaching and student neighborhood experiences brought to mind the famous quote from Shakespeare's *Hamlet*, where Hamlet suggests to Horatio that there are limits to theoretical knowledge. Hamlet states: "There are more things in heaven and earth, Horatio / Than are dreamt of in your philosophy." *Hamlet*, act 1, scene 5.

18. Salisbury, 1958: 216.

19. Strikingly, most of the student critiques were in line with the unassigned classic assessment by Bordua of the early gang literature. He writes: "All in all it does not seem like much fun anymore to be a gang delinquent. Thrasher's boys enjoyed themselves being chased by the police, shooting dice, skipping school, rolling drunks. It was fun. Miller's boys do have a little fun, with their excitement focal concerns, but it seems so desperate somehow. Cohen's boys and Cloward and Ohlin's boys are driven by grim economic and psychic necessity into rebellion." Bordua, 1961: 136. Most researchers continue to pay respect to the early gang researchers, with critical assessments of how their work influenced their own and others in the field. Among the most representative of these are Moore, 1978; Vigil, 1988; Hagedorn, 1998; and Brotherton, 2015.

20. This racial slur, used this way, is toxic. We quote it because we believe the reader needs to know what was said, not what we might have liked them to say. Speakers and writers need to take responsibility for their words.

21. Pauley, 1973: 5.

22. In the mid-1970s, the ethnographic research Quicker did on female juvenile gangs in East Los Angeles demonstrated solid evidence of their existence. But his students at CSUDH were primarily from South Los Angeles.

23. Klein (1967, 1971) had worked with a number of these groups, evaluating programs to reduce delinquency among them. He used fabricated group names and was not involved in ethnography.

24. Experts are not created equal: there is a hierarchy. During the 1980s and 1990s, when the media was rife with reports on gang activity, establishing police "gang experts" was done haphazardly, notably because expertise was without any specific qualifications. A police "expert" might be a veteran of a gang task force, or it might be an officer

who had been in a patrol car for a day in a gang area and had learned a few hand signs and some of the street argot. When a police expert would speak to a community group, their use of street argot, gang hand signs, some sensational photos, and their role as a police gang expert was "Oh my gosh" inspiring, and they were rarely challenged. But in an academic setting, where there were student experts, the police faced a different challenge. Now on an equal footing in a classroom with "the man," students were especially critical. They often knew more than the officers and more than the officers had needed to know with the community groups they were able to impress. Bird was one of the experts the police gang experts found they needed to defer to. Several years after our class, when Bird was a California Youth Authority counselor, he attended a gang conference where one of the LASD officers who had spoken in Quicker's class was in attendance. The officer recognized Bird and made a point of seeking him out to apologize for stating things that were inaccurate. Bird graciously accepted his apology.

25. Batani-Khalfani, 1984.

26. Since Bird's (1984) paper on the Slausons was written, there is Alonzo's (2004, 2010) work and the documentaries by Sloan (2005) and Peralta (2009). Bird was featured in the 2005 film, while he and Kumasi are key participants in the 2009 film. Bird has also been the focus of Mack's YouTube videos: "Bird—Soldier of the Streets of Los Angeles." YouTube, *Kev Mack Videos*. Parts 1–4: February 23–March 1, 2018.

27. Rice and Christensen, 1965.

28. Klein, 1971.

29. Klein (2007: xiv) agrees with the necessity of studying the complexity of the communities gangs come from and their group nature.

30. Jankowski, 1991.

31. Howell and Moore, 2010

32. Valdez, 2009: 197–212.

33. Alonzo, 2004, 2010; Vigil, 2002.

34. Sloan, 2005; Peralta, 2009.

35. This selection of Kev Mack videos is suggestive; there are many others to also choose from: "Cat Carson talks History of Crips and Compton." October 9, 2017; "K.M.V.3.1.1 Eastside Blood Stone Villains in South Los Angeles 52 56 57." December 13, 2019; "OG Sinbad—Inglewood Family Gangster Bloods (Part 1 of 3)" January 27, 2017; "Lil Caesar—Inglewood Family Part 1." March 26, 2018; *Kev Mack Videos*, YouTube.

36. See Davis, 1990: 293.

37. Smith, 2006: 241.

38. This apt phrase has been borrowed from Lindenmeyer, 1970.

39. Ibid.: 55–57.

40. Fraser, 2015.

41. Brotherton (2015: 4–14); also elaborates on how an ignorance of history will doom us to misunderstanding the current situation.

42. Ibid.: 8–18.

43. Soja, 1989: 204, demonstrates that the Rebellion was not the "fulcrum of change" that many claimed it was but played a supporting role as a result of deindustrialization; the major fulcrum of change had already been taking place.

44. Alonzo, 2004: 663.

45. Klein, 1971: 22.

46. As Tom Wicker (1968: v–vii) has noted, the late 1960s was a period of "one nation, divided." Following the Watts Rebellion, cities all over the country—from Tampa to Atlanta to Newark to Detroit, and beyond—had exploded in racial violence, leaving

many people dead and property in ruin. White America was afraid but clueless. Wicker continues: "What white Americans have never fully understood—but what the negro can never forget—is that white society is deeply implicated in the ghetto. *White institutions created it, white institutions maintain it, and white society condones it.*" Ibid, vii. Wicker's emphasis.

47. Davis and Wiener, 2020.
48. Davis, 1990: 113.
49. Davis, 1990; Alonzo, 2004, 2010.
50. Sides, 2006.
51. Soja, 1989: 197.
52. Flamming, 2005: 4–36.
53. Sides, 2006: 8.
54. Davis, 1990: 126, 296.
55. Mills (1959b) and Brotherton (2015: 130, 131) emphasize the *big picture* as a perspective that tries to understand social phenomena as part of a larger whole. Thus, to understand gangs in America, they must be considered "within the broader political, social, economic, and cultural domain," Brotherton (2015: 131) within which they exist. To isolate them, and to not consider their history, is to miss the impact of the forest on the tree.
56. Fraser, 2015.
57. We're taking a bit of poetic license with this descriptive term to refer to the way gang pathologists look at gangs, a group that Brotherton (2015: 168) so appropriately takes to task for their "prejudiced gaze."
58. Dick Gregory, in his *Nigger: An Autobiography*, writes in his dedication: "Dear Momma—Wherever you are, if you ever hear the word "nigger" again, remember they are advertising my book."
59. Brotherton, 2015.

INSIDERS BECOME OUTSIDERS: METHODOLOGY

1. We may have set a new record for data collection, having gone on even longer than the eighteen years Tim Black (2009) spent on his excellent research. We never stopped our research after the formal data collection period ended but continued to talk to people, revisits and new, as questions arose that we needed first-person help in answering.
2. Hagedorn, 1988, appendix 1: 171–180.
3. Moore, 1991: 31–35.
4. Brotherton, 2015: 86–87.
5. We explained to all our respondents that we were writing a book and were given permission by them to include any information that we learned from them in it. They agreed to let us use their street names. We tried to keep our discussions with them informal and relaxed, but we also kept control by doing most of the questioning and answering their questions as necessary with information as required.
6. The most likely reason they would have known little is because they hadn't been in the neighborhood long enough. They could have heard stories but had little way of knowing the accuracy of them. Bird knew who knew what.
7. Tapia, 2017: 13–14.
8. Digital copies of old files didn't exist in the late 1980s and early 1990s, but microfiche did. Gathering historical information from them was a tedious process that

often-produced material without the complete references we would have liked, but it was research Quicker's students pursued it with enthusiasm.

9. Jankowski, 1991: 12.

10. Contreras (2013) is a notable exception to being an outsider. But even he recognized that large ideological differences had emerged between him and the street people he used to hang out with given his vast educational distance from them.

11. Everyone might have known about Bird's integrity, but not everyone was willing to cooperate. Bird had, after all, been a major figure in the communities, loved by many but still hated by a few.

12. Black (2009: xxvi–xxviii) discusses an incident he had with a police officer in a Springfield, Massachusetts, bar during his fieldwork. He was more assertive with the officer than the position Quicker took, although Black later realized he might have erred with his style. Safety should always be a top priority among ethnographers, lest an error might lead to an incomplete. In South Los Angeles, on a street at night, one could easily be shot by being too confrontational with police. Discretion was paramount, especially when dealing with the LAPD or LASD, when one's presence was out of the ordinary.

13. Hagedorn, 1998: xv.

14. Liebow, 1967: 8–10.

15. Miller and Riessman, 1961.

CHAPTER 1

1. Moore, 1991: 39.

2. Hagedorn, 2008: xxxi.

3. Thrasher, 1966: 36.

4. We concur with Hagedorn (1998: 38), who contended that a historical perspective shows gangs differed over time, and disagree with Miller (1976), who argued that gangs had changed little.

5. We have borrowed this apt phrase from Kolbert, 2020: 61. She uses it in reference to a report on COVID-19, showing that there is a historical connection between the phrase and the plagues of the early centuries in Europe. Fittingly, a Philadelphia newspaper described that city as being "gang-plagued" from 1836 to 1878. Spergel, 1995: 7. In an undated issue of *The Dispatcher: The Official Publication of the Association for Los Angeles Deputy Sheriffs*, a special edition issue was published when Gil Garcetti was District Attorney. It was titled, "Battling the Plague of Gangs in Our Community." Associating *gang* with *plague* gives gang an unequivocal onus.

6. Hagedorn (1988: 57) was spot-on when he argued that most of the research on gangs is "fundamentally concerned with understanding why gang members are delinquent, not with understanding how and why they formed and their function within a community." Of course, since Hagedorn made this statement, there have been many solid ethnographic studies conducted on gangs in various cities, which have focused on why they formed and how they function. Our study is designed to join this genre.

7. There have been some notable exceptions to the research designed to control or to punish Los Angeles gangs, focusing instead on how gangs formed and functioned. For East Los Angeles gangs, see Moore, 1978, 1991; and Quicker, 1983; for South Los Angeles, see Alonzo, 2004, 2010; Cle "Bone" Sloan, 2005; and Stacy Peralta, 2009; and for other Los Angeles gangs, see Vigil, 1988, 2002.

8. Edgerton (1987), from the foreword to Vigil, 1988: x.

9. Malcolm W. Klein and his associates, who have conducted a significant amount of research on Los Angeles gangs as well as on gangs elsewhere, beginning in the late 1960s, are generally associated with this ahistorical quantitative school of gang control, for which Walter B. Miller was a prime spokesperson. Valdez (2009) and Valdemar (2007) are examples of law-enforcement researchers who take this position. Law-enforcement blogs and bulletins on gangs have proliferated over the past decade, primarily focusing on ways to control them.

10. Flamming, 2005: 2. Flamming contends that the "official birth" of "modern" Los Angeles didn't occur until over one hundred years later, in the late 1880s, with the real estate boom.

11. Weatherwax (1976: 20) writes that Los Angeles was founded by forty-four people, twenty-eight of whom were "negroes." His contention supports Flamming's, implying that many of the original founders were Spanish, Black, and mixed blood. The City began as a melting pot of ethnicities and races.

12. Katz (1987: 117, 118) writes that intermarriage between Whites and Indians, and Blacks and Mexicans, in the "sparsely settled" "outlying Mexican province" that in 1850 became California, was not unusual.

13. McWilliams, 1988: vii.

14. Both Nadeau (1948: 63–70) and Carey McWilliams (1988: 91–92) provide great detail on the causes and nature of this massacre.

15. The City of Los Angles is not only massive, but outside the city limits are subcities and suburban areas that help to define the Southern California region. Soja (1989: 191) argues that the urban region is defined by "a 60-mile circle around the center of the city." Utilizing this designation, that means one could get in one's vehicle in the city center, drive an hour in any direction at 60 mph, and still be in the City.

16. Rand, 1967: 4.

17. These data come from McWilliams, 1988: 12; Soja, 1989: 194; laalmanac.com/geography/ge10.php. 1998–2021 Los Angeles Almanac.

18. Soja, 1989: 191, 195.

19. Rand (1967: 53) contended that middle-class Angelenos needed "four wheels to be effective." If you were poor, Negro, Mexican, or old, the groups that had limited access to vehicles, it was tough to be or to remain middle-class.

20. In the documentary *Crips and Bloods*, the narrator uses a twenty-five-mile north-to-south expanse to designate LA gang territory, with Hollywood in the north and Imperial Highway in the south. Our conceptualization of downtown being the northernmost boundary of the gangs we discuss is flexible because some of them were a bit north, east, and west of downtown. While the boundary markers discussed by our respondents more or less conform to those established more formally, our point is that South Los Angeles, wherever it has been described, is an expansive area. South Los Angeles is nominal for our analysis, not rigidly definitive.

21. Cities such as Inglewood, Lennox, Hawthorne, and Compton are not incorporated into Los Angeles, although they are part of the South Los Angeles's street gang's history.

22. In one of the most infamous Los Angeles murder cases, the nude, bisected body of Elizabeth Short, nicknamed the "Black Dahlia," was found in 1947 in one of these empty lots, the apparent victim of Los Angeles gangster Bugsy Siegel. Wolfe, 2000. Although the City's street gangs had nothing to do with this homicide, the body was found in the west side of their neighborhood, called *Black* and connected to a *gangster*. Is this a semantics issue?

23. Soja, 1989: 194.
24. Smith, 2006: 28.
25. Sides (2006: 58, 59) writes that Los Angeles rivaled New York and Chicago as the leading industrial producer in the nation and that Los Angeles County was the largest manufacturing county in the United States.
26. Flamming, 2005: 5.
27. Sides, 2006: 2–8, 38, 39.
28. Brotherton, 2015: 120.
29. Paul Feldman, "Neighborhoods—In L.A., It's All in a Name." *Los Angeles Times*, June 18, 1989; Part I: 1, 30, writes, "The term 'South-Cental Los Angeles' came into vogue, they say, after the Watts riots of 1965—in part, perhaps, as a means of easing inflamed emotions."
30. Brotherton, 2015: 110.
31. R. J. Smith, 2006: 197.
32. Los Angeles news media regularly use *South Central* to refer to the City's gangland. Crews and Montgomery (2001) title a chapter of their book on juvenile violence "From South Central to Next Door . . ." for their discussion of gangs. The 1992 Oliver Stone film, *South Central*, humanized people living there but did little to limit the term as a pathologizing trope.
33. Flamming, 2005: 97. Regardless of its proper name of South Central Avenue, most neighborhood people refer to it as Central Avenue.
34. *Thomas Brothers Street Guide: Los Angeles County*. Los Angeles, 1955.
35. Anderson, 1999.
36. A refreshing change from using *South Central Los Angeles* was taken by Horne, 1997, when he used *South Los Angeles* in his retrospective examination of the 1965 Watts Rebellion.
37. R. J. Smith (2006), in a study of the birthplace of West Coast Black music, culture, work, and racism along South Central Avenue and the surrounding communities in the 1940s, titles his book *The Great Black Way*. His deep appreciation of the Avenue's cultural contributions and his well-written text make his book a must read for those seeking a deeper understanding of what the Avenue meant in the lives of South Los Angeles Blacks.
38. Smith, 2006: 4.
39. For an analysis of the complex dynamics of the history of Central Avenue, see Flamming, 2005: 92–125. Bunch (1990: 110–111) contends that the Avenue was a "miniature Harlem," because of the musicians, literati, Black professionals, and the multitude of Black-owned businesses. Miniature Harlem or not, any consideration of Black life in Los Angeles is incomplete without recognition of the Avenue's influence.
40. McWilliams, 1988: 326.
41. Flamming, 2005: 98, 99.
42. Ibid.: 8, 306–308.
43. Flamming's descriptions of middle-class Black Angelenos did not apply to people in Watts.
44. Smith, 2006: 5.
45. Ibid.: 13–15; Flamming, 2005: 284–286. John Somerville said of his hotel, "It was the finest hotel in America catering to Black people." Flamming, 2005: 287.
46. Flamming, 2005: 262.
47. Smith, 2006: 14. Davis (1990: 214) refers to Slauson Avenue as the "White Wall."
48. Soja, 1989: 197.

348 / Notes to Chapter 1

49. Davis, 1990: 214.

50. The Red Cap was also known as the Red Car, a highly efficient and inexpensive people mover used regularly by residents along the Avenue north of Watts to get around the City, especially to jobs and home.

51. Smith, 2006: 14.

52. McWilliams (1988: 325) indicates that after 1916, Black migrants who settled in Watts were poor, rural, and uneducated from Mississippi, Georgia, and Alabama. Glasgow (1981) and Horne (1997) concur.

53. Glasgow, 1981: 6.

54. Ibid.: 37–38.

55. Sides, 2006: 125–129.

56. Fluidity included Black and Chicano movement from downtown areas, those north, and Boyle Heights, as our map suggests. While most of our focus is on areas south of downtown, people and influence flowed in multiple directions.

57. The Harbor Freeway, which connects the Port of Los Angeles to downtown and Pasadena, was completed in stages from 1934 to 1970. The section running through South Los Angeles was completed in 1954. For much of its life, it was CA 11 (1934–1978) but is now called the 110 Freeway. We refer to it as the Harbor Freeway because that was the term commonly used by our respondents.

58. There continues to remain controversy over the geographical boundaries of "Eastside" and "Westside." Paul Thorton, "L.A. Geography Lesson," *Los Angeles Times*, February 22, 2014: A 11. We want to note that during the period we are writing about, there were designated East-Side and West-Side gangs in South Los Angeles. These were distinct from the gangs that arose in East Los Angeles.

59. Flamming, 2005: 93.

60. Ibid.: 377–378.

61. To further complicate the geographical picture, the City of Los Angeles is made up of 153 "communities," which are often incorrectly referred to as "cities." Some of these communities have their own zip code, contributing to the perception they are a city rather than a community. Boyle Heights, South Los Angeles, and Watts are communities of the City of Los Angeles, while East Los Angeles is an unincorporated area of the County of Los Angeles. Florence-Firestone is a Los Angeles City "district" but not a named community *laalmanac.com*/cities/ci93.htm.

62. When gang members from South Los Angeles and East Los Angeles encountered one another, it was typically in a juvenile justice holding facility, such as a California Youth Authority institution or a Los Angeles County probation camp. Sometimes they would meet at a continuation school, a nonresidential facility for juveniles in trouble at a public school.

63. Bird's contention on the interaction of South Los Angeles and East Los Angeles gangs is that some South Los Angeles groups often went into the East Los Angeles groups' territory but that the reverse happened infrequently, if at all. As evidence of a South Los Angeles gang's incursion into East Los Angeles, Bird cited the case where Mariano J. took some South Los Angeles gang members, from Florence, into East Los Angeles to retaliate, because Mariano J. had been jumped on at Jackson School (a continuation school) in Boyle Heights by some East Los Angeles gang members.

64. The LAPD's and LASD's relative size to other policing agencies is taken from their respective websites.

65. Endore, 1978; McWilliams, 1988; and Mazon, 1984.

66. McWilliams, June 21, 1943.

67. See Bogardus, 1943; Moore, 1978, 1991; Frias, 1982; Quicker, 1983; Mazon, 1984; and Harris, 1988.

68. Rand (1967: 102) raised the issue of Los Angeles's "unmeltable" racial groups in 1967.

69. Wilson, 1980.

70. The Southern Poverty Law Center has been publishing reports on hate and racism in the United States for many years, showing that it has grown over that time. Its 2019 report documents the significant increase in the amount of hate groups and racial violence that has occurred since Donald Trump became president. According to this report, California has more hate groups than any other state in the union. Racism and hate in our country have never been stronger; nor those who advocate it, prouder.

71. Glasgow, 1981: 11.

72. West, 1993.

73. Hagedorn, 2008: 61.

74. Hagedorn, 1998.

75. Vigil (1988: 5) writes how much more difficult it was for Mexican Americans and Mexicans than Europeans to blend because they were more "visually distinct." Bogardus also made this point in 1943. Blending in, especially for certain European groups, was often incomplete. Demeaning Polish jokes, for example, could be told to people of Polish descent, who had no accent or whose last name might not reveal their heritage, because the joke teller might just assume that the listener was a "regular" White person. Quicker, whose mother's parents were first-generation Polish immigrants, experienced this in college.

76. Contreras, 2013: 96, 97.

77. Korla Pandit, an African American, didn't pass for White; he passed for Indian, a less despised group than Black people. Smith, 2006: 222–255.

78. John Redd, a light-skinned African American musician, changed his name to Juan Rolando, becoming, with the sweep of a pen, a Mexican musician, allowing him to play in clubs that were off limits to Blacks. Ibid.: 226–227. For many years, correctional systems didn't have a category for Latino inmates and counted them as White. There has always been a category for Black inmates.

79. Sides, 2006: 48. Both Blacks and Mexicans were heavily discriminated against in Los Angeles. Black, however, is a racial category, while Mexican is an ethnic category. Members of either group, who could pass for White, had it easier than those who could not.

80. Smith, 2006: 139–159. Sides (2006: 98) notes that 70,000 Black residents were "crowded" into Bronzeville by the War's end.

81. Rand, 1967: 102.

82. Sides, 2006: 14.

83. Davis, 1990: 104.

84. Sides, 2006: 21. Flamming (2005: 271–275) writes that two of the beaches Black Angelenos could use were (1) the "Ink Well," between Pico and Ocean Park Boulevards in Santa Monica, and (2) "Bruce's Beach," in Manhattan Beach.

85. Mosley, 2004: 78.

86. Sides, 206: 1.

87. Flamming, 2005: 334.

88. Ibid.: 310.

89. Ibid.: 308.

90. Ibid.: 334.

91. Kahloon (2020: 77) notes how Ronald Reagan, supported both by Democrats and Republicans, used covert racism in the 1980s by his focus on "welfare queens" to change the national debate from issues of poverty and inequality to "racially coded anxiety."

92. *The Black Panthers: Vanguard of the Revolution* is an award-winning PBS documentary, by filmmaker Stanley Nelson, that was first screened in 2016.

93. We are indebted to Les McCann and Eddie Harris for this term from their mega hit, "Compared to What," played at the Montreux Jazz Festival in Switzerland in 1969.

94. Smith, 2006: 2.

95. Sides, 2006: 16.

96. Flamming, 2005: 5.

97. Flamming (2005: 47–50) contends that many Black migrants who came to Los Angeles during World War I were from San Antonio, Austin, Dallas, New Orleans, and Atlanta, building communities filled with middle-class families.

98. R. J. Smith, 2006: 42. Flamming (2005: 3) writes the City's race relations "got better and worse at the same time."

99. Sides, 2006: 96,97.

100. Flamming, 2005: 261.

101. Sides, 2006: 64–74; and Soja, 1989.

102. Smith, 2006: 93–96.

103. Ibid.: 103–107.

104. Ibid.: 16, 44.

105. Ibid.: 101.

106. While there were conspiratorial elements among these groups, and it was cabal-like sometimes, it was mostly an accepted, uncoordinated ideological commitment among them all to keep Black people out of certain neighborhoods.

107. Sides, 2006: 105–114.

108. A famous and widely circulated 1943 *Saturday Evening Post* front cover, by Norman Rockwell, while not the fist-clenched-making-a-muscle Rosie drawn by J. Howard Miller, was nevertheless a White woman worker, eating a sandwich as she sat with a rivet gun in her lap. There were some iterations of Rosie as a non-White woman, but they were few.

109. Sides (2006), Flamming (2005), and Smith (2006) provide thorough discussions of the various laws that were passed and their effects on hiring practices, labor struggles, and non-White job growth.

110. Smith, 2006: 236–240.

111. Our thanks to Darby Slick, who wrote these words for the song "Somebody to Love," and to Grace Slick, who popularized the song, as vocalist for The Jefferson Airplane.

112. Potter and Kappeler, 1998; Kappeler and Potter, 2005; Derber, 2007.

113. Moore, 1991; McCorkle and Miethe, 2002.

114. Flamming, 2005: 11–12.

115. Rand, 1967: 129–130.

116. Myths die hard. Quicker's twentieth-century/ early twenty-first century students accepted, although may not have fully internalized, continual media driven concepts about gangs and race.

117. Schiesl, 1990: 157.

118. This account is from Mike Davis commenting on the LAPD in Sloan, 2005, and from Davis, 1990.

119. Davis, 1990: 294–296.

120. Rand, 1967: 130–131.

121. Flamming, 2005: 201.
122. Sides, 2006: 108.
123. Sides, 2006: 47.
124. Sides, 2006: 189.
125. Wilson, 1987, 1997.
126. Hagedorn, 1988, 1998.
127. Hagedorn, 2008.
128. Soja, 1989: 208, 204.
129. Soja, 1989: 194, 195.
130. Sides, 2006: 2; Bunch, 1990: 115. Much of the growth in the Black population, as well as in all demographics, was due to the War and the burgeoning growth in defense-related jobs.
131. Sides, 2006: 75–81.
132. Moore, 1991: 14.
133. Soja (1989: 191–192) describes the Los Angeles urban region as comprising the five counties of Los Angeles, Orange, Ventura, Riverside, and San Bernardino. The enormity of this region covers thousands of square miles, from the ocean to the state line.
134. Los Angeles County had a population of 10.4 million on November 20, 2021, according to lacounty.gov/residents/. Los Angeles traffic over the past twenty years has become infamous for its delays and "Sigalerts," or warnings of traffic delays and accidents, which are regularly given on radio stations.
135. Angelenos rarely comply with the speed limit, seeing it more as an annoyance than safety requirement.
136. Sides, 2006: 113.
137. The CIO was an exception to unionizing non-Whites and advocated for unionization on behalf of both Black and Mexican workers. Charismatic labor leader Harry Bridges, of the ILWU in the Bay Area, came to the LA harbor area and tried, with limited success, to get the longshoremen's union to include Black workers. Sides, 2006: 62–64.
138. Ibid.: 57–83.
139. Soja, 1989: 204.
140. Ibid.: 303, 204.
141. Sides, 2006: 70–88. Although numerous laws were passed to prevent housing discrimination, the Los Angeles Urban League identified "twenty-six distinct techniques used by White homeowners to exclude Blacks." Ibid.: 101.
142. Sides (2006: 176) explains that many communities in the periphery continued to discriminate against non-Whites, especially Blacks.
143. Glasgow, 1981: 24–26.
144. Flamming, 2005: 379.
145. Erikson, 1968.
146. Sides, 2006.
147. Sides, 2006: 88–93.
148. Jensen and Rojek, 1998: 4.

CHAPTER 2

1. Kropotkin, 1914: 76–88.
2. Brotherton (2015: 51) notes the "Rousseauian/Hobbesian dichotomy" as parameters in the social sciences to "emphasize the liberal/conservative divide" about ideas on humankind. Our reference to Hobbes is not about this distinction, but it is a statement

on the tenability of whether the Hobbesian contention of a "war of all against all" would have enabled human society to be possible.

3. Ascribed and achieved groups are basic sociological categories described in introductory texts. Ascribed groups include family of origin, gender, and race. These are groups that we have little control over. Achieved groups include educational level, occupation, the Girl Scouts, Democrat or Republican, the Elks, the Lions, or the Slausons—groups that we have more control over.

4. Racial and ethnic group identity became increasingly homogeneous by the 1960s. As the number of people in the community increased, the pool of people groups could develop from increased. South Los Angeles has been a racially and ethnically mixed area from its early years up through now, although demographic shifts, where certain groups have been numerically and culturally dominant at different times, has characterised the area.

5. Will (1953) points out that some groups contained youth who were beyond the legal definition of juvenile. But because he doesn't differentiate between South Los Angeles and East Los Angeles street groups, it is not clear which of these groups he is referring to as having adults. East Los Angeles street groups were known to have members older than eighteen, while in the South Los Angeles groups, it was practically unheard of.

6. A number of gang researchers have demonstrated that the juvenile gangs they studied were affiliated politically or economically with adults and adult groups: Whyte, 1965; Moore, 1991; Vigil, 2002; Hagedorn, 2008.

7. Hagedorn, 1998: 82–84.

8. Brotherton, 2015.

9. The criminal justice perspective on gang definitions is represented well by Klein (1971) and Miller (1975).

10. Thrasher, 1966; Hagedorn, 1998.

11. By "power elite," Mills (1959a: 9–11) refers to three "domains of power": the warlords (or military), the corporation chieftains, and the political directorate, all of whom are ideologically united. Mills eschews the concept ruling class because it is an "economic" term and doesn't allow enough autonomy to the political order and its agents or to the military in power relations. While these three domains are not always on the same page on every issue, they come together on the important issues that shape our society. Mills, 1959a : 277.

12. Mills (1959a) and Domhoff (1967) describe the "Big Picture," which Mills (1959b) articulates elsewhere and many ethnographers subscribe to.

13. Quinney, 1974: 1.

14. Quinney, 1970.

15. There is an extensive theoretical history on the significance of class rule explaining how our society is organized and run according to the interests of the ruling- and upper-class groups: Domhoff, 1967; Miliband, 1969; Mills, 1943, 1952, 1959a; Platt, 1969, and others. Their rule is carried out by various government intermediaries who have been mostly ignored by the control perspective. Recognition of these organizationally heterogeneous, although ideologically homogeneous, elites is central to our perspective on gangs. C. Wright Mills's concept of the power elite provides the explanatory depth and clarity we utilize to understand how class rule helped create the social, political, and economic environment of gangs.

16. Bursik and Grasmick, 1995: 8.

17. Anne-Marie O'Connor and Tina Daunt, "The Secret Society Among Lawmen," *Los Angeles Times*, March 24, 1999.

18. Robert Faturechi, "Secret Clique in L.A. County Sheriff's Gang Unit Probed," *Los Angeles Times*, April 20, 2012.

19. Editorial, "The Tanaka Verdict," *Los Angeles Times*, April 7, 2016: A 14.

20. "Former Undersheriff Sentenced to 5 Years in Prison," *City News Service*. NBCUniversal Media, LLC, June 27, 2016.

21. Schwendinger and Schwendinger, 1985: 44.

22. We will be using the terms *adolescent* and *juvenile* interchangeably since both refer to the same age-based category.

23. In contrast to the controversial definitions of *gang* and *gang related*, the concepts of adolescence and delinquency were readily accepted by all elements of society as an important creation, while their reasons for being necessary were less agreed upon.

24. Bakan, 1971.

25. Platt, 1969.

26. Before the *other America* and the *underclass* had been identified as social phenomena, another similar group, not only older but more durable, called the "dangerous class[es]" had been recognized and proven to be a valuable concept. Krisberg and Austin, 1978: 21. Identification of this class served the interests of the ruling groups, who wanted to hide from the mess their industrialization had made. Concerned about the dangerous class's revolutionary potential, the ruling groups sought to marginalize them, by discrediting them as a group of "parasites" and criminals, "violating the fundamental law of orderly society." The dangerous class was defined as a "morally depraved" group, a "race apart" from themselves, and "detached from the prevailing social conditions." Taylor, Walton, and Young, 1974: 39–40. Lumped into this class were a host of groups often derogatorily referred to as "social junk" or "social dynamite," depending on the group's level of need or potential for violence. Spitzer, 1975. While Spitzer made clear that smaller groups of deviants didn't pose nearly the threat to capitalism that larger groups did, he didn't seem to think deviants, as a group, had revolutionary potential. Later on, John Irwin, focusing on these same groups, called them social "rabble" and identified them as the people filling our nation's jails. Irwin, 1985.

27. Platt, 1969.

28. The first juvenile court was established by the Illinois legislature in 1899. The idea of a children's court was seen as such an epiphanic moment that within twenty-six years of the Illinois law passing, every state in the union, except two, had a court. Krisberg, 2005: 39,40.

29. Bakan, 1971; Krisberg, 2005. The beneficence the juvenile court was to offer was termed *parens patriae*: the court was to act as a kindly and wise parent and help the child become a "better" person.

30. Brown and Larson, 2009.

31. Vigil, 1988: 125.

32. Hall, 2006.

33. Luna et al. (2001) support Hall's hypotheses when they note that brain development is part of the overall physiological maturation process of all humans. An adolescent's brain does not have the same kind of reasoning power an adult brain has, which may result in adolescent tendencies to punch first, talk second.

34. Binder et al., 1988: 64–67.

35. Brown and Larson, 2009.

36. Hall's work has been critiqued as "biological determinism," by Brotherton (2004: 28–29) and for his subsequent "storm and stress" hypothesis in which "the previous selfhood is broken up" and a new individual is born. Jensen and Rojek, 1998: 37. We do

not refute these contentions but suggest that many of Hall's ideas on adolescence being a time of turmoil and aggressive tendencies are accurate. Adolescents may not be "hormone-bound," but they are certainly *hormone-influenced*. Hall's suggestion that all adolescents have these tendencies, regardless of class or race, is an important contribution to recognizing the political implications involved in the application of derogatory names to select groups.

37. Erickson and Jensen, 1991: 281–282.
38. Ibid.: 294–296.
39. Schwendinger and Schwendinger, 1985: xiii.
40. Esbensen and Winfree (2001) make the case that gang researchers who rely on police data often come to conclusions that gang members are worse people than nongang members. See also, for example, Thornberry, 2001; Thornberry et al., 2006.
41. Platt, 1969: 69.
42. Krisberg, 2005: 25.
43. Krisberg and Austin, 1978: 35–37 (emphasis added).
44. Mills, 1943.
45. Galliher and MC Cartney, 1973: 77–90.
46. Liazos, 1972: 103–120.
47. Brotherton, 2015; Fraser, 2015; Hagedorn, 1998, 2008.
48. Fearn, et al., 2001: 330–343; Bjerregaard, 2006: 381–393.
49. Davis, 2008: xii.
50. Kappeler and Potter, 2005: 216–220. John DiIulio's theory of the juvenile "superpredator," although later discredited by research and publicly distanced by DiIulio, led to a 1996 bill in the U.S. House of Representatives called the Violent Youth Predator Act, as well as to numerous state lawmakers using this theory to pass their own punitive juvenile legislation. DiIulio's theory was speculative and fear based but effective in worrying the public and getting politicians to act.
51. Moore, 1991: 1–5.
52. Fleisher, 2001: 100–103.
53. Decker and Van Winkle, 2001: 19–20.
54. Fraser, 2015: 13.
55. Vigil, 1988: 148.
56. Pearson, 1983: 193–195.
57. Ibid.: 191, 192.
58. Schwendinger and Schwendinger, 1985: 4–5.
59. Ibid.: 42–44.
60. Pearson, 1983: 188.
61. Ibid., 82–83.
62. Fraser, 2015: 9.
63. For early New York gangs, see Riis, 1970, and Asbury 1970; for early Philadelphia gangs, see Spergel, 1995: 7; and for early Chicago gangs, see Thrasher, 1966.
64. Beirne and Messerschmidt, 2011: 33–43.
65. Decker and Kempf-Leonard (1995: 21) write, "There is no such legal term as gang" and that responses to gang activities are based on "socially constructed definitions."
66. Kenneth Bell, an official with the Los Angeles County District Attorney's Office, in an effort to define gangs, writes, in an official publication of the Los Angeles County Sheriff's Department, that a gang is "a group of young men or women who don't agree with society's way of life. They have created their own value and support system that feels normal to them. Their actions often lead to crime." Bell, n.d.: 44. A gang definition

like this is precisely what Quinney (1970: 104–105) was emphasizing in his theory on the social reality of crime: the "ideological orientations of or values of policemen provide a basis for selective law enforcement. . . . Discretion is basic to law enforcement." Police discretion is permitted maximum "interpretational latitude" with a definition as broad as this, allowing "selective law enforcement" to impose a gang label on almost any group they choose.

67. Sellin and Wolfgang, 1964: 71.
68. Decker and Kempf-Leonard, 1995: 14.
69. Spergel, 1995: 15.
70. Moore, 1998: 4–6.
71. Knox, 1998: 133.
72. Bursik and Grasmick, 1996: 12.
73. Durkheim, 1966.
74. The classic work on the political implications of definitions of gang homicides is Maxson and Klein, 1995: 32. They updated their work a few years later to assess the effects of drugs and found the same discrepancies they had found in their earlier work. Maxson and Klein, 2001: 173–185.
75. The LAPD may be a coconspirator in helping Los Angeles gain its title of gang capital of America, since they appear more likely than agencies in other parts of the state "to identify certain classes of homicides as being gang related," giving Los Angeles a biased boost. See Tita and Abrahamse, 2006: 273.
76. Quicker recalls a similar phenomenon occurring in Los Angeles in the early 1980s when the City was bidding for the 1984 Olympics, which it eventually got. In an effort to hold down the appearance of any gang violence, the City hired suspected gang members during the Olympics to serve as ushers and security. As reported in the media, gang-related offenses continued to be low both before and during the Olympics.
77. Hagedorn, 1998: 21–22.
78. Webb and Katz, 2006: 353.
79. Spergel, 1995: 17.
80. Hagedorn, 2008: 135.
81. Fraser, 2015: 38, 6.
82. Kappeler and Potter, 2005: 48–50.
83. Sellin and Wolfgang (1982: 22) offer a similar criticism of studies on delinquency. They write that textbooks and research papers will acknowledge data weaknesses in the first paragraph "and then go on to ignore."
84. 1973 is the start date given for CRASH, later becoming TRASH for *Total Resources Against Street Hoodlums*, on Wikipedia: en.wikipedia.org/wiki/Community_Resources_Against_Street_Hoodlums. Retrieved December 5, 2021.
85. Winton, 2016.
86. Alpert, 2020.
87. Fraser, 2015: 12.
88. Brotherton, 2015: 168.
89. In Quicker's gang courses, students would frequently find fault with research findings from Moore, 1978, 1991; Quicker, 1983; and Vigil, 1988, 2002, which suggested that gangs often provided surrogate family support for the juveniles. The problem, as one student so succinctly expressed it, was that gangs were such horrible groups while families were such honorable ones so that even using the two concepts in the same sentence was offensive, much less arguing that gangs could assist in socialization the family couldn't or wouldn't do.

90. Reiman, 1979.
91. Ibid.: 44–65.
92. Quinney, 1970: 56.
93. Reasons, 1973.
94. Quoting Conquergood's gang research, Brotherton (2015: 105) notes how well Conquergood understands the power of the term *gang* to cathect middle-class fears, by conjuring notions of "disorder, disintegration, and chaos," demonizing gang members as predatory and pathological, prepared to do indescribable harm to decent people.
95. Brotherton and Barrios, (2004: 28) note that gang "appears as an analytical concept in narrative descriptions of marginalized youth and deviant subcultures in the Los Angeles based work of Bogardus (1926) and the Chicago studies of Thrasher (1927)." The term appeared earlier in the work of Riis (1892: 215), in New York, where he contended that the failure of institutions to properly deal with immigration and poverty pushed the "unbridled" boys to the street, where their "nature" resulted in the gang.
96. Tapia, 2017: 10–11.
97. Brotherton, 2004: 157.
98. Brotherton, 2015: 105.
99. Brotherton, 2015: 111.
100. The objection to being referred to as a gang was not entirely universal. Frank M., who was a member of Clanton Street, had this to say about the group: "We called ourselves a gang. It was the Clanton Street gang; that's what it was. We called ourselves the 18th Street gang." (This 18th Street group was within Clanton's area and probably a clique of Clanton.) Then he added that when he and his homeboys became eighteen or nineteen years old, they "were past the gang stage and into parties and stuff." They formed "social clubs," like the Esquires, to give parties with girls invited. The Esquires dissolved after a couple of years because the male members got married and started families. The gang was a stage in the development of their lives, not a life commitment.
101. Spergel (1995: 12) confirms Roslyn's suspicions with his assertion that criminal-justice definitions of gangs, the definitions that inform the media, are "almost exclusively based on a negative perception."
102. The Businessmen was the name of one of the South Los Angeles groups that the Group Guidance Program worked with.
103. This statement is adapted from Quinney's second proposition of his theory of crime. Quinney, 1970: 16–17.
104. Jankowski's description of gangs as relatively formal structures, with well-defined leadership involved in rational exchange relationships with its members, included Los Angeles gangs. Jankowski, 1991: 21–34. We found nothing of this genre in South Los Angeles. While the street groups there represented tremendous variety, with many of them being quite amorphous, none had the bureaucratic organization he describes.
105. The Florencitas were a female affiliate of the Florence street group.
106. Moore, 1991: 25.
107. Vigil, 1988: 90–91.
108. Keiser (1969) uses the term *organization* to refer to the Chicago street group he studied, presumably because *gang* seemed to be an inappropriate word to describe it.
109. Keiser, 1969: 1, 17.
110. Pye, "Brown Sees Delinquency Cub Progress," *Los Angeles Sentinel*, March 21, 1963.
111. Rice and Christensen, 1965.
112. Rodriguez, 1993: 41.

113. Keiser (1969: 40) finds that the Vice Lords used the term *set* too but in a somewhat different context. *Set* for them meant a party, while in South Los Angeles it could also mean who is on the scene at this momemt. Dawley (1992: 33) uses the term *set* to refer to the Vice Lords' group.

114. Former Watts gang member turned LAPD informant Louis Tackwood (1973: 70–76) uses *set* and *club* as well as *gang* almost interchangeably in his book when he references the groups he ran with on the streets in the 1960s.

115. Spergel, 1995: 9–12.

116. An entire cottage industry of articles on the virtues and use of self-report data was born after Ivan Nye and James Short's classic 1957 article on this new and more "accurate" method of data collection. See especially Elliott and Ageton, 1980, and Hindelang et al., 1979.

117. Schwendinger and Schwendinger, 1985: xi.

118. Fraser, 2015: 13.

119. Bursik and Grasmick, 1995: 9.

120. Pepinsky and Jesilow (1984) offer an excellent account of the role of myths in promoting false ideas about a variety of accepted beliefs about crime. Myth 3, "Some groups are more law abiding than others," and myth 6, "Rich and poor are equal before the law," are especially relevant to our analysis.

121. We adopt this term from Stephen E. Ambrose's 2001 book *Band of Brothers*. Of course, the street groups were not military organizations, but they did "delight" in the "comradeship" of their homeboys, like the soldiers.

122. From Webster's, 1999: 562, definition of a "fraternity."

123. A "road dog" was your best friend. He, and it was always a "he," was the person who rode shotgun when you drove, or permitted you that status when he drove.

124. Moore, 1978: 53.

125. Hagedorn, 1988: 82–86.

126. It was the earlier groups who most frequently referred to themselves as *clubs* or *social organizations*, while those appearing from the early and mid-1950s to mid-1960s usually referenced themselves as *sets*.

127. Cloward and Ohlin, 1960. Vigil (1988: 172) updates Cloward and Ohlin's theory of the three subcultures by arguing that because they lacked a historical perspective, they missed the possibility that cliques from the gang might appear as any one of these subcultures, depending on the time it was studied.

128. We prefer the term *street group* as most descriptive of the early South Los Angeles groups. Brotherton's preference for *street organization* does not accurately portray the South Los Angeles groups. Some were organized well enough to be referred to this way, but others were not. Tapia (2017), in his study of San Antonio barrio gangs, seems most comfortable with the term *group* rather than *gang* to refer to the early groups there.

CHAPTER 3

1. The existence of pre-Crip-and-Blood gangs in South Los Angeles has been documented in numerous newspaper articles, as well as by such authorities as Emory Bogardus (1926, 1929, 1943), LASD gang expert Wes McBride (1985) and again with Robert K. Jackson (1985), by gang researchers Rice and Christensen (1965), as well as by the Attorney General's *Report on Youth Gang Violence in California* in 1981, and by Los Angeles County District Attorney, Ira Reiner (1992), in *Gangs, Crime and Violence in Los Angeles*.

2. See Bing, 1991: 148–149; Reiner, 1992: 4–5; Shelden et al., 2001: 8–13.

3. Los Angeles is home to one of the most respected gang researchers in the field, Malcolm Klein. Klein's work in understanding gang structures and the effectiveness of gang-prevention programs both in Los Angeles and around the country is significant. Klein, 1967, 1971. His early work with South Los Angeles gang-prevention programs and street workers helped establish a fundamental understanding of program effectiveness. But Klein's goals were neither to study individual gangs of South Los Angeles nor to study their origins. Klein's work was not intended as ethnography.

4. Most of the histories on early Black Angelenos neglect any mention of gangs. Davis (1990) is an exception, as is Smith (2006), who primarily relied on Davis's depictions.

5. Quicker received a grant from California State University Dominguez Hills to hire four students to do a content analysis of all the Los Angeles newspapers and national magazines—from 1930 to 1970—for articles pertaining to early Los Angeles gangs. The students looked through original copies and microfiches, making copies of any relevant article with one or more of the following terms in them: *gang, youth, teen, juvenile, delinquency, juvenile crime, group violence, mobs, prevention, racism, population changes, and job bias*. It is from this analysis that we have drawn our information for the media's treatment of Los Angeles juvenile gangs.

6. We use the term *Mexican* to refer to the Latin population living in Los Angeles during our study period because most Latinos in South Los Angeles then had Mexican roots. This term was commonly used by residents as well, and it simplifies naming this ethnic group. Sides (2003: 220) offers similar reasons for his use of the term *Mexican* in his work; it is more accurate. The term *Chicano* was also in use in South Los Angeles to refer to this same group. We will use that term as well when it is appropriate in the context. Morales (2020: 28), in his review of Fernandez's book *The Young Lords*, indicates that the Young Lords' use of the term *Latino* was one of the first public uses of the term. The first non-Mexican heritage Latino from South Los Angeles that Bird met was in Los Angeles County Jail in 1965. He was a young Salvadorian male. While there may have been other non-Mexican Latinos in South Los Angeles before 1965, they were probably few.

7. McWilliams, 1943: 819.

8. Turner and Surace (1956), Vigil (2002: 68), and Howell (2010: 11) also note the role played by the police and media in demonizing the zoot suiters, while these groups excused the military and citizen mobs that attacked them.

9. McWilliams, 1950: 570.

10. Ibid.

11. "Cluff was president of the Western Chemical and Manufacturing Co.—Making Asbestos Products," *Los Angeles Times*, December 7, 1953.

12. Ibid.

13. "Gangsters, Wanton Gang Violence: Powder Puff Treatment Given Rise to Gangsterism," *Los Angeles Times*, December 11, 1953.

14. Taylor, Walton, and Young, 1974: 40; Quinney, 1970.

15. "Problem of Ending Gang Threats: Stiff Prison Sentences Necessary," *Los Angeles Times*, December 9, 1953.

16. "Public Menace: Gangs Surpassed Previous Lawless Outrages," *Los Angeles Times*, December 8, 1953 (emphasis added).

17. "Cluff Case: Self Expression Overemphasized, Punishment Underemphasized," *Los Angeles Times*, December 8, 1953.

18. "New Crimes by Youth Gangs Bring Boost in Police Force," *Los Angeles Times*, December 16, 1953.

19. Moore, 1978; Vigil, 1988.
20. Krisberg, 1978: 36.
21. "Cluff Case: Self Expression Overemphasized, Punishment Underemphasized," *Los Angeles Times*, December 8, 1953; and "Gangsters, Wanton Gang Violence: Powder Puff Treatment Given Rise to Gangsterism," December 11, 1953.
22. *Los Angeles Herald*, May 18, 1955.
23. Vigil (1988: 2) notes that a Los Angeles city official unapologetically echoed the control perspective position with these comments on the city's gangs: "We don't want to understand the problem, we just want to stop it."
24. McWilliams, 1988: 322–323.
25. Clanton Street today is a one-block-long, east-west street in the Los Angeles County strip between the cities of San Gabriel and Temple City. This short street is some ten miles from downtown, where the original Clanton Street was. The original Clanton street group took its name from the downtown Clanton Street, a four-block-long street just south of 14th Street. The original no longer exists, having been renamed 14th Place before 1950, most likely because the City felt it could weaken the gang by renaming its namesake street.
26. Starbuck et al. (2001) identify a "new" gang formation they referred to as "hybrid gangs." They are "characterized by mixed racial and ethnic participation within a single gang" or an individual involved in multiple gangs. These hybrid gangs are different from the mixed-racial and ethnic gangs Thrasher found in Chicago, the authors claim. Mixed South Los Angeles street groups were similar to what Thrasher found.
27. Macy Street used to run between Alameda Street and the Ramona Freeway, now the 101 Freeway. It has been renamed East Cesar E. Chavez Avenue.
28. Bob Will, "Gangs Operate in Specific Districts: Major Groups and Boundaries of Their Areas Well Classified," *Los Angeles Times*, December 18, 1953, writes that the Macy Street gang had members in their late teens and early twenties, who "have been involved in many felonious attacks against women." John S. didn't remember it that way. He recalled that the group could be "rowdy," but they were generally respectful toward women.
29. Ibid. Bird remembered seeing a mural on a wall in 1976, near Temple Street's territory, that read: "Temple Street, 1923–1976."
30. Jackson and McBride, 1985. The Boozies have also been termed the "Boosey," the "Boosie," and the "Boozy" gang, by other researchers. Miller, 1988: 1; Eldridge, 1985: 14; and Bird. Since many proper nouns were mostly spoken and rarely written in the early days, spelling variations are to be expected.
31. Jackson and McBride, 1985: 40.
32. Attorney General, 1981: 21.
33. Miller, 1988: 2.
34. Ibid. Mayor Bradley knew Frank Miller by name, having picked him up a few times when Bradley was an LAPD officer and Miller was a juvenile. Bradley would bring him home and warn him to stay out of trouble.
35. Miller (1988) was one of the few to remember the Boozies as being more violent. He wrote that when they "crashed parties," people could get hurt. He recalled an occasion when a party crashing became violent enough that someone was killed. He believes this incident ended the Boozie's existence as a group.
36. The 20s neighborhood was mostly along Central Avenue, from 20th Street on the north to 29th Street on the south. Although this is one of the oldest Black neighborhoods in Los Angeles, it was never all Black. The older street-group members we interviewed

were all aware of the nightlife along the Avenue. They thought it was a positive thing for Los Angeles and the Black community but didn't participate themselves, most likely because none of them were twenty-one years old and able to drink legally, and most didn't have the resources to afford the clubs.

37. The 18th Street clique that emerged in the 1930s in South Los Angeles should not be confused with the current gang of the same name. The first 18th Street group was small, about twenty members, half of whom were Chicano, with three Chinese and the remainder Black. The current 18th Street gang, reputed to be one of the largest gangs in Los Angeles, is all Latin and is not a continuation of the first 18th Street gang.

38. Eldridge, 1975: 11.

39. Smith's *The Great Black Way* describes a cultural "renaissance" along Central Avenue during the 1940s.

40. Watts was a distinctive area in many ways. It was the first significant Black community outside of downtown, it had most of the large post–World War II housing projects, it was traditionally one of the poorest areas in the City, and it was geographically distant from other parts of the City. It was not uncommon for street-group members outside of Watts to differentiate among the various street groups in Watts by specific names: Farmers, Huns, and so on. If the groups were from Watts, they often just referred to themselves as "Watts."

41. Santa Barbara Avenue was renamed Martin Luther King Jr. Boulevard.

42. Gladiator territory was Figueroa to Western and Santa Barbara to Gage.

43. The Coliseum in Rome, Italy, where Roman gladiators fought, inspired South Los Angeles's Gladiators, living near the Los Angeles Coliseum, to refer to themselves as the *Roman Gladiators*, or just *Gladiators*, perhaps trying to capitalize on the moxie of this namesake.

44. The clique names of *baby, little, junior, midget, pee wee,* and others were used by the sets to designate cliques younger than the preceding cliques.

45. Knox, 1998.

46. Ibid.

47. Geis, 2001: x.

48. Knox, 1998: 127–137.

49. Ibid.

50. We thank Kelefa Sanneh (2015: 110) for this apt discussion of the manipulative power of statistics.

51. Lewis, 1956. The emergence of more street groups would logically follow from the presence of more people.

52. Alonzo (2010: 165) adds that the LAPD did not start collecting "complete statistics on gang-related crime until 1985."

53. O'Conner, 1953: A14.

54. Will, 1953a: 2, and 1953b.

55. Sherman, 1963: 1.

56. Ivory, 1960. With parameters on the number of gangs as wide open as "130 to 311," it seems fair to assume that no one really knew how many there were but were trying to cover their contentions with an underestimate and an overestimate, just in case.

57. Shadow, 1960.

58. Neff, 1961a, 1961b. Before 1965, there were no fully Asian, or "Oriental," street groups in South Los Angeles. When Asians joined street groups, the groups were mixed with other races.

59. Sherman, 1963: C5.

60. This large number, five thousand, is a guesstimate by Bird of the total number of juveniles who considered themselves Slausons. It does not mean the number of youth who had been initiated. It includes those who were and many who simply claimed the name Slauson because they lived in the community, and no one stood in their way to say otherwise.

61. The uncertainty about Watts is due to our relative dearth of firsthand accounts. The Watts sources we did speak with had solid information about the things they had been personally involved in but felt less comfortable speculating about activities outside their experience. We felt that some of the generalizations we heard from our Watts sources might have been speculative but not necessarily inaccurate.

62. Most Watts street-group members lived in government-subsidized housing projects, while the families of the groups north and west of them lived in owner-occupied, detached single-family homes. The Watts residents were more dependent on government programs than residents in the Florence-Firestone District, suggesting economic inequality between them. The insularity of living together in a project made movement outside the project less important and no doubt contributed to their sense of in-groupness.

63. Two other wars, the Korean War and the Vietnam War, occurred during this period and are addressed later.

64. Eldridge, 1975: 2.

65. Although migrant Black families were a major contributor to the demographic changes in South Los Angeles after World War II, large numbers of people from other ethnic groups were also part of the influx. The nature of the demographic change and how it affected South Los Angeles is considered further in chapter 9.

66. Ibid.: 2.

67. Batani-Khalfani, 1984: 4.

68. Short (1982: 332) has argued that the Chicago, Boston, and New York gangs of the 1960s were relatively apolitical, even though some tried to go "conservative" and change their public image. They were motivated more by criminality than by politics in their decisions. He generalizes about gangs everywhere, contending that "the appeal of Black Nationalism was compromised by (perceived) failure by some of the groups to deliver on 'promises' and by the established norm of hostility toward other groups and retaliation for real or imagined injury." His characterization is a good example of the difficulty involved when generalizing beyond populations not studied. Black Nationalism had a profound effect on some South Los Angeles street-group members, unlike what Short reports to have occurred within the groups he references.

69. Alonzo, 2004: 668.

70. Kumasi, in Peralta, 2009, makes Hoover's position on the Black Power movement crystal-clear.

71. O'Connor, 1953: A14.

72. "Stabbing of Pair in back: Hoodlumism, Irresponsible Elements," *Los Angeles Sentinel*, September 12, 1946; "5 Raped Her: Gang of Five Forced Her Into Car," *Los Angeles Sentinel*, September 26, 1946. The *Los Angeles Sentinel* was the major Black newspapers in Los Angeles during this period, reporting news for and about Blacks in the City. It is not surprising that some South Los Angeles residents referred to it as the "Snitchnel" because of its reporting on neighborhood activities.

73. "Latest Dual Slaying Makes 11 in 12 Years," *Los Angeles Herald and Express*, August 8, 1951; *Time*, October 14, 1946; and *Newsweek*, August 29, 1949, and February 20, 1950: 59.

74. "Inquest Blames Youth in Slaying: 4 Face Charges," The *Los Angeles Times*, December 4, 1954.

75. We found no evidence that a Black mafia, as identified by Francis Ianni (1975) in New York, involving ethnic succession of non-White gang members to organized crime, occurred in Los Angeles.

76. Bob Will, "Youthful Gang Activities: Thefts and Fights Often End in Deaths," *Los Angeles Times*, December 16, 1953.

77. Ibid.

78. According to Bird, the generation of Mexican youth in South Los Angeles during the 1950s and 1960s primarily spoke English. Their parents spoke Spanish but wanted their children to acculturate by speaking English rather than Spanish. The music that played from the open windows of dwellings or autos before 1965 was primarily soul music or rhythm and blues, performed by Black musicians to a receptive audience of Black and Mexican Angelenos.

79. Hagedorn (1998, 2008) has made the case for the power of industrialization and of deindustrialization contributing to the growth in gangs, the seriousness of their crimes, and their violence.

80. Barmaki, 2019.

81. "Police, Youth Riot: Disturbance on Beach," *Los Angeles Times*, June 21, 1958; "Three Musclemen Jailed for Brawling at Beach," *Los Angeles Times*, June 13, 1954; "Gang Fight on Beach Broken Up by Police," *Los Angeles Times*, June 7, 1954.

82. This quote comes from the following three sources: "Homer Ray Johnson, 147 E. 77th Street, Ganged upon and Severely Stabbed in the Abdomen and the Lower Part of His Back," *Los Angeles Times*, December 25, 1958; "Youth Shot and Knifed in Hoodlum Battle," *Los Angeles Times*, June 27, 1954; "Four Persons Involved in a Gang Fight During Which an El Toro Marine Was Stabbed to Death Were Filed on by the District Attorney," *Los Angeles Sentinel*, July 3, 1958: 1.

83. "Teen School Gang Arrested," *Los Angeles Sentinel*, February 19, 1959.

84. Tannenbaum, 1938; Lemert, 1951; Schur, 1971.

85. "Compton and El Jardin Sit Together to Map Truce," *Los Angeles Times*, January 29, 1954.

86. The early 1950s was a period when the media in other large cities, like New York, also rediscovered gangs. They found their gang constituents to be similar to what their colleagues in Los Angeles described—usually minority and lower-class. Gangs were reported to be violent and dangerous, suggesting threats to all who encountered them. Kramer and Karr, 1953: 194–202. Leading national authorities like FBI director J. Edgar Hoover and Bertram Beck, director of the Juvenile Delinquency Project of the U.S. Children's Bureau, tried to confirm with statistics and by testimony what the newspapers were already claiming: gang delinquency was occurring throughout the country, like a "tidal wave," engulfing agencies and filling jails. Ibid.: 206–207. Films about gangs, like *The Wild Ones* and *Blackboard Jungle*, were released for widespread public consumption. *West Side Story*, a play that later became a hit film, was also released. The public was involved in an official blitzkrieg that not only presented them with the phenomena of gangs but whacked them upside their heads with it, so they wouldn't forget.

87. Yablonsky (1967) stands out as the classic promoter of the idea that gang members, and especially their leaders, are social aberrations.

88. Bernstein, 1964: 37.

89. Ibid.: 37–38.

90. Bernstein's negative characterizations of gang members reminded us of Friedrich Nietzsche's famous remark: "Objectivity and justice have nothing to do with one another."

91. Mike Davis indicates that the early Black community press saw White gangs as evidence of an nascent gang problem in South Los Angeles. He wrote that the Black press gave repeated references to "gangs of White youth who terrorized Black residents along the frontiers of the southward-expanding Central Avenue ghetto" and perhaps gave rise to Black street gangs as a defensive response to their violence. Davis, 1990: 293. Davis's source was the *Eagle*, Los Angeles's progressive Black newspaper, which we did not examine. We examined the early issues of the *Los Angeles Sentinel*, a widely circulated newspaper in the Black community, and found little mention of White gangs. This finding was consistent with what we found in other Los Angeles newspapers. We are not refuting the existence of White gangs in South Los Angeles as discussed by Davis but suggesting that the major media sources rarely if ever mentioned them. Our research supports Davis's findings that White street groups existed and that they terrorized Black residents. In a 1946 *Los Angeles Sentinel* article, there was mention of a White "Venice gang"—a group, it turns out, that was more likely a mob of White racists beating up Black youth than a street gang. This was probably the general case for most early White gangs, even if they had a name. They were more often ad hoc groups that formed to prey on Black youth than they were like the street groups' non-White youth had.

92. We found an article that discussed the formation of "Japanese-American" gangs near downtown. It was written after a sixteen-year-old Japanese juvenile was shot and killed following a "street brawl between three groups of teen-agers of Japanese ancestry." Besides focusing on the incident, the article was also concerned with why it happened, since the Japanese are so "law-abiding," and what the community planned to do about it, Hartt, *Los Angeles Examiner*, June 2, 1958.

93. Durkheim, 1966a.

94. Erikson, 1966.

95. Brotherton (2004: 27) notes the term *gang* was tied historically to agricultural society before it was tied to early capitalism.

96. Fraser, 2015: 4–6.

97. Brotherton, 2004: 27–28.

98. Barnhart, Robert K., *The Barnhart Concise Dictionary of Etymology: The Origins of American English Words*. Unabridged edition, Harper Resource Pub., NY, 1988. Also, Onions, C.T., ed., *The Oxford Dictionary of English Etymology*. Oxford University Press, NY, 1966.

99. Fraser, 2015: 13–15.

100. The original Bowery Boys, forming in New York City in the mid-1850s, were groups of White nativist adults who fought repeatedly with other White immigrant groups, most notably the Irish. A semifictionalized account of them was provided in the 2002 Martin Scorsese film the *Gangs of New York*. The Bowery Boys of the mid-1940s and 1950s were a group of actors playing troublesome kids.

101. Some noteworthy studies using official data, of the many that have been conducted, that have found commonalities among gangs wherever they are found are Thornberry, 1982; Thornberry et al., 1995; Klein, 2006; and most of the publications of the National Youth Gang Survey.

102. Esbensen and Winfree Jr., 2001: 110.

103. Alonzo, 2004, 2010.

104. Coinciding with the metamorphosis of gangs from foreign Whites to non-Whites was the overall increase in the number of poor Black people. Brown (2009: 215) notes that the "complexion of poverty" darkened, as "poverty became associated with urban inner-city Blacks." As Black people became poorer and more numerous, they swelled the ranks of the underclass making groupings of Black juveniles more visible.
105. Moore, 1978: 48; Vigil, 1988.
106. Hagedorn, 2008: 115.
107. Anderson, 1990: 167.
108. Hagedorn, 2008: 54–55.
109. Moore, 1991: 137.
110. Brotherton, 2008.
111. Fraser, 2015: 6–11.
112. Decker and Pyrooz, 2011, 2015; Pyrooz et al., 2017.
113. Fraser, 2015: 32.
114. Hagedorn, 2008: 21.
115. Ibid.: xxxii.
116. Anderson, 1999: 66.
117. Moore, 1991: 17.
118. Fraser, 2015: 16.
119. Brotherton, 2015: 168.
120. "Gee, Officer Krupke." Song from *West Side Story* film, 1961.
121. A good example of the control perspective can be found in the California Council's (1986) *State Task Force on Youth Gang Violence*.
122. Lopez (2007) writes that the STEP Act was part of an "undeclared war" on gangs by the criminal justice system, designed more to bring harm to rather than help to gang members.
123. From *California Penal Code*, "Chapter 11: Street Terrorism Enforcement and Prevention Act," 186.20–186.36 (chapter 11 added by stats. 1988, ch. 1256, sec. 1).
124. A cottage industry of paid "expert witness" testimony, already in existence before the STEP Act, might have been enhanced as a result of it. Public defenders and private attorneys, where possible, try to convince juries with testimony from "gang experts" that the juvenile is not a gang member, while prosecutors bring in their own experts to prove otherwise.
125. While crime has been a part of American society since its founding, it has taken on a new life with the creation, in the twentieth century, of assorted and well-funded federal and state agencies to enforce rules against it and support publications about it.
126. Jensen and Rojek, 2009: 7.
127. Jensen and Rojek, 1998: 2.
128. Although juvenile crime and gangs consistently ranked high when students were asked about the greatest threats to our society, there seemed to be a relationship between how highly they were ranked and what the media had been reporting. The more coverage juvenile crime had had in the months before Quicker conducted his class surveys, the higher the students ranked juvenile crime as a threat.
129. Esbensen, 1993.
130. A comprehensive criminology text on the many forms crime takes, is by Piers Beirne and James Messerschmidt, now in its sixth edition.
131. A primary reason for juvenile absence from white-collar crime is opportunity. Sutherland's ([1949] 1961: 9) classic definition of white-collar crime as "a crime commit-

ted by a person of respectability and high status in the course of his occupation" excludes most juveniles, because they usually don't have occupations.

132. Coleman, 2006.

133. Kappeler and Potter, 2005. These deaths from corporate negligence do not reflect the millions of workers who are injured or made ill on their jobs due to preventable corporate irresponsibility. As Reiman (1979) so aptly phrases it: "Work may be dangerous to your health." When working conditions are dangerous and sometimes fatal, corporations, if caught, get to slide with little more than a slap on the hand and a Boy Scout promise not to do it again. Corporations are, after all, a part of the power elite.

134. Clark, 1970: 38.

135. Mills, 1952.

136. Coleman, 2006: ix. White-collar crime has undergone many reconceptualization's since its introduction and has variously been termed *crimes of the elite, crimes of the powerful, organizational crime, occupational crime, corporate crime,* and *crimes of privilege*. Shover and Wright, 2001. Often excluded from these crimes are political crimes. Beirne and Messerschmidt (2011: 335–368) argue that many criminologists don't even recognize the category of political crime, but when they do, it is usually to acknowledge crimes committed against the state and not by the state. They further contend that crimes by the state, like corruption and political repression, and transnational crimes, such as state-sponsored terrorism, can seriously undermine our social order and need to be considered if we are to understand the big picture of crime.

137. Kappeler and Potter, 2005: 149.

138. Coleman, 2006. When Sutherland first used the term *white-collar crime* in his 1939 presidential address to the American Sociological Society (now changed to the American Sociological Association because of acronym challenges), he raised eyebrows and ire because of the principled stand he took and the defiance he posed to powerful interest groups. In some circles, his audacity had him cast as "un-American," according to Coleman (Ibid: 2).

139. Alterman, 2020: 10–11.

140. Lamoureux, 2019.

141. Schwendingers, 2014.

142. Ibid.

CHAPTER 4

1. Thrasher (1966) contends that the gangs he studied began as play groups, which is not contradicted by our observation but supplemented. The original Slausons weren't "playing" with each other at the Park; they were *hanging out*. South Los Angeles groups that started as play groups were often groups playing a team sport.

2. Moore (1991: 61) notes that one-third of the males in the East Los Angeles street groups she studied reported that they "enjoyed" fighting. In South Los Angeles, the rewards associated with fighting were considerable. As Thrasher (1966) contends, esprit de corps was an important one. Moore's quote, "We would fight if somebody would pick on us, and we would fight to the end, but we wouldn't go around looking for a fight," could have easily come from one of our respondents.

3. We call this "Collette's Law." It is named after Collette Vazquez of the Los Angeles County Probation Department, who introduced the concept in lectures to my classes. She asserted that an explanation of any social phenomenon can be both generally correct

and specifically false. Regardless of how much variance a particular explanation may account for, there are always some parts that remain exceptions. Such an understanding helps to account for the anomalies of social life.

4. Keiser (1969: 1–18) writes that the Vice Lords are called a "nation" rather than a gang. This term was also used to refer to another large Chicago group of the 1960s, the P. Blackstone Nation. Formerly the Blackstone Rangers, the P. Blackstone Nation was an amalgamation of numerous gangs from all over the South Side of Chicago who had come together under this one banner. McPherson, 1969. Unlike Chicago, South Los Angeles never had this kind of organization among its street groups before 1970.

5. Klein, 1971: 65–66.

6. Hagedorn, 1988: 86.

7. Vigil, 1988: 92–96.

8. For many South Los Angeles sets, clique names were often a prefix that suggested size, like *big* or *little*, or age, like *senior* or *junior*. In fact, these designations represented clique sequencing. The *bigs* or *seniors* were older than the *littles* or *juniors* in their respected sets and came first. The *littles* came before the *babies* or *midgets*, but the *babies* were no more babies than the *midgets* were short. The *babies* were usually near the age the *bigs* were when the *bigs* got started, but just developed afterward.

9. There were few clear differences between a set and a clique. The terms could be used interchangeably, with cliques of founders often calling their group *sets*. Groups that had multiple cliques recognized their clique as a clique of a larger set with various levels of allegiance.

10. This was not the case for most of the predominantly Mexican sets in Los Angeles, whose names continued after 1965. Vigil (1988: 88–90) provides a solid account of how this happened for Los Angeles's Mexican American gangs.

11. If a set had more than one age cohort, it had cliques.

12. While the concept of family is often idealized as an endearing, warm, and cozy place, safe from conflict and exploitation, research suggests that many families do not live up to these standards but are in fact places of violence and mistreatment. Referring to their street group as "family" in South Los Angeles meant that members believed, or hoped, that their group might be closer to the ideal. Often the street groups did not meet these standards either, being more like real extended families than the ideal.

13. Klein, 1971; Hagedorn, 1988; Vigil, 1988.

14. A notable exception to this generally occurring phenomenon was the Renegade clique of Slauson. Usually, they were referred to as the Slauson Renegades.

15. Cliques were not equally committed to neighborhood rules. The Renegades, as their name implies, were semiapostates (Apostates being an alternate name for them), a part of Slauson but less committed to neighborhood norms than other cliques.

16. To last four or five years without developing cliques was a bit unusual but probably not unique.

17. The 1957 date is the year the Senators first got their "jackets." They were long purple coats that came down to their ankles, with the person's nickname on it and made out of material similar to high school letterman jackets.

18. The Senators' waning meant that they became inactive, while many of their members remained in the community as adults. In the early 1990s, a group from the Temple Street area calling themselves the Senators was around, but they had no relationship to the group that formed in the mid- to late 1950s.

19. The South-Side is another term used to refer to South Los Angeles. Mexican sets that came from the South-Side were distinctly different from those that came from East

Los Angeles. Almost all those youth in South Los Angeles who came from Spanish-speaking families were born of Mexican or Mexican American parents. The two most commonly used terms to refer people of this ethnicity then were *Mexican* and *Chicano*. The terms were used interchangeably, especially by the mid-1950s. We will use their terminology here.

20. While homogenization became the norm in South Los Angeles, it was not unusual to find a bit of diversity on occasion. The car clubs, for example, were different. Their membership was primarily adult, almost all were of the same race, and their interests revolved around customized cars.

21. *Florencita* is the Spanish feminine use of *Florence*. Although Florencitas referred to females from the Florence area, there was also a movie theater on Florence Avenue, east of the Fox-Florence Theater, named the Florencita Theater, that was in existence before the Florence set formed. This theater's name influenced Linda C. and her friends' choice of a name for their group.

22. A factor contributing to the "we're all in this together" feeling was the timing of the founding of both Florence and the Slausons. Both began about the same time, in the late 1940s, as Black and Mexican families, often with GI loans, moved into the same sea of White hostility.

23. Bird, for one, had girlfriends, some of whom he was quite serious with, who were Chicana and Japanese as well as Black.

24. While race and culture were primary differences between Blacks and Mexicans, another notable difference was the way they referred to the same neighborhood, often referring to it with different names. For example, *Aliso Village* was the term Blacks used to refer to the Aliso housing complex, while the Mexicans referred to that area as *Flats* or *Primera Flats*, because they were on First Street and the building had flat roofs.

25. Clanton was a neighborhood, just south of downtown, from about 7th Street to the streets in the 20s. It was named after Clanton Street, now renamed 14th Place. Sets or cliques from this neighborhood, which included Clanton Street and Mateo Street, went to the same junior high school together, Lafayette Junior High. Maple Street was a set from a junior high on 25th Street and was an enemy to the Clanton groups. Disagreements and fights among them were usually not over racial matters.

26. 18th Street is a street in the former Clanton neighborhood that has no relationship to the 18th Street currently in existence. The current group, beginning in 1964, now has groups all over the City known as 18th Street and is reputed to be one of the largest gangs in Los Angeles.

27. Bird noted that there were always a handful of Black and Mexican racists on either side but that they were kept in check by the others. There were individuals who, when they fought, fought over racial matters. But this was the exception.

28. Florence Avenue is a major east-west street that runs through South Los Angeles and would be 72nd Street if it was numbered. On the west side of Central Avenue, it is West Florence and East Florence is on the east side. The South Los Angeles neighborhood Florence Avenue runs through had a large Italian population before the 1950s, which probably had something to do with its name. When the Italians moved out and Mexicans moved in, the pronunciation of the Avenue changed among some residents from *Florence* to *Florencia*.

29. Although rare in the early Mexican sets, female club affiliation with male sets and their own set formation occurred in the 1950s in South Los Angeles. Moore doesn't mention female sets in her mid-1960s to mid-1970s research on East Los Angeles but does cite Quicker's 1974 research on East Los Angeles Chicana gangs. Moore, 1978: 47. In

his 1970s–1980s research on Chicano gangs in Los Angeles, Vigil also does not mention female sets, even though he too cites Quicker's 1983 research. Vigil, 1988: 101, 153. This suggests that although both Moore and Vigil were aware of Chicana groups, they may not have been as salient as the male groups. In later research, Moore (1991: 53) notes that gangs were "male-oriented groups," with conflicting opinions among males and females of how females were treated.

30. Moore (1978) and Vigil (1988) use "klika" interchangeably with clique in their research on Chicano gangs. LASD sergeant Joseph Guzman, in an undated paper, uses "clika" and "clica" in referring to the Chicano gang. Bird noted that clica is probably correct since the letter *k* in Spanish is used with about the same infrequency as *x*. We use "clique" to keep it simple.

31. The original Florence cliques of the 1950s were Big, Little, Baby, Midget, Tiny, Cherry, and Little Toakers. Big Florence was also known as the Toakers.

32. Diminutive clique references like *little, baby, midget, tiny*, and so on meant younger, not smaller.

33. In the 1980s, Florence still had a clique with a similar-sounding name as the Toakers, although with a different spelling; in the 1980s, it was Tokers.

34. The Spanish word for the number thirteen is *trece*, but the South-Side Chicanos would spell thirteen *trese*. It sounds similar, although misspelled from the Spanish. South-Side street-group members didn't have access to spell check, didn't write a lot, and numerous words would be spelled phonetically rather than dictionary influenced. This point takes on added significance when we later explain the origin of the name *Crips*.

35. Currently, Latino gangs in Southern California refer to themselves as *sur*, for south. They also use 13 as a reference point, while Northern California Latino gangs are referred to as *norte* and use the number 14. There are numerous hypotheses on why the various numbers were adopted, although nobody seems to be quite sure. One of the most tenable explanations is that the numbers refer to letters of the alphabet, which in turn signify something about the gangs. The thirteenth letter of the alphabet, for example, is *m*, which could stand for *marijuana* or, possibly, *murder*. The fourteenth letter of the alphabet is *n*, which, serendipitously or planned, signifies *norte* or *north*.

36. A number of researchers have shown there are multiple reasons for street-group formations in addition to the classic conflict model explained by Thrasher, 1966. See in particular Moore, 1991; Hagedorn, 1998; Vigil, 2002; Brotherton and Barrios, 2004; and Tapia, 2017, for a solid assortment of some of those reasons, with critiques of the theorists of the 1950s and 1960s.

37. The term *homie* in South Los Angeles originally referred to people who came from one's usually out-of-state home area. Commonality was immediate in their new land once they discovered they were from the same state, city, or town and might have known or been related to some of the same people. *Homie* was a reference to an in-group.

38. Membership in these groups was flexible enough for juveniles to join, leave, and then rejoin without repercussions. An intermittent member, like Frank M., was not uncommon. Because Frank M. was good with his fists, he was sought after, and he was loyal. Even during the times he was not a member, he would still assist members when they needed him if he felt their cause was just.

39. The accosters would overwhelm through numbers, strength, or both. There was no point in potential aggressors starting something they might lose.

40. It was a *he* and not a *she* who was taken advantage of this way in unfamiliar neighborhoods. Females had a different role in contributing to street-group conflict, as we show later.

41. Thrasher, 1963: 25–26. Hagedorn's (1988, 1998) research on Milwaukee gangs noted that conflict, as Thrasher theorized, was important in the founding of Milwaukee's gangs but that it was one of four reasons why gangs began there.

42. *J-Flats* was an abbreviation for *Japanese Flats*, a neighborhood adjacent to the Temple Street neighborhood, where there were a lot of Japanese people. The Black Juans came out of J-Flats while the Senators came out of the Temple Street neighborhood.

43. Bird recalled seeing the Black Juan name carved in the cement around North Virgil Avenue, north of Melrose Avenue, in the early 1960s.

44. The refrain that the Businessmen "took care of business" has also been offered as an explanation for their name. While this may be an ex post facto account, it could also be the case.

45. Barry Wa. And Barry Wh. Were Junior Businessmen. The first Barry was a notorious street fighter, while the second one became a famous R & B singer.

46. It's not clear why these cliques left the scene so quickly, but there are two clues: first, they were never that well organized to begin with and didn't have much group identity; and second, most of the Seniors wound up in prison.

47. Upon its dissolution, a number of youth from the Cavaliers went to various other existing clubs, like the Pueblos, the Boss Bachelors, and the Slausons, in addition to the Gladiators and the Businessmen.

48. Continuing Gladiator name association with the Coliseum, one of their leaders took the nickname "Spartacus" and another took the name "Demetrius." This large sports arena on Figueroa Street near the University of Southern California has been an important architectural landmark since its opening in 1923 and a very fitting influence for a juvenile street group to base its name on.

49. The Slauson Flips, emerging after the Babies, were a clique whose athletic abilities and gymnastic skills were instrumental in name choice.

50. Researchers and the police will frequently go into a community and see the names of various cliques and sets written on walls and sometimes assume these groups still exist. Graffiti has a longer life expectancy than many of its producers have, although there may still be members of the group around who continue to identify with it.

51. Under the right circumstances, juveniles could switch sets throughout their educational careers. Fremont High School, for example, was a melting pot for a number of middle schools that contained their own sets. Very few John Muir Middle School Gladiators went there. Carver Middle School, which sent a number of students to Fremont, was home to the Businessmen and the Ross Snyders. Changing schools, especially if the change was due to the juvenile's family's moving, was an acceptable reason why juveniles from a set in a previous neighborhood might change to a set in the new one.

52. Lincoln Park is northeast of downtown and of the Interstate 10 and Interstate 5 freeways. This park is tucked into the triangle formed by North Mission Road on the north, Valley Boulevard on the south, and Soto Street on the east. Memorial Day attracted a lot of South-Side and Compton juveniles to the park to celebrate.

53. To *jam* someone meant to get in their face, to challenge or to confront them.

54. In 1989, we spoke with one of the toughest leaders of the Gladiators, Freddy B., a "hellified fighter" in his time. Freddy B. had fallen on hard times. He had developed a drug problem, had no job, and was physically diminished from his prime. Unlike Bird, his leadership period was short-lived, as was the time the Gladiators remained on the streets as a viable set. Another Gladiator named Floyd was one of the Gladiators Bird had the most respect for because "he always stood up for the Gladiators regardless of where he was." Bird had fought with him, in a fight that was so memorable that others

wanted to see them go at it again. It never happened because in 1965 Floyd was killed by someone at a party.

55. Howard and McCord's (1969: 53–57) description of Watts as a "Black island" might be interpreted to suggest that Blacks were the only race living in Watts then. A number of our respondents remembered there having been Mexican families living in Watts since its early history. During the 1950s and 1960s, Watts was predominantly but not exclusively Black.

56. Some respondents claim the normalization of the nickname "Mudtown" to refer to Watts was due to the large percentage of Black people living there, as well as to the unpaved streets. Bay Bay moved from Watts to Slauson, became a Slauson, and then moved with his family to Hawthorne in 1959. He started referring to the section that he moved to, which was not predominantly Black, as "Little Watts," because many streets there were not paved either.

57. This racial slur, used this way, is toxic. We quote it because we believe the reader needs to know what was said, not what we might have liked them to say. Speakers and writers need to take responsibility for their words.

58. Sides, 2006: 19; Bunch, 1990: 115.

59. McWilliams, 1988: 325.

60. Sides, 2006: 17–19.

61. Tita and Abrahamse, 2006: 269.

62. Bunch, 1990: 115.

63. Hewitt, 1981: 13.

64. This was Jordan High School. With both junior high and high school there, grades 7–12, it quickly became overcrowded.

65. In spite of the negative reputation the Watts street groups had, they were still referred to as *clubs* most of the time by those familiar with them. Babel, a member of the Watts Orientals, told us, "We were a club, a set," not a gang.

66. The Watts projects were a maze of streets and walkways that provided a protective environment from external threats to the juveniles living there. Outsiders could easily get caught up in the labyrinth and then hurt before they could find their way out.

67. Hacienda Village in Watts, built in 1942, was renamed Gonzaque Village in 2000.

68. The Farmers later changed their name to the Excellos, a name they took from the wine of a similar name.

69. While many of the Farmers lived in Palm Lanes and Jordan Downs, numerous other Farmers did not, giving them a ubiquity that no doubt made them more visible and enhanced their reputation.

70. "Nickerson Gardens," *Wikipedia*, https://en.wikipedia.org/wiki/Nickerson_Gardens.

71. The D'Artagnans were not a Watts set. Their territory was just west of Central Avenue, on the western boundary of Watts, off of Avalon Boulevard. They had many things in common with Watts, which, like adjacent patches in a quilt, had threads merging into each other. We call them "Watts oriented" because of the significant influence the Watts sets had on them.

72. Procello and Lang, 2011: vii.

73. Riis was closed in 1965 and then reopened as Mary McLeod Bethune Junior High School, named after the civil rights activist, which it continues to operate as today.

74. This perception of a *different cut* pertained to juveniles from the various junior high schools that came to Fremont. The Watts youth were seen as the rowdiest, perhaps most uncouth of all. Their families were financially less well off than those in the

Florence-Firestone area, and they lived in congested housing projects rather than single-family homes. These circumstances may have contributed to their more "disrespectful" behavior.

75. Woodrow C., a deputy probation officer, who was a former Watts resident and street-group member, contended that the Farmers set was a dominant and ubiquitous Watts street group, at least for a while, during the 1950s. Observing his older brother, who was a Farmer, and his homeboys, Woodrow C. argued that the Farmers "took over, occupying almost all of Watts." The other groups remained but didn't show any fealty nor consider themselves cliques of the Farmers. There were just a lot of Farmers, perhaps as many as 1,800 at their height, whose presence was felt throughout the community. Ron E., a fireman with the Los Angeles Fire Department, who grew up near Watts, remembered the Farmers as the most "feared and most violent" gang in Watts. While short-lived, from 1956 to 1959, their distinctive clothing style of work bib-overalls could conveniently hide various weapons, like hammers, in the many pockets.

76. Bird indicated that a large number of male juveniles lived between Hooper and Central Avenues in the Slauson neighborhood. Fights there, whether individual or group, "could bring whole families out on you," as both participants and observers.

77. Currently, the members of the Slausons who are still alive are in their sixties, seventies, and early eighties yet continue to proudly identify themselves as Slausons. Several times a year, they hold dances and picnics, put on by the Slauson Village Society. These are usually attended by hundreds of people, from different high schools and various other sets. Not all present are Slausons, but they all recognize who the Slausons were and the positive things their existence meant for the neighborhood. Quicker has been an invited guest to many of these functions since the 1990s, witnessing their communality firsthand. In contrast to the deep sense of community still existent among those in the Slauson neighborhood, by 1988, and quite probably earlier, the Farmers of Watts had not only ceased to exist as a group, but former members were reluctant to identify themselves as such. Woodrow C. contended that this is because these members had never "internalized" enough of the values espoused by the Farmers to carry them into adulthood.

78. McWilliams (1988: 325) writes that Watts was "made up largely of migrants from rural areas in Mississippi, Georgia, and Alabama."

79. Moore (1991: 47) notes the significance of historical periods in joining the East Los Angeles gangs she studied: cliques of the 1950s "recruited" youth fifteen and younger, while cliques of the 1970s recruited older youth.

80. Porous boundaries more likely existed in the earlier years, becoming less porous as the neighborhoods aged and became more populated. More people and greater transience meant that neighborhoods had more strangers with unknown motives. More guns, with a greater willingness to use them, meant that "shoot first, ask later" became easier.

81. When Bird was thirteen years old in 1956, he witnessed N. D.'s boldness when he came up from Watts to 68th Street and Central Avenue, the heart of the Slausons' neighborhood, by himself, looking for Roach, who had done something in Watts that N. D. was pissed off about. Bird said that N. D. had to have "nuts as big as monster balls" to come alone into an enemy neighborhood. The thirty to forty Slausons on the corner when he showed up there gave him distance and respect for his daring.

82. These examples add to the understanding that joining a street group was an act of choice rather than compulsion. Compulsion, Brotherton (2015) points out, has been theorized in the pathologizing perspective.

83. Hunter Hancock was a DJ on KGFJ during the 1950s and 1960s that played primarily the blues, the boogie woogie, rhythm and blues, bebop, and other music by Black

artists. He had an ear for music and would play tunes by unknowns who later became famous, such as Johnny Otis and Jesse Belvin.

84. Besides the big four of Cohen, Cloward and Ohlin, and Miller, other theorists, such as Dale Kramer and Madeline Karr (1953), Herbert Bloch and Arthur Niederhoffer (1958), and Lewis Yablonsky (1962), were there but received less attention. Although they too offered general theory to explain the existence of gangs and why juveniles joined, the dearth of attention paid to these theorists was less likely due to the tenability of their claims than it was to their weaker political positions. Cloward and Ohlin's theory, especially, was praised by other important researchers, particularly James F. Short (1965), and by then attorney general Robert Kennedy. Such high-level praise was influential in making large amounts of grant money available to researchers who applied Cloward and Ohlin's theories to action programs that sought to stop or at least reduce gang delinquency. Mennel, 1973: 197. In addition, Lloyd Ohlin, James F. Short, Fred Strodtbeck, and Robert Merton were all members of the Grants Review Committee of the National Institute of Mental Health during its initial year of operation in 1963 and could exert considerable influence on research proposals that used the theories most friendly to their ideologies. Galliher and McCartney, 1973: 84.

85. Almost every researcher pays homage to the big four theorists, noting applicable areas to the groups the researchers studied, but mostly noting explanatory deficiencies. Hagedorn's (1998) critique of these theorists is comprehensive.

86. There has been much discussion among gang researchers of the designations of "core" and "fringe" members. Klein (1971: 70) writes, "This distinction is almost universally employed by gang workers the country over." A primary differentiating point is that core members have "more personal deficits," including lower IQs and lower impulse control. Klein, Maxson, and Miller, 1995: 189. Although we do not use these designations, and they are not equivalent to the regulars and lames we do discuss, we did not find personality deficiencies differentiating regulars from anyone else.

87. Some males got special treatment because of who they were. If they had relatives, like brothers or cousins who were regulars or had sisters who may have been a set member's girlfriend, they were given "passport papers." They were left alone, not bothered or harassed as they went about their business. As a variation, Ameer said the Businessmen had juveniles who were called "fifteen-minute Businessmen." These were youth who were granted various "services" by the Businessmen without the requirement of joining.

88. Regulars in South Los Angeles were different from those described in Vigil, 1988: 66. He found regulars to be committed gang members with more "destructive patterns" of behavior over a longer period, while we found that regulars were committed to the neighborhood.

89. A lame nowadays might be called a *nerd*, a term not used in those days.

90. Kerns is a Santa Ana, California, beverage company that makes a sweet, noncarbonated fruit-based drink. Called Kerns, the beverage was a name brand and popular among some set members in the 1960s.

91. Nehi was also a flavored soft drink, around since 1924, which later became RC Cola. It never had quite the panache among South Los Angeles youth that Coke or Kerns had.

92. To *bogart* something, like a marijuana joint, meant to take more than your share. According to https://www.urbandictionary.com/define.php?term=Bogarting, March 04, 2011, the term *bogart* is derived from Humphrey Bogart's last name. Bogart often had a cigarette hanging out of his mouth, never drawing on it and never smoking it. He just held it there: thus "don't bogart the joint," or hold on to it too long.

93. "Sin Street" was East 73rd Street, between Central and Hooper Avenues. It was a unique area for reasons to be explained later.

94. There were differences between joining South Los Angeles street groups from joining those in East Los Angeles. Moore (1991: 47–49) points out those gang members were "recruited" to join.

95. Strain theory, as explained by Cohen (1955) and Cloward and Ohlin (1960), contended that juvenile subculture formation was a "sour grapes" response to not having the opportunity to join the middle class. Gangs were their second choice.

96. David Matza's 1964 classic, *Delinquency and Drift*, discusses the mechanisms juveniles use to rationalize their involvement in delinquency. Some of these are conscious decisions, where others are less so. Together they neutralize the juvenile's commitment to social constraints, permitting him to "drift" into delinquency. Falling into a street group was like this, although without the emotional struggles of "neutralizing" assorted "cultural restraints." South Los Angeles juveniles did drift into street groups, but the drift was much more of an easy slip or fall than it was a mental battle with legal proscriptions.

97. Before 1952 many Slausons, when identifying where they were from, would often just say "We from the Park," without specifically identifying which park. When necessary, they would explain, but most who asked already knew "the Park" meant Slauson Park. By 1952 the Slausons began saying they were from Slauson, or Slauson Park.

98. Thornberry (2001b: 34–42), by way of introducing some of his own research, gives a solid literature review of other researchers' consideration of the personality problems juveniles have who join gangs. He argues that youth who are at risk of becoming gang members are defective individuals who are having problems with proper institutions. Elsewhere, he and others write that the deviant individual with problems will find the gang more attractive than individuals who have their lives better together. Thornberry, 2006: 32. This was not the case for South Los Angeles street-group members, who couldn't be distinguished from nonmembers by psychological adjustment.

99. A couple minutes is a lot of straight-up whooping. Keep in mind that rounds in professional boxing matches are only three minutes, with both parties swinging and then taking time to posture. "Float like a butterfly, sting like a bee," Muhammed Ali's oft quoted phrase, was a dance meant to buy the fighter some time during those three minutes when he wasn't being hit or hitting.

100. Portrayals of gangs as violent places and joiners as being so desperate to get in they willingly subject themselves to the gangs' codes of violence are commonplace among myth and research. The 1993 film *Blood in Blood Out: Bound by Honor*, partially filmed in East Los Angeles and San Quentin Prison, contributed much to the myth of gang violence. The film was controversial, with one review claiming it was three hours of "cartoonish" violence and another saying it was "the most powerful and important film of the decade"—both reviews appeared in the *Los Angeles Times*. Kenneth Turan, "Capsule Review: 'Bound by Honor' Fails as an Epic," *Los Angeles Times*, May 21, 1993; Mim Eichler, "'Bound by Honor': A Wake-Up Call to Audiences," *Los Angeles Times*, May 24, 1993. More than half my students believed the film to be accurate. Decker and Van Winkle (1996: 174–175) document the violence associated with joining the gangs they studied, where almost three-quarters of joiners were *beaten in*, and some were required to shoot strangers. Vigil (2004), while noting that "jump-ins," with fighting among gang members, has become part of the initiation for some Chicano gangs, also argued that they don't involve attacks on strangers. Fleisher (2001: 102) makes it clear that violent rites of passage are not unique to inner-city gangs, with anthropological

folklore documenting such rituals in many places. Violence, real or mythologized, draws the attention of voters and can be used to manipulate, especially to advance the control perspective's agenda on the need to regulate gangs by any means necessary.

101. Clear as the rules may have been as to where it was appropriate to hit the prospect, there was always the wayward punch, the one that wasn't supposed to be, that landed on the prospect's face: "Oops, sorry!" It was accidental but on purpose.

102. Vigil (1988: 103–105) writes that initiations among the Los Angeles street groups he studied were a way to "weed out the weak and uncommitted." Initiations were a way to demonstrate manliness.

103. Weber, 1965: 326.

104. Vigil, 1988: 106–109. Thornberry (2001b: 34) writes that a number of longitudinal studies have shown that most gang members stay in the gang less than a year. We didn't find this to be generalizable with the Slausons or other South Los Angeles street groups, although most of the girls' clubs were relatively short-lived.

105. Even within this tightly knit group, there were unnamed subcliques. These were small groups of two to four juveniles who would hang out together daily. They'd meet at school, at the Park, at the skating rink, or at any number of other neighborhood locales, to fuss, cuss, and discuss. These were your "road-dogs" or your "ace-koom-boon." These terms referred to your closest buddies, your best friends, the ones who always had your back while you had their's. Only on special occasions would the entire clique gather for something. Vigil, 1988, notes the importance of dyads and triads as the most common associations and that the entire group would only gather on special occasions.

106. Baby Slauson, at its peak, might have had as many as five hundred members claiming affiliation. There was "no way" you could get to meet everybody much less decide if you liked them. The subcliques were groups of people you knew, liked, and wanted to hang out with.

107. "Partners" in this case didn't necessarily mean friends; it meant *associates*.

CHAPTER 5

1. Bird was high-sidin', bragging, when he wrote this.

2. Bird gave credit for originating the concept of "Slaus Angeles" to Jerome, who, in 1959, in a letter written to a girl, wrote "Slaus Angeles" as her city address. When asked why he changed the name of the city to Slaus Angeles, thus potentially rendering the letter undeliverable, Jerome reasoned that by putting "Zone 1," the postal zone of her street address, on the letter, the postman would find the correct address. The postman did, and she received the letter. While the USPS didn't begin using zip codes until 1963, early postmen knew their routes and many of the people on them, so the mail was often correctly delivered even if it had variations in the actual addresses.

3. Slauson Park, located at 62nd Street and Hooper Avenue, was officially called James E. Slauson Park then, but it was later renamed to Mary McLeod Bethune Park, which it continues as today. Many of the juveniles who later became Big Slausons—like Ted Coleman, Jim Davis, "Bo Hog," Norris Carrier, Robert Strauss, and Thomas Henderson—had begun hanging in the Park by 1948, which some have contended marked the "official start" of the set. They called themselves the Slauson Park Boys. A number of other Park juveniles, like Frank Johnson and Don Story, were from a club called the Pueblo Players. This group was originally from the Pueblo Del Rio housing project but had moved from there to the Florence-Firestone District. They remained Pueblo Players, although they were friendly with the Slausons.

4. The year 1952 is the accepted date the Slausons officially started. It is difficult to get an accurate estimate on the size of the first group of Slausons. Bird said that he never saw more than ten Big Slausons in his life but believed there were more.

5. Rice and Christensen, 1965: 43, 44, 111.

6. Manchester/Firestone Boulevard is a continuous east-west street that changes names: it is Manchester on the west side of Central Avenue and Firestone on the east side.

7. The Watts Towers were built between 1921 and 1954 by the Italian construction worker Simon Rodia. He eventually became tired of community opprobrium, gave the property away, and moved out of the neighborhood. The property was condemned by the City in 1955. It then went into a state of limbo until the City and State rescued it in the mid- to late 1970s. Given this history of disjunction with the Towers, it is easy to see why the Watts groups might have had trouble identifying with them and why the Slausons claim of superiority, because they had the blimp, was defensible.

8. "High-siding" was a form of assertive boasting.

9. Slauson was a neighborhood in its own right, but many people who lived there had relatives and friends who lived in Watts, as well as in other parts of the City. While the neighborhood developed into a tight-knit community, it was very much interconnected with the other large Black communities in the City. There were webs of group affiliations throughout these communities.

10. Bernstein, 1964: 40–42; Short and Strodtbeck, 1965: 185–198; Mattick and Caplan, 1967: 114–119; Klein, 1970: 91–99.

11. Yablonsky, 1962; 195–199. Few researchers have agreed with Yablonsky, while Klein (1971: 92) pointedly states that "leaders are not sociopaths or psychopaths."

12. Weber, 1965: 324–365.

13. Bendix, 1962: 301.

14. Denial of being a leader wasn't universal among the notables but significant enough that we are referencing those who showed authority as notables rather than as leaders.

15. A "shot caller" is a relatively new term, showing up in the late 1990s to early 2000s to refer to leaders in prison or in street gangs who are deemed similar to mafia capos.

16. Weber (1965: 363–367) writes that charisma is "unstable" and cannot be "learned or taught."

17. The Businessmen and the Slausons were tolerant of each other. The request to Chinaman was not an attempt at a hostile takeover but recognition that he was a leader and someone whose presence could enhance their group.

18. While Klein (1971: 96) might refer to Chinaman as a "hesitant leader," the term does not accurately describe him. Chinaman certainly recognized his leadership abilities and acknowledged that he was a leader and a founder of the Slausons, but he never boasted. For him, the Slausons were more like a family. He believed that the Slausons were a group of neighborhood friends drawn together for various reasons, who mutually aided one another. His charisma earned him reverence.

19. As noted, the term *bogarting* was adapted from film star Humphrey Bogart.

20. Roach and Jerome were not blood relatives but were so tight with each other that Roach referred to him as his brother.

21. A younger Slauson named O. C., whose views on this issue were representative of other Slausons, called them, "Slauson Village, the body of our neighborhood."

22. Poop had a different view of Roach's position in Little Slauson. Poop felt that Roach wanted to be the leader, but he and another Little Slauson named Treetop didn't accept Roach as such. Poop said, "We was all leaders," but nobody could "tell us what

to do." Poop's rejection of Roach as leader led to four fights between them, with Roach winning all of them. They finally stopped fighting after Roach became interested in one of Poop's sisters, and Poop accepted Roach as "sergeant of arms" (sergeant at arms).

23. Bird's admiration for Roach and Chinaman was a form of the street socialization Vigil, Moore, and Hagedorn discuss, but it was not an alternative to family socialization.

24. Poop indicated that "peer pressure" facilitated his joining of Slauson. When Poop was a Cavalier, so was another juvenile named Monroe Jones. Poop's sister Nedra started going with Monroe, who then became a Gladiator. Bobby Moore, the leader of Baby Slauson, also liked Nedra and was Poop's friend. Moore and Monroe fought over Nedra about the same time the Cavaliers were splitting up and Poop's family was moving into the Slausons' neighborhood, putting Poop in a situation where he had to make a choice. He chose Slauson.

25. According to Poop, the reason Chinaman and his homeboys went to Watts in the first place had to do with a girl from the Slauson neighborhood who was dating a guy in the Yellowjackets, a Watts set. It turns out that one of the Slauson homeboys liked her and wanted to teach her Watts boyfriend a lesson. As Poop related: "They wanted to whoop the girl's boyfriend and everybody associated with him. . . . They went out there to straighten things out, to take care of business, and got straightened out." The straighteners were straightened.

26. In many respects, there was an ephemeral nature about Big Slauson. Although their name is part of neighborhood lore, they didn't coalesce as a group for an extended time. The names of many of its members may have been known to some of the older Slausons, but only a few of them could identify individual Big Slausons. Bird said: "I still ain't met everybody who they call Big Slauson. I've heard names, I probably seen the guys for the last thirty years, but I don't know who they are."

27. Bird eschewed being called a leader of Slauson, regardless of his activities and the opinions of his homeboys. But even non-Slausons recognized his influence, as evidenced by the comment of the president of the Baby Businessmen, Ameer: "If it wasn't for Bird, these Slausons woulda been nothing." Ameer also added that Bird "was the most intelligent of the gangbangers."

28. Of the hundreds of members of the Slausons that Quicker interviewed, spoke to, or hung out with, they—without exception—acknowledged Bird as the seminal source of information about their neighborhood. While they certainly may have had experiences he wasn't privy to, they concurred that Bird was their unofficial spokesperson. It was commonly accepted that he was aware of more details about the group, with the ability to accurately recall and report them, than any other person.

29. Weberian theory, as in Weber, 1965: 367, notes that charisma can only be awakened and tested, as it was with Bird.

30. This racial slur, used this way, is toxic. We quote it because we believe the reader needs to know what was said, not what we might have liked them to say. Speakers and writers need to take responsibility for their words.

31. A number of youths in South Los Angeles took the name Bird or variations of it. Within the Slausons, others who were younger and saw Bird as a role model emulated him by taking modifications of his name as their nicknames. Among these were Little Bird and Baby Bird. Later on, after Little Bird got out of prison and had gotten bigger than Bird, he was referred to as Bird II. According to Bird, every neighborhood had a Bird, including many in the Mexican neighborhoods. The great jazz saxophonist, Charlie Parker, was also known as Bird. There is, however, only one Bird from Slauson.

32. Roach's tactical skills are an example of the "exceptional qualities" that Weber (1965: 362) writes are characteristic of charismatic leaders.

33. Bird was a charmer. He was admired by many girls for the same characteristics that endeared him to the neighborhood, an admiration he returned to the girls he liked, with an allure many found irresistible.

34. Corroborating Bird's perspective was Billy P., a California Youth Authority agent born in 1935 and raised in South Los Angeles. He felt that the Slausons were a "second-generation gang," not really coming into power until the mid- to late 1950s. According to him, Watts was "in control" before the rise of the Slausons.

35. During a discussion with Bird and some others, Little Bird asked Bird, "How come you would never run from anybody?" Bird responded: "I would fight anybody, everybody, any time. I have never been afraid of anybody." In the almost forty years that Quicker has known Bird, he has never seen him back down, even when confronted by dudes twice his size. This includes Daryl F. Gates, who Bird and Quicker met at a gang conference when he was chief of the LAPD and who did not intimidate Bird.

36. According to Bird, Set Seven was a clique composed of youth from various neighborhoods that included the Renegades, Huns, Compton, and others, who considered themselves players and hustlers. Some members from this group were into ill-gotten gains. They stole foreign sports cars, like Austin-Healy's and MGs, and burglarized laundromats.

37. Bird was not fond of Charles Wright. He had fought with and whooped Wright in September 1961, about nine months before he was shot on March 13, 1962. Bird's shooting was connected to the whooping he had administered to Wright.

38. The D'Artagnans street group was adjacent to Watts but outside its boundaries. They were west of Watts and were friendly with some of the Watts sets. Many D'Artagnans had previously lived in Watts, forming the D'Artagnans after their families had moved out. Since the juveniles forming this group had had a Watts history and were now together in a different neighborhood, starting a new in-group was easy. They already had a lot in common.

39. Bird's shooting was commemorated in the *Sentinel* with these words: "Youth Shot 5 Times in Gang Rumble," *Los Angeles Sentinel*, March 15, 1962: A3. The article mistakenly noted he was hit five times, when it was three.

40. The Slauson V was a hand sign made with the first two fingers held vertically to form a V. It signified "Slauson Village" or "the Villa." Bird showed his defiance to Watts and support of Slauson to the crowd by throwing the V with his fingers as he was being carried out on the stretcher.

41. Bird's father had great customizing skills, remaking a number of cars into classic-looking vehicles that Bird proudly drove. This Chevy had a Carson top: "A removable, one-piece, non-folding, padded and upholstered top typically made for and used on Kustom Cars and hot-rod automobiles. . . . They are often referred to as having a 'rakish' appearance; dashing, stylish, disreputable, very cool," https://allstarupholsterymn.com/carson-tops/.

42. The word *fiendish* was a term often used to refer to something that was "way out," "far-out," or "cool," like a "big dog" (a person of influence). It could mean clever or creative in an outlandish sort of way. The idea of the Bat Machine was inspired by the comic book hero Batman, who roamed Gotham City in his Bat Mobile.

43. "Trust" that charismatic leadership is providing proper direction for the group, as Weber (1965: 328) theorized, is exemplified by Bird's directive here.

44. Little Bird is Bird's cousin Kumasi, who, at over six feet tall, muscular, tough, and just out of the penitentiary, had a "cold temper and attitude. He was young and crazy." He was also furious that Bird had been almost killed in a cowardly way and was ready to exact revenge. Baby Bird was Bird's cousin Paul, who was a "maniac." In his last offer, Bird was trying now to keep this issue "all in the family."

45. Weber, 1965: 367.

46. Bendix, 1962: 300.

47. Walter Miller (1970: 355) makes similar observations on gang leadership, in his 1950s field research, when he discusses the "focal concerns" of gang members. He emphasizes the importance of both "smartness" and "toughness," with smartness being most important, as key qualities, for the "ideal leader." Bird was the embodiment of these two factors.

48. Brown, 1992: 118.

49. Bunchy later became a Black Panther in the Los Angeles chapter and was shot to death in 1969 on the UCLA campus in a political-type assassination. Davis and Wiener (2020) provide a much-needed examination of Bunchy's political work in Los Angeles and the circumstances surrounding his assassination.

50. Bird was in three different cliques: the Babies, the Warlords, and the Midgets. He left the Babies for the Warlords and the Warlords for the Midgets. He joined the Midgets with Dudley B., who was a few years older than him and had been a Little Slauson.

51. While such mobility was possible and did occur, most juveniles stayed with one clique.

52. Later on, the Renegades became the Apostates, a name that continued to reflect their independence and differences with Slauson.

53. Boptown was on the west side of Main Street, between 70th Street and 67th Street, deep in the Slauson neighborhood.

54. More than fifteen girls, with little more than five years between the oldest and the youngest, lived on Sin Street when it was named.

55. An additional source of pride for the Slausons was the dance craze called the "Slauson Shuffle," which Dick Clark showcased on *American Bandstand* in 1963. The moves in this dance were begun by Tommy Hughes in 1962 at a Slauson hangout, the Savoy Skating Rink, when he started improvising steps—on skates—to the music being played. David Arnold and others from the 80s block of streets in the Slauson neighborhood came to Wallace's hamburger stand and contributed terpsichorean skills to the moves by dancing off of a tune. Diane Foster asked them what they called the dance, and they said, "The 80s Shuffle." She said, "This is Slauson, it is 'The Slauson Shuffle,'" and Bird cosigned the name. As the dance became more popular in South Los Angeles, Lark and others from Slauson concurred: "There ain't gonna be no 80s Shuffle. If anything it's gonna be the Slauson Shuffle."

56. The symbol of the Lions Club International is a circle with a large *L* in the center and a lion's head on each side of the circle. The symbol for the Benevolent and Protective Order of Elks is an elk's head in a circle with *B.P.O.E.* inscribed in the circle surrounding the head. The Rotary International has a machinery gear as its symbol, with *Rotary* inscribed on the top and *International* inscribed on the bottom of the circle within the gear. The Slausons and other street groups were following a well-established tradition in America of creating symbols to identify their group.

57. There were certainly other street groups that came into existence in neighborhoods with characteristics similar to those of the Slauson neighborhood. But each neighborhood where pre-1965 street groups emerged also had their own distinctive character-

istics, giving shape to the specific groups that developed there. Similar generalizations could be made about them, which would then require specifics.

58. One of the most prominent hangouts and meeting places for juveniles from all over South Los Angeles was the Savoy Skating Rink, on 78th Street and Central Avenue, in the middle of the Slauson neighborhood. Youth would gather there to socialize. While there were a variety of different street groups that hung out there, "everybody kept a cool head," according to Probation Officer W. C. He believed the presence of security guards, who had an understanding of the street groups, plus the acceptance by the juveniles that this was neutral ground helped to keep things peaceful.

CHAPTER 6

1. Geis, 2001: xi–xii.
2. One of the best early critiques of gang theory was by Bordua, 1961. A more recent and comprehensive iteration by Bursik and Grasmick, 1995b, evaluates gang theory and research in the context of neighborhood dynamics.
3. Wilson, 1980, 1987. While Wilson's use of the term *underclass* brought the concept into the mainstream, it didn't originate with him. The Nobel Prize–winning economist Gunnar Myrdal (1960, 1963) used the term to describe a class of dispossessed people existing in the United States as a result of economic inequality.
4. There are many nongang members and nongang groups within the underclass, with gang members making up a small percent of that group. Vigil writes: "The small percentage of barrio youth who become affiliated with a gang are generally members of the underclass and are affected by the realities of this way of life before entering the streets." That is, these youth come from troubled families, have problems with school, and have poor job opportunities, notes Vigil, 1988: 27. In a historical analysis of San Antonio's juvenile street Chicanos, Tapia (2017: 142) adds, they have "devolved into the underclass over the last several decades," as a result of various structurally based "policy paradigms," with the current generation of juveniles suffering the most.
5. Brotherton and Barrios (2004: 34–35), commenting on the research by Hagedorn (1988) and Moore (1991).
6. Harrington, 1964: 20–21.
7. Krisberg and Austin, 1978: 21.
8. Taylor, Walton, and Young. 1974: 39–40.
9. Spitzer, 1975. While Spitzer made clear that smaller groups of deviants didn't pose nearly the threat to capitalism that larger groups did, he didn't seem to think deviants, as a group, had revolutionary potential.
10. Irwin, 1985.
11. We gratefully give credit to Harrison E. Salisbury (1958: 117) for this marvelously apt term.
12. *Father Knows Best* began as a radio serial in 1949, lasting until 1954, when it became a popular TV sitcom until 1960. The show involves a White, middle-class, midwestern family that manages to sort through the myriad of problems the family and children encounter by relying on the father's wise council and the mother's patience and clear reasoning. It was promoted as the type of family that all of America could have, if they would just try. This program was a media mirage, promoting a fantasy internalized by many.
13. Early researchers reasoned that the lower-class groups were the greatest contributors to the most dangerous types of delinquency, thereby justifying their theoretical

analyses of them. Even if that were the case, to accept that there might be gangs outside the lower class would have rendered their theories weak and perhaps unacceptable.

14. Whyte, 1943: 150–153.
15. Rice and Christensen, 1965: 82–84.
16. Ibid.: 75–92.
17. Salisbury, 1958: 109.
18. Cohen, 1955: 44; and Cloward and Ohlin, 1960: 12n8.
19. Schwendinger and Schwendinger, 1985: 44.
20. Ibid.: 92–104.
21. Self-report studies' innovation was to distribute anonymous questionnaires to lower- and middle-class groups of students, inquiring about involvement in assorted delinquent acts, regardless of whether they had been caught or not, reasoning that the promise of anonymity would make them honest.
22. A colleague of Quicker's who grew up in Pasadena during the 1950s and 1960s knew of a number of youth who lived in San Marino, California, and attended Huntington Junior High School and San Marino High School. San Marino is a mostly White and wealthy city in Los Angeles County that in 2014 was ranked the third most expensive city in the County to live in. Many of the youth he knew there hung out in groups that were chronically delinquent. They would engage in dangerous street racing in fast, expensive cars and hold parties in private homes when parents weren't there, with lots of alcohol and drugs present, where date rape occurred regularly. They would vandalize mailboxes set on posts by the curb and vandalize the fronts of homes for revenge on those who might have wronged them. Their actions, when the San Marino police got involved, were handled quietly. Their delinquencies did not become part of the public record and rarely made it into the newspapers.
23. Sanders, 2016; and Howell and Griffiths, 2018.
24. The lower class regularly gets criticized for hiding things from the police, because they are not forthcoming when crime in the community is being investigated. The criticism that they "see no evil, hear no evil, speak no evil" is even more easily applied to a middle-class community where covering up crime is facilitated by official compliance. Cover-ups are a benefit of class privilege.
25. Campbell, 1984: 9–32, 266.
26. Females were mostly ignored by the seminal theoreticians of the 1950s and early 1960s—Miller, Cohen, and Cloward and Ohlin—in their efforts to explain gang delinquency. The theoreticians and researchers Lewis Yablonsky (1962) and Bloch and Niederhoffer (1958) treated female influence as nonexistent. The early field researchers, Asbury, Thrasher, Whyte, and then Miller (1973) mentioned females, had a few comments on their relations with the males, and sometimes described their crimes. Some, like Whyte (1965: 25), found that a few of the girls even had their own organizations, called "clubs," such as the Aphrodite Club. Salisbury (1958) recognized that it is almost impossible to discuss the activities of young males without also considering young females but viewed the girls' role as more tangential than central. The Rice and Christensen (1965) report recognized that girls were an important part of gang life in Los Angeles.
27. Sikes, 1997; Chesney-Lind and Hagedorn, 1999; Miller, 2001; Chesney-Lind and Shelden, 2004; Peterson, 2014; and Campbell, 1984: 8–22, provide important assessments of the positions on girls and gangs taken by the early researchers.
28. Chesney-Lind and Shelden (2004: 69) maintain that in 1991 girls who were labeled as gang members still committed fewer and less serious offenses than males did.
29. Ibid.: 64, 65.

30. Quicker's 1974 research is reprinted in Chesney-Lind and Hagedorn, 1999: 48–56.

31. In 1927, Thrasher (1999: 15–24), while writing that girls lacked the "gang instinct," was concerned about the "immoral gang," occurring when girls joined boys' gangs; "stag" and "shag" parties and the "moral frontier" were all a consequence of female associations. Robert Rice wrote in 1963 that "sexual promiscuity is practically a built-in trait of girls who associate with gang boys." Rice, 1999: 42. Short and Strodtbeck (1965: 240–243) were concerned with the oversexed nature of "negro" gang boys and the "loud, crude" group of "sexually active," cursing, poorly fixed hairstyles, with "no pride in the way they dress," girls who hung out with the boys. Brown (1977: 59) notes that female gang members were less attractive than nongang members, who joined for attention they couldn't get elsewhere. While sartorial styles were issues of concern about both genders, a concern with male attractiveness and sexuality were not.

32. Chesney-Lind and Hagedorn, 1999: 8.

33. Moore, 1991; Vigil, 1988, 2002.

34. Sikes, 1997: xv; Campbell, 1984: 5.

35. Peterson, 2014: 271.

36. Chesney-Lind and Shelden, 2004: 69.

37. Moore, 1991: 8.

38. Peterson, 2014: 272. In the foreword to Jody Miller's 2001 book, Klein questions how it's possible that gang researchers missed this so obviously large number of gang girls and then credits Miller for her serious research that addresses this group (xi).

39. Chesney-Lind and Shelden, 2004: 67, 68.

40. Ibid.: 68–70.

41. Sikes (1997: 5) notes another possibility for the variance of data on the number of gangs and how violent they might be: police manipulation. She cites an example of how the LADP exploited female gang data in the early 1990s to gain a salary boost.

42. This apt phrase is borrowed from Anthony Lane, "Playing Politics: 'Boys State' and 'Red Penguins,'" *The New Yorker*, August 17, 2020: 70.

43. We chose these numbers because at times during the day, the boys did things among themselves or by themselves, and the same held for girls, thus requiring an adjustment on the clichéd "24/7."

44. Peterson (2014: 271) notes various examples of research that demonstrate girls did hang around with gang members without being members themselves, recognizing some girls might falsely claim membership.

45. We did not encounter any situations involving lesbian or homosexual relationships; if they existed, they were not talked about.

46. Although media articles on female involvement in gang-related activity appeared before 1963, they were not given the dramatic descriptions Callan provided in her writing.

47. Sherman, *Los Angeles Times*, April 23, 1963, Sect. II: 1, 8.

48. Fishman (1999: 73, 74) writes that the New York–based Vice Queens "manipulated the boys into fighting over real or alleged insults." *Manipulated* is a strong word and denies *agency* to the recipient. Manipulation was the cause of fights among South Los Angeles juveniles, sometimes, but *influenced* is a more accurate characterization of what usually happened when boys fought over girls.

49. Peterson, 2014: 274, 275.

50. Although they didn't interview any girls for their report, Rice and Christensen (op. cit. 1965: 31) state that "most, but not all," Los Angeles gangs had a girls' group associated with them. Chesney-Lind and Shelden (op. cit. 2004: 67, 68) note some have

claimed that each male gang in Los Angeles has one or more female groups associated with it, but they contend these claims may be highly exaggerated.

51. Brotherton and Salazar-Atias, 2003: 195; Hagedorn, 1998; Campbell, 1984. Peterson (op. cit. 2014: 277) writes that G.R.E.A.T. found that 77 percent of girls "were members for one year or less." *Gang Resistance Education And Training*. See www.great-online.org/GREAT-Home for details.

52. To suggest that something lasted a "minute" is not to be taken literally. It's figurative meaning: lasting for a short time.

53. Chesney-Lind and Shelden, op. cit. 2004: 69.

54. Kumasi, a Slauson Flip, noted that the Charlenettes were a group of eight to twelve girls who were "fighters." One girl even had a rep for fighting men. "They were all pretty but tough," he claimed. They were also noted for helping their man in a fight by jumping in to aid him in whooping his opponent. Their leader was Big Helene.

55. *El* is the masculine Spanish reference that when used with *Playgirls* was grammatically incorrect. Proper grammar would have used the feminine *La*, but *El* was the way it was.

56. The female clubs noted here are not intended as a complete list but rather as indicative. While there were quite likely others, their inclusion would not be expected to change any of our analysis.

57. For large groups with long histories, like the Slausons, it was not surprising that younger members might not have met any of the older girls, having met only a few of the older guys, if they were lucky. For other street groups, like the Senators and the Senates, the alleged female affiliate may have never existed or, if it did, only briefly.

58. Sherman, 1963c: 3.

59. Rice and Christensen, 1965: 39–40.

60. Ibid.: 40, 112.

61. Callan, 1963a, 1963b.

62. Campbell (op. cit. 1984: 8, 28–30), among other researchers, writes that girls' interest in sex led them to be labeled as "sex objects" and that much research on girls has a prurient interest in their sexuality, while boys are spared any such inquiry.

63. The research to portray gang youth as youngsters with psychological problems was not limited to females. In 1962, Lewis Yablonsky tried to make this point stick to male gang members. In his book, *The Violent Gang*, the "violent gang" is his third of three gang categories. It was organized, Yablonsky, 1962: 147–148, contends, to meet the special needs of the emotionally disturbed youth who join. His "working hypothesis" was, "The violent-gang structure recruits its participants from the more sociopathic youths living in the disorganized-slum community" (189). Special attention was reserved for the leader of this gang, the "core sociopath," who, hiding behind a "mask of sanity," was five to ten years older than the youth in his gang (209). While Yablonsky's theories may have been viewed as extreme by some, they had enough traction to influence many into thinking he might be correct enough in his claims of deep psychological problems (why else would a juvenile join an anti-social group like a gang?) to show that gang juveniles had at least some of these problems or at the very minimum were psychologically quite different from nongang juveniles. Clearly there were juveniles in South Los Angeles who may have had psychological issues, just as there were juveniles in every community, race, and class with psychological problems. But these problems were no more characteristic of gang than nongang juveniles, male or female. Of course, with no psychological tests used then as now to make this determination, one person's speculation is as good as the next.

64. Moore, 1991; Miller, 2001.
65. Klein and Maxson, 2006.
66. Esbensen et al., 2010.
67. Miller, op. cit. 2001: 35.
68. Chesney-Lind and Shelden (op. cit. 2004: 78, 79) find that girls joined gangs in Hawaii to hang out and have fun. Peterson (op. cit. 2014: 278) notes that having fun is a consistent finding in the qualitative research on why girls join gangs.
69. The Conservative Young Ladies' name is a reflection of their general orientation to be conservative, both in dress and mannerisms. They were also youthful entrepreneurs who wanted to give parties and make money from them.
70. The Monza girls' club took its name from the Chevy Corvair Monza: a small, sporty car introduced by Chevrolet in 1960. Girls in this club had Monzas or close buddies who did, suggesting enough familial wealth to give the girls independence from males through car ownership.
71. It was important for street-group males to assess how many girls were at a party before they decided whether it was worth their while to attend. "How many *heads* and how many *ribs* are there?" was a common question. *Heads* referred to the guys, while *ribs*—as in the biblical reference to women, Adam's rib—referred to the girls. The choice of these referents was not a reflection of any religiosity among the Slausons as much as it was a statement on breadth of knowledge; and they liked the way it sounded.
72. A hoopty was a large older car, often painted to stand out and look cool. Hoopties had voluminous back seats. In this case, Bird and his homeboys had arrived at the party with the following hoopties: a 1937 Pontiac, a beige 1939 Buick, a yellow 1940 Buick, and a 1940 Packard. These young Slausons were "styling"; they were out looking for fun. Many 1950s Buicks were called *hogs*, while 1955 and 1956 Buicks, which had large trunks, were also called *booty backs*, "'cause it look like a big ol' booty."
73. Moore (1991: 94) notes too the double standard in place for girls from the earlier sets, where they had restrictions placed on them the boys didn't have.
74. Chesney-Lind and Shelden (2004: 65) note the recurring themes in female gang research of the girls being depicted as tomboys or "sexual chattel." Neither of these were the case for girls in South Los Angeles.
75. Chesney-Lind and Shelden (2004: 66) also note the theme of girls as weapons carriers in much of the literature. This theme is more complex than either a "yes, they were" or "no, they weren't" assessment provides.
76. Sheila was also very capable of holding her own if challenged. As Bird asserted, "She'd slap all the spit out of your mouth."
77. A primary fear for young women in the community was rape. Although it was uncommon, it was not unknown. A term for it then was a "gruesome," which generally referred to a gang rape. Sheila believed that having interpersonal connections, especially with males, helped prevent rape. In her words: "If you didn't know somebody, you stood a chance of getting a gruesome, or being raped."
78. Female incarceration was so rare that we have no data on what males would do if their girlfriends were in prison.
79. Additionally, many girls had part-time jobs that denied them the time they would need to hang out. Babysitting and domestic work took up a considerable amount of the spare time they otherwise might have had.
80. Childrearing was not shared equally between the sexes. A baby brought responsibility that both parents understood, but both also knew that primary responsibility resided in the mother. While this arrangement was a case of "gender inequality," and of

women and men behaving in "gendered ways," as discussed by Miller (2001, 7, 8), it was not unique to South Los Angeles; nor was it unique to street groups.

81. Contrary to Fishman's (1999: 77) findings about the New York–based Vice Queens, South Los Angeles girls were not at the "sexual disposal" of the boys. Girls were available and open for romance but eschewed abuse. This is not to deny its occurrence but to recognize it was not the norm.

82. Another way serious make-out sessions were characterized was as "huggin', muggin', and fuggin'." Although the last term was a reference to intercourse, it may have been as much wishful thinking as it was a reality. "Grindin'" was "workin' it," suggesting a bit more physical action yet not intercourse.

83. There were girls for whom the term "looseness" was appropriate; they liked to party and get familiar with the guys on a regular basis, traditions be damned. A binary of "Madonna" and "promiscuous" is not accurate: there was a continuum of sexual activity, with these stereotypes as mythical bookends.

84. We found no data on girls refusing to date a guy because of his set membership.

85. When dating and romance were discussed, it was always male with female.

86. Moore (1991: 82) provides an authoritative summary of the literature that suggests girls who join gangs do so because of a plethora of problems at home, including encouragement from family members to join gangs. We did not find this to be the case in South Los Angeles. Parents there were more concerned about their daughter's well-being than they were with supporting her deviance. South Los Angeles neighborhoods are characterized well by Moore's findings that "the cliques of the 1950s were more closely integrated with the conventional barrio structures and norms" than later groups were. Ibid.: 69.

87. Moore (1991: 75) finds that gang boys in East Los Angeles had a similar preference for conventional girls. Chesney-Lind and Shelden (2004: 88) add to Moore's findings with other research.

88. Moore's (1991: 76) research on East Los Angeles juveniles' dating patterns coincided with patterns found in South Los Angeles.

89. Campbell (1984: 31) writes that males' fighting over females was manly, but females' fighting over males was unfeminine.

90. Girls' involvement in gang wars, where they carry weapons and fight other girls or even fight enemy boys, as Brown (1977: 60) poses, is a compelling exaggeration. But as Chesney-Lind and Shelden (2004: 75) contend, most female researchers have found girls don't "seek out violence" but will fight if they have to. South Los Angeles's girls were far more inclined to be observers than participants in street fights.

91. Bird mentioned a girl fight he witnessed once where the girls began grabbing at each other's blouses and bras, tearing them so that their breasts were exposed. Other witnesses, enjoying the show, prevented anyone from breaking it up. This was an uncommon occurrence, but in the hands of a skilled news spinner, it could become the norm. Add in some weapons and, whether they were used or not, the piece develops or acquires front-page potential.

92. Big Annie had a reputation for taking no nonsense from either males or females. She was large, "the biggest girl I had ever seen in my life," according to Roslyn, and "nice looking," according to Bird. One time, as Roslyn explained, "We were at a party and some Slausonette girls came to the party, and some other girls got to actin' crazy. Big Annie was there, and she cleared the party out. The party was over! Okay, there was some discrepancy, and she handled the business, jumped on a couple girls and a couple

guys too. Pulled a couple guys out of the car, and I had never seen anything like this before." Big Annie was not the norm.

93. This term comes from a Latina probation officer Quicker used to invite to lecture in his classes. She claimed that Chicanas would often hang with their man through the most troubling of times when she loved him.

94. Nedra's brother Larry—a tough, no-nonsense dude in his own right—most likely didn't know about the abuse she was experiencing. If he had known, there's a good chance he would have hurt Mac.

95. Our inability to find perceived exploitation among females may not be a universal neighborhood norm, because in any large grouping there will be differences of opinion. None of the women we spoke to or knew about expressed a concern about being exploited by males. Males no doubt did things the girls didn't like, appreciate, or approve of, but these things were not interpreted as being taken advantage of. Rape should not be minimized; it was regularly on the minds of many young women and an unequivocal example of exploitation.

96. Vigil (1988: 123) adds that, for males, cruising in another barrio and looking for girls was exciting but dangerous, since males in the barrio cruised in would take umbrage at the outsiders.

97. Woodrow C. singled out Jordan High School because it was in Watts and dominated by a group called the Farmers. They were especially aggressive, he argued, a behavior that led to more fights than there would have been had their attitudes been more accommodating.

98. Record hop aggressiveness in Watts may have been due to its attraction of a different crowd. Pittsburgh, who was involved with the Watts sets before she was involved with Slauson, thought there were differences between the two groups in the way they treated females. The Watts dudes "didn't think anything of embarrassing their girlfriends in front of a crowd," she claimed; it was something they would do "at the drop of a hat." Watts girls "didn't seem to have any self-esteem," she thought. The Slausons were more like "gentlemen . . . less rough, less exploitive, and more protective of their women." The Slauson girls were "classier" too, she contended, dressing better than and behaving less rowdy than Watts girls.

99. Linda C., a founding member of the Florencitas, said there were group proscriptions, shared by both the girls and guys, about dating guys from neighborhoods other than Florence. These proscriptions were weaker among the primarily Black sets.

100. Females, as exploited weapons carriers for males, have a long history in gang research. See Peterson, 2014: 271; Brown, 1977: 59; Fishman, 1999: 73, 74; Chesney-Lind and Shelden, 2004: 66.

101. From Sherman, 1963c: 1, quoting a police inspector. The second quote is from Callan, 1963a: 3.

102. Although the LAPD hired its first policewoman in 1910 and had thirty-nine of them by 1937 (lapdonline.org/women-in-the-lapd), throughout the 1950s, policewomen primarily worked as matrons in the jail system, and rarely had any field assignments. "Are Women Better Cops?" *Time*, February 17, 1992. The LASD didn't have female deputies on the streets until the early 1970s. See pinterest.com/lacountysheriff/100-years-of-lasd-female-deputies.

103. A number of our respondents made reference to girls in Watts not only being rowdier than girls in other parts of South Los Angeles but more dangerous too. This opinion was supported by some probation officers who were familiar with Watts. Since

Watts was a more socially and economically deprived community, it is likely that girls there had behavioral differences that distinguished them from other groups in South Los Angeles. It would nonetheless be surprising if Watts girls behaved at the levels depicted by the media.

104. It's likely the changes occurring in the South Los Angeles neighborhoods were not uniform, neither within the neighborhoods nor among the street groups.

105. Bird asserted that Mexican girls have held razor blades in their hair since the late 1950s and early 1960s. Certain hairstyles favored by these girls facilitated hiding small objects.

106. Researchers have contended that the women's liberation movement had little to do with street gangs: Chesney-Lind and Shelden, 2004: 95; Campbell, 1984: 23. We concur but suggest that as the outside world changed, breaking traditional barriers of gendered roles, so too were the neighborhoods reflective of some of those changes.

107. Hagedorn (1998: 47–49, 236–237) clarifies his critique of earlier studies ignoring racism by pointing out that Moore (1978) and Vigil (1983) are notable exceptions, acknowledging racism's importance in their analysis. Since Hagedorn's (1988) critique, other researchers have given more serious attention to racism.

108. Conot (1967: lx), in his study of the Watts Rebellion, writes: "The Los Angeles riot brought into focus the massive pattern of segregation in urban areas—a segregation so vast it dwarfs that of the south. . . . The most residentially segregated cities of the nation are *Los Angeles* [sic], Cleveland, and Chicago."

109. Two comprehensive historical accounts of how Los Angeles's racism dominated the City through the 1960s are Sides, 2006; and Flamming, 2005.

110. Bunch (1990: 121) argues that the bonds of racism held the Black community together. For Los Angeles in particular, he contends that "restrictive housing covenants ensured that rich and poor shared the same residential spaces, stores that refused to allow black shoppers to try on shoes guaranteed that Afro-Americans would patronize black-owned enterprises, and the continued lack of political clout encouraged the support of community action or self-help organizations."

111. Black psychiatrists Grier and Cobbs (1968) note that "Black rage" in America has been fueled by perceptions of "inferiority," cultural loss, and the violence of racism.

112. In *Bastards of the Party* (2005), Sloan provides visual documentation of the cohesive forces for Black Angelenos. With photos of Black migrants from Mississippi, Georgia, and Texas arriving on the train called *The Argonaut*, to Los Angeles's Union Station after World War II, he comments that they came and traveled all this distance *together*, to arrive *together*, to face their future *together*.

113. Woolworths and S. H. Kress were large department stores (much like 2020 Target is) in many communities in America before 1965. S. H. Kress became a target for civil rights demonstrations during the 1960s because of its refusal to seat Black customers at its lunch counters.

114. Davis, 1990: 293.

115. Alonzo, 2004: 664.

116. Alonzo, 2010: 142.

117. The term *spook* is a derogatory term used to refer to Black people. This racial slur, used this way, is toxic. We quote it because we believe the reader needs to know what was said, not what we might have liked them to say. Speakers and writers need to take responsibility for their words.

118. Vigil (1988: 92–98) writes that the idea of barrio youth groups banding together following the "palomilla" custom has a long history in the Mexican barrios and was a major contributor to clique formation.

119. Alonzo (2010: 142) argues that the Devil Hunters, from Aliso Village in East Lost Angeles, started as a "direct response to the Spook Hunters." Bird noted some inaccuracies in this statement. First, Aliso Village is in Boyle Heights, not East Los Angeles, and the demographic of East Los Angeles was primarily Chicano, with no Black street groups. Secondly, the Devil Hunters were a clique from Aliso who chose their name because of the racist nature of the Spook Hunter name, but they did not organize as a response to the White racists.

120. Bird discussed numerous confrontations that he and other Slausons had with White individuals and with groups including the Spook Hunters, who are noted by Davis (1990) and Alonzo (2004, 2010). The Slausons had already formed and adopted their name before these battles. While the White groups were insidious, they were not omnipresent, and confrontations were not an everyday occurrence.

121. Quoted in Lindenmeyer, 1970: 7.

122. The direct and indirect effects of racism are clearly explained in written material by these authors: James Baldwin, Eldridge Cleaver, Angela Davis, Richard Wright, and Malcolm X.

123. Bird notes that almost all sets in the 1950s and 1960s had some heterogeneity. Both the Slausons and Florence had a few White male members.

124. The few White juveniles in the non-White sets before 1965 were culturally non-White.

125. Although racial and cultural homogeneity came to characterize 1950s and 1960s street groups, almost all of them, Bird emphasized, had membership anomalies, with smatterings of other races and ethnicities. Many also had phenotypical White members, such as White Boy Victor from Aliso and Fish from Florence, whose light complexations hid their racial and ethnic origins.

126. White people did not have a monopoly on racism. As Bird clarified: "There was always a handful of racists on each side." But before 1965, the racism that most significantly affected the in-groupism of South Los Angeles non-Whites came from Whites.

127. James Baldwin, in his novel *Go Tell It on the Mountain* (1952/1953), makes clear the psychological impact of racism was every bit as damaging on Richard (one of Baldwin's protagonists) as the physical was, with both synergistically contributing to his suicide. Words do as much damage as deeds; sticks and stones will break bones, but so will words.

128. A number of researchers have noted that street groups are sometimes home-like sanctuaries, providing resources that are often unavailable at home: Moore, 1978; Quicker, 1974, 1983; and Vigil, 1988.

129. In his multiple works, Vigil has unequivocally made the case for social marginalization contributing to and perpetuating gang membership. See Vigil, 1988, 2002.

130. This racial slur, used this way, is toxic. We quote it because we believe the reader needs to know what was said, not what we might have liked them to say. Speakers and writers need to take responsibility for their words.

131. Of course, this action was not judicious; it was, as Little Bird surmised, racist.

132. This experience characterizes too what Ralph Ellison (1952) meant when he wrote *Invisible Man*. Bird and his homies' insignificance made them "invisible."

133. Vigil (1988: 56–58) writes that "blatant racism" was uncommon at school but that "remedial" classes, academic tracking, selective counseling strategies, and teachers' reluctance to teach in non-White schools clarified the schools' agenda.

134. Not all police were racist. But most of the interactions South Los Angeles juveniles had with them had blatant to subtle racial overtones. Since every person we interviewed who discussed their juvenile encounters with the police mentioned race as

being an issue, and racism was not condemned within the large law-enforcement agencies, it seems evident that racism was a dominant ideology. Some police, as individuals, did treat the juveniles fairly and with respect, but this was rare.

135. More detailed accounts of police racism in Los Angeles are provided by Davis, 1990; Flamming, 2005; Rand, 1967; and Davis and Wiener, 2020. One of the most powerful historical analyses of police in the United States and their function in support of capitalist growth is *The Iron Fist and the Velvet Glove* (Bernstein et al., 1977). Their account makes clear that the LAPD and LASD were following patterns of oppression that were similar to departments in other cities.

136. Davis, 1990: 126.

137. Katz (1988: 6) discusses the "America Rule," where U.S. interrogators would pin the label "Vietcong" on all people they interrogated to enable their belief that the interrogated were all enemy. The LAPD appeared to use a similar tactic by imposing a police record of some sort on any non-White person they stopped to interrogate.

138. There were a few Black police officers on the streets before 1965, but they were scarce. During the 1965 Watts Rebellion, of the 205 police assigned to South Los Angeles, only 5 of them were Black. And of those in the Department who were Black, none had made it past the rank of lieutenant (en.Wikipedia.org/wiki/Los_Angeles_Police_Department).

139. When Tom Bradley retired from the LAPD, he was a lieutenant with a law degree. He practiced law until he was later elected mayor of Los Angeles, serving from 1973 to 1993.

140. Frank M. is calling Tom Bradley "mayor" out of respect, not because he was mayor at the time he was stopping Frank M. in the streets.

141. Poop had been arrested before this incident occurred, but because he had a number of aliases, he thought he might escape a hassle here if he used one of them.

142. Frank M. heard later that the cop pummeling the youth just hated Japanese and may not have needed any other reason to beat him. Certainly, there may have been other reasons Frank was unaware of.

143. Although the juvenile who had been beaten was Japanese, not White, the racial distinction might have been lost in the police translation of events.

144. Numerous chroniclers of Mexicans in Los Angeles and elsewhere in the United States have noted their unfair treatment by the police was usually due to racism. See Mazon, 1984; Moore, 1970; and Rodriguez, 1993.

145. The Georgia Street LAPD station was located where the Los Angeles Convention Center now stands. The station was notorious among South Los Angeles youth as a place where they could expect an "ass whoopin'" regardless of the charges.

146. Before 1965, the population of Baldwin Hills, regulated by restrictive land covenants, was home to a large number of medical doctors. Since the covenants' removal, the area has become highly diverse—from drug dealing areas near Coliseum Street and Martin Luther King Boulevard to one of the wealthiest majority-Black communities in the United States, sometimes called the "Black Beverly Hills." Baldwin Hills now is vastly different from what it was.

147. There were bad White people on television, too, but just never any good non-White people.

148. Before 1965, the Native Americans that were on TV were always portrayed as bad guys, except, of course, for the Lone Ranger's sidekick, Tonto. In the Tarzan films, the Africans had that dubious distinction too: they were always the bad guys.

149. Sportsman Park was renamed Jesse Owens Park after the four-time gold-medalist James Cleveland (Jesse) Owens.

150. There were probably Spook Hunter groups in areas not mentioned here, since they were diverse, springing up when Whites clashed with non-Whites.

151. In 1957, when Bird was fourteen and on his way to a club meeting with some of his peers, a carload of seventeen- to eighteen-year-old Spook Hunters showed up, stopped the car, and were preparing to jump out on the young Slausons when the unexpected happened. This was a Thursday, it was club meeting day, it was close to meeting time, and Bird and his group were near Slauson Park, where the meeting would be held. Other Slausons were also on their way to the meeting around this time and nearby to Bird's group, including Roach and a group of Little Slausons, who were about the age of the Spook Hunters. As the Spook Hunters were jumping out of the car, they caught a glimpse of Roach's group fast approaching and knew they didn't want any part of the bigger Slausons. The Spook Hunters split. If an observer did not have the full story, one interpretation of the parts they did have might have been as follows: the racist Spook Hunters were intimidating the Slausons through conflict into organizing to fight them, and the Slausons were meeting to figure out how best to do that, rather than the coincidence it was.

152. Miller (1969) provides a broad description of two White gangs, with cliques, that existed in "Port City" from the Civil War days through the late 1950s. He describes them as middle- to lower-class, very criminal, and quite well organized but does not mention racism. This organizational genre for White groups was absent from South Los Angeles before 1965.

CHAPTER 7

1. Spergel (1995: 98–100) provides a balanced summary of the literature on the importance of status for gang members.

2. *Cojones* is Spanish for "balls" or "testicles." For a male juvenile to show he had cojones is to show that he had courage.

3. Moore (1978: 40) has noted the importance of a "fair fight" among the homeboys she studied in the pre-1970 barrios of East Los Angeles. Vigil (1988: 129) notes too the value of fair fights among the Chicano cliques he studied. It was a "one on one" fight, "without weapons." Moore (1991: 60) writes later that the demise of the fair fight after the early 1970s was accompanied by a rise in the use of weapons. This occurred in South Los Angeles as well.

4. Moore, 1991: 60.

5. Riesman, 1966: 15.

6. The cultural attitude of what it required to be a "man," during this period, was expressed unequivocally by one of the black leaders at the Attica Prison uprising in 1971, where thirty-one inmates and nine hostages were killed by state troopers shooting from the prison walls, as their attack became immanent. In Cinda Firestone's 1973 documentary, *Attica*, the inmate leader defiantly proclaims: "If I cannot live like a man, I can at least die like one."

7. There were at least two different kinds of shooters in the neighborhood: killers and those who shot over people's heads. The first kind were the most dangerous—and most rare—but the latter were more frightening because the next shot or the one after that might not be over one's head.

8. Some words, such as this one, are toxic slurs when used by White people. When used by Black people, the word takes on different meanings, depending on the user's intent, and are understood within the in-group as both appropriate and necessary.

9. There is considerable controversy over the effect of television's influence on facilitating juvenile violence. Huston et al. (1992) find that by the time children are eighteen years old, they will have seen 200,000 acts of violence on television, including 40,000 murders. While a case can be made that this influence is not causal, it is hard to deny that it is at least influential.

10. A proficient wolfer would use general or specific insults about the insecurities of the wolfee to make his point. The central focus was on the wolfee's mother, but his daddy, auntie, puppy dog, goldfish, his physical proportions, the way he walked, or anything else that could be used to demean was fair game. The creativity of the skill is evident in these examples: "Your daddy's a bald-headed faggot, who's so bald-headed you could see a fly land on his head and it's gonna break his neck.... Your mama's so cross-eyed when she cries, tears run down her back.... The bitch is so skinny when she walk down the street on a rainy day, she walk between rain drops.... Your mama's so skinny when she takes a bath, she's got to put on skis to keep from goin down the drain.... Your mama's so fat she got to get out the bed to turn over." Wolfing didn't always have to rhyme, accomplishing the task just as well through its wit.

11. *Petty* is objectified by definition and then differentiated from *serious*. But *petty* is a subjective term. What may appear as petty to an observer may not have been considered at all petty to the participants.

12. Keiser (1969: 29, 30) writes that fights between rival out-groups in Chicago were called a "gangbang." Sanders (1994: 85–107) notes the use of this term among the San Diego gangs he studied. The term was not in common use among the early South Los Angeles sets.

13. Jasper, the president of the Senators, used the term *gunslin* to refer to these set-versus-set gang fights. His description of them made them sound rough but not dangerous: "I used to go out gang fighting, you know, gunslin, and I'd come home—and just me and my mom stayed together. I'd come home, I'm not bullshitting, I'd come home, jacket tore off, beer all over the front of it, and she'd look up and see me, and she'd say, 'I see you made it,' and turn over and go back to sleep." It was not that she didn't care as much as it was an understanding that there was little, at that moment, she could do about it. *Gunslin*, as used by the juveniles in the pre-1965 sets, was not the same as *gun slinging*.

14. "Shots Fired As Teen Gang War Flares on W'Side," *Los Angeles Sentinel*, June 6, 1957.

15. "Gang Fight Broken By Police: 'Minor Gang Fight; Homemade Black Jack, No Other Weapons," *Los Angeles Times*, June 7, 1954.

16. "Rival Gangs Erupt in Bloodiest Fight in Years: Beer Openers, Knives, Chains, and Bottles," *Los Angeles Times*, January 15, 1956.

17. "Easter Miracle—None Hit," *Los Angeles Sentinel*, April 18, 1963.

18. The penitentiary meant either federal or state prison for adults. The "YA" referred to the California Youth Authority institutions, a type of state prison for juveniles. "Camp" meant juvenile probation camp. Camps were residential facilities for juveniles, adjudicated of less serious crimes than YA. Camps were operated by the county.

19. Tackwood (1973: 81) suggests that Watts lacked the unifying philosophy that characterized the Slausons' neighborhood. Since Watts was an area composed of multiple housing projects, their street groups were organized within the individual projects, not a more unified whole like the Slausons were.

20. Tackwood, 1973: 81.

21. Bird's reference to "Manual" is Manual Arts High School.

22. The existence of and threat to use guns on this occasion does not contradict the come-from-the-shoulders ethic. These Slausons had gone over into hostile territory to face—they weren't sure how many—enemies on a mission to rescue their women. They had internalized the shoulders ethic but were not stupid, wanting to make certain that a rescue mission didn't turn into their own massacre. Comin'-from-the-shoulders could be trumped by pragmatism.

23. There were few South Los Angeles street groups that were completely racially or ethnically homogeneous. The groups are most accurately characterized as consisting of predominantly one race or ethnic group.

24. We did not interview any White gang members of these racist groups. We relied on what our respondents said about them and how they were portrayed in the media. Both of these sources referred to them as "gangs." It is their term we use to reference them. The White gang's reason for existing was to look for and then antagonize or attack Black gang members when they discovered them "slippin'." That is, the White gangs assaulted the Black juveniles when they found the Blacks unprepared, either at strategically inopportune moments or when the Blacks were outnumbered.

25. Hamm, 1993.

26. Interset fights between individuals over personal matters happened too. And when they did, they were likely to spread beyond the individuals and involve the sets.

27. Percy M. was one of the Slausons' philosophers, known for this witticism: "Today is the tomorrow I was thinking about yesterday."

28. We borrow this subheading from several films of a similar name, although ours is no fantasy.

29. By many current definitions, this fight between N. D. and Roach, who were both street-group members, would be termed a "gang fight." Their fights had little to do with their set memberships. They were personal, the result of animosities between two individuals, from different neighborhoods, who just didn't like each other, although they had mutual respect for one another.

30. While claiming that he had "heart" can be used to describe the courage Floyd showed, a more colloquial expression was to say, "He had balls."

31. We are not suggesting that after 1965 this type of violence stopped; it didn't. It most likely got worse as the data on increased violence suggest.

32. It could be argued that Poop not only used the phone as a weapon to harm his adversary but then grabbed a bat as soon as he could get to one, both of which may have violated the come-from-the-shoulders ethic. Consider this: the phone was thrown in a moment of rage, while the bat was grabbed because Poop most likely would have been whooped without it by the guy. Poop suffered no criticism from his homeboys for his actions. He had stood up to a much stronger adult adversary and prevailed, albeit with a little help from a solid friend. If either Poop or the man had had a more lethal weapon available, would either have used it? This is, of course, an *academic question*; we don't know, but we can speculate.

33. Fine's Market has since been replaced by a childcare center.

34. Miller (1970: 356–357) writes about "fate"—having good luck or being jinxed—as a "focal concern" of the lower class. His concept of fate is different than our concept of luck. Luck is not an ascribed trait; nor is it a permanent quality, as Miller implies that fate is. Luck is something we all have, at various moments in our lives: good sometimes, bad at other times.

35. Wiseman (2003) and Smith (2016) lend credibility to the value of luck, with studies analyzing how the improbable can become the possible.

36. Rice and Christensen, 1965: 50, 51.

37. I thank Bill Page, who provided immeasurable editorial assistance in the preparation of this manuscript, for this astute suggestion to rename the concept of luck to make it sound more academically appropriate.

38. In Woody Allen's 2006 film *Match Point*, the value of luck in life is made dramatically clear when Chris avoids a murder charge because of the direction a gold ring, inadvertently bounced off a railing, lands. Like a tennis ball, teetering on the top of a net, ready to fall: fall on one side, you win, but fall on the other side, she wins.

39. Presley et al., 1979: 95.

40. "Teen Gangs Flare," *Los Angeles Sentinel*, August 15, 1963.

41. Blumenstein (1995) suggests that the proliferation of drugs in communities during the 1980s was the primary cause of the mini arms race that took place there. As drugs spread and became more lucrative, he theorized, drug sellers became targets for robbery. They were believed to have either drugs or money and sometimes both. They were visible and vulnerable as they stood on street corners to market their product. When a robber presented a gun as a threat, the sellers easily gave up their product or money. Since sellers were marketing a controlled substance to begin with and therefore involved in a crime, they couldn't report the robbery to the police, so they bought guns to defend themselves. Would-be robbers learned quickly that the drug sellers were liable to be armed, so they brought even more powerful weapons to the scene. Residents, who became aware of these dynamics and concerned about their own safety, bought guns too to prevent their victimization as they went about their lives. Thus, drugs flooding into the neighborhoods created a necessity for guns. Both those involved in the drug trade and those not involved armed themselves. The wave of drugs and guns is what led to an increase in violence, according to Blumenstein.

42. "Local Groups Battle: Fists, Stabbing,"*Los Angeles Sentinel*, July 4, 1946; "Stabbing of Pair—in Back, Hoodlumism, Irresponsidble Elements," September 12, 1946.

43. "75 Jailed in Drive-by Crime Prevention Officers During Relays," *Los Angeles Times*, May 22, 1954.

44. "Letting Neighborhoods Run Down," (loafers and pimps are problem, but not gangs) *Los Angeles Sentinel*, March 19, 1959.

45. "One May Die From Using Pills," *Los Angeles Times,* June 23, 1954.

46. Zip guns were crudely constructed homemade guns. They were usually made with trimmed-down—to about three inches—automobile radio antennas as barrels. Chrome and segmented antennas existed on most of the motor vehicles in the 1950s and 1960s and could be easily broken off the vehicle when left extended. Zip guns might have a wooden handle, typically with rubber bands to activate the hammer. Some zip guns had barrels made from drilling a quarter-inch hole in a half-inch cylindrical metal rod, to provide greater strength and increased accuracy. The stronger barrel reduced the likelihood of an explosion, but only slightly. Zip guns used a .22 caliber "short" cartridge and were capable of shooting one round at a time. If they fired, zip guns were notoriously inaccurate, and misfiring was common. They required two hands to use and so much time to prepare for use that an opponent could easily disarm the shooter. The zip gun was about as dangerous for the shooter to use as it was for his intended target.

47. "Mother Mourns 'Quiet' Victim of Gang Fight," *Los Angeles Times*, November 30, 1954.

48. "Gang Fight Broken by Police: Homemade Blackjack, No Other Weapons,"*Los Angeles Times*, June 7, 1954; "One May Die: Found 410 Gauge, Bayonet, Butcher Knife," June 23, 1954; "200 Teen-agers Battle With Fists, Clubs and Knives at Hollywood High," September 16, 1954; "Jail 6 Watts Youths: Knives and Bricks Used," *Los Angeles Sentinel*, April 18, 1957; "Shots-Teen Gang War: 3 Shots, Use of Clubs and Chains," *Los Angeles Sentinel*, June 6, 1957; "Teen School Gang Arrested: Brassknuckles, Chain, Razor," February 19, 1959; "25 Held in Wild Gang Battle: Challenged to Fight with Jackhandles, Clubs, Iron Bars," *Los Angeles Examiner*, December 29, 1957; "138 Youth Gangs Flourish in LA: Minature Armies with Pipes, Wrenches," *Los Angeles Herald & Express*, April 16, 1953.

49. "Youth Gang Shooting Jails 6: Arsenal—Rifles, Zip Guns, Shot Guns, Molotov," *Los Angeles Examiner*, April 28, 1957. Miguel D., a probation officer with the Group Guidance Gang Prevention Program, recalled a case where an effort was made by the police to label one gang member a pyromaniac for throwing a Molotov cocktail at a building. Miguel D. felt that the police wanted to make an example out of him and cast pejorative aspersions on the gang by using an inflammatory term to describe him.

50. "$1 Dice Game Bet Results in Death—.270 Mauser Rifle," *Los Angeles Sentinel*, August 17, 1967; "Compton Murder: 26 Year Old Murders 24 Year Old with M-14 Rifle," April 4, 1968. (This was the first example of so powerful a weapon in South Los Angeles.)

51. A "Saturday Night Special" was the nickname for a cheap gun that was often considered to be inaccurate and unreliable. The gun was frequently a greater danger to the shooter than it was to the target, because it could misfire, leaving the shooter without a weapon and a now pissed-off intended target.

52. There were two stores in South Los Angeles before 1965 that carried an assortment of guns for sale: Western Surplus, on 85th Street and Western Avenue, and Lee's Gun Shop, on 79th Street and Broadway, just a couple blocks from the 77th Street LAPD substation. Cash transactions facilitated sales.

53. The source of neighborhood guns was broader than this. The High Priest, from the Village Assassins of Slauson, noted that he and some others had been involved in a burglary at a gun store where "we got more weapons," indicating that burglary was sometimes a viable way to obtain a gun. It was less common to commit home burglaries to steal guns.

54. "Local Groups Battle: Fists, Stabbing," *Los Angeles Sentinel*, July 4, 1946; "Stabbing of Pair: Hoodlumism, Irresponsible Elements," *Los Angeles Sentenel*, September 12, 1946; "Gang War: 3 Whites Rob and Kill Black Man in His Home," *Los Angeles Sentenel*,. October 2, 1947.

55. Before 1970, the statistics on community violence were not systematically ascribed to gangs or to gang members because these data were not being kept by the LASD or LAPD. Determining whether gang members were involved in a suspected crime or if the violence was gang related before this date involved sophistry from whoever was making these decisions.

56. While most textbooks on juvenile delinquency and criminology confirm that there were significant increases in violent and property crime in the United States during the 1960s, both among juveniles and adults, the discussion about this provided by Beirne and Messerschmidt, 2006, is particularly compelling. Also, Graham and Gurr (1970) offer well-researched analyses on the history of American violence, how it has changed, what changed it, and what we might be able to do about it.

57. See Simmel, 1955, for the theoretical significance of the concept "web of group affiliations," for social solidarity.

58. We have included some people here who died after 1965, both because of key roles they played in the neighborhood street groups and to show that they didn't die from gang violence.

59. In their first edition of *The Modern Gang Reader*, Maxson and Klein (1995: 24–32) provide an important analysis on how the amount of gang crime in a given city is a function of definition. They show that the amount of gang crime reported by the police is easily and readily changed just by manipulating definitions.

60. Treetop was a talented Fremont High School basketball star. While his death was reported in the newspaper, his set status was not, making it appear as a killing due to jealousy: "Dad of 5-Weeks Slain at SLA Party," *Los Angeles Sentinel*, May 24, 1962. Jealousy and set status were both factors, although Bird knew that set status was the primary one.

61. Horseshoe was a star football player in high school and got an award for the "most improved youth in LA." "They gave him a plaque and a gold chain." In his later years, he got into drugs and alcohol quite heavily before he died. His body was found with bullet holes in it in an alley. No one quite knows why he was killed or who killed him, but the suspicion is that it probably had to do with gambling.

62. A comprehensive analysis of drive-by shootings is provided by Sanders (1994: 65–84). He uses both historical background and theoretical analysis to explain them.

63. "18 Youth Arrested in Street Melee," *Los Angeles Times*, April 26, 1954. (Battle was from a group in a car with a street group.)

64. "Gang Style Shooting," *Los Angeles Sentinel*, August 19, 1954. (This may be the first Los Angeles drive-by among juveniles.)

65. Around the time that the Slausons began, organized adult criminal gangster units, led by Mickey Cohen, showed up too and shared turf within the Slausons' neighborhood. The area around 68th Street and Central Avenue, one of Cohen's prime locations, was a hostile place for street-group juveniles as well as other people of color. Mickey and his crew seemed intent on excluding Black residents from everything, including patronizing the crew's local businesses. One day in the 1950s, Chinaman and Melvin Ayers got into a fight at this location with some of Mickey's crew over racial issues. The fight established a balance between the groups and served to reduce tension between them. But there was no love lost. There is no evidence that *ethnic succession*—the transitioning of minority juveniles into existing White organized criminal groups—that Ianni, 1975, found in New York happened among the South Los Angeles set members.

66. Pinker, 2011.

CHAPTER 8

1. "Mopery" comes from the word *mope*, meaning "to be gloomy, listless, or dispirited." It was a term commonly used back in the day, usually by a parent to a child: "Y'all quit that mopin' around and find something to do," was their common refrain.

2. Bird was a well-known figure on the streets in the 1960s, suggesting the stop was not random. A key to Bird's survival in this tough environment was that he knew when he could be a smart-ass and when he needed to hold his tongue. This was a moment for the latter.

3. Some of the time the broader term *crime* will be used to refer to the law-breaking street youth were involved in rather than the specific term *juvenile delinquency*, which is the legal term for juvenile law breaking. We do so to simplify and to avoid problems of

focus, as we discuss crime in general and that committed by set members, some of whom may have been older than eighteen when they broke the law.

4. There is an argument by the sociologist Michael Males (2002) that crime was worse in the 1960s than the late 1990s. Males quotes LAPD chief Bernard Parks' comments on 1960s Los Angeles youth crime as "rarely did we see violent crime" by teens. (Parks was chief from 1997 to 2002.) Then Males writes: "Contrary to Parks' claim, L.A. law enforcement records show youth rape, murder and felony arrest rates today [2002] are well below their 1960s levels when juveniles committed a far higher proportion of serious crimes." We concur with Parks: delinquency, especially serious delinquency, was less in the 1960s than in the late 1990s.

5. We use the masculine pronoun here because it was men, and occasionally older teen males, who were involved in these games. Females shared the winnings and tolerated the losses, but they did not play the games.

6. When street gambling and prostitution occurred among street-group members, they occurred mostly among older juveniles and young adults.

7. Jensen and Rojek (1998: 89) write that rates of juvenile delinquency "may have been even higher in the years before nationwide estimates were first compiled in the 1930s" than they are currently. They contend "that the 1870s—the reconstruction period following the American Civil war—may have been the most violent period in American history." This contention does not lend support to Males's argument that juvenile delinquency rates were higher in Los Angeles in the 1960s than in the late 1990s. There were few juveniles in Los Angeles before 1900, and Reconstruction did not play a significant role in city development.

8. Those interested in learning more about Los Angeles's immoral and illicit history can find a plethora of books and articles via a simple online search. While none of these accounts takes juveniles as either a primary or even a secondary focus, some of the more interesting crime drama books include Lew Irwin, *Deadly Times: The 1910 Bombing of the Los Angeles Times and America's Forgotten Decade of Terror* (2013), a non-fictional account of terrorism in Los Angeles; Paul Lieberman, *Gangster Squad: Covert Cops, the Mob, and the Battle for Los Angeles* (2012), a classic Los Angeles crime noir tale on the takedown of Mickey Cohen; and Walter Mosley, *Devil in the Blue Dress* (1990), a crime novel set in 1948 Watts. Mosely has written numerous novels on crime in Los Angeles during the late 1940s through early 1960s, with a deft touch and deep understanding of Black life then.

9. Jensen and Rojek (1998: 4) write that "a full understanding of delinquency and youth crime requires that we recognize them as *one* dimension of a larger problem." Youth problems do not just drop out of the sky but are part of a larger social context that includes adult criminality, a far more pervasive and dangerous phenomenon than juvenile delinquency.

10. "Delinquents Increasing, Says Kiwanis President: New Form of Savagery in Epidemic Stage, Declares Service Clubs International Head," *Los Angeles Times*, December 31, 1953.

11. "New Crimes Youth Gangs," *Los Angeles Times*, December 16, 1953.

12. Juvenile gangs are part of the overall fear of crime Americans have had for a long time. Fears are heightened by "moral panics," generated by a variety of structural forces that benefit from the fear, like the media. Kappeler and Potter (2005: 48–50) introduce another powerful force, "the crime-industrial complex," with a direct economic interest in perpetuating these fears. Moore (1991: 7) notes how these fears also lead to "a diffuse fear of all minorities."

13. "Urges Larger L.A. Juvenile Hall Staff," *Los Angeles Herald & Express*, December 6, 1927.

14. "Outlines Juvenile Delinquency Curb," *Los Angeles Herald & Express*, October 7, 1937.

15. "Delinquency Increase in LA," *Los Angeles Herald & Express*. May 14, 1942.

16. "Nab 80 Boys, Girls in Youth 'Roundup': Police Open War Against Juvenile Delinquency," *Los Angeles Herald & Express*, August 30, 1941.

17. Dick O'Connor, "Hunt Thrills in Dope, Wild Knife Brawls,"*Los Angeles Herald & Express*, April 14, 1953.

18. Ibid., 7.

19. Ibid., 1, 7.

20. Editorial on Brutal Hoodlumism, " Silent Death By Rat Pack 'Homicide,'" *Los Angeles Herald & Express*, December 12, 1953.

21. Bob Will, "Gang Activities: Thefts and Fights Often End in Deaths," *Los Angeles Times*, December 16, 1953.

22. Bob Will, "Age Range From 9 to 30 Years: No Initiation—They Live by Code," *Los Angeles Times*, December 17, 1953 (emphasis added).

23. Dick O'Connor, "Veteran Officer Tells Faith in Youth, Causes for Juvenile Violence," *Los Angeles Herald & Examiner*, April 17, 1953.

24. The nature of South Los Angeles communities was suspicion of any outsiders; whether political agitator or otherwise, they would have been suspect. "You just couldn't walk into a neighborhood and start influencing people," Bird noted. Strangers in a community of color, especially White strangers, were usually assumed to be police. Communists or communism, as portrayed by the media and understood by the community, were thought of as a White person's realm. As Bird commented, "I wasn't even aware there were any Black communists until I was in college." A stranger in the community would either be encouraged to leave or shunned unless a local spoke up for them. Even then, the stranger's ability to influence the political or criminal actions of any group members was next to impossible. "Who the fuck are you, and why are you saying this crazy shit?" is the most likely response an outsider would have gotten had they been there trying to stir up the community. Such claims, as Stein tried to make, may have augmented the pejorative perception of street groups to those who knew nothing about them, but they were not rooted in reality.

25. Short, 1973.

26. Street-group connections to the Black Power and Civil Rights movements are discussed in Chapter 9.

27. "25 Youths Held in Wild Gang Battle," *Los Angeles Examiner*, December 29, 1957.

28. "Youth Gang Shooting Jails Six," *Los Angeles Examiner*, April 28, 1957.

29. "One Beaten, 6 Held in Youth War," *Los Angeles Examiner*, June 5, 1957.

30. "5 Gang Youth Held in Stabbing,"*Los Angeles Times*, March 2, 1954, Part 1.

31. "200 Teens Battle," *Los Angeles Times*, September 16, 1954.

32. "75 Jailed—75 Juveniles Arrested," *Los Angeles Times*, May 22, 1954.

33. "Trail of Lawless: LA Most Crime Ridden of Nation's 3 Biggest Cities," *Newsweek*, March 16, 1959: 24.

34. "Who the Teen Killers Are: The Gangs of New York," *Newsweek*, September 14, 1959.

35. Don Neff, "County Has 336 Teen-Age Gangs," *Los Angeles Times*, July 6, 1961.

36. The UCR have their own group of critics, who make good points regarding inherent weaknesses in their data. See Beirne and Messerschmidt, 2006: 31–44.

37. The pre-1965 data had other problems in addition to those above. First, while UCR data were available in 1930, they were not published as a yearly summary by city until 1934—the date we begin this table. Second, the category currently termed "Forcible Rape" was termed "Rape" in 1934–1936, before disappearing as a UCR category from 1937 through 1957 in the reported city data. When it reappeared again in 1958, it was retermed "Forcible Rape." Third, in some years, the category "Manslaughter by Negligence" was included, and in some years, like 1935 through 1957, it was not. It reappeared in 1958–1965 and was gone afterward. Since this category is not relevant to our analysis, we have omitted it. Fourth, we saw no benefit to including all the years between 1934 and 1965 here, so we selectively chose years that would best represent the broadest yet most accurate picture of crime in the City without the tedium of listing all the years. Finally, because the UCR data indicate crime for the entire city of Los Angeles—a complex, demographically diverse area—these data provide no clue as to what areas in the City the crimes were committed in or who was actually involved. Therefore, we do not know how many of these offenses were committed by juveniles nor whether they were set members nor where they may have lived. Although critiques of the weaknesses of UCR data are many, the data add a necessary dimension to our efforts to gain an overall perspective on crime.

38. Since yearly *crime rates* using the UCR are mostly nonexistent between 1934 and 1965, important questions can be raised about the crime increases: Did the population just become more criminal, or were the increases in crime the result of the increased number of people around who, even if they maintained the same level of criminality, would add more crime just by their presence? Either of these scenarios would explain the increases in the total number of crimes—and we suspect both had an effect.

39. Kinard et al., 1964: 13.

40. Sides, 2006: 218.

41. "Homicides in LASD Jurisdiction: 1960–2012," Los Angeles County Sheriff's Department—Department Crime Statistics: 1960–2012, white paper, January 09, 2012.

42. As an example of social change preceding an increase in criminality, consider the following scenario. In the early years of South Los Angeles, with fewer people and slower neighborhood growth, people knew their neighbors. They were friendly with them or might have been related to them. With more rapid demographic growth, new neighbors would be in and out before bonds of familiarity and trust had time to develop. With neighbors one knows and trusts, windows can be left open and doors left unlocked, but with neighbors one doesn't know, to leave windows and doors unattended would be to do so at one's peril.

43. An agenda for a law-enforcement agency might be similar to the following: if a police department wants to expand, wants more officers and new equipment, they will reach this goal more easily by justifying their requests with a show of more crime in their jurisdiction than they would by showing less crime.

44. In his study of violent crime among juvenile gangs in an "eastern metropolis," Walter Miller (1966: 96) finds that "violence was not a central preoccupation," that the violent crimes that were committed "were of the less serious variety," that the crimes were rarely "cruel or sadistic," and that the "violence was seldom 'senseless' or irrational." This is similar to the violence we found among the pre-1965 South Los Angeles street groups.

45. Hard drugs on the street included various pills, barbiturates, angel dust, and heroin. Although cocaine is a hard drug, it was mostly absent and thus unfamiliar. Resi-

dents had heard about it and read about it but had seen very little of it in the community. We omitted inclusion of cigarettes, alcohol, or marijuana as hard drugs, even though, pharmacologically, they are drugs and, for the first two, proven dangerous.

46. Death from an overconsumption of alcohol did occur, though mostly indirectly. For example, Lafayette from the Slausons said his older brother died from cirrhosis of the liver, a condition related to overconsumption. Various siblings, friends, and parents of other respondents were among those who had also died from alcohol-related maladies—that is, "gettin' drunk and bein' stupid."

47. "Hard stuff" to John S.'s peers could be any illegal drugs other than marijuana but primarily referred to heroin and cocaine. The film actor Bela Lugosi was addicted to morphine and methadone and died from an overdose in 1956.

48. By the early 1970s, cocaine was quite evident, with several respondents mentioning they had not only seen it at various social functions but were offered an opportunity to try it.

49. The 1950s and 1960s were periods when smoking cigarettes, or at least giving the appearance of smoking by having an unlit cigarette hang out of your mouth, "Bogart style," was considered the essence of cool. TV's the "Marlboro Man," posing with a cigarette in his mouth while he sat on his horse, was considered a man's man. We have seen photographs of, and are personally aware of, male juveniles who didn't smoke but were posers, with cigarettes hanging out of their mouths.

50. Before 1965, marijuana had major legal as well as moral penalties associated with use, possession, and sales. Much of the professional literature held that it was a "gateway drug" to serious addiction, deviant malevolence, and more potent drugs like heroin. Solomon, 1966. The 1937 Marijuana Tax Act made possession of "even a minute quantity of the herb" punishable by five years in prison, a $2,000 fine, or both. Ibid.: xv. Howard Becker's (1966) classic ethnographic study on marijuana refuted many of the professional opinions and concluded that those who used the herb were not psychological misfits but were an assortment of musicians, blue-collar workers, and professionals, who used it recreationally for pleasure. We add juvenile street-group members to this list of pleasure users and note that Becker was not alone on his stance as the research in Solomon's 1966 treatise attests.

51. Helmer, 1975.

52. Holloway, 2021: 7.

53. There is evidence to suggest there were exceptions to the claims of a few drugs. Some South Los Angeles juveniles not only used hard drugs but used them to excess. The president of the Baby Businessmen, for example, remembered seeing, when he was in high school, another student come into a classroom "so full of red devils that he was slobbering on the teacher's desk." It is most likely that Chinaman's experiences, coming at an earlier period than the president of the Baby Businessmen's, are a reflection on the dissimilarities of drug availability between two different periods.

54. Bird does recall a 1950s–1960s clique from Florence called the Toakers, which was a different clique than the Tokers, a 1990s Florence clique. The original Toakers and Little Toakers may have taken their name from the term *toke* or *toak*, verbs used to indicate taking a drag from a marijuana joint. This clique could have taken their name to reflect their association with marijuana use, or the name might have been an example of the "wish fulfillment" Thrasher discusses, or, less likely, it might have had nothing to do with marijuana or any other drug.

55. "Dope Peddling Suspect Shot," *Los Angeles Times*, June 10, 1954.

56. "One May Die," *Los Angeles Times*, June 23, 1954; five seventeen-year-olds were nabbed with "thousands of sedative pills."

57. "Police War on Narcotics Jails 7," *Los Angeles Sentinel*, December, 17, 1953.

58. "LA Teen Gangs Feed US Dope Rings," *Los Angeles Times*, July 21, 1963.

59. *Peeling the grape* is a colloquialism of the 1960s, which meant imbibing in wine. Beer, malt liquor, and a bit of hard alcohol, which were also consumed, could fall under this concept.

60. A contrary position on the debilitating effects of drugs came from Whit, the vice president of the Royal Aces, describing the athletic prowess of the legendary "baddest dude" in South Los Angeles, Horseshoe: "Horseshoe tell you about, he wouldn't play a game of football unless he drank him a short dog wine first." Legends do, after all, have to be maintained. Most neighborhood athletes took the position of Barry Wa. from the Junior Businessmen, who said: "We wasn't on no drugs when we was comin' up. We was good athletes; we was good students."

61. Nedra, a sister to one of the Little Slausons, who married a person who later became a drug dealer, is an example of a drug-using woman. She said that her husband was "crazy, really," and that he used to regularly tell her that he was born too late. "Al Capone and John Dillinger were his idols, the kind of people he wanted to be like." A self-described "pill head," she noted that people used to come by their house regularly to buy "bennies." "Them 'dexes' man, I'd take one of them, and I was wired up for three days. I'd try anything once, you know, except heroin," she exclaimed. Her history with drugs went from 1959 to 1968. "Dexes" is street vernacular for dextroamphetamine, a prescription drug used to treat ADHD and narcolepsy. Linda, from Florence, another drug-using woman, said: "All my old mans were drug addicts, and they didn't want me to get influenced. One time, the guy I was with—he was a drug addict—he always told me, 'There's one drug addict in this family, and that's me.'" But she did smoke marijuana: "I been smoking weed since I was twelve years old."

62. We did not find evidence of the "retreatist subculture" made infamous by Cloward and Ohlin (1960: 178–184) in *Delinquency and Opportunity*. Although the juveniles who used drugs knew each other, shared information on access to various drugs, and appeared to enjoy getting wasted together, there was scant evidence of the richer subcultural attributes discussed by Cloward and Ohlin to distinguish them. But there were differences in drug use among the users, with only a few being addicts.

63. This was a figurative minute that meant for a short time, not a literal minute.

64. Vigil (1988: 95) notes how "dyadic" and small-group interactions characterized a barrio he studied, including a threesome who slipped away from a party to have consensual sex before returning. Drug usage among South Los Angeles street groups was organizationally similar.

65. Two reasons why cocaine was most likely not prevalent in South Los Angeles before 1965 were because it was expensive and it required an indoor setting to consume. At one hundred dollars per gram for a vial of cocaine powder, it was considered a "rich man's" drug. Since it only came in powder form then, it required a place without wind (preferably indoors), so it could be chopped into fine particles with a razor blade and then snorted through a tube. Few youth had either the financial means for purchase of the drug or the indoor location for consumption.

66. The "ass whoopin'" administered by the cheated drug purchaser to the seller was a warning to not cheat this purchaser again. Killings by street juveniles, due to a bad drug transaction, were virtually unknown before 1965.

67. In the 1940s, when Lefon was coming of age, Central Avenue was the "business and entertainment mainline" of Los Angeles.

68. Driving under the influence of alcohol (DUI) is an offense that is punishable by a fine, jail time, or both. None of our respondents mentioned it as a factor in their lives. The police data, because of inadequacies noted elsewhere, were not much help in providing further clarity.

69. A discovery, by adults, of consensual sex among minors was often the result of a pregnancy, which in some families was not taken lightly.

70. The offense causing some of the greatest moral repugnance was child molestation. As Florence set member Rick C. said, "Molesters got chased out of town. They wouldn't be tolerated."

71. Another woman told us about an incident that had happened to her when she was thirteen years old, leaving her with permanent emotional scars. She explained how her mother used to bring home strange men to party with, in a small apartment that the thirteen-year-old shared with her brother. One night, one of those men attempted to "grab" her while she was lying in her bed but was stopped by her mother and brother. She thought he was going to rape her and was terrified by the encounter.

72. It would be quite easy to express shock at the South Los Angeles communities' acceptance of behavior, which from a twenty-first-century perspective many would be comfortable calling out as rape. "How could such behavior be tolerated?" might seem to be appropriate contemporary responses. Yet this response reeks of hypocrisy. As events at a 2012 Steubenville, Ohio, middle-class neighborhood party among football players and their female admirers show, community tolerance of questionable sexual activity continues to exist, but is mediated by race, class, and technology; the behavior is similar. There is not a new moral high ground existent today among middle-class White communities that was absent in South Los Angeles before 1965. The Steubenville event might never have been reported on, or the perpetrators held accountable, if it had not been for Twitter. People in the community had already looked the other way. But an electronic bust by a persistent investigator may have revealed the tip of an iceberg of sexually aggressive behavior there that many in the staid community wanted to believe had melted. See Ariel Levy's (2013) poignant analysis of the Steubenville events for a better understanding of how the initially hidden circumstances of this middle-class rape unfolded.

73. Auto parts were also a relatively common item to be stolen, but were usually a larceny rather than a robbery.

74. Some words, such as this one, are toxic slurs when used by White people. When used by Black people, the word takes on different meanings, depending on the user's intent, and are understood by those within the group as both appropriate and necessary.

75. There were too many years between Chinaman and Lafayette, in addition to Chinaman's prison time keeping him off the streets, for him to have served as a mentor to Lafayette. They both responded similarly to opportunities, at different times, to join the Slausons and to rob banks.

76. From Cloward and Ohlin's (1960: 161–171) perspective, the existence of a "criminal subculture" is one of the three variations delinquent gangs can take. Our research demonstrated such a subculture was absent from the street groups of South Los Angeles before 1965.

77. Vigil, 1988, 2002.

78. Glasgow's (1981) research and our field research show Watts to have continuing urban disarray that persists in distinguishing it.

79. Neighborhood silence in South Los Angeles was different from the neighborhood silence that Salisbury (1958) discusses occurs in middle-class communities, but the results are similar. Police records are a reflection of community class standards more than they are an accurate statement on community crime. Pepinsky and Jesilow (1985: 47–57) argue that it is a myth that "some groups are more law abiding than others." Middle- and upper-class groups are just more effective at hiding what they do and in keeping it from being perceived as dangerous as what lower-class groups do. Ibid.: 58–65.

80. Being labeled a "snitch" or a "rat" was to be put in an unenviable situation. These were among the most odious of titles that could be applied, resulting in community shunning.

81. Since the very nature of neighborhood hidden criminality defies official measurement, other unobtrusive methods to measure how extensive it actually was are required before further comments on how much there was can be made.

82. This statement may appear to contradict our earlier point about a set member's money being his to do with as he chose. In fact, it's a corollary: someone who has experienced a windfall, especially if he had previously been relying on others, might be expected to reimburse his earlier benefactors, perhaps with a bit of interest, because what's here today could quite easily be gone tomorrow. If one gets needy again, after a windfall that was not at least partially shared, who's going to help if the windfall disappears?

83. Kumasi was formerly known as "Little Bird."

84. Wilson (1987) refers to this group as the "truly disadvantaged," an urban ghetto underclass. Marxists refer to this group as "superfluous people," the *lumpenproletariat*, and theorize that its creation and disenfranchisement is an inevitable part of capitalist production. Marx, 1887; Braverman, 1974.

85. After being used up by their slickster bosses, the thugs became what John Irwin (1985) refers to as "social junk," or superfluous people.

86. See Braverman, 1974.

87. Quinney, 1970.

88. Some probation officers had a different view on purse snatching, believing it happened more frequently than the set members claimed it did. One set member reluctantly admitted he was once involved in a purse snatching. An older juvenile encouraged him, when he was eleven or twelve years old, to snatch the purse of an older woman. He did and was caught by the police. The experience both embarrassed and frightened him so much that he never did it again. Since there was little that was honorable about snatching purses, we suspect it was one of those offenses that, when it happened, involved no boasting, thus minimizing the number of people who knew it had occurred. When there was a purse snatching, it usually took place in a neighborhood other than one's own. It's possible that purse snatching occurred at a greater frequency than our respondents admitted, although we have little reason to think that it did. It was certainly not a set-sanctioned activity.

89. Describing the victim as a nonresident without neighborhood ties does not mean we are excusing the crime. By implication, targeting her was a rational act—she had money, and it was a far less serious offense, by community standards, than a snatching involving someone's mama.

90. Street gambling was sufficiently lucrative that foul play from law enforcers could occur. In an ethnographic research paper for a seminar that he took with Quicker, Frank Miller (1988: 7) wrote that big dice games would get raided by police plainclothesmen, who would approach the group inconspicuously. Once a large enough pile of cash being

wagered was on the ground, the cop would throw his badge on it, scaring the bettors into fleeing. "The cop would [then] take the money and leave without arresting anyone."

91. This probation officer was certainly aware of the more serious robberies occurring in the neighborhood but wanted to note that all robberies and robbers were not equal.

92. These data come from the FBI's *Crime in the United States PDFs 1930–1969*. Sorting by age and city was not available for the data reported in Table 8.1.

93. A case could be made that burglary and larceny are serious offenses and are not to be taken lightly. We do not take them lightly. Our points are (1) these are property crimes, involving no physical harm to the victims; and (2) in comparison to homicide, they are nonserious. In fact, from 1934 to 1965, the top five offenses each year that juveniles were arrested for were nonserious. They included the following behaviors: disorderly conduct, vandalism, vagrancy, suspicion, drunkenness, liquor laws, and auto theft. These data could suggest that juveniles steal primarily to have the economic or transportational wherewithal to enjoy themselves.

94. An additional issue faced those detained for curfew who had responsible parental figures was parental response. Anyone under eighteen who was on the streets after 10:00 P.M., without an accompanying adult, was in violation of the curfew. Bird argued that the police would often pick you up shortly after 10:00 P.M. and then wait a few hours, until after your parents had retired for the evening, before phoning them—at a time the police knew would wake them. This was double trouble. Bird explained: "They'd [police] wait till one in the morning and call your mother up and tell her to come get you, knowing she had to be to work or get up for work at six [A.M.]. See, they might get you at five minutes after ten [P.M.] and hold you down there and wait, let your mother be sleeping real good and in her dreams, and then call up and say, 'Mrs. Williams, we have your son down here. Would you like to come pick him up?' She say, 'Oh yeah, I'm gonna pick him up, um hum, yeah; I'll be down there in a minute, um hum.' Then, when they come to get you, man, you'd a rather stayed in jail!"

95. Katz, 1988.

96. Some crime can be fun, but this theft was not done for fun. Certain thefts, especially when the thieves were making a break for it, could be a thrill. If they got away, they could later laugh and talk about the excitement, but these unintended experiences were not motivators.

97. Cohen's (1955) hypothesis on the *nonutilitarian* nature of delinquent theft is not supported by our research.

98. *Need* varied considerably among those who stole. Stealing "poop-stained drawers" certainly reflected a different level of need than those who took car parts to make their cars more stylish.

99. One of the most notable examples of male involvement in shoplifting came from Lefon, of the Serfs car club, who admitted that he and his homeboys would steal "screws" for their cars from "Mr. Greenberg's hardware store." Curiously, Mr. Greenberg didn't seem to mind, because "he understood. We were kids." Later on, he even sold Lefon his second vehicle, a 1957 pickup truck, which pleased Lefon immeasurably.

100. Mary Owen Cameron, in her 1964 study titled *The Booster and the Snitch*, divided shoplifters into these two categories, boosters and snitches, according to whether they stole in order to resell the merchandise later (the booster) or stole for personal use (the snitch). She identified the booster as the professional and the snitch as the amateur. Our respondent wanted to make it clear she knew the difference and was an amateur.

101. Let us not lose sight of the important role that writing, drawing, or carving on natural or man-made structures has had throughout human history. From the early cave dwellers to the civilizations of the world to the American GIs in World War II who wrote, "Kilroy was here," humans have had a long history of marking up all sorts of structures with *art* or *graffiti*—however the observer might choose to term it.

102. Bird remembered where many of these cement markings were, and we visited over a dozen of them in our field forays.

103. Early graffiti artists did not have the availability of paint spray cans to use for their designs, adapting instead what was available. While chalk was used, its impermanence never gave it much popularity. A remarkably good product, practically designed for the street artist's needs, was Shinola shoe polish. This was a long-lasting liquid polish that came in numerous colors. It even came with a convenient applicator that, although made for shoes, had just the proper proportions for writing on walls. Bird used Shinola with great aplomb.

104. Some lock-up facilities, especially for juveniles, were brutal punishments in themselves. Ameer and Bird both mentioned a facility for juveniles who were sixteen years old or older, called the "Georgia Street Jail," where the Los Angeles Convention Center now sits. This facility did deter. Ameer described a time he spent there like this: "We got busted in the summer. This is how chickenshit they were there, man; this is outright cruel. It was a hundred degrees when we got busted. It was a hot summer, and they turned the heater on. Literally, they turned the heater on us!" Bird concurred: "Georgia Street was chickenshit."

105. The key difference, Rick C. opined, between those who went to jail and those who did not was whether they had money for a lawyer. Those who were unable to afford an attorney were assigned a public defender. In Rick C.'s case, being poor, he received public defenders that would "psych" him into accepting time whether he was guilty or not. Rick C. was down for his set and would not snitch. While he was no angel, his street morality often prompted him to plead guilty when he was innocent. In his words: "There were times when I was arrested that I did not do the crime. My buddy did, but I couldn't tell on him. But the cops would say, 'Okay, you're goin'.' And here would come my so-called public defender and say, 'Well, there's only one thing I can do for you, you know. You take this year and a half, and we'll put you on probation, and that's the best we can do. Sorry, guy.' I ain't got no money; what am I gonna do? All my cases would've been beat; they [the police] never even showed up in court against me. My stuff got solved before court. My mind was made up as soon as I hit the cell door: 'Well, let's see. I'll take two [years], if that's what they offer. I'll take a year; I need the rest anyway.'"

106. Before 1965, the majority of people locked up from the community were males. While it was not unheard of for females to be locked up, it was rare. Female imprisonment's effect on the community was considerably less than that of the males because so few females were institutionalized then.

107. Katz (1988: 6–8) offers an analogy to LAPD stigmatizing black juveniles with a criminal record, whether deserving or not, called the "American Rules." During the Vietnam War, American interrogators would brand Vietnamese interrogees "Vietcong," whether they were or not, to make them by definition the enemy and thereby easier to brutalize with interrogation techniques. Stigmatizing Black juveniles this way, but as criminals, made it easier to hold and interrogate them and find them guilty, particularly if they had a record.

108. Ianni, 1975.

109. Taylor, 1990.

110. Hagedorn, 2015.

111. In 1971, Janis Joplin released her hit song "Mercedes-Benz," on her album *Pearl*. The refrain, "Oh, Lord, won't you buy me a Mercedes-Benz," was a testament to the ideological commitment of Americans to their righteous claims on materialism.

112. Veblen, 1953.

113. Merton, 1964: 139. The classic article by Robert K. Merton, "Social Structure and Anomie," was first published in 1938 and has under gone many extensions and revisions up to the ninth printing in his revised and enlarged edition (Merton, 1964: 121), which is our reference.

114. Beginning with Cloward and Ohlin's (1960) subcultural archetypes, based on Merton's theory, many delinquency and gang researchers used a narrower interpretation of innovation, applying it only, or at the least primarily, to causes of delinquency and gang formation among lower- or working-class juveniles. Merton's concept of innovation became politicized and lost direction.

115. The *captains of industry* are corporate leaders, industrialists, capitalists, and associates. Their criminality was discussed in detail by Josephson (1962), who referred to them as "robber barons."

116. Merton, 1964: 141.

117. *Living large* is a post-1970 street term meaning showing off by your display of material things: *sparkle plenty* (gold and jewelry), a nice car, expensive clothes, and other luxuries.

118. The idea that in America, "success, wealth and power" are part of the American Dream, while the legal means to get them are not, is a core issue contributing to deviance in Merton's theory. The anomic nature of American culture as a prime contributor to crime was one of Merton's most important theoretical formulations.

119. In an unsung autobiography on the excitement that crime can provide compared to a "boring" job, John Mac Isaac (1968) demonstrates how and why he is happiest when engaged in certain illegal hustles.

120. We heard no reference to homosexuality among our respondents and are therefore unable to comment on it.

121. In the 1960s, Timothy Leary's mantra of "Tune in, turn on, and drop out" was an ode to the virtues of drug use. While this mantra may have had less influence in South Los Angeles communities than it did among middle-class youth, he was nevertheless expressing youthful American values.

122. A disclaimer: we are the messengers, not the advocates, for deviance that might be fun. "Bud" is a colloquial term for marijuana, as "grape" is for wine.

123. We found limited evidence of drug addiction and more evidence of those with alcohol problems. The medical research on addiction is unequivocal: many of those who become addicted have serious issues that lead to further health and social disabilities.

124. In his insightful research on the importance of blue-collar jobs for community stability in urban areas, Wilson (1997) analyses the devastating effects job loss produces.

125. "Enough," as it is used here, is subjective. Those who seemed satisfied the money they earned enabled them to do and have the things they needed were less likely than those who felt otherwise to engage in appropriative crime. As the Chinese philosopher Lao Tse once stated: "He who knows when he has enough is rich." (This quote and philosopher's name came from an interview Quicker conducted with Min S. Yee in the late 1990s.)

126. As with so many generalizations, we found one very notable exception to this notion of set members fighting more frequently than nonset members: Horseshoe. As

discussed, he was one of the most pugnacious of South Los Angeles's youngsters, with a reputation that stretched across most of the area, yet he never joined a set. Although he was courted by many sets, he preferred his lone-wolf independence to set membership.

127. Durkheim, 1966: 39–75.
128. Clark, 1970: 35.

CHAPTER 9

1. A comprehensive account of Los Angeles's 1960s history is provided by Mike Davis and Jon Wiener (2020) in their *Set the Night on Fire*.
2. Davis, 1990: 296.
3. Davis and Wiener, 2020: 207–208.
4. Soja, 1989: 159–162.
5. Mari, 2020: 32.
6. By "elders," we mean those who were juveniles in the 1950s and early 1960s. While they were hardly old, they were elder to the young juveniles who were coming up on the street. The term *elder* differentiates them from the youngsters.
7. Massoglia and Uggen (2010) provide a review of the literature, as well as analyzing their own important research on the necessity of juveniles to mature out of delinquency to become adults. Maturing out of street groups seems to involve some of the same processes. The pre-1965 street-group members recognized that the proper transition to adulthood involved leaving their street activities behind.
8. On several occasions, Quicker was invited by a probation officer he knew in the Department's Specialized Gang Supervision Program to attend annual county programs on gangs. The programs were jointly held in the 1980s by the Los Angeles County Department of Probation and Sheriff's Department. They consisted of various lectures, with slide presentations, and discussions on what the two departments knew about gangs, what they were doing and planning to do to combat them, and how they could cooperate to achieve their goals. Program admission was by invitation only. It was here that Quicker got an insiders' look and learned of the Sheriff's Department's belief that Crip groups existed in certain western European countries, although this is hardly a secret now.
9. Sides (2006: 218) writes: "The growth rate of the Black population in Los Angeles from 1940 to 1970 was 1,096 percent." Poe (1965: 426) notes that the "Negro" population in Los Angeles increased "eight-fold" from 1940 to 1965, or from 75,000 to 600,000. According to the Kerner Commission Report (1968: 243–248), there was a doubling of the Black population from 1950 to 1968. The McCone Commission (1969: 3) wrote that the "negro population" in Los Angeles "exploded" from 1940 to 1965, increasing "tenfold." By whichever statistic is used, the demographic transformation of South Los Angeles was unprecedented, and social reordering was a consequence of the times.
10. Soja (1989: 217) contends that a resurgence of migration since 1960 from Mexico into Los Angeles "has added at least a million residents to the existing population and helped to shade into the regional map a nearly ubiquitous Spanish-speaking presence." Further, he notes, "In what may be the record for in-migration from a single country, nearly 400,000 Salvadorans are estimated to have moved to Los Angeles since 1980."
11. Soja, 1989: 208–221.
12. Herbers, 1970: xiii. The second quote here comes from the back jacket cover of this same book.
13. Curiously, the LASD and LAPD were not officially categorizing crimes as "gang related" until 1976 for the LASD and the early 1980s for the LAPD. Could the media have

known something in the 1960s that the large law-enforcement agencies didn't, or were they just in a creative mood, identifying as gang crimes offenses that the police agencies hadn't yet confirmed?

14. Some examples from the *Los Angeles Sentinel*: August 24, 1962; "Teen Gang of 20 Battles Police," September 7, 1962; "Teens Wreck Watts Café Over Burger," July 29, 1965; "Bullets, Gas Bombs Rout Party Guests," police describe as gang activity. From the *Los Angeles Times*: December 14, 1960; "South Area LA Hit for Crime," one third of Los Angeles's crime is from the southern section of the City, a mecca for mass migration. December 31, 1960; "City Shows Increase All Major Crimes," juvenile delinquency up 16.8 percent.

15. Klein, 1971: 50.

16. Davis and Wiener, 2020: 39.

17. Berman, 1963: 1, 8.

18. Klein, 1971: 50.

19. In his classic on the origins of the juvenile justice system, Anthony Platt (1969) documents the hypocrisy of the early interventionists and provides insights into the primarily insurmountable issues they faced trying to reform the juveniles. The Group Guidance Program and the Ladino Hills Project—also in Los Angeles but in this case trying to change "Mexican-American gangs" (Klein, 1971)—faced problems similar to what Platt had found. Mennel (1973) adds to Platt's analysis on the problems of reform practices and argues that revitalized families and community government were keys to making positive changes among juveniles. Mennel's suggestions were not followed in Los Angeles.

20. Sides, 2006: 168.

21. Davis and Wiener, 2020: 117.

22. Ron Eldridge (1985: 22), who lived and worked in South Los Angeles during the 1960s, believed the Vietnam War had a large impact on Black gangs. He writes: "One of the biggest reasons why Black gangs declined was Vietnam. Joining the armed forces and the draft wiped out whole neighborhoods of gang and would be gang members. Some members enrolled in school to avoid the draft." A more definitive analysis of the effect of this War on gangs is warranted because of the difference in conclusions between what we found and what Eldridge contends.

23. McAdam and Moore (1989: 267–274) offer a penetrating analysis of where the Black Power movement drew its strength, why the movement declined, and the dramatic effect its decline had on Black communities throughout America.

24. Churchill and Vander Wall, 1990; Davis and Wiener, 2020.

25. Black Panther Party, 1966.

26. Kumasi, a.k.a. Little Bird, is Bird's cousin.

27. By doing "something," Kumasi meant help with the Free Breakfast for Children Program and with the health clinics set up to get people with sickle-cell anemia assistance. It gave people with idle time on their hands a feeling they were important, they were valuable, and that they were involved in relevant contributions to their community.

28. For a well-researched and readable account of the Panthers and U.S. history in Los Angeles, see Davis and Wiener, 2020. They note the roles of John Floyd and Ayuko Babu in the early Los Angeles chapter formation and the details involved in Bunchy's takeover. Ibid.: 286–287.

29. Bunchy did not have a lot of time on the street to organize after his release from prison—somewhat less than a year and a half. Bird noted he was released in the fall of 1967. He was killed on January 15, 1969. Davis and Wiener, 2020: 441–443. During the

time Bunchy ran the teen post and recruited for the BPP, Bird was mostly off the street as a result of various incarcerations. But because he had many contacts on the streets, Bird was well aware of what was happening.

30. Teen posts were government-sponsored programs designed to keep juveniles out of trouble. Usually held in an indoor setting and offering counseling services and after-school and evening activities, the posts were popular for a while in the 1960s.

31. Not everyone was as enamored of the Panthers as many of the neighborhood juveniles were. Number one on the list of Panther detractors was law enforcement: LAPD chief Daryl Gates said that they were really after power for themselves, not the people; FBI director J. Edgar Hoover described them as "the greatest threat to the internal security of the country." Churchill and Vander Wall, 1990: 77. Gates wrote they were "hoodlums," who took checks from "wealthy patrons," which was why the Panthers didn't have to rob and steal. Further, he believed that they were "mean" and "violent" and mostly "feared" by neighborhood people. Gates, 1992: 135. Although many in the neighborhood did not view the Panthers as highly as some of the youth did, we found no evidence to support Gates's claims. The FBI created and exploited antagonism existing between the Panthers and US. Their COINTELPRO, or counterintelligence program, took the Black Power and Civil Rights movements as prime focuses, trying to "disrupt" or "neutralize" them. Beirne and Messerschmidt, 2006: 236. Churchill and Vander Wall (1990: 42–99) are even more critical of the FBI's role in attempting to extinguish the BPP. Citing the congressional investigation called *The FBI'S Covert Action Program to Destroy the Black Panther Party* and to destroy all other Black Power groups, including Dr. Martin Luther King's civil rights efforts, the authors document the illegal activities the FBI used to achieve this goal. They released "disinformation" to the press; sent forged letters to both the Panthers and to US purporting the letters to be from the other group, which were designed to humiliate and antagonize the group they were sent to; used infiltrators and agents provocateur; fabricated evidence; and engaged in assassinations. Given this material, it would not be difficult to make the case that the FBI was at least indirectly involved in Bunchy's death.

32. The Slauson sartorial style, which preceded and influenced the Panthers, was also designed to make a statement. Among the garments worn by Slausons were fine-looking leather jackets.

33. Gardell, 1996.

34. Black Muslims were viewed as threats by the LAPD, who continually harassed their recruiters on the streets. Davis and Wiener, 2020.

35. A Los Angeles County Sheriff's Department white paper, prepared by Deputies Rick Graves and Ed Allen of the Juvenile Operations Bureau, titled *Black Gangs and Narcotics and Black Gangs* (no date of publication but obtained by Quicker in the 1980s), recognizes that Raymond Washington "started the Crip gang" but then holds that the Crips "started in the West Los Angeles area" (1). We disagree with their contention of Crip origins in West Los Angeles. Raymond grew up on East 76th Street, between Stanford Avenue and Avalon Boulevard. He attended the 79th Street Elementary School and Edison Junior High School and began high school at Fremont, which was basically across the street from his house. He was kicked out of Fremont and then attended Washington High School on West 108th Street and Denker Avenue, on the West-Side, in an unincorporated area of Los Angeles County. Raymond quite likely found some followers at Washington High, but he spent his early years—his street-group affiliation years—on the East-Side, deep in the Slauson neighborhood. The Crip group that he formed came out of the Slauson neighborhood.

36. While Raymond Washington was old enough to have been a member of one of the last Slauson cliques, he wasn't. He became an Avenue as his first street group of choice.

37. "Number one boy" is not a derogatory title but means "sidekick" or partner. It does not mean a subordinate. Craig C. was an OG (original gangster) Crip and one of the toughest. He was a "loverboy," a "pretty boy," and a regular companion of Raymond's. Shortly after Craig C. was killed in 1976, Bird ran into Raymond again, this time on 78th Street and Central Avenue. Raymond's physical change, from Bird's first encounter with him when he was fifteen, until 1976, was dramatic. As Bird recalled: "He's five feet eight inches tall, two hundred pounds, you know. He's buff: bow leg with no shirt on and wearin' Levis. He's walkin' down the street sayin', 'Who shot a hole in my dog, my road dog?' and blah, blah, blah. And I'm leanin' on the car talking to one of my homeboys, Wolford F. And Wolford said, 'Yeah, that's Raymond.' And I said, 'Raymond who?' He said, 'Raymond Washington.' And by that time, Raymond had become a household name." Raymond had changed so much that Bird didn't recognize him, although he knew who he was.

38. The United Slaves Organization, or US, founded by Ron Karenga in 1965, had a somewhat different political ideology than that of the Black Panther Party. Davis and Wiener, 2020. The distrust between US and the Panthers was used by the FBI to weaken the Panthers.

39. It's not clear how many set members became involved in the Black Power movement. Since the Black Panther Party's original platform wasn't announced until October 1966, their neighborhood influence came after the Watts Rebellion. The president of the Baby Businessmen noted that none of his homeboys became Panthers because the Businessmen had "no respect" for them, but some Businessmen did become Muslims. The Black Power movement, most likely, had a limited impact on South Los Angeles sets before 1965, although it was a significant factor in the overall changes influencing the community.

40. Ameer felt that the Muslims and US got along because both were cultural groups. US was teaching its members Marxism by having them read Franz Fanon's *Wretched of the Earth* and works by Malcolm X, Che Guevara, and Mao Tse-tung. He felt that the Panthers were revolutionaries. Ameer's judgment of the BPP lends further support to the significant diversity of opinion existing in the community among the street-group members. One size did not fit all.

41. While a number of Renegades followed Bunchy into the Panthers, there were, according to Bird, "a whole lot of them that didn't become Panthers." Bunchy led, but he didn't dictate.

42. Although the details of Bunchy's assassination remain murky, they are explained well by Davis and Wiener (2020).

43. Brown, 1970: 51.

44. Smith, 2006: 87–89.

45. Poe, 1965: 429.

46. Howard and McCord, 1969: 57.

47. Ibid.: 58.

48. Gates, 1992: 102–103.

49. Ibid.: 118.

50. Poe, 1965: 430.

51. Howard and McCord, 1969; Flamming, 2005.

52. The LAPD leadership was not alone in its condemnation of the rioters as social misfits and as the primary cause of the riot but was ideologically joined by others in

the City power structure. Notable among this group was Catholic cardinal Francis McIntyre, a "mean-spirited" and "vindictive man." He denounced the rioters as "inhuman, almost bestial." He in turn was supported by the *Tydings* political columnist George Kramer, who "added that reports of police abuse were only an old Communist canard." Davis, 1990: 333.

53. This racial slur, used this way, is toxic. We quote it because we believe the reader needs to know what was said, not what we might have liked them to say. Speakers and writers need to take responsibility for their words.

54. Conot, 1967: 250. There were numerous law-enforcement agencies involved in trying to contain the Rebellion. These included the LAPD, the LASD, and the National Guard. The greatest racial animosity toward the rioters came from the LAPD, followed by the LASD. The McCone Commission Report (1969: 28), ranking community bitterness of law enforcement, adds that "many Negroes felt that he [LAPD chief Parker] carries a deep hatred of the Negro community." The Commission Report notes: "Generally speaking, the Negro community does not harbor the same angry feeling toward the Sheriff or his staff as it does toward the Los Angeles police" (28).

55. LSMFT (Lucky Strike Means Fine Tobacco) was originally an acronym created to advertise cigarettes before the LAPD racialized it during the Rebellion.

56. Conot, 1967: 40.

57. Fogelson (1969) made it clear that all social classes of Black Angelenos resented the indignities of racism they had been experiencing and felt the "riot" was justified. In Fogelson's analysis, the Watts Rebellion was a manifestation of "problems of race even more than class." Fogelson, 1969: 123.

58. Davis and Wiener, 2020: 237.

59. Ibid.: 226.

60. McCone, 1969: 1–2.

61. Davis and Wiener, 2020: 233.

62. Conot (1967: 226–234) has a chapter in his book on the Businessmen's involvement in the Rebellion but with few details. Davis and Wiener (2020: 215, 217) mention a gathering of gangs in the Jordan Downs projects and the Businessmen getting attacked in South Park. We speculate that one reason for the dearth of materials on street-group involvement is related to the overall dearth of materials on South Los Angeles street groups in general. But there could be other reasons.

63. Conot, 1967: 244.

64. As Bird noted, the Slausons in particular were "there for a cause, not because. We knew what we were doing."

65. This expression is adapted from Peter Finch in the classic 1976 film *Network*.

66. The D'Artagnans named themselves after the fourth musketeer of *The Three Musketeers* film. Some of them did misspell their name as the "Dartallians." Two reasons for the different spelling of set and member names are, first, set members spoke the names far more often than they wrote them, thus leaving a scant written record; second, when names were written down by law enforcement or the media, they often guessed at the spelling, writing it phonetically.

67. Yablonsky, 1966: 10.

68. Conot, 1967: 255–262.

69. "Kumbaya" is the name of a Joan Baez folk song, emphasizing people coming together in a peaceful fashion to overcome their differences.

70. Horne, 1997, makes the spontaneity of the 1965 Rebellion clear.

71. Howard and McCord, 1969: 64–67.

72. Conot, 1967: 417–419. Davis and Wiener (2020) go into important detail on the failure of social programs for the Watts community and the increased power gains for the police brought on by the Rebellion.

73. Other than a few hustles by some of its members, the pre-1965 street groups were not into illegal pursuits that could provide a steady source of income. To continue being a street-group member at twenty was not only imprudent; it was also a way to stay poor. The juveniles were now emerging into adulthood with options outside their street group taking priority over street life. Street groups for the pre-1965 members were for youthful endeavors, with little to offer them as adults. Nevertheless, some media reports, such as Bob Will's "Age Range from 9 to 30 Years: No Initiation—They Live by Code," (*Los Angeles Times*, December 17, 1953), mention a range that goes well beyond the juvenile years for gang involvement. But it is not always clear whether these reports are referring to South Los Angeles street groups or to those in East Los Angeles, where some members of the East Los Angeles street groups were adults.

74. Both boys were Bird's sons, but the woman they were with was the birth mother of one.

75. The term *gunselin* was used by pre-1965 street groups to refer to their rowdier types of activity. Fights, partying, chasing women, and establishing reputations characterized this style. While guns may have been part of this, it was uncommon. Gunselin was the name for behavior carried on with peer associates in the pursuit of common group-sanctioned goals. It had a fitting ring.

76. Bird made it clear that the Gladiators and Watts remained adversaries to Slauson throughout the 1960s. "We kept tearin' Gladiators' asses up until 1969," he noted and then added, "There are some people who just don't like each other."

77. Ameer recalled one skirmish that occurred between the youngest clique of Businessmen, called the Unborns, and the Pueblos in 1968. Afterward, some Pueblo elders spoke to some Businessmen elders about keeping their youngsters in check. This discussion was effective in avoiding further altercations.

78. *Players* is another name for street hustlers. Since demographic growth continued to change the community, the existence of more juveniles on the street made their hustling more visible. One group of players—about eight guys—coming out of the Renegades' territory had a notable member named Dusty. Dusty's brother was Jerry C., Raymond Washington's "road dog."

79. *Slippin'* meant you had screwed up and were caught at it. It often occurred when someone was on the street and unprepared for or not paying attention to developments that subsequently had a negative impact on them. It could also mean an error in judgment, thinking a person was all right who wasn't.

80. Klein (1995: 304–312) has explained how the new gang-suppression tactics of the criminal-justice system, emerging from deterrence theory, functioned in Los Angeles. Presciently, he warned that "the straightforward suppression programs may backfire." Ibid.: 310. They did.

81. Fearn et al., 2001: 331–332.

82. While the police played a central role in the get-tough suppression tactics of the criminal-justice system, with "Operation Hammer" as a very visible example, they were hardly alone. The tactics were systemwide. Within the courts, the district attorney's "Operation Hardcore" was designed to make sure that "bad" gang members were convicted and then received plenty of time. Krisberg, 2005: 164–168. "Gang enhancement" penalties—if it's "proven" that you are a gang member, you automatically get more time

for it—added time to already draconian sentences. Prisons and jails became home, forever longer periods, to ever larger numbers of street-group members. Almost impossible parole requirements—associate with gang members, violate parole, and get returned to prison—guaranteed recidivism rates would be high. In addition, California entered a law-and-order period in 1966 with the election of Ronald Reagan as governor. He readily fulfilled his campaign promises to get tough on crime, when—with little hesitation—he called in the National Guard on University of California protestors. None of these kick-their-butt and take-no-prisoner changes boded well for inner-city youth, as enhanced state suppression made their plights even more difficult.

83. We use the terms *originals* and *elders* to refer to two different groups of street-group members. The originals, among the Slausons, were youth like Chinaman, Roach, Bunchy, and Bird, and those who were their peers. They were there at the beginning or shortly thereafter. An elder was a pre-1965 street-group member who was acknowledged by an original as being part of their street group. All originals were elders, but not all elders were originals. The concepts are not mutually exclusive ranks categorizing all pre-1965 street-group youth but are reference points.

84. There are two Black South Los Angeles street groups that kept a part of their original names past 1965: the Outlaws and the 20s. The 20s neighborhood is from 20th Street through 29th Street. Both groups formed in the oldest Black neighborhoods in Los Angeles, from downtown to Jefferson Boulevard along Central Avenue. Beginning in the 1930s, when these groups formed as social clubs, into the early twenty-first century, the groups using these names transformed more than the names did. The Outlaws became the Outlaw Bloods, while the 20s became the Roman 20s and then the Rollin' 20s.

85. Data from other sets like the Businessmen, which still had some neighborhood juice, suggested similar patterns. Where the sets of elders were less unified, neighborhood anomie was greater, facilitating an even easier development of the new street groups.

86. The McCoy Boys' name was a family name. Many of their members were from a family of "real tough suckas," with McCoy as a surname, noted Bird. The McCoys, Shacks, and 76th were all from the Slauson neighborhood.

87. None of the pre-1965 street groups ever used the term *boys* in their name. The term was demeaning to them, a reminder of the inferior status they had been assigned by White people. To be referred to as "boy" was derisive, a remnant of the racism they had struggled against. The new groups were not offended by this association.

88. Some of the antagonisms that developed among the new street groups had causes similar to those of the pre-1965 groups. However, it would be a mistake to fail to recognize that additional reasons for disagreements also emerged along with the major social and economic changes affecting their communities.

89. The Avenues of South Los Angeles should not be confused with the Avenues of Highland Park. Bird contended that the Highland group began before 1960 and had no connection to the South Los Angeles group, whose name was sanctioned by Charles W., a Renegade. The sanction wasn't necessary, but it didn't hurt to have an elder say, "Yeah, all right, that's cool."

90. Bob M., a director of Roosevelt Park in the 1960s, remembered first hearing about the Avenues in 1964. He knew they considered this park their hangout, and they believed they "controlled" it during their time.

91. Teddy Bear was another founder of the Avenues. One of the best-known members of the group was Stanley "Tookie" Williams, who later became a Crip. Tookie was

convicted of murder and executed on December 13, 2005. He left behind a mixed legacy of violence and antigang children's books, books he wrote to try to keep young people out of gangs.

92. The Avenues did not find the comin'-from-the-shoulders ethic particularly applicable to themselves. Looking tough, instead of demonstrations of toughness, was the Avenues' path to identity.

93. "Sherm" was street vernacular for PCP, or phencyclidine. A synthetic drug, originally developed as an anesthetic, it is known to produce visual and auditory hallucinations in users. "Phencyclidine," Drug Enforcement Administration, Diversion Control Division, Drug and Chemical Evaluation Section, March 2020.

94. In 1987, during a lecture to one of Quicker's classes, Sergeant T. of the Compton Police Department Gang Unit reiterated that the Crips had taken their name from the British film *Tales from the Crypt*.

95. Maltin, 1989: 1046.

96. Before the film *Tales from the Crypt* appeared, there were other popularized uses of *crypt*. William M. Gaines published a horror comic book series titled *Tales from the Crypt* from 1950 to 1955. Gaines also introduced another horror comic series titled *Crime Patrol*, which changed to *The Crypt of Terror*, and had the "Crypt-Keeper" as the host of both of these series. Since these comic books predate the Crips, it is both chronologically and logically possible they could have taken their name from one of these comics. But that is not the way this myth of the Crips' name was explained in the 1980s. https://en.wikipedia.org/wiki/Tales_from_the_Crypt_(comics).

97. About the same time as the Crips' origins, a drug called "kryptonite," which just might have been some "strong-ass weed," existed in the community. There is little doubt this drug was used by some of the juveniles. In higher concentrations, the drug could be quite powerful, inducing a pleasant euphoric state. While the Superman connection is melodramatic, the evidence that the Crips took their name from a drug association is speculative. Quite likely, the name Crip and the drug kryptonite became so entangled that their actual connection has been lost. It has become convenient to explain the Crips' origin as related to the drug's existence. But this is not where their name came from.

98. The Crips have been referred to as the "Cripplers," by various sources including some of Quicker's students. Crip groups have probably held on to this characterization because it conveniently helps promote them as fierce doers of great harm. Regardless, their ability to cripple opponents was not how the name began.

99. Quicker heard the term *Cowards run in packs* from a police officer in the LAPD CRASH unit in 1984. Mike Davis writes that the term *Continuous revolution in progress* was discussed by Donald Bakeer in a paper he wrote. Bakeer was a teacher at Manual Arts High School and was told this by an OG Crip. Davis, 1990: 298, 299.

100. A cursory Google search of "Black argot" reveals a plethora of resources—articles, dictionaries, histories, current usage, and innovations—with significant material on Black linguistic creativity.

101. Of course, Black people are not the only ones to use slang or this term, but they did shorten it to "crip."

102. It also made geographic sense for Raymond to not stay with the Avenues. The Avenues emerged in the Renegade neighborhood, while Raymond lived near 76th Street and Avalon Boulevard, in the heart of the Slauson neighborhood. These neighborhoods had a historical estrangement that had not been resolved during Raymond's time.

103. Bird knew Raymond to be a "head-up fighter," preferring fists to guns, which added to his juice among his peers.

104. Another story holds that Tony S. was the first person to call Raymond a crip when he saw him on 76th Street and Wadsworth Avenue, all banged up and on his way to visit a girl he liked.

105. Neighborhood lore often has numerous variations of the same tale, and this tale is no exception. Jerry C., who was Raymond's road dog, told us that Raymond injured his arm and had it in a cast, while he (Jerry C.) had injured his leg. This tale holds that they both had been in a fight with some Avenues and were whooped up badly enough to require bandages, crutches, and casts, making them appear disabled. All of the accounts, from those who were there, conclude that Raymond and his associates were called crips because they were visibly, although temporarily, crippled from their injuries. One name frequently connected with Raymond Washington at the fight and with the founding of the Crips is Raymond Burns. The two Raymonds knew each other because they were both in Bunchy's teen post. But Burns was a year or two Washington's senior and thus not exactly a peer, according to Bubbles S., who was also a member of that teen post. Bubbles explained that Burns became an Avenue but was never a Crip. Ameer reported that by 1989, Raymond Burns had left street-group life altogether to become a Muslim.

106. Cureton, 2009; Howell and Moore, 2010: 12.

107. Davis and Wiener, 2020.

108. One group's rowdiness is another's idea of fun. This is especially the case for intergenerational assessment of these concepts. Adults regularly exaggerate the gravity of the misdeeds of contemporary juveniles while underestimating the gravity of their own.

109. None of the new groups that came out of the Businessmen or Gladiator neighborhoods became cliques of these sets either, for many of the same reasons the new groups didn't become Slauson cliques. Ameer claimed the new groups weren't interested in becoming a clique of the Businessmen. He opined: "It wasn't that they [the Businessmen] didn't allow it; they [the new groups] didn't pick it up. It [becoming a Businessman] wasn't feasible."

110. Ameer confirmed that the new groups' inability to embrace the Businessmen's ideology or their lack of interest in doing so were reasons why the groups didn't become Businessmen.

111. Some members of the new sets were relatives—sons, little brothers, nephews, cousins—of those from the earlier sets. Although not part of the early sets, they were family and probably lived close enough to the members to observe them and learn ideology the early set members had tried to hide.

112. Different phrases have become associated with the Crips in an effort to show how dangerous they were. Self-promotion suggests that the Crips most likely began the phrase. Sometimes these phrases were created elsewhere and then adopted by the Crips. One of those phrases is "Walkin' triple and lookin' to cripple." Bird recalled this phrase being in use since at least the early 1960s and quite likely earlier. It was used in the old Los Angeles County Jail by the jail trustees, who would be lining up the inmates outside their cells to prepare for the approaching jailers' inspection. As the jailers came walking, the trustees would begin with, "Walkin' double, lookin' for trouble," followed by "Walkin' triple and lookin' to cripple." The Crips may have used these phrases to suit their image, but they were not the originators.

113. In the *Crips and Bloods* (2009) documentary, the narrator observes, "Much of the knowledge on how they formed has been taken to the grave." This passage suggests death has deprived us of much information. While true, this shouldn't be interpreted to mean that we are therefore unable to know or to figure out how they formed. We were

able to speak to many of those who did know about formation, because they were there, while the Kev Mack YouTube videos provide an important supplement.

114. Davis, 1990: 301.
115. Ibid.: 300.
116. Krikorianwrites.com, 2014.
117. Bird spoke with a number of the individuals who had participated in the fight at the Palladium to get the details on what had actually happened from their perspective. He found that the antagonisms generating the fight had been around a long time, because the high schools the groups identified with had been historic rivals. The fight was not personal. The juvenile who was killed had been with a group of youth from the West-Side. As their group was leaving the Palladium, they noticed another group across the street that they recognized as being from the East-Side—by the Fremont High School letter jackets a couple of the juveniles were wearing. Unfriendly words were exchanged between members of the groups, resulting in a fight during which the lawyer's son, who was from the West-Side, was killed. Afterward, the media reported that the fight was over a robbery to steal a leather coat. While it is possible that a leather coat was stolen during the melee, the coat was not the reason for the altercation—the reason was high school rivalry between the groups. Leather coats had been a symbol of pride among Black males since at least 1964, when some Slauson notables started wearing them. Some of these leathers had been ripped off from Wilson's House of Suede, a major retailer at the time of fine leather garments. When the Panthers arrived in 1966, they also started wearing leather jackets, as a symbol of strength and beauty. The Crips and Avenues saw the Slausons and Panthers wearing the cool-looking leathers and wore them as well. A number of Crips and Avenues who had leather coats had stolen them from individuals on the street. The Slausons and Panthers considered it wrong to steal from individuals, while taking them from a large retailer, as some Slausons had done, was acceptable.
118. Quoted in Krikorianwrites.com, 2014.
119. Ibid.: 3.
120. Davis and Wiener, 2020: 625–630.
121. Personal communication with Kumasi, November 4, 1989.
122. Kev Mack, in his many documentary videos, shows how the Crip name became adopted by various already existing street groups, by assorted means that ranged from intimidation to imitation. He demonstrates how newer groups easily created a group name with something Crip in it. This selection, on South Los Angeles, are from YouTube, *Kev Mack Videos*: "Too Pretty Kenney: Original Corner Poccet Crips," May 9, 2018; "History of Compton Crips-Part Two," June 5, 2018; "Presto from Corner Poccet Compton Crips-Part 2," November 29, 2019; "Jackamoe-Campanella Park Piru Origins and History of Comtons Piru 1970s," February 6, 2018.
123. Mertonian theory, of local and cosmopolitan, has given form to our analysis. Merton, 1964: 387–420.
124. Hagedorn, 2008.
125. Mari, 2020: 32.
126. One reason Vietnam vets had a greater chance of going to prison than their World War II counterparts was the greater availability of drugs in the jungles and cities where they fought and in the neighborhoods they returned to. Many vets returned addicted to heroin, a drug they'd found plentiful in Vietnam. Heroin eased the pain of war, there and at home. For these vets, unable to get clean, prison awaited. An essential analysis of heroin and its history, political implications, effect on, and consequences for the U.S. military can be found in McCoy's (1972) well-researched analysis.

127. Aviv, 2017, provides an insightful discussion of the various negative effects racism, imprisonment, and the denial of legitimate opportunity has had on the lives of Black males, their families, and their communities, as experienced by a former BPP member.

128. Hinton and Cook (2021: 2.1), in a major contribution, have shown how all elements of government have historically used the American "anti-black punitive tradition" to create a criminal justice system whose central focus has been control of Black people through criminalizing and mass incarceration.

129. And great fortunes continue to be made in America by wealthy and shrewd businesspeople and professionals willing to bend and break the law. Keefe, 2017, for example, documents how the opioid crisis, dominating American society in 2017, was directly tied to the Sackler family's Purdue Pharma Company's promotion of OxyContin as a nonaddictive pain reliever, knowing full well that their marketing was contradicted by their research. Mendacity has and continues to generate and maintain fortunes.

130. It has been noted that behind every fortune in America lies a crime. More accurately, there were probably numerous crimes and criminals behind those fortunes. In his essential analysis of the capitalists who built America, Josephson (1962) quite adroitly shows that none of them were beyond breaking the law when it got in the way of profits. Termed *The Robber Barons*, Josephson's analysis of their misdeeds was published during the height of the Great Depression in 1934. Crime for profit helped build America, and it has helped build the Crips and Bloods. But because crime is class based, as Reiman (1979) explains, the "rich get richer and the poor get prison," when involved.

131. The 1990 film *Heat Wave*, directed by Kevin Hooks, about the Watts Rebellion, and reported on by Bob Richardson, the first Black reporter for the *Los Angeles Times*, notes that there were 364 "gang homicides" in Watts in 1989.

132. Bird noted that *blood* is a word that was around long before Terry's (1984) book on Blacks serving in Vietnam was published. It meant "brother," through kinship or friendship, and perhaps both. The same is true for the term *cuzz*. It might mean "cousin" but also a brother. Both of these words are terms of endearment for a cherished other soul. The first Blood gang was the Pirus from Piru Street in Compton. Most street groups in the original Crip neighborhoods of South Los Angeles had been enemies to most Compton street groups for years. It is therefore not surprising that the new groups coming up in Compton would, at least initially, decline to call themselves Crips. *Cuzz* and *Blood* are both old terms that express an affiliation more like family—deeper than just friendship. Blood is a logical choice for the groups following in the wake of the Crips, especially so because of its historical association with Black culture. As is true almost everywhere in gang research, care must be exercised in issuing broad generalizations. While Blood was a logical choice for the Pirus and other Compton cliques, there also arose groups of Compton Crips—a variation on what appeared to be a general rule. Social phenomena do the damnedest things. They just refuse to follow the rules and fit into the categories we social scientists so carefully establish for them.

133. Peralta, 2009.

APPENDIX

1. Bird recalled that during the time he was a student at Riis, members of various sets would sit around on the campus playground in exclusive groupings. The largest group was always composed of the multiple sets from Watts.

2. We are not so presumptuous to assume we have created a complete list of all the many groups that existed in South Los Angeles prior to 1965. Besides being around for

short periods, perhaps as briefly as a semester, group names were so capricious that two or more names might have existed for the same or mostly the same group of youth at mostly the same time. We have tried to accurately locate neighborhoods, high schools, racial and ethnic composition, and periods. Other reasonable researchers may find fault; after all, opinions on these issues, even then, varied. Census data here don't exist.

Bibliography

Alonzo, Alejandro A., "Racialized Identities and the Formation of Black Gangs in Los Angeles." *Urban Geography* 24, no. 7 (2004): 658–674.
Alonzo, Alex. "Out of the Void: Street Gangs in Black Los Angeles." In *Black Los Angeles: American Dreams and Racial Realities*, edited by Darnell Hunt and Ana-Christina Ramon, 140–167. New York: New York University Press, 2010.
Alpert, Adrienne. "LAPD Gang Reports Investigation." *Los Angeles Times* (online), February 17, 2020.
Alterman, Eric. "The American Berserk: Accurately Describing the Trump Presidency Stretches the Limits of our Imagination." *The Nation*, May 4–11, 2020, 1–11.
Ambrose, Stephen E. *Band of Brothers*. 2nd ed. New York: Simon & Schuster, 2001.
Anderson, Elijah. *Code of the Street: Decency, Violence, and the Moral Life of the Inner City*. New York: W. W. Norton, 1999.
———. *Streetwise: Race, Class, and Change in an Urban Community*. Chicago: University of Chicago Press, 1990.
Angelou, Maya. *The Heart of a Woman*. London: Virago, 1986.
Asbury, Herbert. *The Gangs of New York: An Informal History of the Underworld*. New York: Capricorn Books, 1970. (The original edition by Alfred A. Knopf was published in 1927–1928.)
Aviv, Rachel. "Surviving Solitary." *New Yorker*, January 16, 2017, 54–67.
Bakan, David. "Adolescence in America: From Idea to Social fact." *Daedalus* 100, no. 4 (Fall 1971): 979–995.
Baldwin, James. *Go Tell It on the Mountain*. New York: Delta, 1952–1953.
———. *Notes of a Native Son*. New York: Beacon, 1984.
Barmaki, Reza. "On the Origin of 'Labelling Theory': Frank Tannenbaum and the Chicago School of Sociology." *Deviant Behavior* 40, no. 2 (2019): 256–271.
Barnhart, Robert K. *The Barnhart Concise Dictionary of Etymology: The Origins of American English Words*. Unabridged edition. New York: Harper Resource, 1988.

Batani-Khalfani, Akil S. *The History of Slauson Village: The Organized Gang Set.* Unpublished class paper, California State University Dominguez Hills, 1984.
Becker, Howard S. "Becoming a Marijuana User." In *The Marijuana Papers*, edited by David Solomon, 34–65. Indianapolis: Bobbs-Merrill, 1966. (Like many classics, this is an adaption of an original article, which first appeared in the *American Journal of Sociology* 59 [November 1953]: 235–242.)
Beirne, Piers, and James W. Messerschmidt. *Criminology: A Sociological Approach.* 5th ed. New York: Oxford University Press, 2011.
Bell, Kenneth M. "The Black Gang Phenomenon." *The Dispatcher: The Official Publication of the Association for Los Angeles Deputy Sheriffs*, special edition, "Battling the Plague of Gangs in Our Community," 44–51, n.d. (Date unknown, but Gil Garcetti [1992–2000] was Los Angeles County district attorney at the time of publication.)
Bendix, Reinhard. *Max Weber: An Intellectual Portrait.* New York: Doubleday Anchor, 1962.
Berman, Arthur. "Juvenile Gangs' Peace Talks Held Incentive to Violence." *Los Angeles Times*, April 1, 1963, 1, 8.
Bernstein, Saul. *Youth on the Streets: Work with Alienated Youth Groups.* New York: Association, 1964.
Bernstein, Susie, Lynn Cooper, Elliott Currie, Jon Frappier, Sidney Harring, Tony Platt, Pat Poyner, Gerda Ray, Joy Scruggs, and Larry Trujillo. *The Iron Fist and the Velvet Glove: An Analysis of the U.S. Police.* 2nd ed. Berkeley, CA: Center for Research on Criminal Justice, 1977.
Binder, Arnold, Gilbert Geis, and Bruce Dickson. *Juvenile Delinquency: Historical, Cultural, Legal Perspectives.* New York: Macmillan, 1988.
Bing, Leon. *Do or Die.* New York: Harper Collins, 1991.
Bjerregaard, Beth. "Antigang Legislation and Its Potential Impact: The Promises and Pitfalls." In Egley et al., *Modern Gang Reader*, 318–393.
Black Panther Party. "What We Want: What We Believe." White paper in *Black Panther Party Platform and Program*, October 1966.
Black, Timothy. *When a Heart Turns Rock Solid: The Lives of Three Puerto Rican Brothers on and off the Streets.* New York: Vintage Books, 2009.
Bloch, Herbert A., and Arthur Niederhoffer. *The Gang: A Study in Adolescent Behavior.* New York: Philosophical Library, 1958.
Blumenstein, Alfred. "Youth Violence, Guns, and the Illicit Drug Industry." *Journal of Criminal Law and Criminology* 86, no. 4 (1995): 10–36.
Bogardus, Emory S. *The City Boy and His Problems.* Los Angeles: House of Ralston, Rotary Club of Los Angeles, 1926.
———. "Gangs of Mexican-American Youth." *Sociology and Social Research* 28 (September 1943): 55–66.
———. "Second Generation Mexicans." *Sociology and Social Research* 13 (1929): 276–283.
Bordua, David J. "Delinquent Subcultures: Sociological Interpretations of Gang Delinquency." *Annals of the American Academy of Political and Social Science* 336, no. (1961): 119–136.
Braverman, Harry. *Labor and Monopoly Capital: The Degradation of Work in the Twentieth Century.* New York: Monthly Review, 1974.
Brotherton, David C., and Luis Barrios. *The Almighty Latin King and Queen Nation: Street Politics and the Transformation of a New York Street Gang.* New York: Columbia University Press, 2004.

———. "Beyond Social Reproduction: Bringing Resistance Back in Gang Theory." *Theoretical Criminology* 12, no. 1 (2008): 55–77.
———. *Youth Street Gangs: A Critical Appraisal.* London: Routledge, Taylor & Francis, 2015.
Brown, B. Bradford, and James Larson. "Contextual Influences on Adolescent Development." In *Handbook of Adolescent Psychology*, Vol. 2. New York: John Wiley & Sons, 2009.
Brown, Dee. *Bury My Heart at Wounded Knee: An Indian History of the American West.* New York: Holt, Rinehart and Winston, 1970.
Brown, Elaine. *A Taste of Power: A Black Woman's Story.* New York: Anchor Doubleday, 1992.
Brown, Richard Maxwell. "Historical Patterns of American Violence." In *Violence in America: Historical and Comparative Perspectives*, rev. ed., edited by Hugh Davis Graham and Ted Robert Gurr, 19–48. Beverly Hills, CA: Sage, 1979.
———. "Historical Patterns of Violence in America." In *The History of Violence in America*, edited by Hugh Davis Graham and Ted Robert Gurr. New York: Bantam Books, 1970.
Brown, Waln K. "Black Female Gangs in Philadelphia." In Chesney-Lind and Hagedorn, *Female Gangs in America*, 57–63.
Bunch, Lonnie G. "A Past Not Necessarily Prologue: The Afro-American in Los Angeles." In *20th Century Los Angeles: Power, Promotion, and Social Conflict*, edited by Norman M. Klein and Martin J. Schiesl, 99–130. Claremont, CA: Regina Books, 1990.
Bursik, Robert J., Jr., and Harold G. Grasmick. "Defining Gangs and Gang Behavior." In Klein, Maxson, and Miller, *Modern Gang Reader*, 1995a, 8–13.
———. "The Effect of Neighborhood Dynamics on Gang Behavior." In Klein, Maxson, and Miller, *Modern Gang Reader*, 1995b, 114–124.
California Council on Criminal Justice. *State Task Force on Youth Gang Violence, Final Report*, Sacramento, January 1986.
California Office of the Attorney General. *Report on Youth Gang Violence in California.* Prepared by the Attorney General's Youth Gang Task Force, Sacramento, CA, 1981.
Callan, Mary Ann. "Girl Gangsters Thrive on Hate." *Los Angeles Times*, August 12, 1963b, B1, B8.
———."Lives Smashed in Girl Gangs." *Los Angeles Times*, August 11, 1963a, B1, B3.
Cameron, Mary Owen. *The Booster and the Snitch.* New York: Free Press, 1964.
Campbell, Anne. *The Girls in the Gang.* New York: Basil Blackwell, 1984.
Chambliss, William J. *On the Take: From Petty Crooks to Presidents.* Bloomington: Indiana University Press, 1988.
———."The Saints and the Roughnecks." In *The Children of Ishmael*, edited by Barry Krisberg and James Austin, 294–308. Palo Alto, CA: Mayfield, 1978.
Chambliss, William J., and Richard H. Nagasawa. "On the Validity of Official Statistics: A Comparative Study of White, Black, and Japanese High-School Boys." *Journal of Research in Crime and Delinquency* 6 (1969): 71–77.
Chambliss, William J., and Robert Seidman. *Law, Order, and Power.* 2nd ed. Reading, MA: Addison-Wesley, 1982.
Chesney-Lind, Meda, and John M. Hagedorn, eds. *Female Gangs in America: Essays on Girls, Gangs and Gender.* Chicago: Lake View, 1999.
Chesney-Lind, Meda, and Randall G. Shelden. *Girls, Delinquency, and Juvenile Justice.* 3rd ed. Belmont, CA: Wadsworth, 2004.

Churchill, Ward, and Jim Vander Wall. *Agents of Repression: The FBI's Secret Wars against the Black Panther Party and the American Indian Movement.* Boston: South End, 1990.

Clark, Ramsey. *Crime in America: Observations on Its Nature, Causes, Prevention and Control.* New York: Simon and Schuster, 1970.

Cliff, Jimmy. *The Harder They Come.* LP recording, originally released on Island ILPS 9202, July 7, 1972.

Cohen, Albert K. *Delinquent Boys: The Culture of the Gang.* New York: Free Press, 1955.

Cohen, John. *The Essential Lenny Bruce.* New York: Ballantine Books, 1997.

Coleman, James William. *The Criminal Elite: Understanding White-Collar Crime.* 6th ed. New York: Worth, 2006.

Conot, Robert. *Rivers of Blood, Years of Darkness.* New York: Bantam, 1967.

Contreras, Randol. *The Stickup Kids: Race, Drugs, Violence, and the American Dream.* Berkeley: University of California Press, 2013.

Cox Richardson, Heather. *How the South Won the Civil War: Oligarchy, Democracy, and the Continuing Fight for the Soul of America.* New York: Oxford University Press, 2020.

Crews, Gordon A., and Reid H. Montgomery Jr. *Chasing Shadows: Confronting Juvenile Violence in America.* Upper Saddle River, NJ: Prentice Hall, 2001.

Cureton, Steven R. "Something Wicked This Way Comes: A Historical Account of Black Gangsterism Offers Wisdom and Warning for African American Leadership." *Journal of Black Studies* 40 (2009): 347–361.

Davis, Mike. *City of Quartz: Excavating the Future in Los Angeles.* London: Verso, 1990.

———. "Foreword." In Hagedorn, *A World of Gangs*, xi–xvii.

Davis, Mike, and Jon Wiener. *Set the Night on Fire: L.A. in the Sixties.* London: Verso, 2020.

Dawley, David. *A Nation of Lords: The Autobiography of the Vice Lords.* New York: Anchor Books, 1973.

Decker, Scott H. "'I'm Down for a Jihad': How 100 Years of Gang Research Can Inform the Study of Terrorism, Radicalization and Extremism." *Perspectives on Terrorism* 9 (February 2015): 104–112.

Decker, Scott H., and Kimberly Kempf-Leonard. "Constructing Gangs: The Social Definition of Youth Activities." In Klein, Maxson, and Miller, *Modern Gang Reader*, 14–23.

Decker, Scott H., and David C. Pyrooz. "Gangs, Terrorism, and Radicalization." *Journal of Strategic Security* 4 (October 2011): 151–166.

Decker, Scott H., and Barrik Van Winkle. "The History of Gang Research." In *Modern Gang Reader*, 2nd ed., edited by Miller, Maxson, and Klein, 15–21. Los Angeles: Roxbury, 2001.

———. *Life in the Gang: Family, Friends, and Violence.* Cambridge: Cambridge University Press, 1996.

Deming, W. Edwards. *Statistical Adjustments of Data.* New York: Dover, 2011.

Derber, Charles. *The Wilding of America: Money, Mayhem, and the New American Dream.* 4th ed. New York: Worth, 2007.

Dillon, Michelle. "Talcott Parsons and Robert Merton, Functionalism and Modernization." In *Introduction to Sociological Theory: Theorists, Concepts, and Their Applicability to the Twenty-First Century*, 156–157. New York: Wiley, 2013.

Domhoff, G. William. *Who Rules America?* Englewood Cliffs, NJ: Prentice-Hall, 1967.

Douglass, Frederick. In *The New Yale Book of Quotations*, edited by Fred R. Shapiro. New Haven: Yale University Press, 2021.

Durkheim, Emile. *The Division of Labor in Society.* Toronto: Free Press, 1966a. (Original English publication by Macmillan, 1933.)

———. *The Rules of Sociological Method.* New York: Free Press, 1966. (Original English publication by the University of Chicago, 1938.)
Egley, Arlen, Jr., Cheryl L. Maxson, Jody Miller, and Malcolm W. Klein. *The Modern Gang Reader.* 3rd ed. Los Angeles: Roxbury, 2006.
Eldridge, Ronald. "The Dark Circle: A Historical Look at Black Street Gangs in Los Angeles." Unpublished class paper, California State University Dominguez Hills, 1975.
———. "Los Angeles Street Gangs: Fist to Uzi." Unpublished class paper, California State University Dominguez Hills, 1985.
Elliott, Delbert S., and Suzanne S. Ageton. "Reconciling Race and Class Differences in Self-Reported and Official Estimates of Delinquency." *American Sociological Review* 45 (1980): 95–110.
Ellison, Ralph. *Invisible Man.* New York: Signet, New American Library, 1952.
Endore, Guy. *The Sleepy Lagoon Mystery.* Los Angeles: Unidos Books and Periodicals, 1978.
Erikson, Erik H. *Identity, Youth, and Crisis.* New York: W. W. Norton, 1968.
Erikson, Kai T. *Wayward Puritans: A Study in the Sociology of Deviance.* New York: John Wiley & Sons, 1966.
Erickson, Maynard L., and Gary F. Jensen. "Delinquency Is Still Group Behavior! Toward Revitalizing the Group Premise in the Sociology of Deviance." In *Juvenile Delinquency: Classic and Contemporary Readings,* edited by William E. Thompson and Jack E. Bynum, 281–296. Boston: Allyn and Bacon, 1991.
Esbensen, Finn-Aage, David Huizinga, and A. W. Weiher. "Gang and Non-Gang Youth: Differences in Explanatory Factors." *Journal of Contemporary Criminal Justice* 9 (1993): 94–116.
Esbensen, Finn-Aage, Dana Peterson, Terrance J. Taylor, and Adrienne Freng. *Youth Violence: Sex and Race Differences in Offending, Victimization, and Gang Membership.* Philadelphia: Temple University Press, 2010.
Esbensen, Finn-Aage, and L. Thomas Winfree Jr. "Race and Gender Differences between Gang and Nongang Youths." In Miller, Maxson, and Klein, *Modern Gang Reader,* 106–120.
Fearn, Noelle E., Scott H. Decker, and G. David Curry. "Public Policy Responses to Gangs: Evaluating the Outcomes." In Miller, Maxson, and Klein, *Modern Gang Reader,* 330–343.
Federal Bureau of Investigation. *Crime in the United States.* Department of Justice, Uniform Crime Reporting Program, Washington, DC, 1930–1969.
Felson, Marcus. *Crime and Nature.* Los Angeles: Sage, 2006.
Fernandez, Johanna. *The Young Lords: A Radical History.* Chapel Hill: University of North Carolina Press, 2019.
Fishman, Laura T. "Black Female Gang Behavior: An Historical and Ethnographic Perspective." In Chesney-Lind and Hagedorn, *Female Gangs in America,* 64–84.
Flamming, Douglas. *Bound for Freedom: Black Los Angeles in Jim Crow America.* Berkeley: University of California Press, 2005.
Fleisher, Mark. "Inside the Fremont Hustlers." In Miller, Maxson, and Klein, *Modern Gang Reader,* 94–103.
Fogelson, Robert M. "White on Black: A Critique of the McCone Commission Report on the Los Angeles Riots." In *Mass Violence in America: The Los Angeles Riots,* edited by Robert M. Fogelson, 113–143. New York: Arno Press and the New York Times, 1969.
Fraser, Alistair. *Urban Legends: Gang Identity in the Post-Industrial City.* London: Oxford University Press, 2015.
Frias, Gus. *Barrio Warriors: Homeboys of Peace.* Los Angeles: Diaz, 1982.

Galliher, John F., and James L. MC Cartney. "The Influence of Funding Agencies on Juvenile Delinquency Research." *Social Problems* 21, no. 1 (Summer 1973): 77–90.

Gardell, Matthias. *In the Name of Elijah Muhammad: Louis Farahhan and the Nation of Islam*. Durham: Duke University Press, 1996.

Gates, Daryl F. *Chief: My Life in the LAPD*. New York: Bantam Books, 1992.

Geis, Gilbert. "Foreword." In Miller, Maxson, and Klein, *Modern Gang Reader*, ix–xii.

Glasgow, Douglas G. *The Black Underclass: Poverty, Unemployment and Entrapment of Ghetto Youth*. New York: Vintage Books, 1981.

Graham, Hugh D., and Ted R. Gurr, eds. *The History of Violence in America: A Report to the National Commission on the Causes and Prevention of Violence*. New York: Bantam Books, 1970.

Gregory, Dick. *Nigger: An Autobiography*. New York: E. P. Dutton & Co., 1965. A Pocket Cardinal Edition.

Grier, William H., and Price M. Cobbs. *Black Rage*. New York: Basic Books, 1968.

Guzman, Joseph. "Hispanic Gang Presentation." *P.O.S.T Gang Awareness Course*. Undated paper. (Guzman is a sergeant with the LASD, OSS Street Gangs.)

Hagedorn, John M. *The Insane Chicago Way: The Daring Plan by Chicago Gangs to Create a Spanish Mafia*. Chicago: University of Chicago Press, 2015.

———. *People and Folks: Gangs, Crime and the Underclass in a Rustbelt City*. Chicago: Lake View, 1988.

———. *People and Folks: Gangs, Crime and the Underclass in a Rustbelt City*. 2nd ed. Chicago: Lake View, 1998.

———. *A World of Gangs: Armed Young Men and Gangsta Culture*. Minneapolis: University of Minnesota Press, 2008.

Hall, Stanley G. *Adolescence: Its Psychology and Its Relations to Physiology, Anthropology, Sociology, Sex, Crime, Religion and Education*. Hong Kong: Hesperides, 2006. (Originally published by Appleton, in 2 vols., 1904.)

Haller, Mark. "Bootleggers and American Gambling, 1920–1950." In *Gambling in America*, edited by Commission on Review of National Policy toward Gambling, 102–143. Washington, DC: U.S. Government Printing Office, 1976.

Hamlet. Act 1, Scene 5. Kidadl Team. "40 Famous Hamlet Quotes by William Shakespeare." Kidadl.com, November 4, 2021.

Hamm, Mark S. *American Skinheaads: The Criminology and Control of Hate Crime*. Westport, CT: Praeger Series in Criminology and Crime Control Policy, 1993.

Haney, B., and M. Gold. "The Juvenile Delinquent Nobody Knows." *Psychology Today*, September 1973, 49–55.

Harrington, Michael. *The Other America: Poverty in the United States*. New York. Macmillan, 1964.

Harris, Mary G. *Cholas: Latino Girls and Gangs*. New York: AMS, 1988.

Helmer, John. *Drugs and Minority Oppression*. New York: Seabury, 1975.

Herbers, John. "Special Introduction." In *The History of Violence in America: A Report to the National Commission on the Causes and Prevention of Violence*, edited by Hugh D. Graham and Ted R. Gurr, xiii–xix. New York: Bantam Books, 1970.

Hewitt, Mary Jane. "The Long Black Line." In *Los Angeles, 1781–1981*, edited by Larry L. Meyer, 12–17. San Francisco: California Historical Society, 1981.

Hindelang, Michael J., Travis Hirschi, and J. Weis. "Correlates of Delinquency: The Illusion of Discrepancy between Self-Report and Official Measures." *American Sociological Review* 44 (1979): 995–1014.

Hinton, Elizabeth, and DeAnza Cook. "The Mass Criminalization of Black Americans: A Historical Overview." *Annual Review of Criminology* 4 (2021): 261–286.
Holloway, Kali. "Justice Long Due: The MORE Act Is Necessary—but Not Enough." *The Nation*, January 11–18, 2021, 7–8.
Hooks, Kevin, dir. *Heat Wave*. Los Angeles: Avnet/Kerner Productions, 1990.
Horne, Gerald. *Fire This Time: The Watts Uprising and the 1960s*. Charlottesville, VA: Da Capo, 1997.
Howard, John, and William McCord. "Watts: The Revolt and After." In William McCord, John Howard, Bernard Friedberg, and Edwin Harwood, *Life Styles in the Black Ghetto*, 52–68. New York: W. W. Norton, 1969.
Howell, James C., and Elizabeth Griffiths. *Gangs in American Communities*. 3rd ed. Newbury Park, CA: Sage, 2018.
Howell, James C., and John P. Moore. "History of Street Gangs in the United States." Bureau of Justice Assistance, OJJDP. *National Gang Center Bulletin* 4 (May 2010).
Huston, Aletha C., Halford H. Fairchild, and Edward Donnerstein. *Big World, Small Screen: The Role of Television in American Life*. Lincoln: University of Nebraska Press, 1992.
Ianni, Francis A. J. *Black Mafia: Ethnic Succession in Organized Crime*. New York. Pocket Book Edition, 1974.
"The Infamous Hollywood Leather Jacket Murder." Krikorianwrites.com/blog/?tag=Palladium. December 1, 2014.
Irwin, John. *The Jail: Managing the Underclass in American Society*. Berkeley: University of California Press, 1985.
Ivory, Dolores. "Crime Comes of Age." *Los Angeles Sentinel*, January 28, 1960.
Jackson, Kenneth T. *The Crabgrass Frontier: The Suburbanization of the United States*. New York: Oxford University Press, 1985.
Jackson, Robert K., and Wesley D. McBride. *Understanding Street Gangs*. Sacramento, CA: Custom, 1985.
Jankowski, Martin S. *Islands in the Streets: Gangs and American Urban Society*. Berkeley: University of California Press, 1991.
Jensen, Gary F., and Dean G. Rojek. *Delinquency and Youth Crime*. 3rd ed. Prospect Heights, IL: Waveland, 1998.
———. *Delinquency and Youth Crime*. 4th ed. Long Grove, IL: Waveland, 2009.
Josephson, Matthew. *The Robber Barons: The Great American Capitalists, 1861–1901*. New York: Harcourt, Brace, & World, 1962. (Originally published in 1934.)
Kahloon, Idrees. "The Leveler: Thomas Piketty Goes Global in 'Capital and Ideology.'" *New Yorker*, March 9, 2020, 75–78.
Kappeler, Victor E., and Gary W. Potter. *The Mythology of Crime and Criminal Justice*. 4th ed. Long Grove, IL: Waveland, 2005.
Katz, Jack. *Seductions of Crime: A Chilling Exploration of the Criminal Mind—from Juvenile Delinquency to Cold-Blooded Murder*. New York: Basic Books, 1988.
Katz, William Loren. *The Black West*. 3rd ed. Seattle: Open Hand, 1987.
Keefe, Patrick Radeen. "Empire of Pain: The Sackler Family's Ruthless Promotion of Opioids Generated Billions of Dollars—and Millions of Addicts." *New Yorker*, October 30, 2017, 34–49.
Keiser, R. Lincoln. *The Vice Lords: Warriors of the Streets*. New York: Holt, Rinehart and Winston, 1969.
Kerner, Otto. *Report of the National Advisory Commission on Civil Disorders*. New York: Bantam Books, 1968.

Kinard, John, James Cantlen, Raymond Robinson, Robert W. Fults, Arthurs G. Coons, and Joseph E. Haring. *Migration and the Southern California Economy.* Report no. 12, Southern California Research Council, Occidental College, Los Angeles, CA, 1964.

King, Charles. *Gods of the Upper Air: How a Circle of Renegade Anthropologists Reinvented Race, Sex, and Gender in the Twentieth Century.* New York: Doubleday, 2019.

Klein, Malcolm W., ed. "Attempting Gang Control by Suppression: The Misuse of Deterrence Principles." In Klein, Maxson, and Miller, *Modern Gang Reader,* 304–312.

———. *Chasing after Street Gangs: A Forty-Year Journey.* Upper Saddle River, NJ: Pearson Prentice Hall, 2007.

———. *Juvenile Gangs in Context: Theory, Research, and Action.* Englewood Cliffs, NJ: Prentice-Hall, 1967.

———. "Street Gangs: A Cross-National Perspective." In Egley et al., *Modern Gang Reader,* 104–116.

———. *Street Gangs and Street Workers.* Englewood Cliffs, NJ: Prentice-Hall, 1971.

Klein, Malcolm W., and Cheryl L. Maxson. *Street Gang Patterns and Politics.* New York: Oxford University Press, 2006.

Klein, Malcolm W., Cheryl L. Maxson, and Jody Miller, eds. *The Modern Gang Reader.* 1st ed. Los Angeles: Roxbury, 1995.

Knox, George W. *An Introduction to Gangs.* 4th ed. Chicago: New Chicago School Press, 1998.

Kolbert, Elizabeth. "The Spread: How Pandemics Shape Human History." *New Yorker,* April 6, 2020, 58–61.

Kramer, Dale, and Madeline Karr. *Teen-Age Gangs.* New York: Henry Holt, 1953.

Krisberg, Barry A. "Gang Youth and Hustling: The Psychology of Survival." In *The Children of Ishmael,* edited by Barry Krisberg and James Austen, 243–257. Palo Alto, CA: Mayfield, 1978.

———. *Juvenile Justice: Redeeming Our Children.* Newbury Park, CA: Sage, 2005.

Krisberg, Barry A., and James Austen. *The Children of Ishmael: Critical Perspectives on Juvenile Justice.* Palo Alto, CA: Mayfield, 1978.

Kropotkin, Petr. *Mutual Aid: A Factor of Evolution.* Boston: Extending Horizons Books, 1914. (Originally published in 1902, the 1914 edition was made possible by Ashley Montagu.)

Lamoureux, Aimee. "The Rise and Fall of Boss Tweed's Tammany Hall." Allthatsinteresting.com/boss-tweed-tammany-hall, September 3, 2019.

LEAA/OJP Retrospective: 30 Years of Federal Support to State and Local Criminal Justice. U.S. Department of Justice, Office of Justice Programs, Washington, DC, 1996.

Lemert, Edwin. *Social Pathology.* New York: McGraw-Hill, 1951.

Levy, Ariel. "Trial by Twitter." *New Yorker,* August 5, 2013, 38–49.

Lewis, Robert. "The Negro Migration to Los Angeles 1900–1946." *Negro History Bulletin,* February 1956, 110–113.

Liazos, Alexander. "The Poverty of the Sociology of Deviance: Nuts, Sluts, and Preverts." *Social Problems* 20, no. 1 (1972): 103–120.

Liebow, Elliot. *Tally's Corner: A Study of Negro Streetcorner Men.* Boston: Little, Brown, 1967.

Lindenmeyer, Otto. *Black History: Lost, Stolen, or Strayed.* New York: Avon Books, 1970.

Lopez, Jose M. *Gangs: Casualties in an Undeclared War.* 2nd ed. LGR Publishers, 2007.

Los Angeles Sheriff's Department. *News Advisory Document: LASD Statistics: 1960–2012.* lasdnews.net/CrimeStats/cms1_189076.pdf, 2017.

Luna, Beatrice, Keith R. Thulborn, Douglas P. Munoz, Elisha P. Merriam, Krista E. Garver, Nancy J. Minshaw, Matcheri S. Keshavan, Christopher R. Genovese, William F. Eddy, and John A. Sweeney. "Maturation of Widely Distributed Brain Functions Sub-serves Cognitive Development." *NeuroImage* 13 (2001): 786–793.

Lyman, Michael D., and Gary Potter. *Organized Crime*. Upper Saddle River, NJ: Prentice-Hall, 2004.

Mac Isaac, John. *Half the Fun Was Getting There*. Englewood Cliffs, NJ: Prentice-Hall, 1968.

Malcolm X. "The Ballot Or The Bullet." In *From The Movement Toward Revolution*, edited by Bruce Franklin, 13–21. New York: Van Nostrand Reinhold, 1971.

Males, Michael. "The New Demons: Ordinary Teens," *Los Angeles Times*, April 21, 2002, M6.

Maltin, Leonard. *Movie and Video Guide*. New York: Signet, 1997.

Mari, Francesca. "A Lonely Occupation: The Homeless People Guarding Empty Houses in a Broken Real-Estate Market." *New Yorker*, December 7, 2020, 30–35.

Marx, Karl. *Capital*. Vol 1. Moscow: Progress, 1887.

Massey, Douglas S., and Nancy A. Denton. *American Apartheid: Segregation and the Making of the Underclass*. Cambridge: Harvard University Press, 1993.

Massoglia, Michael, and Christopher Uggen. "Settling Down and Aging Out: Toward an Interactionist Theory of Desistence and the Transition to Adulthood." *American Journal of Sociology* 116, no. 2 (September 2010): 543–582.

Mattick, Hans W., and Nathan S. Caplan. "Stake Animals, Loud Talking, and Leadership in Do-Nothing and Do-Something Situations." In *Juvenile Gangs in Context: Theory, Research, and Action*, edited by Malcolm W. Klein, 106–119. Englewood Cliffs, NJ: Prentice-Hall, 1967.

Matza, David. *Delinquency and Drift*. New York: John Wiley & Sons, 1964.

Maxson, Cheryl L., Arlen Egley Jr., Jody Miller, and Malcolm W. Klein. *The Modern Gang Reader*. 4th ed. New York: Oxford University Press, 2014.

Maxson, Cheryl L., and Malcolm W. Klein. "Defining Gang Homicide: An Updated Look at Member and Motive Approaches." In Miller, Maxson, and Klein, *Modern Gang Reader*, 173–185.

———. "Street Gang Violence: Twice as Great, or Half as Great?" In Klein, Maxson, and Miller, *Modern Gang Reader*, 24–32.

Mayer, Harold. *The Inheritance*. Amalgamated Clothing Workers of America, 1964. www.laborheritage.org/product/inheritance.

Mazon, Mauricio. *The Zoot-Suit Riots: The Psychology of Symbolic Annihilation*. Austin: University of Texas Press, 1984.

McAdam, Doug, and Kelly Moore. "The Politics of Black Insurgency 1930–1975." In *Violence in America: Protest, Rebellion, and Reform*, vol. 2, edited by Ted Robert Gurr, 255–285. Newbury Park, CA: Sage, 1989.

McBride, Wes. 1985. "Street Gangs a Specialized Law Enforcement Problem: A Law Enforcement Perspective and Response." Peace Officers Association of Los Angeles County Paper, January 1985.

McCone, John A. "Violence in the City—an End or a Beginning?" Report by the Governor's Commission on the Los Angeles Riots. In *Mass Violence in America: The Los Angeles Riots*, edited by Robert M. Fogelson, xi–109. New York. Arno Press and the New York Times, 1969.

McCoy, Alfred W. *The Politics of Heroin in Southeast Asia*. New York: Harper Colophon Books, 1972.

McGovern, George S. "The Colorado Coal Strike, 1913–14." In *American Violence*, edited by Richard Maxwell Brown, 122–126. Englewood Cliffs, NJ: Prentice-Hall, 1970.
McIntosh, Mary. "The Growth of Racketeering." *Economy and Society* 2, no. 1 (1973): 35–69.
McPherson, James Alan. "Chicago's Blackstone Rangers." *Atlantic Monthly* 223, no. 5 (pt. 1) and 6 (pt. 2) (May and June 1969). www.theatlantic.com/magazine/archive/1969/05/chicagos-blackstone-rangers-i/305741/.
McWilliams, Carey. "Nervous Los Angeles." *The Nation*, June 10, 1950, 570–571.
———. *Southern California: An Island on the Land*. Salt Lake City: Gibbs-Smith, 1988. (Originally published in 1946.)
———. "The Zoot-Suit Riots." *New Republic*, June 21, 1943, 818–820.
Mennel, Robert M. *Thorns and Thistles: Juvenile Delinquents in the United States, 1825–1940*. Hanover, New Hampshire: University Press of New England, 1973.
Merton, Robert K. "Social Structure and Anomie." In *Social Theory and Social Structure*, 131–160. London: Free Press of Glencoe, 1964.
Miller, Frank. "Black Gangs: A Seminar Paper for Dr. J. Quicker." Unpublished seminar paper, California State University Dominguez Hills, May 19, 1988.
Miller, Jody, Cheryl L. Maxson, and Malcolm W. Klein, eds. *The Modern Gang Reader*. 2nd ed. Los Angeles: Roxbury, 2001.
Miller, S. M., and Frank Riessman. "The Working Class Subculture: A New View." *Social Problems* 9, no. 1 (Summer 1961): 86–97.
Miller, Walter B. "Lower Class Culture as a Generating Milieu of Gang Delinquency." In *The Sociology of Crime and Delinquency*, 2nd ed., edited by Marvin E Wolfgang, Leonard Savitz, and Norman Johnson, 351–363. New York. John Wiley and Sons, 1970. (Originally published in the *Journal of Social Issues*, 1958.)
———. "The Molls." *Society*. November/December 1973, 32–35.
———. *Violence by Youth Gangs and Youth Groups as a Crime Problem in Major American Cities*. Monograph for the National Institute for Juvenile Justice and Delinquency Prevention, Washington, DC, 1975.
———. "Violent Crimes in City Gangs." *Annals of the American Academy of Political and Social Science* 364 (March 1966): 96–112.
———. "White Gangs: Leadership and the Struggle between 'Good' and 'Evil' Endure." *Transaction*, special issue, "The Anti-American Generation," 6, no. 10 (September 1969): 11–26.
———. "Youth Gangs in the Urban Crisis Era." In *Delinquency, Crime, and Society*, edited by James F. Short, 91–122. Chicago: University of Chicago Press, 1976.
Mills, C. Wright. "Diagnosis of Our Moral Uneasiness." In *Power, Politics, and People*, edited by Irving Horowitz, 330–338. New York: Ballantine Books, 1952.
———. *The Power Elite*. New York: Oxford University Press, 1959a.
———. "The Professional Ideology of Social Pathologists." *American Journal of Sociology* 49 (1943): 165–180.
———. *The Sociological Imagination*. New York: Oxford University Press, 1959b.
Moore, Joan W. "Gangs and the Underclass: A Comparative Perspective." Introduction to John M. Hagedorn, *People and Folks: Gangs, Crime and the Underclass in a Rustbelt City*, 2nd ed., 3–17. Chicago: Lake View, 1998.
———. *Going Down to the Barrio: Homeboys and Homegirls in Change*. Philadelphia: Temple University Press, 1991.
———. *Homeboys: Gangs, Drugs, and Prison in the Barrios of Los Angeles*. Philadelphia: Temple University Press, 1978.

Morales, Ed. "The Roots of Organizing: The Young Lords Revolution." *The Nation*, April 6, 2020, 25–32.
Myerhoff, Howard L., and Barbara G. Myerhoff. "Field Observations of Middle Class 'Gangs.'" In *Juvenile Delinquency*, edited by William E. Thompson and Jack E. Bynam, 309–320. Boston: Allyn and Bacon, 1991. (Originally published in *Social Forces* 42 (March 1964): 328–336.)
Myrdal, Gunnar. *Beyond the Welfare State*. New Haven, CT: Yale University Press, 1960.
———. *Challenge to Affluence*. New York: Random House, 1963.
Nadeau, Remi A. *City Makers: The Men Who Transformed Los Angles from Village to Metropolis during the first Great Boom, 1868-76*. New York: Doubleday, 1948.
Neff, Don. "Cars Give Teen-Age Gangs Range and Speed in Crime." *Los Angeles Times*, July 5, 1961, pt. 3, 1–8.
———. "County Has 336 Teen-Age Gangs." *Los Angeles Times*, July 6, 1961.
Nelli, Humbert S. *The Business of Crime*. Chicago: University of Chicago Press, 1987.
Nirenberg, David. "The Impresarios of Trent: The Long and Frightening History of the Blood Libel." *The Nation* (Nov. 30/Dec. 7, 2020):32–36.
Nye, Ivan F., and James F. Short Jr. "Scaling Delinquent Behavior." *American Sociological Review* 22 (1957): 326–331.
O'Connor, Dick. "138 Gangs of Youthful Rowdies Flourish on Streets of Our City." *Los Angeles Herald and Examiner*, April 16, 1953, A14.
Onions, C. T., ed., *The Oxford Dictionary of English Etymology*. New York: Oxford University Press, 1966.
Pauley, Walter E. "Juvenile Gangs and Their Activity in South Central Los Angeles." Unpublished paper, submitted in partial fulfillment of the requirements for Sociology 269, California State University Dominguez Hills, 1973.
Pearson, Geoffrey. *Hooligan: A History of Respectable Fears*. London: Macmillan, 1983.
Pepinsky, Harold E., and Paul Jesilow. *Myths that Cause Crime*. Cabin John, MD: Seven Locks, 1985.
Peralta, Stacy, dir. *Crips and Bloods: Made in America*. Los Angeles: New Video Group, 2009.
Peterson, Dana. "Girlfriends, Gun-Holders and Ghetto Rats? Moving beyond Narrow Views of Girls in Gangs." In Maxson, Egley, Miller, and Klein, *Modern Gang Reader*, 271–281.
Pinker, Steven. *The Better Angels of Our Nature: Why Violence Has Declined*. New York: Viking, Penguin, 2011.
Platt, Anthony M. *The Child Savers: The Invention of Delinquency*. Chicago: University of Chicago Press, 1969.
Poe, Elizabeth. "Nobody Was Listening." In *Los Angeles: Biography of a City*, edited by John Caughey and LaRee Caughey, 426–430. :Berkeley: University of California Press, 1977.
Polsky, Ned. *Hustlers, Beats, and Others*. New York: Doubleday and Company, 1969.
Potter, Gary W., and Victor E. Kappeler. *Constructing Crime: Perspectives on Making News and Social Problems*. Prospect Heights, IL: Waveland, 1998.
Presley, Robert, Ruben Ayala, John Garamendi, Milton Marks, Newton Russel, David J. Townsend, Fritz Zimmer, and Barbara Hadley. *Juvenile Gangs*. California Legislature, Senate Select Committee on Children and Youth, Los Angeles, CA, November 5, 1979.
Procello, Richard, and Steven J. Lang. *Running for Success: An Anthology of Fremont High School Track History, 1950s-1980s*. Los Angeles: Grace, 2011.

Pyrooz, David C., Gary LaFree, Scott H. Decker, and Patrick A. James. "Cut from the Same Cloth? A Comparative Study of Domestic Extremists and Gang Members in the United States." *Justice Quarterly* 35, no. 1 (2018): 1–32.

Quicker, John C. "The Chicana Gang: A Preliminary Description." In Chesney-Lind and Hagedorn, *Female Gangs in America*, 48–56. (This article was the second edition of a paper presented at the Pacific Sociological Association annual meeting in 1974.)

———. "A Consideration of the Relationship of 'Punitiveness' to Delinquency as Developed in Opportunity Theory." *Journal of Criminal Law and Criminology* 64, no. 3 (September 1973): 333–338.

———. "The Effect of Goal Discrepancy on Delinquency." *Social Problems* 22, no. 1 (1974): 76–86.

———. *Homegirls: Characterizing Chicana Gangs*. San Pedro, CA: International Universities Press, 1983.

———. *Seven Decades of Gangs: What Has Been Learned, What Has Been Done, and What Should Be Done*. Prepared for the California Commission on Crime Control and Violence Prevention, contract no. C82-5, 1981.

Quicker, John C., and Akil Batani-Khalfani. "From Boozies to Bloods: Early Gangs in Los Angeles." *Journal of Gang Research* 5, no. 4 (1998): 15–22.

Quicker, John C., and Janet Schmidt. "A Contribution to the Critique of Bourgeois Criminology: The Case of Criminal Sentencing." *Insurgent Sociologist* 7, no. 3 (Summer 1977): 62–69.

Quinney, Richard. *Criminal Justice in America: A Critical Understanding*. Boston: Little, Brown, 1974.

———. *The Social Reality of Crime*. Boston: Little, Brown, 1970.

Rand, Christopher. *Los Angeles: The Ultimate City*. New York: Oxford University Press, 1967.

Reasons, Charles E. "The Politicizing of Crime, the Criminal and the Criminologist." *Journal of Criminal Law and Criminology* 64, no. 4 (December 1973): 471–477.

Reiman, Jeffrey H. *The Rich Get Richer and the Poor Get Prison: Ideology, Class, and Criminal Justice*. New York: John Wiley & Sons, 1979.

Reiner, Ira. *Gangs, Crime and Violence in Los Angeles*. Los Angeles: Office of the District Attorney, 1992.

Report on Youth Gang Violence in California. Sacramento: Attorney General's Youth Gang Task Force, 1981.

Rice, Robert. "A Reporter at Large: The Persian Queens." In Chesney-Lind and Hagedorn, *Female Gangs in America*, 27–47.

Rice, Roger E., and Rex B. Christensen. *The Juvenile Gang: Its Structure, Function, and Treatment as Perceived by the Gang Leader*. Los Angeles County Probation Department Research Office Report No. 24, 1965.

Riesman, David. *The Lonely Crowd*. New Haven, CT: Yale University Press, 1966. (Originally published in 1950.)

Riis, Jacob A. *The Children of the Poor*. New York: Garrett Press, 1970. (Originally published in 1892.)

Rodriguez, Luis J. *Always Running: La Vida Loca; Gang Days in L.A.* New York: Touchstone, 1993.

Sale, R. T. *The Blackstone Rangers: A Reporter's Account of Time Spent with the Street Gang on Chicago's South Side*. New York: Random House, 1971.

Salisbury, Harrison E. *The Shook-Up Generation*. New York: Harper & Brothers, 1958.

Sanders, Bill. *Gangs: An Introduction*. New York: Oxford University Press, 2016.
Sanders, William B. *Gangbangs and Drive-bys: Grounded Culture and Juvenile Gang Violence*. New York: Aldine De Gruyter, 1994.
Sanneh, Kelefa. "Drunk with Power: What was Prohibition Really About?" *New Yorker*, December 21 and 28, 2015, 105–110.
Schiesl, Martin J. "Behind the Badge: The Police and Social Discontent in Los Angeles since 1950." In Norman M. Klein and Marten J Schiesl, *20th Century Los Angeles: Power, Promotion, and Social Conflict*, 153–194. Claremont, CA: Regina Books, 1990.
Schur, Edwin M. *Labelling Deviant Behavior*. New York: Harper and Row, 1971.
Schwendinger, Herman, and Julia Schwendinger. *Adolescent Subcultures and Delinquency*. New York: Praeger Special Studies, 1985.
———. "Defenders of Order or Guardians of Human Rights." *The Free Library*. Social Justice, March 2014. (Originally published in *Issues in Criminology* 5, no. 2 [Summer 1970]: 123–157.)
Sellin, Thorsten, and Marvin E. Wolfgang. *The Measurement of Delinquency*. New York: John Wiley and Sons, 1964.
"Shadow of Gang Fight: 2000 Car Clubs May Get Setback." *Los Angeles Times*, April 1, 1960.
Shelden, Randall G., Sharon K.Tracy, and William B. Brown. *Youth Gangs in American Society*. Belmont, CA: Wadsworth, 1997.
Sherman, Gene. "Girl Gangs Create New L.A. Problem." *Los Angeles Times*, April 23, 1963c, Metro, 1, 3.
———. "Juvenile Gangs Pose Two Distinct Problems in L.A." *Los Angeles Times*, April 21, 1963a, Metro, 1, 5.
———. "Juvenile Gangs Puzzle Experts." *Los Angeles Times*, April 22, 1963b, 1, 8.
Short, James F., Jr. "Gangs and Politics: Images and Realities." In *Negley K. Teeters Symposium on Crime in America*, edited by Mary Jane Hageman, 42–50. Oneonta, NY: Hartwick College, 1973.
———. "Youth, Gangs and Society: Micro- and Macrosociological Processes." In *Juvenile Delinquency: A Book of Readings*, 4th ed., edited by Rose Giallombardo, 329–342. New York: John Wiley and Sons, 1982.
Short, James F., Ramon J. Rivera, and Ray A. Tennyson. "Perceived Opportunity, Gang Membership and Delinquency." *American Sociological Review* 30, no. 1 (1965): 56–67.
Short, James F., and Fred L. Strodtbeck. *Group Process and Gang Delinquency*. Chicago: University of Chicago Press, 1965.
Shover, Neal, and John Paul Wright, eds. *Crimes of Privilege: Readings in White-Collar Crime*. New York: Oxford University Press, 2001.
Sides, Josh. *L.A. City Limits: African American Los Angeles from the Great Depression to the Present*. Berkeley: University of California Press, 2006.
Sikes, Gini. *8 Ball Chicks: A Year in the Violent World of Girl Gangsters*. New York: Anchor Books, 1997.
Simmel, Georg. *Conflict and the Web of Group Affiliations*. New York: Free Press, 1955.
Sloan, Cle "Bone," dir. *Bastards of the Party*. Hill District Media, 2005. www.blackpowerproductions.com/item/Bastards-of-the-Party-DVD-133.
Smith, Gary. *What the Luck? The Surprising Role of Chance in Our Everyday Lives*. New York: Overlook Press, Peter Mayer, 2016.
Smith, R. J. *The Great Black Way: L.A. in the 1940s and the Lost African-American Renaissance*. New York: Public Affairs, 2006.

Soja, Edward W. *Postmodern Geographies: The Reassertion of Space in Critical Social Theory.* London: Verso, 1989.
Solomon, David, ed. *The Marijuana Papers.* Indianapolis: Bobbs-Merrill, 1966.
Southern Poverty Law Center. *The Year in Hate and Extremism: 2019.* Report from the Southern Poverty Law Center, Montgomery, AL, 2019.
Spergel, Irving A. *The Youth Gang Problem: A Community Approach.* New York: Oxford University Press, 1995.
Spitzer, Steven. "Toward a Marxian Theory of Deviance." *Social Problems* 22, no. 5 (June 1975): 638–651.
Starbuck, David, James C. Howell, and Donna J. Lindquist. "Hybrid and Other Modern Gangs." (Juvenile Justice Bulletin. Youth Gang Series) Washington, D.C.: U.S. Department of Justice, *OJJDP*, December 2001.
Sutherland, Edwin H. *White Collar Crime.* New York: Holt, Rinehart and Winston, (1949) 1961.
Sweezy, Paul M. *The Theory of Capitalist Development.* New York: Modern Reader, 1970.
Tackwood, Louis E. *The Glasshouse Tapes: The Story of an Agent Provocateur and the New Police-Intelligence Complex.* New York: Avon Books, 1973.
Tannenbaum, Frank. *Crime and the Community.* Boston: Ginn, 1938.
Tapia, Mike. *The Barrio Gangs of San Antonio: 1915–2015.* Fort Worth, TX: TCU Press, 2017.
Taylor, Carl S. *Dangerous Society.* East Lansing: Michigan State University Press, 1990.
Taylor, Ian, Paul Walton, and Jock Young. *The New Criminology: For a Social Theory of Deviance.* New York. Harper Torchbooks, 1974.
Terry, Wallace. *Bloods: An Oral History of the Vietnam War by Black Veterans.* New York: Ballantine Books, 1984.
Thomas Brothers. *Street Guide Los Angeles County.* Thomas Bros. 1955.
Thornberry, Terrance P. "Membership in Youth Gangs and Involvement in Serious and Violent Offending." In Miller, Maxson, and Klein, *Modern Gang Reader,* 164–172.
———. "Race, Socioeconomic Status and Sentencing in the Juvenile Justice System." In *Readings in Juvenile Delinquency,* edited by Dean G. Rojek and Gary F. Jensen, 86–90. Lexington, MA: D. C. Heath, 1982.
———. "Risk Factors for Gang Membership." In Miller, Maxson, and Klein, *Modern Gang Reader,* 34–42.
Thornberry, Terrance P., Marvin D. Krohn, Alan J. Lizotte, and Deborah Chard-Wierschem. "The Role of Juvenile Gangs in Facilitating Delinquent Behavior." In Klein, Maxson, and Miller, *Modern Gang Reader,* 174–185.
Thornberry, Terrance P., Marvin D. Krohn, Alan J. Lizotte, Carolyn A. Smith, and Kimberly Tobin. "The Antecedents of Gang Membership." In Egley et al., *Modern Gang Reader,* 30–42.
Thrasher, Frederic M. *The Gang: A Study of 1,313 Gangs in Chicago.* Chicago: University of Chicago Press, 1966. (Second impression of the 1963 abridged ed., originally published in 1927.)
———. "Sex in the Gang." In Chesney-Lind and Hagedorn, *Female Gangs in America,* 1–26.
Tita, George, and Allan Abrahamse. "Gang Homicide in LA, 1981–2001." In Egley et al., *Modern Gang Reader,* 269–282.
Tuck, Ruth D. "Behind the Zoot-Suit Riots." *Survey Graphic,* August 1943, 313–336.
Turner, Ralph H., and Samuel J. Surace. "Zoot-Suiters and Mexicans: Symbols in Crowd Behavior." *American Journal of Sociology* 62 (July 1956): 14–20.

Valdemar, Richard. "The Structure of Gangs." *Police: Law Enforcement Solutions: Police Magazine* blog, June 27, 2007. www.policemag.com/authors/338077/richard-valdemar.

Valdez, Al. *Gangs: A Guide to Understanding Street Gangs.* 5th ed. San Clemente, CA: Law Tech Publishing Group, 2009.

Vaz, Edmund W., ed. *Middle-Class Juvenile Delinquency.* New York: Harper & Row, 1967.

Veblen, Thorstein. *The Theory of the Leisure Class.* New York: Mentor, 1953. (Originally published in 1899 by Macmillan.)

Vigil, James Diego. *Barrio Gangs: Street Life and Identity in Southern California.* Austin: University of Texas Press, 1988.

———."Chicano Gangs: One Response to Mexican Urban Adaptation." *Urban Anthropology* 12, no. 1 (1983): 45–68.

———. *A Rainbow of Gangs: Street Cultures in the Mega-City.* Austin: University of Texas Press, 2002.

———. "Street Baptism: Chicano Gang Initiation." In *American Youth Gangs at the Millennium*, edited by F. Esbensen, S. G. Tibbetts, and L. Gaines, 218–228. Long Grove, IL: Waveland, 2004.

Vold, George B. *Theoretical Criminology.* New York: Oxford University Press, 1958.

Weatherwax, John M. *The Founders of Los Angeles.* 2nd ed. Los Angeles: Aquarian Spiritual Center, 1976.

Webb, Vincent J., and Charles M. Katz. "A Study of Police Gang Units in Six Cities." In Egley et al., *Modern Gang Reader*, 349–360.

Weber, Max. *The Theory of Social and Economic Organization.* New York. Free Press, 1965. (The original translation from the German was published by Oxford University Press in 1947.)

Webster's New World College Dictionary. 4th ed. New York: Macmillan General Reference, 1999.

West, Cornel. *Race Matters.* Boston: Beacon, 1993.

Whoriskey, Peter. "As Drug Industry's Influence over Research Grows, so Does the Potential for Bias." *Washington Post*, November 24, 2012.

Whyte, William F. *Street Corner Society: The Social Structure of an Italian Slum.* Chicago: University of Chicago Press, 1965. (Originally published in 1943.)

Wicker, Tom. "Introduction." In Otto Kerner, *Report of the National Advisory Commission*, v–xi.

Will, Bob. "Age Range from 9 to 30 Years; No Initiation—They Live by Code." *Los Angeles Times*, December 17, 1953, 2. (This was a six-part series, December 16–21, written by Will in 1953 for the *Los Angeles Times*.)

Wilson, William Julius. *The Declining Significance of Race: Blacks and Changing American Institutions.* 2nd ed. Chicago: University of Chicago Press, 1980.

———. *The Truly Disadvantaged: The Inner City, the Underclass, and Public Policy.* Chicago: University of Chicago Press, 1987.

———. *When Work Disappears: The World of the New Urban Poor.* New York: Vintage Books, 1997.

Winton, Richard. "Gang Database Is Plagued with Errors, Auditor Finds." *Los Angeles Times*, August 12, 2016, B7.

Wiseman, Richard. *The Luck Factor: Changing Your Luck, Changing Your Life; The Four Essential Princples.* New York: Miramax, 2003.

Wolfe, Donald H. *The Black Dahlia Files: The Mob, the Mogul, and the Murder that Transfixed Los Angeles*. New York: Regan Books, 2000.

Yablonsky, Lewis. *The Violent Gang*. Baltimore: Penguin Books, 1967. (Reprint of the 1966 edition used here. Originally published in 1962.)

———. "Watch Out Whitey: Negro Youth Gangs and Violence." *New Republic*, January 1, 1966, 10–12.

Index

adolescence, 44–46, 48–50, 354n66. *See also* juveniles
aircraft industry, 38, 75
Alameda Industrial Corridor, 23, 36–37
Alameda Street, 26
alcohol, 249, 263–266, 273–274, 285
Aliso Village/Flats group, 335, 339
Alonzo, Alejandro, 8, 10, 83, 198
Alpert, Adrienne, 53
Alpine group, 334
Alterman, Eric, 86
Ambassadors, 73
Ameer (Baby Businessmen), 55, 71, 73, 77, 102–103, 113–114, 181, 185, 225, 228, 250, 266, 305–306, 324–325, 372n87
Anderson, Elijah, 24, 83–84
Anslinger, Harry, 264–265
Asbury, Herbert, 4, 83, 86–87
athletics, 121, 206
Avalon Boys, 319
Avenues group, 10–11, 320–321, 324–326, 336, 411n89

Bakan, David, 44
Ballou, Robert, Jr., 328–329

Barry Wa. (Junior Businessmen), 56, 73, 118–121, 207, 214–215, 249, 284–285, 287–288, 291, 369n45
Bartenders, 336
Bastards of the Party (Sloan), 11, 31, 322–323, 343n26
Batani-Khalfani, Akil S. "Bird": academic research on the Slausons, 7; access to subjects and, 15; altercation with Frank Gentry and, 137–138; Baby Slausons and, 130–131; Chinaman and, 135; early life of, 133; Kev Mack interview and, 9; marriage of, 144; nickname and, 134; pictured, *163*, *167*, *168*, *169*; Raymond Washington and, 305–306; relationship with Quicker, 6–7; reputation of, 112, 134–137, 139–140, 143–144, 146; Roach and, 135–137, 139; role of in the Slausons, 131–132, 139–140, 143–144, 146–148, 160–161, 376n28; shooting of at Manchester Theater, 141–143; Sin Street set and, 152–154; stabbing at Jefferson High School of, 144–146; Watts sets and, 140–141. *See also* methodology; Slausons
Bebop Winos, 70, 336
Bell, Ken, 328, 354n66
Bernstein, Saul, 81

Black Angelenos, 24–27, 29, 34–38, 197, 301. *See also* racism; South Los Angeles; Watts
Black Juans/Wongs, 70, 101–102, *164*, 336, 369n42
Black Panther Party (BPP): as alternative focus for juveniles, 77; "Bunchy" Carter and, 304–305; Cleaver and, 20; coexistence with emerging late 1960s and 1970s groups, 319; detractors of, 407n31; in South Los Angeles, 304, 306, 325, 408n39
Black Power movement: aftermath of Watts Rebellion and, 313; as alternative focus for juveniles, 76–77, 260; destruction of, 330; effect in criminal justice system and, 77; effect of in South Los Angeles, 303–304; housing discrimination and, 303
Black women, 39, 75. *See also* gender
Block, Herbert, 4
Blocks group, 340
Blood Alley group, 336
Blood Brothers, 336
Bloods, 2, 11, 77–78, 331
Boot Hill group, 336
Boozies, 69–70, 99, 117, 334, 359n35
Boss Bachelors, 128
Boss 50s, 338
Boy Scouts, 49, 203–204
Bradley, Tom, 207
Bronzeville, 29, 35
Brotherton, David, 9–10, 12–13, 53–54, 82–83, 172, 178
Brown, Bradford, 46
Brown, Edmund G., 2
Brown, Elaine, 148
Brown, Richard, 307
Buddha Bandits, 70, 337
Buddha Spooks, 70, 337
Bursik, Robert, 43, 60
Businessmen: about, 340; associated groups of, 103; Baby Businessmen, 55, 73, 102–103; Calvin's stabbing of Bird and, 145; Cavaliers and, 128; Chinaman and, 102, 127, 293; club structure and, 102–104; conversions to Islam and, 306, 408n39; current lives of, 8; female cliques and, 179; fifteen-minute Businessmen, 372n87; fighting between groups and, 228; Gladiators and, 103; hand signs and, 159; initiations and, 118–119, 121; Junior Businessmen, 73, 102–103; origins of, 71; rival Roman 20s and, 103; Senior Businessmen, 73, 102–103; Slausons' Chinaman and, 103; smaller sets of, 103

C-14 group. *See* Clanton Street group
CalGang database, 53
California Fair Housing Act (Rumsford, 1963), 302–303
California Highway Patrol (CHP), 1–2
California Real Estate Association, 302–303
California State College Dominguez Hills, 1, 317
California Street Terrorism Enforcement and Prevention Act of 1988, 85, 364n122, 364n124
Callan, Mary Ann, 177, 180
Campanella Park Boys, 319
Campbell, Anne, 176
Canal Boys, 319
Caravans car club, 339
cars: Bird and, 144; Boozies and, 70; drug use and, 272; economic opportunity and, 346n19; individual fights and, 233; Los Angeles culture of, 22; materialism and, 295; Serfs car club, 73; Watts street groups and, 74
Carter, Alprentice "Bunchy," 148, 151, 304–307, 325, 330
Carver Park Boys, 319
Castleberry, Glen, 70
Cavaliers, 103, 128, 369n47
Cavemen (LASD), 44
Central Avenue, 24–27, 287, 292, 347n37, 347n39
Chambliss, William, 175
Chesney-Lind, Meda, 176, 178–179
Chestnut, Ralph (Little Slausons), 136–137
Chiefs car club, 337
Chinaman (Slausons), 112, 116, 129–131, 135, 139, 146–148, 158, 218, 232–234, 251, 279, 290–291, 303, 375n18
Choppers 12, 337
Christensen, Rex, 5, 8, 57, 124, 180, 241
Chubby Dukes, 112–113
cigarettes, 268, 398n49
Civil Rights movement, 76–77, 121–122
Clanton Street group, 68–69, 99–100, 117–118, 285, 334, 359n25
Clark, Ramsey, 86
class: emphasis on in early literature, 171, 196; gang moniker and, 80; gangs into clubs theory, 173; theoretical approaches

and, 171–175; upper- and middle-class delinquency and, 173–175; use of the "dangerous classes" and, 172, 353n26
Cleaver, Eldridge, 19–20, 304
cliques: adoption of other culture among sets in, 94–96; age and, 91, 148, 366n8, 368n32; Florence and, 98–99; loyalty to larger group and, 91–92; numbering of, 99; role of in street groups, 89–91; sets vs., 91–92, 366n9; Slausons and, 148–150; social context and, 91, 374n105
Cloward, Richard, 4, 61–62, 171
Cluff, William D., 65
Coachmen car club, 337, 339
Coasters, 337
cocaine, 264, 399n65
Cohen, Albert, 4, 171, 174
Cohen, Mickey, 292
Coleman, James, 86
Colonia Watts, 108
colors, 331
comin'-from-the shoulders ethos: ability to take a beating/showing heart and, 214–215; attractiveness to opposite sex and, 216; guns and, 220–221; hand-to-hand fighting and, 213; Horseshoe and, 217–218; masculinity and, 214–215, 238–239; reputation and, 215–216; role models and, 218–220; taking responsibility for one's actions and, 217
communism, 260
Compton, 26, 124, 307, 319
Compton Police Department, 56
Compton Varrio Tres group, 337
Connoisseurs, 102, 336
Conot, Robert, 308–309, 312, 386n108
Conquergood, Dwight, 54
Conservatives car club, 339
Conservative Young Ladies, 181–183, 383n69
Constituents, 337
Contreras, Randol, 29
corporate violence, 86
crime: bank robbery, 279–280; Bloods and Crips commitment to, 77–78; curfew violations, 287–288; Department of Justice figures and, 261–263, 262t, 287; deterrence and, 296–297; drug dealing, 270–273, 330–331, 342n16; drug-related, 273; forced sex and, 273–275; graffiti, 157, 289; hard drugs and, 267–272; as individual practice, 280, 285, 298; lack of meaningful data on during studied period, 256–257, 259–261; marijuana and, 263–264, 271–273; organized crime, 292; petty thefts, 288–290, 402n93; police data on, 280–281, 397n37; population growth of Los Angeles and, 261–262; portrayal of juvenile in media, 256–261; probation officers on, 286–287; purse snatching, 284–285, 401n88; racist beliefs about Black tendency toward, 34–36; reasons for, 292–296; robbery, 246–247, 277–280, 285; ruling groups and definitions of, 43; shoplifting, 289; "slicksters" and, 283–284; spontaneous violence and, 275–277; street gambling, 285–286, 395n5, 401n90; street scams, 285; as transgressive behavior, 295–296; types of crime studied, 256; unclear definitions of "gang-related," 261; white-collar, 86, 365n136, 365n138
Crime Control Act of 1968, 2
criminal justice system: Black Panther Party and prison and, 306; Black Power movement and, 77; California Youth Authority institutions, 390n18; change from deterrence to suppression model and, 330, 410n82; crime data and, 50–51; cycle of incarceration and, 290–291; effect of Watts Rebellion on, 313, 317; formalization of gangs and, 331; girls and, 176; incarceration in South Los Angeles and, 290–292, 403n105; juvenile statutes and, 45; political aims of, 54; racism and, 84, 206–209; role of luck and, 240–241; treatment of juveniles as labor and, 46–47; utility of petty crime for, 284
"Crip Constitution" (Danifu), 322–323
Crips: adoption of name and new groups, 328–329, 405n8, 414n122; Bunchy Carter and, 325; Castle Crips, 326; colors and, 331; commitment to crime and, 77–78; emergence of, 77, 300–301; ideology of, 11–12; Kitchen Crips, 326; media prominence and, 326–328; myths surrounding, 321–323; name of, 323–324; origins of, 12; Palladium incident and, 327–328, 414n117; slang and, 323–324; Slausons and, 325–326; Tookie of, 328–329, 411n91; Tweedy Bird of, 326, 329;

Crips *(continued)*
  Raymond Washington and, 304–306, 320, 324–325, 329, 407n35, 408n37; Watts Rebellion and, 2; Wattstax music festival and, 328
Crips and Bloods: Made in America (Peralta), 37, 122, 346n20
Crown 40s, 70, 338
Crusaders, 73
curfew violations, 287–288, 402n94

Daddy Rolling Stones, 70, 128, 336
Danifu, 322–323
Dante, 315–316
D'Artagnans, 108, 141, 309–310, 340, 370n71, 409n66
Davis, Mike, 9, 11, 31, 35, 48, 198, 299
Dawley, David, 57
Deckard, Eula and Jule, 32
Decker, Scott, 48, 51
deindustrialization, 11, 36–38, 198, 329–330
delinquency, 45–46
Del Vikings, 179
Devil Hunters, 387n119
Diamond Street group, 334
DiIulio, John, 48
Dirty 30s, 70, 337
Dodge City group. *See* Businessmen
Dogtown group, 339
Domhoff, G. William, 43
Dominators, 337
Don Juans, 55, 73, 102, 240, 336
drugs: cocaine, 264, 399n65; dealing of, 270–273, 330–331, 342n16; gendered use of, 273, 399n61; hard drugs and, 267–271, 397n45, 398n53; heroin, 269–270, 272; juvenile drug use and, 263–264; lowriders and, 272; marijuana, 263–264, 271–273, 398n50; parental disapproval and, 272; religion and, 297; social stigma and use of, 269–270; as transgressive behavior, 296; unreliability and, 267–269; variation among individuals, 272–273; Vietnam and, 414n126
Du Bois, W.E.B., 1
Dutchmen car club, 337

East Los Angeles, 10, 27–28
East Side Clover group, 334
Edgerton, Robert, 21
Egyptians, 340

18th Street group, 69, 335n3, 360n37
Eldridge, Ron, 75
El Hoyo Soto, 337
Elm Street group, 108, 337
Emerald Street group, 334
Erikson, Erik, 82
Esbensen, Finn-Ange, 83
Eskimo Radiator Company, 124
Everett, Big Freddy, 310–311
Evil Angels car club, 339
Excellos, 337

families, 297–298
Farmers, 5, 71, 108, 179, 340, 371n75
Federal Bureau of Investigation, 77, 157–159, 250, 261–263, 273, 303, 407n31
female affiliates: ability to stop fights of, 194; biases against study of as members of gangs, 176; early research and, 175–176, 380n26, 380n28, 381n31; effect of group membership on girls, 178; female cliques and, 178–179, 184; female gang estimates, 176; fighting and, 188, 382n54; gender norms and, 183–184; girls clubs, 177, 180–183; holding weapons and, 194–195; media portrayal of girls in street groups, 177, 193–194; nonmembers, 181; police data and, 176; protection from street groups for related, 178; Quicker's work on female gangs and, 176; rape and, 274, 383n77; reason for joining for, 179–181; relational advantages for, 184–187; romantic expectations and, 186–187; "social injury" vs. "liberation" hypotheses about gang membership and, 178; transition to more active role in fights, 195–196. *See also* gender; girls; romantic relationships
Ferrero, John, 66
1st Flats group, 335
Flamming, Douglas, 25, 27, 30, 38
Fleisher, Mark, 48
Florence 13. *See* Florence group
Florence-Firestone District: Black migration into, 75–76; ethnography of, 25–26; Florence and, 93; policing district and, 28; Slausons and, 71, 93
Florence group: about, 340; Big Florence, 98; cliques of, 98–99, 368n31; female cliques and, 179; Florence Midgets, 74, 98–99; Little Florence, 98; Mariano from,

96; numbered cliques in, 99; origins of, 96–98; pictured, *166, 168*; Rowdy Frank of, 98–99; size of, 74; truce with Slausons and, 96, 124

Florencitas, 93–94, 96–98, 367n21

forced sex, 273–275, 383n77

Forsythe, Donald T., 257

Frank M. (Clanton), 68–69, 94–95, 100, 117–118, 183–184, 197, 205–210, 215–216, 219–220, 227, 243, 270, 293, 356n100

Fraser, Alistair, 48, 50, 52–53, 60, 82–83

fraternities, 43, 50

Frye, Marquette and Ronald, 310

gangs: authors' use of term and, 60–62, 357n128; biases against study of girls in, 176; Chicago vs. Los Angeles crime-related definitions and, 51; class bias and label of, 80; Cluff incident and attention to, 66; construction of defining statistics and, 50–52; as cultural other, 82–84; difficulties in defining, 42–43, 50–52; early coverage and, 63–64; estimating numbers and, 71–74; existing ethnography of, 8–9; focus on class and, 171–172, 171–175; focus on occasional violence and, 48–49; "gang wars" and, 226–229; identifiable name and label in press of, 80; importance of structural/historical context in study of, 9–11; labeling of groups as, 9, 42; labeling of police as, 44, 55; media and post-Cluff incident labeling of, 78–82; other named groups of adolescents and, 49–50; proportion of offenses committed by juvenile, 85–87; racial context and, 82–84; racism's role in formation of, 11, 196–197; reaction of street group members to designation, 54–56, 356n100, 370n65; self-reported data and, 59–60; skewed crime data and, 50–52, 72; stigma of term, 54–56; superpredator label and, 49; theory and origins of, 4; "Twead Ring" and, 87. *See also individual groups*; street groups

"Gangs and Adolescent Subcultures" class, 6–7

Gangs of New York, The (Asbury), 86–87

"gangsta culture," 329–331

gang sweeps, 51

Garcetti, Eric, 53

Gardell, Matthias, 305

Gates, Daryl, 308, 407n31

Geis, Gilbert, 72, 171

gender: childrearing duties and, 383n80; crime and, 289; drugs and, 273; female associates and norms of, 183–184; incarceration and, 403n106; violence and, 239–240. *See also* female affiliates; girls

Gentry, Frank, 137–138, *166*

Gibson, John S., Jr., 66

girls: comin'-from-the-shoulders ethos and attractiveness to, 216; forced sex and, 273–275, 383n77; gender norms and, 183–184; jealousy and, 191–193, 224–225; shoplifting and, 289. *See also* female affiliates; romantic relationships

Gladiators: about, 340; association with Business men and, 103; Baby Gladiators, 103; Del Vikings and, 103; Descendants and, 103–104; Dudley B. (Slausons) vs. Floyd (Gladiators) fight and, 235; female cliques and, 179; fighting between groups and, 228; Floyd of, 235, 369n54; former members of the Cavaliers and, 128; hand signs and, 159; history of, 102–104; origins of, 71; Slausons and, 104–107, 124, 230–231; United Slaves Organization (US) and, 306–307; younger cliques and, 103–104

Glasgow, Douglas, 25, 28, 38

Glass House Tapes, The (Tackwood), 229

Golden Earrings, 70, 336

Goodyear Blimp, 124–125

Goodyear Rubber Company, 76, 124

graffiti, 157, 289

Grandees, 340

Grasmick, Harold, 43, 60

GREAT database, 176

Great Migration, 11, 23

Gregory, Dick, 13, 313, 344n58

Griffiths, Elizabeth, 175

Group Guidance Project, 8, 55, 81, 173, 215, 302

guns. *See* weapons

Hagedorn, John, 9, 15, 28, 36, 42, 51–52, 61, 83, 90, 130–131, 172, 178, 196

Hall, G. Stanley, 45–46

Hamm, Mark, 231

Hampton, Fred, 330

hand signs, 159–160
Happy Valley group, 337
Harbor Freeway, 27, 348n57
Harrington, Michael, 172
Hazard group, 336, 339
Head Hunters, 100–101
heroin, 269–270, 272
Hickory Street group, 108, 337, 340
Highway Men car club, 339
Himes, Chester, 32
History of Violence in America, The, 301–302
Holton, Karl, 258
Hoover, J. Edgar, 35, 77, 260, 362n86, 407n31
Horseshoe, 112–113, 217–218, 235–236, 251, 394n61
housing discrimination, 33, 38, 302–303
housing projects, 26, 75, 107–108, 111–112
Howard, John, 107, 307
Howell, James, 8, 175
Huns (Watts), 5, 71, 108, 141, 310, 339

industrialization, 36, 44–45; demographic growth and, 11
industrialization-deindustrialization paradigm, 36
in-groupism/out-groupism, 38, 42, 322–323, 331
Irwin, John, 172
Islam, 303, 305–306

Jackson, Robert, 69
Jankowski, Martin, 8, 10, 18
Japanese Angelenos, 29, 34
Jardin group, 108, 339
Jensen, Gary, 39
Juvenile Justice and Delinquency Prevention Act (1974), 52
juveniles: criminal justice penalties and, 84–85; Group Guidance Program and effect on, 302; history of named groups of, 49–50; human tendency to form groups and, 42; incarceration and, 290–292; as inheritors of adult creations, 39; Parker's policies toward, 35; proportion of offenses committed by, 85–87; racism from police and, 206–209; racism in schools and, 204–206; self-reported data on gangs and, 60. *See also* adolescence; street groups

Kappeler, Victor, 86
Katz, Charles, 52
Katz, Jack, 288
Keiser, R. Lincoln, 57, 89–90
Kempf-Leonard, Kimberly, 51
Khans car club, 339
Klein, Malcom, 8, 10, 48, 51, 61, 90, 175, 179–180, 302, 358n3
Knox, George, 71–72
Korean War, 37, 75
Krisberg, Barry, 67
Kropotkin, Petr, 41
Ku Klux Klan, 25, 107, 206
Kumasi, 56, 93–94, 96–98, 122, *167*, 184, 194, 224–225, 283–284, 304, 328, 330, 332, 401n83

Lafayette street group, 334
LaHunter, 236–237
Largo group, 337
larrikins, 50
Larson, James, 46
Latin Gents car club, 339
Law Enforcement Assistance Administration (LEAA), 2
Liazos, Alexander, 47
Little Bird. *See* Kumasi
Little Scarlet (Mosely), 30
Los Angeles: association with Slausons of, 6–7; constructed South Central Los Angeles label and, 24; East vs. South gangs, 10; gang emergence and structural conditions in, 9; geography of, 22–23; Great Migration and, 11, 23; manipulation of gang statistics and, 52–54; massacre of Chinese residents by White vigilantes and, 22; population growth and, 301; pre–Watts Rebellion beliefs about, 1; Quicker student interview of, 5; racial history of, 21–22; structural changes after Watts in, 2; World War II and, 23; Yorty's rejection of federal poverty funds and, 299. *See also* East Los Angeles; racism; segregation; South Los Angeles; Watts neighborhood
Los Angeles City Council, 51, 66
Los Angeles County Probation Department, Group Guidance Project, 8, 55, 81, 173, 215, 302
Los Angeles County probation report (1965, Rice and Christensen), 5, 8

Los Angeles County Sheriff's Academy, 49
Los Angeles County Sheriff's Department (LASD), 7, 28, 44, 49, 53, 308
Los Angeles Herald Examiner, 72, 78, 258, 260, 327
Los Angeles Police Commission, 66
Los Angeles Police Department (LAPD): beliefs about Black peoples' inherent criminality, 34; Black officers and, 207; Black Power movement and, 303; Tom Bradley and, 207; California Highway Patrol (CHP), 1; Chinaman's story of individual fight with police officer from, 232–233; Cluff incident and, 65–66; Community Resources Against Street Hoodlums (CRASH) gang unit, 7, 53; early hiring of Black in Los Angeles, 1; female officers and, 194, 385n102; female street group data and, 381n41; gang sweeps and, 51; groups within labeled as gangs, 44, 55; Jim Crow culture and, 31; in John Quicker's classes, 2; manipulation of gang statistics, 53; William H. Parker of, 11, 31, 35, 53, 65–66, 206, 302, 308, 409n54; racism in, 11, 31, 35, 206–209, 308, 387n134; research process and, 19; rise of attention to Crips and, 326–328; solidification of gang ties and, 4; South Los Angeles and jurisdiction of, 27–28; treatment of status crimes and, 287–288; Watts Rebellion and, 308
Los Angeles Sentinel, 226–227, 242, 248
Los Angeles Times, 44, 65, 72–73, 78, 177, 226, 260, 327
Low Riders car club, 339

MacIver, Robert, 173–174
Mack, Kev, 9
Macy Street group, 68, 334
Majestics, 108, 340
Malcolm X, 77, 122, 303, 330
Maple Street group, 68
marijuana, 263–264, 271–273, 398n50
Mary McLeod Bethune Park, 320
masculinity, 214–215, 238–239. *See also* comin'-from-the-shoulders ethos
Mateo Street group, 68–69, 334
materialism, 294
Maxson, Cheryl, 51
McBride, Wes, 53, 70

McCord, William, 107, 307
McCoy Boys, 10–11, 319, 411n86
McGroarty, John, 35
McWilliams, Carey, 22, 64
media: all-White gangs and, 363n91; Cluff incident and use of gang term, 78–79; coverage of guns in street fighting, 242–243; estimating numbers of street groups and, 72–74; on fighting between neighborhood groups, 226–227; focus on violence in 1960s and, 302; gang activity between 1965 and 1970 and, 10; on girls in street groups, 177; minimal attention to gangs before Watts Rebellion of, 63–64; portrayal of juvenile crime and, 256–261; on racial makeup of street groups, 73; rise of Crip coverage in, 326–328; ubiquity of racism in, 210; use of term gang and, 78; Zoot-Suit Riot response and, 28
Men of Status car club, 339
Merton, Robert, 294
methodology: access to subjects and, 15; disruptions due to researchers' identities, 18–20; East vs. South Los Angeles trends and, 16; efforts to correlate meaning of material between researchers and, 20; interviews, 15–18, 344n5; period of study, 15; police interviews and, 18; questions asked and, 15–16; research locations, 16–17, 19–20; subjects and, 16–18; supplemental materials, 18; types of crime studied, 256
Mexican residents: class bias and, 64–65; criminal justice system and, 84; media labeling of groups as gangs and, 79; Mexican as term and, 358n6; Parker's comments about, 35; racism and, 64–65, 79, 208; racism experienced by vs. experiences of Black Angelenos, 29, 349n78; response to Cluff incident and, 65–67, 74, 79; Zoot-Suit Riot response and, 28, 64
Middle-Class Juvenile Delinquency (ed. Vaz), 174
Migration and the Southern California Economy, 261
military service, 75, 121, 303
Miller, S. M., 20
Miller, Walter, 4, 59–61, 171
Mills, C. Wright, 12, 13, 43, 47, 86
Ministers, 337

Modern Gang Reader, 175
Molokans, 67–68
Mongolians, 337
Monson, Craig, 320, 324
Monza Club, 181, 383n70
Moore, Bobby, 130, 139, 146–147, 150
Moore, Joan, 12, 34, 48, 51, 57, 61, 83–84, 172, 176, 178, 216
Moore, John, 8
Mosely, Walter, 30
motherhood, 3, 39. *See also* gender
Mutual Aid (Kropotkin), 41
Myerhoff, Howard and Barbara, 174

National Advisory Committee on Criminal Justice Standards and Goals (1976), 59
National Crime Victimization Survey, 50
National Urban League, 1
National Youth Gang Center, 52
Nation of Islam, 305–306
Nation of Lords, A (Dawley), 57
Naughty 40s, 70, 337
N. D. (Watts), 110–112, 233–234, 251
Needle, Jerome, 61
neighborhood schools, 104, 109–110, 138–139, 152, 192–193, 204–206, 225, 367n25, 369n51
New Republic, 64
Newsweek, 260
Newton, Huey, 304
Nidiffer, Rose, 241
Niederhoffer, Arthur, 4
Nifty 50s, 70, 337
"Nuts, Sluts, and Preverts" (Liazos), 47

Ochentas, 337
O'Connor, Dick, 72
Office of Juvenile Justice and Delinquency Prevention (OJJDP), 52
Ohlin, Lloyd, 4, 61–62, 171
organized crime, 292
Orientals, 108, 340
Outlaws, 103, 337

Pachucos, 57
Palm Lanes group, 337
Palomar group, 108, 339
Pandit, Korla, 29, 349n77
Park Boys, 102
Parker, William H., 11, 31, 35, 53, 65–66, 206, 302, 308, 409n54

Pearson, Geoffrey, 49–50
Peralta, Stacy, 9, 37, 122
Peterson, Dana, 176
Pirates (LASD), 44
Piru Boys, 319
Platt, Anthony, 44–45, 47
Poe, Elizabeth, 307
police. *See* Compton Police Department; Los Angeles County Sheriff's Department (LASD); Los Angeles Police Department (LAPD)
Polk, Kenneth, 174
Poop (Wild Willie Poo Poo), 92–93, 119, 129–130, 139, 196, 205, 207–208, 221, 237–240, 246–247, 268–271, 275–279, 294–295
Potter, Gary, 86
Procello, Richard, 370n72
public transportation, 22, 25, 37
Pueblo Players, 336
Pueblos, 103, 128, 336
Purple Hearts, 336

Quarter group, 339
Quicker classes, 2–7, 12
Quinney, Richard, 43, 54, 284

racism: in aircraft industry, 38; Black Americans and, 28–30; Black Angelenos and, 25, 29–31, 196; Black migrants and, 23, 25; Cluff incident and, 66–67; de facto segregation and, 30; economics and, 30; gang panics and, 48–49; gang understanding and, 83; history of Los Angeles and, 11; Japanese Angelenos and, 29; lack of treatment of in literature on LA gangs, 9; Los Angeles Police Department (LAPD) and, 4–5, 11, 31, 35, 206–209, 308, 387n134; Los Angeles real estate and, 26, 29–30, 32–34, 196; Mexican Angelenos and, 29, 64–65; neighborhood schools and, 204–206; other youth group opportunities and, 203–204, 206; police and, 206–209; racial in-groupness and, 201–203; racially motivated all-White street groups, 211; racial violence, 31–32, 198–201, 231, 307, 349n70; racist beliefs, 34–36, 203; in South Los Angeles neighborhoods, 11; theoretical literature and, 4; training programs and, 38; treatment of drug

use among non-Whites and, 264–265; ubiquity of, 210; Watts Rebellion and, 308–309; White migrants from South and, 30–31; White understanding of in Los Angeles, 30; World War II and, 33–34; Zoot-Suit Riot response and, 28, 64. *See also* Los Angeles
Ramona Gardens group, 336, 339
Rand, Christopher, 22, 29
rape, 273–275, 383n77
Rattlesnakes (LASD), 44
real estate, 11, 26, 29–30, 32–34, 38, 196
Reasons, Charles, 54
Rebel Rousers, 179, 181–182, 337
record hops, 114, 191–193, 385n98
Regents car club, 337
Regnery, Alfred, 85
Reiman, Jeffrey, 54
religion, 249, 296–297. *See also* Islam
Renegades, 141, 151–152, 306
respondents: Big, 157, 224; Billy P. (probation officer), 73, 112, 250, 377n34; Bob M. (park director), 321, 324; Cardell (Slausons), 117–118, 315; Chili (Gladiators), 31; Cordell (Slausons), 296–297; Davetta (Warnette), 189–191; Donny H., 215, 247, 324; Ed B., 116–117, 153–154, 241–242, 290; Eugene (Slauson), 141–142, 146, 251; E. V. (LAPD officer), 265; Geronimo (Jasper, Senators), 92, 99–102, 116, 119–120, 179, 185, 188, 219; Harry S., 76; High Priest (Lafayette, Slauson), 58, 120, 123, 187–188, 222, 246; Jasper (Geronimo, Senators), 92, 99–102, 116, 119–120, 179, 185, 188, 219; Jerry C., 325; John S., 68, 263–264; Lafayette (High Priest), 58, 120, 123, 187–188, 222, 246, 252–253, 279, 314; Lefon A. (Serfs), 73, 272, 280, 402n99; Lieutenant T. (Compton Police Department), 56; Linda C (Florencitas), 56, 93–94, 96–98, 184, 194, 224–225; Miguel D. (from Group Guidance Project), 55, 215, 244, 265; Miller, Frank, 69–70, 359n35; Nedra (Warnettes), 180–181, 187–189, 193, 201; Oliver Cool (Slausons), 120, 156, 214; One, 264; Percy M., 232, 292–293; Pittsburgh Slim, 154–156; R. C. (Florence), 296; Rick C. (Florence), 74, 94, 98–99, 188, 193, 195, 209, 290–291; Rickie H., 222–223; Roslyn (Slausons), 55, 58, 184, 188, 266, 291, 314; Sergeant T. (Compton Police Department), 319; Sheila D., 184–185, 194–195, 383n76, 383n77; Skillet, 211; Ted W. (Boozies), 69, 71, 197–198; Whit (Royal Aces), 94, 217, 236, 240, 243–244, 269, 280; Willie C., 116, 296–297; Woodrow C. (W. C., probation officer), 121–122, 158, 191–194, 247–249, 314, 371n77. *See also* Ameer (Baby Businessmen); Barry Wa. (Junior Businessmen); Chinaman (Slausons); Frank M. (Clanton); Kumasi; Poop (Wild Willie Poo Poo); Roach (Slauson)
Rice, Roger, 5, 8, 57, 124, 180, 241
Rich Get Richer and the Poor Get Prison, The (Reiman), 54
Riesman, David, 218
Riessman, Frank, 20
Roach (Slauson), 112, 135–137, 139, 147, 152, 154, 158, *169*, 233–234, 251, 315–316
Road Devils car club, 339
robbery, 246–247, 277–280, 285
Rob Roys, 334
Rodriguez, Luis, 57–58
Rojek, Dean, 39
Roman 20s, 70, 103, 128, 228, 236–237, 337
Roman 103s, 337
Roman Pearls, 337
romantic relationships: domestic abuse and, 189–190; double standard with respect to group affiliation, 188; expectations for, 184–187; jealousy and fighting around, 191–193; marriage, 187; parental reactions to, 188; pregnancy and, 187; premarital sex and, 187; romantic expectations and, 186–187
Roosevelt, Franklin D., 33
Ross Snyder group, 338
Royal Aces Social Group, 55, 73, 94, 102, 178–179, 240, 336
Royal Deuces, 102, 336
Royal Genies, 108
Royal Syndicators, 338

"Saints and the Roughnecks, The" (Chambliss), 175
Salisbury, Harrison, 4, 173–174
Sanders, William, 175
Saracens, 340
Satan's Saints car club, 339
Schiesl, Martin, 34

Schwendinger, Herman and Julia, 44, 46, 49–50, 60, 87, 174
Seale, Bobby, 304
segregation, 11, 30, 33–34, 386n108
Sellin, Thorsten, 51
Senators, 92, 99–102, 119–120, 179, 338
Senior Businessmen, 73
Serfs car club, 73, 272, 280, 339
Set Seven, 141
7th Street group, 335
76th Boys, 319
Shack Boys, 319
Shandus, 340
Shelden, Randall, 176, 179
Sherman, Gene, 73, 177
shoplifting, 289
Short, James, 48, 174, 260
Sides, Josh, 11, 26, 29, 37, 261–262
Sikes, Gini, 176
Sin Town, 71, 340
Sir Valiants, 108, 340
Slauson Avenue, 25–26
Slauson neighborhood: Boptown part of, 152; "crip" slang and, 322–323; economic industry in, 124; Goodyear Blimp and, 125; size of, 124; Slauson Village moniker of, 125, 128; Zip Code and, 124
Slauson Park, 123–124, 319–320
Slausons: about, 340, 340n6; Apostates, 179; Avenues and, 325–326; Baby Slausons, 74, 131–132, 150, 374n106; Big Slausons, 117, 130–131, 376n26; Black Panther Party (BPP) and, 304–305; Bunchy Carter and, 148, 151, 304–307, 325, 330; Chinaman and Businessmen and, 102, 127, 293, 375n17; cliques of, 148–152; confrontation at Manchester Theater with D'Artagnans, 141–143; confrontation of Baby Businessmen about Bird's stabbing, 145–146; Crips and, 325–326; current lives of, 8; "dirty" reputation of, 154–157; Dudley B. (Slausons) vs. Floyd (Gladiators) fight and, 235; Eugene (Little Slauson), 141–142, 146, 318; female cliques, 179; fight between Roach and N. D., 233–234; Flips, 104–105, 149, 369n49; Florence-Firestone District and, 71; former members of the Cavaliers and, 128; founding of, 129–131, 375n4; Gladiators and, 104–107, 124, 230–231; hand signs and, 159, 377n40; initiations and, 117–120; Jerome of, 128, 139, 146; Junior Slausons, 74, 117; leadership and, 125–126; legacy of, 160–161; Little Flips clique, 120; Little Renegades, 104–105, 149; Little Slausons, 119, 130–131; Robert Manual and, 150; Marvin M. and N. D. of Watts and, 110–111; membership during the 1960s and, 318–319; migration between cliques and, 148–150; Bobby Moore and, 130, 139, 146–147, 150; moving on of early members, 316–318; neighborhood schools and, 138–139, 152; Oliver Cool and, 120, 156, 214; Onionhead and, 106, 140; pictured, 164, 165, 166, 167, 168, 169; post-Rebellion economic opportunities for, 317; PotTea, 318; racial makeup of, 70, 340; Renegades, 141, 151–152, 306, 320, 366n14–15; rivalries with Watts groups, 108–111, 124, 228–229, 310–311; robberies and, 157–158; Senior Slausons, 74; sets and cliques and, 91–92; Sin Street set and, 152–154; Skillet, 211; "Slauson Shuffle" and, 155–156, 378n55; Slauson Village Society, 371n77; strength of, 12; swastikas and, 157–159; territory of, 123–125; Terry of, 304–305; truce with Florence and, 96, 124; Village Assassins clique, 74, 120; Warlords of Baby Slauson, 91, 150; Watts Rebellion and, 310–312. *See also* Batani-Khalfani, Akil S. "Bird;" Chinaman (Slausons); Poop (Wild Willie Poo Poo); Roach (Slauson)
Sleepy Lagoon murder case, 8, 28, 64, 78
Sloan, Cle "Bone," 9, 11, 31
Smith, R. J., 9, 23
Soja, Edward, 22, 23, 299
Soul on Ice (Cleaver), 19
South Los Angeles: Black Power movement and, 303–304; camaraderie among Blacks and, 197; pathologizing South Central Los Angeles label and, 24; decline of incomes in 1960s in, 299; demographic changes of 1960s and, 301; demographic layout of, 24–27; emerging groups from late 1960s and 1970s, 319; "gangsta culture" and, 329–331; geographical layout of, 22–23; hostilities between street groups from Watts and, 108; influx of drugs and, 330–331; maturation of early street group members in, 300; migration of Blacks to, 74–75; racial

in-groupness and, 201–203; racism in neighborhoods of, 11, 196–198; rape and, 274–275; religious values and, 249
Spartans, 340
Spergel, Irving, 51, 52, 59–60
Spook-a-Pinos, 70
Spook Hunters, 211, 338, 387n119, 387n120
Stapleton, William, 61
State Street group, 334
Stein, Ben, 260
street gambling, 285–286
Street Gangs and Street Workers (Klein), 8
street groups: adoption of other culture among sets in, 94–96; alcohol and, 249, 263–266, 273; all-White groups, 211; assessment of neighborhood members by group, 115–116; authors' terminology and, 60–62; crime as an individual action and, 280, 285, 298; drugs and alcohol and, 263–271; emergence of in South Los Angeles, 63; emerging in late 1960s and 1970s, 319; as ephemeral part of members' lives, 314–315; estimating numbers and, 71–74; ethics of children and, 315–316; families ties and, 97; female cliques and, 178–179; girls clubs and, 178; hand signs and, 159–160; hard drugs and, 267–271, 397n45, 398n53; high-sidin' and, 224; in-group associations, 101–102; initiations into, 117–120, 373n100, 374n102; internal organization of into age groups and sets/cliques, 89–92; leadership and, 125–126, 279; luck and, 240–242, 279, 391n34; marijuana and, 263–264, 271–272; masculinity and, 214–215, 238–239; members with reputations allowing for free mobility in, 112–113; Mexican sets and, 92–94; migration between cliques and, 119, 148–150, 368n38; mobility and, 104; moments of warmth and, 235–237; neighborhood schools and, 104, 109–110, 138–139, 152, 192–193, 367n25, 369n51; neighborhood ties and, 249–250; numbered cliques in, 99; out-group conflict and, 100–101; race and diverse, 94–96; racial in-groupness and, 201–203; racially diverse, 93–94, 101–102; reaction to gang designation of, 54–56, 356n100; reasons for formation of, 99–100, 365n1; reasons for membership, 114–117; regular non-members, 116–117, 121–122; religious values of neighborhoods and, 249–250; research on female street groups, 175–176; role models and, 218–220; self-reported data and, 59–60; serious injury and killings, 248–250; set designation, 58–59; terms of for the groups, 56–59; thieves and, 290; truces, 96; violence between neighborhood groups and, 226–229; Watts Rebellion and, 309–313, 409n62; white members, 94, 209; White violence/discrimination as one reason for joining, 198–201; wolfin' and, 222–223; women and crossing of borders, 113–114. *See also* comin'-from-the-shoulders ethos; gangs; *individual groups*
street scams, 285
Strodtbeck, Fred, 48
Superior Trays car club, 339
Swamp Boys, 56, 338
Swamps, 340
Syndicators, 336

Tackwood, Louis, 229
Tampico Spice, 124
Tanaka, Paul, 44
Tapia, Mike, 17, 54
Taste of Power, A (Brown), 148
Taylor, Carl, 292
teen posts, 77
Temple Street group, 68, 334
terrorist groups, 84
Theory of the Leisure Class (Veblen), 294
38th Street group, 335
39th Street group, 338
32nd Street group, 336
Thornberry, Terrance, 178
Thrasher, Frederic, 4, 42, 71–72, 83, 130–131
Tortilla Flats group, 338
training programs, 38
Tree Tops group, 339
Treintas, 338
T-Timers car club, 338
Turbans, 340
Turks, 340
Twead, William "Boss," 87

United Slaves Organization (US), 306–307, 408n38, 408n40

U.S. Department of Justice, 47
U.S. Riot Commission Report, 309

Valdez, Al, 8
Valiants group, 108, 340
Van Dykes car club, 339
Van Winkle, Barrik, 48
Vaz, Edmund W., 174
Vazquez, Collette, 365–366n3
Veblen, Thorsten, 294
Vice Lords (Chicago), 57, 89–90; division into age groups and cliques, 89–90
Vietnam War, 303, 330, 414n126
Vigil, Diego, 8, 45, 48, 57, 90, 119, 176
Vikings (LASD), 44
Village Assassins, 74
Vineyards, 159–160, *164*, 338
violence: between different groups/neighborhoods, 226–231; drive-by shootings, 252–253; escalation of, 252–253, 395n4; gang-related vs. non-gang-related, 251; hand-to-hand, 213–214; high-sidin' and response of, 224; increase in 1960s of, 301–302; individual fights and, 231–235; influx of drugs and, 391n41; intragroup fighting and, 225–226; jealousy over girls as source of, 191–193, 224–225; luck and, 240–241; moments of warmth amid, 235–237; more serious fights, 237–240; police violence, 250; race and, 230–231; reasons for fighting, 221–222, 230–231; role of the gun and, 220–221, 239–240; school rivalries and, 225; serious injury and killings, 248–250; snipin' (fighting for hire), 223–224; spontaneous, 275–277; Watts and Slausons groups, 228–229; wolfin' as a type of, 222–223. *See also* comin'-from-the shoulders ethos; weapons
Voodoo Men car club, 339

wards of the court, 45
Warlords, 179
Washington, Raymond, 304–306, 320, 324–325
Waters, Frank J., 66
Watts Labor Community Action Committee, 197
Watts neighborhood: assessing crime in, 281–282; Black street groups and, 108; borders of, 108–109; decline of incomes in 1960s in, 299; diverse roots of, 107; early Mexican sets and, 108; estimating numbers of streets groups within, 74; ghettoization of, 26, 107–108; government housing projects and, 75, 107–108, 111–112; hostilities between street groups from south LA and, 108; media coverage of street groups and, 76; pre-World War II and, 26; racist real estate practices and, 33–34; rivalries with Slauson of street groups in, 108–111
Watts Rebellion: Black Power movement and, 76–77; Crips and Bloods and, 63; deindustrialization and, 36; magnitude of, 309; racism and, 308–309; South Los Angeles gangs and, 2; street groups and, 309–313, 409n62; structural issues underneath, 10; *U.S. Riot Commission Report*, 309; violence leading up to, 307–308; as watershed moments in race relations, 1
Watts sets: Bird and, 140–141; Black street groups and, 108; early Mexican sets and, 108; emerging groups from late 1960s and 1970s, 319; fight between Roach and N. D., 233–234; George C., 318; government housing projects and, 107–108, 111–112, 199, 361n62; hand signs and, 159; Islam and, 306; names of, 360n40; pictured, *164*; Renegades and, 151–152; rivalries with Slauson of street groups and, 108–111, 124, 310–311; Sin Town, 157; Watts Rebellion and, 310–312
weapons: availability of, 244–248, 393n52–53; customs around gun use and, 245–246, 249–250; escalation over time in, 241–243, 252–253; gasoline bombs (Molotov cocktails), 243, 247, 252; guns, 220–221, 239–245, 252–253, 303; knives, 233, 242–244; large-bore shotguns and, 243; media reports about, 213; other weapons, 243, 247; passing through borders with, 244–245; use of in robbery, 246–247; varying use of by clique, 246; zip guns, 392n46
Webb, Vincent, 52
West Adams District, 27
West, Cornel, 28
West Jefferson District, 27
West Side Boys, 319
White Angelenos, gang label and, 81–82

white-collar crime, 86, 365n136, 365n138
White Fence group, 334
White migrants, Jim Crow culture and, 30–31
Whyte, William, 4, 173
Wiener, Jon, 299
Willowbrook 13, 338
Willowbrook area, 26
Willowbrook Boys, 319
Wilson, William, 28, 171–172
Winfree, L. Thomas, Jr., 83
Winton, Richard, 53

Wolfgang, Marvin, 51
wolfin', 222–223
women, 33–34. *See also* Black women; female affiliates; gender
World War II, 23, 29, 33–34, 37, 75

Yablonsky, Lewis, 4, 120, 125, 311
Yellowjackets, 73, 108, 130, 336
Yorty, Sam, 11, 299
Youth Gang Task Force, 69

Zoot-Suit Riots, 8, 28, 64, 78, 307

John C. Quicker is Emeritus Professor of Sociology at California State University, Dominguez Hills, and the author of *Homegirls: Characterizing Chicana Gangs*.

Akil S. Batani-Khalfani is a South Los Angeles Street Sage. He is a former Youth Correctional Counselor for California Youth Authority and a former Youth Gang Counselor for the Los Angeles Community Youth Gang Services.